RACE, CRIME, and the LAW

Randall Kennedy
RACE, CRIME, and the LAW

Randall Kennedy received his undergraduate degree from Princeton University and his law degree from Yale Law School. A Rhodes Scholar, he served as law clerk to Supreme Court Justice Thurgood Marshall. He is a professor at Harvard Law School and lives in Dedham, Massachusetts.

RACE, CRIME, and the LAW

RANDALL KENNEDY

Vintage Books
A Division of Random House, Inc.
New York

FIRST VINTAGE BOOKS EDITION, APRIL 1998

*Grateful acknowledgment is made to the following for permission to reprint previously
published material:*

The Final Call: Excerpt from "The Million Man March Pledge." Reprinted by
permission of The Final Call.

The New York Times: Excerpt from "Growing Up to Fear the Law" by Brent Staples. Copyright © 1991 by The New York Times Co. Reprinted by permission of
The New York Times.

Dorothy E. Roberts and Harvard Law Review: Excerpt from "Punishing Drug Addicts Who
Have Babies" by Dorothy E. Roberts (104 *Harvard Law Review* 1420, 1991). Copyright ©
1991 by Dorothy E. Roberts. Copyright © 1991 by the Harvard Law Review Association.
Reprinted by permission of Dorothy E. Roberts and *Harvard Law Review*.

The Library of Congress has catalogued the Pantheon edition as follows:
Kennedy, Randall, 1954–
Race, crime, and the law / Randall Kennedy
p. cm.
Includes bibliographical references and index.
ISBN 0-679-43881-5
1. Discrimination in criminal justice administration—United
States. 2. Afro-Americans—Civil rights. 3. Afro-American
criminals. I. Title.
KF9223.K43   1997
345.73´05—dc21

Vintage ISBN: 0-375-70184-2

Author photograph © Harvard University
Book design by Laura Hough

Random House Web address: http://www.randomhouse.com/

Printed in the United States of America
10 9 8 7

For my darling wife, Yvedt Lové Matory

Contents

Foreword

THIS BOOK EXPLORES the bitterly contested crossroads where race relations intersect with the rules that govern the apprehension, trial, and punishment of criminals. Many people are interested in that intersection but lack a detailed understanding of it. This book attempts to supply that understanding by explaining and evaluating resolutions to the most important legal controversies that arise when legislative, administrative, or judicial policies or decisions are challenged on the grounds that they are racially unjust. Everyone plays a role in and is affected by these controversies. That is a principal reason why this book is written for a general audience as well as specialists. But among those who play especially prominent roles (e.g., legislators, attorneys, and police officers), judges receive the largest share of attention in these pages. They (followed closely by prosecutors) are the officials upon whom society most relies to protect the integrity of criminal law as it is administered in courtrooms, our houses of justice.

I pursue a variety of aims. The first is to show the existence of neglected common ground between combatants of competing ideological camps. This effort is animated by a sense that inherited debates between liberals and conservatives about the race question in criminal law have become increasingly sterile. It is also animated by a belief that useful prescriptions for problems as complex as those generated by the large, rambunctious, multiracial society of the United States can arise only from thinking that frees itself of reflexive obedience to familiar signals.

My second aim, closely related to the first, is to recount, make vivid, and explain the history that causes a substantial number of Americans, particularly African-Americans, to perceive the criminal justice system with suspicion, if not antagonism. To accomplish this aim, I focus first on how authorities have declined to protect blacks from criminality and second on how authorities have racially mistreated black suspects, defendants, and convicts. There is significance to this sequence. An important theme of this book is that blacks have suffered more from being left unprotected or underprotected by law enforcement authorities than from being mistreated as suspects or defendants, although it is allegations of the latter that now typically receive the most attention.

At the same time that I highlight the history of racial injustice, I note an insistent current in that history that has significantly shaped American legal institutions—the tradition of struggle *against* racial injustice. It is important to know the story of the nine black youngsters dubbed the Scottsboro Boys who were wrongly convicted of rape in Alabama in the 1930s, after trials in which due process was mocked by blatant prejudice. It is also important to know, however, that state and federal judges saved the Scottsboro Boys from execution by establishing legal norms that now benefit all persons tried in American courts.

My third aim is to provide useful guidance in grappling with an age-old question in American life: When, if ever, is it defensible to engage in racial discrimination? By racial discrimination I simply mean using race as a criterion for treating one person or group differently from others. At the end of the twentieth century, racially discriminatory decision-making remains influential though controversial. For example, nothing has poisoned race relations more than racially discriminatory policing pursuant to which blacks are watched, questioned, and detained more than others. Defended on the grounds that blacks commit a disproportionate share of street crimes relative to their share of the population, the race line in policing creates cycles of resentment. Many law-abiding blacks resent the racial discrimination to which they are subjected because it makes them pay for fears generated by criminals with whom they are lumped by dint of color. Many of them voice their resentment by attacking as "racists" those who view blackness as a proxy for an enhanced risk of criminality. That charge, in turn, deepens the anger of those who view it as yet another way of denying that blacks, too, bear some responsibility for the sorry state of American race relations.

Another example of the controverted legal status of the race line emerges in debates over the propriety of proposals designed to enlarge the presence of blacks on juries. These proposals include requiring officials to make race-dependent calculations in changing the venue of a trial and setting aside a minimum number of seats for black jurors.

A third area in which the race line appears is in appeals to racial sentiments by participants in criminal trials—"playing the race card." One example of playing the race card is the attorney who seeks to elicit from jurors feelings of racial solidarity as in "we whites [or blacks] have got to stick together." Another example is the attorney who seeks to elicit from jurors feelings of racial animus as in "don't believe this witness because she's black [or white] and those people lie."

I oppose racial discrimination by public officials in all but the narrowest of emergencies. Hence, in contrast to the ascendant case law, I conclude that officials should generally be prohibited from using the race of a person as a proxy for an enhanced risk that this person is engaging in crime. I condemn attorneys' appeals to racial sentiments and argue that the legal system should do more to deter them. Similarly, because I seek to radically minimize those occasions on which officials or private individuals may properly discriminate racially in their treatment of others, I oppose proposals requiring racially mixed juries. Many proponents of such proposals want to create juries that "look like America." I want, by contrast, to create a legal system that looks beyond looks. As long as the process of choosing the jury has been kept free of racial selectivity and care is taken to exclude from jury service anyone, regardless of race, whose judgment is likely to be unfair, there is nothing inherently wrong with an all-white jury deciding the fate of a black defendant or an all-black jury deciding the fate of a white defendant.

My fourth aim is to shed light on the difficult problem of uncovering racial discrimination when a policy makes no reference to race and its authors deny having acted with a racial motive. To do so, I examine allegations of racial discrimination in decisions to prosecute women for endangering their babies through illicit drug usage, the design and enforcement of laws which punish crack cocaine offenses more harshly than powder cocaine offenses, and the administration of capital punishment. Throughout this discussion, I show that all too many commentators make exaggerated claims for results they prefer, denying evidence and arguments that contradict, or at least complicate, the positions they espouse. Many of those who charge, for example, that racial discrimination accounts for the differential punishment of crack and powder offenses deny the undeniable—that crack cocaine is distinguishable from powder cocaine in respects that can appropriately be considered by legislators. By the same token, many defenders of the death penalty reject out of hand evidence suggesting that, in a substantial number of instances, age-old racial habits assert themselves in the process of condemning certain criminals to death. I argue that the stubborn unwillingness of courts to acknowledge racial selectivity in capital punishment is an ongoing scandal that later generations will condemn.

Although this book speaks broadly to the regulation of race relations in the administration of criminal law, the racial conflict upon which it mainly focuses is the white–black confrontation. This is the conflict that has served as *the* great object lesson for American law, the conflict that has given birth to much of the federal constitutional law of criminal procedure, and the conflict that remains the most pervasive and volatile point of racial friction within federal and state courthouses. This is not to say that other racial conflicts are insignificant; to the contrary, they have shaped the law in important ways. Where appropriate, I discuss them. More than any other racial divide in America, however, it is the racial frontier separating whites from blacks where the difficulties have proven hardest to overcome.*

---

*I use the term "white" conventionally and uniformly throughout the book. I use a number of terms synonymously with "black," including "Negro" and "African-American." If I mean to refer to a group that contains various nonwhite people, I sometimes use the term "colored" or "people of color." I view all of these necessarily imprecise terms as equally acceptable. For interesting commentary on racial nomenclature, see Harold R. Isaacs, "A Name to Go By," in *The New World of Negro*

. . .

I began this book at the suggestion of Erroll McDonald of Pantheon Books. I am thankful that he has been so patient and supportive as I worked to complete it. Altie Karper carefully shepherded it through production. Mr. Benjamin Sears carefully, diligently, and cheerfully typed the manuscript. Judge Henry Kennedy, Jr., provided constant encouragement and excellent advice, as he has with all of my endeavors.

I owe a large debt to many students and colleagues at various institutions who have listened to or read earlier versions of what follows. Especially helpful were classes that I taught at the Florida State University School of Law as a holder of the Tobias Simon Chair, seminars in which I participated at the Boston University School of Law at the invitation of Professor Tracey Maclin, and talks in which I tried out ideas at the American Enterprise Institute, the Center for Equal Opportunity, the University of Pittsburgh School of Law, and the Washington College of Law at American University. Professors Albert W. Alschuler, Barbara Allen Babcock, Daniel Bell, Steven Duke, Paul Gewirtz, Nathan Glazer, Samuel R. Gross, Adam Jay Hirsch, Yale Kamisar, Nancy J. King, Sanford Levinson, Glenn Loury, Tracey Maclin, Tracey Louise Meares, john a. powell, Jamin Ben Raskin, David Rudovsky, Stephen Schulhofer, Jordan M. Steiker, and David A. Strauss generously commented on several chapters, as did my friends Brad Berenson, Stephen B. Bright, Harry Downs, Pope McCorkle III, George Packer, Harvey Silverglate, and Christopher Stone.

I owe my greatest debt to Harvard Law School, my workplace for the past decade. Under the leadership of James Vorenberg and Robert C. Clark, the Harvard I have known provides a wonderful environment for scholarship. Scott Brewer, Richard H. Fallon, Jr., Charles Fried,

---

Americans (1963); Sterling Stuckey, "Identity and Ideology: The Names Controversy," in *Slave Culture: Nationalist Theory and the Foundations of Black America* (1987); Ben L. Martin, "From Negro to Black to African American," 106 *Political Science Quarterly* 83 (1991); Kendall Thomas, "*Rouge et Noir* Reread: A Popular Constitutional History of the Angelo Herndon Case," 65 *Southern California Law Review* 2599 n.2 (1992).

Philip B. Heymann, Daniel J. Meltzer, Charles Ogletree, Richard Davies Parker, Todd D. Rakoff, Michael Sandel, David L. Shapiro, Carol S. Steiker, Lloyd L. Weinreb, and David B. Wilkins are among my Harvard colleagues who offered notably helpful assistance. Absolutely essential, moreover, was the help given to me by the extraordinary staff of the Harvard Law School library, particularly Dale Alan Diefenbach, Joan Duckett, David Goldman, Michael Jimenez, Janet C. Katz, Naomi Ronen, Philip Satterfield, Aparna Sen, and Terry L. Swanlund. Students, too, provided crucial aid in terms of research, proofing, and editing. Among those who significantly improved this book through their efforts are Richard Banks, Reginald Brown, Jennifer Cabranes, Debra Dickerson, Mark Fleming, Sam Kaplan, Jennifer Martinez, Russell Robinson, Tina Perry, Cathleen Price, Andy G. Schopler, Peter G. Smith, Karl Sun, Tania Tetlow, and James Trilling.

Finally, I want to express my heartfelt appreciation to my dear wife, Yvedt Lové Matory. This book is dedicated to her.

RACE,
CRIME,
and the
LAW

1.

The Race Question in Criminal Law:
Changing the Politics of the Conflict

Creating Common Ground

ANYONE SEEKING TO influence the administration of criminal law must reckon with the complex and ferocious racial politics that surround the subject. I want, therefore, to speak immediately to contending ideological camps about the race question in criminal law and clear space for a shared discussion that will uncover common grounds for action.

The first of the four camps to which I address myself has made the control of street crime primarily through punitive measures a high priority on its political agenda. Demanding that attention be paid to the misery inflicted by crime, devotees of this camp have insistently raised the banner of "law and order." At the national level, this camp was, for three decades, dominated by the Republican Party. Presidents Richard Nixon, Ronald Reagan, and George Bush each used to great effect the claim that they would be tougher on crime than their opponents.[1] Their electoral success prompted imitation. Bill Clinton is only the most prominent of many Democrats who have gone to considerable lengths to prove themselves capable of being as tough as Republicans on crime.[2] As a result, this first camp—the law and order camp—has become thoroughly bipartisan.[3]

Various aims, beliefs, and sentiments have played a role in animating the law and order camp. For some politicians, the law and order slogan has served as a thinly veiled code with which to signal sympathy for and solidarity with whites upset by the social, political, and cultural changes brought about by the upheavals of the 1960s, particularly the Civil Rights Revolution.[4] I have little hope of communicating my message to those for whom law and order are code words designed primarily to appeal covertly to anti-Negro prejudice. I do believe it possible, however, to reach those drawn to law and order rhetoric because they are afraid of being victimized, seek reassurance that the government will do its utmost to protect them, and desire to express outrage at street criminals, especially those who repeatedly commit violent offenses. I share that fear, anxiety, and anger and therefore want to remove impediments to the enforcement of decent law and order. One major impediment is the conviction of many people that the law enforcement system is overwhelmingly racist. Although the precise dimensions of this attitude are unclear, within African-American communities it is certainly appreciable. This attitude causes some black attorneys to eschew joining prosecutors' offices because they feel that doing so will entail "selling out" and working for "the Man."[5] It causes some black citizens to decline to cooperate with police investigations. Even more alarmingly, it prompts some black jurors to be unreasonably skeptical of police testimony from law enforcement authorities or even to refuse to vote for convictions despite proof beyond reasonable doubt of defendants' guilt.[6]

To change this attitude and the conduct it generates, action will have to be taken to rectify injustices that nourish feelings of racial aggrievement. To improve the effectiveness of police and prosecutors, high priority should be given to correcting and deterring illegitimate racial practices that diminish the reputation of the law enforcement establishment. Proponents of law and order, then, should be in the forefront of those who insist that officials respect authoritative rules prohibiting racial misconduct and who demand that the legal regime effectively discipline officials who fail to comply. Proponents of law and order should acknowledge what cannot sensibly be denied: that to an extent that is significant, albeit hard to identify, declining but nonetheless regrettable, illicit racial discriminations continue to adversely affect the administration of criminal law. Remarkably, some devotees of law and order occasionally deny the obvious, as did Professor John J. DiIullio, Jr., when he asserted that data on the administration of capital punishment "disclose no trace of racism"*—a matter about which I shall have much to say below. (See pp. 311–350.) For a campaign of law and order to succeed, it must apply not only to ordinary persons but to the guardians of law and order as well.

A second important camp in American politics is populated by people passionately dedicated to limiting governmental power. This camp is convinced that, if left unchecked, officials will virtually always tend to overstep their authority. Insistence upon checking governmental power is deeply rooted in American political culture and embraced in different forms by an array of ideological types. While one faction in this camp insists mainly upon checking governmental power with respect to taxation and the regulation of business enterprise, another insists mainly upon checking governmental power with respect to freedom of expression, governmental intrusion on life-style, police investigations, and criminal punishments. My message here is aimed primarily at the former faction, libertarian conservatives,[7] as opposed to libertarian liberals.

I accept the premise that citizens need always be alert to the danger of governmental abuse and corruption. I simply urge libertarian conservatives to apply more generally their intolerance for governmental tyranny.[†] That intolerance should make them especially sensitive to

---

*See John J. DiIullio, Jr., "My Black Crime Problem and Ours," *City Journal* (Spring 1996).

[†]It is noteworthy that members of Congress who recently harshly criticized federal law enforcement officials accused of overreacting to paramilitary organizations, many of which openly espouse white supremacist views of the most extreme sort, mobilized sufficient political backing to bring about changes in FBI personnel and practices and also to stymie the Clinton administration's efforts to enact broad antiterrorism laws. See, e.g., Steve Daley, "House Rivals Unite to Soften Anti-Terror Bill," *Chicago Tribune*, March 14, 1996; Charles V. Zehren, "A Year After Oklahoma City—Unkept Promises—Still No Pact on Anti-Terror Bill," *Newsday*, April 15, 1996.

One is entitled to wonder whether the response of right-wing members of Con-

racial misconduct. After all, in the United States, the epitome of governmental arrogance and undisciplined power is the police officer, prosecutor, juror, or judge who mistreats people on racial grounds, confident that his or her conduct will remain unchecked because of the racial status of the abused. Bitter experience has repeatedly shown, moreover, that where bigotry flourishes, corruption is also likely to prosper. Since federal and state constitutional and statutory provisions outlaw many types of invidious racial discrimination, those who disregard these restrictions become practiced in the art of lying. Lying, once loosed, is hard to cabin. Officials who deceitfully disregard laws prohibiting racial discrimination will tend also to disregard other boundaries. The classic example, of course, is the former Los Angeles police officer Mark Fuhrman, whose deceitful coverup of his racist language, actions, and attitudes played such a large and notorious role in the murder prosecution of O. J. Simpson.[8]

A third camp is that constituted by people who claim to disavow *all* types of racial discrimination. This camp marches under the banner of the color-blind constitution. Its primary target of late has been that form of racial discrimination known as "affirmative action," race-targeted policies expressly designed to help racial minorities.[9] Opponents of affirmative action reject the argument that racial discrimination favoring minorities should be treated differently than racial discrimination favoring whites. They insist instead upon formal symmetry, treating whites and blacks precisely the same, on the grounds that, as Justice Clarence Thomas puts it, "government-sponsored racial discrimination based on benign prejudice is just as noxious as discrimination inspired by malicious prejudice. In each instance, it is racial discrimination, plain and simple."[10]

One might think that those who attack affirmative action because of their commitment to the idea of a color-blind Constitution would also oppose policies that permit racial discrimination by law enforcement officers. This, however, has not been so. The Reagan administration at-

---

gress would have been different had the paramilitary groups in question been mainly black instead of mainly white. (On repression of black political organizations, see pp. 107–113.)

tacked race-based affirmative action on color-blind grounds but supported permitting race-based peremptory challenges as a tool of litigation.[11] Subsequently, critics of affirmative action have written voluminously about the dangers posed by racially-weighted means to advance the interests of blacks in employment and electoral politics. Most of these same critics are silent about the pervasive use of race by police in making determinations of suspiciousness.

This inconsistency suggests that some in the color-blindness camp tend to act opportunistically with respect to the matter of racial discrimination, complaining seriously about it only when racial distinctions hurt, or are perceived to hurt, whites. One way that this camp could begin to dispel this skepticism would be to apply rigorously in the context of criminal law their asserted commitment to antidiscrimination. This would entail supporting efforts aimed at uprooting racial discriminations that are already prohibited but still widely practiced, for example, the racially discriminatory peremptory challenge (see pp. 193–230). It would also entail backing reforms aimed at outlawing wrongful racial discriminations that are presently permitted by law, for example, police acting on the belief that black skin signals a higher risk of criminality (see pp. 136–167).

The fourth camp to which I address myself is that peopled by those dedicated specifically to advancing the interests of blacks. I embrace this camp's admirable labors on behalf of America's paradigmatic racial pariah, the Negro. I suggest, though, that many of those within this camp ought to be more careful in making allegations of racial discrimination. Clearly there exists racial unfairness in the administration of criminal law; considerable space in this book is allocated to detailing and criticizing this deplorable reality. It is important, though, to define the problem carefully. Whereas others all too often ignore or minimize racial injustices, some activists in this fourth camp all too often make formulaic allegations of racial misconduct without even bothering to grapple with evidence and arguments that challenge their conclusions.[12] Those who do this not only damage their own credibility; worse, they undermine the credibility of all who protest against racial wrongs.

I have in mind, for instance, the controversy over Tawana Brawley, a black teenager who alleged in November 1987 that she had been abducted and raped by six white men (several of whom were, she claimed, police officers).[13] A New York State grand jury concluded, on the basis of overwhelming evidence, that Brawley's allegations were groundless. Yet some people within the fourth camp, evincing an almost religious desire to believe Brawley, continue to credit her story despite compelling evidence that she lied. Others conclude that, in Barbara Omolade's words, "No matter what the actual facts were in the Tawana Brawley case, in a society which believes a black woman cannot be raped because of her 'nature,' it is impossible to sort out the truth or the lie of her story."[14] Still others concur with William Kunstler who declared that "It makes no difference anymore whether the attack on Tawana really happened" because "it doesn't disguise the fact that a lot of young black women are treated the way she said she was treated. [Her lawyers, Alton Maddox and Vernon Mason] now have an issue with which they can grab the headlines and launch a vigorous attack on the criminal justice system."[15] Such disregard for facts and exploitation of antiracist sentiment reduce the stature of those who sink to such tactics as well as the credibility of future allegations of racial injustice.

Loose, inaccurate, demagogic allegations of racial misconduct backfire in other ways as well. Because wrongful racial discrimination has been widely stigmatized, converting charges of such behavior into serious threats to reputation, many people will fight harder against such charges than other complaints, for instance complaints that the person is mistaken or even foolish. Thus, allegations of racial discrimination sometimes have the unintended consequence of stiffening the resolve of opponents to continue policies that they might otherwise consent to discontinue. Inaccurate or false allegations undoubtedly accentuate this response.

Poorly conceived allegations of racial misconduct also spread harmful confusion.* Consider, for example, how racial paranoia has con-

---

*Edward Banfield once noted that a serious danger of overemphasizing prejudice as a direct cause of blacks' troubles is that doing so "may lead to the adoption of futile and even destructive policies and the non-adoption of others that might do great good." He went on to say that "the other, perhaps more serious danger . . . is that it raises still higher the psychic cost of being Negro. . . . It is bad enough to have to suffer real prejudice . . . without having to suffer imaginary prejudice as well." See *The Unheavenly City: The Nature and Future of Our Urban Crisis*, 86 (1970).

tributed to stifling intelligent debate over drug policy. Some commentators and activists condemn the war on drugs as "genocide" because blacks constitute a disproportionate number of those subjected to arrest, prosecution, and incarceration for illicit drug trafficking.[16] Others condemn proposals for decriminalizing drug use on the grounds that decriminalization would amount to "genocide" because racial minorities would constitute a disproportionate number of those allowed to pursue their drug habits without deterrent intervention by the state.[17] This is sheer demagoguery that causes discussions over drug policy to degenerate into contests over who can shout "genocide" more quickly or loudly. No one has come forward with credible evidence to suggest that American drug policy is *really* genocidal,[18] that is, designed to eradicate a people. But that does not restrain the use of this rhetoric even by people of substantial public standing such as Lee Brown, the former "drug czar" of the Clinton administration. Dismissing Surgeon General Joycelyn Elders' suggestion that decriminalization ought at least to be studied, Brown retorted that legalization would be "the moral equivalent of genocide,"[19] a statement that offers a dismal example of a broad tendency to misuse key words—"racism," "lynching," "holocaust"—that warrant special care in order to preserve their meaning and impact.

A proper appreciation for words is not the only casualty of the intellectual sloppiness that has impeded analysis of racial issues in the administration of criminal law. Another is the proper interpretation of statistics. Statistics can be a powerful tool for uncovering racial misconduct.[20] Too often, however, activists in the fourth camp (along with journalistic and scholarly supporters) automatically insist, simply on the basis of observable racial disparities, that officials are engaged in making invidious racial discriminations.[21] They seem unaware that a racial disparity is not necessarily indicative of a racial discrimination.[22] A disparity is often evidence of discrimination. But one must keep in mind that a racial disparity may stem from causes other than disparate treatment. A disproportionate number of blacks in a jail *might* signal that police are racially discriminating in making arrests. On the other hand, the racial demographics of the inmate population may reflect that more blacks than whites are engaging in prohibited conduct which leads them to be arrested. If that is so, the racial disparity stems not from biased decision-making on the part of the police but from some other cause. Often that cause will be related to racial wrongdoing. Real differences in behavior may stem, to some extent, from deprivations imposed upon individuals who live in the depressed, isolated, criminogetic settings in which large numbers of blacks reside as a consequence of historic racial oppression.[23] It is important, however, to distinguish between racial discrimination engaged in by police and real differences in behavior caused by conditions partially shaped by racial oppression. It is important to avoid wrongly stigmatizing police officers; their work is too essential to be hobbled by mistaken charges. It is also important insofar as the specificity which comes from making distinctions will facilitate efforts to reach a comprehensive understanding of what accounts for the remarkable prevalence of blacks in jails and prisons.

A closely associated problem is determining whether, or for whom, a given disparity is harmful. Some critics attack as "racist" the policy under which people who traffic in crack cocaine are more harshly sentenced than people who traffic in powder cocaine, since crack's clientele is overwhelmingly black and powder's clientele includes more whites. But is the black population *hurt* when traffickers in crack cocaine suffer longer prison sentences than those who deal in powdered cocaine or *helped* by incarcerating for longer periods those who use and sell a drug that has had an especially devastating effect on African-American communities? (For more on this issue, see pp. 364–386.) Some critics attack as racist urban curfews that regulate youngsters on the grounds that such curfews will disproportionately fall upon minority youngsters. But are black communities *hurt* by curfews which limit the late-night activities of minors or *helped* insofar as some of their residents feel more secure because of the curfews? Some critics attack as racist police crackdowns on violent gangs because such actions will disproportionately affect black members of gangs. But are black communities *hurt* by police crackdowns on violent gangs or *helped* by the destabilization of gangs that terrorize those who live in their midst? Some critics attack as racist prosecutions of pregnant drug addicts on the grounds that such prosecutions disproportionately burden blacks. But, on balance, are black communities *hurt* by prosecutions of pregnant women for using illicit drugs harmful to their unborn babies or *helped* by interventions which may at least plausibly deter conduct that will put black unborn children at risk? (For more on this issue, see pp. 352–364.) How can "hurt" and "help" be measured and distinguished? And what branch and level of government is best positioned to make and respond to such measurements? Often ignored or even repressed by leading figures in the fourth camp, these questions need to be raised and answered.

In my view, it is often unclear whether a social policy that is silent as to race and devoid of a covert racial purpose is harmful or helpful to blacks as a whole since, typically, such a policy will burden some blacks and benefit others. This makes it difficult to determine whether the policy represents a net plus or minus for African-Americans as a group. That is one (often overlooked) reason why, in the absence of persuasive proof that a law was enacted for the *purpose* of treating one racial group differently than another (or some other clear constitutional violation), courts should permit elected policymakers to determine what is in the best interest of their constituents. Courts must demand that officials respect the rights of all persons, regardless of race. In deciding whether rights have been infringed, however, courts should be careful to avoid conflating the interests of a subdivision of blacks—black suspects, defendants, or convicts—with the interests of blacks as a whole.

Like many social disasters, crime afflicts African-Americans with a special vengeance; at most income levels, they are more likely to be raped, robbed, assaulted, and murdered than their white counterparts.* Thus, at the center of all discussions about racial justice and criminal law should be a recognition that black Americans are in dire need of

---

*According to the U.S. Justice Department's 1993 National Crime Victimization Survey report, blacks were more victimized by crimes of violence than whites at every income level except for the poorest income bracket (annual household income less than $7500). More striking is that whereas white victimization rates *declined* as income increased, black victimization rates *rose* at the higher income levels. According to the survey, whites in the highest income bracket ($75,000 or more) were the least victimized by crimes of violence (with a rate of 36.3 crimes per 1000 persons). By contrast, blacks in the highest income bracket were the most victimized group (with a rate of 104 crimes per 1000 persons). See U.S. Department of Justice, Criminal Victimization in the United States, *1993—A National Crime Victimization Survey Report* 23, 26–27 (May 1996). See also Andrew Hacker, *Two Nations: Black and White, Separate, Hostile, and Unequal,* 179–98 (1992); Harold M. Rose and Paula D. McClain, *Race, Place, and Risk: Black Homicide in Urban America* (1990); John J. DiIulio, Jr., "The Question of Black Crime," 117 *The Public Interest* 3 (1994).

protection against criminality. A sensible strategy of protection should include efforts to ameliorate the social ills that contribute to criminality, including poverty, child abuse, and the deterioration of civic agencies of social support. A sensible strategy of protection should also include, however, efforts aimed toward apprehending, incapacitating, deterring, and punishing criminals. To accomplish those essential tasks requires a well-functioning system of law enforcement. Yet, too often, those in the fourth camp are unduly hostile to officials charged with enforcing criminal laws, insufficiently attentive to victims and potential victims of crime, and overly protective of suspects and convicted felons.

Some will question my decision to allocate considerable space and energy to a critical engagement with the fourth camp. After all, it is relatively weak politically. Represented at its best by the likes of Jesse Jackson, the National Association for the Advancement of Colored People, and the Congressional Black Caucus, the fourth camp is largely marooned on the left end of the American political spectrum. Although marginal within American political culture at large, this camp's dominant views regarding race relations and the administration of criminal law exert considerable influence within African-American communities.[24] To understand those views one must consider the association of crime with blackness and African-Americans' reactions to this debilitating linkage.

African-American Responses to the Association of Crime with Blackness: Toward a New Politics of Respectability

Many groups in America have been vilified by allegations that they harbor "racial instincts" for certain types of criminality.[25] Commentators and politicians have long stigmatized Italian-Americans, for instance, by associating them with the Mafia.[26] Jews, too, have been stigmatized as peculiarly susceptible, on account of their "race," to certain forms of criminality. Early in this century, officials and commentators drew attention to "Jewish crime" in the predominantly Jewish Lower East Side of Manhattan, wielding statistics of social pathology in a fashion calculated to smear Jews with an innuendo of racial debility.[27]

The racial reputation of blacks, however, has been uniquely besieged.* Some defenders of slavery pointed to blacks' alleged racial propensity to engage in crime as a justification for enslaving them. A century ago, belief in the racial tendency of Negroes to commit horrendous crimes was so strong that respected intellectuals defended lynching as a necessary mode of discipline. "Have American Negroes Too Much Liberty?" Charles Henry Smith asked in 1893. Yes, he replied, because of their *racial* penchant for scurrilous crimes, especially rape.[28] The idea that blacks are racially predisposed toward criminality, or at least certain sorts of crime, continues to shadow discussions of race relations and crime. It helps to explain the common use of the term "black crime" long after the disappearance of references to "Jewish crime" or "Italian crime."[29]

The historically besmirched reputation of blacks, however, is not the only force that encourages a perceived association of Negroes with criminality. Influential as well are two other phenomena. One is a popular fixation on crime. Although crime is undoubtedly a "real" menace, sellers of news and politicians who stand to benefit from increasing the anxieties of voters have often exaggerated the scope of that menace.[30] The other phenomenon is that a notably large proportion of the crimes that people fear most—aggravated assault, robbery, rape, murder—are committed by persons who happen to be black.†

---

*As Gunnar Myrdal observed, "[The Negro's] name is the antonym of white. As the color white is associated with everything good, with Christ and the angels, with heaven, fairness, cleanliness, virtue, intelligence, courage, and progress, so black has, through the ages, carried associations with all that is bad and low . . . the Negro is believed to be stupid, immoral, diseased, lazy, incompetent, and *dangerous*—dangerous to the white man's virtue and social order." *An American Dilemma: The Negro Problem and Modern Democracy*, vol. 2 (Twentieth Anniversary Edition), 98, 100 (1944 [1964]).

†Some observers suspect that racial prejudice plays a role in selecting which types of crime become the targets of public outrage and disgust. Why, they ask, do politicians attack street crime—murder, rape, robbery, burglary, and the like—so much more ferociously than white-collar crime—insider trading, bank fraud, anti-trust offenses, and so forth. See, e.g., Richard Delgado, "Rodrigo's Eighth Chronicle: Black Crime, White Fears—On the Social Construction of Threat," 80 *Virginia Law Review* 503 (1994). Racial prejudice in its many guises is a sufficiently powerful presence in American life that this hypothesis cannot be immediately discounted as wholly im-

These phenomena reinforce one another. Racist perceptions of blacks have given energy to policies and practices (such as racial exclusion in housing, impoverished schooling, and stingy social welfare programs) that have facilitated the growth of egregious, crime-spawning conditions that millions of Americans face in urban slums and rural backwaters across the nation.[31] A substantial number of voters both fear and resent the so-called "undeserving" poor, particularly those among them who are colored, a sector of the population that many perceive as especially dangerous and unworthy.[32] When voters, politicians, judges, and other shapers of public policy perform the rough calculations of costs and benefits that structure their decisions, undervaluation of the worth and promise of people with dark skins explains, to some degree,

---

plausible. I doubt, though, that racial prejudice accounts for much, if any, of the priority that most people give to street crime over white-collar crime. Differences in public response are most likely attributable to differences in the nature of the offenses in question as opposed to differences in the racial demographics of perpetrators. The racial discrimination thesis would be stronger if it revealed a sizable population (of any hue) that was more fearful of white-collar crime than street crime. Absent that showing, it seems to me likely that differentiation between street and white-collar crime is rooted in a sensible perception that the harm wrought by the former is more personally threatening than harms wrought by the latter. Explaining why most Americans are less concerned about tax fraud than robbery, Christopher Jencks notes that "[u]nlike robbery, tax evasion has no individual victims. It forces the rest of us to pay higher taxes than we otherwise would, but it does not create . . . the same sense of personal violation. . . . Given a choice, almost everyone would rather be robbed by computer than at gunpoint." Jencks, *Rethinking Social Policy: Race, Poverty and the Underclass* 93 (1992).

Furthermore, while there is a deeply and widely held impression—one that I share—that the judicial system treats white-collar offenders with discriminatory and wrongful leniency because of their status, important scholarship challenges that belief. See David Weisburd, Stanton Wheeler, Elin Waring, and Nancy Bode, *Crimes of the Middle Class: White-Collar Offenders in the Federal Courts* (1991); Stanton Wheeler, Kenneth Minn, Austin Sarat, *Sitting in Judgment: The Sentencing of White-Collar Criminals* (1988); David Weisburd, Elin Waring, and Stanton Wheeler, "Clan, Status, and the Punishment of White-Collar Criminals," 15 *Law and Social Inquiry* 223 (1990); Stanton Wheeler, David Weisburd, and Nancy Bode, "Sentencing the White-Collar Offender: Rhetoric and Reality," 47 *American Sociological Review* 641 (1982).

why it is that in so many areas the interests of colored people receive unequal attention.

On the other hand, the disproportionate prevalence of African-Americans in the population of street criminals functions to create or exacerbate racial prejudice by providing grounds for viewing blacks in general with heightened suspicion. As Thomas and Mary Edsall observe, "For many white voters living in major cities, no issue is more divisive than crime, and no issue more undermines the prospects for lessening the racial stereotyping that forms the basis of prejudice.[33] Consider, for example, the person who, responding to racial cues, avoids young black men while walking alone in urban areas at night. This person may resort to this self-protective maneuver without racial hostility and knowing that his strategy is overly inclusive, causing him to avoid many virtuous people who mean him no harm. He may do this knowing that his action, in conjunction with similar actions by others, will harm young black men by stigmatizing and isolating them. But he may pursue his policy nonetheless, mainly for two reasons. One is that, if he has calculated accurately, his policy will indeed provide him with greater security. The second is that his policy costs him less than plausible alternatives. One alternative might be to purchase a car. But perhaps he has no money for that. Another alternative would be to pay no mind to race and seek self-protection only when the actual (as opposed to the feared) conduct of others warrants such a response. But the cost of waiting and individualizing one's judgment may be diminished security; sometimes it is too late to avoid a person when he finally gives you concrete reasons for doing so.

Jesse Jackson memorably exhibited the way in which such calculations can influence even those who are fervent champions of black advancement. "There is nothing more painful for me at this stage in my life," he stated in 1994, "than to walk down the street and hear footsteps and start to think about robbery and then look around and see it's somebody white and feel relieved."[34]* The reason he felt relief was not that

---

*Consider also the following comments. The first is by Theodore A. McKee, a black judge on the United States Court of Appeals for the Third Circuit:

> If I'm walking down a street in Center City Philadelphia at two in the morning and I hear some footsteps behind me and I turn around and there

he prefers whites or dislikes blacks. He felt relief because he estimated that he stood a marginally greater risk of being robbed by a black person than by someone white.

The calculation that prompted Jackson to feel relief is a large part of what makes the linkage between blackness and criminality so far-reaching in its destructive ramifications—from strategies of self-help by which individuals (blacks as well as whites) fearfully avoid African-Americans (particularly men) in public spaces,[35] to decisions to discriminate against African-Americans on the grounds that they are more likely than others either to scare off customers or to prey upon the businesses that hire them,[36] to refusals to sell houses to blacks for fear that crime will follow and destroy neighborhoods,[37] to legal doctrines which authorize law enforcement officials to view blackness itself as a predictor of wrongdoing (see pp. 136–163),[38] to appeals in political campaigns that are clearly designed to both incite and address anxieties that stem not simply from fear of criminality in general but fear of the criminality of blacks in particular.[39] The association of crime with blackness is

---

are a couple a young white dudes behind me, I am probably not going to get very uptight. I'm probably not going to have the same reaction if I turn around and there is the proverbial Black urban youth behind me. Now if I can have this reaction—and I'm a Black male who has studied martial arts for twenty some odd years and can defend myself—I can't help but think that the average white judge in the situation will have a reaction that is ten times more intense.

Quoted in Linn Washington, *Black Judges on Justice: Perspectives from the Bench*, 71 (1994).

The second story is recounted by Professor Jean Bethke Elshtain:

Several years ago, my daughter Heidi was a student at the Pratt Art Institute in a pretty tough Brooklyn neighborhood. She called me, very upset, and said she was afraid she was becoming a racist. She said that when she saw a cluster of young black men together on a street-corner, she crossed over and tried to avoid them. She also told me there had been some muggings and assaults—in fact, a few months after she called, a friend of hers at Pratt was murdered. I told her that I didn't think she was becoming a racist but rather dealing with the realities of the environment in which she lived where certain precautions have to be taken.

See "Race and Racism: American Dilemma Revisited," *Salmagundi*, nos. 104–105, 24 (1994–1995).

thus of great importance. As long as it exists, efforts to advance the fortunes of African-Americans will remain heavily encumbered.

Many blacks are aware of the burdens placed upon them because of the fears, resentments, and stereotypes generated in part by the misdeeds of black criminals. From this awareness stems a deeply rooted impulse in African-American culture to distinguish sharply between "good" and "bad" Negroes.* Every community erects boundaries demarcating acceptable from unacceptable conduct. What makes this commonplace activity distinctive among blacks is the keenly felt sense that it implicates not only the security of law-abiding blacks vis-à-vis criminals but also the reputation of blacks as a collectivity in the eyes of whites. This urge to differentiate between "good" and "bad" Negroes is an important feature of what Professor Evelyn Brooks Higginbotham has termed "the politics of respectability."[40]

The principal tenet of the politics of respectability is that, freed of crippling, invidious racial discriminations, blacks are capable of meeting the established moral standards of white middle-class Americans. Proponents of the politics of respectability exhort blacks to accept and meet these standards, even while they are being discriminated against wrongly (in hypocritical violation of these standards). They maintain that while some blacks succeed even in the teeth of discouraging racial oppression, many more would succeed in the absence of racial restrictions. Insistence that blacks are worthy of respect is the central belief animating the politics of respectability. One of its strategies is to distance as many blacks as far as possible from negative stereotypes used to justify racial discrimination against all Negroes.

---

*Factions within other minority groups have also promoted politics of respectability. This is certainly true of Jews. Early in this century, when the criminality of some Jews provided the occasion for anti-Semitic diatribes hurtful to all Jews, certain Jewish leaders responded by criticizing bigoted overgeneralizations and—more relevant to the immediate point—acting against Jewish criminals. In 1912, Jewish philanthropists in New York quietly established a Bureau of Social Morals, which collected incriminating evidence on Jewish criminals and criminal organizations and turned it over to local prosecuting authorities. See Howard M. Sachar, *A History of the Jews in America*, 171–172 (1992).

Blacks of a wide variety of ideological persuasions have assimilated into their programs the politics of respectability. Hence W.E.B. DuBois urged "the Best" blacks to "guide the Mass away from [the] contamination and death of the Worst."[41] S. Willie Layton, a leading figure of the women's movement in the black Baptist church, declared to her colleagues, "The misfortune not to be judged [on the same terms as whites] behooves us to become more careful until we have gained a controlling influence to contradict the verdict already gone forth."[42] More recently, the potency of the politics of respectability was dramatically illustrated by the organizers of the Million Man March who voiced a desire to uplift the racial reputation of African-American men.*

Deeply rooted in African-American political culture, the politics of respectability is also prone to excesses that have limited its attractiveness. First, some of its proponents have displayed an undue fear of antagonizing whites. Here I think of black opponents of the civil rights movement in the late 1950s and early 1960s. Among the most ruthless enemies of civil rights activists on some college campuses, for example, were anxious black administrators.[43]

Second, the desire of some blacks to be seen as respectable has been so overwhelming that it has impelled them, pathetically, to shun anything that might remotely be associated with "bad Negroes"—from dark skin, to political activism, to cultural artifacts such as jazz, soul music, and rap.[44] Third, concern for respectability has led some analysts to underestimate the power of the forces which push people subject to severe deprivation toward criminal conduct. Properly rejecting the notion that poverty strips people of all choice to avoid crime, these analysts unduly minimize the extent to which poverty and its vicious companions reduce the amount of choice available to black impoverished youngsters.

---

*Illustrative of this feature of the Million Man March was the Million Man March Pledge which declared, in part: "I, ———, pledge that from this day forward I will strive to improve myself spiritually, morally, mentally, socially, politically, and economically for the benefit of myself, my family and my people. . . . I, ———, pledge that from this day forward I will never raise my hand with a knife or a gun to beat, cut, or shoot any member of my family or any human being except in defense." *Million Man March/Day of Absence: A Commemorative Anthology*, 29 (Haki R. Madhubuti and Maulana Karenga, eds., 1996).

Fourth, some proponents of the politics of respectability have neglected the webs of commonality that connect criminals to law-abiding members of communities. Crime war "hawks" sometimes forget, as Glenn Loury observes, "that the young black men wreaking havoc in the ghetto are still 'our youngsters' in the eyes of many of the decent poor and working class black people who are often their victims."[45] Fifth, obsession with racial reputation has, on occasion, prompted an egregious toleration of racist attacks which, by implication, threaten *all* black people and not simply the "bad Negroes." The most dramatic illustration of this tendency was the position taken by some black intellectuals and civic leaders around the turn of the century with respect to lynching, a subject to which I shall return later (see pp. 41–63). Many blacks condemned lynching unequivocally, but some, traduced by their yearning for respectability, endorsed the theory of lynching's apologists. In 1899, commenting on the rising toll of lynchings, the 71st Annual Conference of the African Methodist Episcopal Zion Church in Philadelphia unanimously condemned "those worthless negroes whose shiftlessness leads them into the commission of heinous crimes."[46] Alluding to the lynching of a black man accused of rape, the Reverend George Alexander McGuire stressed the horror of the alleged crime while offering no critique of the lawless reaction. Speaking to an audience of African-Americans at a high school graduation in 1903, McGuire declared that they must "ostracize such brutes in their own race."[47]

Despite the mistakes of some who have enthusiastically championed the politics of respectability, its core intuitions are sound, two of which are particularly pertinent currently. One is that the principal injury suffered by African-Americans in relation to criminal matters is not overenforcement but underenforcement of the laws. Whereas mistreatment of suspects, defendants, and criminals has often been used as an instrument of racial oppression, more burdensome now in the day-to-day lives of African-Americans are private, violent criminals (typically black) who attack those most vulnerable without regard to racial identity. Like many activities in America, crime tends to be racially segmented; four-fifths of violent crimes are committed by persons of the same race as their victims.[48] Hence, behind high rates of blacks perpetrating violent crimes are high rates of black victimization. Black teenagers are nine times more likely to be murdered than their white counterparts. While young black men were murdered at the rate of about 45 per 100,000 in 1960, by 1990 the rate was 140 per 100,000. By contrast, in 1990 for young white men the rate was 20 murder victims per 100,000.[49] One out of every twenty-one black men can expect to be murdered, a death rate double that of American servicemen in World War II.[50] Such figures place the now-mythic beating of Rodney King in a somewhat different light than it is typically put. As Gerry G. Watts acidly comments, "Racist white cops, however vicious, are ultimately minor irritants when compared to the viciousness of the black gangs and wanton violence."[51]

Of course, even if violent, racially motivated wrongdoing by police is lesser in quantity than violent wrongdoing engaged in by criminals, the peculiar character of official wrongdoing—the fact that its authors are officers of the state sworn to uphold the law—accentuates its malevolent force and influence. Moreover, racist discrimination by law enforcement officers has often played a role in creating the conditions that make blacks more vulnerable than whites to destructive criminality. For one thing, throughout American history, white officials have tolerated black-on-black crime ("what do you expect of *those* people") while zealously punishing black-on-white transgressions. Still, the main point stands: In terms of misery inflicted by direct criminal violence, blacks (and other people of color) suffer more from the criminal acts of their racial "brothers" and "sisters" than they do from the racist misconduct of white police officers.

A second core intuition of the politics of respectability is that, for a stigmatized racial minority, successful efforts to move upward in society must be accompanied at every step by a keen attentiveness to the morality of means, the reputation of the group, and the need to be extra-careful in order to avoid the derogatory charges lying in wait in a hostile environment. These are among the reasons that Thurgood Marshall, working on behalf of the National Association for the Advancement of Colored People, carefully investigated the circumstances surrounding a case before he would represent a person charged with committing a crime. Initially, he allowed the NAACP to represent only defendants whom he believed to be innocent. In 1943, for example, Marshall declined to represent a black sixteen year old who had been sentenced to death for rape and who had participated in a jail break. In Marshall's view the youngster was "not the type of person to justify our intervention."[52] Later, Marshall loosened his policy and represented defendants even if he believed them to be guilty as long as he also believed that they had been denied a fair trial. At no point, however, did he take the position that racism excuses thuggery when perpetrated by blacks.[53] Marshall sought to right miscarriages of justice, not excuse, much less canonize, criminals who happen to be black.

It should be clear by now that I am recommending a politics of respectability, albeit a version that steers clear of the excesses noted above. Some readers will undoubtedly object on the grounds that, however modified, the politics of respectability smells of Uncle Tomism. It may have been a necessary concession earlier, they concede, but championing the politics of respectability today, they charge, is an anachronistic error. Obviously I disagree. In American political culture, the reputation of groups, be they religious denominations, labor unions, or racial groups, matters greatly.[54] For that reason alone, those dedicated to advancing the interests of African-Americans ought to urge them to conduct themselves in a fashion that, without sacrificing rights or dignity, elicits respect and sympathy rather than fear and anger from colleagues of other races. The politics of respectability, for example, would have cautioned against the triumphalist celebrations that followed the acquittal of O.J. Simpson on the grounds, among others, that such displays would singe the sensibilities of many, particularly whites, who perceived the facts of the trial differently. Acting based on the notion that blacks need not be attuned to the way they are perceived by others has adversely affected the racial reputation of African-Americans, facilitating indifference to their plight.

Racial bigotry has been and remains a significant pollutant within the administration of criminal justice. At the same time, bigotry also provokes protests that have prompted salutary reforms. Several of the most basic protections enjoyed by all Americans, for example, the right to an attorney when charged with a serious offense, the right to be free of torture, and the right to a trial absent mob intimidation, are protections that arose in response to the racially motivated mistreatment of black defendants (see pp. 92–107).

Not all reactions against racist misconduct have been so benign. The toxins of racism have also generated antibodies that are destructive. One is a tendency to deny troublesome realities. This explains why some observers, even in the face of overwhelming evidence, deny claims that blacks commit a disproportionate percentage of street crimes.[55] Some deniers maintain that the apparent disproportionate prevalence of black street criminals is an illusion created by news and popular entertainment media. Others maintain that an exaggerated image of the black man as criminal stems from a racially discriminatory criminal justice apparatus that systematically disadvantages black men by watching them more closely than whites, by arresting them more frequently under circumstances in which whites are not arrested, and by treating them more harshly than similarly situated whites.

The deniers have a point. First, racial discrimination by law enforcement officials does probably distort, at least to some extent, the racial demographics of arrests and imprisonment. Racially discriminatory arrests and investigations probably do play some small role in the racial demographics of crime statistics. Second, racists do and will use evidence of disproportionate rates of criminal activity by blacks to argue against racial egalitarianism. White supremacists, for example, have repeatedly used such evidence to attack desegregation.[56]

Derogatory attacks cannot be responded to effectively, however, by denying facts that cannot sensibly be denied. As Representative Barney Frank writes, "Whenever something is obvious and has a significant impact on people's lives, those who try to make believe it does not exist cede control of the debate to those who are willing to talk about it."[57] That relative to their percentage of the population, blacks commit more street crime than do whites is a fact and not a figment of a Negrophobe's imagination.* Although blacks constitute only around 12 percent of the national population, in 1992, 44.8 percent of all persons arrested for violent

---

*This proposition has ceased to be controversial among most careful students of crime in America. Compare Michael Tonry, *Malign Neglect: Race, Crime, and Punishment in America*, 3 (1995), and Elliott Currie, *Confronting Crime: An American Challenge*, 152–160 (1985), with James Q. Wilson and Richard J. Herrnstein, *Crime and Human Nature*, 461–468 (1985). This racial disproportionality is not new. It has been evident throughout much of this century. See, e.g., Roger Lane, *Roots of Violence in Black Philadelphia*, 1860–1900 (1986), and Charles E. Silberman, *Criminal Violence, Criminal Justice*, 159–167 (1978).

crimes were black. Blacks made up 55.1 percent of those arrested for homicide, 42.8 percent of those arrested for rape, and 60.9 percent of those arrested for robbery.[58] Even after one makes a reasonable discount to offset some degree of racial discrimination in law enforcement, a strikingly large disproportionality remains.

Incarceration rates are more probative of actual criminal activity than arrest rates since the processes that surround convictions and plea bargains, albeit far from perfect, are still more protective than those which surround mere arrest.[59] It is significant, then, that the statistics showing disproportionate arrests of blacks are mirrored by statistics showing disproportionate imprisonment. By the early 1990s, blacks outnumbered whites in American prisons. In 1990, for every 100,000 whites, about 289 were in jail or prison. For every 100,000 blacks, about 1,860 were in jail or prison.[60]

Reports by victims of crime describing those who robbed or attacked them corroborate these patterns. Here, too, of course, there is room for error, bias, and deceit to distort an accurate portrayal of reality. Susan Smith, the white woman who accused a black man of abducting her children (although she herself killed them), and Charles Stuart, the white man who accused a black man of killing his wife (although Stuart himself almost certainly committed the murder) are two well-known examples of false reports by purported victims of crime.[61] It is unlikely, however, that falsehoods account for the large racial disparities evident in the cumulative portrait produced by victimization reports. Such reports typically made by ordinary citizens with nothing to gain by lying confirm the pattern revealed by official reports of arrest and incarceration rates,[62] a pattern in which the percentage of street crimes perpetuated by blacks is considerably greater than the percentage of blacks in the population at large.[63] Posing the question, "Is racial bias in the criminal justice system the principal reason that proportionately so many more blacks than whites are in prison?," Professor Michael Tonry, a leading liberal expert on sentencing, answers rightly: "The main reason that black incarceration rates are substantially higher than those for whites is that black crime rates for imprisonable crimes are substantially higher than those for whites."[64]

Given the deprivations blacks have faced, it should come as no surprise that, relative to their proportion of the population, blacks are more likely than whites to commit street crimes.[65] The legacy of legal racism, modern discrimination, and the failures of government to provide opportunities to the disadvantaged have combined to create criminogenic conditions in which too many black Americans are forced by circumstances to live. That is a reality indifferent to the embarrassment of those ashamed of the criminality that poor economic, social, cultural, and moral conditions spawn. Shame has more to do with denying the true extent of criminality perpetrated by blacks than has hitherto been recognized. Some deniers are simply embarrassed by the criminal conduct that plays such an obviously large role in many African-American communities. Acknowledging the prevalence of that misconduct and its consequences is essential, however, to educating and mobilizing the political will necessary to address the nation's criminogenic social problems.

In stressing the need to address the socioeconomic as well as the moral conditions that spawn criminality, I minimize neither personal responsibility for criminal acts nor the need to punish criminality. Rather, I posit the need to forswear either/or dichotomies that avoid the complications posed by complex realities. Society faces both real racism and real criminality, a long-term need to address socioeconomic inequities and a short-term need to provide for public safety *now*, a crisis in individual moralities and a crisis of social justice.

Some observers have been driven to doubt the very possibility of a racially just system of law within the United States. Suspicion and anger have pushed them to identify law enforcement completely with oppression and even to embrace vicious criminals as heroic rebels. In his classic *An American Dilemma*, Gunnar Myrdal glimpsed this dynamic at work at mid-century in the American South:

> The Negroes . . . are hurt in their trust that the law is impartial, that the court and the police are their protection, and, indeed, that they belong to an orderly society which has set up this machinery for common security and welfare. They will not feel confidence in, and loyalty toward, a legal order which is entirely out of their control and which they sense to be inequitable and merely part of the system of caste oppression. Solidarity then develops easily in the Negro

group, a solidarity against the law and the police. The arrested Negro often acquires the prestige of a victim, a martyr, or a hero, even when he is simply a criminal.[66]

Now, at the close of the twentieth century, despite notable reforms, this dynamic is still at work. It largely explains why many blacks rallied around the gang of boys who raped a white jogger in New York's Central Park,[67] around Marion Barry, the mayor of Washington, D.C., who was caught red-handed smoking cocaine,* around Alcee Hastings, the federal district court judge who, based on allegations of corruption, was ousted from office by the U.S. Senate (only to be subsequently elected to the House of Representatives),[68] around Damian Williams and the other hooligans who gained notoriety when they were filmed beating a hapless white truck driver (Reginald Denny) in the early hours of the Los Angeles riot of 1992,[69] and around Mike Tyson, the boxing champion, when he was imprisoned for rape.[70] This dynamic was also glaringly present in the response to the prosecution of O.J. Simpson, the football star tried for murdering two whites, including his former wife, in the most widely publicized trial in American history.[71] Before the murders, Simpson ignored, and was largely ignored by, most blacks. After Simpson was indicted, however, and even more after his attorneys claimed that he had been framed by at least one racially prejudiced police officer, many blacks perceived Simpson as the embodiment of all black men and accordingly rallied to his cause.[72] One black celebrant of Simpson's acquittal spoke for scores of others when, describing his understanding of the case, he stated bluntly:

[A] black man was charged with killing a white woman—a blond white woman at that . . . —and the court said he didn't do it. Hell,

*Paul Butler, a former prosecutor, states that there were blacks, including himself, in the U.S. Attorney's Office in Washington, D.C., who privately hoped that Marion Barry would be acquitted because they believed that their office's prosecution of the mayor was racist. Butler has subsequently called upon black jurors to engage in jury nullification in cases involving black defendants charged with nonviolent crimes. See Paul Butler, "Racially Based Jury Nullification: Black Power in the Criminal Justice System," 105 *Yale Law Journal* 677 (1995). For my critique of Butler, see pp. 295–310.

that's worth celebrating. We never win *anything*. I don't care if he did do it. This is a victory for all those brothers sitting in jail right now 'cause the system got its foot on their necks.[73]

The inversion of values which martyrizes criminals stems in part from the crisis of legitimacy that afflicts the administration of criminal law. For a long time, criminal law—not simply the biased administration of law but the law itself—was the enemy of African-Americans. In many places, for several generations, it was a crime for blacks to learn to read, to flee enslavement, or to defend themselves, their families, or their friends from physical abuse. It was a crime, in sum, for blacks to do all sorts of things deemed to be permissible or admirable when done by others. More recently, during the civil rights era, African-Americans violated criminal laws (although many of these "laws" were subsequently invalidated) to uproot the Jim Crow system. That is why so many African-Americans lionized in black communities have had "criminal" records. The list includes Martin Luther King, Jr., Robert Moses, Fannie Lou Hamer, Rosa Parks, and John Lewis. By using the criminal law against these and others involved in resisting racial oppression, officials have destabilized the moral meaning of conforming to law and violating it. That is why being a "good," law-abiding Negro came to be associated with acquiescence to oppression, why James Baldwin wrote in 1966 that "to respect the law in the context in which the Negro finds himself is simply to surrender...self-respect,"[74] and why being a "crazy," law-breaking "bad nigger" came to be associated with laudable rebelliousness.[75]

For many blacks, Professor Regina Austin observes, "there has historically been a subtle admiration of criminals who are bold and brazen in their defiance of the legal regime of the external enemy."[76] Robert Wideman, presently serving a life sentence for felony murder, vividly expresses this sentiment. Applauding black criminals, Wideman states:

We can't help but feel some satisfaction, seeing a brother, a black man, get over on these people, on their system without playing by their rules. No matter how much we have incorporated these rules as our own, we know that they were forced on us by people who did not have our best interests at heart.... [We black people] look at [this gangster or player or whatever label you give these brothers] with some sense of pride and admiration. . . . We know they represent rebellion.[77]

His sentiments are shared by a substantial number of Americans. Precisely how many is difficult to say. That the numbers are significant, however, is clear. One sees reflections of this sentiment in such things as expressions of admiration for "the spook who sat by the door," the fictional black terrorist hero in a novel of racial revenge set in the 1960s, in the applause for the character "Super Fly," the black drug dealer who "stuck it to The Man" in one of the leading "blacksploitation" films of the 1970s, in the popularity of "gangsta rappers" who create groups like the Lenchmob Crew, companies like Death Row Records, and songs like "Cop Killer," the fashionableness of the "cool pose" by which many young men attempt to assert their masculinity by adopting a defiant, confrontational, "badman" style of conduct, and in expressions of popular support voiced for people like Larry Davis (an alleged murderer who wounded several police officers in a highly publicized shootout with police in New York City).[78]

Sympathetic to this perspective is a distinctive racial critique of the criminal justice system according to which the legal order is pervasively infected by a systematic racial bias that nullifies its legitimacy. Proponents of this argument portray the police as colonial forces of occupation, prisons as centers of racist oppression, and the law as merely the white man's law. As articulated by one proponent of this critique, the white power structure "constructs crime in terms of race and race in terms of crime" and thereby creates a "racial ideology of crime that sustains continued white domination of blacks in the guise of crime control."[79] Such claims reinforce hostility toward the agencies of crime control, sympathetic identification with convicts, and a commitment to policies aimed at constraining as much as possible the powers of law enforcement authorities. Proponents of this view point to the history of criminal law in the United States as justification for their position. They assert, rightly, that racial bigotry suffuses this history. That is why I devote much of this book to an exploration of the history of racial oppression in the administration of criminal law. The burden of the past weighs upon us.

Some commentators proceed, however, as if there has been *no* progress in American race relations, as if there exists little difference between the laws, practices, and beliefs prevalent during the eras of slavery and *de jure* segregation and those prevalent today, as if African-Americans have completely failed in efforts to participate in shaping and implementing government policy, as if black legislators, mayors, attorneys, judges, jurors, and chiefs of police do not exist. But, of course, there has been substantial, beneficial change in race relations. One development in particular highlights this point. Until recently, playing the "race card" almost always meant whites exploiting racial power. Now, in enough circumstances to make the matter worth discussing, playing the race card also refers to blacks effectively exploiting racial power (see pp. 295–310). Now black attorneys face the question whether they should seek to elicit the racial loyalties of black jurors or judges on behalf of clients. Now black jurors and judges face the question whether they should respond to such appeals. These facts illustrate that, while racial animus against blacks still strongly grips American society, circumstances have indeed changed. My exploration of race relations in the administration of criminal law attempts to give due recognition to this ongoing transformation. Indeed, it is precisely because of the conflicting, ambiguous tendencies in American law and politics that a reconsideration of the race question in American criminal justice is especially urgent.

2.

History:
Unequal Protection

"Goodness gracious, anybody hurt?"
"No'm, killed a nigger."
—Mark Twain, *Huckleberry Finn*

DELIBERATELY WITHHOLDING PROTECTION against criminality (or conduct that should be deemed criminal) is one of the most destructive forms of oppression that has been visited upon African-Americans. The specter of the wrongly convicted black defendant rushed to punishment by a racially biased process is haunting and shall be attended to below. As bad as that problem has been though, even worse is racially selective underprotection. This form of discrimination is worse because it has directly and adversely affected more people than have episodic misjudgments of guilt. Racially selective underprotection is also worse in the sense that society is not as well equipped to combat it. Even before the abolition of slavery, officials everywhere acknowledged, at least in principle, that government is obliged to punish for crimes only duly convicted persons, regardless of race. Much more difficult to establish has been the idea that government is obliged to protect blacks from crime on the same terms as it protects whites.

The Failure to Protect Slaves from Murder and Assault and Battery in Antebellum America

The racial policy of withholding protection from blacks has its roots in slavery. The slave, William Goodell aptly observed, "is under the *control* of law, though *unprotected by* law, and can know law only as an enemy, and not as a friend."[1] Racial status and slave status, though typically overlapping, were not identical. By the time of the founding of the United States, virtually all slaves were black, although not all blacks were slaves. There did exist a small cadre of free blacks. State governments, however, frequently treated free blacks and enslaved blacks similarly because whites decided that keeping the latter securely in thrall entailed degrading the status of the former.[2] Part of the strategy for denigrating all blacks involved depriving them of legal protections against conduct that was deemed criminal when visited upon whites. Hence, in the slave South (the locus of the great mass of the black population in antebellum America), officials decriminalized violence inflicted upon blacks to the extent thought necessary to assert and preserve white supremacy. Throughout the antebellum period, the law shielded slaveowners from criminal liability for killing a slave if death resulted from violence administered for the purpose of subduing resistance or imposing discipline. As Andrew Fede observes, "Legislators expressly deprived slaves who were violently abused by whites of the protections of the common law of crimes by passing exculpatory acts that granted both slave masters and whites who were strangers to the slave legal rights to beat, whip, and kill bondsmen."[3] In 1798, for example, a North Carolina statute declared the killing of a slave to be a felony, but then added that the statute should not extend "to any person killing . . . any slave in the act of resistance to his lawful owner or master, or any slave dying under moderate correction."[4] In 1860, the Mississippi Supreme Court similarly condoned a master's killing of his slave to achieve submission. Reversing the manslaughter conviction of a master who had killed his slave during a dispute over the slave's method of performing a chore, the court remarked that if a slave resists, "then the master may use just such force as may be requisite to reduce his slave to obedience, even to the death of the slave, if that become[s] necessary . . . to maintain his lawful authority."[5]

Although courts did find on occasion that masters committed

crimes by killing slaves, such instances were notably rare. To be convicted, a master had to do something that was egregiously cruel even by the highly permissive standards of the slave regime. The brutality of Simeon Souther rose to this level. In 1850, in Hanover, Virginia, Souther was convicted of murdering Sam, one of his slaves, during the course of punishing him for drunkenness. According to the General Court of Virginia:

> [Sam] was tied to a tree and whipped with switches. When Souther became fatigued with the labour of whipping, he called upon a negro man of his, and made him cob Sam with a shingle. He also made a negro woman of his help to cob him. And after cobbing and whipping, he applied fire to the body of the slave; about his back, belly and private parts. He then caused him to be washed down with hot water, in which pods of red pepper had been steeped. The negro was also tied to a log and to the bed post with ropes, which choked him, and he was kicked and stamped by Souther. This sort of punishment was continued and repeated until the negro died under its infliction.[6]

Anything less than this level of barbarity was likely to be forgiven or regarded as part of a master's prerogative. Furthermore, even in those rare cases where the killing of a slave did result in the conviction of an owner, the severity of the punishment was often less than would have been inflicted had the victim of the violence been white. Souther, for example, was sentenced only to five years' imprisonment for his horrific murder of Sam.

Over time, the law became more protective of slaves, particularly with respect to persons other than their owners. Initially, some states refrained from imposing serious criminal penalties against violence directed at slaves regardless of the slave's relationship to the perpetrator. In the South Carolina slave codes promulgated between 1712 and 1740, even the willful and malicious killing of a slave by a stranger without claim to the slave's labor amounted to no more than a misdemeanor punishable by a fine and an obligation to compensate the deceased slave's owner. Later, statutory and judge-made law imposed higher levels of punishment. In 1821, the South Carolina legislature made the willful, malicious, and deliberate killing of a slave a capital offense. Although several motivations combined to produce this and similar reforms, one of the most important was a desire to protect slaveowners' economic investment in their human property against the depredations of resentful poor whites. As a South Carolina judge put the matter (albeit in a somewhat different context), "It can never be considered politic to subject a valuable species of property to the disposal of any unprincipled, unfeeling man in society."[7]

Slaves, however, never received the full measure of protection that the common law afforded to whites. Consider, for example, *State* v. *Tackett*,[8] a case in which the North Carolina Supreme Court reversed the conviction of a white man prosecuted for murdering a slave. The conflict between the deceased slave and the defendent stemmed from an illicit sexual relationship between the defendant and the wife of the slave, a free black woman. At trial, the defendent sought to introduce evidence that the slave was "a turbulent man . . . insolent and impudent to white people."[9] The judge, however, excluded this testimony and instructed the jury that the case "was to be determined by the same rules and principles of law as if the deceased had been a white man."[10] The supreme court decided that this standard and the evidentiary ruling to which it gave rise were erroneous:

> It exists in the nature of things, that where slavery prevails, the relations between a white man and a slave differs from that, which subsists between free persons; and every individual in the community feels and understands that the homicide of a slave may be extenuated by acts, which would not produce a legal provocation if done by a white person.[11]

According to the court, although neither words of reproach nor an insulting gesture would excuse the killing of a white person, such a killing might well be excused if such speech or conduct was offered by a "turbulent and disorderly" slave.[12]

The law governing other sorts of violence against slaves mirrored the evolution of the law governing homicide. Over time, slaves were accorded increasing protection against nonfatal assaults. Slaves even received additional protection against sadistic owners; several states eventually passed laws prohibiting masters from inflicting "cruel or unusual" punishments upon slaves. Like the law of homicide, however, the law of assault and battery deprived slaves of the protections accorded to whites.

Consider *State* v. *Mann*, perhaps the best known of all the cases relating to slavery and criminal law.[13] The defendant, John Mann, leased from an owner a slave named Lydia. During her period of bondage to Mann, Lydia committed what the North Carolina Supreme Court describes as "some small offense, for which the [D]efendant undertook to chastise her."[14] The court does not specify what sort of chastisement was attempted but does indicate that Lydia tried to run away. When she disregarded Mann's order to stop, he shot and wounded her. Mann was indicted and convicted for assault and battery, a remarkable event given the difficulties that authorities faced in bringing criminal prosecutions against whites for inflicting violence upon blacks. The North Carolina Supreme Court, however, unanimously reversed the conviction in an opinion written by Judge Thomas Ruffin, one of the most respected jurists in nineteenth-century America. "The enquiry here," Ruffin asserted, "is whether a cruel and unreasonable battery on a slave, by the hirer, is indictable."[15] Ruffin's answer was no:

> We cannot allow the right of the master to be brought into discussion in the Courts of Justice. The slave, to remain a slave, must be made sensible that there is no appeal from his master; that his power is in no instance, usurped; but is conferred by the laws of man at least, if not by the law of God.[16]

Unless expressly directed by the legislature, the courts should refrain from criminalizing even a cruel and unreasonable battery on a slave by a hirer because, according to Ruffin, the only thing that could create the obedience that slavery required was "uncontrolled authority over the body."[17] "The power of the master," he argued, "must be absolute, to render the submission of the slave perfect."[18]

The formalities of law should not be confused with what actually happens. Just because the legal order gave whites, particularly owners, broad leeway to brutalize slaves without fear of prosecution and punishment does not mean that whites characteristically did so. There were, after all, forms of social control other than law which regulated whites' behavior. These included conscience, regard for reputation, a desire to protect economic investment, and a sense that the overall protection of the slave system was best accomplished by showing slaves that the master class had a sense of honor.[19] These controls filled, to some degree, the vacuum created by the decision to withhold from slaves the protection afforded by law to free persons. These informal sources of discipline undoubtedly made the lives of slaves less miserable and desperate than they might otherwise have been. "It may be said with truth," W.E.B. DuBois observed, "that the law was often harsher than the practice."[20] Still, the dismal historical fact is that in many jurisdictions the law explicitly permitted slaves to be killed under circumstances in which it did not permit the killing of other human beings—a discrimination whose consequences continue to trouble America.

The Failure to Protect Slaves from Rape in Antebellum America

It is unclear to what extent black Americans are aware of the various ways in which their forebears were deliberately pushed outside the protections of the criminal law during the slavery era in order to make them more fully dependent upon whites. With respect to at least one type of violence, however, many black Americans are acutely conscious that their forebears were victimized by a policy of nonprotection. W.E.B. DuBois decried the "red stain of bastardy which two centuries of systematic legal defilement of Negro women [has] stamped upon [blacks]."[21] Malcolm X spoke of how he "learned to hate every drop of that white rapist's blood that is in me."[22] In the writings of Toni Morrison, Patricia Williams, and bell hooks, among others, the rape of slave women surfaces time and again as an unredressed violation.[23] From a very different vantage on the cultural spectrum, the rapper Ice Cube indicates in his songs that the memory of the widespread raping of slave women continues to rankle in the consciousness of a younger generation of African-Americans.[24]

The decision to leave slave women unprotected by criminal law accentuated their vulnerability to sexual abuse.[25] Sometimes the abuse was perpetrated by other slaves,[26] a fact highlighted by an appalling case decided by the High Court of Errors and Appeals for the State of Mississippi in 1859. In *George (a slave)* v. *The State*,[27] a male slave was convicted and sentenced to death for having had "carnal knowledge of a female slave, under ten years of age." His conviction was overturned on appeal. Asserting that slaves have no rights under the common law, Judge William L. Harris declared that courts must look to legislation alone to discover what rights a slave might have. Since no statute specifically protected slave girls or women from rape, no law was violated by inflicting sexual violence upon them. "We are satisfied," Harris declared, "that there is no act which embraces either the attempted or actual commission of a rape by a slave on a female slave."[28]

Subsequently, the Mississippi legislature enacted a statute that offered at least some protection to slave girls. It provided that "the actual or attempted commission of a rape by a negro or mulatto on a female negro or mulatto, under twelve years of age, is punishable with death or whipping, as the jury may decide."[29] The narrowness of the legislation, however, underscores the extent to which officials in the slave states, even when focusing on the problem of sexual abuse, discriminated against female slaves. The new law only prohibited rape committed on female slaves under the age of twelve; those who were older remained outside the protection of the criminal law. Moreover, the new law prohibited rape perpetrated only by "a negro or mulatto"; it was silent with respect to rape attempted or committed by whites.

White men often imposed themselves sexually upon slave women.[30] Rape and kindred forms of sexual exploitation by white men were the dangers that gave rise to Harriet Jacobs' haunting observation, based on her own experience as the victim of a sexually abusive master, that while "slavery is terrible for men . . . it is far more terrible for women." As Jacobs put it, "superadded to the burden common to all, [slave women] have wrongs, and sufferings, and mortifications peculiarly their own."[31]

Although the experience of slavery was suffused with the sexual abuse of slave women by their masters and other white men in authority over them, the law remained mute on the subject. That is because, as a definitional matter, the law did not view as a crime the rape of slave women by white men.[32] Consider the case of Celia, a teenager who, in June 1855, was pregnant for the third time as a result of the sexual assaults of her seventy-five-year-old owner.[33] After warning Robert Newsom, a successful farmer, that she would defend herself against any further assaults, Celia killed Newsom when he again tried to rape her. In the ensuing prosecution, a Missouri trial judge, affirmed by the state supreme court, refused to allow a jury instruction that the homicide could be excused or extenuated by the fact that Celia was seeking to defend herself. Instead, the trial judge told the jury that Celia should be found guilty of murder if she did, in fact, strike and kill Newsom, even if he "was in the habit of having intercourse with [her] . . . and went to her cabin on the night he was killed to have intercourse with her or for any other purpose."[34] After the judge erased the possibility of an excuse founded on self-defense,* the jury convicted Celia. The judge sentenced her to death but delayed the execution until the birth of Celia's child. After Celia gave birth to a dead baby, she was hanged.†

Free black women received a bit more protection than their enslaved sisters. For example, on at least six occasions between 1790 and 1833, Virginia authorities tried slaves for raping free black women.[35] That did not mean that free black women who were victims of sexual assaults were treated the same as white women. Reversing the conviction of a slave accused of raping a woman whose race was unmentioned in an indictment, the Tennessee Supreme Court ordered a new trial on the grounds that the indictment failed to note that the victim was a *white* woman. "Such an act committed upon a black woman," Judge Nathan Green observed, "would not be punished with death." The whiteness of the victim "gives to the offence its enormity."[36] Furthermore, the absence of cases involving white men suggests that on this score the free black woman was almost as unprotected as the enslaved black woman, especially insofar as blacks were precluded from testifying against whites.

Reconstruction and the Origins of Federal Intervention to Protect Blacks

During and after the Civil War, elevating the status of blacks by arming them with the protection of the criminal law proved to be an extraordi-

---

*The jury could have voted to acquit notwithstanding the judge's instruction and the incriminating evidence. It did not do so, however, either as a matter of choice or as a matter of ignorance. For discussions of race relations and jury nullification see pp. 59–66, 295–310.

†Regarding a more recent case of a black woman, Joan Little, who killed a white man who was attempting to assault her sexually, see James Reston, Jr., *The Innocence of Joan Little: A Southern Mystery* (1977); Fred Harwell, *A True Deliverance* (1979). Unlike Celia, Little was acquitted.

narily difficult endeavor. It was impeded by the reluctance of many whites in the North to change radically the nation's antebellum constitutional order and by the resistance of many whites in the South to any change at all.

An example of the reluctance pervasive among Northern whites is the protracted struggle that erupted during the Civil War over efforts to enact a federal law permitting blacks to testify against whites in federal courts regardless of limitations imposed by state laws. Many federal courts excluded blacks as witnesses because these courts adopted the rules of evidence of the states in which they were located. If the law of a given state denied blacks the right to testify against whites, federal courts in those states followed suit.[37]

In all of the Southern states and in several of the Northern ones, blacks (regardless of their status as slaves or freedpeople) were barred from testifying against whites.[38] "No matter how pure the character," the Ohio Supreme Court asserted in 1846,

> yet, if the color is not right, the man can not testify. The truth shall not be received from a black man, to settle a controversy where a white man is a party. Let a man be Christian or infidel . . . let him be of good character or bad; even let him be sunk to the lowest depths of degradation; he may be a witness in our courts if he is not black.[39]

Behind this exclusion was the widespread belief that, as a matter of racial character, blacks are mendacious and that it would therefore be unjust to use their racially tainted testimony in circumstances that put at risk the property or liberty of whites.[40]

This legal disability drastically undermined blacks' security; absent white witnesses, blacks could be swindled, assaulted, or killed with impunity.* The murder of William Johnson illustrates the point. In 1851 in

---

*Blacks are not the only people of color who have been excluded from the witness stand on the basis of race. A California statute enacted in 1850 provided that "no Black, or Mulatto person, or Indian, shall be allowed to give evidence in favor of, or against, a White man." *People* v. *Hall*, 4 Cal. 399 (1854). Under this law, a white man successfully annulled his conviction for murder on the grounds that it had been obtained in violation of the statute when Chinese witnesses were allowed to give testimony against him. Although the statute did not expressly mention people of Chinese

New Orleans, Johnson, a prosperous, slaveowning free Negro, got into a dispute with a white neighbor, whom he sued for trespass. In response, the neighbor killed Johnson. Prosecution, however, proved unavailing because the only witnesses to the murder were Negroes—Johnson's son and one of his slaves.*

In 1862, two years into the Civil War, U.S. Senator Charles Sumner proposed a law barring racial discrimination against black witnesses in federal court. He argued, in part, that this reform would allow loyal blacks to testify against disloyal whites for purposes of identifying those who had participated in rebellion against the Union. Sumner's proposal was rejected on the grounds that it would disturb the traditional and proper relationship between states and the federal government. Sumner responded by saying that the states should be permitted to keep their racially discriminatory rules of evidence. "They are beyond [the federal government's] control," he conceded. But he pleaded with his colleagues to bring the federal courts which were within their control "at last within the pale of civilization."[41] Only after three defeats and two years of agitation was Sumner able finally in 1864 to push through Congress a bill which enabled blacks to testify in all federal courts.[†42]

---

ancestry, the California Supreme Court ruled that they were embraced by the term "black." That term, the court ruled, "exclude[d] every one who is not of white blood." Ibid., 403. Elaborating further on reasons to exclude Chinese in particular from the witness box, the court asserted that their "mendacity is proverbial" and that they are "a race . . . whom nature has marked as inferior." Ibid., 405.

*On occasion the exclusion of blacks from the witness box directly harmed whites. Charged with murder, a white man sought to prove that he acted in self-defense by introducing the testimony of three black children, the only witnesses to the incident. The court, however, barred their testimony. See *Dupree* v. *State*, 33 Ala. 380 (1859). *See* generally Daniel J. Flanigan, "Criminal Procedure in Slave Trials in the Antebellum South," in *The Law of American Slavery*, 184–185 (Kermit L. Hall, ed., 1987).

†Inveighing against the racial exclusion, especially insofar as it barred free blacks as well as slaves from the witness box, Senator Sumner declared that "it would be difficult to point out any law, the spawn of cruelty or tyranny in ancient or modern times, exceeding in atrocity that by which a free population is thus despoiled of protection on account of color." U.S. Congress Senate Committee on Slavery and the Treatment of Freedmen. *Equality Before the Law in the Courts of the United States.* S. Rep. No. 25, 38th Cong., 1st Sess. at 10 (1864).

The most significant example of Southern whites' resistance to elevating the legal status of blacks after the Civil War was their unwillingness to recognize blacks' rights to protection against violence. Throughout the 1860s and 1870s, congressional hearings, newspaper accounts, and magazine articles were filled with stories featuring blacks who were beaten, murdered, raped, or robbed by angry, resentful, racist Southern whites whom local authorities were either unwilling or unable to restrain or punish. According to Eric Foner, Reconstruction's foremost historian, "the wave of counterrevolutionary terror that swept over large parts of the South [during Reconstruction] lacks a counterpart either in the American experience or in that of the other Western Hemisphere societies that abolished slavery in the nineteenth century."[43]

In an effort to reassert control, whites beat or killed African-Americans for such "infractions" as failing to step off sidewalks, objecting to beatings of their children, addressing whites without deference, and attempting to vote. At least one-tenth of the black members of state constitutional conventions in the South were victimized by racially motivated violence, including seven who were murdered. Educated blacks were especially targeted for punishment. In Georgia, Ku Klux Klansmen killed Washington Eager because he could read. They also destroyed a teacher's library, declaring that they "just dare[d] any other nigger to have a book in his house."[44] In the Freedmen's Bureau's record of the thousand reported murders of blacks by whites in Texas between 1865 and 1868 are incidents like the following: One victim "did not remove his hat"; another "wouldn't give up a whiskey flask"; one white man "wanted to thin out the niggers a little"; another wanted "to see a d———d nigger kick."[45]

On occasion, flareups of racially motivated violence singed more than individual blacks and engulfed whole communities. In Memphis, Tennessee, rioting whites killed forty-six blacks, raped five black women, and destroyed scores of black-owned dwellings, churches, and schools.[46] In New Orleans, rioting whites killed thirty-four blacks (and three of their white Republican allies).[47]

The problem extended far beyond the immediate perpetrators of this violence. It included authorities who were unable or unwilling to defend blacks or to punish white criminals. It was "almost an impossibility," one Southern judge remarked, "to convict a white man of any crime . . . where the violence has been against a black man."[48] "My own opinion," remarked General Philip Sheridan, "is that the trial of a white man for the murder of a freedman in Texas would be a farce."[49]

Attacks upon blacks (and their white reformist allies) prompted Northern whites to go further than they might otherwise have gone toward arming African-Americans with civil and political rights (an irony replicated in the 1960s). Hence, although racially motivated violence is often minimized in the nation's historical consciousness, its presence and reactions to it are among the most important of the factors that have influenced the evolution of American legal institutions. A desire to protect blacks against concerted white terror was among the motivations for Congress to initiate passage of the Fourteenth and Fifteenth amendments to the U.S. Constitution, to pass legislation to enforce these new federal constitutional rights, and to create a new cabinet-level sector of government, the Department of Justice.[50]*

For a brief period, federal intervention considerably reduced racially motivated violence, thus enabling African-American men to participate actively in the governance of Southern politics and society. The most dramatic episode of federal prosecution of the Ku Klux Klan took place in the Piedmont counties of South Carolina in 1871–1872.[51] The outrages perpetrated there were egregious even by the standards of that time and region. Two stand out. In one incident, five hundred masked men broke into a Union County jail and lynched eight black prisoners. In another, seven Klansmen beat a black Reconstructionist, Amzi Rainey, in front of his family and then raped and shot his eldest daughter, acts that local officials refused to prosecute. President Ulysses S. Grant proclaimed a "condition of lawlessness," dispatched troops to quell it, and suspended the writ of habeas corpus. Troops occupied the region and arrested hundreds of suspects while thousands of others fled. Dozens of Klansmen pleaded guilty or were convicted at trials (usually

---

*The Fourteenth Amendment (1868) provided blacks with citizenship and the equal protection of the laws. The Fifteenth Amendment (1870) prohibited states from excluding persons from the vote on the basis of race. Among the several Reconstruction laws enacted primarily to protect blacks was the Ku Klux Klan Act of 1871 which contained provisions that are of continued major importance. See, e.g., 42 U.S.C. § 1983 (1994).

before predominantly black juries). The man principally responsible for this campaign, Attorney General Amos T. Akerman, poignantly recorded both its success and limitations. "Though rejoiced at the suppression of KuKluxery even in one neighborhood," he wrote in a letter to a friend, "I feel greatly saddened by this business. It has revealed a perversion of moral sentiment among the Southern whites which bodes ill to that part of the country for this generation."[52]

Akerman's pessimism was warranted; white supremacist violence eventually triumphed. It both contributed to and reflected the weakness of Reconstruction administrations which fell in one state after another, so that by 1877 virtually the entire South had been retaken—"redeemed"—by the political forces that had championed the Confederacy. Many factors account for this turnabout: reformers' tentativeness and confusion in the face of unprecedented circumstances; the persistence and ruthlessness of Southern whites committed to reimposing a strict racial hierarchy; the federal government's undeveloped administrative infrastructure; the fatigue and racism of Northern whites; and widespread allegiance to a conception of federalism opposed to the activist role that the federal government would have been required to play in order to insure the rights newly granted to blacks. The consequences were terrible and long-lasting. When Reconstruction came to an end, a remarkable effort to provide blacks with the equal *protection* of the laws gave way to a rigid pigmentocracy that, once again, deprived African-Americans of basic human rights.

"Real Lynching": The Failure to Protect Blacks in the Age of Segregation

Those who destroyed Reconstruction demanded unchallenged white supremacy. Of the many methods used to realize this aim, the most striking was lynching. Like certain other terms that denote extreme actions that have been almost universally deplored—"genocide" comes to mind—the term "lynching" has suffered from metaphorization. Commentators and politicians have used the term metaphorically in circumstances that have clouded its meaning and diminished its significance. President Ronald Reagan, among others, complained that Judge Robert Bork was "lynched" when the Senate blocked his elevation to the

Supreme Court.[53] Justice Clarence Thomas claimed that he was subjected to a "high-tech lynching" by the Senate Judiciary Committee when it inquired into allegations that he had mistreated a subordinate.[54] Ben Chavis asserted that he was the victim of a "lynching" when the NAACP fired him as its leader.[55]

As used here, "lynching" refers to a killing done by several people acting in concert outside the legal process to punish a person perceived to have violated a law or custom.[56] The focus, in other words, is on *real* lynching.[57]

Between 1882 (when reliable data were first collected) and 1968, at least 4,743 people were lynched in the United States.[58] The majority of reported lynchings—73 percent—occurred in the South, and the majority of these were inflicted upon blacks. Whereas 1,297 whites were among those lynched, the toll for blacks ran to 3,446, or 72.7 percent. The worst states were Mississippi (539 black victims), Georgia (492 black victims), Texas (352 black victims), Louisiana (335 black victims), and Alabama (299 black victims). Although 1901 marked the last time that the toll of black victims exceeded 100—at least 105 blacks were lynched that year—it was not until the mid-1930s that the number of black lynching victims consistently dipped beneath 10 per year.[59]

To provide a glimpse of the atrociousness of lynching—its ritualistic brutalities, flagrant carelessness, mass hysteria—I offer the following excerpts from "The Story of One Hundred Lynchings," a document published by the NAACP in 1919 "to make vivid the facts of lynching in the United States."[60]

TEXAS 1895

News has been received of the lynching of a Negro in . . . Madison County on Tuesday night. He was accused of riding a horse over a little white girl and inflicting serious injuries on her. Later developments go on to show that the mob got hold of the wrong negro. The guilty one made his escape. *Chicago Tribune*, November 22, 1895.[61]

GEORGIA 1899

Sam Hose, a Negro farm laborer, was accused of murdering his employer in a quarrel over wages. He escaped. Several days later, while he was being hunted unsuccessfully, the charge was added that he raped his employer's wife. He confessed the murder, but refused, even under duress, to confess the other crime.

The following account of the lynching is taken from the *New York Tribune* for April 24, 1899:

"In the presence of nearly 2,000 people, who sent aloft yells of defiance and shouts of joy, Sam Hose (a Negro who committed two of the basest acts known to crime) was burned at the stake in a public road. . . . Before the torch was applied to the pyre, the Negro was deprived of his ears, fingers and other portions of his body. . . . Before the body was cool, it was cut to pieces, the bones were crushed into small bits and even the tree upon which the wretch met his fate was torn up and disposed of as souvenirs.

"The Negro's heart was cut in several pieces, as was also his liver. Those unable to obtain the ghastly relics directly, paid more fortunate possessors extravagant sums for them. Small pieces of bone went for 25 cents and a bit of the liver, crisply cooked, for 10 cents."

No indictments were ever found against any of the lynchers.[62]

FLORIDA 1901
Will Wright and Sam Williams, charged with being implicated in a murder, were lynched without trial in jail at Dade City, by a mob of thirty or more men. Sheriff Griffin refused to give up the keys and they broke down the outer door. Unable to break down the steel doors of the cells, they opened fire through the steel bars, shooting both the Negroes to death.

The Coroner's jury found that they came to their death at the hands of "parties unknown." *New York Tribune*, February 7, 1901.[63]

DELAWARE 1903
George White, a Negro, accused of rape and murder, was taken out of jail at Wilmington, Del., dragged to the scene of his alleged crime and forced to confess. He was tied to a stake, burned and riddled with bullets, even as he was being burned. The Chamber of Commerce of Wilmington, which met a few days later, refused to pass a resolution condemning the lynching but passed one against forest fires. *New York Tribune*, June 23, 24, 1903.[64]

MISSISSIPPI 1904

Luther Holbert, a Doddsville Negro, and his wife were burned at the stake for the murder of James Eastland, a white planter, and John Carr, a Negro. The planter was killed in a quarrel which arose when he came to Carr's cabin, where he found Holbert, and ordered him to leave the plantation. Carr and a Negro, named Winters, were also killed.

Holbert and his wife fled the plantation but were brought back and burned at the stake in the presence of a thousand people. Two innocent Negroes had been shot previous to this by a posse looking for Holbert, because one of them, who resembled Holbert, refused to surrender when ordered to do so. There is nothing in the story to indicate that Holbert's wife had any part in the crime. *New York Tribune*, February 8, 1904.[65]

TENNESSEE 1906

Ed Johnson, a Negro, convicted of rape and sentenced to be hanged, was granted an appeal by the Supreme Court of the United States. Johnson was in jail at Chattanooga, Tennessee. A mob broke down the jail door, took him out and hanged him. *New York Tribune*, March 20, 1906.[66]

ARKANSAS 1910

Pine Bluff, Ark., March 25—Resenting alleged improper conduct on the part of Judge Jones, a Negro, and a young white woman, a mob of forty men gathered at the county jail here tonight, overpowered the jailer and his deputies, and hanged the Negro. Special to *The Chicago Tribune*, March 26, 1910.[67]

OKLAHOMA 1911

At Okemah, Oklahoma, Laura Nelson, a colored woman, accused of murdering a deputy sheriff who had discovered stolen goods in her house, was lynched together with her son, a boy about fifteen. The woman and her son were taken from the jail, dragged about six miles to the Canadian River, and hanged from a bridge. The woman was raped by members of the mob before she was hanged. *The Crisis*, July, 1911.[68]

Apologists for lynching justified it on several grounds. Some contended that certain crimes were so heinous—for example, the rape of a white woman by a black man—that they demanded punishment more swift and sure than the regular legal process could offer. Others argued that lynching was a necessary supplement for a criminal justice system that all too often permitted the guilty to avoid punishment altogether or to suffer too little for their misdeeds. Others focused on the special threat assertedly posed by blacks. According to one popular theory, blacks had undergone a salutary civilizing process through enslavement that was tragically ended by emancipation. By the end of the nineteenth century, the "good" Negroes who had once been slaves were being supplanted by "bad" Negroes who had never known slavery. Freed from the discipline of enslavement, blacks were reverting to their natural, primitive, brutish ways. Proponents of this view argued that in order to secure the protection of whites, especially white women, from this aggressive, "new" Negro, resort would have to be made to special means, including lynching.

A related belief was that black men lusted after white women with such powerful longing that ordinary means of control were insufficient. According to the white supremacist intellectual Philip Alexander Bruce, white women so arouse black men that they are moved "to gratify their lust at any cost and in spite of every obstacle."[69] Indeed, the alleged need to deter and avenge rapes perpetrated by black men against white women became the *principal* rationale for lynching. Clarence H. Poe expressed the belief of many observers when he wrote in *The Atlantic Monthly* in February 1904, "It was with rape that lynching begins."[70]

The claim that a Negro had murdered a white person constituted the single most widely used excuse for racially motivated lynchings. The claim that a Negro had raped a white woman, however, represented the most emotionally potent excuse.[71] The white supremacist Jim Crow South suffered from what W. J. Cash termed a "rape complex."[72] A constant refrain in countless speeches and editorials was that lynching constituted a brutal necessity to keep the Negro "beast" at bay. "Governor as I am," Ben Tillman of South Carolina confessed in 1892, "I would lead a mob to lynch the negro who ravishes a white woman."[73] U.S. Senator Theodore Bilbo of Mississippi commented that often lynching was the only "immediate and proper and suitable punishment" for blacks who dishonored white womanhood.[74] U.S. Senator William Van Amberg of Mississippi boasted that once he had personally led a lynch mob against a black man accused of having killed a white woman. "I led the mob which lynched Nelse Patton," the former senator declared, "and I am proud of it. I directed every movement of the mob and I did everything I could to see that he was lynched. Cut a white woman's throat? . . . Of course I wanted him lynched."[75]

Lynchings were a powerful tool of racial control, an ever-present threat that resided in the shadows of practically all white–black interactions. Richard Wright made this point in his memoir *Black Boy* when he recalled his coming of age in the 1920s:

> The things that influenced my conduct as a Negro did not have to happen to me directly; I needed but to hear of them to feel their full effects in the deepest layers of my consciousness. Indeed the white brutality that I had not seen was a more effective control of my behavior than that which I knew.[76]

What rape is to women, lynchings were to blacks: a constant threat shaping daily decisions from choice of demeanor to choice in clothing.

Among Southern whites, lynching was widely perceived as a *legitimate* action. What Professor Neil McMillen says of white Mississippians was true more broadly: "Whether upper or lower class, [whites] did not generally regard lynching as a lawless act. It was understood as law enforcement by informal means, a community-sanctioned extension of the criminal justice system."[77] Leading white journalists, churchmen, and politicians either passively ignored or actively justified lynching. If it is necessary for every Negro in the State of Mississippi to be lynched, Governor James Vardaman declared, "it will be done to maintain white supremacy."[78] Cole Blease, governor of South Carolina, received the finger of a lynched black in the mail and planted it appreciatively in the gubernatorial garden.[79]

Not all Southern politicians applauded lynchings. Some repudiated mob murder in strong terms. Recommending antilynching legislation to the Mississippi legislature (a recommendation that was rejected), Governor A. H. Longino declared, "The honor of Mississippi and the good name of her Christian civilization demand the suppression of mob violence which . . . is the most demoralizing, brutalizing, and ruinous species of lawlessness known to any brave and free people."[80] Indeed, opponents of lynching were sufficiently numerous and influential to enact eventually some form of antilynching law in virtually all of the Southern states. These laws included provisions for making participation in lynching a crime, employing military force to guard prisoners, changing venue in circumstances in which mob violence posed a threat, calling special terms of court in order to promptly try defendants, removing vulnerable prisoners to more secure places of incarceration, fining counties or cities in which lynchings occurred, and removing from office delinquent law enforcement officials.[81]

For the most part, however, these laws went unenforced. Redress was doomed by the reluctance or unwillingness of officials to prosecute, witnesses to cooperate, or juries to convict. Writing in 1933, Professor James Chadbourn calculated that only about 0.8 percent of lynchings in the United States since 1900 had been followed by convictions of any lynchers.[82]

Lynching in African-American Politics and Memory

It would be difficult to exaggerate the importance of lynching in the development of African-American political consciousness. The threat lynching posed served as a focal point around which black communities mobilized themselves. The most significant black protest organization in American history, the National Association for the Advancement of Colored People (NAACP), was born as a direct result of efforts to combat racially motivated mob violence. In August 1908, in Springfield, Illinois, a white mob frustrated by its inability to lynch two Negroes charged with rape instead killed two other blacks who were unlucky enough to cross its path. The mob also injured scores of people and burned and looted black-owned homes and businesses. This was done, ironically, in the midst of preparations to honor the centennial of the birth of Springfield's most famous son—Abraham Lincoln.[83] Two details of this sickening episode warrant special notice. The riot was fueled by a *false* charge of rape by a white woman against a black man, a scenario that has led to terrible mischief throughout American history. Second, white handkerchiefs were placed outside of homes and businesses to signal that whites lived in or owned the premises and should therefore be spared by the white mob. A similar practice came to the fore sixty years later when blacks, or people seeking to be identified as blacks, placed "Soul Brother" signs on property menaced by black rioters.

After witnessing the riot up close as a journalist, William E. Walling pleaded for a revival of the movement to elevate the status of African-Americans, a plea that was answered by a small cadre of reformers (including W.E.B. DuBois, William Dean Howells, Mary White Ovington, Oswald Villard, and John Dewey) who soon thereafter founded the NAACP.[84] For the first four decades of its existence, the NAACP's primary activities consisted of investigating, publicizing, and denouncing lynchings. It also campaigned for the enactment of a federal statute that could effectively punish racially motivated mob murder. The NAACP lobbied on behalf of over two hundred antilynching bills proposed to Congress.[85] Although three passed the House of Representatives, none progressed further because of stubborn opposition from white supremacist senators whose willingness to use the filibuster prevented any antilynching legislation from ever reaching a vote in the Senate.[86] The hostility of the Southern white political bloc was so potent that even during the New Deal, President Franklin Delano Roosevelt refused to back any federal antilynching bills. Unwilling to risk the political dangers that would have attended his support, FDR dodged the issue; lynching was, in his view, simply too hot to touch.[87]

Along with the unpunished raping of black women, lynching stands out in the minds of many black Americans as the most vicious and destructive consequence of racially selective underprotection. Its importance and resonance is reflected in the large extent to which lynching has been represented, explored, and memorialized by black writers including Charles W. Chestnut, Paul Lawrence Dunbar, Jean Toomer, Langston Hughes, Richard Wright, James Baldwin, Toni Morrison, David Bradley, and John Edgar Wideman.[88] Nothing has more eroded confidence in the criminal justice system than the long history of willful refusals to punish white antiblack vigilantes.* Nothing has more embit-

---

*"Lynching's legacy, and the failure of the nation to stop it, haunts Americans today. . . . The history of lynching and white America's cultivation of the myth of black men as 'beast-rapists' may help to explain why blacks' reactions to recent media spectacles involving black men accused of crimes against white women is often so different from the reactions of whites to these same events." Barbara Holden-Smith, "Lynching, Federalism, and the Intersection of Race and Gender in the Progressive Era," 8 *Yale Journal of Law and Feminism* 31, 34 (1996).

tered discussions of the criminal justice system than the recognition that among those who have insistently demanded "law and order" are those who have been unwilling to take effective action to deter antiblack racially motivated crimes. Nothing has more nourished dreams of racial revenge than the knowledge that buried in American history are scores of black victims of lynching whose murderers, though known, escaped punishment.

Federalism and Opposition to National Measures Against Racially Motivated Violence

Some people opposed federal antilynching legislation because of genuine constitutional concerns. They argued that the federal government lacked authority to regulate criminality perpetrated by private persons, even if their crimes were racially motivated. According to this argument, a proper respect for federalism requires the central government to stay its hand in order to permit the states to police criminal misconduct.* In 1918, even Moorfield Storey, the president of the NAACP, had doubts about the constitutional legitimacy of federal antilynching legislation.[89]

Reasons for genuine doubt had roots that reached back to the Civil War. In the aftermath of the war, unionists were divided over the extent to which the federal government should be empowered to protect the newly freed slaves against their former masters. Each of the Reconstruction constitutional amendments became the occasion for hard-fought struggles over this issue, as did each of the civil rights laws enacted to enforce those amendments. Even after these provisions were enacted, moreover, debate over their meaning continued (and persists).[90]

It is important to emphasize the contentiousness, complexity, and confusion that attended the Reconstruction amendments and enforce-

---

*Many proponents of this argument failed to acknowledge that local law enforcement often connived in the commission of lynchings. They also failed to acknowledge that even in those cases in which local law enforcement officials did try fellow whites for racially motivated violent crimes, all-white juries typically refused to convict even in the face of overwhelming evidence of guilt. Only one of the perpetrators of the Springfield lynching and race riot was convicted, and that person confessed his guilt. A similar story recurred time and time again.

ment legislation in order to modify the widely held but simplistic belief that "the promise" of Reconstruction was "betrayed" by a Supreme Court that perpetrated a "judicial coup d'état" by either invalidating civil rights laws or interpreting them narrowly.[91] Far more than is generally appreciated, the Supreme Court's race-relations decisions between the 1880s and the 1950s reflect not a betrayal of Reconstruction-era promises but a reflection of the limitations imposed by those ambiguous promises.[92] As Professor Michael Les Benedict observes, "Every Reconstruction-era effort to protect the rights of citizens was tempered by the fundamental conviction that federalism required that the day-to-day protection of the citizen had to remain the duty of the States."[93]

A string of decisions reversing convictions of violent white supremacists tried pursuant to federal criminal civil rights laws are among the rulings for which the Supreme Court has been harshly criticized. One was *United States* v. *Cruikshank*, which stemmed from "the bloodiest single act of carnage in all of Reconstruction."[94] In 1872, in Colfax, Louisiana, during and after a battle between contending political factions, opponents of Reconstruction killed about 280 blacks, many of whom were unarmed or in the process of surrendering.[95] Pursuant to the Enforcement Act of 1870, the federal government indicted ninety-seven people, although it succeeded in bringing to trial only nine and convicting only three. These three were convicted of depriving blacks of various rights assertedly protected by the federal constitution. The Supreme Court, however, voided their convictions on a variety of grounds, including the failure of the prosecution to charge the defendants with acts punishable by federal authority. Although the prosecution described the actions of the defendants and described the racial identities of the parties involved, it failed to charge explicitly that the defendants attacked the victims because of their race. Absent a specific allegation of racial motive, the Court declared, the conduct objected to represented behavior that could be criminalized only by the state and not by the federal government.

The Supreme Court has been roundly condemned for *Cruikshank* and its discouraging effect on federal prosecutors. Blame, however, lies at least equally with the Presidency and Congress. Even considering the novelty of the Reconstruction criminal statutes it is still true that federal prosecutors performed poorly in bringing their case against Cruikshank and company. Congress, moreover, failed twice. It failed initially to take the radical steps required to protect the newly freed slaves and instead enacted confusing half-measures. Worse, in light of the continuing campaign of racially motivated violence and the lessons generated by adverse judicial opinions, Congress failed to correct, clarify, and strengthen the legislation it had previously enacted. Having expended considerable effort in the 1860s and 1870s to protect blacks against racially motivated violence, Congress subsequently abandoned the issue and has never comprehensively revisited it.

Absent new constitutional amendments or legislation, Supreme Court jurisprudence continued to impede prosecutions of those charged with engaging in racially motivated violence. Two cases are particularly illuminating: *Hodges* v. *United States*[96] and *Screws* v. *United States*.[97]

Hodges stemmed from the federal prosecution of a mob of whites in eastern Arkansas who, in 1903, ousted blacks from jobs at a lumber mill by threatening to kill them. The whites were indicted for violating a federal statute which made it a crime for two or more persons to conspire "to injure, oppress, threaten, or intimidate any citizen in the free exercise or enjoyment of any right or privilege secured to him by the Constitution or laws of the United States."[98] The government alleged that the defendants had violated a federal statute, which gave to all persons "the same right . . . to make and enforce contracts . . . as is enjoyed by white citizens."[99] The government further argued that the constitutional authority for this statutory grant was the Thirteenth Amendment to the Constitution. The government's theory, essentially, was that by forcibly ejecting the black workers from their jobs for racial reasons, the white gang was subjecting the blacks to a vestige of slavery. In the words of Attorney General (and soon to be Supreme Court Justice) William H. Moody:

> If the Negro who is in our midst can be denied the right to work, and must live on the outskirts of civilization, he will become more dangerous than the wild beasts. . . . He will become an outcast lurking about the borders and living by depredation. There is but one refuge from that condition, and that is to put himself back under some chosen master in the condition of slavery itself.[100]

The Supreme Court had previously established that the Fourteenth Amendment gave no general authority to the federal government to punish racially motivated crimes perpetrated by private parties against other private parties. The Fourteenth Amendment, the Court insisted, protected individuals only against wrongful conduct by state actors (i.e., government officials), not private actors. Prior to *Hodges*, though, the Court had hinted that it might be willing to recognize the Thirteenth Amendment as a source of constitutional power from which the federal government could properly punish racially motivated violence perpetrated by private persons. An early and vivid articulation of this view was offered by Justice Joseph P. Bradley:

> The war of race, whether it assumes the dimensions of civil strife or domestic violence, whether carried on in a guerrilla or predatory form, or by private combinations, or even by private outrage or intimidation, is subject to the jurisdiction of the government of the United States.[101]

In *Hodges*, however, the Court made clear that, in its view, the Thirteenth Amendment did not empower the federal government to respond broadly to "the war of race." All that amendment empowered the federal government to do was prevent and punish enslavement. What befell the blacks in Arkansas, the Court reasoned, was not enslavement but merely common crimes that were the responsibility of the state and not the federal government. The Court therefore vacated the convictions on the grounds that the federal government had exceeded its jurisdiction.

A second example of the Supreme Court's hostility toward assertions of federal jurisdiction to protect citizens against wrongful violence is *Screws* v. *United States*. Justice William O. Douglas's rendition of the underlying facts of the controversy is worth quoting:

> This case involves a shocking and revolting episode in law enforcement. Petitioner [Claude] Screws was sheriff of Baker County, Georgia. He enlisted the assistance of petitioner Jones, a policeman, and petitioner Kelley, a special deputy, in arresting Robert Hall. . . . The arrest was made late at night at Hall's home on a warrant charg-

ing Hall with theft of a tire. Hall, a young negro about thirty years of age, was handcuffed and taken by car to the court house. As Hall alighted from the car ... the three petitioners began beating him with their fists and with a solid-bar blackjack about eight inches long and weighing two pounds. They claimed Hall had reached for a gun and had used insulting language as he alighted from the car. But after Hall, still handcuffed, had been knocked to the ground they continued to beat him from fifteen to thirty minutes until he was unconscious. Hall was then dragged feet-first through the court-house yard into the jail and thrown upon the floor dying. An ambulance was called and Hall was removed to a hospital where he died within the hour.... There was evidence that Screws held a grudge against Hall and had threatened to "get" him.[102]

Sheriff Screws had told an FBI agent that Hall was a "biggety negro" who "considered himself to be a leader among the colored people in the community."[103] What may have triggered Sheriff Screws' lethal anger was Hall's temerity in retaining an attorney to recover a pistol that Screws had seized. Screws received a letter from the attorney the day that he arrested Hall and was heard to say that "he was going to go and get the black [SOB] and ... kill him."[104]

After the killing, state authorities brought no charges against Screws and his accomplices. After four months of state inaction, the federal government intervened, charging Screws et al. with willfully depriving Hall of, among other things, the right to be free of deprivation of life without due process of law. The government did not charge that the defendants had mistreated Hall on a racial basis. Rather, the government presented the prosecution as a simple police brutality case, albeit one with obvious racial overtones. A jury convicted the defendants, who were then sentenced by the trial judge to a $1,000 fine and a three-year prison term.

The Supreme Court, however, overturned the convictions. Three justices—Felix Frankfurter, Owen J. Roberts, and Robert H. Jackson—voted to reverse the convictions mainly on federalism grounds. They decried the action giving rise to the prosecutions, declaring that the killing "rendered these lawless law officers guilty of manslaughter, if not of murder, under Georgia law."[105] Yet they insisted that only Georgia had the power to punish the defendants. Indeed, they scolded the federal government for intervening. "Instead of leaving this misdeed to vindication by Georgia law," they asserted, "the United States deflected Georgia's responsibility by instituting a federal prosecution."[106]

Frankfurter, Roberts, and Jackson were egregiously mistaken. They suggested that the federal government impatiently pushed the local Georgia law enforcement authorities aside. As noted above, however, only after it was clear that the local and state officials would not be bringing any prosecutions against these flagrantly "lawless lawmen" did the federal government intervene. This bloc of justices also wrote that "the practical question is whether the States should be relieved from responsibility to bring their law officers to brook for homicide, by allowing prosecutions in the federal courts for a relatively minor offense carrying a short sentence."[107] In fact, however, that was not at all the practical question posed by the federal government's effort to do something about the murder of Robert Hall. The real question was what the American legal system should do when state officials fail to discipline their fellow officials in circumstances like those surrounding Hall's death. To that question, Frankfurter, Roberts, and Jackson had nothing useful to say.

Five other justices also voted to annul the conviction of Screws et al. They did so on the grounds that the trial judge had defined too vaguely the crime for which the defendants were convicted. This conclusion permitted the federal government to try again to convict Screws et al., albeit under a narrower reading of the law.

Justice Frank Murphy alone argued in favor of affirming the convictions:

> It is an illusion to say that the real issue in this case is the alleged failure . . . to warn the state officials that their actions were illegal. The Constitution, [the relevant federal statute], and their own consciences told them that. . . . The significant question, rather, is whether law enforcement officers . . . shall be allowed to violate with impunity the clear constitutional rights of the inarticulate and the friendless. Too often, unpopular minorities, such as Negroes, are unable to find effective refuge from the cruelties of bigoted and ruthless authority. States are undoubtedly capable of punishing their officers who commit such outrages. But where, as here, the states are

unwilling for some reason to prosecute such crimes, the federal government must step in unless constitutional guarantees are to become atrophied.[108]

Upon retrial, Sheriff Screws and his accomplices won acquittals. Several years later, Screws won election to the Georgia State Senate.[109]

There were, then, as we have seen, genuine reasons for a legislator to be concerned about the constitutionality of federal antilynching legislation. At the same time, for many opponents of this legislation, constitutional doubts were only a supplemental reason for opposition. The primary reason was anti-Negro prejudice. Particularly instructive is the rhetoric of certain politicians and their willingness to subordinate their commitment to federalism in the face of other federal legislation that also arguably encroached upon the police power of the states.

During congressional debate in 1922 over a bill proposed by Representative Leonidas Dyer of Missouri "to assure to persons within the jurisdiction of every State the equal protection of the laws, and to punish the crime of lynching,"[110] Southern opponents steadfastly asserted that such legislation was both futile and unwise. When "the criminal element of the Negro race" commits "the diabolical crime of rape upon the white women," Representative James Buchanan of Texas declared, "lynching follows as swift as lightning, and all the statutes of State and Nation cannot stop it."[111] Echoing Buchanan, another Texan, Representative Hatton Sumners, proudly asserted that Southern white men "have never yielded to the courts . . . or to laws established by legislatures the protection of their women."[112]

The Dyer bill was unwise, according to its opponents, because the lynching problem was attributable not to the lynchers but to blacks, a people Buchanan described as the "race most addicted to the tragic infamy" of rape.* "We are going to protect our girls and womenfolk from these black brutes," remarked Representative Thomas Upton Sisson of

---

*Repeating an idea often expressed by white supremacists, Buchanan argued that lynching did not show hatred for or even prejudice against blacks. The Negro race, he maintained, had "long enjoyed its distinction as the most favored race protégé ever coddled and petted by the sentimental sacrifice of an indulgent people." Blacks brought lynchings upon themselves by committing the "hellish outrage that fires the spirit of retaliation." See Holden-Smith, "Lynching," 55.

Mississippi. "When these black fiends keep their hands off the throats of the women of the South then lynching will stop."[113] "You men from the North," Representative John Rankin of Mississippi complained, "have never known what it means to live in a state of constant dread for the safety of your loved ones." In the South, however, a person comes to learn that "the shadow of the Negro criminal constantly hangs . . . like the sword of Damocles over the head of every white woman . . . and [that] no one knows just when or where it is going to fall." Rankin suggested that even debating the Dyer bill was having evil effects. "Four assaults were committed on white women by Negro brutes during the first week of [the bill's] consideration by this House," he charged.[114] Warning of terrible consequences that would ensue in the event of enactment, Representative Finis Garrett of Tennessee declared that the Dyer bill ought to be renamed "a bill to encourage rape."[115] Senator T. H. Caraway of Arkansas elaborated upon this theme. "The truth of the matter," he claimed, was that "a society known as the society for the protection of the rights of colored people wrote this bill. . . . These people had but one idea in view, and that was to make rape permissible, and to allow the guilty to go unpunished if that rape should be committed by a negro upon a white woman of the South."[116]

This rhetoric is indicative of widespread sentiments that played an important role in blocking proposals for federal antilynching legislation. Instructive, too, was Congress's inconsistency in dealing with legislation that encroached upon the police powers of the states. Twelve years before the defeat of the Dyer bill, Congress passed the White Slave Traffic Act, popularly known as the Mann Act (after its sponsor Representative James R. Mann of Illinois). The Mann Act made it a felony under federal law to transport knowingly any woman or girl across state lines for prostitution "or any other immoral purpose."[117] According to its sponsors, the legislation was aimed at eradicating "the business of securing white women and girls and of selling them outright, or of exploiting them for immoral purposes."[118] The bill encountered considerable resistance, almost all of which stemmed from federalism concerns. Complaining that the Mann Act would unconstitutionally encroach upon the states' police powers, Representative William Richardson of Alabama insisted that morals are "in the supreme control of the State" and beyond delegation to the federal government.[119] In this instance, however, a limiting vision of federalism proved less compelling than the specter of white women being sold into debauchery.

Proponents of the Mann Act constantly deployed the imagery of race to solidify support. They named "white women" as the intended beneficiaries of the legislation. They also mobilized support by evoking the specter of purchased interracial sex. Finally, Representative Mann argued in favor of his bill by comparing the white slave trade with the Negro slave trade and finding the former a much weightier problem. "Congress would be derelict in its duty," he declared, "if it did not exercise [its power], because all of the horrors which have ever been urged, either truthfully or fancifully, against the black-slave trade pale into insignificance as compared to the horrors of the so-called 'white slave traffic.' "[120]

Although some congressmen continued on federalism grounds to oppose the Mann Act, the number who did so were insufficient to defeat it. Some who might have opposed the bill were undoubtedly persuaded by sentiments of the sort voiced by Representative Thetus W. Sims of Tennessee, who told his colleagues, "Pass this law, take care of the girls, the women—the defenseless—and let the courts say whether or not the law is unconstitutional."[121] Moreover, even those who fought against the Mann Act declined to attack it with the die-hard ruthlessness with which foes of federal antilynching legislation attacked the Dyer bill.

There are probably a variety of reasons that help to explain the divergent fates of the Mann Act and the Dyer bill. One of the most salient, however, had to do with the racial identities of those envisioned as primary beneficiaries. The idea of protecting white women from sexual exploitation sufficiently stilled anxieties over federalism concerns to permit the passage of the Mann Act. The idea of protecting black citizens from mob violence did not have the same pull; to the contrary, that very idea impelled a substantial number of congressmen to vote *against* the Dyer bill.

The passage of the Mann Act was not an isolated development. It formed part of a pattern that helps to explain, among other things, the first federal narcotics law, the Harrison Narcotics Act of 1914,[122] and a federal statute enacted in 1912 that prohibited the interstate transportation of prizefight films.[123] Federalism concerns might well have been mobilized against both of these bills, but in neither case did major opposition arise. The Harrison Act won passage easily, facilitated by testimony that cocaine use increased Negroes' penchant for violent crime, particularly the commission of rape upon white women. Similarly, anxieties over federalism created no substantial barrier to enacting a ban on interstate transportation of prizefight films. The specific purpose of this ban was to prevent publicizing the exploits of Jack Johnson, the first black heavyweight boxing champion. That Johnson beat his racial "superiors" was itself troubling to many whites. That he married a white woman made him intolerable. Congressman William Francis Murray of Massachusetts questioned the propriety and necessity for federal legislation inasmuch as states could and did regulate prizefights and the showing of prizefight films. "I wonder what it is," he mused, "that causes men from the Southland, who in this Hall have always insisted upon the doctrine of State rights, to arise and urge with such great seriousness that legislation of this kind be passed?"[124] Of course, the answer, or at least a very large part of it, is obvious. The desire to maintain white supremacy substantially explains the inconsistency that Representative Murray noted.

Neither inconsistency nor anxieties over federalism appear to have mattered much in Congress; the House unanimously passed the prizefight bill. Outside the Congress, though, especially in black communities, observers keenly appreciated the difference that race clearly made in lawmaking. A front-page cartoon in the *Chicago-Defender* on July 10, 1910, reflected the feelings of many blacks. Entitled "The Strong Arm of the American Law," the cartoon pictures Sheriff Uncle Sam tossing a promoter of prizefighting into a paddy wagon while three men clearly marked as lynchers run away undisturbed.[125]*

---

*African-American journalists not only decried the inconsistency of Congress on the federalism issue, they also decried the sensibilities of people who loudly objected to the showing of prizefights on film but who silently tolerated lynchings. According to the editorial writer of the *Baltimore Afro-American Ledger*:

> There is entirely too much hipocrisy [sic] about the whole thing. Men in every station in life are holding up their hands in holy horror. Ministers are denouncing [prizefight films] from the pulpit, prominent men are speaking against it on the rostrum and in the newspapers, and it is being talked of everywhere. . . . If half of the protest against the showing of these pictures

Racially Motivated Violence during the Twilight of the Jim Crow Era: The Emmett Till Case

Midway through the twentieth century the American legal regime at both the state and federal levels displayed notable failings in terms of protecting blacks against racially motivated violence. On one hand, the laws enacted for this purpose during Reconstruction were crippled by ambiguity, underuse, restrictive interpretation, and invalidation. On the other hand, proposals for new, clearer, potentially more effective, federal laws were consistently stymied, primarily by the political opposition of Southern white supremacists who even succeeded in rejecting a bill crafted during World War II to provide federal protection "from assault or killing . . . [to] persons in the uniform of the [United States]," legislation prompted by several cases of racially motivated maimings and murders of African-American servicemen.[126]

Despite failures to enact federal antilynching legislation or to enforce state antilynching laws and what remained of the Reconstruction-era federal civil rights laws, the number of lynchings declined during the 1940s and 1950s. Between 1930 and 1939, 119 blacks were reported lynched. Between 1940 and 1949, the number fell to 31. Between 1950 and 1959, the number fell to 6. None were recorded between 1952 and 1954, and only one between 1956 and 1959.[127] A number of factors account for the decline. Many blacks migrated from the South to the North and from rural areas to urban areas, moves which provided black migrants with greater insulation against racist terror. Freed from disenfranchisement at "home," blacks who moved north encouraged politicians to press for federal intervention. This in turn prompted some white supremacists to dissuade violence-prone neighbors from committing acts of terrorism that might open the door to increased federal oversight. Another factor was a changing moral climate in the South and the nation as a whole, which prompted growing numbers of people to view racially motivated violence as intolerable. This stemmed to some extent

---

were made against the lynching fever now abroad in the land, lynching would stop.
Holden-Smith, "Lynching," 75 (quoting editorial, *Afro-American Ledger*, August 6, 1913).

from the humanitarian pleadings of reformers (especially in the wake of Hitler's grotesque crimes), to some extent from Southerners who wanted to modernize their region and understood that newspaper stories about "nigger killing" were bad for business, and to some extent from internationalists who perceived the importance of the newly emerging colored nations to the struggle between the capitalist nations and the communist nations for global supremacy; unredressed lynchings, after all, fit poorly into America's portrayal of itself as the virtuous leader of the Free World.[128]

Justified fear of racially motivated violence, however, continued to exercise a profound influence over the everyday lives of blacks throughout the South and in other areas of the country as well. Confirmation of the prudence of such fear was provided by the infamous murder of Emmett Till.[129] In August 1955, Emmett "Bobo" Till, a fifteen-year-old boy who had been raised in Chicago, was sent to vacation with relatives in Tallahatchie County, Mississippi. Unaware of the racial etiquette of the Jim Crow South, Till answered "yeah" and "naw" to white men instead of the expected "yassah" and "nawsah." He also did two other things that violated the Deep South's prevailing racial customs. First, he kept the photograph of a white girlfriend from Chicago in his wallet and boasted of having sex with her. Second, acting on a dare, he went into a store in Money, Mississippi, and asked the cashier—a young white married woman—for a date and whistled at her.

A few days after the incident in the store, the woman's husband, Roy Bryant, and his brother-in-law, J. W. Milam, went to the cabin where Till was staying under the care of his elderly uncle, Moses Wright. Wright testified that he pleaded with Bryant and Milam to spare Till, that he told them that he had himself chastised the boy, and further that Till "ain't got good sense. He was raised up yonder. He didn't know what he was doing."[130] The entreaties, however, were to no avail.

In a paid interview that Bryant and Milam gave to a journalist after their acquittal, they said that they had initially planned only to beat Till.[131] They decided to kill him when he failed to beg for mercy or show remorse and continued to boast of his sexual intimacies with white girls in Chicago. After they both pistol-whipped Till, Milam shot him once in the head. Then Bryant and Milam threw him into the Tallahatchie River with a heavy fan tied around his neck to weigh him down.

When Till's body was discovered and Bryant and Milam were identified as his likely killers, state politicians, leading editorialists, and local police condemned the murder. Governor Hugh White urged a "vigorous prosecution" and claimed that "Mississippi deplores such conduct."[132] The *Jackson Daily News* termed the slaying "a brutal senseless crime . . . one which merits not one iota of sympathy for the killers."[133] Sheriff Harold Clarence Strider arrested Bryant and Milam, a prosecutor sought an indictment, and a local grand jury complied with the request, prompting a local black newspaper to praise "white men [willing to take] this step against other white men for a crime against a Negro."[134]

Soon, however, a reaction set in that made convicting the defendants virtually impossible. So long as Till's murder was approached as an isolated matter of individual morality, some white supremacists were at least willing to consider condemning the defendants. However, when enemies of the Jim Crow regime linked the murder to the overall system of segregation, many of these same white supremacists took the position that they would rather overlook the crime than give any victory to proponents of racial equality. The more that "outside agitators" such as officials of the NAACP condemned the murder as a characteristic outgrowth of the segregationist way of life, the more wagons began to circle around Bryant and Milan. For example, although Sheriff Strider had inititally appeared intent upon bringing the defendants to justice, he eventually became a witness for the defense.

At trial, Emmett Till's mother positively identified her son's body, and his uncle, overcoming tremendous fear, positively identified Bryant and Milam. The prosecutor contended that although Till may have deserved a whipping, he was "entitled to his life."[135] The defendants admitted abducting Till but claimed that they released him unharmed on the belief that they had probably seized the wrong person. Their attorneys focused on the fact that no eyewitness had come forward to link the defendants to any killing, and Sheriff Strider speculated on the witness stand that the whole affair might be an NAACP plot to disgrace Mississippi and win attention for itself. He went on to conjecture that the badly decomposed body pulled from the Tallahatchie River might not even be Till's body but the corpse of someone else. Confronted with the fact that a ring on the finger of the recovered body bore the initials of Till's father, one defense attorney contended that some sinister group had planted it on the corpse to further a conspiracy against the good people of Mississippi. Summing up the case, he asserted to the jury that he was sure that, despite outside pressures, "every last Anglo-Saxon one of you has the courage to free [the defendents]."[136]

As indicated by the defense counsel's comment, the jury was all-white, even though blacks constituted 63 percent of the approximately thirty thousand residents of Tallahatchie County. Its monochromatic hue was not accidental. Local officials simply refused to allow blacks to participate in local government either as jurors or voters.

On September 23, 1955, after an hour and seven minutes of deliber-ation, the jury acquitted the defendants. One juror remarked, "If we hadn't stopped to drink pop, it wouldn't have taken that long."[137] Other jurors claimed later that the sheriff-elect of the county had sent them word to delay the verdict to make the trial "look good."[138]

The farcical nature of the acquittal was compounded by subsequent events, three of which are particularly noteworthy. First, although Bryant and Milam had initially confessed to abducting Till—and thus committing the crime of kidnapping—a grand jury impaneled after their acquittal for murder declined to indict them for the wrongful ab-duction. Second, although the acquittal was correctly viewed abroad as a scandal (one German newspaper editorialized that it demonstrated that "the life of a Negro in Mississippi is not worth a whistle"),[139] in the South many whites viewed the trial as a vindication. Despite unwel-come agitation, the *Memphis Commercial Appeal* editorialized, "the processes of the law [were] followed in full."[140] Third, the international spotlight that was focused on Mississippi's administration of criminal law during the trial of Emmett Till's murderers accomplished little in the short term for local blacks. Two months after the trial, an inebriated white cotton-gin manager named Elmer Kimbell pulled up to a gas sta-tion in Glendora, Mississippi, and asked the attendant for a full tank of gas. It just so happened that the car belonged to J. W. Milam, one of Kimbell's best friends. A black employee, Clinton Melton, complied. Harsh words were exchanged when Kimbell changed his mind and de-cided that he wanted only two dollars' worth of gas. Angered, Kimbell drove off, got a gun, returned, and fatally wounded Melton with two shots to the head. Kimbell was tried in the same building as Till's mur-derers and with the same result. Despite the testimony of three eyewitnesses, an all-white jury voted for acquittal. "There's open season on the Negroes now," an observer remarked to David Halberstam, one of the few reporters to cover Kimbell's trial. "They've got no protection, and any peckerwood who wants to can go shoot himself one, and we'll free him."[141]

Racially Motivated Violence and the Civil Rights Movement

Civil rights activists who challenged segregation during the period 1955–1970 raised to new levels of visibility the legal issues surrounding the regulation of racially motivated violence.[142] In the five years following the Supreme Court's 1954 decision in *Brown* v. *Board of Education* invalidating de jure segregation in public schools, white supremacists engaged in 210 recorded acts of racially motivated violence. The list includes 6 murders, 29 assaults with firearms, 44 beatings, and 60 bombings.[143]

Activists encountered violence whenever they pushed hard for reform. In 1961, E. H. Hurst, a white Mississippi state representative, shot and killed Herbert Lee because the latter, a black resident of Amite County, sought to register potential Negro voters. A coroner's jury accepted Hurst's claim that he had killed Lee in self-defense, a claim initially corroborated by a black eyewitness, Louis Allen. Allen was later shot to death after telling federal officials that he had lied to the coroner's jury out of fear that he, too, would be murdered if he told the truth—that Hurst had killed Lee in cold blood.[144] In 1962, Sheriff Cull Cambell beat with a walking stick C. B. King, an attorney who visited a jail near Albany, Georgia, to check on the condition of civil rights protesters. Admitting that he had "knocked the hell" out of King, the sheriff justified his conduct by declaring: "I'm a white man and he's a damn nigger."[145] In 1963, Byron De La Beckwith, an outspoken racist, killed Medgar Evers, field secretary of the Mississippi NAACP, right outside of his home.[146]

Despite clear evidence that Southern officials were generally unwilling or unable to protect civil rights activists, the federal government maintained a largely hands-off posture. Restrained by a narrow conception of "federalism," a desire to minimize the anger of white Southern politicians, and deference to the old-fashioned bigotry of powerful officials (most notably, J. Edgar Hoover, the longtime director of the FBI), representatives of the federal government looked on passively while civil rights activists were beaten or harassed by white supremacists who often acted with the approval, if not the aid, of local police.[147] Eventually, the federal government was moved to intervene. The case, however, that prompted a more active federal presence itself vividly illustrates the phenomenon of racially selective *under*-protection.

Frustrated by widespread apathy and the stubborn resilience of the Jim Crow system, activists decided in 1964 that they would have to find a provocative way to highlight its oppressive racial practices. They settled upon the idea of sending scores of *white* reformers into the Deep South. They believed that white activists would better attract the attention of other whites, including white shapers of opinion and policy. Leaders of the black freedom struggle also thought that a few white casualties of white supremacist violence would elicit a greater response from the national government than had been forthcoming as a response to the maimings and killings of black protesters.[148]

These intuitions were vindicated. When two whites, Andrew Goodman and Michael Schwerner, were reported missing, along with a black activist, James Chaney, many politicians displayed unprecedented attentiveness. Voicing the sentiments of many within the civil rights community, the wife of one of the missing white men declared, "It's tragic that white northerners have to be caught up into the machinery of injustice and indifference in the South before the American people register concern." Rita Schwerner went on to say that she suspected that, "if Mr. Chaney, a native Negro Mississippian, had been alone at the time of the disappearance, this case, like many before it, would have gone completely unnoticed."[149]

Goodman, Chaney, and Schwerner had been caught up in a veritable whirlwind of brutality. They were killed during the course of responding to the burning of a church by Klansmen. The Klansmen were angered by the congregation's willingness to allow civil rights activists to use its building as a "freedom school." On their way to the gutted church, Goodman, Chaney, and Schwerner were arrested, purportedly for speeding, by Deputy Sheriff Cecil Price. After spending several hours in jail, they were released, only to be stopped again by Price, who then turned them over to the gang of Klansmen that murdered them and hid their bodies.

The disappearance of Goodman, Chaney, and Schwerner prompted a massive response at the highest levels of the federal government. Eventually their bodies were found and, with the assistance of paid informants, their killers identified. State officials, however, never prosecuted anyone for the murders. They claimed that they were prevented from doing so because the FBI refused to share with them essential evidence. For good reason, however, the FBI refused to cooperate. Local law enforcement officers were not acting in good faith but were, instead, intent upon unmasking the FBI's informants and thwarting any punishment of the suspects.[150]

The inaction or opposition of local prosecutors would ordinarily have put an end to efforts to inflict a just punishment upon the wrongdoers. This time, however, the national government marshalled all its resources to obtain convictions under federal law. Difficulties abounded, two of which are particularly significant. One stemmed from the federal district judge who presided over the case, Harold Cox, a notorious segregationist who, reading precedent as narrowly as he could, dismissed many of the criminal counts lodged against the defendants.[151] The Supreme Court, however, reversed Cox, reinstated the charges, and remanded the case for trial.[152] This set the stage for a second difficulty: persuading an all-white jury in the Deep South to punish white men for criminally inflicting violence on a "biggety" Negro and "nigger-loving" whites.

Jury nullification in the service of white supremacy had long posed a hurdle to those who attempted to extend to blacks the equal protection of the laws. By "jury nullification," I refer to a refusal to convict despite belief beyond a reasonable doubt based on proper evidence that the defendant committed the offense for which he is charged. Even as other weapons of the segregation regime began to disintegrate in the 1960s, nullification retained considerable strength. All-white juries acquitted the accused killers of Lemuel Penn notwithstanding the confession of a participant,[153] acquitted the accused killers of Viola Liuzzo despite the eyewitness testimony of an informant and other incriminating evidence,[154] and acquitted the accused killers of Jonathan Daniels and James Reeb despite the absence of any reasonable doubt concerning their culpability.[155] "You cannot whip us," a Mississippi segregationist district attorney confidently declared to Attorney General Robert F. Kennedy in 1964, "as long as we have the right of a jury trial."[156] (For discussion of jury nullification in a different context, see pp. 295–310.)

A strong case was made against the assailants of Goodman, Chaney, and Schwerner. It included testimony from paid informants, several of whom were police officers and members of the Klan at the time of the killings, as well as testimony from participants in the crime. Perhaps the most memorable single piece of testimony came from one participant who described how one Klansman begged his colleagues to "save one for me" and then bitterly complained when the one they saved for him to kill was James Chaney. This defendant was said to have groused that his associates "didn't leave me anything but a nigger."[157]

To counter the prosecution's evidence, the defense made a naked appeal to racism and regional resentment. One defense attorney asked a prosecution witness whether Schwerner had tried "to get young male Negroes to sign statements agreeing to rape a white woman once a week during the hot summer of 1964."[158] Although Judge Cox rebuked the attorney for asking this question without any evidentiary basis, defense counsel continued to make racist appeals, asking, for instance, whether "colored women" had stayed in Schwerner's apartment and what the murdered men thought about integration in the schools.[159] (For discussion of law relating to racial appeals by attorneys, see pp. 256–310.)

The all-white jury initially deadlocked but then agreed to convict seven of the defendants—including the lawmen—while acquitting seven. Some observers attached to the verdict large symbolic import. According to the *New York Times*, it was proof of a "quiet revolution . . . a slow, still faltering but inexorable conversion to the concept that a single standard of justice must cover whites and Negroes alike."[160] Some support for the *Times'* assertion came from results in other federal prosecutions. Although efforts to try violent white supremacists faltered in state courts, in federal courts juries convicted the killers of Samuel Penn and Viola Liuzzo. On the other hand, racially motivated violence aimed at the civil rights movement remained a constant threat throughout the 1960s, particularly in the South. In Mississippi in January 1966,

Klansman killed Vernon Dahmer, an NAACP official, by firebombing his home. State prosecutors succeeded in obtaining convictions against four of the perpetrators, but others escaped convictions in two separate trials because of deadlocked juries that appear to have been hamstrung by a small number of white jurors who refused to vote to convict despite overwhelming evidence of guilt.[161]

Frustrated by what they perceived as a paucity of legal authority to respond adequately to racially motivated violence, officials of the Johnson administration proposed legislation in 1966 aimed at enlarging federal jurisdiction. This legislation, codified in the U.S. Criminal Code as Section 245, was one of the last pieces of federal civil rights legislation during the Second Reconstruction.

The major innovation of Section 245 is that it criminalizes certain activities whether or not the perpetrator is an official or otherwise acting under color of law. Die-hard segregationists in Congress attacked the legislation, arguing that it violated established norms of federalism. This complaint, however, has been consistently rejected by lower federal courts, although the Supreme Court has never ruled on the issue.

The activity criminalized by Section 245 is of two sorts. First, it subjects to possible punishment "whoever, whether or not acting under color of law, by force or threat of force" willfully prevents any person from voting, participating in any program provided by the federal government, working for the federal government, or serving as a juror in any federal court.[162] Second, Section 245 subjects to possible punishment whoever willfully interferes with any person because of his race and because he is or has been attending any public school, enjoying any benefit provided by the state, applying for or enjoying any employment opportunity, serving or seeking to serve on a jury, or using any vehicle or otherwise travelling in interstate commerce.[163]

Three aspects of this legislation are relevant to our concerns. First, Section 245 encountered sufficient opposition to delay its enactment until two years after it was initially proposed, notwithstanding the highly publicized acts of racially motivated violence and state inaction or complicity described above. Many of the same federalism arguments that had been used previously to oppose federal antilynching statutes were used again to block an even narrower grant of federal authority. To be sure, things had changed between the 1920s and the 1960s. Gone were the speeches openly lauding antiblack terrorism, but opposition by segregationists and their ideological allies remained intact.

Second, when political pressure mounted to the extent that it appeared that the proposed legislation might pass Congress despite resistance, opponents insisted that the bill include an antirioting provision aimed at punishing black militants who were blamed for inciting "the long hot summers" of the years 1965–1967, when rioting engulfed hundreds of urban black ghettos across the United States. "Urban civil disorders," Michael Belknap notes, "bothered the House [of Representatives] more than attacks on blacks and civil rights workers."[164]

Third, the murder of Martin Luther King, Jr., on April 4, 1968, is what finally propelled the bill, the Civil Rights Act of 1968, to enactment. King's assassination, like that of Malcolm X, is seen by many blacks as yet another example of racially selective underprotection on the part of the government (or, worse, racially selective governmental murder). King and Malcolm X, the two most famous leaders of black liberation struggles in America during the 1960s, were both assassinated while under close surveillance by federal law enforcement agencies (a subject about which more will be said in chapter 3). This fact has buttressed the idea that there exists a broad racist conspiracy—"the Plan"— against blacks guided by powerful forces within and outside of government.[165] There exists, however, no substantial evidence that with respect to either King or Malcolm X government officials at any level conspired in their assassinations.[166]

Ironically, given the origins of Section 245, one cannot be sure that its provisions would have applied even to King's assassination. That is because its provisions are so narrow. An illustration of its unduly limited reach (as well as the *continuing*, albeit diminished, problem of racially motivated violence) is provided by an ugly episode which transpired in April 1980, in Chattanooga, Tennessee. Three Klansmen, on their way to burn crosses in a predominantly black neighborhood, shot and wounded five elderly black women. The Klansmen were acquitted of all criminal charges by a jury in state court but forced to pay damages to their victims in a subsequent federal civil suit. No federal criminal prosecution was brought because the Justice Department concluded that the victims' activities at the time of the shootings (standing upon a public sidewalk and watering a plant on privately owned property) did not fall within the spectrum of activities defined by Section 245.[167] Even now, in other words, federal statutory law remains deficient in terms of criminalizing racially motivated violence.[168]

The Failure to Protect Blacks from Common-Law Criminality: The Problem of Black-on-Black Victimization

Thus far, this chapter has mainly focused on ways that governments have failed, often by design, to protect blacks from racially motivated violence perpetrated by whites. Now the focus shifts to ways in which governments have failed, again often by design, to protect blacks from "ordinary" criminality, much of it perpetrated by blacks. During the antebellum period, criminal law in the slave states explicitly withheld protection from slaves with respect to many offenses. Hence, when a slave woman was raped, the law recognized no criminal violation (see pp. 34–36). Although the Fourteenth Amendment to the federal constitution supposedly prohibits states from continuing such practices, many officials have disregarded it. Describing law enforcement in Mississippi during the age of Jim Crow, Neil R. McMillen concludes that, "for the rape or murder of a person of his own race, the black defendant was far more likely than his white counterpart to confront an indulgent prosecutor willing to exchange a guilty plea for life imprisonment."[169] "Such permissiveness," McMillen notes, "seemed to condone intraracial black lawlessness and offered inadequate protection for black life and property."[170] Many whites explicitly said as much. "We have very little crime," a white person in Natchez, Mississippi, boasted. "Of course, Negroes knife each other occasionally but there is little *real* crime. I mean Negroes against whites or whites against each other."[171] Commenting on why news of black-on-black homicides went unreported in local, white-owned newspapers, one editor remarked, "It is like dog chewing on dog . . . the white people are not interested in the matter. Only another dead nigger—that's all."[172]

Although a heinous black-on-black crime might provoke a stiff punishment, often in cases of even serious offenses some extra factor was needed to elicit the attention and efforts of white law enforcement officials when the crime was black on black. Seeking the death penalty for a murder, a Mississippi prosecutor did not simply state to the jury that the facts warranted the defendant's execution. Rather, he asserted that capital punishment was in order because the defendant, a "bad nigger," had killed "a good nigger," by which the prosecutor meant, in his own words, "a white man's nigger."[173] Explaining the jury's death sentence, defense counsel remarked: "The average white jury would take it for granted that the killing of a white man's nigger is a more serious offense than the killing of a plain, every-day black man."[174] David Sykes, a black man, was sentenced to death for murdering George McIntosh, another black man. In calling for—and obtaining—a death sentence, however, the Mississippi prosecutor did not focus the jurors' attention on the actual crime that was committed. Rather, the prosecutor focused the jurors' attention on a crime that *might* be committed in the future against white folks. According to the prosecutor, the defendant murdered in order to gain access to the murdered man's wife. In his argument to the jury, though, the prosecutor did not base his plea for a conviction and punishment on the dastardliness of *that* misdeed. Rather, he based his argument on the grounds that, absent a conviction and death sentence, the defendant "might rape some of the white women of the country."[175]

In *An American Dilemma*, Gunnar Myrdal reported in 1944 that this same attitude was prevalent throughout the South:

> The leniency in punishment of Negro crime against Negroes has repeatedly been pointed out ... by white Southerners as evidence of the friendliness of Southern courts towards Negroes.... Yet the Southern Negro community is not at all happy about this double standard.... Law-abiding Negroes point out that [criminal Negroes] ... are a danger to the Negro community. Leniency toward Negro defendants in cases involving crimes against other Negroes is thus actually a form of discrimination.[176]

Since Myrdal's observation, changes in law, customs, and sentiments have rearranged substantially the ground rules of racial interaction. Perceptions persist, however, that law enforcement authorities take more seriously crimes against whites than crimes against blacks. Persistent also are events and trends that lend support to that perception. Consider a case decided sixty-eight years after the prosecution of David Sykes mentioned above. In the course of prosecuting Marshall Andre Kelley for rape, a district attorney in California felt moved to say in a closing argument to the jury: "Think about the consequences of letting a guilty man . . . go free. Because maybe the next time it won't be a little black girl from the other side of the tracks; maybe it will be somebody that you know."[177] The district attorney explicitly suggested, in other words, that if the rape of the black victim in the case was insufficient to trigger an appropriate response, then the vision of the same defendant—a black man—raping a white victim might better concentrate the jurors' minds.

Large numbers of blacks are convinced that, in general, law enforcement authorities value the safety and well-being of whites more than that of blacks. In 1968, the Report of the National Advisory Commission on Civil Disorders, also known as the Kerner Report, stated:

> The strength of ghetto feelings about hostile police conduct may even be exceeded by the conviction that ghetto neighborhoods are not given adequate police protection.
>
> . . . [S]urveys have reported that Negroes in Harlem and South Central Los Angeles mention inadequate protection more often than brutality and harassment as a reason for their resentment toward the police.[178]

A quarter-century later, many blacks share this same perception. To them, concentrations of drug abuse and criminal violence are not impersonal incidents of socioeconomic dynamics but rather the consequences of purposeful designs to deprive blacks of legal protections and the benefits that flow from them. This is the view of Minister Louis Farrakhan, who declares, "The epidemic of drugs and violence in the black community stems from a calculated attempt by whites to foster black self-destruction."[179] His perception that the criminality besetting black communities is abetted by a shadowy conspiracy of white power elites is embraced by a substantial number of African-Americans. Reporting in 1990 on the prevalence of conspiracy theories among black Americans, Jason DeParle noted in the *New York Times* that "a quarter of the blacks polled said that the government deliberately makes sure that drugs are easily available in poor black neighborhoods in order to harm black people."

Much of this conspiracy-minded rhetoric is inflated by paranoia. No one has brought forth any substantial proof evidencing "a deliberate" governmental effort currently to harm black people, and the plausibility of such a scheme is nil. At the same time, there does exist a kernel of truth in the general complaint that, in all too many instances, networks of decisionmakers—journalists, police, prosecutors, legislators, voters, etc.—respond differently—more attentively—when whites rather than blacks are victimized by crime or other injurious activity.

When a white, young, affluent woman was raped by as many as twelve colored youths in New York's Central Park in 1989, her agony became a front-page news story for several days. The same week that she was raped, twenty-eight other cases of sexual assault were reported in New York, seventeen of which involved black women as victims. They all received much less media attention than the jogger. None involved the number of rapists implicated by the jogger case. Still, several of them, too, involved horrifying facts that might have distinguished them from the "normal" run of criminality to which big city dwellers have become largely inured.[180]

One must be careful to avoid speaking with undue confidence about inferences regarding law enforcement that are drawn from the character of media coverage. First, even if media coverage suggests racial selectivity, that does not necessarily mean that law enforcement officials are responding in a racially selective manner. Second, even when it is the case that a crime featuring a white victim receives considerably more media and police attention than similar crimes featuring black victims, there remains the possibility that other, nonracial factors may be playing a role in the differential treatment—the relative youth or affluence of the victims, the activities in which they were engaged when assaulted, or the locations at which the crimes occurred. It might be, for instance, that, regardless of race, a person raped in Manhattan has a much better chance of receiving prominent coverage in the pages of the *New York Times* (and thus, perhaps, an enhanced amount of attention from law enforcement officials) than a person raped in any of New York City's outer boroughs. In all likelihood, however, differing degrees of public attention will result in differing amounts of actual investment in investigations and prosecutions. It makes sense to suppose that local law enforcement officials will probably allocate more of their scarce resources to the crime that is a page-one *cause célèbre* than to the crime that never makes it past the back pages of the local press. Moreover, there exists credible evidence that in at least some locales race continues to account for part of the differential treatment observed.

In 1988, a study in Dallas, Texas, indicated that rapists whose victims were white were punished more severely than those whose victims were black or Hispanic. According to the *Dallas Times Herald*, which commissioned the study, the average prison term for a man convicted of raping a black woman was two years, whereas the average term for raping an Hispanic woman was five years and for raping a white woman ten.[181] Again, there is need to sound a note of caution about attributing causal significance to race when it is one of many variables that are difficult to distinguish from one another. Unless researchers are careful to account for variables often correlated with race, it will remain impossible to know precisely what causes differential treatment. For instance, unless researchers take into account the possibility that the criminal justice system sentences more harshly persons accused of raping strangers than persons accused of raping acquaintances, what appears to be a difference stemming from race may be a difference stemming from contrasting reactions to stranger rapes as opposed to acquaintance rapes (assuming that stranger rapes are more likely to be interracial and acquaintance rapes intraracial). Unfortunately, the value of the *Dallas Times Herald* study is lessened precisely because it did not explore the character of the relationship between victims and perpetrators.

After one acknowledges the limitations of statistical correlations, however, there remains the patterns plus anecdotal evidence which adds plausibility, if not probability, to the fear that legal systems continue to regard the victimization of black women with less concern than the victimization of white women. Summarizing the results of his investigation of the processing of rape cases in Indianapolis, Indiana, in the period 1978–1980, Professor Gary LaFree concluded that the administration of criminal justice there still contained "vestiges of an older sexual-stratification system that punishes men accused of rape according to the race of the victim-offender dyad. Cases involving black offenders and white victims were treated the most seriously, while black intraracial cases were treated the least seriously."[182] Exploring the reasons for this, Professor LaFree hypothesized that, among other factors, racial distance inhibits jurors from identifying as fully with certain victims as with others. "Our interview with jurors," he writes, "suggested that part of the explanation for [them being more inclined to vote for acquittal in black-victim cases] was that jurors—many of whom were middle-class whites—were influenced by stereotypes of black women as more likely to consent to sex or as more sexually experienced and hence less harmed by the assault."[183]

The best-documented large-scale illustration of racially selective underprotection is also the most chilling, for it arises in the context of capital punishment. Writing in 1940, Charles Mangum, Jr., suggested that "it should occasion no great surprise [if data indicated], especially in interracial homicide and sex crimes, a decided tendency toward a longer or more severe sentence where the victim was white and a lighter punishment when the victim was colored." He refrained, however, from alleging the actual existence of racially selective sentencing practices because "most of the instances which have been unearthed in an effort to prove that such unfairness really exists are so complicated by the presence of other social phenomena as to be practically useless in an attempt to show that the injustice was due to racial distinction alone."[184] Since Mangum's study, scholars in various disciplines have produced a steady flow of increasingly sophisticated empirical studies on race and capital sentencing. Most of them strongly suggest that, because of race, defendants who kill whites are more likely to be sentenced to death than defendants who kill blacks.[185] The most comprehensive of these studies investigated the disposition of over two thousand murder cases in Georgia between 1973 and 1979. It found that even after accounting for every nonracial variable that might plausibly have mattered, the odds of being condemned to death were 4.3 times greater for defendants who killed whites than for defendants who killed blacks, a variable nearly as influential as a prior conviction for armed robbery, rape, or even murder.[186] (For more on racial discrimination in the application of capital punishment, see chapter 9.)

One might think that such statistics would prompt blacks to be drawn to demands for "law and order." Many are on the grounds that black communities are especially in need of effective public law enforcement services since blacks far more than whites live in settings that make them particularly vulnerable to robbery, rape, murder, and the overall destruction of social life that occurs in areas in which street crime flourishes. Many more would associate themselves with demands for law and order if they did not fear racially prejudiced misconduct by law enforcement officials. History reinforced by persistent contemporary abuses gives credence and force to this fear. It is to the story of racially unjust treatment of suspects, defendants, and prisoners that I now turn.

3.

History:
Unequal Enforcement

With reason, African Americans tend to grow up
believing that the law is the enemy.
—Brent Staples

THUS FAR I have focused on ways in which African-Americans have suffered from racial policies that deprive them of equal protection against
criminality. Now I shall focus on the ways in which the legal system has
discriminated against blacks officially deemed to be suspects, defendants, and convicts.

The Black Defendant During the Slavery Era

Prior to the Civil War, many jurisdictions made slaves into "criminals"
by prohibiting them from pursuing a wide range of activities that whites
were typically free to pursue.[1] Authorities enacted criminal statutes barring slaves from learning to read, leaving their masters' property without a proper pass, engaging in "unbecoming" conduct in the presence of
a white female, assembling to worship outside the supervisory presence
of a white person, neglecting to step out of the way when a white person
approached on a walkway, smoking in public, walking with a cane,
making loud noises, or defending themselves from assaults.[2] Governed
by a separate law of crimes, slaves were also subjected to a separate

brand of punishment. Slaves, for example, were subjected to capital punishment for a wider range of crimes than any other sector of the population. Virginia, for instance, defined seventy-three capital crimes applicable to slaves but only one—first degree murder—applicable to whites.[3]

Racial discrimination in punishment stemmed from a variety of beliefs, some of which conflicted. On the one hand, white masters, recognizing that blacks reacted to enslavement with the same impulse to revolt as other humans, imposed harsher codes of punishment to ensure control. On the other hand, whites imposed greater punishments out of a sense that blacks, as primitive, wild, inferior beings, were fundamentally different from whites, and thus in need of more coercive social control. "The more debased or licentious a class of society is," Judge Ruffin asserted for the North Carolina Supreme Court, "the more rigorous must be the penal rules of restraint."[4]

The law of slavery imposed differences not only in degrees of punishment but also in the character of punishment. Long after maiming, branding, ear cropping, whipping, castration, and other sorts of physically injurious punishments had waned as an approved method of chastising whites, they remained available for the correction of slaves.[5] Because of humanitarian and financial reasons, the worst of the maiming punishments were probably resorted to sparingly. Whipping, on the other hand, was an oft-used device for correction. Justifying whipping, the Florida Supreme Court observed that "the degraded caste should be continually reminded of their inferior position, to keep them in a proper degree of subjection to the authority of the free white citizens."[6]

Discriminated against in terms of substantive criminal law and in terms of punishment, slaves were also discriminated against in terms of procedural rules. As noted previously, slaves were prohibited from testifying against or contradicting whites in court. Moreover, in some jurisdictions, such as Virginia, South Carolina, and Louisiana, slaves were tried before special tribunals—slave courts—designed to render quick, rough justice. Affirming the conviction of a slave charged with assaulting a white man, the Louisiana Supreme Court acknowledged the lowered expectations that surrounded the proceedings accorded to slaves charged with crime. "The law," the court observed, "does not demand on the trial of slaves, in the tribunals established for that purpose, an observance of the technical rules which regulate criminal proceedings in

the higher courts [reserved for adjudicating cases involving free peo-
ple]." The court based its decision and reasoning in part on a statutory
provision which expressly stated that "no [slave] proceedings . . . shall be
annulled or impeded by any error of form."[7]

As burdensome as the criminal law was for slave defendants, in certain ways it placed them in a better position than either their free black
contemporaries or some of their emancipated descendants. First of all,
as human property, slaves represented an investment that their white
masters were typically interested in protecting. Masters stood to lose financially if slaves were convicted of serious crimes for which they could
be beaten, incarcerated, transported out of state, or executed. The state
did compensate owners for slaves it executed—much as the state pays
owners of land for property it condemns through eminent domain. But
levels of compensation varied widely. In certain locales, owners faced
stark undercompensation.[8] This helps to explain why some owners
were willing to go to the considerable expense of paying attorneys to
represent their slaves; it was worthwhile financially to defend their human property against serious criminal charges.

Another factor that placed slave defendants in a better position than
that occupied by many of their emancipated descendants was the confidence felt by the white master class prior to the Civil War. Secure in
their hegemony, surrounded by a legal order openly, unapologetically,
and formally committed to white supremacy, the most elite sectors of
the antebellum master class sometimes judged slaves with remarkable
punctiliousness. In a study of appellate courts in nine Southern states between 1830 and 1860, Professor A. E. Keir Nash discovered that black
defendants received reversals of convictions in 136 of 238 appeals. These
cases disclose a striking exactitude in procedural matters.[9] When prosecutors erred in drawing up indictments of slaves, appellate judges reversed convictions even in circumstances in which it would have seemed
rather easy to fudge the matter. In the 1840s, for example, both the Alabama and Tennessee supreme courts reversed convictions for rape because of the failure of prosecutors to specify in the indictments that the
victims were white, even though at trial the prosecution offered ample
proof of this fact as well as the slaves' guilt.[10] When juries were improperly constituted, even in cases where actual guilt appeared to be clear,
appellate courts reversed convictions. The Supreme Court of Alabama,
for example, overturned a guilty verdict against a slave charged with

murdering a white man on the grounds that one of his jurors had only a share in an undistributed estate of slaves, whereas state law required a juror in a case against a slave to be a full owner of at least one slave.[11]

In notable instances, appellate courts in the slave South reversed convictions of slaves based on involuntary confessions, holding that evidence obtained through coercion was insufficiently trustworthy to be relied upon. In *Ann* v. *State*, for example, a slave was charged with killing her master's baby.[12] Immediately following the baby's death, the master struck the defendant and threatened to shoot her. A day later, the defendant confessed to two overseers. The state argued that the confession had been properly admitted into evidence because the defendant was no longer in imminent danger of violence when she confessed. The Tennessee Supreme Court, however, rejected the state's argument, holding that, under the circumstances, the confession could not be viewed as truly voluntary:

> in the case of a timid girl, of tender age, ignorant and illiterate, a slave and in chains, whose life had been threatened by her master, and against whom the hand of everyone, even those of her own color and condition, seems to have been raised . . . the law . . . conclusively presumes that an influence was exerted upon the mind of the prisoner.[13]

This exclusion of the slave's confession was by no means idiosyncratic. The Mississippi Supreme Court ruled that magistrates in that state were obliged not only to warn defendants, including slaves, that their statements could be used against them but also that they had a right to remain silent. The court also ruled that magistrates were under a duty to make sure that prisoners, whatever their status, *understood* those warnings.*

---

*Also revealing is a case from North Carolina involving the prosecution of a free black man who was convicted of violating a state law which forbade blacks from carrying firearms, *State* v. *Jacobs*, 50 N.C. 256 (1858). The defendant appealed his conviction on the grounds that his privilege against self-incrimination had been denied because the trial court had insisted that he make himself available for display to the jury. The prosecution wanted the jury to see for itself that the defendant was black. The North Carolina Supreme Court reversed the conviction, holding that the trial

Though surprisingly exacting, rulings such as these were of sharply limited significance. The perceived misdeeds of blacks were mainly dealt with outside of courtrooms. Except for the most serious crimes, it was unusual for the control of slaves by masters to be superseded by the control of slaves by judicial authorities. Moreover, regardless of the punctiliousness of certain antebellum Southern appellate judges, *all* of them, even the most exacting, were complicit in the maintenance, justification, and enforcement of an abominable institution. Still, it is fascinating and instructive to see the paradoxes, gaps, and surprises that emerge in the law of slavery. Dedicated to the protection of slavery, some appellate courts of the Old South also displayed a simultaneous dedication to a strict observance of legal rules. Indeed, in terms of procedural fairness, black defendants charged with serious, interracial crimes were better off before the abolition of slavery than for a long time afterward. As we have seen, prior to the Civil War, in a substantial number of cases, state appellate courts attempted to ensure that slaves were accorded the procedural rights promised to them under existing law, even when doing so entailed reversing convictions of clearly guilty defendants. By contrast, after the Civil War, Southern state appellate courts became notorious for ignoring violations of black defendants' rights and for scheming to prevent redress of such violations by federal courts. In 1844, the Mississippi Supreme Court was willing to reverse the conviction of a slave tried on the basis of a confession obtained without direct threats or promises but made while a hostile crowd milled outside the jail where he was kept.[14] In 1935, the same court was willing to uphold the conviction of black men sentenced to death for murdering a white man on the basis of confessions obtained by torture.[15]

---

court had wrongly compelled the defendant to furnish evidence against himself. The attorney general of North Carolina argued that, under state law, defendants were required to be present at their trials. The supreme court countered that this law could be satisfied without compelling the defendants to stand or sit within view of the jury. What the court appeared to have in mind was permitting the defendant to be present in the courtroom but out of sight to the jury, perhaps behind a partition.

Free Blacks and Suspected Runaways
during the Slavery Era

In antebellum America, blacks of all types—the free, the enslaved, and those of disputed status—were discriminated against racially by the criminal law. Three areas of controversy are especially illuminating: the fight over the Negro Seamen Acts, the scope of rights of free Negroes in the North, and the struggle over the Fugitive Slave Act.

The Negro Seamen Acts show vividly the extent to which the slave South subjected *all* blacks, not just slaves, to racially oppressive criminal laws. These laws provided that any blacks on board a ship in a South Carolina or Louisiana harbor would be imprisoned throughout the period during which the ship remained in harbor. Enacted after discovery of plans for a slave rebellion in South Carolina, these laws were intended to insulate the slave population from the "contagion of liberty" that might be spread by free black seamen. The laws did not criminalize any conduct on the part of the black seamen; rather, the laws criminalized their very presence. The Negro Seamen Acts, moreover, not only directed that blacks aboard vessels be imprisoned. They also stipulated that the captains of such vessels pay for the imprisonment and that, in the event of a captain's default, the black seamen would be sold into slavery.

Massachusetts attempted to challenge the constitutionality of the South Carolina Negro Seamen statute. It claimed that this law violated the privileges and immunities clause of the federal constitution by depriving black citizens of Massachusetts of the respect that was their due as citizens even in the harbors of South Carolina. Massachusetts' claim, however, never made it to court. First the Massachusetts legislature sought to engage a South Carolina attorney to challenge the statute. But no attorney in South Carolina was willing to take the case. The Massachusetts legislature then sent its own attorney to South Carolina to investigate the possibility of bringing a suit. However, after only a few days there, he was forced to flee when it became clear that his safety was in danger and that South Carolina officials would do nothing to protect him.[16]

The Negro Seamen laws represented just one of many actions taken by slave states to reduce the status of free blacks. Every slave state except Delaware barred free Negroes from testifying against whites in court.[17]

At one point, Georgia denied free blacks the right to a jury trial, decreeing instead that they be tried, like slaves, before a local justice of the peace. Slave jurisdictions specifically criminalized certain conduct if engaged in by free blacks. Hence, in various locales, it was a crime for free blacks to entertain slaves, meet in groups of more than seven, attend school, or hold church meetings.[18] Unsurprisingly, states distinguished whites from free blacks for purposes of punishment. For example, whereas some slave states subjected whites to fines or prison terms for crimes such as harboring runaway slaves, they subjected free blacks to the additional penalty of whipping.[19]

Blacks in the North generally faced a better situation than their counterparts in the South. This stemmed in large part from the gradual abolition of slavery in the North during the first thirty years of the nineteenth century.[20] Northern blacks were not subjected to a separate, inferior court system as were slaves and free blacks in some parts of the South. Nor were they subjected to surveillance as close and aggressive as that imposed upon blacks in the South, where the entire white community was directed to serve as a police force on guard against slave uprisings. Nor were they subjected to as many insulting prohibitions.

Blacks in the North, however, did face racial discrimination.[21] Although considerable work remains to be done delineating the precise racial character of the antebellum administration of criminal law in the North, it is safe to suppose that black suspects and defendants were prejudiced insofar as they faced officials steeped in the Negrophobia that dominated white Northern public opinion in those years. "It is hardly possible," an observer noted at the 1846 New York state constitutional convention, that Negroes "should have an impartial trial. Hated, trodden upon, and despised, they had not the means to procure counsel to defend themselves against false and malicious charges, and false witnesses; and too often, an accusation against them was equivalent to conviction."[22] Moreover, just as certain Southern states criminalized the presence of black seamen, so too did certain Northern jurisdictions criminalize the presence of Negro emigrants. Illinois, Indiana, and Oregon incorporated into their constitutions clauses barring the further admission of Negroes. Although these bans went largely unenforced, they did give rise to at least a few prosecutions, such as the conviction in 1856 in Indiana of an African-American man who brought his fiancée into the state to marry her. Upholding the conviction, the Indiana Supreme Court declared sternly that it was the state's policy "to exclude any further ingress of negroes, and to remove those already among us as speedily as possible."[23]

Since the Civil War, champions of racial equality have looked to the federal government, particularly the federal courts, for help. Prior to the Civil War, the situation was reversed; for blacks, state legislatures and courts were the better forums. Although the great majority of Northern whites perceived blacks as a racially inferior caste, many also disliked slavery and, even more, resented efforts by white Southerners to spread proslavery mores and practices across the nation. This resentment, allied with abolitionist sentiments, provided the basis for what came to be known as "personal liberty laws," which gave some degree of protection in the North to free blacks and fugitive slaves. Personal liberty laws required masters to petition state officials to seize alleged runaway slaves, stipulated procedures to be followed for the purpose of verifying the claims of masters, and criminalized noncompliance. Such laws represented an instance in which allegiance to state's rights furthered the interests of blacks. Supporters of the personal liberty laws insisted that states had the right to regulate the activities of slaveowners hunting runaway slaves within their jurisdictions.[24] The Supreme Court disagreed, however, ruling in *Prigg* v. *Pennsylvania*[25] that under the federal constitution states did not have the authority to regulate slaveowners pursuing their fugitive human property. Later, moreover, Congress and the president enacted a statute, the Fugitive Slave Act of 1850,[26] which created a federal bureaucracy to aid slaveowners in the capture and return of runaway slaves.[27]

Congress omitted from the Fugitive Slave Act "nothing which the utmost ingenuity could suggest as essential to the successful enforcement of the master's claim to recover his fugitive slave."[28] The act created a cadre of commissioners who were empowered to appoint deputies to execute warrants issued for the apprehension of persons accused of being fugitive slaves. The act also authorized the commissioners and their deputies to enlist the aid of bystanders or posses to enforce the act. The act stipulated that a commissioner would be paid a fee of $5 in each case in which he determined that a slavemaster was *not* entitled to an alleged fugitive slave, and would be paid a fee of $10 in each case in which he determined that a master was entitled to the accused person. To encourage diligence, the act provided that a $1,000 fine could be imposed upon U.S. marshals who either refused or neglected to execute arrest warrants issued by commissioners. The act also provided that a U.S. marshal would be liable to an owner for the full value of slaves who escaped from custody after arrest. Finally, to streamline the process, the act commanded commissioners to hear and determine cases in a summary manner, meaning that upon receiving "satisfactory proof" of the identity of an accused person, a commissioner was supposed to remand him to the owner's custody without a jury trial, without access to habeas corpus, and without the opportunity to testify on his own behalf.

The Fugitive Slave Act profoundly undermined blacks' sense of security in the North by making any African-American an accusation away from quasi-criminal legal proceedings which were tilted heavily in favor of any person alleging a property interest in a black human. The fear and anxiety it created is poignantly reflected in a handbill dated April 24, 1851:

> Colored People of Boston, One & All, You are hereby respectfully CAUTIONED and advised, to avoid conversing with the Watchmen and Police Officers of Boston . . . [They have been] employed in KIDNAPPING, CATCHING, AND KEEPING SLAVES. Therefore, if you value your LIBERTY, and the welfare of the fugitives among you, Shun them in every possible manner, as so many HOUNDS on the track of the most unfortunate of your race.[29]

Pursuant to the Fugitive Slave Act, approximately three hundred runaways were returned to bondage between 1850 and 1860.[30]

The Black Defendant during Reconstruction

The Civil War and Reconstruction profoundly changed the obligation of state governments to African-American defendants. Before the Reconstruction, states were permitted to discriminate racially against blacks. Even after the Thirteenth Amendment to the federal constitution abolished slavery, some of the former slave states continued to discriminate racially against blacks in an open, formal manner. They passed Black Codes, which included criminal provisions that regulated

Negroes far more closely and harshly than the "regular" law regulated whites. The Mississippi Black Code, for instance, made it a criminal offense for blacks to make "insulting gestures" or to function as ministers of the Gospel without a license from some regularly organized (i.e., white) church. Mississippi, South Carolina, and Alabama continued to make blacks alone eligible for hanging for raping white women. South Carolina created a special court system to adjudicate cases in which blacks were accused of crimes.[31]

Intended to minimize the consequences of the abolition of slavery, the Black Codes had just the opposite effect by nakedly displaying the former Confederate states' desire to keep blacks in bondage. Anger at such intransigence, repugnance for compulsory (as distinct from contractual) labor, fear that overly harsh conditions in the South would drive blacks northward, empathy for the Negro, and a variety of other motivations prompted Congress to enact legislation that canceled the Black Codes. A wide-ranging statute which remains an active part of America's civil rights jurisprudence, the Civil Rights Act of 1866 stipulates that all citizens "of every race and color, without regards to any previous condition of slavery or involuntary servitude . . . shall be subject to like punishment, pains, and penalties."[32] Two years later, Congress reinforced its insistence that local law enforcement authorities treat all persons equally before the same laws. Congress did so by proposing the Fourteenth Amendment to the federal constitution, which obligates states to bestow upon all persons "the equal protection of the laws."

Beneath these formal changes, however, what happened on the ground in terms of the administration of criminal law? Relatively little detailed, systematic information is known about the treatment of black suspects and defendants during Reconstruction. Contrary to legend, blacks did not dominate society, even in those states such as South Carolina and Mississippi where they constituted a voting majority. For the first time, however, blacks did garner an appreciable degree of political power that enabled them to affect the treatment they received from the criminal justice system. In the South they exercised influence as voters, jurors, legislators, magistrates, justices of the peace, sheriffs, police officers, and, in at least one instance, as an elected justice of a state supreme court.[33]

The limited and fragmentary evidence presently available suggests that substantial black political influence diminished the capacity of local law enforcement authorities to wield their power invidiously in ways harmful to Negroes. Comparing the racial demographics of criminal indictments for property offenses in jurisdictions where blacks served on grand juries to those where blacks were excluded, Professor Donald G. Nieman concludes that, in the former, "the presence of black grand jurors limited the capricious impulse of whites to indict those whom they merely suspected of theft."[34]

The influence of black voters and officeholders during Reconstruction also appears to have checked a practice that emerged immediately after the abolition of slavery—the practice of using criminal laws to reimpose involuntary servitude. In 1866, for instance, Alabama made a criminal of "any person who, having no visible means of support, or being dependent on his labor, lives without employment."[35] Although this and other vagrancy statutes were silent as to race, their authors intended and assumed that they would be applied principally, if not exclusively, against Negroes. During Reconstruction, however, such laws were either invalidated, repealed, or ignored. "There is a vagrant law on our statute books," an Alabama newspaper observed in 1870, "but it is a dead letter because those who are charged with its enforcement are indebted to the vagrant vote for their offices."[36]

The Black Defendant during the Era of Segregation: Outrages

After Reconstruction's demise, white authorities uprooted black influence in the administration of criminal justice. The ranks of those running the criminal justice system became, once again, lily-white. Speaking generally about the administration of law enforcement in the South, the Englishman William Archer observed in 1910, "No negro holds a job higher than that of washing spittoons in the Court House."[37]

The reaction against Reconstruction did not succeed in placing blacks and whites formally into wholly different spheres of justice as had been done during slavery and by the postwar Black Codes. What the Mississippi attorney general noted regarding his state applied to the South and the nation as a whole: "There is no . . . law on the statute book that *per se* can be said to be directed by way of discriminating against negroes."[38] Reconstruction, therefore, did partially succeed; after all, even segregation statutes purported to treat blacks and whites equally, albeit separately. In practice, however, the white supremacists who authored and administered the criminal laws of the Jim Crow period openly used the machinery of law enforcement to buttress pigmentocracy.

Three examples illustrate ways in which authorities used criminal law as a tool for disenfranchising blacks, for imposing a humiliating etiquette upon them, and for weakening blacks in labor markets. Several Southern states used the criminal law to rid voting rolls of as many blacks as possible.[39] They made permanent disenfranchisement a consequence of conviction for certain crimes. Facially these provisions were silent as to race. They were enacted, however, specifically to exclude blacks; the authors of the legislation believed that Negroes were especially likely to commit the designated offenses. Noting approvingly that the Mississippi constitutional convention of 1895 "swept the circle of expedients to obstruct the exercise of the franchise by the negro race," the Mississippi Supreme Court observed:

> By reason of its previous condition of servitude and dependence, [the black population] had acquired or accentuated certain particularities of habit, of temperament, and of character, which clearly distinguished it as a race, from that of the whites,—a patient, docile people, but careless, landless, and migratory within narrow limits, without forethought, and its criminal members given rather to furtive offenses than to the robust crimes of the whites. Restrained by the federal constitution from discriminating against the negro, the convention discriminated against its characteristics and the offenses to which its weaker members were prone. . . . Burglary, theft, arson, and obtaining money under false pretenses were declared to be disqualifications, while robbery and murder and other crimes in which violence was the principal ingredient were not.[40]

Other states followed Mississippi's lead, with several of them adding wife-beating to the list of crimes to which blacks were perceived as particularly drawn.

The Supreme Court has adjudicated the constitutionality of such laws twice, once in 1898 in *Williams* v. *Mississippi*[41] and a second time in 1985 in *Hunter* v. *Underwood*,[42] a case from Alabama. In *Williams*, the Supreme Court ruled in favor of the state. Acknowledging that the purpose behind the law was to racially bar blacks from the voting booth, the Court held that "nothing tangible can be deduced from this."[43] First, although state officials declared that they intended to exclude as many blacks as possible, they also declared that they intended to do so within the limitations imposed by the federal constitution. Second, the Court noted that the law itself made no reference to racial distinctions but instead reached "weak and vicious white men as well as weak and vicious black men."[44] Finally, with respect to the legislative purpose, the Court reasoned that "whatever is sinister in [the] intention, if anything, can be prevented by both races by the exertion of that duty which voluntarily pays taxes and refrains from crime."[45] Eighty-seven years later, in *Underwood*, the Supreme Court invalidated a statute similar to the one in *Williams*. The Court did so on the very basis it had previously eschewed—the damning fact that state officials had enacted the disenfranchising law for the purpose of discriminating against black voters.

During the age of segregation, authorities used the criminal law to impose a stigmatizing code of conduct upon Negroes, one that demanded exhibitions of servility and the open disavowal of any desire for equality. Of all the many infractions of this code, none were perceived as more threatening than a black man's desire for sex with a white woman. Anxiety about this perceived threat was channeled into the administration of criminal laws prohibiting sexual misconduct. As we have seen, in many instances mobs did away entirely with even the form of due process by simply lynching Negroes accused of raping white women. In the event that a suspect escaped a real lynching, he often faced the prospect of a "legal lynching": an execution sanctioned by the forms of judicial process absent the substance of judicial fairness.

The pressure that lynchings put on court proceedings is vividly displayed, albeit in a paradoxical way, by an attorney's appeal to a jury in a 1907 Louisiana case in which a black man was charged with burglary and intent to rape a white woman:

> Gentlemen of the jury, this man, a nigger, is charged with breaking into the house of a white man in the nighttime and assaulting his wife, with the intent to rape her. Now, don't you know that, if this

nigger had committed such a crime, he never would have been brought here and tried; that he would have been lynched, and if I were there I would help pull on the rope.[46]

Another illustration of the point is provided by the circumstances surrounding the "trial" of Isaac Howard, Ernest McGehee, and Johnnie Jones in DeSoto County, Mississippi, in 1934, for the rape of a white teenager. The courthouse where the trial took place was surrounded by barbed wire, machine guns, and more than three hundred National Guards equipped with gas masks and fixed bayonets. At one point during the joint trial of all three men, a mob of several thousand whites attempted to overcome the court's defenses. Against the backdrop of this intimidation, the jury deliberated only six minutes before returning the foreordained guilty verdict. The judge immediately condemned the men to execution by hanging and then requested jurors, relatives of the victim, and other whites in the courtroom to disperse the crowd outside in order to avoid any lynchings, since extralegal hangings might aid the passage of the antilynching legislation then pending in Congress, legislation that would, in the judge's view, "destroy one of the South's cherished possessions—the supremacy of the white race."[47]

The white South's rape complex renders suspect the legitimacy of many convictions built upon allegations against black men by white women. Consider two cases which show the way that racial bias not only influenced the informal mechanisms by which laws are enforced, such as decisionmakers' intuitions about a witness's honesty, but influenced as well formal rules of law.

Dorsey v. *The State* arose from the prosecution of a black man convicted of attempting to rape a white woman.[48] On appeal, the defendant challenged the trial judge's instruction to the jury that, as a matter of law, the defendant's race could be taken into account to nullify his assertion that he had only been attempting to obtain the complainant's consent to sexual intercourse. Affirming the conviction, the Georgia Supreme Court ruled that race may properly be considered "to rebut any presumption that might otherwise arise in favor of the accused that his intention was to obtain the consent of the female."[49] In a purely formal sense this rule was race neutral; by its terms it was capable of being applied to any claim of attempted rape across racial lines—the white man charged with attempting to rape a black woman, as well as the black man charged with attempting to rape a white woman. But just as everyone knew that segregation laws were, in fact, brands upon blacks as a race, so too did everyone know that this evidentiary rule was meant to apply only to encounters between black men and white women.[50]

The second case is *McQuirter* v. *State*,[51] which involved the conviction in 1953 in Alabama of a black man for "an attempt to commit an assault with intent to rape."[52] According to the prosecution, the defendant followed a woman down a street, came within two or three feet of her, leaned on a stop sign across the street from her home, and, after his arrest, confided to a police officer that he intended to "get him a white woman that night."[53] The defendant, on the other hand, denied following the complainant or making any gesture toward her. He denied making any confession of a desire to rape or have sex with a white woman and testified that he had never before been arrested.

Two aspects of this case stand out. One is the tenuousness of the evidence relied upon for a conviction. The defendant's only "crime," it appears, was to walk too close to a fearful white woman. The second is the evidentiary rule (similar to the one noted above in *Dorsey* v. *The State*) that the Alabama Court of Appeals referred to without any hint of discomfort. Asserting that there existed sufficient evidence of wrongdoing to warrant permitting the jury to convict, the court declared that in determining the defendant's state of mind "the jury may consider social conditions and customs founded upon racial differences, such as that the prosecutrix was a white woman and defendant was a Negro man."[54] The folklore that black men have a dangerous, virtually ungovernable lust for white women was thus elevated into proper evidence cognizable in a court of law.

During the Jim Crow era, officials also used the criminal law to reimpose involuntary servitude upon blacks. When whites had no pressing need for black workers, Negroes were permitted to move about freely to wring from the labor market whatever wages they could command. When whites needed black workers, however, law enforcement officials, reinforced by a panoply of byzantine statutes, limited competition for labor, deprived Negroes of freedom of movement, coerced them into labor agreements, criminalized breach of contract, and compelled black convicts to work off their "debt to society" by laboring for white employers at rock-bottom prices.

Enticement laws made it a crime to solicit the services of a worker already under contract. The purpose of such prohibitions was to lower the price of labor by diminishing competition for it. Enticement laws were meant to scare away outsiders in search of labor and thereby condemn Negro workers to local labor conditions. "More than any other form of legislation," Professor William Cohen observes, "the enticement acts embodied the essence of the system of involuntary servitude. They re-created in modified form the proprietary relationship that had existed between master and slave."[55] The aptness of Cohen's observation is demonstrated by advertisements such as the following that appeared in Southern newspapers: "NOTICE—I forbid anyone to hire or harbor Herman Miles, colored, during the year 1939. A. P. Dabs, Route 1, Yanceyville, North Carolina."[56]

Reinforcing the enticement laws were statutes which essentially criminalized the status of being unemployed. Alabama, for instance, made a criminal of "any person wandering or strolling about in idleness, who is able to work, and has no property to support him; or any person leading an idle, immoral, profligate life, having no property to support him."[57] These vaguely worded vagrancy statutes pressured black men into signing unfavorable labor contracts by making arrest and jailing the harsh alternative. Vagrancy laws were the employers' labor weapon in reserve; it was not always used, but it was always available. When white employers faced labor scarcities, police would often arrest unemployed blacks to create pools of cheap, exploitable workers. When Savannah, Georgia, was selected in 1910 as the site of the Grand Prix Race of the Automobile Club of America, police officials responded by rounding up what a local newspaper described as "Negro loafers and vagrants" and informing them that those who could not "prove their innocence" would be sent to work on the racecourse.[58] That same year, a Memphis, Tennessee, police court judge promulgated a policy under which Negroes brought before him on vagrancy charges would be permitted to go free provided they would accept jobs offered by farmers needing hands.[59] "There is no excuse for loitering and loafing," warned the Macon, Georgia, chief of detectives, "and we are going to arrest all who do not go to work at once."[60] During the Depression, municipal authorities in Miami, Florida, ran out of money to pay for garbage men. The authorities then began to use Negro prisoners for garbage collection. "Unfortunately," remarked a writer for the *Miami Daily News*, "there weren't enough prisoners of the proper persuasion [i.e., black] available, but that didn't stop the astute officials. They simply sent an SOS to police, who promptly went out and rounded up a hatful of Negro vagrants."[61]

Another way in which law enforcement officials helped to exploit black labor was by leasing prisoners to private employers who assumed the responsibility of guarding and maintaining the inmates. Professor Cohen notes that those who leased prisoners often relegated them to hellish living conditions "which often bore a striking similarity to the most lurid abolitionist stereotypes of slavery."[62] In 1877–1880, of 285 convicts sent to build a railroad in South Carolina, 128, or 44.9 percent, died. Reflecting the view of many whites that blacks had been better off under slavery, the South Carolina warden responsible for these convict-laborers remarked that "casualties would have been less if the convicts were property having a value to preserve."[63]

Yet another method of manacling black workers to poorly paid employment was to threaten them with criminal penalties in the event that they breached their employment contracts. Alabama, for instance, criminalized breach of an employment contract with the intent to defraud the employer.[64] On its face, such a statute appears unobjectionable; after all, the state *should* punish those who intentionally defraud others. The Alabama statute, however, had a different aim. Its purpose was to arm employers and officials with a weapon with which to intimidate or punish recalcitrant workers, particularly black ones. It was, as a U.S. attorney observed, part of an effort "to weave about the ignorant laborer, and especially the blacks, a system of laws intended to keep him absolutely dependent upon the will of the employer and the land owner."[65]

The Black Defendant during the Era of Segregation: Reforms

Blatant racial oppression eventually provoked a strong reaction on two discrete but related fronts. On one, reformers attempted to place federal statutory and constitutional limits on the capacity of states to criminalize conduct. On a second, reformers intent upon guaranteeing minimal decencies of due process to defendants, including Negro defendants, planted the seeds from which emerged the federal constitutionalization of state criminal procedures.

Limiting the Reach of Criminal Law

The central struggle on the first front revolved around states' efforts to shackle black labor. A key episode in this struggle began in 1907, when Alonzo Bailey was convicted and sentenced to 136 days of hard labor under Alabama's false pretenses statute. After approximately a month into a year-long contract, Bailey quit his job as a fieldhand and failed to repay the fifteen-dollar advance he had received from his employer. A local prosecutor contended that this conduct violated Alabama's criminal code, which provided that a prima facie case of fraud could be shown by a breach of contract along with failure to repay any advance given by the employer. The statute further provided that a prima facie violation could not be rebutted by a defendant's own testimony. A number of influential persons, including Booker T. Washington, selected Bailey's case as a vehicle for challenging the constitutionality of this statute. They secretly aided him by providing funds for a first-rate legal defense and eliciting intervention by the U.S. Justice Department.[66]

In 1911, in *Bailey* v. *Alabama*,[67] the Supreme Court invalidated Bailey's conviction, ruling that the Alabama statute violated both the Thirteenth Amendment's prohibition against involuntary servitude and a federal antipeonage statute. In certain ways, the Court's opinion evinced a realistic understanding of Alabama's law and what it meant in the lives of those it menaced. Speaking for the Court, Justice Charles Evans Hughes remarked that the law in question "furnishes a convenient instrument for the coercion which the Constitution and the act of Congress forbid; an instrument of compulsion peculiarly effective as against the poor and the ignorant, its most likely victims."[68] On the other hand, the Court refused to acknowledge openly the racial aspect of the case. The Justice Department's brief reported in some detail that the law in question and similar statutes in Southern states had been enacted "in order to give the large planters . . . absolute dominion over the negro laborer."[69] The Court asserted, however, that it "at once dismiss[ed] from consideration the fact that [Bailey] is a black man."[70] Although the Court claimed that it adopted this position because it could not discern in the record a racially discriminatory administration of the law, a more realistic understanding of the Court's dismissal of the race question in *Bailey* is that the justices were anxious to avoid reigniting the volatile emotions associated with the Civil War and Reconstruction. (The Court's chief justice Edward Douglass White, had served in the Confederate army. The Court's most distinguished justice, Oliver Wendell Holmes, Jr., had served in the Union army.) Instead of frankly facing the fact that in the aftermath of Reconstruction the white South was once again using the criminal law to subjugate black labor, the Court carefully avoided racial issues associated with intersectional strife. "No question of a sectional matter is presented," the Court implausibly asserted. "We may view the legislation in the same manner as if it had been enacted in New York or Idaho."[71]

No one Supreme Court decision uproots immediately a deeply entrenched social practice. Subsequent efforts were required to make *Bailey* stick. Georgia, for instance, retained a law similar to the one struck down in *Bailey* except that the statute contained no rule barring a defendant from making at trial a statement as to his motives. That statute remained in effect until challenged in the 1940s.[72] Still, for all its limitations, *Bailey* was an important decision that lessened the power of businesses in the South to exploit black labor by deploying the criminal law.

The Origins of Federal Regulation of Criminal Procedure

Ensuring minimal federal procedural safeguards for defendants constituted a second front of activity on behalf of blacks oppressed by the administration of criminal law during the age of segregation. Three sets of Supreme Court decisions shed light on this subject: one established a right to a trial free of intimidation by a mob; a second established a right to representation by an attorney when facing the possibility of a death sentence and reasserted the right to be tried before a jury selected without the purposeful exclusion of black jurors; the third established a right to be free of state-inflicted torture aimed at eliciting a confession.

Moore *v.* Dempsey *and the Right to a Trial Free of Intimidation by a Mob*

In 1919, in Phillips County, Arkansas, black cotton farmers attempted to organize themselves and obtain legal representation for the purpose of bettering their position in the local economy. In particular, they sought some way to avoid being cheated by white landowners. This mild degree of assertiveness was viewed by many whites as dangerously revolutionary. One evening, blacks held an organizing meeting in a church, where they were fired upon by a sheriff's deputy. Some of the blacks who were armed fired back, killing the deputy. This precipitated several days of retaliatory violence by mobs of hastily deputized whites, local and state police, and soldiers of the U.S. army. The violence was largely one-sided: approximately 10 whites were killed; the death toll for blacks ran from 200 to 250. Yet blacks were the ones disarmed and detained en masse. Prohibited from moving about in public without passes signed by military authorities, many blacks were refused passes unless they were vouched for by whites. After order was restored or, more accurately, after white authorities were convinced that they had succeeded in snuffing out all traces of organized opposition to white domination, authorities began to initiate criminal prosecutions. Prosecutors did not bring charges against any whites. By contrast, they indicted 122 blacks, obtaining convictions for various crimes; 12 blacks were condemned to death for murder.[73]

The campaign to save the condemned men became a major testing ground for the National Association for the Advancement of Colored People.* Although the NAACP had developed some experience in rep-

---

*The NAACP had intervened before to stop miscarriages of justice. Its first serious case stemmed from the prosecution in 1910 of a black South Carolina farmer named Pink Franklin. Franklin was alleged to have defrauded his employer under a state statute which was essentially the same as that invalidated by the Supreme Court in *Bailey*. Indeed, even prior to *Bailey*, the South Carolina Supreme Court had invalidated this statute. See *Ex parte Hollman,* 60 S.C. 19 (1908). Nonetheless, police sought to arrest Franklin pursuant to it. Early one morning, they charged unannounced into the Franklin family bedroom. Franklin shot and killed one of the officers, later claiming that he did not know the identity of the intruders. Franklin and his wife barely escaped lynching but were indicted for murder. Although Mrs. Franklin was acquitted, Mr. Franklin was convicted and sentenced to death by an all-white jury chosen pursuant to state laws enacted (like those challenged in *Williams* v. *Mississippi*) for the purpose of excluding as many blacks as possible from voting and jury rolls. The U.S. Supreme Court upheld the conviction. *Franklin* v. *South Carolina,* 218 U.S. 161 (1910). Working quietly behind the scenes through its well-placed white officials, the NAACP succeeded first in persuading South Carolina's governor to commute Franklin's death sentence to a sentence of life imprisonment and later in persuading another governor to grant Franklin parole.

resenting criminal defendants, the problems it confronted in Arkansas were considerably larger and more complicated than any it had previously encountered. Currents of aggressive racial animus were running at high tide throughout much of the nation in 1919, amid the tensions brought about by the end of World War I. This atmosphere made it perilous for persons to pursue even low-key advocacy on behalf of blacks. In August 1919, for instance, the NAACP sent its executive secretary, John Shillady, a white social worker, to investigate efforts by Texas officials to oust the organization from the state. When he attempted to visit the governor and attorney general, Shillady was attacked and beaten in Austin by a group of white men that included a local judge and constable. When the NAACP protested and demanded that the assailants be brought to justice, the governor contended that Shillady had been the offender. In a similar spirit, the Austin police maintained that the NAACP should understand that its executive secretary had only been "received by red-blooded white men" who simply disliked having "Negro-loving white men" in the state.[74]

When the NAACP sent its assistant secretary, Walter White, to Arkansas to investigate what had happened there, he too faced life-threatening hostility. Initially, he was protected by two different sorts of disguise. He presented himself as a journalist (instead of an NAACP official) and was perceived as a white man (instead of as a Negro) due to his fair skin, blond hair, and blue eyes. When whites in Phillips County became aware of Walter White's true identity, he was forced to escape hurriedly. "You're leaving mister, just when the fun is going to start," White recalls being told by the conductor of the train on which he made his getaway. "A damned yellow nigger [was] down here passing for white and the boys are going to get him." "No matter what the distance," White later recalled, "I shall never take as long a train ride as that one seemed to be."[75]

White unearthed evidence which proved that the official story of the disturbances—the claim that blacks were engaged in a racial war against the whites—was a big lie intended to cover up the brutality of the police and army and provoke popular revulsion against black defendants. White also publicized the conditions under which the defendants charged with murder were tried: the utter failure of their lawyers to mount any defense; the use of confessions extracted by torture; and the intimidating presence of a mob, which signalled to the court that lynchings would be resorted to if convictions and death sentences did not quickly ensue.

White's efforts paid off. First, remarkably, the NAACP was able to persuade Henry J. Allen, the governor of Kansas, to refuse to extradict to Arkansas Robert L. Hill, a black organizer indicted for murder along with the others condemned to death in Phillips County. Governor Allen refused to extradict Hill on the grounds that, in light of the information revealed by the NAACP's investigations, "he might be tried by racial passion and bitterness" if he were returned to Arkansas.[76]

Second, the NAACP was able to persuade the U.S. Supreme Court to order a lower federal court to issue a writ of habeas corpus to six of the twelve condemned Phillips County defendants. The twelve had been tried in two groups of six each, which became known by the first-named defendants in each party. One group received reprieves from execution through judgments of the Arkansas Supreme Court. That court reversed the initial convictions on the grounds that jurors had failed to specify whether they had found the defendants guilty of first as opposed to second degree murder.[77] When members of that group were retried, reconvicted, and resentenced to death, the Arkansas Supreme Court again reversed, this time on the grounds that the trial judge had wrongly prevented the defense from attempting to prove unconstitutional racial discrimination in jury selection.[78] Finally, in 1923, the Arkansas Supreme Court ordered this group of defendants released from prison on the grounds that the state had excessively delayed their retrial.[79]

The other group of defendants did not receive the benefit of the Arkansas Supreme Court's rulings because, in their case, the juries did specify the degree of murder for which convictions were handed down. They sought federal habeas corpus relief.* The federal district court in

---

*"Habeas corpus" refers to a procedure pursuant to which a court can order an official who holds a person in custody to explain the legal justification for detaining the person. If the court determines that the detention is illegal, it can order the official to release the prisoner. A prisoner is generally entitled to seek federal habeas corpus relief to redress violations of federal rights even though appellate courts have rejected previous appeals of a conviction. For a quarter century, however, the Supreme Court has been steadily narrowing opportunities to obtain habeas corpus relief. For a thorough examination of this complex, unstable subject see James S. Liebman and Randy Hertz, *Federal Habeas Corpus Practice and Procedure* (2d. ed., 1994).

Arkansas, however, turned down their request. The denial was unsurprising because, at the time, federal habeas corpus relief was exceedingly difficult to obtain.

The principal Supreme Court case then governing federal habeas corpus procedures, *Frank* v. *Mangum*,[80] was another monument to bigotry in the administration of criminal law. In May 1913, in Atlanta, Georgia, Leo M. Frank, a (white) Jew, was convicted of murdering Mary Phagan, a (white) Christian who worked in the factory he owned and managed. The trial was tainted by blatant anti-Semitism and took place in an environment that was so close to mob action that the trial judge advised the defendant and his counsel to refrain from attending court when the jury rendered its verdict; the judge feared that they would immediately be hurt if the verdict proved displeasing to the crowd.

Frank was convicted and sentenced to death. Subsequently, the Supreme Court of the United States decided to review a lower court's rejection of his plea for federal habeas corpus relief. Frank argued that he had been deprived of due process of law by mob domination of his trial. The Supreme Court ruled against him on the grounds that Frank had been given a fair opportunity to present his objections to the state's appellate courts and that their conclusions were entitled to great deference from the federal courts. Although Frank later obtained a commutation of the death sentence from Georgia's governor, a mob, enraged by the governor's action, overpowered Frank's jailers and lynched him.[81]*

The Phillips County defendants seeking federal habeas corpus relief shared much in common with Leo Frank. One difference, however, which may have been crucial, had to do with the extensiveness of the re-

---

*In 1986, Georgia pardoned Frank. The Georgia Board of Pardons and Paroles said that it did so because the state had failed to protect Frank and bring his killers to justice. It may also have been prompted to award the pardon because of a statement made in 1982 by a man who claims that as a teenager he had seen Frank's primary accuser carrying the limp body of the girl Frank supposedly murdered. Frank's primary accuser, Jim Conley, was a black man. It is doubtful that, under comparable circumstances, a Christian white man would have been convicted of murder on the testimony of a black man in Georgia in 1913. See "Georgia Pardons Victim 70 Years after Lynching," *New York Times*, March 12, 1986.

view given to the trials by the relevant state appellate courts. The Georgia Supreme Court expressly responded to Frank's claim that the fundamental fairness of his trial had been compromised by popular pressure. By contrast, the Arkansas Supreme Court made no findings with respect to specific charges and simply asserted conclusorily that it could not "assume that the trial was an empty ceremony."[82] That difference in treatment may have been crucial in moving the U.S. Supreme Court to order a lower federal court in Arkansas to hold hearings on the defendants' request for habeas corpus relief. Writing for the Court, Justice Oliver Wendell Holmes maintained that federal interference through habeas corpus hearings ought not be allowed in cases where the state provides defendants with adequate corrective postconviction procedures. "But if [it is true]," Holmes averred,

> that the whole [trial] proceeding is a mask—that counsel, jury and judge were swept to the fatal end by an irresistible wave of public passion, and that the State Courts failed to correct the wrong, neither perfection in the machinery for correction nor the possibility that the trial court and counsel saw no other way of avoiding an immediate outbreak of the mob can prevent this Court from securing to the [defendants] their constitutional rights.[83]

For the defendants, the concrete meaning of the Supreme Court's rather murky opinion was that they were given a reprieve from a looming date of execution and also given the chance to set forth proof of their contentions at a habeas corpus hearing. At that point, however, diplomacy superseded law. In return for agreeing to rescind their request for habeas corpus relief, the defendants were given commutations that permitted them to be released from prison immediately, seven years after they were first convicted.

Moore v. *Dempsey* represented a major triumph for the NAACP. It also marked a major advance in the federal constitutionalization of state criminal procedure and the development of federal habeas corpus relief. As in *Bailey*, the Court refrained from casting *Moore* as a race relations case. There can be little doubt, however, that at least part of what prompted the Supreme Court's intervention was revulsion at the underlying facts of the case, ugly realities that, in Professor Robert

Cover's words, "exemplified the national scandal of racist southern justice."[84]*

The Scottsboro Scandal

The second set of Supreme Court decisions to which we shall turn stems from an incident that has become a major landmark in American race relations and the classic instance of a miscarriage of justice. On March 25, 1931, officials in Scottsboro, Alabama, charged nine black youngsters ranging in age from thirteen to twenty with raping two white women. They were accused of raping Victoria Price and Daisy Bates on board a freight train, after ejecting white men from the car in which the women were riding as hoboes. The evidence against the nine consisted principally of the women's allegations. One of the women, Daisy Bates, later recanted and testified for the defendants. The other, Victoria Price, never recanted but told such contradictory and implausible versions of her alleged rape that it is virtually certain that she lied materially about the entire episode. The flimsiness of the prosecution's case led one judge to annul the conviction of one of the Scottsboro Boys (who was subsequently retried and reconvicted) and prompted several of Alabama's leading newspapers, all of them organs of white supremacy, to oppose the state's plans to execute the defendants. Despite this opposition, however, over the course of the decade, prosecutors tried the Scottsboro Boys on three occasions, each time obtaining convictions. Juries sentenced the defendants to death on several occasions, although in recognition of the weakness of the prosecution's case, one jury sentenced one defendant to "only" seventy-five years in prison as opposed to execution.[85]

The widespread impression that racial prejudice tainted the reliability of the jury verdicts against the Scottsboro Boys is thoroughly merited. The trials were parodies of due process. One trial judge openly

---

*This point is reinforced by a letter that Justice Holmes wrote to Harold Laski four years after *Moore*. Replying to Laski's outrage over the execution of Sacco and Vanzetti, Holmes remarked: "Your last letter shows you stirred up like the rest of the world on the Sacco Vanzetti case. I cannot but ask myself why this so much greater interest in red than black. A thousand-fold worse cases of negroes come up from time to time, but the world does not worry over them." Robert M. Cover, "The Origins of Judicial Activism in the Protection of Minorities," 91 *Yale Law Journal* 1287, 1306 (1982).

disparaged defense counsel in front of the jury, blatantly favored the prosecution with evidentiary rulings, and, when instructing the jury, initially ignored the possibility of acquittal by giving instructions only relating to a finding of guilt. This same judge rejected the defense counsel's argument that blacks had been wrongfully excluded as jurors despite overwhelming evidence to the contrary and, later, refused to strike certain white jurors for cause even when they readily acknowledged that they believed blacks to be racially inferior to whites. According to Judge William Washington Callahan, these whites were acceptable as jurors as long as they did not allow their belief in Negro inferiority to interfere with their judgment.

Most of the racial prejudice that surfaced during the trial was antiblack in character. Judge Callahan, for example, gave a jury the following instruction regarding how it should interpret evidence relating to charges that a black man had raped a white woman:

> Where the woman charged to have been raped, as in this case, is a white woman, there is a very strong presumption under the law that she would not and did not yield voluntarily to intercourse with the defendant, a Negro; and this is true, whatever the station in life the prosecutrix may occupy, whether she be the most despised, ignorant and abandoned woman of the community, or the spotless virgin and daughter of a prominent home of luxury and learning.[86]*

In addition to antiblack prejudice, however, the defendants also suffered from anti-Semitic bigotry aimed at their New York Jewish lawyers, Joseph R. Brodsky and Samuel Leibowitz. During one summation, a county prosecutor turned to the jury and declared: "Show

---

*Two closely related purposes appear to have given rise to this instruction. One was to rehabilitate Victoria Price, who had been shown by the defense to be an unsavory and untrustworthy person. The other was to remind the jury that the trial was part of a larger context of racial struggle, a context in which they, as white men, owed a sacred duty to protect white women from rapacious Negroes. One doubts, though, that the judge needed to send such a reminder; his feelings were already widespread. As one spectator told a reporter for the *New York Herald Tribune*, Victoria Price "might be a fallen woman, but by God she is a white woman." Dan T. Carter, *Scottsboro: A Tragedy of the American South*, 295 (rev. ed., 1969) (quoting *New York Herald Tribune*, November 30, 1933).

them that Alabama justice cannot be bought and sold with Jew money from New York."[87] The trial judge scolded the prosecutor for his "improper" statement but declined to declare a mistrial as the defendants' attorneys requested. A short while later, another appeal to racial prejudice from a different prosecutor—"If you acquit this Negro, put a garland of roses around his neck, give him a supper and send him to New York City"—failed even to elicit an objection, much less a reprimand.[88] (For a discussion of the law governing racial appeals by attorneys, see chapter 8.)

Although there were many injustices that could have served as the predicates for appeals from the convictions of the Scottsboro Boys, two stood out and became the bases of two interventions on the part of the U.S. Supreme Court. One, *Powell* v. *Alabama*,[89] challenged the failure of the state to provide effective assistance of counsel even though it sought to execute the defendants. The other, *Norris* v. *Alabama*,[90] involved the state's purposeful exclusion of blacks from jury service.

Powell stemmed from the first of the prosecutions of the Scottsboro Boys, a trial in which eight were convicted and sentenced to death in a courtroom that one of them described as "one big smiling white face."[91] A mistrial was declared with respect to the youngest defendant because the jury could not decide whether to sentence him to death or to life imprisonment. Although the prosecution asked for a life term for the thirteen-year-old, seven jurors insisted upon sentencing him, too, to the electric chair.

The Alabama Supreme Court affirmed the convictions, but the U.S. Supreme Court reversed on the grounds that the defendants had been denied due process of law. The Court held that the trial judge violated the federal constitution by neglecting to assign counsel to the defendants under circumstances in which such counsel could offer effective representation. The judge did not appoint a specific attorney to represent each of the defendants but instead appointed all of the members of the town's bar to represent the defendants in the event that no private counsel appeared to argue on their behalf. The Supreme Court concluded that this collective appointment of defense counsel failed to give the attorneys named "that clear appreciation of responsibility or . . . individual sense of duty" which is constitutionally required for effective representation in a criminal case.[92] The Court also faulted the trial judge on the grounds that he delayed making any definitive appointment of defense counsel until immediately before the trial began, thereby precluding meaningful preparation.

Powell is a major landmark which established the idea in federal constitutional law that, in at least certain circumstances, states have an affirmative obligation to provide criminal defendants with the rudiments of effective representation. *Powell*, however, provided the Scottsboro Boys with only a brief reprieve. They were quickly retried, reconvicted, and resentenced to death. This time, however, they were saved, remarkably, by their trial judge, who annulled the convictions on the grounds that the testimony of their accuser, Victoria Price, was literally unbelievable.

A third trial ended like the others with convictions and death sentences after the prosecutor warned in his summation that an acquittal would force the white women of Alabama to "buckle six-shooters around their middles" to protect "the sacred parts of their bodies" from rapacious Negroes.[93] The jury delivered guilty verdicts. But the Supreme Court again intervened, this time ruling in *Norris* v. *Alabama* that the reconvictions obtained were invalid because state officials, for racial reasons, had purposefully excluded Negroes from jury service. (For further discussion of *Norris,* see pp. 176–177.)

In the end, Alabama did not succeed in executing any of the Scottsboro Boys. After *Norris,* four of the defendants were once again convicted at tragicomic trials. A black participated in the grand jury that indicted them and twelve blacks were among the hundred potential jurors from which trial juries were chosen. These twelve, however, were not allowed to enter the jury box during the voir dire—the process during which potential jurors are questioned about prejudices that might bar them from service. When one of the blacks inadvertently entered into the area where the white prospective jurors were seated, the presiding judge instructed him to sit with the other Negroes. For understandable reasons, seven of the twelve sought and received permission to be excused from service.* The prosecution used peremptory challenges to strike the other five.†

---

*One observer noted that they left the courthouse "looking anything but regretful." Carter, *Scottsboro,* 341 (quoting *New York Times*, January 21, 1936).

†A peremptory challenge is a device that empowers lawyers to bar potential jurors from service on a jury without explaining the basis of objection. Since the late

Although Clarence Norris was again sentenced to death, two of his codefendants were sentenced "only" to prison terms of seventy-five and ninety-nine years—a substantial victory under the circumstances. As the *Birmingham Age-Herald* observed (exaggerating a bit), such decisions "represent[ed] probably the first time in the history of the South that a Negro has been convicted of a charge of rape upon a white woman and has been given less than a death sentence."[94] Rape charges against the other codefendants were dropped and the death sentence against Norris was eventually commuted. By 1950, all of the Scottsboro Boys had finally gained freedom after serving collectively 104 years of imprisonment for what was, almost certainly, a hoax.[95]

Brown v. *Mississippi*: The Right to Be Free of Torture

Brown v. *Mississippi*[96] marks another miscarriage of justice that was prevented from degenerating into total, irredeemable farce by Supreme Court intervention. On April 4, 1934, in Kemper County, Mississippi, Ed Brown, Arthur Ellington, and Henry Shields, three black farmhands, were indicted for murdering Raymond Stewart, a white farmer. Within two days they had all been tried, convicted, and sentenced to death. The evidence suggesting their guilt were confessions that had been extracted from them by torture. Ellington was severely whipped and hung by a rope to the limb of a tree. Brown and Stewart were beaten with leather straps with buckles attached. In court the defendants repudiated their confessions. When Ellington did so, rope marks were still plainly visible on his neck. The police *admitted* beating them. Asked how severely he had whipped Ellington, one deputy sheriff replied: "Not too much for a negro; not as much as I would have done if it were left to me."[97] Although the jury was instructed that they could take this evidence into account in determining whether to credit the defendants' confessions, it nonetheless rendered guilty verdicts.

The Supreme Court of Mississippi upheld the convictions.[98] With respect to the coerced confessions, the court rested its affirmance on two

---

1980s, lawyers have been prohibited from racially discriminating in their use of peremptory challenges, although many continue to do so regardless of legal norms. For discussion of racially discriminatory peremptory challenges see chapter 6.

grounds, one procedural, the other substantive. First, the court concluded that the trial judge was under no duty to question the admissibility of confessions after they had properly been examined at a preliminary hearing and in the absence of any subsequent challenge by defense counsel. Responding to the argument that the defense attorneys' default should not deprive the defendants of relief given uncontroverted evidence that the confessions had been extracted by torture, the Mississippi Supreme Court declared that "what the appellants request is simply that they be excepted from the procedure heretofore uniformly applied to all litigants. This we cannot do. All litigants, of every race or color, are equal at the bar of this court, and we would feel deeply humiliated if the contrary could justly be said."[99] The Mississippi Supreme Court, in other words, perceived the defendants' claim as one for special treatment and rejected it in the name of equality.

Second, as a substantive matter, the Mississippi Supreme Court concluded that, although the Fifth Amendment to the U.S. Constitution gave individuals a right against compulsory self-incrimination in federal trials, it provided individuals with no such right in state trials. Thus, according to the Mississippi court, even if the defendants' confession had been coerced, admitting it into evidence did not violate the federal constitution since this prosecution took place in a state as opposed to a federal forum.

The Mississippi court's decision triggered two angry dissents. In one, Justice V. A. Griffith graphically described the tortures inflicted upon the defendants, stating that in "pertinent respects the transcript [containing testimony of the hanging and beatings] reads more like pages torn from some medieval account, than a record made within the confines of modern civilization which aspires to an enlightened constitutional government."[100] He scornfully criticized the defendants' "so-called trial," asserted that compared to it the Scottsboro cases were "models of correct constitutional procedure," and remarked that the trial "was never anything but a fictitious continuation of the mob which originally instituted and engaged in the admitted tortures."[101] Appealing openly for reversal by the U.S. Supreme Court, Justice William Dozier Anderson went on to say:

> If this judgment be affirmed by the federal Supreme Court, it will be the first time in the history of that court wherein there was allowed

to stand a conviction based solely upon testimony coerced by the bar-
barities of executive officers of the state, known to the prosecuting
officers of the state as having been so coerced, when the testimony
was introduced, and fully shown in all its nakedness to the trial
judge before he closed the case and submitted it to the jury, and
when all this is not only undisputed, but is expressly and openly
admitted.[102]

The U.S. Supreme Court, in yet another opinion authored by Chief
Justice Hughes, answered Anderson's plea, reversing the Mississippi
court. Hughes maintained that the wrong complained of was so obvious
and fundamental that the trial judge ought to have addressed it
notwithstanding the neglect of defense counsel. Hughes conceded that
under Supreme Court precedent a state did not have to offer to persons
a privilege against self-incrimination.* He argued, however, that because a state may dispense with the privilege against self-incrimination,
or the grand jury, or even a jury, does not mean that the state "may sub-
stitute trial by ordeal. The rack and torture chamber may not be substi-
tuted for the witness stand."[103]

As was true in *Moore, Powell,* and *Norris,* the Supreme Court's intervention in *Brown* did not end the tribulations of the defendants, who
faced a retrial at the hands of the district attorney, John Stennis.† This
confronted them with two dangers: the danger that they might be
lynched; and the danger that they might be convicted and sentenced to
death again, even in the absence of their confessions. To avoid these dangers, a compromise was reached under which the defendants pleaded no
contest to manslaughter in return for a ten-year sentence for Ed Brown,
a five-year sentence for Henry Shields, and a three-year sentence for

---

*Not until 1964, in *Malloy* v. *Hogan*, 378 U.S. 1 (1964), did the Supreme Court rule
that the privilege against self-incrimination is a fundamental right that cannot be violated by state action.

†John Stennis went on to become one of Mississippi's most popular politicians, serv-
ing in the U.S. Senate for forty-one years. He paid no professional or political price
for his part in the wrongful prosecution of the defendants in *Brown.* See Richard C.
Cortner, *A "Scottsboro" Case in Mississippi*, 157–158 (1986); David E. Rosenbaum,
"John C. Stennis, 93, Longtime Chairman of Powerful Committees in the Senate,
Dies," *New York Times*, April 24, 1995.

Arthur Ellington. Reflecting on this arrangement, Roy Wilkins of the NAACP bitterly remarked years later:

> As far as Mississippi was concerned, liberal justice had been meted out. The three field hands were innocent, of course, but then they hadn't been lynched or electrocuted had they? To the Magnolia State, jail terms seemed a small price to exact in return for upholding the honor of Mississippi courts against a meddling Supreme Court in Washington. That was the way things were done down South.[104]

Wilkins's words and the events to which they were addressed should serve as a warning against exaggerating the importance of Court decisions. They can sometimes prevent bad things from happening. In *Brown* (as in *Dempsey*, *Powell*, and *Norris*) the Court's intervention saved the defendants from death. But courts are less capable of making things happen, much less making them happen in a particular way. *Brown* prohibited Mississippi officials from using confessions extracted by torture. It did not stop officials, however, from using the power of a racially discriminatory criminal justice apparatus to extract a compromise from obviously innocent defendants who should never have even been made to stand trial in the first place. Nor could the Supreme Court ensure that officials would abide by the rules it promulgated. Court decisions are not self-executing; to be enforced, they require the cooperation of others. In many locales, officials were antagonistic to federal constitutional norms which challenged the local mores of white supremacy. In many locales, moreover, there existed no effective base from which to launch campaigns on behalf of suspects victimized by racial prejudice. For every Ed Brown or Clarence Norris saved from the electric chair, there were surely others who were either killed or condemned to long terms of imprisonment.[105]

J. Edgar Hoover's Covert War against Black Political Activists

Thus far the focus has mainly been on run-of-the-mill racial discrimination in the administration of criminal law, official bigotry that happened to ensnare unfortunate suspects. Now I shall turn to a string of related episodes in which, for racial reasons, officials targeted for surveillance, "dirty tricks," or prosecution black activists whom they perceived as threats to national security. The one official above all others who animated this campaign was J. Edgar Hoover, perhaps the most revered (and reviled) law enforcement official in all of American history. During his long career, Hoover played an important, often decisive, role in monitoring, hounding, and jailing several of the most important black leaders of the century.[106] A crude racism prompted Hoover to view protest against white domination as itself a danger tending toward treason. He disapproved of any Negro who displayed what he termed "defiantly assertive" ideas about "the Negro's fitness for self-government."[107]

I have already discussed in chapter 2 how Hoover's FBI neglected to protect civil rights activists who faced violent attacks from private persons and local law enforcement personnel. The FBI's hostility, however, extended far beyond malign neglect. The FBI also affirmatively acted against civil rights activists. Three episodes in particular are enlightening: Hoover's campaigns against Marcus Garvey, Martin Luther King, Jr., and the Black Panther Party.

The FBI and Marcus Garvey

During and immediately after World War I, the federal government unleashed the investigatory and prosecutorial power of the Department of Justice upon persons and groups perceived as radical—pacifists, socialists, communists, and proponents of the advancement of the colored peoples of the world. Hence, when the black activist Monroe Trotter attempted to highlight the inconsistency between American rhetoric, especially the asserted wish to make the world safe for democracy, and American practices, especially the mistreatment of colored peoples in the United States and its overseas empire, a youthful J. Edgar Hoover successfully urged the Justice Department's Bureau of Investigation to monitor him. By 1919 the Bureau ("Federal" wasn't added to its title until 1935) had created a network of informants comprised of "reliable Negroes" who reported on every person or organization that preached "equal rights" or "social equality" on behalf of blacks.

Among blacks, the person whom the Bureau monitored most closely was Marcus Garvey, the Jamaica-born founder of the Universal

Negro Improvement Association, the leading black nationalist organization of its time. Hoover denounced Garvey as "the foremost radical
among his race" and, along with other Justice Department officials, attempted to find some way to neutralize his influence.[108] The Justice Department infiltrated the UNIA with black operatives and shadowed
Garvey as he pursued his various activities. First, it attempted to prove
that he had violated federal law by transporting a woman across state
lines for immoral purposes. Then it attempted to prove that he had engaged in income tax violations. When these avenues of inquiry failed to
bear fruit, the Justice Department sought to prove that Garvey had used
the mails to defraud the public in the course of raising funds for a
Negro-owned steamship company, the Black Star Line. Unlike the others, this investigation ended with a conviction.

The government charged that Garvey had violated the law when he
used the mails to solicit investments for an enterprise which he deceitfully described as flourishing, although he knew it to be headed toward
bankruptcy. At trial, Garvey was certainly shown to be careless, domi-
neering, pompous, and overreaching. It is not altogether clear, though,
that he was shown to have had a criminal intent to defraud.[109]

An important element in Garvey's downfall were attacks on him
not only by the government but by black citizens as well, including some
who had initially admired him. Without the aid of blacks who either felt
cheated by Garvey or who intensely opposed him on political grounds,
the government's efforts to jail him would likely have foundered.
J. Edgar Hoover hated "the Black Moses," but so, too, did W.E.B.
DuBois and A. Philip Randolph. Indeed, it was Cyril Biggs, another
black activist, who first brought to the government's attention the possibility of prosecuting Garvey for mail fraud.[110]*

Although Garvey may indeed have been guilty, that guilt was not
the cause of the government's campaign against him but rather a conve-

---

*Commenting on the Garvey prosecution, one black activist remarked, "If all the
rogues are to be sent to the penitentiary, with the sole exception of those who steal
from black people, that would be discrimination against black people, indeed." Judith Stein, *The World of Marcus Garvey: Race and Class in Modern Society*, 205–206
(1986) (quoting William Pickens, "Garvey's Last Stand" [February 1925], Associated
Negro Press, C-304, in NAACP Papers).

nient rationale for it. From the perspective of the FBI, what distinguished Garvey and made him suitable for prison was not so much his allegedly fraudulent activity as his standing as a prominent Negro "agitator."

The FBI and Martin Luther King, Jr.

Forty years after helping to convict Marcus Garvey, J. Edgar Hoover initiated and guided an intensive effort to destroy Martin Luther King, Jr.[111] A combination of factors stoked Hoover's enmity: King's position as the outstanding leader of African-American protest against segregation; his association with leftists; his opposition to the Vietnam War; and his lively extramarital sexual career, a facet of King's persona that may well have titillated Hoover's own tortured sexual obsessions.

With the knowledge and implicit approval of his superiors, including Presidents Kennedy and Johnson, Hoover infiltrated virtually every aspect of King's existence between 1963 and 1968, the last five years of his life. Hoover's agents wiretapped King's phones, bugged his home, office, and hotel rooms, and made into an informant at least one of the employees within King's Southern Christian Leadership Conference. Hoover then disseminated the embarrassing information he gathered to government officials and influential private persons.*

The most extraordinary single event in the FBI's campaign occurred in November 1964, when FBI Assistant Director William Sullivan created an audiotape which contained snippets of bawdy remarks overheard from telephone conversations and the sounds generated by King having sex in a hotel room. Sullivan sent this tape anonymously to King along with a threatening letter which seems to have been intended to make him either withdraw from public life or commit suicide. "There is but one way out for you," the letter concluded. "You better take it before your filthy, abnormal fraudulent self is bared to the nation."[112]

---

*Hoover, for example, relayed derogatory information to high-ranking members of the Catholic hierarchy in an unsuccessful effort to prevent a meeting between King and the Pope. "I am amazed," Hoover privately remarked, "that the Pope gave an audience to such a degenerate." Kenneth O'Reilly, *Racial Matters: The FBI's Secret File on Black America, 1960–1972*, 149 (1989).

The FBI campaign against King illustrates vividly the ugly, perverse, deeply ingrained but covert racial animus that civil rights activists have faced at the highest levels of government. It also nurtured an aversion to the FBI that remains deeply felt across wide reaches of the African-American population.*

The FBI and the Black Panthers

Hoover's campaign to destroy the Black Panther Party was the most lethal of his attacks against black activists. It was part of a program code-named COINTELPRO which stemmed in part, ironically, from efforts to monitor the Ku Klux Klan and other "white hate groups." Although the FBI maintained from its beginnings a watchful eye on black activists of all stripes, in the late 1960s it dramatically increased its surveillance through thousands of informants known as "ghetto listening posts." Exemplifying the breadth of the FBI's coverage was a directive from Hoover in November 1970 which ordered the automatic investigation of *all* college or university black student unions.[113]

Although an invidious racial selectivity influenced the FBI's strategy of surveillance, some of its targets engaged in suspicious or criminal activities that warranted attention from police authorities. This certainly applies to the BPP. Its rhetoric was dangerously provocative, with

---

*A vivid illustration of this aversion is provided by what occurred in 1995, when federal prosecutors charged Qubilah Shabazz, the daughter of Malcolm X, with conspiring to murder Minister Louis Farrakhan, who she (and others) believe was complicit in the assassination of her father in 1965. The charges were based primarily on testimony gathered by an FBI informant. Instead of thanking the FBI, Minister Farrakhan castigated it, asserting that it was simply engaged in yet another effort to undermine black political unity. Many blacks (and others) agreed with him and applauded his response. See "Questions about Plot to Kill Farrakhan Show Blacks' Mistrust of Legal System," *Rocky Mountain News*, January 19, 1995; Mary A. Johnson, " 'Plot' a Ploy, Farrakhan Says; Minister Charges U.S. out to Discredit Him," *Chicago Sun-Times*, January 18, 1995; Clarence Page, "Shabazz Case Shows FBI Can Abuse Powers It Now Has," *Orlando Sentinel*, May 9, 1995. Ultimately, the government and Shabazz reached a settlement; in return for the government's promise to forgo prosecution, Shabazz promised to seek counseling and to stop contending that the government had entrapped her. See Judy Pasternak, "U.S. Settles Case against Daughter of Malcolm X," *Los Angeles Times*, May 2, 1995.

leaders threatening to torch the White House ("I'll burn the mother fucker down") and kill police officers ("Off the pigs!").[114] Moreover, despite the halo of martyrdom that continues often to obscure a clear-eyed view of the BPP, the fact is that a substantial number of those affiliated with it engaged in serious bouts of thuggery, including murder, extortion, arson, and embezzlement.[115]

Still, law enforcement officials were obligated to deal with the BPP in accordance with applicable legal norms, and the FBI, often in complicity with local police agencies, violated this obligation. FBI agents phoned relatives of Panthers claiming, falsely, that the BPP aimed to assassinate them, sent letters to wives telling them that their husbands were having affairs with other women, and spread rumors that BPP personnel were infected with loathsome diseases or serving as informants for police authorities. Two of the FBI's other COINTELPRO activities are particularly noteworthy.

First, the FBI insinuated itself into a violent feud between the BPP and a black nationalist organization, United Slaves, by sending anonymous, poison-pen letters to the two groups that were calculated to increase their violent rivalry. "Our basic policy," one high-ranking FBI official later remarked, "was to divide and conquer."[116] For example, after a shootout between members of the BPP and US in January 1969, the FBI mailed material to the homes of BPP activists that included cartoons in which US members were portrayed as gloating over the corpses of Panthers, while Panthers were portrayed as describing members of US as "pork chop niggers." Subsequently, members of the two groups again shot at one another, causing casualties and at least one death.[117]

Second, the FBI seeded BPP chapters with agents provocateurs who both informed on Panthers and egged them on to commit crimes for which they could be arrested by local police. In Chicago, the FBI paid a career criminal, William O'Neal, to disrupt and inform upon the BPP. Adept at his work, O'Neal became a trusted BPP official whose duties involved making security arrangements for Fred Hampton, the head of the Chicago BPP. Acting pursuant to information supplied by O'Neal, local police attacked Hampton's apartment, killing him and another Panther, Mark Clark, and wounding four of their colleagues. Subsequent investigations have shown that this raid was essentially a planned execution. Panthers who survived it were initially prosecuted for various crimes. Charges against them were dropped, however, when it appeared that trials might reveal the involvement of the FBI. Subsequently, O'Neal continued to inform for the FBI, reporting, for example, on the strategies being contemplated by the attorneys for the Hampton and Clark families. Not until the late 1970s did the FBI connection to the Hampton-Clark killings surface, along with other information that established unequivocally that federal and local authorities had not only violated the rights of those they had targeted but had also covered up those violations. In November 1982, the United States agreed to pay the Hampton and Clark families $1.85 million to settle the matter.[118]

Failures to Protect Blacks against Racially Biased Police Misconduct

In the previous section, I focused on racially motivated efforts to repress disfavored political dissidents. Here I concentrate on racial misconduct arising from routine police work. Relations between black communities and police departments have often been characterized by bitter conflict. Writing in 1944 about conditions in the South, Gunnar Myrdal stated that the police officer "stands not only for civic order as defined in formal laws and regulations, but also for 'White Supremacy' and the whole set of social customs associated with this concept."[119] He also noted that other organs of government, particularly the judiciary, adopted a hands-off approach which implicitly authorized police officers to go beyond their lawful authority to carry out the task of keeping Negroes in their place. Alluding to the unlawful beating, intimidation, and harassment that have been hallmarks of police conduct toward Negroes, Myrdal observed that there was "a strange atmosphere of consistent illegality around the activity of the officers of the peace."[120] Compounding these problems was another: the especially intense racial animus that white police officers seemed to exhibit. "Probably no group of whites in America," Myrdal maintained, "have a lower opinion of the Negro people and are more fixed in their views than Southern policemen. To most of them . . . practically every Negro man is a potential criminal. They usually hold, in extreme form, all other derogatory beliefs about Negroes; and they are convinced that the traits are 'racial.' "[121]

What Myrdal wrote with respect to the Deep South appears to have been applicable also, albeit perhaps to a somewhat lesser extent, to other regions. The report of the special committee authorized by Congress to investigate the East St. Louis riots of 1917 details all manner of racially selective police violence, including at least one instance in which police shot into a crowd of blacks who were huddled together, offering no resistance. This shooting, according to the committee, was "a particularly cowardly exhibition of savagery."[122] Reporting on the Washington, D.C., riots of 1919, Herbert Seligman observed that "the police gave the impression both to Negroes and to white men that they would be the allies of the white men. Although the aggressors were white mobbists . . . ten Negroes were arrested for every white man arrested."[123] The Mayor's Commission report on the Harlem, New York, riot of 1935 noted that "the police practice aggressions and brutalities upon the Harlem citizens" in part "because they are Negroes" and concluded that these attacks "are doing more than anything else to create a disrespect for authority and to bring about mass resistance to the injustices suffered by the community."[124] After investigating the Detroit riot of 1943, Thurgood Marshall pointed out that of the thirty-four persons killed during the riot, twenty-five were Negroes, and that of these seventeen had been killed by police. The police, Marshall observed,

> used "persuasion" rather than firm action with white rioters, while against Negroes they used the ultimate in force: night sticks, revolvers, riot guns, sub-machine guns, and deer guns . . . Negroes killed by police—17; white persons killed by police—none. . . . This record by the Detroit police demonstrates once more what all Negroes know only too well: that nearly all police departments limit their conception of checking racial disorders to surrounding, assessing, maltreating, and shooting Negroes. Little attempt is made to check the activities of whites.[125]

Although there has been considerable change in race relations over the past half-century, some of Myrdal's observations of 1944 remain troublingly relevant today. Two sets of conflicts are illustrative. The first is the string of riots that have periodically exploded in black urban areas over the past thirty years. The second is the series of court cases initiated by plaintiffs seeking judicial regulation of police conduct that is alleged to be both excessively brutal and racially discriminatory.

During the "long hot summers" of the years 1965–1967, riots either caused or contributed to scores of deaths and massive destruction of property. In 1967, for example, riots in 56 cities accounted for 84 deaths, at least 3,800 injuries, and hundreds of millions of dollars in property damage.[126] Citing "deep hostility between police and ghetto communities," the Report of the National Advisory Commission on Civil Disorders (the Kerner Report) declared that "in practically every city that has experienced disruptions since the summer of 1964 . . . abrasive relationships between police and Negroes and other minority groups have been a major source of grievance, tension, and ultimately, disorder."[127] Fueling this sense of aggrievement was the perception, substantially supported in fact, that at least in part for racial reasons police tended to behave in a distinctively rude, overbearing, contemptuous fashion in predominantly black neighborhoods, a manner that gave credence to the notion that, in black communities, police constituted an occupying force rather than a cadre of useful civil servants.[128]

Since the 1960s, riots have continued to explode. Two in particular illuminate the troubling tendency in many jurisdictions to leave unpunished or underpunished police abuse of African-American suspects. The first is the Miami riot of 1980, which claimed eighteen lives and $80 million in property damage.[129] In the fifteen months preceding that riot, "a series of five highly sensitive cases reinforced the belief widely held among blacks that they could never expect to get fair treatment from the [local] criminal justice system." In one incident, five white police officers erroneously raided a home in a drug bust and in the course of so doing called the occupants "niggers" and seriously injured one of them, a black schoolteacher named Nathaniel Lafleur. Although some of the officers involved were suspended without pay, a local grand jury refused to indict any of them for criminal wrongdoing. In a second incident, a white off-duty policeman shot and fatally wounded a black man, Randy Heath, who was urinating next to the wall of a warehouse. The officer stated that he believed that Heath was a burglar. He also claimed that he shot Heath during the course of a struggle, a claim he later recanted. After the shooting, authorities announced that the policeman had been suspended. This was later shown to be false or, at best, inaccurate. One month after the killing, the officer was given a week's leave with pay to attend the National Police Revolver Championship. No criminal charges stemming from the killing were ever lodged against this officer.

In a third incident, a white member of the Florida Highway Patrol sexually molested an eleven-year-old black girl. State prosecutors requested an arrangement under which the officer would be required to seek psychological help and pay for any counseling needed by his victim. The first judge to whom this plea bargain was submitted removed himself from the case but before doing so wondered aloud in open court whether the case would have been prosecuted differently had the victim been white and the perpetrator black. Eventually a second judge allowed an arrangement under which the officer pleaded no contest to the charges and was given three years' probation and directed to pay for any psychiatric care his victim might require—payments he subsequently neglected to make. Eventually, federal officials indicted the trooper. He fled, however, before he could be arrested.

A fourth case involved Johnny L. Jones, Dade County's first black public school superintendent, who was charged with attempting to steal $9,000 worth of gold-plated plumbing fixtures for a vacation home. Tried before an all-white jury whose monochromatic hue was assured by the prosecutor's deployment of peremptory challenges to exclude potential black jurors, Jones was convicted and sentenced to three years in prison. The successful prosecution of Jones became a benchmark for many, particularly blacks, who compared that outcome with the nonexistent or unsuccessful prosecutions of white policemen accused of criminally harming black civilians.

The fifth case was the proverbial straw that broke the camel's back. In the early morning of December 17, 1979, Arthur McDuffie, a thirty-three-year-old black insurance agent was killed as a result of massive injuries to the head inflicted by a group of white police officers. Initially the policemen falsely reported that McDuffie hurt himself by falling off his motorcycle. To cover up what really happened, police officers ran over McDuffie's motorcycle with a squad car and broke all of the glass gauges on the motorcycle with nightsticks. When their lie unraveled, the policemen resorted to the perennially effective excuse that the victim, albeit unarmed, had resisted arrest. Perhaps he did. But even if one gives the self-serving testimony of the accused policemen full credence—quite a concession given the implausibility of a lone civilian actually putting up resistance to police officers in a locale known for police brutality—there is still the matter of the attempted cover-up and the extraordinary extent of the damages that McDuffie suffered, injuries caused by force far beyond anything that could reasonably be expected under the circumstances. Describing McDuffie's fatal injuries, a medical examiner likened them to the consequences of falling from a four-story building and landing head first on concrete.[130]

Four police officers were prosecuted for second degree murder. Arguing that their clients could not receive fair trials in Miami because of local media coverage, defense attorneys successfully moved for a change of venue. The trial was moved to Tampa, Florida, where only a few months earlier a white police officer had been acquitted of criminal charges by an all-white jury in another prosecution stemming from a fatal beating of a young black motorcyclist stopped for a routine traffic violation. At the trial of the officers accused of unjustifiably killing McDuffie, defense attorneys used peremptory challenges to remove all of the potential black jurors. The six-person, all-white jury acquitted the police officers of *all* charges—an acquittal that triggered massive rioting in Miami's predominantly black ghetto area known, ironically, as Liberty City.

The other riot stoked, in part, by failures of the criminal justice system to protect blacks from police misconduct is that which rocked Los Angeles in April 1992, in the aftermath of the acquittal of four white police officers charged with violating state laws when they beat a black man whose name has become synonymous with police use of excessive force—Rodney King.[131] On March 3, 1991, police officers in Los Angeles gave chase to King, whom they reported as speeding. For four miles he eluded them, dangerously racing down streets in residential neighborhoods. Police eventually cornered his car and ordered King and his passengers to alight. According to one perspective, King refused to follow instructions, resisted arrest, and in so doing put the arresting officers in reasonable fear for their safety, thereby justifying the force they used to subdue him. According to King and others at the scene, the police beat him severely without cause.

What distinguished this case from thousands of other police–civilian altercations is that it was filmed: an amateur photographer captured much of the action on tape with a hand-held camcorder. In the eyes of most viewers, the tape largely favored King's version of events. It shows a man on the ground surrounded by police officers who appear to be in no danger but who nonetheless kick and beat King severely.

The spectacle of a black man being beaten without apparent justification by a group of white policemen touched off a national outcry. A state prosecution ensued. As in the McDuffie case, defense attorneys sought a change of venue on the grounds that publicity made it impossible for their clients to receive a fair trial in Los Angeles. The changed venue also mimicked the McDuffie case insofar as the new trial site, Simi Valley, a predominantly white, suburban enclave—the home of the Ronald Reagan Presidential Library—offered the likelihood of a jury that would be considerably more white and considerably more solicitous to the defense than any jury that would probably have emerged had the trial taken place at the original trial site. (For discussion of the law, race, and change of venue, see pp. 245–252.) The Simi Valley jury that heard the case has often been described as all-white. That is untrue; the jury contained an Asian-American and an Hispanic-American. It is true, however, that the jury contained no blacks.

After fifty-five days of trial and seven days of deliberation, the jury acquitted all of the officers of the most serious charges and deadlocked with respect to a lesser charge brought against one of the officers. Almost uniformly condemned, the acquittals sparked several days of furious rioting during which 52 people were killed, 2,383 injured, 500 fires set, a billion dollars in property destroyed, and 16,291 arrests made: the bloodiest, most destructive American riot in the twentieth century.[132]

Several complexities need to be noted regarding the trials of the officers accused of criminal wrongdoing in the violence inflicted on Arthur McDuffie and Rodney King. In both instances, although there is strong reason to believe that the accused policemen acted wrongfully, there is also good reason to believe that in acquitting the defendants the juries did not engage in racist nullification à la the acquittal of Emmett Till's murderers. With respect to McDuffie's assailants, the prosecution badly mismanaged the presentation of its case. Prosecution witnesses gave conflicting testimony. Jurors, moreover, were apparently put off by the possibility that policemen who were granted immunity by the government in return for their testimony may have been more culpable than some of the officers who were tried.

With respect to the Rodney King beating, a substantial argument can be made that that case, too, was simply more complicated than is conventionally acknowledged. First, the vaunted videotape did not show the entire confrontation between King and his assailants but only that part of it which, seen alone, appeared to be incriminating. At trial, defense attorneys focused the jury's attention on the pre-videotape portion of the incident, a period during which even the prosecution conceded that King not only refused to follow police instructions but resisted officers in such a way as to justify their initial use of force against him. Second, although the brief snippets of the videotape that were endlessly replayed on television across the country appeared to show an unambiguous episode of naked brutality, at trial defense attorneys pointed out subtleties that clouded the issue of whether the police assailants harbored criminal intent.[133]

The point here is not to exculpate the assailants of McDuffie or King but rather to avoid a tendency indulged in all too often: the tendency to portray a case as unequivocally emblematic of a particular evil whether or not the specific facts of the case warrant the attribution. The acquittals of those charged with criminally harming McDuffie and King have come to symbolize racist police brutality and a blatant unwillingness of the legal system to discipline such brutality. The facts of the cases, however, do not point unequivocably to this conclusion. In both instances there are alternative explanations that plausibly explain the acquittals. In the case of the McDuffie assailants, prosecutorial ineptitude may well explain the jury's decision. In the case of King's assailants, the actual (as opposed to reported) facts of the entire (as opposed to merely the videotaped) confrontation provided an arguable predicate for the acquittals.

The acquittals in the McDuffie and King cases highlight a fact that was also accentuated by the outcome of the prosecution of O.J. Simpson: the difficulty of obtaining a conviction in complicated criminal cases in which the accused are zealously defended by aggressive counsel. Moreover, those enraged by the outcome of the McDuffie and King cases ought to consider another lesson underscored by the Simpson case: an acquittal is not a declaration of innocence; rather, it is a declaration that the jurors are not persuaded beyond a reasonable doubt that, on the basis of the evidence presented to them, the defendant is guilty. Finally, it should be recalled that, with respect to McDuffie and King, federal authorities brought prosecutions in federal courts for alleged violations of federal civil rights statutes despite the acquittals for alleged violations of state law. Federal prosecution failed in the McDuffie case but succeeded in convicting the officers who assaulted Rodney King. It cannot fairly be said, then, that in these instances law enforcement officials did nothing in the face of substantial evidence suggesting that crimes may have been committed by police officers.

What can be said is that the public attention generated by these cases succeeded in shining a bright light on an area of society that has often been neglected: the disturbing tenor of interracial conflict between police and black civilians. As noted above, investigations following the Miami riots of 1980 documented a troubling pattern of police mistreatment of blacks that had gone unpunished or underpunished. A similar pattern was revealed—or, more accurately, confirmed—by the Independent Commission on the Los Angeles Police Department (the Christopher Commission), which investigated the LAPD in the aftermath of the 1992 riots.[134] Concluding that police use of excessive force was a significant failing that warranted urgent attention, the commission also declared that "the problem of excessive force [was] aggravated by racism."[135] Although the police misconduct or criminality that was documented reached beyond the sufferings inflicted on racial minorities, a recurring theme in the Christopher Commission's report was the corrosive consequence of the racial contempt for blacks (and other colored people) that clearly infused the organizational culture of the LAPD. It is noteworthy that shortly before responding to the call for assistance that brought him face to face with Rodney King, a police officer transmitted a computer message about a domestic dispute in which they had intervened, a dispute involving an African-American couple. Referring to this dispute and associating blacks with apes—an association that has deep roots in European-American culture—the officer stated that the couple's confrontation was "right out of *Gorillas in the Mist*."[136] Confirming the racial connotation of the reference, someone responded with appreciative sarcasm, using a distinctively African-American argot: "hahaha . . . let me guess who be the parties."

The notorious lawlessness of the Los Angeles Police Department was a dramatic instance of a widespread problem: the failure to regulate police satisfactorily. Internal policing of police departments is typically inadequate because police officials (like all officials) are loath to discipline "their own." At the same time, external regulation is rendered difficult because the power of police unions and kindred organizations attracts the support or compels the silence of politicians who nominally govern the police. Opposition mobilized by police organizations has succeeded frequently in stymieing efforts to create civilian review boards empowered to investigate charges of police brutality. Moreover, even where civilian review boards have been established, police have shown themselves adept at "capturing" their supposed monitors.[137]

State and federal laws provide civil causes of action that individuals can bring against officers for money damages. The centrality of racial conflict to the regulation of police is suggested by the fact that the single most important statute available to victims of police brutality is the federal Ku Klux Klan Act of 1871, popularly known as Section 1983.[138]* The deterrent threat of civil litigation typically lacks bite, however, because expense, delay, doctrinal impediments, and the need to be an attractive party who will win the sympathy of jurors—for example, a person uninvolved in crime—often dissuade potential plaintiffs from bringing suit, even though they have, in fact, been brutalized.[139] Of course, in theory, police officials can be prosecuted criminally. But interdependence between police and prosecutors often discourages local district attorneys from pushing police brutality prosecutions vigorously.[140]

Additional impediments to the regulation of police have been raised by the U.S. Supreme Court in two cases whose dismal facts again emphasize the frequent intertwining of racial bias and police misconduct: *Rizzo* v. *Goode* (1976)[141] and *City of Los Angeles* v. *Lyons* (1983).[142] In these cases, the Court needlessly restricted the authority of federal courts to oversee dangerously abusive police departments.

---

*Further accentuating the significance of race in this context are the facts of a watershed case in the history of Section 1983, *Monroe* v. *Pape*, 365 U.S. 167 (1961), (overruled in part by *Monell* v. *New York Dep't. of Social Servs.*, 436 U.S. 658 (1978)). *Monroe* involved a suit in which it was alleged that police in Chicago violated federal law when, without a warrant, they broke into the home of the plaintiffs (six black children and their parents), rousted them from bed, made them stand naked in the living room, showered them with racial epithets, ransacked the house, and took the father to a police station, where he was interrogated for ten hours and denied the opportunity to call his family or an attorney. In *Monroe*, the Supreme Court held that certain abuses by state police officers were subject to suit under Section 1983.

Rizzo arose from litigation initiated by various individuals and community groups who sought to impose federal judicial restraints on the Philadelphia Police Department. The plaintiffs alleged that certain police officers were racially biased, that these officers habitually violated the rights of Negroes and other racial minorities, that these racist misdeeds were well known to police supervisors, and that nothing substantial had been done to deter the continuation of this well-documented misconduct. A U.S. district court judge carefully detailed numerous incidents which provide a virtual catalogue of the types of police mistreatment that have become deeply etched in the popular folklore of African-Americans: flagrant use by officers of the racial epithet "nigger"; resort to deadly force against suspects who could have been subdued by other means; harsher reactions to blacks than to whites engaged in the same conduct; needlessly destructive searches; unwarranted detentions; arrests for nothing more than what police perceived as insufficient deference; and purposeful infliction of public humiliation on political activists seeking to elevate the status of black Americans.[143] Although there existed no formal departmental policy of racial discrimination, the district court concluded that such violations occurred "with such frequency that they cannot be dismissed as rare, isolated instances, and that little or nothing is done by the city to authorities to punish such infractions, or to prevent their recurrence."[144]

The plaintiffs requested the appointment of a receiver for the police department. The district court judge, however, declined to impose upon the police department an outside agency authorized to supervise its reformation. Instead, he decreed that the police department would maintain the authority to supervise itself. All the court demanded was that the Philadelphia Police Department make arrangements to handle citizen complaints in a manner suggestive of authentic responsiveness. Hence, the district court ordered the police to prepare and distribute to the citizenry forms for the submissions of complaints, provide prompt and adequate investigations, offer adjudication by an impartial body, and create an opportunity for both complainants and the police to present their views, followed by notification to the parties of decisions reached.

Although a court of appeals affirmed the district court's decision,[145] the Supreme Court disapproved of even this minimal amount of federal judicial oversight. In an opinion authored by Justice Rehnquist, the Supreme Court held that the district judge's order represented "an unwarranted intrusion by the federal judiciary into the discretionary authority committed [to the defendant police authorities] by state and local law."[146] The Court was by no means united; three justices (Blackmun, Marshall, and Brennan) dissented. The majority, however, made it clear that they intended to reinvigorate limits on federal power that have often impeded those seeking to enforce national standards on behalf of racial minorities.*

The message articulated by *Rizzo* was delivered even more strongly in *City of Los Angeles* v. *Lyons*, a federal civil rights suit brought by a twenty-four-year-old black man.[147] The circumstances which occasioned Adolph Lyons's complaint aptly punctuate the central point of this chapter.

> According to the uncontradicted evidence in the record, at about 2 a.m. on October 6, 1976, Lyons was pulled over to the curb by two officers of the Los Angeles Police Department (LAPD) for a traffic infraction because one of his taillights was burned out. The officers greeted him with drawn revolvers as he exited from his car. Lyons was told to face his car and spread his legs. He did so. He was then ordered to clasp his hands and put them on top of his head. He again complied. After one of the officers completed a patdown search, Lyons dropped his hands, but was ordered to place them back above his head, and one of the officers grabbed Lyons' hands and slammed them onto his head. Lyons complained about the pain caused by the ring of keys he was holding within his hand. Within 5 to 10 seconds, the officer began to choke Lyons by applying a forearm to his throat. As Lyons struggled for air, the officer handcuffed him, but continued to apply the chokehold until he blacked out. When Lyons regained consciousness, he was lying face down on the ground, choking, gasping for air, and spitting up blood and dirt. He had urinated and defecated. He was issued a traffic citation and released.[148]

Lyons's experience was not unique, and even though he suffered pain, humiliation, and physical injury, the situation could have turned out

---

*Given the federalism concerns voiced by the Supreme Court, it is especially noteworthy that among those urging affirmance of the district court was the Pennsylvania Attorney General. 423 U.S. 366 (1976).

even worse for him. Between 1975 and 1982, at least sixteen persons were *killed* by police chokeholds. Of the sixteen, twelve were blacks. In a city where black men constituted 9 percent of the population, black men constituted 75 percent of those killed by chokeholds.[149]

The district court concluded that the treatment accorded to Lyons violated his constitutional rights and, further, that authorizing police to apply chokeholds to civilians in situations in which the police faced no serious threat to themselves "was unconscionable." The court therefore enjoined the LAPD from using chokeholds under circumstances posing no serious threat to officers.*

After the court of appeals agreed with the district courts, the Supreme Court, in an opinion authored by Justice Byron White, held that the federal courts lacked the power to offer injunctive relief—that is, order the LAPD to restrict its use of the chokehold. The defect in Lyons's case, according to the Court, was that he could not show that he stood a real and immediate danger of again being subjected to a chokehold. Absent such a showing, the Court declared, the federal judiciary should decline to intervene. The Court also stated that federalism concerns of the sort it expressed in *Rizzo* provided another, distinct ground for concluding that the federal district court had exceeded its powers. Finally, the Court noted that its ruling did not leave Lyons without a remedy. Though unable to have federal courts modify the LAPD's policy and practice regarding chokeholds, Lyons was free to sue his assailants for money damages for violating his federal civil rights.

Dissenting, Justice Thurgood Marshall (joined by Justices Brennan, Blackmun, and Stevens) argued that, contrary to the majority's claim, precedent did not at all dictate the Court's conclusion, that the majority had actually strained precedent to reach the conclusions it desired,

---

*The court of appeals affirmed the district court, but its order never went into effect. The court of appeals and then the Supreme Court stayed the district court's injunction until local officials were able to attain a final judgment of their appeals. In the meantime, local authorities themselves echoed the district court's conclusions. The Los Angeles chief of police prohibited the use of one type of chokehold under any circumstances, and the Board of Police Commissioners imposed a moratorium on another type of chokehold, unless an officer reasonably perceived himself to be in serious danger. Local officials, however, continued to press their appeal in order to establish that the federal district court did not have authority to order them to modify the chokehold policy.

and that simply allowing suits for money damages was a wholly inadequate way to protect federal rights. Ridiculing the Court, Justice Marshall noted that under *Lyons* "the federal judicial power is now limited to levying a toll" for widespread, systematic violations of federal norms.[150]

Rizzo and *Lyons* reflect the intuition of jurists who believe that complaints against police are exaggerated and that, in any event, the costs imposed by the violations complained of are less worrisome than the social costs imposed by judicial oversight of complex bureaucracies that judges may be in no better position to monitor than local officials. Over the past quarter-century, this intuition has moved federal courts, under the prodding of the Burger-Rehnquist Supreme Court, to defer increasingly to law enforcement officialdom.[151]

Racial Prejudice and the Continuing Problem of Wrongful Convictions: The Case of Clarence Brandley

Alongside racially biased police brutality, the specter of wrongful convictions at trials tainted by bigotry has long haunted the collective consciousness of African-Americans. A striking documentation of the sort of events that have stoked this anxiety is offered by Michael L. Radelet, Hugo Adam Bedau, and Constance E. Putnam in their careful study, *In Spite of Innocence: Erroneous Convictions in Capital Cases* (1992).[152] This study unearths 416 instances between 1900 and 1991 in which it appears likely that erroneous convictions were obtained in prosecutions for which death sentences constituted a potential punishment. Of the 416 cases, 188 involved black defendants. Not every miscarriage of justice touching a black defendant arises from racial discrimination. Blacks, too, are sometimes simply the victims of calamitous mistake. On the basis of the Radelet-Bedau-Putnam study, however, it is clear that in a substantial number of cases, racial bias played a significant, sometimes decisive, role in convicting innocent black defendants. A revealing example is the ordeal of Clarence Brandley.

❧ In the fall of 1980, in Conroe, Texas, Clarence Brandley, a black man, was accused of murdering Cheryl Dee Fergeson, a white student at the high school at which he managed the janitorial services. Some circumstantial evidence supported considering Brandley as a suspect: the absence of a corroborated alibi; statements by co-workers that he had had the opportunity to commit the crime and had acted somewhat suspiciously around the time the murder was perpetrated; the fact that at the time of the murder Brandley was on probation for possessing a sawed-off shotgun he had allegedly used in an effort to coerce a woman into having sex with him. There was, however, exculpatory evidence available as well, though, as we shall see, the prosecution illicitly suppressed much of it.

Brandley's first trial ended with a hung jury; a lone juror on the all-white panel held out for acquittal. Later, that juror claimed that he was called "nigger lover" during deliberations.[153] At a second trial, Brandley was convicted and sentenced to death, again before an all-white jury, the monochromatic complexion of which was no accident. The local district attorney's office had a policy of deploying peremptory challenges to strike all prospective black jurors in any case involving a black defendant.[154]

For six years, Brandley sat on death row as attorneys pursued appeals. Then two things happened. First, new, exculpatory evidence emerged. A woman came forward with testimony that her former husband had confessed to murdering Fergeson. Unaware that Brandley faced trial for the killing, the witness said that she never bothered to report her husband's statement because she thought he was lying. When she found out about Brandley's conviction, she told a lawyer about her information, and he, in turn, advised her to speak with the district attorney who had inherited the case. The district attorney disbelieved her and neglected to inform Brandley's lawyers. Luckily, however, the witness's attorney told Brandley's lawyer about the new development.

Second, Brandley's attorneys unearthed evidence of misconduct on the part of police and prosecutors. Although Brandley's janitorial co-workers should have been viewed as suspects by police, the Texas Ranger who supervised the investigation quickly limited his attention to Brandley and then took action to suppress the cultivation of any evidence that might have cast suspicion on others. He coordinated the testimony of Brandley's co-workers and threatened one of them with jail and physical violence if he declined to follow the coordinated script. The witness who was threatened later swore that his testimony at trial was fraudulent and that the only reason he offered it was fear of the police. He stated that he had seen two janitors talking with the murder victim before Brandley arrived on the scene. Indeed, he declared that he had heard the victim scream for help before Brandley's arrival. State officials knew of this evidence before Brandley's trials but declined to make it known to the defense.

Other acts and omissions on the part of officials are also worth noting. Although a Caucasian pubic hair, not belonging to the victim, was found near the victim's vagina, police officials resisted all efforts to obtain hair samples for comparison from Brandley's co-workers. State officials, moreover, resisted attempts to obtain blood samples from the co-workers despite finding blood inconsistent with Brandley's blood type on the victim's shirt. In addition, despite discovering semen in the victim's vagina, state officials failed to run an analysis of the sample to determine the blood type of the man from whom the semen came.

A Texas district court judge granted Brandley's request for habeas corpus relief, ruling that the state's investigation was "so impermissibly suggestive that false testimony was created, thereby denying [Brandley] of due process of law and a fundamentally fair trial."[55] The judge also found that "the color of Clarence Brandley's skin was a substantial factor which pervaded all aspects of the State's capital prosecution against him, and was an impermissible factor which significantly influenced the investigation, trial, and post-trial proceedings of [Brandley's] case."[56]

Cases like Brandley's are not simply a part of the past. They are also part of the present and the future. Stories surface annually of blacks released from prison after losing years of their lives as a result of wrongful convictions obtained by racially tainted prosecutions.* In addition,

---

*Erroneous convictions tainted by racial prejudice pose an ongoing danger. Four black men, convicted in Illinois for murdering a white couple, were released in 1996 after spending eighteen years in prison. New evidence, witness recantations, and a jailhouse confession overwhelmingly indicated their innocence. See Don Terry, "After 18 Years in Prison, 3 Are Cleared of Murders," *New York Times*, July 3, 1996.

In another case, a black man sentenced to death for murdering a white woman obtained release in 1993 when defense counsel succeeded in unearthing facts that documented severe misconduct by police and prosecutors and that also placed in serious doubt the defendant's guilt. See *McMillian* v. *State*, 616 S. 2d 933 (Ala. Crim.

racially biased miscarriages of justice have strongly influenced American culture, particularly African-American culture. They have helped make many blacks intensely skeptical of police officials, profoundly fearful of the judicial system, and keenly insistent that in the absence of militant, collective demands for justice, white decisionmakers are apt to deal with black defendants with less care than white ones.

There was a time, not long ago, when these sentiments did not much influence the administration of criminal justice since blacks were excluded from positions of decisionmaking responsibility. That situation, however, has changed. To a degree unprecedented in American history, blacks are exercising authority as jurors, attorneys, and judges. The way in which they exercise that authority is powerfully affected, in part, by the memories and sentiments which guide and animate them.[157] For this reason and others as well, the history of racial injustice in American courts will continue to weigh upon future developments.

Race and the Terror of Incarceration

Much of the discussion thus far has focused on racial bias in the investigation and adjudication of criminal disputes. I turn now to racial bias in conditions of incarceration.

Incarceration warrants attention for a variety of reasons. First, historically, incarceration has been a setting in which racial prejudice has been especially prevalent, stubborn, abusive, grotesque, and tolerated. Prior to the Civil War, virtually all imprisoned convicts in the South were whites; black criminals, most of whom were slaves, were typically subjected to corporal punishment and then sent back to labor. As one former slave recalled, "In slavery times jails was all built for the white folks. There weren't never nobody of my color put in none of them. No time . . . to stay in jail; they had to work; when they done wrong they was whipped and let go."[158] After the Civil War, the overwhelming majority of criminals imprisoned in the South were black.[159] The emer-

---

App. 1993). See also Pete Earley, *Circumstantial Evidence: Death, Life, and Justice in a Southern Town* (1995); Bryan K. Fair, "Using Parrots to Kill Mockingbirds: Yet Another Racial Prosecution and Wrongful Conviction in Maycomb," 45 *Alabama Law Review* 404 (1994).

gence of a large population of incarcerated blacks posed a new problem within penal institutions: Should white prisoners lose their racial privilege on account of their status as convicts and be grouped with black convicts? Or would such a demotion be too demeaning even for white felons? Speaking to the National Prison Congress in 1886, a white Southerner embraced the latter position, insisting fervently that whites should not be imprisoned with blacks on the grounds that enforced race mixing would constitute a punishment too cruel to permit. "It is akin," he remarked, "to the torture anciently practiced of tieing [sic] a murderer to the dead body of his victim limb to limb, from head to foot, until the decaying corpse brought death to the living."[160]

All Southern jurisdictions and many outside the South segregated convicts by race.[161] They did so for many reasons. Some officials believed, as noted above, that even white convicts deserved better than to be housed with blacks. Other officials favored segregation out of habit, for purposes of dividing and thereby better controlling inmate populations, or because they believed that, absent segregation, white and black inmates would harm one another. Whatever the motivation, formal racial segregation lasted longer in prisons than any other public institution. The first federal court to adjudicate a challenge to racial segregation in prisons dismissed it summarily in 1959 four years *after* the landmark ruling in *Brown* v. *Board of Education*, concluding that the reasons for abolishing segregation in public schools did not apply to prisons.[162] Only in the late 1960s did federal judges begin to clearly indicate that they would no longer view routine racial segregation in jails or prisons as constitutionally permissible.[163]*

Physical separation of the races was part of a wider set of troublesome racial conditions. Although incarceration for anyone is purpose-

---

*Courts have generally rejected claims that the threat of violence justifies the racial segregation of inmates. See, e.g., *Battle* v. *Anderson*, 376 F. Supp. 402 (E.D. Okla. 1974) *affd in part, revd in part*, 993 F. 2d 1551 (CA 10 1993); *Blevins* v. *Brew*, 593 F. Supp. 245 (W.D. Wis. 1984). In *Rentfrow* v. *Carter*, 296 F. Supp. 301 (N.D. Ga. 1968) five white and five black prisoners petitioned the court to block mandatory desegregation on the grounds that both black and white inmates would violently resist this reform. The court rejected their petition. In at least one case, however, a court has permitted temporary racial segregation for the purpose of avoiding imminent violence. See *Stroman* v. *Griffin*, 331 F. Supp. 226 (S.D. Ga. 1971).

fully miserable, officials have often designedly made incarceration for blacks an especially hellish experience. After the abolition of slavery, incarceration became a "legal" way to subject blacks to servitude. To reduce public expenditures and aid private businesses, Southern officials leased convicts to private employers, who shouldered the burden of feeding, clothing, and confining prisoners in return for the authority to extract their labor. "The lease system," Professor Edward L. Ayers observes, "was tailor-made for capitalists concerned only with making money fast. Labor costs were fixed and low, problems of labor uncertainty were reduced to the vanishing point, lucrative jobs could be undertaken that others would not risk, convicts could be driven at a pace free workers would not tolerate."[164]

Some observers applauded penal slavery for blacks. "To the ignorant negro," T. J. Hill declared in an address to the National Prison Association in 1897, "a term in the penitentiary was without question the best lesson he could obtain in citizenship," since it was there that blacks could learn mining and other skills which would be marketable upon obtaining freedom.[165] Other observers condemned the convict-lease system, as did Fletcher Green in 1949, when he declared that it, among other "southern penal practices . . . left a trail of dishonor and death that could find a parallel only in . . . the prisons of Nazi Germany."[166] In mines, on railroads, and in turpentine camps, convict laborers were literally worked to death in pockets of horrific despotism in which black convicts were especially vulnerable to exploitation.

By the 1920s, most states had gotten rid of the convict-lease system; it proved to be intolerably brutal and prone to corruption. The modes of incarceration that replaced it, however, state-run work farms and chain gangs along with jails and prisons, all tended to re-create the pigmentocracy of "normal" society, which meant, of course, the racial subordination of black inmates. To paraphrase Professor James B. Jacobs, race was, and in many places remains, the most important factor in the prison subculture, determining more than anything else how one "does time."[167] With substantial frequency, race has determined job assignments, levels of discipline, and the tenor of relationships between inmates and between prisoners and guards.

A 1991 decision by federal district judge David G. Larimer highlights the character of invidious racial discriminations in prisons (though it is difficult to gauge comprehensively the extent of the problem). In 1986, black and Hispanic inmates at the Elmira (New York) Correctional Facility sued the prison administration under federal civil rights law, claiming that colored prisoners were routinely discriminated against with respect to housing, employment, and discipline.[168] The plaintiffs showed that, customarily, white inmates received preferential treatment and that when this racial etiquette was breached officials openly and emphatically reasserted it. For instance, when an Hispanic prisoner was sent to the prison library to serve as a clerk, the library supervisor told him to mop floors instead. Similarly, when a black prisoner was assigned to a relatively desirable cell block, a guard made good on his threat to move the inmate's "fat nigger ass out."[169] When black professional staff at the prison sought to intercede (despite their small numbers and social isolation), they, too, became objects of racial insult. A white guard told a black member of the staff that he and his fellow white officers "don't like smart niggers" at the prison.[170] Another black member of the staff had "nigger" and "KKK" and a crude picture of a chimpanzee scrawled on her mailbox.[171]

Judge Larimer held in favor of the plaintiffs. He concluded that "a pervasive atmosphere of racism" infected decisionmaking at the prison and ordered that reforms be undertaken.* That such an order was required is indicative of the continuing presence of racial prejudice in the administration of criminal law, as in all other realms of American life.

Not so long ago, judges declined to intervene in the governance of prisons almost regardless of the character of inmates' allegations. As

---

*Judge Larimer also declared that

> no matter how difficult the task facing prison administrators, racism must play no part in the operation of a prison. Racism is never justified; it is no less inexcusable and indefensible merely because it occurs inside the prison gates. As a society we have made a commitment to equality under the law. This goal has not yet been achieved and perhaps never will be unless those who govern take firm steps to eradicate racism whenever they are able to do so. When racism is proven, federal courts must be especially vigilant to insure that all citizens—even the most unpopular—are guaranteed the equal protection guaranteed by the Constitution.

Santiago v. *Miles*, 774 F. Supp. 775, 778 (W.D. N.Y. 1991).

Professor Michael B. Mushlin observes, "[t]he Constitution did not breach prison walls for over 170 years."[172] Under the "hands-off doctrine," courts refused to hear inmate complaints about prison conditions on the grounds that "it is not the function of the courts to superintend the treatment and discipline of prisoners in penitentiaries, but only to deliver from imprisonment those who are illegally confined."[173] Beginning in the 1960s, however, heightened attentiveness to racial inequality, the dangers of unchecked governmental power, and the special vulnerabilities of prisoners combined to create a prisoners' rights movement that succeeded in substantially limiting the prerogatives of penal bureaucrats.* This movement persuaded the federal judiciary to scrutinize and, if necessary, modify the conduct of jail and prison authorities in order to establish that prisoners retain certain rights that society is bound to respect.

Judicial oversight ameliorated some of the worst abuses that prison-

---

*One event in particular that galvanized support for the recognition and protection of inmates' rights was the hasty, violent squashing of a prisoner rebellion at the Attica (New York) Correctional Institute on September 13, 1971. To recapture a portion of the prison taken over by inmates four days earlier, the governor of New York, Nelson Rockefeller, authorized an armed assault by state police who killed twenty-nine inmates and ten guards who had been taken hostage. Although officials initially claimed that the hostages had been killed by the inmates, these statements were subsequently shown to be lies.

Racial conflict suffused the tragic events at Attica, a prison at which a virtually all-white cadre of officials administered a predominantly colored population of prisoners. After the rebellion was quelled, guards subjected prisoners to brutal reprisals and vicious taunts. Credible testimony indicates that officers addressed black inmates as "niggers" and "coons" and threatened to kill them. See *Inmates of Attica Correctional Facility* v. *Rockefeller*, 453 F. 2d 12, 19 (CA 2 1971). See also *Attica: The Official Report of the New York State Special Commission on Attica* (1972); Malcolm Bell: *The Turkey Shoot: Tracking the Attica Cover-Up* (1985); Tom Wicker, *A Time to Die: The Attica Prison Revolt* (Bison Book Editon, 1994 [1975]).

Although neither inmates nor officials were held criminally liable for actions taken during and after the Attica rebellion (Governor Hugh Carey issued a blanket pardon to everyone implicated in wrongdoing), inmates did succeed in a civil action against certain officials. See Gary Spencer, "Attica Inmates Win $1.3 Million from State," *New York Law Journal*, Oct. 26, 1989.

On the prisoners' rights movement, see Michael B. Mushlin, *Rights of Prisoners* 9–11 (2d. ed., vol. 1, 1993).

ers faced on account of hostility or indifference by corrections officials, including racially motivated official misconduct. In many places, however, conditions of confinement are still horrific. Indeed, some close observers of prison life contend that in certain ways conditions of incarceration are even worse now than before the inception of the prisoners' rights movement.[174] They argue that although reform was essential, the type of reform imposed by judicial intervention eroded the ability of penal authorities to assert order. According to this view, under the old regime, guards did abuse their power, but in doing so at least inhibited inmates from abusing one another. Now, with guards' authority checked, inmates are encouraged either to rebel against their jailers—sometimes leading to massive bloodletting—or, more frequently, to ignore the jailers and prey upon their neighbors—the great danger that faces virtually anyone sentenced to prison.

Whites, too, face horrific conditions in jails and prisons. Although the percentage of whites in jails and prisons has declined substantially over the past forty years,[175] whites still constitute a sizable portion of the inmate population. In 1990, of those persons committed to state prisons, 45 percent were white.[176] White prisoners, like black ones, face far more than legal punishment in prison; they also face illegal dangers, particularly vulnerability to sexual attack by other inmates, an especially chilling danger now given the prevalence of HIV infection in prison populations.[177] Indeed, where they are a racial minority, white inmates are often singled out for sexual attack by their black counterparts, a form of assault that some black assailants view as "payback" for the sexual and other forms of violence that have historically been inflicted upon blacks by whites. Explaining black-on-white rapes in the prison in which he resided, one black inmate remarked, "you guys been cuttin' our b[alls] off ever since we been in this country. Now we're just gettin' even."[178]

Some observers will argue that the indifference, if not hostility, shown by governments at every level toward inmates despite the large percentage of whites in the inmate population negates any suggestion that this indifference or hostility is tainted by illicit racial sentiments. That argument, however, should by no means be viewed as decisive. First, it may be that the politically influential sectors of the society are unaware that whites constitute a large proportion of inmate populations. It is possible, indeed likely, that the imagery of the Negro as criminal has misled some people into believing that blacks (and other people of color) constitute an even larger percentage of incarcerated populations than is actually the case, thereby misleading these same people into erroneously minimizing the number of whites who face danger and misery in jails and prisons. Second, even if voters and their representatives do have an accurate understanding of the racial demographics of inmate populations, that alone does not negate the possibility that racially selective hostility or indifference is at work in affecting public sentiment and thus public policy regarding incarceration. Although whites constitute a large proportion of the prisoner population, white inmates constitute a much smaller percentage of the overall white population than is the case with black inmates. In 1990, for every 100,000 white Americans, 289 were in jail or prison; for every 100,000 black Americans, 1,860 were in jail or prison.[179] It is entirely plausible that the white-dominated political institutions of America would not tolerate present conditions in jails and prisons if as large a percentage of the white population were incarcerated as is the reality facing the black population. It is surely possible, to many likely, that if the racial shoe were on the other foot, white-dominated political structures would be more responsive than they are now to the terrors of incarceration. That possibility should make more alarming the fact that the darkening of jail and prison populations during the past twenty years has been attended by a discernible increase and hardening of antagonism toward the incarcerated. One indication of this increased public hostility is the return of chain gangs and other policies calculated to increase the immiserization of prison life.[180]

It is impossible to say definitively whether attitudes toward the incarcerated would be different if those who are jailed and imprisoned represented as large a proportion of the white population as the jailed and imprisoned represent of the black population. That this hypothesis is at least plausible is itself a damning statement about the state of American race relations. Moreover, apart from the matter of governmental intentions, the plain fact is that deplorable, unlawful conditions in jails and prisons have a distinctively racial *appearance* because such a relatively large percentage of the black population is, has been, or will be incarcerated.[181] At present, jails and prisons are among the most influential institutions of socialization in African-American communities. The extent to which authorities allow these institutions to remain dangerous, destructive, lawless hells is the extent to which authorities strengthen the belief held by an appreciable number of black Americans that the "white man's" system of criminal justice remains their enemy.

4.

Race, Law, and Suspicion:

Using Color as a Proxy for Dangerousness

Fear covers the streets like a sheet of ice.
—Bill Bradley

TWO POWERFUL ANTAGONISTIC attitudes have shaped the decisions that have largely determined the course of American race relations. One, whose influence has been stressed in the two preceding chapters, is marked by an insistence that, at bottom, the United States of America is, and should remain, a white man's country. A second attitude, less influential historically than the first, though strong in its own right, rejects the legitimacy of an official pigmentocracy. It insists that all persons and all groups be accorded equality before the law with no privileged or subordinated castes.

The question whether, or under what circumstances, people should be able to view and act upon race as a mark of increased risk of criminality frames a context in which the struggle between these competing attitudes is intense. But the matter is more complicated than this. For debate over the proper response to that question rages not only between white supremacists and racial egalitarians; it rages as well within the ranks of racial egalitarians, indicating the existence of differing conceptions of racial equality.

Whether the legal system ought to authorize people to take race into account in making calculations about the criminal propensity of others is a vexing question. Attuned to the reported demographics of crime, fearful people of all hues engage in race-dependent strategies either to apprehend criminals or to avoid them. Consider the police officer who detains the young black man disembarking from an airplane because the officer believes that the young man's race is one of the signals indicating that he is probably engaged in drug trafficking. Consider, too, the lone pedestrian who perceives the blackness of an oncoming teenager as part of a reason to cross the street, shift the position of a handbag, or touch the grip of a hidden handgun.

The hypothesized police officer and lone pedestrian each use race as a proxy for an increased risk of criminality. By proxy I mean a trait—in this case blackness—which is (or is believed to be) correlated with some other trait—in this case crime. All of us use proxies a great deal of the time. As Professor Larry Alexander writes, "Day in and day out . . . we react to people based on traits they possess which, though immaterial in themselves, we believe to be highly correlated with those traits in which we are primarily interested."[1] We look to traits, such as having a law degree, as indicators of other traits, such as having expertise in legal matters.

Why do we proceed in this way? Why don't we dispense with proxies and simply look for the qualities with which we are ultimately concerned? One reason is expense. Obtaining information is expensive, so we depend upon various sorts of proxies, such as educational credentials, to lessen the costs entailed in gathering the information we need to make sensible decisions. It would be very expensive to examine for ourselves directly the handiwork of doctors, lawyers, accountants, and so on, so we look to less expensive proxies for competence—degrees, licenses, recommendations. Similarly, it is expensive for a person to determine with his own eyes whether another individual actually has criminal intentions. Doing that might require waiting until the individual pulls a gun and demands what he wants. So we look to proxies to help us calculate at less expense the risk that a given individual is likely to make such a demand—proxies such as gender, age, clothing, posture, accent, and, yes, race.

But is it proper to use a person's race as a proxy for an increased likelihood of criminal misconduct?* Let's begin with the police.[2]

---

*I am not talking about the case in which police act against a person based on a detailed description that includes the suspect's race. In such a case, the person's skin

Police and the Problem of "Reasonable" Racial Discrimination

Public authorities in the United States have long used race as a signal of an increased risk of criminality. Many jurisdictions that permitted slave-holding institutionalized the linkage of blackness with suspiciousness by empowering all whites to demand proof of a black's status as a slave or free person. Since blacks were presumed to be slaves, any black person lacking obvious supervision by a white person was deemed to be suspect, a possible fugitive from bondage. North Carolina attempted to lessen the burden of supervision by requiring that all urban nonslave blacks wear shoulder patches on the outside of their clothing inscribed with the word "free."[3]

Blacks are not the only racial minority to confront racially selective policing. The most dramatic and extensive single episode in which authorities used race as an indicia of potential criminality involved the wholesale detention of persons of Japanese ancestry during World War II. After the Japanese attack on Pearl Harbor brought the United States fully into the war, federal authorities placed all persons of Japanese ancestry who lived on or near the West Coast under military orders, pursuant to which they were subjected to curfew, removed from their homes, and detained in camps. The U.S. Supreme Court upheld the constitutionality of most of these measures against charges that they denied equality before the law to persons of Japanese ancestry.* Speaking for the Court, Justice Hugo L. Black wrote:

---

color is being used no differently than information about the pants or jacket or shoes that the suspect was said to be wearing. When used as part of a detailed description to identify a given individual, the person's race is not so much a category that embraces a large number of people as a distinguishing fact about the identity of a designated person. My concern in this chapter is with the use of racial categories as a probabalistic sorting device used by police and others to demarcate groups of persons who, because of their race, are viewed as more risky than other persons.

*In *Hirabayashi* v. *United States*, 320 U.S. 81 (1943), the Supreme Court upheld a curfew imposed on people of Japanese ancestry. In *Korematsu* v. *United States*, 323 U.S. 214 (1944), the Court upheld the exclusion of people of Japanese ancestry from designated areas. In *Ex Parte Endo*, 323 U.S. 283 (1944), the Court ruled that the Constitution prohibited government authorities from continuing to detain a concededly loyal American citizen of Japanese ancestry.

All legal restrictions which curtail the civil rights of a single racial group are immediately suspect. That is not to say that all such restrictions are unconstitutional. It is to say that courts must subject them to the most rigid scrutiny. Pressing public necessity may sometimes justify the existence of such restrictions; racial antagonism never can.[4]

The Court upheld the restrictions on the ground that public necessity justified them. In the midst of war, there was simply no time to pursue the investigation that would have been required to distinguish between those persons of Japanese ancestry who represented a real risk of subversion and those who could presumably be trusted. "We are not unmindful of the hardships imposed by [the military orders] upon a large group of American citizens," Black declared, but "citizenship has its responsibilities as well as its privileges, and in time of war the burden is always heavier."[5]

Korematsu has been widely criticized as a judicial capitulation to racial prejudice.[6] There was no substantial evidence of subversion by persons of Japanese ancestry. No similarly broad or burdensome restrictions were imposed upon whites whose lineage was German or Italian (though the United States went to war against Germany and Italy as well as Japan).* Moreover, it was well known that racial hatred was one of the important motivations behind the restrictions. The general whose

---

*In dissent, Justice Robert H. Jackson presses this point eloquently:

Had Korematsu been one of four—the others being, say, a German alien enemy, an Italian alien enemy, and a citizen of American-born ancestors, convicted of treason but out on parole—only Korematsu's presence would have violated the order. The difference between their innocence and his crime would result, not from anything he did, said, or thought, different than they, but only in that he was born of different racial stock.

Now, if any fundamental assumption underlies our system, it is that guilt is personal and not inheritable. Even if all of one's antecedents had been convicted of treason, the Constitution forbids its penalties to be visited upon him, for it provides that "no attainder of treason shall work corruption of blood, or forfeiture except during the life of the person attainted." But here is an attempt to make an otherwise innocent act a crime merely because this prisoner is the son of parents as to whom he had no choice, and belongs to a race from which there is no way to resign.

323 U.S. 243 (1994) (Jackson, J., dissenting).

orders the Supreme Court upheld openly declared that in his view all persons of Japanese descent belong to "an enemy race."[7] Justice Frank Murphy rightly observed in dissent that the government had fallen "into the ugly abyss of racism,"[8] a judgment the United States subsequently embraced by passing legislation that formally apologized for its conduct and that paid reparations to many of those who suffered on account of the forced relocations.[9]

Nowadays the question of whether, or in what circumstances, officials may legitimately take race into account in determining the suspiciousness of a person arises in situations such as these:

EPISODE ONE. Police officers in Phoenix, Arizona, stop and question a person because he is sitting in a car outside of an apartment complex, appears to be nervous, moves his car when a marked police car approaches his vehicle, and also because, in an officer's words, "he was a Mexican male in a predominantly white neighborhood."[10]

EPISODE TWO. A drug enforcement agent at the Kansas City, Kansas, airport stops and questions a person because he is "roughly dressed," young, got off a direct flight from Los Angeles, a source city for drugs, walks rapidly from the airplane toward a taxi cab, has two carry-on bags and no checked luggage, and appears to be very nervous. That the person is black is another factor which, along with the others, prompted the agent's action.[11]

EPISODE THREE. In California, at a highway checkpoint thirty miles north of the Mexico–U.S. border, officers of the U.S. Border Patrol subject the driver of an automobile to questioning and search. Their suspicions are triggered, in part, by his apparent Mexican ancestry.[12]

EPISODE FOUR. Police randomly stop, question, and search young black men in a neighborhood in Boston for several weeks. The provocation is a report by a (white) man that his (white) pregnant wife was shot and killed in that neighborhood by a young black man.[13]

EPISODE FIVE. Police in New York City detain and search a clean-shaven, 6 foot 4 inch, 225 pound young black man carrying a briefcase immediately after he alights from a commuter train. They are acting on the basis of an anonymous letter which warned that a 5 foot, 10 inch, trim, mustachioed, black man riding the train routinely carries a gun.[14]

EPISODE SIX. Police receive a credible tip that a white man armed with a bomb is somewhere in an office building. They surround the building and then enter it. The police examine white men more closely than those who are non-white.

Most courts that have confronted the issue have authorized police to use race in making decisions to question, stop, or detain persons so long as doing so is reasonably related to efficient law enforcement and not deployed for purposes of racial harassment. An example is the decision by the Supreme Court of Arizona in *State* v. *Dean*, which stemmed from the incident described above in episode one. In this incident, police acted in part on the basis of a perception that the suspect was "out of place" given his race and the racial composition of the neighborhood in which he was sighted. The Arizona court saw the officers' use of race not as a dubious practice but rather as a "practical aspect of good law enforcement."[15] The court conceded that it would be impermissible for officers to act on the basis of racial or ethnic background *alone*. That, however, was not the case here, where the racial incongruity between the person observed and the area in which he was stopped was only one factor of several that prompted police to act.* The court could have added that the racial incongruity that supplemented police suspicions was presum-

---

*The Arizona Supreme Court stated:

> [The suspect's] ethnic background was only one of several factors which caused the officers to believe that further investigation was necessary. That a person is observed in a neighborhood not frequented by persons of his ethnic background is quite often a basis for an officer's initial suspicion. To attempt by judicial fiat to say he may not do this ignores the practical aspects of good law enforcement. While detention and investigation based on ethnic background alone would be arbitrary and capricious and therefore impermissible, the fact that a person is obviously out of place in a particular neighborhood is one of several factors that may be considered by an officer and the court in determining whether an investigation and detention is reasonable and therefore lawful.

State v. *Dean*, 543 P.2d 425, 427 (Arizona 1975).

ably evenhanded, applying to whites who are "out of place" as well as to people of color who appear to be where they "do not belong."*

Another example of judicial toleration of race-dependent police decisionmaking is the judgment of the U.S. Court of Appeals in *United States* v. *Weaver*, which upheld the validity of the airport stop described above in episode two. "Large groups of our citizens," the Court declared, "should not be regarded by law enforcement officers as presumptively criminal based upon their race."[16] However, the Court went on to say:

> Facts are not to be ignored simply because they may be unpleasant— and the unpleasant fact in this case is that [the DEA agent] had knowledge, based upon his own experience and upon the intelligence reports he had received from the Los Angeles authorities, that young male members of the black Los Angeles gangs were flooding the Kansas City area with cocaine. To that extent, then, race, when coupled with the other factors [the agent] relied upon, was a factor in the decision to approach and ultimately detain [the suspect]. We wish it were otherwise, but we take the facts as they are presented to us, not as we would like them to be.[17]

Another example of judicial deference to racially discriminatory police conduct is *United States* v. *Martinez-Fuerte*,[18] a U.S. Supreme Court decision that upheld the stop described above in episode three. First, the Court concluded that stopping motorists at a permanent checkpoint for brief questioning is of such a minimally intrusive character that it can appropriately be done in the absence of an individualized suspicion that a particular vehicle contains illegal aliens. Second, the Court reasoned that "as the intrusion here is sufficiently minimal that no particularized reason need exist to justify it . . . it follows that the Border Patrol officers must have wide discretion in selecting the motorists to be diverted for [brief questioning]," including the discretion to use apparent Mexican

---

*Police sometimes view whites who are "out of place" with increased suspiciousness. They also sometimes view such people with solicitude, perceiving they must be lost and thus face an increased risk of being harmed.

ancestry as an indicia of suspicion.[19] Third, the Court pointed to results: Of the 820 drivers selected for questioning by the Border Patrol during the eight days surrounding the incident in question, roughly 20 percent were engaged in transporting illegal aliens. What the Court inferred was that "to the extent that the Border Patrol relies on apparent Mexican ancestry . . . that reliance clearly is relevant to the law enforcement need to be served."[20]

In permitting race to be used on a routine basis as a negative signal of increased risk of criminality, *Dean*, *Weaver*, and *Martinez-Fuerte* represent an influential, indeed dominant, view within the judiciary. There is an alternative perspective that has been voiced by some judges. The Court of Appeals of Virginia, for example, has ruled that in the absence of a compelling (as opposed to a merely reasonable) justification, police use of race as a factor in calculating suspiciousness violates the Virginia and federal constitutions.[21] Several federal judges voice a similar view.[22] Most courts that have confronted the issue, however, have concluded that race can appropriately be used as a factor of suspicion in determining the likelihood that a person is engaging in, or has already committed, criminal activity, so long as this use of race is *reasonably* related to law enforcement aims and not a mere pretext for racial harassment.

Some commentators dispute that it is reasonable for police (or anyone else) to use racial indicia—or, more precisely, blackness—in evaluating risks of criminal mischief.[23] They castigate as bigots police officers who see blackness as a signal of a higher probability that an otherwise undifferentiated person has engaged in or will pursue criminal behavior. They mistrust statistics that uniformly indicate that blacks, especially men, are more likely than whites to commit street crimes. They resist the idea that racial discrimination (at least discrimination that adversely affects blacks) can properly be termed "reasonable." They contend that theories of reasonable racial discrimination are mere rationalizations for the mistreatment of vulnerable minorities. When confronting the fact that some blacks, too, are among the defenders of the concept of reasonable racial discrimination, these commentators respond by saying, as did Professor Patricia Williams, that such blacks have "learned too well the lessons of privatized self-hatred and rationalized away the fullness of [their] public, participatory selves."[24]

There is both virtue and vice in this response. Its virtue consists in its resistance to a seductive theory to which many have acquiesced all too easily. Some defenders of so-called "reasonable" racial discrimination neglect to consider certain difficulties embedded in the implementation of it. One difficulty has to do with the fact that misinformation may mar the calculations pursuant to which determinations of suspiciousness are made. If news reports, rumor, and folklore exaggerate the danger that crime poses and misportray blacks' contribution to that danger, then officers acting in reliance on these impressions may react reasonably to the *perceived* situation but unreasonably to the *actual* situation. Hence, before conceding that a given act of racial discrimination is "reasonable," careful attention must be paid to the accuracy of the information used in making such an assessment—an attentiveness that is now often absent.*

A more fundamental difficulty has to do with the values people bring to bear in deciding what is "reasonable." The judgment that a racial discrimination is reasonable depends not only on an evaluation of the discrimination's assistance in apprehending criminals. It also depends on an evaluation of the danger posed by given suspects and assessments of the costs imposed upon innocent people by using the racial criterion in dispute. The more one empathizes with the innocent blacks erroneously detained by racially discriminatory investigation, the smaller will be the range of decisions one views as "reasonable." By the same token, the more distant one feels from those erroneously detained, the larger will be the range of decisions one views as "reasonable." Rea-

---

*Dissenting from the court's affirmation of the police conduct that served as the basis for Episode Two noted above, Judge Richard Arnold complained about the absence of information needed to gauge whether, or the extent to which, blackness actually correlated with a higher risk of drug trafficking. "If we had evidence," Judge Arnold maintained, "that young blacks in Los Angeles were more prone to drug offenses than young whites, the fact that a young person is black might be of some significance." *United States* v. *Weaver*, 966 F.2d 391, 397 (CA 8 1992). Judge Arnold noted, however, that the government had presented no evidence on this point but had simply depended on the judges to resort to their own casual impressions as a basis for decision. Insisting upon a showing of concrete and precise evidence before using race as a proxy, Judge Arnold appropriately scolded his colleagues: "Use of race as a factor simply reinforces the kind of stereotyping that lies behind drug-carrier profiles. When public officials begin to regard large groups of citizens as presumptively criminal, this country is in a perilous situation indeed. Ibid at 397.

sonableness, then, is not a definite, arithmetic, objective quality that is independent of aims and values. It is a concept that is considerably more subtle, complex, malleable, and mysterious than the simplistic model of human decisionmaking relied upon by those who accept at face value the "reasonableness" or "rationality" of conduct that not only expresses controversial moral and political judgments but that also expresses deep-seated, perhaps unconscious, affections, fears, and aversions.[25]

Although critics of reasonable racial discrimination usefully discourage a complacent acceptance of it, some of them also obscure important matters about which clarity is needed. People seeking solutions to America's massive racial problems must resolutely eschew the temptation to prettify ugly realities. Crime and its racial demographics are part of those realities. It does no good to pretend that blacks and whites are similarly situated with respect to either rates of perpetration or rates of victimization. They are not. A dramatic crime gap separates them. In relation to their percentage of the population, blacks on average both commit more crimes and are more often victimized by criminality. The familiar dismal statistics and the countless tragedies behind them are not figments of some Negrophobe's imagination. The country would be better off if that were so. Instead, the statistics confirm what most careful criminologists (regardless of ideological perspective) conclude: In fact (and not only in media portrayal or as a function of police bias) blacks, particularly young black men, commit a percentage of the nation's street crime that is strikingly disproportionate to their percentage in the nation's population.[26]

That is why there are circumstances in which, as a statistical matter, a police officer would be correct in estimating that a man's blackness identifies him as more likely than a similarly situated white person to be involved in criminal wrongdoing. Just as race can signal a heightened risk that a black person will die younger, earn less money, reside farther away from employment opportunities, experience more unpleasant encounters with police, and possess less education than a white person, so, too, can race signal a heightened risk that a black person will commit or has committed certain criminal offenses. This sociological fact does not mean that the legal system ought to permit police to engage routinely in racial discrimination. No sociological fact dictates the proper response to it. At the same time, we need to know what the facts are, whether we like them or not.

Many of those who refuse to concede the instrumental rationality of using race as a proxy for an increased risk of criminality are gripped by a sense that racial discriminations must be stripped of any and all positive features and absolutely demonized. They fear that if they concede that racial discrimination may be rational in certain circumstances, many persons will seize the concession, wrongly generalize from it, and in the process weaken antidiscrimination norms. That fear largely explains the strong tendency to brand *all* racial discriminations that adversely affect blacks and other people of color as the product of irrational bigotry or prejudice.* Like many strategies based on simplification, however, this one incurs a considerable cost, namely, a lessened appreciation of the depth of the difficulties facing American society. One of those difficulties is that irrationality and bigotry are not all that supports racial discrimination. Many decent, enlightened, well-intentioned people engage in racial discrimination because it is often an understandable (albeit wrong) adaptation to a deformed social structure that dimishes blacks and pushes them toward their own anti-social adaptations. Tragically, in other words, from a short-term self-interested perspective, it makes sense for many people to engage in racial discrimination given the many racially correlated stratifications that mark American society. As Cornel West says, race matters.[27]

If taking race into account in making determinations of suspicion is a rational adaptation to the racial demographics of criminality, why not permit police to engage in racial discrimination routinely, as many courts have? The heart of the answer resides in the special significance of racial distinctions in American life and law. *Race is different.* In

---

*Although some jurists (including Justice Clarence Thomas) insist that there exists no difference between affirmative action and segregation, others insist that there exists no difference between rational racial discrimination and bigoted racial discrimination. In both instances, and perhaps for similar reasons, proponents of these positions neglect important distinctions. For a good argument to the effect that champions of racial minorities have erred self-destructively by refusing to acknowledge the phenomenon of rational racial discrimination, see Cass R. Sunstein, "Three Civil Rights Fallacies," 79 *California Law Review* 751 (1991). This same issue re-emerges in the struggle over the use of peremptory challenges in jury selection. (See chapter 6.)

America, the making of racial distinctions has proven to be more destructive and more popularly distasteful than other lines of social stratification.* That is why, at least since the civil rights revolution of the
1950s and 1960s, judges have ruled, pursuant to the Equal Protection
Clause of the Fourteenth Amendment, that mere reasonableness is an
insufficient justification for officials to discriminate on racial grounds.[28]
When officials discriminate on racial grounds, judges have typically demanded "strict scrutiny"—the most intense level of judicial review. Under strict scrutiny, a racially discriminatory governmental action should
be upheld only if it can be supported by reference to a *compelling* justification and only if the government's racial distinction is narrowly tai-
lored to advance the project at hand.[29] When a court administers strict
scrutiny, it shines an intense spotlight on the governmental decisionmaking at issue in order to uncover any covert or unconscious racial biases at work. Strict scrutiny embodies a recognition, born of long and
terrible experience, that the presence of a racial factor in decisionmaking should raise anxiety and signal that the government is likely to be
doing something wrong. As Professor Paul Brest observes:

> Even a glance at history indicates [that] race-dependent decisions
> that are rational and purport to be based solely on legitimate consid-
> erations [such as "good law enforcement"] are likely in fact to rest on
> assumptions of the differential worth of racial groups or the related
> phenomenon of racially selective sympathy and indifference.[30]

In short, under U.S. constitutional law, governmental use of racial distinctions is typically strongly discouraged. It is presumed to be invalid.

---

*For example, the law permits insurance companies to use a wide variety of traits to
guide them in selecting customers and setting rates. Yet state and federal laws uniformly prohibit race from being used as a factor in making actuarial calculations, despite the fact that, from the insurance industry's perspective, it would be a useful
predictive criterion. See Jill Goulding, "Race, Sex, and Genetic Discrimination in Insurance: What's Fair," 80 *Cornell Law Review* 1646 (1995).

American law widely discourages gender discrimination. Federal constitutional
and statutory law, however, give more leeway to gender discrimination than race discrimination. See, e.g., *Rostker* v. *Goldberg*, 453 U.S. 57 (1981) (upholding male-only
draft); 42 U.S.C. 2000e-2(e) (1) (permitting gender discrimination in employment
when gender "is a bona fide occupational qualification").

Yet many courts, including the U.S. Supreme Court, have failed to apply strict scrutiny—or a heightened scrutiny of any sort—to police using race as a factor of suspicion. Instead, courts have broadly *defended* police use of racial proxies by asserting, among other things, that such strategies are "realistic." In *Weaver*, the U.S. Court of Appeals articulated this view, declaring that "facts are not to be ignored simply because they may be unpleasant," by which the court referred to the supposed fact that the suspect's race represented an increased likelihood that he was a courier for crack.[31] Assuming the accuracy of the court's facts—an unwarranted assumption given this court's complacency toward factfinding[32]—its reasoning remains objectionable. The court seems to believe that facts dictate the way in which the legal order should respond. This is erroneous. The legal order always *chooses* how it shall respond to a given set of facts.* Although U.S. constitutional law is inconsistent, it has now typically and rightly chosen to subject to strict scrutiny racial classifications used by public officials. The court of appeals in *Weaver*, however, not only declines to follow the normal path, but declines as well to articulate why it withholds applying heightened scrutiny to racially selective policing. It says that "facts are not to be ignored simply because they are unpleasant." Subjecting racial policing to strict scrutiny, however, would not entail ignoring facts. It would require courts to determine whether, in light of the society's presumptive disapproval of race-dependent decisionmaking, the facts in a given instance are such that drawing a racial line is permissible.

Some courts argue that there is nothing to be concerned about if race is only one of several factors taken into account by police in determining suspiciousness. Indeed, some courts are suggesting that decisions which distinguish between persons on a racial basis do not even constitute racial discrimination when race is not the *sole* or dominant consideration prompting disparate treatment.[33] This is a profoundly wrong view. Even if race is only one of several factors behind a decision, tolerating it at all means tolerating it as potentially the *decisive* factor. In a close case, it is a person's race that might make the difference between

---

*When whites violently resisted desegregation of public schools, some believed that the fact of that resistance dictated suspending desegregation. Fortunately, the Supreme Court *chose* a different response—ordering that officials comply with the Court's interpretation of the Constitution. See *Cooper* v. *Aaron*, 358 U.S. 1 (1958).

being stopped by the police or being permitted to go on about one's business free from governmental intrusion. In a case involving two people engaged in ambiguous behavior, the white person may be left alone while the black person may be intruded upon because her race, perceived as a signal of heightened risk, tipped the balance against her. Few racially discriminatory decisions are animated by only one motivation; they typically stem from mixed motives.[34]* There are, of course, differing degrees of discrimination. For some discriminators, race may be a small consideration; for others, large. The degree of discrimination may have a bearing on its justifiability. But the degree of the discrimination cannot logically have a bearing on the *existence* of the discrimination itself. Taking race into account in a small, marginal, even infinitesimal amount still constitutes racial discrimination.

Judicial precedent largely favors the position I advocate. The Supreme Court has declared, for instance, that the Equal Protection Clause of the federal constitution "does not require a plaintiff to prove that the challenged action rested solely on racially discriminatory purposes."[35] Noting that "racial discrimination is not just another competing consideration," the Court averred that, "when there is proof that a discriminatory purpose has been *a* motivating factor in the decision" [emphasis added], strict scrutiny is imperative.

---

*Although it is unusual for police to use race as the *only* signal of increased risk, there are many instances in which race is used as the overwhelming indicia of suspiciousness. An especially chilling instance involves the Pennsylvania State Police. In 1974, this police department sent to banks a directive which read as follows:

BANK INFORMATION

Take photos of any black males or females coming into bank who may look suspicious:

A   Come in to ask directions
B.   Exchange large bill for small money
C.   Come in for no apparent reason

NOTIFY LOCAL OR STATE
POLICE

A black man who was photographed pursuant to this policy sued the bank and the police. See *Hall* v. *Pennsylvania State Police*, 570 F.2d 86 (CA 3 1978) (allegation states cause of action under federal civil rights laws). See also *United States* v. *Nicholas*, 448 F.2d 622, 624 (CA 8 1971) (black person driving car with out-of-state license plates does not properly create inference of criminality).

Precedent, however, is not entirely on my side. After all, I am criticizing courts, including the Supreme Court, for failing to handle racial policing according to the rules generally applicable under federal constitutional law. Recently, moreover, in the context of disputes over electoral districting, the Supreme Court (mainly pursuant to the thinking of Justice Sandra Day O'Connor) has held that strict scrutiny applies when race is a "predominant" consideration in drawing district lines.[36] The judges I am criticizing might say that this "predominant" consideration idea is essentially the same as that which they have articulated: The use of racial criteria should only trigger strict scrutiny when race is the predominant proxy looked to for purposes of identifying a heightened risk that a person has committed or is about to commit a crime. In short, there already exists some judicial precedent supporting the emergence of new expectations that are more tolerant of formal racial distinctions than alternative understandings of what racial equality demands.

In 1966, in *Justice without Trial*, Jerome Skolnick wrote:

> "In principle . . . police departments . . . are racially unbiased. That is, one would not find in a training manual the idea that blacks should be treated differently in the criminal process than whites, nor even that blacks are apt to exhibit greater criminality than whites. The explicit principle is racial equality.[37]

The principle to which Skolnick referred is now under siege. In 1966, many police officers undoubtedly ignored that principle in their day-to-day activities, but at least their actions were wrong according to the norm Skolnick describes. The great danger posed by the judicial trend I am criticizing here is that it threatens to turn police conduct that should be understood to be legally and morally wrong into conduct that is understood to be legally and morally right.*

Of what, however, am I afraid? Given that as a matter of fact a person's race may signal a statistically higher risk of criminality, why not

---

*American constitutional law is remarkably uneven. At the same time that it has shown increasing tolerance for police using race in making determinations of suspicion, it has shown increasing intolerance for lawyers using race to exclude prospective jurors pursuant to racially discriminatory peremptory challenges. (See chapter 6.)

permit police to take race into account in making determinations of suspicion so long as they do so for purposes of law enforcement and not racial harassment? Several reasons justify prohibiting the police from using racial proxies in their decisionmaking, except in the most extraordinary of circumstances. The first is prophylactic: such a prohibition will diminish the occasions on which police officers will engage in racial harassment under the guise of using racial criteria "reasonably." Exertion of police power for purposes of racial harassment is a social evil that the legal system should attempt to eradicate. A racially prejudiced decision can survive undisturbed all too easily when an officer is pressed only to give a reasonable justification for that decision. Consider, for example, the Border Patrol officer who is prejudiced against *all* people of discernible Mexican ancestry. He could easily give vent to his prejudice by acting in the same manner as the officers whose conduct was upheld by the Supreme Court in *Martinez-Fuerte*. Prejudiced against all Mexican-looking people, such an officer might express his sentiments by using apparent Mexican ancestry as a criterion for selecting those whom he questions. Under the Supreme Court's ruling, however, such an officer need not worry about judicial interference as long as he catches a sufficient number of illegal aliens to make his racially prejudiced strategy apparently efficient and as long as he refrains from openly stating that he targets Mexican-Americans because he dislikes them. A reasonableness standard provides some protection against stupid, candid, or inefficient bigots but virtually none against the depredations of bigots who are savvy, duplicitous, and efficient.

A second, closely related reason for more tightly circumscribing police use of race-dependent criteria is that the current permissive regime nourishes powerful feelings of racial grievance against law enforcement authorities that are prevalent in every strata of black communities. Examining responses of elite blacks to the furor surrounding O.J. Simpson's acquittal, Henry Louis Gates, Jr., relates:

> Blacks—in particular, black men—swap their experiences of police encounters like war stories, and there are few who don't have more than one story to tell. Erroll McDonald, one of the few prominent blacks in publishing, tells of renting a Jaguar in New Orleans and being stopped by the police—simply "to show cause why I shouldn't

be deemed a problematic Negro in a possibly stolen car." Wynton
Marsalis says, "Shit, the police slapped me upside the head when I
was in high school. I wasn't Wynton Marsalis then. I was just another nigger standing out somewhere on the street whose head could
be slapped and did get slapped." The crime novelist Walter Mosley
recalls, "When I was a kid in Los Angeles, they used to spot me all
the time, beat on me, follow me around, tell me that I was stealing
things." Nor does William Julius Wilson wonder why he was
stopped near a small New England town by a policeman who
wanted to know what he was doing in those parts. There's a moving
violation that many African-Americans know as D.W.B.: Driving
While Black.[38]

Similar testimony is offered by Don Jackson. After serving as a police officer for several years, during which time he became the victim
himself of racially selective police mistreatment, Don Jackson penned a
remarkable essay arrestingly titled "Police Embody Racism to My People."[39] Jackson recounts that upon hearing numerous reports of racial
harassment of blacks by police in Long Beach, California, he began to
ride through that community at night without the protection of his police uniform. To document what he encountered, Jackson arranged for
a hidden television camera crew to trail him in a van. While riding
along, breaking no laws, Jackson was pulled over for questioning by two
white police officers who appear to have acted, at least in part, on the basis of Jackson's race. Upon questioning the legitimacy of the officers'
demand, Jackson was beaten and thrown through a plate-glass win-
dow—all of which was filmed. This incident and the controversy surrounding it prompted Jackson to remark that "police have long been the
greatest nemesis of blacks, irrespective of whether we are complying
with the law or not. We have learned," he continued, "that there are cars
we are not supposed to drive, streets we are not supposed to walk. We
may still be stopped and asked 'Where are you going, boy?' whether
we're in a Mercedes or a Volkswagen." The black American, he concluded, "finds that the most prominent reminder of his second-class citizenship are the police."[40]

Similar experiences and feelings are related by journalist Don
Wycliff, who asserts that notwithstanding his middle-class status, and
law-abiding character, he feels "an ambivalence tilting toward antipathy

for the police." He feels that way, he explains, because "a dangerous, humiliating, sometimes fatal encounter with the police is almost a rite of passage for a black man in the United States."[41]

If the police may properly view race as an indicia of suspicion, thereby making people of color more vulnerable to stops and questioning and all that stems from unwanted attention from the police, then it follows that people of color will have more reason than white persons to fear the police, regardless of their compliance with law. That racial minorities are, on average, more likely to be victimized by crime than whites only compounds the problem. The communities most in need of police protection are also those in which many residents view police with the most ambivalence, much of which stems from a recognition that color counts as a mark of suspicion relied upon as a predicate for action—stopping, questioning, patting down, arresting, beating, and so forth. This causes people who might otherwise be of assistance to police to avoid them, to decline to cooperate with police investigations, to assume bad faith or dishonesty on the part of police officers, and to teach others that such reactions are prudent lessons of survival on the streets.[42]

Permitting color to count, albeit only in conjunction with other considerations, as an indicia of suspiciousness also contributes to residential racial separation, one of the most intractable and consequential problems in America.[43] Racially selective policing will help to dissuade blacks from venturing into neighborhoods where they are viewed as being "out of place," "not belonging." Recall the words of Don Jackson: "We have learned . . . that there are . . . streets [on which] we are not supposed to walk."[44]

It is important to distinguish between the brutish officer who uses race as a guide in decisionmaking and the polite officer who uses race as a guide in decisionmaking. Racially selective policing need not entail the malevolent treatment Don Jackson suffered. One can imagine a police officer who, depending on the circumstances, sometimes views whiteness as an indicia of suspiciousness just as he sometimes views blackness as an indicia of suspiciousness and who, in any event, treats all people with as much courteousness as the rigors of law enforcement permit. This policeman, let's call him Officer Friendly, engages in courteous racial discrimination.[45] One can much more easily imagine, however, that racially discriminatory conduct which starts off as courteous will degenerate, that disciplined racial selectivity will give way to undisciplined racial selectivity, and that the emotions that always seem to coalesce around racial distinctions will lead to the sort of conflicts which have often vexed relations between police departments and black communities.

Even many of the Officer Friendlys will unintentionally *exaggerate* the criminality or potential for criminality of African-Americans. They will do so honestly, but they will do so nonetheless. This exaggeration flows from age-old, derogatory images of the Negro as criminal, images that have been revived and deployed in all manner of contexts, from popular entertainment, to scholarship, to political campaigns. The exaggeration is reinforced by the very real fact that a disproportionately large share of the nation's street crimes—robberies, rapes, murders, aggravated assaults—are perpetrated by certain blacks, more specifically, certain young black men. Whatever the source, inflated anxieties about the risks posed by African-Americans (and others, like Mexican-Americans, about whom these comments are relevant) make it likely that, even when police officers are sincerely attempting to use race solely for the purpose of advancing efficient law enforcement, they will err in a disturbingly large number of instances because of exaggerated fears.

Judges should be more skeptical than many have been of the ability of police officers to use race as an indicia of suspicion without making an unacceptably large number of errors whose consequences fall predictably upon innocent black people. Again consider *Martinez-Fuerte*. Rebuffing claims that the Border Patrol's use of apparent Mexican ancestry was impermissible, the Supreme Court stated:

> Less than 1% of the motorists passing the checkpoint are stopped for questioning, whereas American citizens of Mexican ancestry and legally resident Mexican citizens constitute [roughly 16%] of the population of southern California. . . . If the statewide population ratio is applied to the approximately 146,000 vehicles passing through the checkpoint during the eight days surrounding the arrests [at issue], roughly 23,400 would be expected to contain persons of Spanish or Mexican ancestry, yet only 820 were referred to the secondary area. This appears to refute any suggestion that the Border Patrol relies extensively on apparent Mexican ancestry standing alone in referring motorists to the secondary area.[46]

One footnote later, the Court observes, "Of the 820 vehicles referred to the secondary inspection area during the eight days surrounding the arrests [in question], roughly 20% contained illegal aliens."[47] Despite the justificatory aim behind the Court's presentation of these facts, they hardly provide a secure vindication. As Justice William J. Brennan, Jr., noted in dissent, the Court provides no indication of the ancestral makeup of the 1 percent stopped by the Border Patrol for secondary questioning. If, as is likely, this group was made up overwhelmingly of people of discernible Mexican ancestry, this means that an overwhelmingly large number of the innocent people who were questioned were also persons of apparent Mexican ancestry who found themselves placed in the position of proving their legality because of how persons of their racial makeup are widely perceived.

Criticizing the thinking exemplified by *Martinez-Fuerte*, Judge Harry T. Edwards rightly complains, "The real harm done [by permitting police to use race as a proxy for increased risk of criminality] is not fully apparent because we usually do not hear of the cases of the innocent people who are stopped by the police."[48] There are cases in which innocent parties have successfully sued the police for civil rights violations associated with racially discriminatory stops. These usually arise, however, from incidents in which police have behaved violently or with aggravated coarseness.[49] More illuminating are the cases in which innocent parties have not been roughed up but "merely" subjected to the "normal" mistakes that attend the use of racial proxies. Some examples are revealed in an admirably conscientious opinion by U.S. District Court Judge Jim R. Carrigan.

In *United States* v. *Laymon*,[50] Judge Carrigan suppressed incriminating evidence found in the car of a twenty-one-year-old black man from California who was stopped and searched in Eagle County, Colorado, by a police officer who used race as a factor in determining whom to investigate on suspicion of trafficking in narcotics.

Officer James Perry denied that race had played a role in his decision to stop the defendant. Indeed, officer Perry claimed that color blindness prevented him from perceiving the race of the defendant. Based on the officer's record as well as inconsistencies in his testimony, Judge Carrigan disbelieved Perry's assertion.[51] In doing so, Judge Carrigan displayed a fidelity to truthseeking that all too many judges forsake by showing undue deference to police, even when they are clearly lying.[52] Judge Carrigan ruled that officer Perry had insufficient reason to search the defendant's automobile and that the defendant had not given the policeman permission to conduct the search.[53] Revealing the effects of the officer's policy, Judge Carrigan noted what happened when the racial criteria proved to be misleading:

> Jhenita and Janice Whitfield, two young Black women, testified that they were stopped, while driving a car with California plates, for the alleged offense of failing to signal a sufficient distance prior to changing lanes on I-70, a four-lane highway. . . . [T]hey testified that they were forced to stand alongside the highway [with their four infant children] in cold mountain weather for more than forty-five minutes while Perry searched their car, unpacking their luggage and rummaging through all their personal clothing and belongings. No contraband was found, and the only product of this exercise was the anger of these citizens who felt they had been pressured to submit to a search because of their race. Perhaps ironically, one of them had served for years in the military service of the United States and had elected that service as her career.
>
> Byron Boudreaux, a young black male, testified that he was stopped by Perry while driving a car with Oklahoma plates through Eagle County on I-70. Perry and two other officers informed him that they had received an anonymous tip that a man fitting his description was carrying drugs. Boudreaux testified he was detained for approximately forty-five minutes while Perry and other officers searched his car.
>
> Aguinaldo Ferreria, a young Black male, was stopped by Perry while driving a car with California plates through Eagle County on I-70. Perry told him that he fit a description of someone suspected of carrying drugs. Ferreria was detained for about forty-five minutes while Perry conducted his search.
>
> These Black drivers indicated that Perry gave them the impression that the searches would be of the vehicle and would delay them only a few minutes, but the actual searches involved going through all their luggage and personal effects and took far longer.[54]

Judge Carrigan's opinion in *Laymon* usefully highlights the extent to which other judges have typically underestimated the cumulative costs imposed by police use of race as a proxy for suspiciousness. In *Martinez-Fuerte*, for instance, the Supreme Court maintained that the Border Patrol's intrusion on those selected for questioning is "quite limited," involving "only a brief detention of travelers during which all that is required of the vehicle's occupants is a response to a brief question or two and possibly the production of a document."[55] The stories recounted in *Laymon*, however, should prompt skepticism toward Justice Lewis F. Powell's portrayal of quick, courteous, nonthreatening, nonburdensome police interventions. First, at stake for many individuals will be more than simply one stop; at stake will be a lifetime of numerous stops. A person will not cease to be of apparent Mexican ancestry after the first instance of being pulled aside for questioning. In the eyes of the Border Patrol, his looks will continuously mark him as more suspicious than his similarly situated white Anglo counterpart.[56]

Second, the quality of the interaction between officials and at least some of those stopped for questioning is likely to be degraded by everyone's knowledge that race played a role in the decision to question. Officers who begin by seeking to discharge their duties with courteousness will confront people who will resent being stopped in part because of their racial heritage. The people stopped will vent their resentment. The officer—and recall that we are here talking about the initially good, nonracist, courteous officer—will respond in some defensive manner, which will in turn provoke further negative responses from those who feel aggrieved. That, in turn, will further aggravate the officer, leading to a deteriorating relationship that will often create bruised feelings, sometimes generate needless arrests, and occasionally spark violence.[57]

By too easily permitting the police to use race as an indicia of suspiciousness, courts also derogate from the idea that individuals should be judged on the basis of their own, particular conduct and not on the basis—not even *partly* on the basis—of racial generalizations. Race-dependent policing erodes the difficult-to-maintain habit of individualizing persons and strengthens the reflex of lumping people together according to gross racial categories. This reflex has had many disastrous consequences. One is the extra burden it puts upon blacks who want very much to assert responsibility for themselves but confront social impediments that mock their efforts. This burden and a common reaction to it is memorably described in an essay by Anthony Walton entitled "Willie Horton & Me."[58] Walton objects to being treated by police officers and others as a high-risk person because, in part, of his blackness. He relates how he has conscientiously and self-consciously stayed out of trouble and done everything else that should entitle him to the same degree of dignity accorded to his white counterparts. He notes, too, however, that despite his efforts he is "often treated the same as a thug."[59] He concludes that no amount of conformity to accepted standards "will make [him] the trusted American individual," that nothing he does will enable him to escape the automatic negative responses triggered by blackness, that no matter what he does to improve himself, people encountering him on the streets "won't see a mild-mannered English major," but will see instead Willie Horton.[60]

Walton responds with rage to his perception that his efforts to distinguish himself are futile. After admitting that he feels "suckered" for having ever believed that he could escape the reputation of his racial group by dint of his own personal efforts, Walton confesses to feeling a bitterness and a thirst for revenge that should alarm all Americans. "My black Ivy League friends and I," he writes, feel a disgust for mainstream values and institutions that is "infinitely" more contemptuous than the alienation expressed by youth of the black underclass. He and his friends, he claims, are "cynically biding [their] time, waiting for some as-yet-unidentified apocalypse that will enable [them] to slay the white dragon, even as [they] work for it, live next to it, and sleep with it."*

Walton's testimony reflects the sentiments of many who feel deeply insulted because they are targeted for scrutiny at least partly on the basis of their race. Are these people *right*, however, in feeling aggrieved? Should the legal system modify its practices in light of the feelings articulated by Walton and others?

When a Mexican-American motorist is selected for questioning in

---

*Describing her reaction to a salesman who refused, for what she perceived as racial reasons, to open the door to a store from which she desired to purchase a gift, Professor Patricia Williams writes: "I was enraged. At that moment I literally wanted to break all of the windows in the store and *take* lots of sweaters. . . . There was almost nothing I could do, short of physically intruding upon him, that would humiliate him the way he humiliated me." See "Spirit Murdering the Messenger: The Discourse of Fingerpainting as the Law's Response to Racism," 42 *University of Miami Law Review* 127, 128 (1987).

part on the basis of his perceived ancestry, he is undoubtedly being burdened more heavily at that moment on account of his race than his white Anglo counterpart. He is being made to pay a type of racial tax for the campaign against illegal immigration that whites, blacks, and Asians escape. Similarly, a young black man selected for questioning by police as he alights from an airplane or drives a car is being made to pay a type of racial tax for the war against drugs that whites and other groups escape. That tax is the cost of being subjected to greater scrutiny than others. But is that tax illegitimate?

One defense of it is that, under the circumstances, people of other races are simply not in a position to pay the tax effectively. In contrast to apparent Mexican ancestry, neither apparent white nor black nor Asian ancestry appreciably raises the risk that a person near the Mexican border is illegally resident in the United States. Similarly, the argument would run that in contrast to the young black man, the young white man is not as likely to be a courier of illicit drugs. The defense could go on to say that, in this context, race is *not* being used invidiously. It is not being used as a marker to identify people to harm through enslavement, or exclusion, or segregation. Rather, race is being used merely as a signal that facilitates efficient law enforcement. In this context, apparent Mexican ancestry or blackness is being used for unobjectionable ends in the same way that whiteness is used in the affirmative action context: as a marker that has the effect, though not the purpose, of burdening a given racial group. Whereas whites are made to pay a racial tax for the purpose of opening up opportunities for people of color in education and employment, Mexican-Americans and blacks are made to pay a racial tax for the purpose of more efficient law enforcement.*

We need to pause here to consider the tremendous controversy that has surrounded affirmative action policies aimed at helping racial minorities.[61] Many of the same arguments against race-based affirmative

---

*Moreover, while some proponents of affirmative action maintain that, overall, it helps whites as well as blacks by creating a more harmonious society for everyone, so, too, do some proponents of responsible racial discrimination in policing assert that, overall, it helps people of color as well as whites by creating a more secure society. They point out also that enhanced security may well disproportionately help blacks since they are often disproportionately victimized by criminality.

action are applicable as well in the context of race-based police stops. With affirmative action, many whites claim that they are victims of racial discrimination. With race-based police stops, many people of color complain that they are victims of racial discrimination. With affirmative action, many adversely affected whites claim that they are *innocent* victims of a policy that penalizes them for the misconduct of others who also happened to have been white. With race-based police stops, many adversely affected people of color maintain that they are *innocent* victims of a policy that penalizes them for the misconduct of others who also happen to be colored. Many whites claim that a major drawback of affirmative action which makes it more costly than valuable is the fact of their intense resentment against such programs. Many people of color claim that one of the drawbacks of race-based police stops that makes it more costly than valuable is their resentment against such policies.

There exist, however, a remarkable difference in reactions to these racial policies, both of which involve race-dependent decisionmaking. While affirmative action is under tremendous pressure politically and legally, racial policing is not. The Supreme Court has carefully hedged affirmative action by decreeing that such programs must meet the exacting requirements of strict scrutiny. By contrast, in *Martinez-Fuerte* and similar cases, the Supreme Court and other tribunals have barely mentioned the antidiscrimination norms within the Fifth and Fourteenth amendments to the federal Constitution.[62]

Another important dissimilarity between the Court's handling of affirmative action and its handling of race-dependent policing relates to burdening innocent parties. The Supreme Court has been exquisitely sensitive to charges that affirmative action unfairly burdens innocent whites. When it has upheld affirmative action programs it has done so only in situations in which it was convinced that the interests of innocent whites would not be unduly trammeled. More recently, it has typically invalidated affirmative action programs, in part because of a belief that such programs are unfair to whites who themselves played no role in establishing the racial injustices that affirmative action seeks to remedy.[63] By contrast, as we have seen, the Court pays little attention to the burdens imposed on innocent people of color by race-dependent policing.

Whatever one thinks of the conclusions drawn by the Court with respect to affirmative action, at least it begins at the correct starting point for analysis—that race-dependent decisions by officials call for more than ordinary justifications. With respect to race-dependent policing, however, the Court, mirroring public opinion, has made the terrible error of permitting race-dependent decisionmaking to become a normal part of police practice.

Many of those who defend the current regime of race-dependent policing speak as if there existed no sensible alternative. But there is an alternative: spending more on other means of enforcement to make up for any diminution in crime control caused by the reform I seek: prohibiting officers (except in absolutely extraordinary circumstances) from using race as a proxy for increased risk of criminality. Instead of placing a racial tax on blacks, Mexican-Americans, and other colored people, governments should, if necessary, increase taxes across the board. More specifically, rather than authorizing police to count apparent Mexican ancestry or apparent blackness as negative proxies, states and the federal government should be forced either to hire more officers or to inconvenience everyone at checkpoints by subjecting all motorists and passengers to questioning (or to the same chance at random questioning). The reform I support, in other words, does not entail lessened policing. It only insists that the costs of policing be allocated on a nonracial basis.

The law should authorize police to engage in racially discriminatory investigative conduct only on atypical, indeed extraordinary, occasions in which the social need is absolutely compelling: weighty, immediate, and incapable of being addressed sensibly by any other means. I have in mind a real emergency, a situation, like that noted above, in episode six, in which there is clear reason to believe that a violent crime has been or is about to be committed and that the reported characteristics of the perpetrator are such that using racial criteria to narrow the pool of potential suspects clearly increases the ability of the police to apprehend the criminal quickly. This formulation is by no means foolproof. Recall *Korematsu*. Implemented properly, however, this proposal would prohibit officers from using racial criteria as a *routine* element of patrolling. It would prohibit officers from *regularly* placing a race-based question mark over the heads of colored people. It would substantially change the current situation under which there exist separate and unequal rules of privacy for people of color. My proposal still permits race to be taken into account in some narrow circumstances. Under such circumstances, however, no person can rightly feel aggrieved even if he is the suspect of racial discrimination. After all, freedom from official racial discrimination, although dear, is but one of other weighty freedoms that are in tension with one another. Care must be taken to insure that the category of exceptional circumstances remains tightly circumscribed, but if that is done, this species of racial discrimination should be viewed as an unpleasant necessity and not a racial injustice.

Everyone—ordinary citizens, legislators, police officials, judges, and so on—should demand that race play no routine role in decision-making regarding whom to scrutinize for purposes of law enforcement. For judges, this typically would entail declining to count race as a proxy for increased risk of criminality, except in cases in which the government offers a compelling justification to decide differently. It would entail judges typically subtracting race from the array of considerations that can properly be viewed as contributing to the suspiciousness of a person. Thus, in a case in which police would not be legally justified in detaining an individual in the absence of the race factor, a judge should conclude that the detention is illegal. If police would be legally justified in detaining an individual in the absence of the race factor, but the police nonetheless used race in their calculation, the detention would be ruled legal—but the police would also be subject to administrative and legal penalties for having utilized a prohibited criterion. One hopes that the higher circles in the police hierarchy would discipline their underlings for illegal conduct. One also hopes that citizens subjected to wrongful use of racial criteria by police would succeed in suing wrongdoing police officers under federal and state laws enacted to protect the civil rights of citizens.

I am under no illusion that a general prohibition against taking race into account in making determinations of suspicion will provide a cure-all, if only because this reform would likely be underenforced to a large extent. After all, it would often be very difficult to determine whether an officer made a given decision on a racial basis if the officer keeps silent as to the racial aspect of his selectivity and mentions only the non-racial cues that prompted him to act. Some officers would be sufficiently candid to reveal the real bases of their decisionmaking regardless of the legal consequences. Others, upon learning of the applicability of the legal reforms advanced here, would adapt by covering up the real—racial—aspect of their decisionmaking. Courts might be able and willing to identify some cases in which an officer acted against someone in circumstances that permitted no other plausible explanation than that the officer used race as a cue for intervention.[64] Such instances, however, would be rare. In the usual case involving ambiguous circumstances, courts would be unlikely to rule against police officers. Such a ruling would amount not only to holding that an official acted on an unlawful basis. It would also amount to holding that the official lied in explaining the basis for his action. This helps to explain why many judges make such rulings only when they are absolutely sure of their conclusions—a protective posture that enables a considerable amount of illegal discrimination to pass undisturbed.*

Even so, the reform I suggest is worth pursuing. If it became the norm, it would dissuade conscientious law-abiding officials from using criteria they ought not use. It would provide a basis for resourceful attorneys to uncover wrongful racial discrimination even in some cases in which officers attempt to conceal their misconduct. And it would at least compel non–law-abiding officials to use racial criteria covertly, a far cry from the situation today, in which the courts permit the police openly and unapologetically to use a race line for purposes of calculating suspiciousness. There is, I grant, a danger in constructing a constitutional norm that will likely be underenforced to a substantial degree. Underenforcement will further nourish the corrosive cynicism of those who believe that, when it comes to blacks, the system habitually breaks its own promises. The correct response, however, is not to promise less but to work harder to bring the actual conduct of officials into line with appropriate goals. Even when rightful rules are underenforced, they are still worth fighting for because they set the standards for legitimacy, standards which, like magnets, exert a pull that affects the order of things.†

*For an analogous problem in the context of policing the prohibition against racially discriminatory peremptory challenges, see pp. 208–14.

†Here I follow the great nineteenth-century reformer Frederick Douglass. Speaking in favor of an antidiscrimination provision in the Civil Rights Act of 1875, Douglass observed that even if the provision could not be enforced, it would still be useful as "a

The Private Person and
Self-protective Racial Discrimination

What about private actors who are not engaged in commercial activities presently regulated by the state—the person walking home at night who uses racial cues as a guide to conduct: when to be on guard, cross the street, shift the position of a handbag, run for the nearest open door? The issue here is not whether to extend governmental regulation to embrace these activities. The political backing for such an effort would be virtually nonexistent because of a widely shared intuition that there ought to exist certain zones of privacy that are left undisturbed by the state and also because of a concomitant fear of overweening state power. Regulation backed by state power, however, is not the only form of regulation. Another important regulatory force is reputation—the evaluation of a person by his or her peers and the general public.

Many black men complain bitterly about people fearfully avoiding them.* Rivaling the prevalence of angry stories about being stopped by police for "driving while black" are angry tales told by black men who recount the numerous times they have been unable to obtain service from cabbies.† Some describe the experience as if it were the 1990s

---

banner on the wall of American liberty, a noble moral standard, uplifted for the education of the American people. . . . This law though dead, did speak." See Philip S. Foner, *The Life and Writings of Frederick Douglass*, IV: 401 (1955). See also "Note, Judicial Right Declaration and Entrenched Discrimination," 94 *Yale Law Journal* 1741 (1985); "Note, Making the Violation Fit the Remedy: The Intent Standard and Equal Protection Law," 92 *Yale Law Journal* 328 (1982).

*Phillip Martin's observation is representative:

> As I was leaving my Cambridge, Massachusetts apartment in a running suit . . . a white couple walking by glanced at me [and] abruptly crossed the street. When I looked back, I noticed that they had recrossed the street a block away. I know both working class and college educated men who have experienced similar disrespectful fear, regardless of what they were doing at the time.

Phillip O. Martin, "Understanding Black Rage," 2 *Reconstruction*, no. 1, 12 (1992). See also Ellis Cose, *The Rage of a Privileged Class*, 93–100 (1993).

†For a useful collection of anecdotes as well as a helpful description of the federal law that is arguably applicable to racial discrimination in taxi service, see Loren Page Ambinder, "Dispelling the Myth of Rationality: Racial Discrimination in Taxicab

equivalent of being excluded from a lunch counter. Jake Lamar recounts a particularly poignant anecdote. On a rainy night in Manhattan, he twice tried hailing cabs for himself and his date, only to be disregarded by cabbies who stopped for whites nearby. Only when Lamar's date, a white woman, sought alone to hail a cab did a driver stop.[65]

Should we criticize these drivers for taking self-protective albeit racially discriminatory action? Racially discriminatory self-protective action by private persons reinforces existing mistrusts and resentments and circulates them throughout the various spheres of society, public as well as private. After all, an individual does not become an altogether different person when he dons the uniform of a police officer; reflexes that he develops and exhibits in his private life are likely to reemerge, particularly under conditions of stress, in his public, professional pursuits. On the other hand, in comparison to other contexts, the injury done by racially discriminating *private* individuals is likely to be less than that inflicted by *public* officials. A private person walking down the street is not an agent of the state, much less a guardian of law and order. This is not to say that the actions of private pedestrians and entrepreneurs are inconsequential; as mentioned above, many blacks are painfully aware that other citizens avoid them on a racial basis out of fear. That conduct, though, has far less public backing than the legally authorized conduct of police officers. Furthermore, private parties are typically in a far more precarious situation than the police officer who is linked to a bureaucracy able to call upon significant resources for the protection of their agents. Often facing danger alone, private parties warrant the solicitude due to persons who find themselves severely restricted in terms of choice. For these reasons, we should certainly admire private parties who refrain from using racial proxies for self-protection. For the same reasons, though, we should sympathize with, and thus qualify our criticisms of, those who do resort to racially discriminatory

---

Service and the Efficacy of Litigation Under 42 U.S.C. § 1981," by *George Washington Law Review* 342 (1996).

See also West, *Race Matters* at xv ("After the ninth taxi refused me, my blood began to boil."); Kevin M. Brown, "The Shades of Racism," *Washington Post*, May 7, 1993 ("Whenever the moment comes to hail a cab, I'm ridden with anxiety. My stomach knots and my blood boils.")

cues as a stratagem of self-defense. They, like everyone, are caught up in a large tragedy that will require more than individual good will and bravery to resolve.*

What, however, about the pistol-packing lone pedestrian who, encountering persons he considers dangerous, shoots his gun at them in part because their race increased his fear, triggering a lethal response? This question calls to mind the prosecution of Bernhard Hugo Goetz, a much-celebrated and much-reviled figure in late twentieth-century America.[66]

On December 22, 1984, in New York City, a group of four black youths were riding a subway train. Goetz, a white man, entered the train and soon after doing so was approached by one, or perhaps two, of the youths. They asked him for five dollars. After the request was repeated—or perhaps because it was a demand—Goetz pulled a pistol and emptied it into the youths. Charged with a variety of crimes, including attempted murder, Goetz asserted that he had acted in self-defense.

The prosecution did not allege that Goetz's actions were racially motivated. It simply charged that he had committed an assault without

---

*My sympathy for nonbigoted private persons who resort to racially discriminatory conduct for purposes of self-defense does not stretch so far as to exempt them from applicable antidiscrimination laws. If cabbies are given a personal safety excuse for failing to abide by antidiscrimination laws, why not employers or landlords?

Some commentators urge repealing many, if not all, antidiscrimination laws that regulate private parties. See, e.g., Dinesh D'Souza, "The 'Rational' Discrimination of Cab Drivers," *Washington Times*, Oct. 21, 1996; Richard Epstein, *Forbidden Grounds: The Case Against Employment Discrimination Laws* (1992). Down their proposed road lay moral and political disaster.

One way to deal with the problem of physical danger faced by cabbies and other entrepreneurs has already been suggested spread the costs of security on a non-racial basis. As Reginald J. Brown observes, "if taxi drivers are especially attractive targets for criminals, the morally just response is to pursue solutions that make taxi drivers less attractive targets while spreading the costs of doing so broadly among the entire taxi-riding population." Taxis could, for example, be outfitted with debit card readers or other methods of payment that would eliminate the need for cabbies to carry large amounts of cash. Letter to the Editor, *Washington Times*, Oct. 27, 1996. One potential benefit of cost-spreading is that it might educate the white majority about problems disproportionately faced currently by people of color.

justification. Likewise, the defense did not assert that Goetz had properly taken race into account in deciding how to respond to the youths' demand. Without referring to race at all, it argued that given the defendant's past—several years earlier he had been robbed by youngsters and permanently injured—and given the totality of the particular situation—a lone rider surrounded by four young men demanding money on a New York City subway—Goetz reasonably believed himself to be in danger and responded in an excusable manner. Race, however, lurked beneath the formal arguments. The prosecution sought to insinuate that Goetz acted at least in part due to racial bias against blacks. The defense sought to insinuate that, under the circumstances, taking race into account in making a split-second determination of the danger at hand was excusable.

Because the racial aspect of the case was never permitted to become a formal part of it, no ruling was ever made on whether race could properly be included as part of a claim of self-defense. By acquitting Goetz of attempted murder (although he was convicted of a gun possession offense), the jury, some believe, answered that question in the affirmative (at least if the shooter is white and those shot are black).[67] Whatever *that* jury's answer, however, the answer should be that the race of the shooter and the shot is legally irrelevant to a proper judgment as to whether or not a person acted properly in defending himself. Giving legal recognition to racially differentiated concepts of proper conduct—the black reasonable person, the white reasonable person, and so on—will encourage the creation of racially distinct mores, reactions, beliefs, and intuitions. I oppose that project. As I argue throughout this book, I aim to facilitate the emergence of a polity that is overwhelmingly indifferent to racial differences, a polity that looks beyond looks. Bringing to bear that long-range goal on the immediate racial question posed by the Goetz case means excluding race as a proper element in a person's calculation of danger when that person unleashes violence and seeks an excuse for doing so from the legal system on the ground of self-defense.[68]

5.

Race and the Composition of Juries:
Setting the Ground Rules

THE REGULATION OF race relations in jury selection is a large, complicated, and volatile subject that is dominated by three issues. One is identifying wrongful racial exclusion from jury service. How should the legal system proceed, for example, when a defendant alleges that a prosecutor has peremptorily challenged a prospective juror because of her race but the prosecutor denies the charge, saying that age, or place of residence, or ideology prompted the challenge? The second issue is establishing appropriate remedies. How should the legal system proceed if racial discrimination infected the process of selecting a grand jury that indicted a defendant who was subsequently convicted by a fairly chosen trial jury? The third issue is determining whether jurisdictions should be permitted to racially discriminate in order to promote or insure the presence on juries of underrepresented racial minorities. How should the legal system respond when a judge, in deciding a trial's venue, takes into account the racial composition of alternative sites or when officials in a county with a small black population decide that they want to implement a policy requiring every jury of twelve to seat at least two blacks?

In this chapter and the two that follow, I describe and evaluate how courts deal with these issues. I advance the same position I advocated in the preceding chapter's discussion about the use of race as a proxy for risk. I maintain that, except in the narrow instance of an emergency, courts should prohibit officials from drawing racial distinctions between persons. I therefore urge courts to be more attentive than they currently are to covert racial discrimination and more consistent and emphatic in remedying those violations that they do recognize. Similarly, I urge courts to eschew the use of racial criteria for jury selection even when the purpose of doing so is putatively "inclusionary" rather than "exclusionary," putatively helpful rather than harmful to historically disadvantaged racial minorities. The issue is a close one; I concede that there are substantial reasons for permitting racial criteria for purposes of ensuring racially integrated juries. Ultimately, though, these reasons are insufficiently strong to overcome what should be a vibrant, powerful, and vigorously protected presumption in the constitutional law of American race relations: that in governmental affairs race can play no proper role in distinguishing between persons (absent absolutely compelling cause to the contrary).

Establishing the Prohibition Against Racial Exclusion in Jury Selection

Prior to the Civil War, only one state, Massachusetts, permitted blacks to serve on juries.[1] During Reconstruction, African-American men in some Southern jurisdictions regularly served.[2] In other locales, however, officials continued to bar African-Americans. Sometimes the exclusion was handled covertly. In 1876, for instance, an African-American newspaper complained, "We have been told for eight years past [that] the names of colored men have been in the jury box . . . [but] not one colored man's name has ever been drawn."[3] Sometimes, though, the exclusion was open, formal, and unapologetic. As late as 1873, West Virginia enacted a statute that expressly limited jury service to white males over the age of twenty-one.[4]

The Supreme Court dispelled much of the uncertainty surrounding the legal status of blacks as jurors in two cases decided in the 1880s, *Strauder* v. *West Virginia* and *Neal* v. *Delaware*.[5] These cases marked the first occasions on which the Supreme Court applied the Fourteenth Amendment to race relations.

Strauder arose from efforts to defend "a colored man" who was convicted of murder by a jury from which West Virginia law had excluded all blacks.[6] The defendant argued that the West Virginia statute violated the Fourteenth Amendment's injunction that the states must provide to all persons the equal protection of the laws. The Supreme Court agreed and reversed his conviction.

The Court observed that, although the words of the Fourteenth Amendment were merely negative,

> they contain a necessary implication of a positive immunity, or right, most valuable to the colored race,—the right to exemption from unfriendly legislation against them distinctively as colored,—exemption from legal discriminations, implying inferiority in civil society, lessening the security of their enjoyment of the rights which others enjoy, and discriminations which are steps towards reducing them to the condition of a subject race.[7]

The Court concluded that the West Virginia statute limiting jury service to whites was a prohibited discrimination that inflicted two distinct harms. One was a harm done to the entire black population. According to the Court:

> The very fact that colored people are singled out and expressly denied by a statute all right to participate in the administration of the law, as jurors, because of their color, though they are citizens, and may be in other respects fully qualified, is practically a brand upon them, affixed by the law, an assertion of their inferiority, and a stimulant to that race prejudice which is an impediment to securing to individuals of the race that equal justice which the law aims to secure to all others.[8]

The Court perceived a second harm that primarily hurt black defendants. "It is not easy to comprehend," the Court declared, "how it can be said that while every white man is entitled to a trial by a jury . . . selected without discrimination against his color, and a negro is not, the latter is equally protected by the law with the former."[9] Although the Court did not say so expressly, the underlying logic of its argument seems to have been that a racial bar to colored jurors undermines the equal protection due to colored defendants by depriving them of something that white defendants are permitted: at least the *chance* to have people of their race judge their actions. "How can it be maintained," the Court asked rhetorically, "that compelling a colored man to submit to a trial for his life by a jury drawn from a panel from which the State has expressly excluded every man of his race, because of color alone, however well qualified in other respects, is not a denial to him of equal legal protection?"[10]

In *Strauder* it was easy to determine the presence of state officials' purposeful discrimination; the state explicitly announced its racial exclusion. Determining whether purposeful discrimination exists in the absence of such an announcement has generated a huge volume of litigation. The Supreme Court first addressed this problem in *Neal v. Delaware*.

Neal arose from a black man's rape conviction. He was tried by an all-white jury in Delaware, where officials conceded that no blacks had ever served on juries. The issue was whether the state had excluded black jurors on the basis of race—a constitutional violation under *Strauder*—or whether the defendant had wound up with an all-white jury for some reason other than purposeful racial exclusion. The Delaware Supreme Court held that the defendant's jury was all-white not because of an illicit intention to exclude qualified black jurors but because there existed few, if any, blacks who were qualified to sit on juries. According to Delaware's chief justice: "That none but white men were selected is in nowise remarkable in view of the fact—too notorious to be ignored—that the great body of black men residing in this State are utterly unqualified by want of intelligence, experience, or moral integrity to sit on juries."[11]

The tack taken by Delaware's chief justice is wholly unsurprising. In *Strauder*, after declaring that the Fourteenth Amendment prohibited discrimination based on race, the Court noted that the amendment did not prohibit other sorts of discriminations. States may, the Court observed, "confine the selection [of jurors] to males, to freeholders, to citizens, to persons within certain ages, or to persons having educational qualifications."[12] Although it is unlikely that the Court aimed to suggest to states ways of evading its own ruling, the Court's observation dramatically highlighted the extent to which states, by erecting certain nonracial barriers to jury service, could effectively (albeit indirectly) exclude many potential black jurors. Delaware's chief justice perceived this, arguing that the state had not excluded blacks on the basis of race—a prohibited criterion—but rather on the basis of allowable, nonracial qualifications—"intelligence," "experience," "moral integrity."

The U.S. Supreme Court responded by holding that Delaware had indeed engaged in racial discrimination against blacks in the selection of jurors. It intuited that, among the 20,000 blacks in Delaware in the 1870s, there must have been at least a few qualified to serve as jurors. Speaking for the Court, Justice John Marshall Harlan stated that it was an untenable presumption to suppose "that such uniform exclusion of [Negroes] from juries, during a period of many years, was solely because . . . the black race in Delaware were utterly disqualified, by want of intelligence, experience, or moral integrity."[13] Instead, in the absence of a persuasive explanation to the contrary, the Court inferred that Delaware officials intended to select only whites.

The Submergence of the Black Juror

Although *Strauder* established the constitutional right of blacks to be free of racial exclusion in jury selection, state officials in many locales consistently disregarded this right until rather recently.* For an insight into the pervasiveness of this wholesale racial exclusion, no document is more illuminating than Gilbert T. Stephenson's *Race Distinctions in American Law*, published in 1910. To determine whether blacks actually

---

*In 1875 Congress criminalized racial discrimination in jury selection:
> No citizen possessing all other qualifications . . . shall be disqualified for service as a grand or petit juror in any court of the United States, or of any State on account of race, color or previous condition of servitude; and whoever, being an officer or other person charged with any duty in the selection or summoning of jurors, excludes or fails to summon any citizen for such cause, shall be fined not more than $5,000.

18 U.S.C. §243 (1994). This provision, however, has never been effectively enforced. The case law offers only one instance of a prosecution under this statute. See *Ex Parte Virginia*, 100 U.S. 330 (1880).

served on juries in the South, Stephenson sent a questionnaire to the clerk of court in every Southern county in which blacks constituted at least half of the population. The following are characteristic responses:

Alabama—County No. 1, 10,000 white people, 13,000 Negroes: "Negroes are not allowed to sit upon juries in this county. It sometimes happens that names of Negroes are placed in our jury-box by mistake on the part of the jury commissioners, and are regularly drawn to serve as jurors; this, however, is a very rare occurrence. Once in the past four years, a Negro was drawn as a grand juror (by mistake) who appeared and insisted upon the court's impanelling him with other jurors, which was done in accordance with law, the court having no legal right to discharge or excuse him. My recollection is he served two days, when he was taken out at night and severely beaten, and was then discharged by his own petition by the court. This will convey to your mind that negro jurors are not very wholesomely regarded and tolerated in this county."[14]

Georgia—County No. 1, 5,000 white people, 24,000 Negroes: "No Negroes serve on our jury. There are no Negro names in the jury box."[15]

Georgia—County No. 10, 2,500 white people, 4,000 Negroes: ". . . There has never been a Negro juror to serve in this county nor any other county surrounding this to my knowledge. . . . I am, satisfied if one should be put on any jury that the white men on would flatly refuse to serve at all. . . ."[16]

North Carolina—County No. 2, 11,000 white people, 19,000 Negroes: "I will say that Negroes do not serve on the jury in this county and have not since we, the white people, got the government in our hands."[17]

South Carolina—County No. 4, 18,000 white people, 41,000 Negroes: . . . "We are careful and painstaking in making our lists; therefore, we never allow a Negro to serve for the reason of the general moral unfitness, and general depravity."[18]

These responses make clear that racial exclusion was a multilayered problem beyond the ability of courts alone to fix. It both reflected and contributed to a societal crisis, a fundamental breakdown in law and order, the depth of which is highlighted by considering the obstacles that stood in the way of reform.

Consider a black defendant facing the prospect of being tried by a jury from which officials excluded blacks. The first thing that such a defendant would need is an attorney. Attorneys, however, cost money, and many black defendants charged with crimes were unable to afford an attorney. *Powell* v. *Alabama*[19] and cases in its wake partially abated that difficulty by imposing an affirmative duty on states to provide indigent defendants with counsel when facing serious criminal charges.[20] The problem of challenging racial exclusion involved more, however, than access to an attorney. Attacking racial exclusion required a lawyer with the ability and the willingness to attack a central feature of white supremacy. Many attorneys, dependent on the good will of whites, were unwilling to jeopardize their careers for the sake of clients, notwithstanding the importance of the rights and interests at stake. Moreover, some attorneys chose to forgo making jury discrimination claims on the grounds that their clients would ultimately suffer even if they prevailed on the discrimination issue because, in the event of a conviction, white prosecutors, judges, and jurors would punish them more severely for disturbing racial customs.* In 1959, a panel of federal court of appeals judges took judicial notice that "lawyers residing in many southern jurisdictions rarely, almost to the point of never, raise the issue of systematic exclusion of Negroes from juries."[21]

---

*In response to a questionnaire that the *Yale Law Journal* sent to Southern lawyers in 1963, one Alabama defense attorney vividly revealed the social pressures that dissuaded him from challenging the exclusion of Negroes from juries. Noting that he, too, actively participated in the exclusion of blacks, this attorney wrote: "If I accepted a Negro for jury duty and put him on with 11 white men I would prejudice the white men against me and my client." See Note, "Negro Defendants and Southern Lawyers: Review in Federal Habeas Corpus of Systematic Exclusion of Negroes from Juries," 72 *Yale Law Journal* 559, 565 n. 25 (1963). See also *Whitus* v. *Balkcom* 333 F.2d 496 (CA 5 1964), cert. denied, 379 U.S. 931 (1964) ("we know what happens when a white attorney for a Negro defendant raises the exclusion issue in a county dominated by segregation patterns and practices: both the defendant and his attorney will suffer from community hostility").

Even if one could find an attorney who was willing and able to challenge racial discrimination in jury selection, yet another impediment loomed: finding a judge willing to acknowledge discrimination brought to his attention. One might have hoped that *Neal* v. *Delaware* signalled a willingness on the part of the Supreme Court to peek beneath formalities to determine whether, in fact, officials conducted themselves according to the dictates of the Reconstruction amendments. After all, *Neal* could be read to stand for the proposition that a long absence of Negroes from juries in a given locale is itself prima facie evidence of racial discrimination that, unrebutted, suffices to establish a constitutional violation. But many judges overlooked or ignored *Neal* or interpreted it with crippling stinginess.[22] In *Royals* v. *State*,[23] the Supreme Court of Florida declined to find discrimination despite testimony from a deputy sheriff that he could not remember any blacks serving as jurors in twenty-seven years. That evidence appears to have been overcome in the judge's mind by the simple statement of a jury commissioner that he did not discriminate against blacks. In *Welch* v. *State*,[24] the Oklahoma Criminal Court of Appeals declined to find discrimination notwithstanding the uncontroverted assertion that for more than ten years no Negro had sat on a jury in any court in the county where the defendant was tried. The court ruled this evidence of uniform absence to be irrelevant. The defendant, it maintained, "cannot predicate error upon discriminations against his race in other cases, extending over a period of previous years."[25] Rather, "the question is was there such discrimination in this particular case?"[26] The court concluded that the defendant had failed to show the presence of discrimination in *his* case, relying heavily, it appears, on the declarations of the jury commissioners, who stated "very positively that [in the process leading to the defendant's trial] no one was rejected for jury service on account of race."[27]

The U.S. Supreme Court permitted, indeed encouraged, such decisions by showing unwarranted deference to state courts that were obviously hostile to discrimination claims.[28] On occasion between 1881 and 1935 the Supreme Court reversed a conviction when a state court prevented defendants from even attempting to prove that officials had racially excluded blacks from a jury.[29] If state courts handled black defendants with a modicum of procedural nicety, however, the Supreme Court generally refused to intervene. After *Neal* v. *Delaware*, the Supreme Court did not again use sensible inferences to disagree with the factual holding of a state court in a jury discrimination case until *Norris* v. *Alabama*.[30]

Norris arose from one of the prosecutions of the Scottsboro Boys. (See pp. 100–104.) Describing the county in which Clarence Norris had been retried, reconvicted, and resentenced to death, Chief Justice Charles Evans Hughes observed that "no negro had served on any grand or petit jury in that county within the memory of witnesses who had lived there all their lives."[31] Attempting to rebut the allegation of purposeful racial exclusion, state officials made two claims. First, they asserted that they had placed the names of some Negroes on jury lists. Second, they maintained that the absence of Negroes from juries was not attributable to racial discrimination. Unsurprisingly, the Alabama Supreme Court ruled in favor of the prosecution. The U.S. Supreme Court, however, resuscitating *Neal*, refused to be bound by the factual holdings of the state court.

The Court concluded that officials fraudulently added the names of blacks to the grand jury rolls *after* the selection of the grand jury that indicted the Scottsboro Boys. It reached this conclusion partly on the basis of testimony offered by a handwriting expert and partly on the basis of its own examination of the jury rolls in question. Referring to the forgery, Justice Willis Van Devanter was heard to whisper at the oral argument, "Why it's as plain as punch" that the names had been forged.[32]

More importantly, the Supreme Court refused to defer to the Alabama court's conclusion that the absence of blacks from the Norris jury was attributable to causes other than a design to exclude blacks. To make out the case for racial discrimination, the defense presented evidence showing that blacks had been absent from juries for a long time and that there were blacks qualified for jury service. Defense attorneys called to the witness stand a variety of gainfully employed and law-abiding blacks, including a plasterer, a Pullman porter, an owner of a drycleaning establishment, and a trustee of local Negro schools, who had never been approached for jury service. The defense sought to prove that the blacks were as educated as, if not better educated than, the whites who had been approached.[33] The prosecution responded by arguing that the jury commissioner had found no blacks suitable for jury service. As the jury commissioner put it: "I do not know of any negro in Morgan County over twenty-one and under sixty-five who is generally reputed to be honest and intelligent and who is esteemed in the community for his integrity, good character and sound judgment."[34] The Supreme Court decided, however, that in light of the testimony given by the defendant's witnesses, "we find it impossible to accept such a sweeping characterization of the lack of qualifications."[35] Broadening the point, the Court noted that if "mere general assertions by officials of their performance of duty were to be accepted as [an] adequate justification for the complete exclusion of negroes from jury service, the [Fourteenth Amendment] . . . would be but a vain and illusory requirement."[36]

Norris v. *Alabama* is rightly celebrated for repudiating both racial discrimination and the fraud local officials perpetrated in order to cover it up. The decision is also appropriately applauded for reviving the doctrine that the long-term absence of blacks from juries in jurisdictions with sizable black populations itself constitutes a prima facie case of discrimination which the state can rebut only by presenting specific evidence indicating a nonracial reason for their absence. Within twelve years of *Norris*, the Supreme Court reversed convictions in five cases in which black defendants had been sentenced to death by all-white juries in counties where blacks had been absent as jurors for decades.[37]

In *Hale* v. *Kentucky*,[38] a black man was convicted for murder and sentenced to death in a county where no Negro had served on a state grand or petit jury for at least thirty years. In the absence of any attempt by the state to offer a nonracial reason for this result, the Supreme Court, citing *Norris*, reversed the conviction. In *Smith* v. *Texas*,[39] a black man was indicted for rape by an all-white grand jury and then tried by an all-white petit jury, which convicted and sentenced him to death. Although 3,000–6,000 Negroes were deemed eligible for grand jury service in the county in question, *no* Negroes served on any grand juries in the year prior to Smith's indictment. Reversing the conviction, the Supreme Court ruled that, absent a strong explanation, these numbers raised an inference of improper racial discrimination.

In *Smith*, the Court took another important step as well. The state argued that the jury commissioners had not meant to engage in racial exclusion but had simply overlooked blacks since the commissioners were unacquainted socially with Negroes. This was a potentially potent argument, depending on how narrowly or broadly one defines racial discrimination. The state was saying that its officials had not barred blacks with racial intent but had, without racial intent, simply failed to select any blacks. In *Smith*, however, the Court rejected that argument and insisted that, to avoid racial exclusion, jury commissioners would have to take affirmative measures to identify qualified black jurors. "Where jury commissioners limit those from whom grand juries are selected to their own personal acquaintance," the Court declared, "discrimination can arise from commissioners who know no negroes as well as from commissioners who know but eliminate them."[40]

Two years later, in *Hill* v. *Texas*,[41] the Supreme Court revisited this point, overturning another conviction on grounds of jury discrimination. It labeled as discriminatory jury commissioners "who neither know nor seek to learn whether there are in fact any qualified" Negroes available for jury service." *Smith* and *Hill* suggest that, at least in contexts in which blacks had long been absent from juries, the Court believed that jury commissioners had an affirmative duty to acquaint themselves with blacks who would qualify for jury service—a proposition that anticipates aspects of the debate over affirmative action that is currently so contentious.

These rulings represented the advanced guard of antidiscrimination law in the 1930s and 1940s and put state courts on notice that the total exclusion of blacks from grand and petit juries would put convictions at risk of reversal. It is important, though, to recognize the limits of these rulings. First, some officials continued to exclude blacks, secure in the knowledge that a defendant would rarely be able to attract the Supreme Court's attention.[42] Second, some officials who did heed the Court's rulings merely moved from racially excluding *all* blacks to racially excluding *almost all* blacks. They resorted, in other words, to tokenism. Remarkably, on several occasions, the Supreme Court openly tolerated their ploy. In *Akins* v. *Texas*,[43] for instance, the Court faced a situation in which a black defendant, convicted and sentenced to death for murder, challenged the legitimacy of a grand jury system in which officials quite clearly limited black involvement to one Negro per grand jury. A jury commissioner stated: "We had no intention of placing more than one negro on the panel."[44] A second acknowledged: "I did not have any intention of putting more than one [Negro] on the list."[45] A third stated: "Yes, sir, there were other negroes' names mentioned besides the one we selected; we did not go talk to them; we liked this one, and our intentions were to get just one negro on the grand jury, that is right."[46] The Court rejected the defendant's challenge. Justice Frank Murphy rightly observed in dissent, however, that "Clearer proof of intentional and deliberate limitation on the basis of color would be difficult to produce."[47]

Local officials did not begin substantial reform of racially discriminatory practices until the 1960s. The Fifth Circuit Court of Appeals was particularly important in this process. Far more than the Supreme Court, the Fifth Circuit impressed the lesson upon recalcitrant officials in the Deep South that evasion of constitutional standards would no longer be tolerated.[48] Pursuant to repeated and insistent prodding by the Fifth Circuit, state courts began to get the message. Reversing the conviction of a black defendant tried by an illegally constituted, all-white jury, the Supreme Court of Mississippi told local judges and jury commissioners in 1966 that they simply must heed federal requirements. "We recognize," the Mississippi justices declared, "that in some counties compliance with these constitutional requirements may present difficulties, but they must be surmounted if the criminal laws are to be effectively administered."[49] That same year, a lower court in Mississippi threw out all forty-four indictments returned by a grand jury from which blacks had purposefully been excluded, because it was likely that any convictions obtained pursuant to those indictments would be overturned on appeal. Determined to insulate from reversal the likely conviction of a black defendant accused of raping a white woman, a trial judge in Texas appointed a Negro jury commissioner (a first) as part of an effort to ensure the validity of the grand jury that indicted the suspect.[50]

Responses to increasingly rigorous judicial oversight varied, however, and not all were positive. The worst and luckily the rarest reaction involved recourse to lynching. Accused of raping a white woman, Charles Mack Parker was snatched from jail in Mississippi in 1959 and shot by a mob that feared that his anticipated conviction would be overturned on appeal by courts that would insist upon a jury selection free of racial exclusion.[51]

Another response was a new round of tokenism aimed at maintaining as much of the white supremacist status quo as possible while avoiding judicial intervention. Some officials permitted the participation of only as many blacks as were thought necessary to camouflage efforts to minimize the number of blacks serving on juries. *Amadeo* v. *Zant*[52] provides a vivid and relatively recent example. In November 1977, Tony B. Amadeo was sentenced to death for murder in Putnam County, Georgia. During the course of appeals, defense counsel discovered that the Putnam County district attorney and jury commissioners had established a scheme to minimize the number of blacks and women on the jury lists. In a handwritten memorandum, the district attorney, Joseph Briley, asked the jury commissioners to place only enough blacks and women on the master lists to rebut any potential charges of discrimination. Reversing a Court of Appeals decision, the U.S. Supreme Court held that Amadeo was entitled to a new trial.

Overview of Current Jury Selection Procedures

Current controversies involving the regulation of race relations in jury selection take place against the backdrop of a complex set of laws governing jury formation. Although state laws vary widely, they contain certain common features. Local officials periodically create a list of names and addresses of residents in a given jurisdiction. This list is the basic pool of names officials use when they seek potential jurors. In most jurisdictions, the list of registered voters serves as the primary source of names for the jury list. Some states, though, rely on a "key-man" system of selection, under which leading citizens of the community, such as aldermen, bankers, and ministers, submit lists of prospective jurors to jury commissioners, who then generate a source list.[53]

In jurisdictions using voter registration lists as their source for names, authorities seek to learn more about prospective jurors by mailing them questionnaires. Typically, authorities will only consider those people who both return the questionnaires and provide information which indicates that they meet statutory requirements for jury service. Requirements may include such criteria as possessing an ability to understand English and a record free of felony convictions. In locales using the key-man system, authorities are empowered to use personal knowledge to exclude individuals deemed to be unqualified for jury service because they lack "intelligence," "uprightness," or "good character."

People who make it through these screens are summoned to court, where they form groups of prospective jurors called venires. From venires, officials direct prospective jurors to either grand juries, the entities that decide whether to indict suspects, or trial juries, the entities that decide whether a defendant is guilty beyond a reasonable doubt. Prospective grand jurors face relatively little further screening, although judges often limit their selection of grand jury foremen to those jurors whom they believe will be good leaders. Prospective trial jurors face a more involved screening process. Two legal devices may exclude a member of a venire from service on a trial jury (also known as a petit jury). One is the strike for cause. A lawyer may move that a prospective juror be stricken for cause if there is something about that person—for example, he has made up his mind about the defendant's guilt, is prejudiced against persons of the defendant's race, is a close relative of the defendant or victim—which clearly raises doubts that he could impartially evaluate the evidence and apply the law relevant to the case in question.[54] A second device is the peremptory challenge which empowers attorneys to exclude potential jurors without having to justify their action. Although an attorney must convince a judge to dismiss a juror for cause and must presumably articulate a good reason for exclusion, an attorney may dismiss a juror with a peremptory challenge without offering any reason whatsoever (though, as we shall see, the discretionary nature of the peremptory challenge has been increasingly limited over the past decade). Attorneys obtain knowledge about prospective jurors through *voir dire*, a process during which the attorneys or the judge pose questions designed to reveal conflicts of interest, sources of prejudice, or other information bearing upon a person's fitness to serve on a jury in a given case.[55] Attorneys often base their motions to strike for cause and their peremptory challenges on what they learn from the voir dire.

The procedure for jury selection in federal courts is similar, although more streamlined and transparent. It is governed by the Jury Selection and Service Act of 1968, which provides that "all litigants in federal courts entitled to trial by jury shall have the right to grand and petit juries selected at random from a fair cross section of the community."[56] The JSSA explicitly rejects the key-man system. It requires officials to generate lists of potential jurors from voter registration lists, which may, if needed, be supplemented by other sources to obtain jury pools containing a fair cross-section of the community. The JSSA leaves it up to the federal courts to determine whether, in a given instance, a voter list must be supplemented in order to obtain jury pools that meet the fair cross-section requirement.

Racial Discrimination and Qualifications for Jury Service

One factor that has undoubtedly encouraged some officials to try to evade the prohibition against racial discrimination in jury selection is that the U.S. Supreme Court has steadfastly refused to invalidate per se subjective qualifications for jury service—"intelligence," "good character," "sound judgment"—behind which racial discriminations can hide. The leading case, *Carter* v. *Jury Commission of Greene County*,[57] deals with Alabama's key-man system.

Carter is notable in several respects. It is a civil rather than a criminal case. Instead of being brought by a defendant attacking the legitimacy of his conviction, the case was brought by blacks who alleged that they were qualified for jury duty but had never been summoned because of a policy to minimize black participation. As part of their proof, the plaintiffs noted a suspicious pattern of racial demographics for jury service in their county. Although blacks constituted three-fourths of the county's population in 1960, between 1961 and 1963 they constituted only 7 percent of prospective jurors. In 1967, four years after a federal judge had ordered local officials to cease their discriminatory conduct, blacks constituted only 32 percent of prospective jurors, although by then blacks constituted about 65 percent of the county's population.[58] In *Carter*, the Supreme Court affirmed a lower court's finding that local officials were continuing to discriminate on a racial basis and that the plaintiffs were entitled to relief against racial exclusion. This marked the first occasion on which the Supreme Court expressly held that prospective jurors suing on their own behalf were entitled to be free of racial exclusion.

The federal district court instructed the jury commissioners to desist from racially excluding blacks from the jury roll, directed them to compile a new jury list, and ordered them to submit the new list to the court with information about the selected prospective jurors, including their race, and the method of selection. The plaintiffs, however, wanted more than this. They also wanted the court to invalidate Alabama's key-man system, with its reliance on vague, subjective judgments. They emphasized that jury selection in Greene County demonstrated a persistent practice of illegal racial discrimination despite previous federal court orders directing the cessation of such conduct. They also argued that so long as the key-man system existed, black citizens would be forced to attack its misadministration county by county, a process that would impose a heavy burden not only upon the plaintiffs but upon court dockets as well. Essentially, the plaintiffs claimed that the key-man system, with its decentralized, highly discretionary character, created a process so susceptible to racial discrimination that it should be invalidated, especially in light of past misuse.

The district court, however, refused to invalidate the key-man system, and the Supreme Court affirmed the refusal. In rejecting the plaintiffs' argument, the Court pointed to several considerations, the first being precedent: it had "long been accepted that the Constitution does not forbid the States to prescribe relevant qualifications for their jurors."[59] In *Strauder* itself the Court had stressed that although the Fourteenth Amendment prohibited racial qualifications, it did not prohibit the states from prescribing other qualifications for jurors.[60] Second, to rebut any suggestion that the system at issue in *Carter* was a peculiarly Southern arrangement, the Court noted that several states, including Northern ones, limited jury service pursuant to vague, subjective requirements, such as being "intelligent" or "well informed." Third, while recognizing that "overwhelming proof"[61] showed that the local officials sued in *Carter* had abused their statutory discretion in preparing jury rolls, the Court refused to conclude that such discretion was incapable of being used properly.[62] Responding to the plaintiffs' fear that a failure to invalidate the Alabama key-man system would simply leave the same bigoted officials able to begin a whole new round of racial exclusion the day after the Supreme Court's ruling, Justice Potter Stewart asserted, "The federal courts are not incompetent to fashion detailed and stringent injunctive relief that will remedy any discriminatory application [of the key-man system] at the hands of the officials empowered to administer it."[63]

Did the Court rule rightly in permitting the continuation of Alabama's key-man system? On the one hand, there is nothing racially discriminatory per se about limiting jury service to people with "intelligence" or "good character." Applied in good faith and without racial prejudice, these admittedly vague standards will presumably exclude and include people of all hues. Furthermore, as a general matter, courts presume good faith in the enactment and administration of state law. Judges grant officials a rebuttable presumption that they will do the right thing. On the other hand, one can confidently assume that in some places the key-man system's vague criteria will not be applied in good faith. Moreover, the subjectivity of the criteria invite and obscure abuse. Furthermore, when abuses are suspected, it is expensive to reveal their existence in court.

I conclude that, as a prophylactic measure, the Supreme Court should have invalidated the key-man system. First, the key-man system has a baleful history in many locales. It has often been used as a device to exclude people illicitly from the jury box. Second, the subjectivity of the criteria used by the arbiters of key-man systems invites abuse. Third, the legitimate aims of a key-man system can be obtained by procedures less vulnerable to invidious manipulation. For example, if a state wants knowledgeable jurors it can impose an objective test to screen for the knowledge desired. At a certain point, a procedure becomes so subject to corruption and so expensive to monitor that it should be adjudged incompatible with federal constitutional requirements. Just as the Court has invalidated overly vague licensing arrangements that permitted local authorities to indulge their personal whims in deciding whom to permit to parade,[64] so too should it have invalidated the key-man system.[65]

Although the Supreme Court has failed to abolish the key-man system in the states (though the JSSA abolished the procedure in the federal judiciary), it has rightly subjected the key-man regime to a high level of skepticism. A significant example is *Castaneda* v. *Partida*,[66] a case in which a Mexican-American defendant attacked the validity of his conviction for burglary with intent to rape on the grounds that racial discrimination had reduced the number of Mexican-Americans on the grand jury that indicted him. Although Mexican-Americans constituted about 79 percent of the county's adult population, only about 39 percent of those summoned for jury duty were Mexican-American during the eleven years prior to Partida's indictment. Despite this disparity, several considerations cut against the defendant's claim. Most importantly, in the county where he was tried, Mexican-Americans played a prominent role in the administration of criminal law, including the defendant's own case. The judge who appointed the jury commissioners was Mexican-American; three of the five jury commissioners were Mexican-American; 52.5 percent of the grand jurors the year Partida was indicted were Mexican-American; five of the twelve grand jurors who returned the Partida indictment, including the foreman, were Mexican-American; and seven of the twelve petit jurors who found Partida guilty were Mexican-American.* Because of the extensive participation of Mexican Americans at every level of the case, including the formation and deliberation of the grand jury, several Justices rejected the defendant's discrimination claim. Yet the Supreme Court nonetheless ruled for the defendant. A feature of the case that pushed a slim majority toward that judgment was the presence of the key-man system and an apprehension that the key-man system "is susceptible of abuse as applied," especially inasmuch as Spanish surnames are readily identifiable.[67] Thus, while refraining from invalidating

---

*Justice Lewis F. Powell, Jr. made much of the political dominance exercised by Mexican-Americans in the county in which Partida was tried. "The most significant fact in this case," he declared, "is that a majority of the jury commissioners were Mexican-American." *Castaneda* v. *Partida*, 430 U.S. 482, 515 (1977) (Powell, J., dissenting). Justice Marshall, however, responded that

> members of minority groups frequently respond to discrimination and prejudice by attempting to disassociate themselves from the group, even to the point of adopting the majority's negative attitudes towards the minority. Such behavior occurs with particular frequency among members of minority groups who have achieved some measure of political success and thereby have gained some acceptability among the dominant group.

Ibid., 503 (Marshall, J., concurring). Marshall has a good point. The phenomenon he identifies animates the bad side of the politics of respectability (see pp. 12–21). Powell, however, was surely correct in suggesting that the dominant presence of Mexican-Americans at least lessened the plausibility of Partida's racial discrimination charge. The presence of racial minorities in decisionmaking forums does not preclude racial discrimination against them but does attentuate that possibility—a position that Justice Marshall often embraced in other contexts.

the key-man system outright, the Court has clearly impugned its reliability.

Remedies for Racial Discrimination
in Selecting Grand Juries

Another aspect of *Castaneda* warranting attention is that the defendant
obtained the reversal of his conviction and thus a new trial because
the Supreme Court determined that racial discrimination invalidated
the grand jury that indicted him. In *Strauder*, the Court inaugurated the
practice of annulling convictions in cases involving racial discrimination
in the selection of the trial jury. In *Castaneda*, however, the Court annulled a conviction even though the defendant had been found guilty by
a trial jury that was presumably valid. Some jurists have objected to paying such a high price to enforce the norm against invidious racial discrimination at the grand jury level. One was Justice Robert Jackson,
who voiced his view memorably in 1950 in a dissenting opinion in *Cassell* v. *Texas*.[68] In *Cassell* there was no question regarding the legitimacy
of the trial jury that convicted the defendant of murder. The only question was what should ensue in light of the finding that state officials had
purposefully excluded blacks from the grand jury that indicted the defendant. To Jackson, the defendant was not entitled to have his conviction reversed for two reasons. First, the illegal racial discrimination did
not harm the defendant in the sense of depriving him of a fair trial. Any
harm visited upon the defendant at the grand jury stage was mooted, in
Jackson's view, by the defendant's subsequent conviction before a presumably legitimate trial jury: "It hardly lies in the mouth of a defendant
whom a fairly chosen trial jury has found guilty beyond reasonable
doubt, to say that his indictment is attributable to prejudice."[69] The trial
verdict shows, Jackson asserted, that whatever the effect racial exclusion
had on the grand jury's deliberations, the predominant influence must
have been evidence of the defendant's guilt.

The second reason behind Jackson's objection to reversing convictions because of illegally constituted grand juries is that, in his view,
such reversals are unneeded to enforce the prohibition against racial exclusion in jury selection. Racially discriminatory officials could be more
suitably disciplined, he thought, either by prosecutors bringing criminal

actions or aggrieved black prospective jurors bringing civil actions against the offending officials. "The Negro's right to be selected for grand jury service is unquestionable and should be directly and uncompromisingly enforced," Jackson declared. He doubted, however, "if any good purpose will be served in the long run by identifying the right of the most worthy Negroes to serve on grand juries with the efforts of the least worthy to defer or escape punishment for crime."[70]

Thirty-six years later, the issue reappeared in *Vasquez* v. *Hillery*. This case arose from the conviction for murder of Booker T. Hillery in 1962. In 1985, in habeas corpus proceedings, Hillery's lawyers sought reversal of the conviction on the grounds that he had been indicted by a jury from which blacks had been excluded. Although a number of Justices echoed Justice Jackson in arguing that racial discrimination in the formation of a grand jury should not void a conviction, a majority disagreed. Speaking through Justice Marshall, the Court cited precedent, the weightiness of the transgression at issue, and the belief that racial discrimination during grand jury formation could affect the type of indictment brought against a defendant as reasons for voiding Hillery's conviction. The Court, however, only faintly suggested the best reason behind its conclusion. That reason has less, if anything, to do with the actual harm that racial discrimination inflicts upon a defendant than with a broader aim concerning which the defendant is only an expedient vehicle. That broader aim is to deter future constitutional violations, the same goal that primarily animates the famous exclusionary rule, which excludes from consideration at trial evidence obtained in violation of the Fourth and Fifth amendments to the Constitution.[71]

It would be preferable to reach this goal without offering to guilty defendants the windfall of a new trial. Alternatives, however, are unlikely to be as effective. Civil actions of the sort brought in *Carter* are rare; potential jurors who are discriminated against in jury selection are typically unaware of their wrongful exclusion. Prosecutions of local officials are dependent on U.S. attorneys who, heretofore, have shown little or no interest in resuscitating federal criminal prohibitions against racial discrimination in jury selection. Defendants could sue. There are, however, strong reasons to doubt the efficacy of such suits. First, criminal defendants are strikingly handicapped as a class of plaintiffs. Many defendants will forgo suing because of ignorance of their rights, lack of resources, and fear of police reprisals. Others will be dissuaded from suing because of a realistic apprehension that, because of prejudice against convicted or even merely accused lawbreakers, they will stand little chance of prevailing at trial. Second, all sorts of doctrines and customs provide heavy insulation to individual officials. Broad grants of immunity shield many officers, particularly judges and prosecutors. Moreover, the deterrent effect of even successful suits is undermined by the fact that governments will typically indemnify government officials for legal bills, settlements, and adverse judgments. For these and other reasons, Professor Daniel J. Meltzer rightly concludes that civil suits are unlikely to provide "a meaningful set of controls on unlawful activity by law enforcement officials."[72]

In light of the weakness of alternative deterrent devices, the Court is right to maintain its long-established policy of reversing convictions whenever defendants succeed in showing that purposeful racial exclusion played a part in the shaping of grand or petit juries. This policy does impose a heavy cost; the public pays dearly when persons who have committed crimes delay, minimize, or evade punishment for reasons having nothing to do with their culpability. As the opening up of southern juries demonstrates, however, there is reason to believe that annulling convictions will, in the long run, prove to be more helpful than harmful. Referring to the hoped-for consequences of the Court's strategy, Justice Marshall aptly observed, "If grand jury discrimination becomes a thing of the past, no conviction will ever again be lost on account of it."[73]

Racial Discrimination and the Selection of Grand Jury Foremen

To a large extent, federal equal protection jurisprudence with respect to racial exclusion from grand and petit juries is attractively clear: Purposeful exclusion of blacks is a violation remedied by annulling any conviction associated with it. Spoiling the clarity, however, is the case law arising from a subspecies of racial exclusion at the jury box—the exclusion of blacks from the position of grand jury foreman.

In *Rose* v. *Mitchell*,[74] the Supreme Court assumed without deciding that a defendant convicted in a Tennessee state court would be entitled to a new trial if the defendant could show that the judge excluded blacks from consideration for the post of grand jury foreman. By contrast, in *Hobby* v. *United States*,[75] the Court refused to grant a new trial to a defendant even assuming that racial discrimination had precluded the possibility of a black person serving as the foreman of the grand jury that indicted him. This was not an assumption founded on an unlikely scenario. Prior to trial, the defendant produced evidence indicating that *none* of the fifteen grand juries impaneled over a seven-year period between 1974 and 1981 in the U.S. District Court in the Eastern District of North Carolina had a black or a woman as foreman.[76]*

The Court distinguished *Hobby* from *Rose*. It drew attention to the fact that, in *Rose*, *black* defendants alleged that blacks were excluded from consideration as the grand jury foreman, whereas in *Hobby* a *white* defendant alleged that blacks and women were excluded from consideration as the grand jury foreman.[77] More important to the Court, however, was the distinction between the functions of grand jury foremen in Tennessee courts as opposed to federal courts. In Tennessee courts, the grand jury foreman is an additional member of the grand jury. In federal courts, the foreman is selected from among the grand jurors. Racial discrimination in the selection of a grand jury foreman therefore affects the composition of the grand jury in Tennessee courts but not in federal

---

*The Court says at one point that "no factual evidence was presented . . . on the issue of discrimination; instead, petitioner relied upon inferences to be drawn from the failure to select a women or Negro as foreman of the grand jury for the seven years studied." 468 U.S. 339, 342–343 (1984). This statement shows the Court doing all that it can to minimize the significance of embarrassing facts. The absence of blacks and women as grand jurors over a seven-year period *is* "factual evidence." It is not necessarily determinative evidence; perhaps there was some nonracial reason for this longstanding tendency of U.S. district court judges to choose only white men as foremen. But the statistical information offered was surely "factual evidence" which justifiably raises eyebrows and suggests racial discrimination in the absence of a good explanation to the contrary.

Cases in which courts have ruled that judges did engage in racial discrimination in the selection of grand jury foremen include *Guice* v. *Fortenberry*, 722 F.2d 276 (CA 5 1984); *Johnson* v. *Puckett*, 929 F. 2d 1067 (CA 5 1991), *cert. denied*, 112 S. Ct. 274 (1991); *State* v. *Moore*, 404 S.E.2d 845 (N.C. 1991).

courts. Moreover, in Tennessee, the foreman is charged with assisting the district attorney in investigating crime, whereas in the federal system the prescribed duties of the grand jury foreman are considerably more circumscribed. Based on these distinctions, the Supreme Court reasoned that, although a change in personnel might actually affect the course of a prosecution in a Tennessee case, a change in the identity of a grand jury foreman in a federal case would almost certainly not affect the outcome.*

Ruling against the defendant in *Hobby*, the Court embraced the argument rejected in *Vasquez* that redressing racial exclusion by annulling a conviction imposes too heavy a cost upon society in circumstances in which it is unlikely that the racial exclusion at issue actually prejudices a verdict. The Court in *Hobby* readily recognized "that purposeful discrimination against Negroes or women in the selection of federal grand jury foremen is forbidden by the Fifth Amendment to the Constitution."[78] The Court concluded, however, that racial discrimination of this limited sort does not warrant reversing a conviction. With respect to racial discrimination in the selection of a federal grand jury foreman, the Court asserted that "less Draconian measures will suffice to rectify the problem."[79]

As suggested earlier, the Court's resolution of *Hobby* is inconsistent with its resolution of other racial discrimination cases involving juries. If actual prejudice to a trial outcome is the Court's touchstone, then it should go much further toward the protection of convictions than it has been willing to go. As Justice Jackson noted in *Cassell*, it is unlikely that an untainted grand jury would come to a different conclusion than

---

*Foremen on federal grand juries perform a more significant role than the Court intimated. Even if the foreman's post on a federal grand jury is less important than on certain state grand juries, that does not mean that the federal post is of negligible significance. As Justice Marshall noted in dissent, the foreman's post in a federal proceeding "enables, indeed requires, a person to be first among equals within the grand jury room." *Hobby* v. *United States*, 468 U.S. 339, 357 (1984). Moreover, the Court's portrayal of the federal foreman's position as an empty, wholly ceremonial position is hardly consistent with district judges' testimony that they invested considerable effort in selecting suitable persons as foremen who could lead the grand jury. Ibid., 357–358.

a tainted grand jury in a case strong enough to obtain a guilty verdict from a presumably valid trial jury.* That being so, the same reasoning that pushed the Court to decline to reverse the conviction in *Hobby* would seem to require the Court to decline to reverse automatically convictions in any case involving racial exclusion from grand juries. Unwilling to upset precedent, however, the Court did what it often does: it compromised. It finally gave vent to the sentiments Justice Jackson expressed in *Cassell*, but only in the context of challenges to the selection of federal grand jury foremen.

The Court's compromise in *Hobby* is unfortunate and unsatisfying. Although the Court claimed that some means other than reversal of convictions would suffice to address the unconstitutional racial exclusion of blacks from consideration as grand jury foremen in federal criminal cases, the Court notably failed to suggest effective alternative remedies. It seems that the justices in the majority implicitly believed what other jurists have stated explicitly, namely that calling attention to the racial discrimination will be sufficient to prompt judges to reform their conduct.[80] If that prognosis proves incorrect, however, the Supreme Court's *Hobby* decision will have deprived the federal judiciary of an important weapon in the fight against illegal racial exclusion. This risky disarmament is especially noteworthy given the identity and position of the assumed wrongdoers and their relationship to the Supreme Court. The persons assumed in *Hobby* to have excluded blacks (and women) from consideration as grand jury foremen were, as Justice Marshall emphasized, *judges* of the U.S. District Court, figures residing squarely "within the four corners of the federal judicial process, an area uniquely amenable to [the Supreme] Court's influence."[81] The identity of the assumed wrongdoers should have received much more acknowledgment than it did from the Court. As Marshall observed, judges are "supposed to be the very embodiment of evenhanded justice." Therefore, the idea that a judge, of all officials, would

---

*On the other hand, perhaps Jackson overemphasizes the *presumed* validity of the petit jury in a case in which racial discrimination has tainted the selection of the grand jury. Perhaps the presence of racial discrimination in selecting the grand jury should be enough to impugn the validity of related trial jury proceedings.

discriminate on the basis of race and sex in selecting grand jury foremen is extraordinarily disquieting. . . . For it is unlikely that a judge
who engages in racist and sexist appointment practices will confine
his prejudicial attitudes and actions to the area of foreman selections.
More likely is that the presence of unconstitutional discrimination in
that area is but a portion of a widespread region of tainted decisionmaking.[82]

In the aftermath of *Hobby*, the federal constitutional law governing
what to do about racial discrimination in the selection of grand jury
foremen is unsatisfactory. In many places, it is unclear whether a defendant is entitled to reversal of a conviction because of racial discrimination in the selection of grand jury foremen.[83] Moreover, as we have seen,
a dubious rationale characterizes the line drawing that distinguishes
those circumstances in which relief is forthcoming from those in which
relief is denied.

The legal system deals poorly with racial discrimination in other
phases of jury selection. One of the most important of these involves the
operation of peremptory challenges, to which we now turn.

6.

Race and the Composition of Juries:
The Peremptory Challenge

THE PEREMPTORY CHALLENGE empowers attorneys to exclude potential jurors without having initially to articulate the basis for the exclusion. This chapter examines two controversies that have affected the usage of this important weapon. The first involves conflict over the legitimacy of the trial-related, racially discriminatory peremptory challenge. The Supreme Court largely resolved this matter when it prohibited all racially discriminatory peremptory challenges. The second controversy involves the problem of enforcing this prohibition, a problem that reveals the large extent to which racial discrimination is practiced despite formal legal disapproval. As in chapter 3, here, too, one encounters racial discrimination that often stems from sentiments other than mere bigotry. Just as many police officers believe that race matters for purposes of more efficiently apprehending criminals, so, too, do many lawyers believe that race matters for purposes of shaping a jury favorable to their client. My attitude toward lawyers' use of racial proxies in deploying peremptory strikes is the same as my attitude toward police use of racial proxies in fighting crime. I oppose the practice, applaud the Supreme Court's prohibition of it, and urge judges to be more vigorous in their enforcement of the antidiscrimination standard that has been established.

Swain v. Alabama: Authorizing the Racially Discriminatory Peremptory Challenge

Swain v. Alabama[1] is the best starting point for analyzing the constitutional status of the racially motivated peremptory challenge. Swain arose from the 1962 prosecution of a black man convicted and sentenced to death by an all-white jury for raping a white woman in Talladega County, Alabama.[2] Although 26 percent of the people then eligible for jury service in the county were black, no African-American had sat on a trial jury since at least 1950. Typically, a small number of blacks were included on grand juries—two sat on the grand jury that indicted Robert Swain—and on the panels from which trial juries were chosen. When it came time to select the jury that would actually decide a case, however, prosecuting attorneys and sometimes defense attorneys used peremptory challenges to exclude all of the blacks who were potential jurors.*

---

*On some occasions black defendants specifically directed their attorneys to strike black jurors. See Swain v. Alabama, 380 U.S. 202, 225 (1965). Perhaps they did so believing that black jurors would seek to curry favor with white jurors by being tougher than the whites on black defendants. Perhaps they did so when they were accused of victimizing blacks out of a belief that black jurors would regard such criminality more seriously than white jurors.

In 1910, a jury commissioner in a Mississippi county observed that as a rule the few blacks who qualified for jury service (and somehow escaped racial exclusion) were "much more inclined to convict Negroes charged with crime than . . . [were] the white jurors" with the result being that "Negro defendants always challenge Negro jurors." Gilbert Thomas Stephenson, Race Distinctions in American Law, 261 (1969 [1910]). A jury commissioner in a Louisiana county reported a similar impression, stating that Negro jurors tended to "inflict capital punishment more readily than [whites] and generally want all law enforced, especially against bad men of their own race, as they know this is their best protection." Ibid., 259.

According to one experienced student of trial practice, "it is a common experience for criminal defense lawyers who represent black clients to find many situations in which whites are less biased toward a black defendant than a member of his own race." See Barbara Allen Babcock, "Voir Dire: Preserving 'Its Wonderful Power,'" 27 Stanford Law Review 545, 554–555 n.30 (1975). A recent echo of this impression can be heard in Currin v. State, 638 N.E.2d 1319 (Ind. Ct. App. 1994), in which a judge refused to permit a black defendant on trial for robbery to peremptorily excuse the sole black prospective juror in the venire. The judge noted that "experienced defense

In Swain's case, the prosecution struck all six of the blacks who might have been jurors. Although Swain's attorneys objected, the trial judge ruled against the defendant's constitutional challenge. The Supreme Court of Alabama and the U.S. Supreme Court affirmed this decision.

Speaking through Justice Byron White, the Supreme Court concluded that there was nothing in the Constitution that required a judge to examine the motives behind a prosecutor's use of peremptory challenges so long as he was using them as a weapon of litigation and not as a screen for categorically excluding blacks (like the statute that was invalidated in *Strauder*). According to Justice White, "[t]he presumption in any particular case must be that the prosecutor is using the State's challenges to obtain a fair and impartial jury to try the case." He went on to say that this "presumption is not overcome and the prosecutor therefore subjected to examination by allegations that in the case at hand all Negroes were removed . . . because they were Negroes." Any other result, White maintained, "would establish a rule wholly at odds with the peremptory challenge system as we know it" because, historically, peremptory challenges could be exercised for any reason whatsoever. Therefore, White concluded, "it is permissible to insulate from inquiry the removal of Negroes from a particular jury."[3]

Justice White offered several justifications for the Court's holding. The Court respected the peremptory challenge's "very old credentials." It feared that subjecting the prosecutor's peremptory challenges to scrutiny under the Equal Protection Clause would entail "a radical change in the nature and operation of the challenge" because it "would no longer be peremptory, each and every challenge being open to examination." The Court also maintained that striking jurors on the basis of race in pursuit of a winning litigation strategy posed no equal protection violation since, presumably, members of any group are similarly vulnerable to exclusion "whether they be Negroes, Catholics, accountants or those with blue eyes."[4]

The Court recognized the danger that prosecutors might deploy

---

counsel strike mature blacks, if they have a black defendant for a client, more readily than they would strike anyone else." Ibid., 1321. This special perceived (and actual) hostility of some blacks toward black defendants is another reflection of the politics of respectability.

peremptory challenges to exclude blacks "from juries for reasons wholly unrelated to the outcome of the particular case on trial," namely, to deny Negroes as a class "the same right and opportunity to participate in the administration of justice enjoyed by the white population." This use, the Court declared, would violate the Constitution. In outlining what would signal an impermissible use of peremptory challenges, however, the Court set forth an exceedingly heavy evidentiary burden. White wrote that a Fourteenth Amendment problem might arise only if a prosecutor "in case after case, whatever the circumstances . . . is responsible for the removal of Negroes . . . with the result that no Negroes ever serve on petit juries."[5]

Many people misunderstand the Court's ruling in *Swain*. First, the Court held that prosecutors could legitimately take race (or anything else) into account in peremptorily excluding potential jurors for trial-related reasons. Hence, the Court wrote that "it is permissible to insulate from inquiry the removal of Negroes from a particular jury on the assumption that the prosecutor is acting on acceptable considerations related to the case he is trying, the particular defendant involved and the particular crime charged."[6] Second, the Court indicated that a prosecutor could not use racially discriminatory peremptory challenges for reasons unrelated to winning a given case. With respect to this aspect of *Swain*, however, the Court constructed a high evidentiary bar that defendants would have to surmount in order to substantiate any claims of illicit prosecutorial racial discrimination.

All of the justices agreed that the trial-related peremptory challenge should be exempt from constitutional scrutiny no matter what the alleged motivation behind such a challenge. Three justices, Earl Warren, William O. Douglas, and Arthur Goldberg, dissented, however, with respect to the question of whether, in *Swain* itself, the state had used peremptory challenges as something akin to a law categorically barring blacks from trial juries. The dissenters argued that, absent rebuttal by the state, the defendant had established a constitutional violation based on the long absence of *any* blacks on trial juries in the county. Speaking for the dissenters, Justice Goldberg argued that the Court missed the reality of the situation in Talladega County by separating the process of creating jury venires from the process of exercising peremptory challenges. Goldberg argued that these two phases of jury selection should be viewed together as a dynamic, interactive whole. When so viewed, Goldberg asserted, it became clear that "the total exclusion of Negroes from juries in Talladega County resulted from the interlocking of an inadequate venire selection system . . . and the use of peremptory challenges."[7] In Goldberg's view, the state was engaged in minimizing the number of blacks available in jury pools and then consistently using peremptory strikes to remove this small number of potential black jurors from being seated on actual trial juries. Goldberg did not dispute that lawyers should be permitted to deploy peremptory challenges for *any* reason (including racial reasons) as a matter of trial strategy. He contended, however, that regardless of the process used, whenever blacks were kept off trial juries for a long period of time, the state should have to rebut the inference that blacks' absence is due to racial discrimination that is unrelated to trial strategy.

Because the Supreme Court sought to protect the peremptory challenge as a tool of litigation, it raised the evidentiary bar that defendants would have to jump in order to prevail in a racial discrimination challenge. By contrast, Goldberg believed that no special evidentiary rules should apply simply because peremptory challenges were part of the apparatus of exclusion. In his view, the same reasoning that led to reversal in *Norris* v. *Alabama* should have led to reversal in *Swain* v. *Alabama*. Goldberg's reliance on *Norris* is poignant. Thirty years earlier, immediately following the Supreme Court's second intervention in the Scottsboro Boys case, the *New York Times* reported that "a Negro on a trial jury is as rare as ever in the deep South. . . . In both criminal and civil cases . . . Negroes . . . can be—and are—easily eliminated by one or both sides through [peremptory challenges]."[8]

The Struggle to Stigmatize the Racially Discriminatory Peremptory Challenge

Swain "effectively isolated from judicial review a device susceptible of extraordinarily efficient use in the Southern States' effort to perpetuate the all-white jury." The practice of routinely striking black prospective jurors, however, was not limited to the South; prosecutors deployed it throughout the country, particularly in serious criminal cases featuring black defendants. Critics of *Swain* rightly viewed the ruling as a blow to efforts to desegregate the nation's courthouses. They therefore mobilized efforts to evade or reverse it.[9]*

Judge Jon O. Newman initiated the first judicial movement toward reform in 1976 in *United States* v. *Robinson*.[10] This case arose from the prosecution for embezzlement of two codefendants, one of whom was black. Near the end of jury selection, defense counsel objected to the fact that the federal prosecutor had used peremptory challenges to strike all four of the Negroes on the jury panel. Judge Newman asked the prosecutor whether he wanted to state a nonracial reason for challenging the four blacks. The prosecutor declined to respond. Judge Newman then gave the defense permission to analyze records regarding the impaneling of juries in federal cases in Connecticut during the previous two years. The defense found that eighty-two blacks sat on jury panels and that prosecutors exercised peremptory challenges to strike fifty-seven of them, an exclusion rate of 69.5 percent. In cases involving white defendants, the exclusion rate for black jurors was 52.2 percent. In cases involving black or Hispanic defendants, the exclusion rate was 84.8 percent. Of seventy-three analyzed trials, blacks served as jurors in only thirteen cases—18.1 percent—and in ten of these cases only one black juror served. Based on these findings, Judge Newman concluded that "prosecutors' challenges alone [had] had a substantial impact in reducing the frequency of juries with at least one Black, and increasing the frequency of all-White juries," that "in a large number of instances Black veniremen were challenged because they were Black," and that "the pattern of government peremptory challenges of [Blacks had] now reached an excessive point that call[ed] for the exercise of [the] Court's supervisory power over the conduct of criminal trials in [the] District."[11]†

Judge Newman ordered the seating of the four blacks who had been peremptorily struck. He also ordered the U.S. Attorney's Office to sub-

---

*This campaign focused mainly on the prosecutorial use of racially discriminatory peremptory challenges. Later I shall discuss problems surrounding defendants' use of racially discriminatory peremptory challenges. (See pp. 214–27.)

†By "supervisory power," Judge Newman meant the inherent authority of a judge to impose fair standards for the administration of justice as distinct from authority based on expressly federal statutory or constitutional law.

mit reports periodically on the racial demographics of its use of peremptory challenges.

Judge Newman's attempted end-run around *Swain* was short-lived. Obtaining an unusual form of appellate review, the U.S. Attorney's Office elicited a reversal from the Second Circuit Court of Appeals that harshly chastised Newman.[12] His decision, the Court of Appeals remarked, "cannot but have an immediate and continuing detrimental impact on the administration of criminal justice" because, "among other things[,] it is likely to bring about interminable delays . . . as the result of constant defense challenges . . . every time a Black is peremptorily challenged" by a prosecutor.[13]

The next attack against *Swain* came from the ranks of state courts. Although states are bound to follow the Supreme Court's interpretation of the Constitution, they can impose upon themselves greater burdens than those imposed by federal norms. In 1978 and 1979, the highest state courts in California and Massachusetts imposed upon their state prosecutors a heavier burden than that imposed by *Swain*.

The California breakthrough stemmed from *People* v. *Wheeler*,[14] a prosecution of two black men accused of murdering a white man in the course of a robbery. During jury selection, the prosecution peremptorily struck each of seven prospective black jurors. An all-white jury convicted the defendants. The defendants alleged that the peremptory strikes were racially motivated and that the prosecution's actions deprived them of the right, given by the state constitution, to be tried by a jury drawn from a representative cross-section of the community. The California Supreme Court held in favor of the defendants and reversed their convictions. The Court concluded that under the state constitution it could not countenance "the decimation of . . . jurors by peremptory challenges on the ground of group bias alone."[15] The Court ruled that when the defense makes a prima facie case that the prosecution has used peremptory challenges in a racially discriminatory fashion, a trial judge must require the prosecution to rebut the charge. The state attorney general had argued that the California courts should follow the U.S. Supreme Court, but the California Supreme Court expressly declared that "the rule of *Swain* v. *Alabama* is not to be followed."[16]

A year later, in *Commonwealth* v. *Soares*,[17] the Massachusetts Supreme Judicial Court also rebuffed *Swain*. The occasion for doing so arose from convictions of three black men accused of murdering a white Harvard College student in downtown Boston during an altercation between the defendants and members of the Harvard football team. The trouble began when several of the Harvard men encountered two black women in Boston's "combat zone" and discussed the buying and selling of sexual favors. Later, upon discovering that one of their wallets was missing, the men chased the women. Several black men then intervened. According to witnesses, a number of the black men shouted various threats, including, "We're going to cut you white m[other] f[ucker]s."[18] One of the Harvard men was mortally wounded by knife punctures to his chest.

At trial, thirteen blacks were in the pool of eligible jurors. Over objections, the prosecutor eliminated twelve with peremptory challenges. The one black who was not challenged was subsequently designated by the judge as foreman of the jury that proceeded to convict the accused.

Reversing the convictions under the Massachusetts Declaration of Rights, the Supreme Judicial Court declared that if it failed to prohibit the use of peremptory challenges to exclude jurors because of their membership in particular, defined groups, it "would leave the right to a jury drawn from a representative cross-section of the community wholly susceptible to nullification." The state attorney general argued that trial-related racially discriminatory peremptory challenges should be permitted because members of given racial groups are statistically more likely to harbor beliefs unfavorable to the prosecution in certain types of cases. The Supreme Judicial Court agreed that "no human being is wholly free of the interests and preferences which are the product of his cultural, family, and community experience." It concluded, however, that "nowhere is the dynamic commingling of the ideas and biases of such individuals more essential than inside the jury room."[19]

After *Wheeler* and *Soares*, some observers thought that state court decisions might provide the basis for a widespread disavowal of *Swain*. Yet during the five years following *Soares*, no other state courts imposed state constitutional limits on peremptory challenges. During that period, at least nineteen states decided to follow *Swain*.[20]

Justice Thurgood Marshall launched the third attack on *Swain*.[21] He did so by using the dissent from the denial of certiorari.[22] Parties seeking review in the Supreme Court do so by petitioning for a writ of certiorari. This writ is granted or denied at the discretion of the justices. Four must vote to grant the petition in order for a case to be reviewed by the Court. When a justice feels strongly that the Court has wrongly denied a writ, he or she will write a dissent from denial of certiorari. A frequent dissenter from denials of certiorari, Marshall's dissents in cases involving peremptory challenges were among his most influential.

Marshall began his campaign on May 31, 1983, when, joined by Justice William J. Brennan, he dissented from the Court's denial of certiorari in three cases, including *McCray* v. *New York*.[23] Michael McCray was black. The person who accused him of robbery was white. McCray was initially tried before a racially mixed jury that was unable to reach a verdict. According to McCray's attorneys, the three blacks on the jury voted for acquittal.[24] At a second trial, the prosecutors used peremptory challenges to exclude all seven of the blacks who sat on the panel of prospective jurors. The resulting all-white jury convicted McCray. Citing *Swain*, the New York state courts affirmed the conviction, ruling that the prosecutor had no obligation to explain the racial pattern of the peremptory challenges he deployed.[25]

In his dissent from denial of certiorari, Justice Marshall pointed out that *Swain* had been the subject of scathing criticism. The aspect of *Swain* that he found most troubling was the notion that prosecutors should be permitted to deploy racially discriminatory peremptory challenges absent unvarying racial exclusion. Marshall did not see the sense in permitting *some* racial discrimination by a prosecutor, so long as he refrained from discriminating all the time "in case after case whatever the circumstances": "Since *every* defendant is entitled to equal protection of the laws and should therefore be free from the invidious discrimination of state officials, it is difficult to understand why several must suffer discrimination . . . before any defendant can object."[26]

Marshall needed to convince two other justices besides himself and Justice Brennan in order to force a reexamination of *Swain*. He failed to do so with his *McCray* dissent. He did, however, obtain something for his effort. His dissent prompted Justice Stevens, joined by Justices Blackmun and Powell, to write an opinion in which he stated that his vote to deny certiorari did not reflect disagreement with Marshall's appraisal of the importance of the underlying issue, but was simply a judgment that the issue was not yet ripe for the Court's reexamination.

Observing that there existed no conflict between federal courts and that only two state courts had deviated from *Swain*, Justice Stevens concluded that, in his view, "it is a sound exercise of discretion . . . to allow the various States to serve as laboratories in which the issue receives further study before it is addressed by this Court."[27]

Four months later, Marshall again urged his colleagues to reconsider *Swain*. In *Gilliard* v. *Mississippi*,[28] he dissented from the Court's denial of certiorari in a case in which a black man pleaded guilty to a murder-robbery. At a sentencing trial, seven blacks were among those eligible for jury service. The prosecution peremptorily challenged all of them. Somehow an additional black ended up among the prospective jurors, but the prosecution struck him too. In the end, the prosecutor used peremptory challenges to remove *all* the Negro prospective jurors and *only* the Negro prospective jurors. The trial judge dismissed the defense attorney's objections. Citing *Swain*, he ruled that there existed no basis for questioning the prosecutor's conduct. An all-white jury then heard the evidence and sentenced the defendant to death in proceedings affirmed by the Mississippi Supreme Court.

When the U.S. Supreme Court declined to review *Gilliard*, Marshall wrote a dissent from denial of certiorari that was addressed directly to Justices Stevens, Blackmun, and Powell:

> When a majority of this Court suspects that . . . rights are being regularly abridged, the Court shrinks from its constitutional duty by awaiting developments in state or other federal courts. Because abuse of peremptory challenges appears to be most prevalent in capital cases, the need for immediate review in this Court is all the more urgent. If we postpone consideration of the issue much longer, petitioners in this and similar cases will be put to death before their constitutional rights can be vindicated. Under the circumstances, I do not understand how in good conscience we can await further developments.[29]

He failed, however, to persuade his colleagues to move.

Seven months later, grouping together several death penalty cases, Marshall again dissented from denial of certiorari.[30] In one of these cases, prosecutors sought the death penalty after a black defendant pleaded guilty to murder. Blacks constituted 22 percent of the jury pool. The prosecution used eleven of its twenty peremptory challenges to exclude the blacks. Ultimately, an all-white jury condemned the defendant to death.[31]

Sounding a note of desperation, Marshall wrote that these cases presented the Court with additional opportunities to protect criminal defendants against racially discriminatory jury selection procedures. "Again today," he pleaded, "I urge my colleagues to grant certiorari on what I believe to be one of the gravest and most persistent problems facing the American judiciary today."[32]

A month later, Justice Marshall again dissented from a denial of certiorari.[33] Wesley Eric Harris, a black man, was indicted in Harris County, Texas, for sexually assaulting a white woman. He had no criminal record. He claimed to have been at home at the time the crime was committed. There were no witnesses to the alleged assault, and no physical evidence linked Harris to the alleged offense. The case came down to whether the jury would accept the white woman's identification or believe the black man's denial. After an extensive voir dire, eight blacks remained on the jury panel. The prosecution removed each of them with peremptory challenges. An all-white jury then proceeded to convict Harris. Bemoaning his inability to persuade the Court to reexamine the legitimacy of *Swain*, Marshall asserted that cases like *Harris* showed that prosecutorial abuse of peremptory challenges had grown to "epidemic proportions."[34]

Although it might have seemed at that moment that Justice Marshall's efforts had borne little fruit, in fact, his efforts had already helped to set into motion events that would soon force the Court to revisit *Swain*. After the Supreme Court denied certiorari to *McCray* on direct review of the case from the New York state courts, the defendant's attorneys sought habeas corpus review in the federal courts. The lawyers repeated the arguments voiced by Justice Marshall and pointed to the statement by Justices Stevens, Blackmun, and Powell, which suggested their uncertainty about the continued vitality of *Swain*. That action prompted federal district judge Eugene H. Nickerson to break away from *Swain*'s grip. In *McCray*, he granted relief to the defendant pursuant to the Equal Protection Clause.[35] A divided panel of the Second Circuit Court of Appeals affirmed Judge Nickerson, albeit on a basis different than the one he had articulated.[36] Attempting to avoid a direct confrontationwith *Swain*, the Second Circuit based its decision not on the Equal Protection Clause but rather on the Sixth Amendment.* According to Judge Amalya Kearse, a prosecutor's racially discriminatory peremptory challenges violate the Sixth Amendment because that provision stands for the proposition that "justice is best served by a jury that represents a cross-section of the community, not one from which cognizable groups have been systematically eliminated because of their group affiliation."[37]

This ruling created the conflict within the federal judiciary that had previously been absent. Despite superficially genuflecting to *Swain*, *McCray* actually subverted it. Furthermore, after *McCray*, another court of appeals rebelled against *Swain* while others rallied behind it.[38] To re-establish order, the Supreme Court was forced to revisit the rules governing the peremptory challenge as Thurgood Marshall had demanded.

Batson v. *Kentucky*: *Swain* Reconsidered

The Supreme Court clarified matters in 1986 in *Batson* v. *Kentucky*.[39] James Kirkland Batson was a black defendant convicted of burglary and receipt of stolen goods. His jury pool included four blacks. Over objection, the prosecutor used four of his six peremptory challenges to remove all four of the blacks. Batson was then tried and convicted by an all-white jury.

Although the only federal issue adjudicated by the state court in *Batson* was the propriety of the prosecutor's conduct under the Sixth Amendment, and although the Supreme Court granted certiorari to consider the Sixth Amendment issue, the Supreme Court decided the case on federal equal protection grounds. The Court clearly wanted to revisit *Swain*. In an opinion written by Justice Powell, the Court held that, contrary to what it had previously ruled, the Equal Protection Clause prohibits *all* racially discriminatory peremptory challenges by prosecutors. *Batson* withdraws permission for prosecutors to use race as

---

*The Sixth Amendment provides that "in all criminal prosecutions the accused shall enjoy the right to a speedy and public trial, but an impartial jury of the State and district wherein the crime shall have been committed."

a basis for peremptorily striking potential jurors, even if a prosecutor sees removing blacks as the best way to obtain a jury most sympathetic to the state's side in a given case.

Two beliefs animated the *Batson* decision. One was that prosecutors had overused racially discriminatory peremptories—that they had too often exercised their privilege in a sloppy, unthinking, reflexive manner. This point comes through most clearly in a concurring opinion by Justice White, *Swain*'s author. According to White, *Swain* itself "should have warned prosecutors that using peremptories to exclude blacks on the assumption that no black juror could fairly judge a black defendant would violate the Equal Protection Clause."[40] Since, in his view, many prosecutors had ignored this warning, he was now prepared to abandon *Swain* and to join in establishing a new evidentiary rule that would be considerably less protective of the prosecutorial peremptory strike.

The second belief animating *Batson* eclipses the first. This belief is that racial discrimination by the government in the exercise of peremptory challenges is not only bad when used to disenfranchise black potential jurors consistently but also when used as a trial-related tactic in a single instance. "A single invidiously discriminatory governmental act," the Court maintained, "is not immunized by the absence of such discrimination in the making of other comparable decisions."[41] Citing Justice Marshall, it asserted that "to dictate that several must suffer discrimination before one could object . . . would be inconsistent with the promise of equal protection for all."[42]

To effectuate its newly pronounced ban on all racially discriminatory peremptory challenges, the Court created a process that involves several steps. The first step entails the defendant establishing a prima facie case that the prosecution is using its peremptory challenges in a racially discriminatory fashion. A prima facie case means an allegation supported by facts that, if left unrebutted, give rise to an inference that the allegation is true. Among the facts that might give rise to an inference of discrimination are a pattern of strikes against jurors of a given race or the prosecutor's statements and questions during voir dire. When the defendant can make out a prima facie case, the burden shifts to the prosecution to come forward with a nonracial explanation for its challenges. When the prosecutor offers a nonracial explanation, the defendant can, of course, then seek to show that the nonracial explanation is a mere pretext. Ultimately, though, the defendant must persuade the judge that race played a part in the prosecutor's decision to strike the juror in question.[43]

Two justices dissented in *Batson*. Chief Justice Warren E. Burger suggested that racially motivated peremptory challenges might well be justified, even under strict scrutiny, the most intense level of judicial oversight, because the unregulated peremptory challenge had long been understood as "essential to the fairness of trial by jury."[44] Justice Rehnquist reasserted the argument from *Swain* that trial-related racially motivated peremptories did not violate the Constitution insofar as potential jurors of all racial groups were subject to the same treatment. "Crudely stereotypical" peremptory challenges "may in many cases be hopelessly mistaken," Rehnquist noted, but so long as everyone was subject to them, he reasoned, they could not be properly viewed as invidiously discriminatory.[45]

While Burger and Rehnquist concluded that *Batson* went too far, Marshall concluded that *Batson* did not go far enough. In a concurring opinion, he maintained that banning racially motivated peremptory challenges while permitting peremptory challenges in general would fail to satisfactorily address the problem. Basing his observations on the experience of California and Massachusetts in the aftermath of *Wheeler* and *Soares*, Marshall contended that defendants would be able to establish a prima facie case only in the most obvious instances of discrimination. He complained that in the states that had already prohibited racially motivated peremptories, "prosecutors are left free to discriminate against blacks in jury selection provided that they hold discrimination to an 'acceptable' level."[46] In the event that a defendant was able to make out a prima facie case, Marshall feared that a smart, duplicitous prosecutor would easily be able to offer nonracial explanations that most judges would be unwilling to reject as pretextual. Marshall suggested, moreover, that an even more subtle and difficult problem would reside in the prosecutor who unconsciously discriminates racially and then, erroneously but in good faith, denies that he discriminates. Marshall hypothesized, for example, the prosecutor who unconsciously, though genuinely, views a black prospective juror as "distant" or "sullen," even though he would not attribute those traits to a similarly situated white person.[47] Convinced that the ban against racial discrimination in prosecutorial peremptory challenges could not be satisfactorily enforced, and stressing that peremptory challenges are not constitutionally required, Marshall argued that the Court should disallow prosecutorial peremptory challenges altogether (leaving the way clear for state and federal governments to eliminate the defendant's peremptory challenge).

All of these approaches to the racially discriminatory peremptory challenge are problematic. Considered together, they suggest why conflict over the peremptory challenge continues to cast a heavy pall over criminal litigation.

The Burger–Rehnquist defense of *Swain* is wrong. Burger emphasized that educated observers over a long span of time have praised the peremptory challenge as a device for excusing jurors who are in fact biased against a party though not biased in a sufficiently clear way to be struck for cause by a judge. To Burger this function was so valuable that it passed the test of strict scrutiny on the grounds that it advances a compelling state interest—affording litigants fair trials—in the least bothersome way available.

Two considerations undermine Burger's argument. First, much of the historical support for the peremptory challenge refers to the peremptory challenge when used by the *defense*. At issue in *Batson* was the *prosecutorial* exercise of peremptory challenges, a function that is less supportable than the defendant's exercise of the peremptory challenge.[48] Second, notwithstanding Burger's suggestion to the contrary, neither defense nor prosecutorial peremptory challenges are constitutionally required;[49] they owe their existence solely to custom or statute, which means, presumably, that a jurisdiction could decide to make do without any peremptory challenges. If a jurisdiction could get rid of peremptories altogether without violating constitutional requirements, it is hard to see how keeping the peremptory challenge free of increased regulation could plausibly be seen as something so "compelling" as to trump the constitutional ban against racial discrimination.

Rehnquist argued that *Swain* did not invidiously discriminate against blacks because, after all, any person from any group was subject to racially discriminatory strikes—whites, yellows, reds, and browns as well as blacks. Rehnquist's argument is hauntingly reminiscent of segregationist logic which reasoned that governmental bans on interracial fornication, marriage, or transportation did not invidiously discriminate against blacks because whites, too, were burdened by the same laws.[50] The Court has rightly rejected Rehnquist's logic. It has done so on the grounds that, notwithstanding the appearance of symmetry, "neutral" race lines typically obscure a reality in which blacks are actually and purposefully held in their "place" by such racial distinctions. More fundamentally, it has rejected Rehnquist's tolerant approach to race-neutral racial lines on the grounds that *all* governmental racial lines are troublesome and in need of extraordinary justification.[51]

There are also difficulties with Justice Marshall's suggested approach to the peremptory challenge. These problems can better be examined, however, after considering the experience of the courts in attempting to enforce *Batson*.

The Problem of Enforcing *Batson*

Despite *Batson*, prosecutors continue to deploy racially motivated peremptory challenges.[52] Few officials have openly admitted doing so.[53] Circumstantial evidence, however, points to a substantial amount of noncompliance. Judges have found violations of *Batson* in scores of cases. Surveying all reported decisions of federal and state courts between April 30, 1986 (the date of the *Batson* decision) and December 31, 1993, Professor Kenneth J. Melilli uncovered 165 cases in which judges determined that prosecutors had violated *Batson*.[54] This figure amounts to a little over 10 percent of the 1,101 cases in which criminal defendants alleged that prosecutors were using racially discriminatory peremptory challenges.

The blatant lying by public officials in some of these cases is rather sobering. Consider *People v. McDonald*,[55] a case featuring three black men prosecuted for kidnapping and rape. At trial, the prosecution exercised sixteen of its peremptory challenges to remove *all* of the blacks in the pool of potential jurors. An all-white jury then proceeded to convict the defendants. Although *Batson* had not been announced at the time of the *McDonald* trial, it was available by the time the defendants appealed their convictions. Pursuant to a Supreme Court ruling on retroactivity,[56] the Supreme Court of Illinois decided that the defendants should have an opportunity to prove a *Batson* violation. The defendants easily established a prima facie case given the noticeable pattern of the prosecution's strikes. At that point, the prosecution was asked if it could give nonracial reasons for its peremptory challenges. Inasmuch as the prosecution had been initiated prior to *Batson*, it would have been understandable for the prosecutor to have stated candidly that, relying on long-established precedent, he had for trial-related but racially discriminatory reasons peremptorily challenged the black jurors. That, however, is not how the prosecutor responded. Instead, he attempted to offer nonracial reasons for his strikes.

The prosecutor's explanations were transparently false. In several instances, he struck blacks who displayed a trait to which he claimed to object while refraining from striking whites who shared the same trait. For example, the prosecutor claimed to have challenged a thirty-four-year-old black man because of his youth. Yet he refrained from challenging an eighteen-year-old white man. The prosecutor claimed to have peremptorily challenged a black potential juror on the grounds that she had had prior jury service. Yet he refrained from challenging a white man who had previously served on two juries. The prosecutor claimed to have challenged a sixty-three-year-old black man on the basis of his advanced age. Yet, the prosecutor refrained from challenging a sixty-seven-year-old white man. The Supreme Court of Illinois agreed with the trial judge that despite the prosecutor's denials, he had, in fact, engaged in racial discrimination in exercising his peremptory strikes.

A Georgia case, *Gamble* v. *State*,[57] resulted in a similar outcome. In *Gamble*, the prosecutor used all of his peremptories to remove all of the potential black jurors in the trial of a black defendant who was convicted and sentenced to death for murder by an all-white jury. Although the prosecutor offered nonracial reasons for his challenges, the courts found them insufficient to rebut the defendant's prima facie case of discrimination. As in *McDonald*, some of the prosecutor's stated rationales were belied by his inconsistent treatment of blacks and whites. The prosecutor claimed to have struck a black juror because of mental inadequacy—the prosecutor stated that the juror "appears to have the intelligence of a fencepost."[58] In reversing the conviction, however, the Supreme Court of Georgia noted that one white juror whom the prosecution refrained from challenging was illiterate while another described himself as being "a little slow." The prosecutor claimed to have struck a black prospective juror named McGruder because she had stated during voir dire that she knew of a friend or member of her family who had abused alcohol or drugs and also because the prosecutor said that he recalled having previously prosecuted someone named McGruder. The Georgia Supreme Court observed, however, that several whites who served on the jury without challenge also knew members of their families or friends who had abused alcohol or other drugs. As for the prosecutor's alleged concern that the black juror might be related to someone he had previously tried, the Court noted that the prosecutor had failed to ask whether, in fact, any such relationship existed.

In *McDonald*, *Gamble*, and scores of similar cases, prosecutors not only racially discriminated but also lied to courts about doing so. This underscores a phenomenon that surfaces repeatedly throughout this book: the intimate link between wrongful racial discrimination and deception by public officials. Where one finds the former, one generally finds the latter. Even more disturbing than the cases in which prosecutors have lied unsuccessfully, however, are those cases in which their deceptions have prevailed. These "successes" indicate not only misconduct on the part of prosecutors but also failure or, worse, corruption, on the part of judges.

To invalidate a peremptory challenge under *Batson*, the defendant must convince a judge of two things. First, he must persuade the judge that the prosecutor's strikes raise a prima facie inference of purposeful racial discrimination. The Supreme Court did not give any clear guidance with respect to this matter. As Professor Albert W. Alschuler observes, the Court "left lower court judges at large to determine when 'things look bad.' "[59] Judges have rather consistently deemed things to "look bad" when a prosecutor uses peremptory challenges to strike *all* of a substantial number of potential black jurors, especially if the prosecutor refrains from striking whites. In more ambiguous contexts, though, the case law is mixed. Some courts have been rather demanding of the prosecution, ruling that a prima facie case is established any time that the percentage of peremptory strikes used against potential jurors of a certain race is appreciably greater than the percentage of the jury panel that consists of people of that race.[60] Other courts have been remarkably lax, ruling that the presence on a jury of *any* blacks who could have been struck negates any inference that the prosecutor acted on racial grounds with respect to black jurors whom he did strike.[61]

Second, even if a defendant persuades a judge to find a prima facie case of discrimination, the defendant must then persuade the judge that the nonracial rationale offered by the prosecutor is erroneous or pretextual and that racial bias is the real reason behind the peremptory strike at issue. The transparently false explanations noted above reveal prosecutors who were sloppy, stupid, or inexperienced. By contrast, a skillful, well-prepared, experienced prosecutor who wishes to offer a pretext can often succeed in crafting a neutral explanation that will satisfy judges. That is so because, in the absence of direct evidence, it is frequently unclear whether a prosecutor peremptorily challenged a potential juror on account of race or on account of some other, nonracial, consideration (e.g., age, occupation, demeanor, perceived intelligence, residence, marital status, or previous adverse involvement with the criminal justice system). Some of these explanations correlate strongly with race. Previous adverse involvement with the criminal justice system is one of the most commonly cited explanations prosecutors give for striking black potential jurors. Given that a relatively large percentage of the black population has been arrested or convicted or is closely related to someone who has been arrested or convicted, this rationale for striking jurors could serve as an efficient pretext for what are, in fact, racially discriminatory strikes. Some explanations, moreover, are so subjective as to be virtually beyond verification, as when a prosecutor claims that he struck a juror because the juror seemed inattentive, headstrong, or hostile. In the face of these difficulties, defense counsel must go beyond persuading a judge that the prosecutor acted unreasonably or superstitiously or otherwise badly. He must persuade the judge that the prosecutor struck a juror, at least in part, because of race.[62]

Another reason that helps to explain why prosecutors succeed in racially discriminating, despite *Batson*, is that judges tend to give the benefit of the doubt to prosecutors. This tendency results partially from the difficulty of accurately delineating motive. It also stems partially from the special status accorded to prosecutors by judges who see them not only as attorneys but as government officials who should and do represent broader interests than private counsel. Because prosecutors are often seen as quasi-judges, their actions receive extra deference. This tendency to give prosecutors facing a *Batson* challenge the benefit of the doubt also has to do with the nature of the judicial finding at stake. When a judge rules against a prosecutor in this setting, he rules not only that the prosecutor wrongly discriminated; he also rules that the prosecutor was either mistaken about or lying about his motives. Many judges will refrain from reaching such an embarrassing conclu-

sion in the absence of overwhelming evidence. This hesitancy infor-
mally raises the evidentiary burden and further limits the circumstances
under which judges deem prosecutors' explanations to be erroneous or
pretextual.

These considerations clarify why judges have ruled in favor of prosecutors in cases in which a realistic view of the evidence points toward a
different conclusion. *Branch* v. *State*,[63] a murder case in which a prosecutor used six of his seven peremptory challenges to remove six of the
seven black potential jurors, provides a good example. Claiming that he
had tried a case three weeks previously in which the same prosecutor
had used all seven of his strikes to eliminate all of the black potential jurors, the defense attorney raised a *Batson* objection to the prosecutor's
conduct. At a hearing, the prosecution offered nonracial explanations
for each of the six strikes. It claimed that it struck one juror because he
was a scientist and would therefore put too much pressure on the prosecution. It claimed it struck another because he was similar in age and appearance to the defendant and might have had a relationship to a person
arrested in an unrelated criminal case several months earlier. The prosecution claimed it struck a third juror because she had been unemployed
and had a "dumbfounded or bewildered look on her face." It claimed it
struck a fourth juror because it believed that employees of the company
where the prospective juror worked had been inattentive as jurors on
previous occasions and that some employees at that company were currently the subjects of criminal investigations. It claimed it struck a fifth
prospective black juror because he was unkempt and gruff. The prosecution said that it struck a sixth black prospective juror because she was
a single woman around the same age as the defendant, because it feared
that she "might feel as though she were a sister . . . and have some pity"
on him, because she frowned indicating that she might be in a bad
mood, and because her demeanor indicated more sympathy to the defense than the prosecution.

Attacking these explanations, the defense attorney mainly objected
to the broad, amorphous character of the prosecutors' stated rationales:

> Judge, [i]f you believe that junk and if you uphold this jury, what
> you are saying . . . [is that the Justices of the Supreme Court] wasted
> their time. . . . [I]f you are going to [accept these explanations] then

that just gives the government prosecutors, who have been living a lie so long that they now believe that they have never done anything wrong as far as discriminating against blacks, a license to come in and give you some junk like they just gave you. . . . They eliminated one person because they had a frown on their face. . . . [T]hat can be a reason? Then forget about *Batson*.[64]

In response, the judge ruled in favor of the prosecutors. "I think they are credible persons, I trust these men," he remarked, "when they tell me something as court officers."[65] One would like to share the judge's confidence. One should not, however, in the face of facts that make it highly improbable that the prosecution's peremptory strikes would have been the same if the jurors at issue had been white instead of black. It is not impossible that, regardless of race, the prosecutors would have struck six of the seven prospective black jurors. It is sufficiently unlikely, however, especially in light of the prosecutions' vague explanations, that one can properly reject *Branch*'s conclusion.[66]

Similarly dubious is *State* v. *Jackson*,[67] a case in which a prosecutor used five peremptory challenges to remove four blacks and one white from a jury that ultimately contained eleven whites and one black. Asked to explain her strikes, the prosecutor stated that she sought to obtain jurors who were "stable, government oriented, employed, and had sufficient ties to the community, and a mind-set, if you will, that would . . . pay more attention to the needs of law enforcement than the fine points of individual rights." She then sought to justify specifically the strikes in question. The prosecutor said that she struck one black prospective juror because she was unemployed and had previously served as a student counselor at a university, a position that bothered the prosecution because it was "too liberal a background."[68] The prosecution said that it struck another black prospective juror because she, too, was unemployed and, through her demeanor, had displayed hostility or indifference. By contrast, two whites who were unemployed were seated without objection by the prosecution.

Again, one cannot be absolutely sure of the correct outcome in a case such as this. One should give due deference to the trial judge who was in a position to see directly the indescribable subtleties—the revealing tenor of a witness's voice or the telling steadiness of a witness's gaze—

that cannot be captured by summary descriptions of the gross facts of a case. When one has given all due deference, however, one still has difficulty believing that, had these prospective jurors been white, the prosecutor would have struck them just the same.

As in *McDonald*, the defendant in *Jackson* was tried before the *Batson* ruling. At that time, it would have been legally permissible for the prosecutor to have used her peremptory strikes in a racially discriminatory way to further her litigation strategy. One can understand the feeling of frustration that a prosecutor and judge might feel when faced with the possibility of reversing the conviction of a murderer on the basis of a Supreme Court holding that did not exist when the defendant was tried. One can also understand the temptation to "fudge" in such a case, to accept a prosecutor's story when that story is untrue. Fudging is, in all likelihood, what happened in *Jackson*. A concurring opinion by a justice of the North Carolina Supreme Court supports that impression. The justice agreed with his colleagues to affirm the trial judge's ruling in favor of the prosecution. He was also moved to promise, however, that he and his colleagues "will review with a scrupulous eye" explanations for peremptory challenges after the making of a prima facie case in order "to thwart the remnants of the past pernicious practice of excluding blacks from juries for no other reason than for the color of their skin."[69] In part a call to enforce *Batson*, this statement is also a sign of bad conscience, a muted acknowledgment that the evasion of *Batson* had already begun.

Race and the Defendant's Use of Peremptory Strikes

Thus far, the peremptory challenge has been portrayed as the villain of the drama, a creature of unbridled discretion that, in the hands of white prosecutors and white defendants, has often been used to sustain racial subordination in the courtroom.* For many who agree with this por-

---

*Earlier we saw white defendant police officers use peremptory challenges to clear venires of all-black prospective jurors. The most vivid example was the McDuffie case. (See pp. 116–17.) There are many others. One of the most chilling of these was the 1980–1981 episode that featured a state and federal criminal prosecution in

trayal, however, a dramatic switch occurs when the discussion turns to the regulation of peremptory strikes by *black* defendants. Discussion at the highest level of the judiciary turned to that subject in a roundabout way in 1990. The occasion was a case, *Georgia* v. *McCollum*,[70] that featured the prosecution of three whites for beating and assaulting a black couple in Dougherty County, Georgia. Before jury selection began, the prosecution moved to prohibit the defendants from racially discriminating in their exercise of peremptory challenges. The prosecution feared that the defense would use their peremptory strikes to exclude all of the black potential jurors. The trial court rejected the prosecutor's motion and was later upheld by the Supreme Court of Georgia.

In an opinion authored by Justice Harry Blackmun, the Supreme Court ruled that the Equal Protection Clause prohibits defense counsel as well as prosecutors from using race as a basis for peremptorily challenging jurors. The Court rejected the argument that, because defendants are private actors, they are beyond federal constitutional restraints since the Constitution applies only to governmental action.[71] The Court held that constitutional limitations should attach to a defendant because, in exercising a peremptory challenge, he wields a power, given by the government, to help choose "a quintessential governmental body"—the jury.[72] When a government confers on a private person the power to choose the government's employees or officials, the Court concluded, " 'the private body will be bound by the constitutional mandate of race neutrality.' "[73]

The Court did not address the claim that the defendant has an especially intense, immediate, and personal stake in a criminal trial, a stake that arguably justifies permitting him to strike jurors for racial reasons barred to government attorneys.[74] Rather, the Court emphasized that the defendant's interest was only one of three interests to be considered. Another interest was that of potential jurors to participate in the administration of justice. Although an individual juror, the Court declared, does not have a right to sit on any particular jury, he does have a

---

North Carolina against members of the Ku Klux Klan who killed five members of the Communist Workers Party in a grisly event largely captured on film. Two all-white juries from which all potential black jurors were peremptorily struck acquitted the Klansmen. See Paula DiPerna, *Juries on Trial* 171–173 (1984).

right to be exempt from exclusion from a particular jury on account of race. The Court maintained that "regardless of who invokes the discriminatory challenge, there can be no doubt that the harm is the same—in all cases, the juror is subjected to open and public racial discrimination."[75] A third competing interest, according to the Court, is that of the entire community in barring conduct that undermines public confidence in the integrity of criminal proceedings. In Justice Blackmun's words, the "selection procedures that purposefully exclude African Americans from juries [be it at the hands of the State or the defense] undermine that public confidence—as well they should."[76]

Although the facts of *McCollum* did not squarely present the question of whether a *black* defendant should be permitted to discriminate racially in using peremptory challenges, several courts have concluded that the answer is no.[77] But the prospect of depriving black defendants of a device with which they could more likely ensure the seating of at least some blacks on their juries creates a fascinating and unlikely alliance between Justice Sandra Day O'Connor, Justice Clarence Thomas, and the NAACP Legal Defense and Educational Fund (LDF). All three decry disabling black defendants from peremptorily challenging whites for the purpose of opening up space on juries for blacks. Observing that "conscious and unconscious racism can affect the way white jurors perceive minority defendants . . . [and that there] is substantial reason to believe that the distorting influence of race is minimized on a racially mixed jury,"[78] Justice O'Connor proceeded to quote affirmatively from the amicus curiae brief submitted by the LDF:

> The ability to use peremptory challenges to exclude majority race jurors may be crucial to empanelling a fair jury. In many cases . . . [t]he only possible chance the defendant may have of having any minority jurors on the jury that actually tries him will be if he uses his peremptories to strike members of the majority race.[79]

For his part, Justice Thomas maintained that "black criminal defendants will rue the day that this Court ventured down this road that inexorably will lead to the elimination of peremptory strikes."[80]

In fact, though, the seeming alliance between O'Connor, Thomas, and the LDF was likely a mirage. After all, neither O'Connor nor Thomas expressly urged that black defendants be treated differently, more permissively, than white ones, and given their stance toward racial affirmative action it would have been very surprising had they done so.*

Rather, they argued that it was improper for the Supreme Court to use the federal constitution to preclude *any* defendant from using peremptory challenges in the way he saw fit. It was probably only for ironic effect and rhetorical flair that they buttressed their main point with the supplemental claim that constitutional regulation of defendants' peremptory challenges would also, indeed especially, have negative consequences for black defendants.

LDF went further, arguing that even if white defendants were prohibited from using racially motivated peremptory challenges, such a limitation ought not be imposed on black defendants.[81] LDF maintained that in many black-defendant cases in which white prospective jurors are peremptorily challenged by defense counsel, the purpose is not "to rid a jury of all members of a particular racial group because of animosity towards them . . . but rather to include persons who would otherwise not sit."[82]

LDF's position is predicated on a belief at odds with the portrayal of

---

*After all, both Justices O'Connor and Thomas have been in the forefront of jurists who insist that all racial distinctions, including so-called benign racial distinctions, be subjected to strict scrutiny. Justice Thomas, moreover, has insisted that all racial distinctions, whatever their intentions, are equally noxious. Given his views, it is surprising to see Justice Thomas suggest that the particular perspective of "black" defendants should have any normative bearing on the constitutional law governing peremptory challenges. His expressed solicitude for black defendants (as opposed to any other type of defendant) seems out of character with his general insistence that the law (including judges) treat all persons the same regardless of race.

That Justice O'Connor is primarily interested in containing the state action doctrine rather than defending a conception of racial fairness is shown by her statement

> That the Constitution does not give federal judges the reach to wipe all marks or racism from every courtroom in the land is frustrating to be sure.
> But such limitations are the necessary and intended consequence of the Fourteenth Amendment's state action requirement.

McCollum, 505 U.S. at 69 (O'Connor, J., dissenting). Justice O'Connor, in other words, threw into her dissent any and every argument against the Court's decision, including arguments that were in tension with one another. This is by no means unusual. Often Supreme Court opinions are merely a new set of briefs, distinguished from advocates' briefs mainly by the power of their authors.

the racially discriminatory peremptory challenge that was popularized by opponents during the campaign against peremptories targeting *black* prospective jurors—the portrayal of the racially discriminatory peremptory challenge as necessarily malevolent. Justice Marshall, for example, invariably pictured the racially discriminatory peremptory challenge as either a consequence of a categorical aversion to blacks serving as jurors or a pernicious disbelief in the capacity of black jurors to be impartial, at least in cases with black defendants. Hence, in his *Batson* concurrence, Marshall referred to racially discriminatory peremptory challenges as a "shameful practice" that will be difficult if not impossible to detect and deter because of "conscious or unconscious racism."[83] Subsequently, he suggested that, when a potential juror is peremptorily struck for racial reasons, that juror is being told that his race makes him "too stupid or too biased to serve on a particular jury."[84] Justice Powell presented a similar portrait of the racially discriminatory peremptory, as if only a lawyer deluded by bigotry or racial stereotyping would choose to racially discriminate in shaping a jury. Writing for the Court in *Batson*, Powell invoked the unflattering image of the prosecutor who challenges potential jurors "on the assumption that black jurors as a group will be unable impartially to consider the State's case against a black defendant."[85]

It is simplistic to believe, however, that racially discriminatory peremptory challenges merely reflect prejudice, animosity, or unthinking habit. Bigotry or reflexive allegiance to certain stereotypes surely explains why some attorneys racially discriminate in their use of peremptory challenges. On the other hand, many attorneys, prosecutors as well as defense counsel, racially discriminate in their deployment of peremptory challenges because they reasonably believe that doing so redounds to the benefit of the side they represent. Here again emerges the phenomenon of strategic as opposed to prejudiced racial discrimination. (For other discussion of strategic racial discrimination, see chapter 4.)

Demonizing the racially discriminatory peremptory strike as merely a product of "racism" retards understanding of what prompts attorneys to continue a practice the courts have prohibited. Racial prejudice explains some peremptory challenges. Opponents of the racially discriminatory peremptory challenge have more to worry about, however, than racial prejudice. They also have to contend with the desire of attorneys to prevail—the desire of prosecutors to convict those whom they believe to be guilty of crime and the desire of defense counsel to provide their clients with zealous representation.* Precisely because of the perceived virtuousness of this desire, it may pose more of an impediment to uprooting racially discriminatory peremptory challenges than hostile prejudice or ignorant stereotyping.

The situation of a prosecutor trying a case that turns on the contested testimony of a police officer illustrates the point. That prosecutor is going to want jurors who are most likely to credit the officer's version of events. In light of the poor reputation of police officers in many black communities, it would make sense for the prosecutor to take race into account in seeking as prosecution-minded a jury as possible. More specifically, in the absence of countervailing facts, it would make sense for this prosecutor to peremptorily challenge as many blacks as he could. If a prosecutor learned facts about a particular black juror that suggested that he would likely be equally or even more prosecution-minded than potential white jurors, the prosecutor would be well advised to refrain from striking that particular black candidate. If the prosecutor struck such a juror even in the face of such evidence, he would most likely be showing himself either to be a bigot or the captive of a stereotype. Absent such facts, however, the prosecutor's racially discriminatory conduct might well reflect intelligent strategic decision-making. After all, jury selection in the context of the adversary process is part of a competition. The opposing attorneys do not simply want impartial jurors. They each want jurors who will give their side an edge.†
As Professor William T. Pizzi notes, many, if not most, of the jurors struck by peremptory challenges "will be struck because one of the

---

*Judge Leonard D. Wexler notes that many attorneys confronted with a rule prohibiting them from using racially discriminatory peremptory challenges "will be under enormous pressure to lie regarding their motives. . . . Indeed, it is even possible that an attorney will lie to himself in an effort to convince himself that his motives are legal." *King* v. *County of Nassau*, 581 F.Supp. 493, 501–502 (E.D.N.Y. 1984).

†Here it bears noting that some observers criticize the prosecution in the O. J. Simpson case for having declined to peremptorily challenge black women who were prospective jurors despite information from a jury consultant indicating that, viewed collectively, black women would be less likely than other sectors of the population to vote for conviction. See Jeffrey Toobin, *The Run of His Life: The People v. O. J. Simpson*, 189–194 (1996). However, to have followed the promptings of the jury consultant and strike black women would have constituted a violation of *Batson*. Cf.

lawyers believes that he can obtain [another] juror who will be easier to persuade of the merits of his side of the case. A prosecutor will obviously try to get people on the jury who will be easiest to convince of the merits of the prosecution's case while the defense will try to get jurors who are likely to be sympathetic to the defendant or the defendant's plight."[86]

To return to the issue of whether black defendants should be permitted to use racially discriminatory peremptory challenges, it should now be plain that some of the rhetoric used by those favoring such permission is sentimental obfuscation. The black defendant who uses peremptory challenges to exclude whites in the hope of obtaining blacks on his jury is not doing so in order to empanel a fair jury or to enlarge opportunities for blacks to participate in self-government through jury service. The defendant is doing so because he thinks that that strategy will give him a better chance of escaping conviction. That is an understandable motivation, but one that we should see for what it is—a self-interested rather than societal concern.

A feature of the defendant's motivation, however, is sharpened by a fear that does relate to a fundamental societal concern—a concern about the deficiency of methods by which the legal system purports to protect defendants against racial bias in the jury box. The most important of these methods is voir dire—the process of questioning that elicits information pursuant to which prospective jurors are dismissed for cause, struck by peremptory challenges, or seated on the jury that will decide a defendant's fate.[87] Although voir dire might be effective at times in unearthing important information about jurors,[88] it is often carried out in ways that minimize the possibility of useful information gathering. In many cases, for instance, voir dire is conducted by a trial judge who directs a few broadly worded questions to an entire panel of prospective jurors. Since biases of various sorts have been widely stigmatized, a prospective juror may be dissuaded from revealing a prejudice before an assemblage of fellow citizens.* Since some biases are unknown to those

---

Christopher Darden with Jess Walter, *In Contempt* 169 (1996) ("It is hard to stomach the hypocrisy of those people who criticize Johnnie Cochran for 'playing the race card,' yet would have had . . . [the prosecution] avoid black jurors").

*Commenting on a defense attorney's insistence upon asking prospective jurors in a death penalty case whether they could render a fair verdict irrespective of the black

who harbor them, it may require more than a casual question or two to unearth traces of the prejudice. It may require concerted, repeated, forceful probing that many judges are unwilling or unable to pursue. At present, however, rules of procedure permit judges considerable control over the content of questions at voir dire and over who gets to pose them. In many jurisdictions, judges can decide to conduct the voir dire themselves without any participation by the attorneys, a situation that frequently begets superficial questioning.[89] Superficial questioning is detrimental because it lessens the possibility of gathering information that may disqualify a juror for cause or permit an attorney in considering his peremptory challenges to reach conclusions based on evidence as opposed to stereotype.

The Supreme Court has ruled that, under certain circumstances, the constitutional requirements of due process and the provision of an impartial jury demand that judges permit inquiry into whether prospective jurors harbor racial prejudice. In *Ham* v. *South Carolina*,[90] for example, the Court reversed a conviction for illegal possession of marijuana after a trial judge declined to ask jurors any questions related specifically to prejudice against Negroes.* The defendant was a black civil rights activist who charged that he had been framed by law en-

---

defendant's race, Professor Albert W. Alschuler responds sarcastically: "One doubts that Lester Maddox, Orville Faubus, George Wallace, Theodore Bilbo or anyone else would have responded to the proposed question by confessing a bias likely to affect his or her resolution of a capital murder case." "The Supreme Court and the Jury: Voir Dire, Peremptory Challenges, and the Review of Jury Verdicts," 56 *University of Chicago Law Review* 153, 160 (1989). Professor Sheri Lynn Johnson is similarly skeptical, noting wryly that "when the distinguished white-haired, black-robed judge seated above the jurors (and below the American flag) asks 'Do you have any racial prejudice that will prevent you from rendering a fair verdict?' honest responses may be . . . inhibited." "Black Innocence and the White Jury," 83 *Michigan Law Review* 1611, 1675 n. 348 (1985).

*Defense counsel asked the trial judge to ask the panel of prospective jurors the following race-related questions:

    1. Would you fairly try this case on the basis of the evidence and disregarding the defendant's race?

    2. You have no prejudice against Negroes. Against black people? You would not be influenced by the use of the term "black"?

Ham v. *South Carolina* 409, U.S. 524, 525 n. 2.

forcement officers who were "out to get him" because of his racial politics. The Supreme Court held that, on these facts, the trial court was obliged to make some inquiry about the possible racial bias of potential jurors.* The Court emphasized, though, that the nature of the inquiry would be left up to the discretion of the trial judge.

It appeared initially that *Ham* might mean that judges were constitutionally obligated to make or permit inquiries into racial prejudice in any case involving allegations of an interracial crime. That would have been a sensible, uniform, predictable policy whose basis was well articulated by U.S. District Judge Joseph L. Tauro:

> Voir dire examination focused directly on the issue of racial bias is the ultimate means for jogging a venireman's conscience to the point that an acknowledgment of some latent bias might be revealed. It is not a perfect method for ferreting out prejudice, but it is the best we have. And so when a defendant in a case involving allegations of interracial violence requests voir dire interrogation, on the question of racial bias, his request should be granted. He is presumed to be innocent, and is entitled to the best protection the courts have available to ensure that bias and prejudice are not factors in his trial.[91]

Instead of permitting the establishment of a clear per se rule, however, the Supreme Court needlessly complicated matters. In *Ristaino* v.

All that the trial judge was willing to ask prospective jurors were the following questions:
1. Have you formed or expressed any opinion as to the guilt or innocence of the defendant, Gene Ham?
2. Are you conscious of any bias or prejudice for or against him?
3. Can you give the State and the defendant a fair and impartial trial?
Ibid., 526. n. 3.

*The defendant also claimed that the trial judge was constitutionally obligated to inquire whether prospective jurors were biased against bearded people since he wore a beard. The Supreme Court ruled, however, that the trial judge did not have to make inquiries into prejudice against beards. See *Ham*, 409 U. S. at 527–528. Justices William O. Douglas and Thurgood Marshall dissented on the issue of the beard, arguing that the defendant was entitled to inquire into anti-beard animus. As Justice Douglas rightly noted: "Taken as an affirmative declaration of an individual's commitment to a change in social values, nonconventional hair growth may become a very real personal threat to those who support the status quo." Ibid. at 530.

Ross,[92] the Court reversed the U.S. Court of Appeals for the First Circuit which had granted federal habeas corpus relief to a black prisoner convicted in a Massachusetts state court for various crimes of violence against a white security guard. *Ham*, the Supreme Court stated, did not stand for the proposition that a defendant was entitled to pose inquiries into racial prejudice in any case involving allegations of interracial crime. Rather, according to the Court, *Ham* merely dictated that only in special circumstances when "[r]acial issues [are] . . . inextricably bound up with the conduct of the trial," must a judge permit direct inquiries into racial prejudice.[93] To complicate matters more, the Court conceded that "the wiser course [for a trial judge is generally] to propound appropriate questions designed to identify racial prejudice if requested by the defendant." Indeed, the Court remarked that it would have required as much from a federal judge.[94] *Ristaino* v. *Ross*, however, was a state court case and the Supreme Court concluded, out of deference to federalism that it should grant state courts more leeway than federal courts in running their affairs.

A decade after *Ristaino* v. *Ross*, the Supreme Court returned to the problem of racial inquiries in voir dire, further muddying the field. In *Turner* v. *Murray*,[95] the Court encountered a situation in which a black man was charged with murdering a white jeweler during the course of a robbery. Defense counsel requested that the trial judge ask prospective jurors a list of questions including the following:

> The defendant, Willie Lloyd Turner, is a member of the Negro race. The victim, W. Jack Smith, Jr., was a white Caucasian. Will these facts prejudice you against Willie Lloyd Turner or affect your ability to render a fair and impartial verdict based solely on the evidence?[96]

The judge declined to ask this question and instead asked prospective jurors in groups of five: "Do any of you know any reason whatsoever why you cannot render a fair and impartial verdict in this case, either for the defendant or for the Commonwealth of Virginia?" All answered "no." A jury of eight whites and four blacks, with one of the blacks serving as the jury foreman, then proceeded to convict Turner and sentence him to death.

A federal court of appeals, relying upon *Ristaino*, held that the defendant was not constitutionally entitled to an inquiry into prejudice and therefore affirmed the conviction and death sentence. The Supreme Court delivered a bewildering compromise. It affirmed the conviction, saying that with respect to the guilt phase of the trial, Turner's case was indistinguishable from *Ristaino*. However, the Court vacated Turner's death sentence. It held that because "the risk of racial prejudice infecting a capital sentencing proceeding is especially serious in light of the complete finality of the death sentence," a defendant accused of an interracial capital crime "is entitled to have prospective jurors informed of the race of the victim and questioned on the issue of racial bias."[97]

This compromise attracted sharp attacks from opposite sides. On one side, Justice Powell (joined by Justice Rehnquist) argued that, despite the possibility of a death sentence, there were no special circumstances present in the *Turner* case to create a constitutional obligation upon the trial judge to make inquiries into racial prejudice if, in his sound discretion, he believed that such inquiries were not required for an effective voir dire. Justice Powell complained, moreover, that the Court's new per se requirement "amount[ed] to a constitutional presumption that jurors in capital cases are racially biased" and that such a presumption "unjustifiably suggest[ed] that criminal justice . . . is meted out on racial grounds."[98] His complaint is ridiculous; one wishes that he had been as vigilant in rectifying cases of racial bias as he was in assuaging the hurt feelings of those whom he perceived as wrongly accused of racial bias. The Court did not presume that the prospective jurors were racially biased. Rather, it recognized a point that cannot intelligently be denied: that in the United States, not to mention Virginia (a state steeped in a notably harsh history of racial oppression), there is an enhanced risk that racial prejudice may affect the judgment of prospective jurors in an interracial murder in which a death sentence is a possible punishment. (For discussion of race relations and the death penalty, with special attention to Virginia, see pp. 312–16.) In light of that enhanced risk and the peculiar finality of capital punishment, the Court prudently concluded that inquiries into racial prejudice must be made in the event that defense counsel request them.

The real problem with *Turner* is highlighted by Justice Brennan (joined by Justice Marshall) who objected to the Court's unwillingness to vacate the conviction on the same grounds that it vacated the death sentence. "Although clearly half right," Justice Brennan observed, the

Court "is even more clearly half wrong."[99] Justifying its decision to vacate the death sentence, the Court alluded to subtle prejudices that might have been revealed by a voir dire that included at least some inquiry into racial attitudes, biases that might have inclined a juror to be more willing to sentence Turner to death. Justice Brennan noted, however, the Court's failure to explain why these same possible biases should be of such less concern at the guilt phase as opposed to the sentencing phase of the trial to warrant affirming the conviction but vacating the punishment:

> Might not those same racial fears that would incline a juror to favor death not also incline a juror to favor conviction? . . . Does the Court really mean to suggest that the constitutional entitlement to an impartial jury attaches only at the sentencing phase? Does the Court really believe that racial biases are turned on and off in the course of one criminal prosecution?[100]*

The Supreme Court's decisions governing the obligation to make inquiries into racial bias during voir dire have created one per se rule (in interracial capital cases defendants are entitled to inquiry) and a series of fact-specific decisions that are difficult to decipher and apply. As a result, practices vary, mainly in the wrong direction. A regrettably tiny number of state courts have embraced the rule that the Supreme Court should have adopted—the proposition that defendants are entitled to probe for racial bias in any case involving interracial violent crimes.[101] Many more states grant the leeway offered to trial judges by *Ristaino* and require special circumstances before mandating that judges accede to defense requests for probes into racial prejudice. Some of these states,

---

*The end of Justice Brennan's stirring dissent warrants notice:

> The Court may believe that it is being Solomonic in "splitting the difference" in this case. . . . But King Solomon did not, in fact, split the baby in two, and had he done so, I suspect that he would be remembered less for his wisdom than for his hard heartedness. Justice is not served by compromising principles in this way. I would reverse the conviction as well as the sentence in this case to insure compliance with the constitutional guarantee of an impartial jury.

Turner v. Murray, 476 U.S. 28, 44 (1986) (Brennan, J., dissenting).

reading *Ristaino* narrowly, permit judges to decline to probe for racial bias even in contexts that scream for such attention. The South Carolina Supreme Court's decision in *State* v. *Jones*[102] is illustrative. In that case a black man was convicted of various offenses, including rape. The alleged assailant's victims were white women. His defense counsel requested that the trial judge ask prospective jurors: "Would the fact that the defendant is black make it more difficult for you to render a verdict in his favor than if he was white?"[103] The judge refused, and instead asked, "Are you conscious of any bias or prejudice against the defendant?," and similarly broad questions, none of which mentioned racial bias specifically.* In light of the notorious history of racial injustice heaped upon black men accused of sexual crimes against white women, one might have thought that a judge would feel obliged to make sure that no plausible objection could be raised to proceedings involving this most volatile, delicate, and wrenching of all interracial criminal dramas. What makes the fight over voir dire in some of these even more puzzling is the modesty of the defendants' requests. Clearly judges should govern voir dire and reject questions that are needlessly burdensome or intrusive. But in *Jones* and similar cases the defendants' requests were minimal and should have been accommodated. All they were asking was that judges permit some, albeit small, probing into racial attitudes so that information elicited might permit the more intelligent deployment of peremptory challenges and other strategies.† The stubbornness with which judges at every level have fought to protect their discretionary turf against even a minimal amount of defendant entitlement reflects poorly on the judiciary.

Voir dire as practiced is a deficient method of protecting defendants

---

*The judge also asked, "Do you have any reason why you could not sit as an impartial juror?" and "Can you give the defendant a fair and impartial trial, based upon the law and the facts of the case?" *State* v. *Jones*, 233 S.E. 2d 287, 289 (S.C. 1977).

†Professor Alschuler cautions, however, that information gathering is not the only use to which lawyers put voir dire. Attorneys also use it to impress upon prospective jurors certain ideas that they want jurors to remember. See "The Supreme Court and the Jury" at 158–159. However, opening up voir dire to the point of permitting questions that offer some realistic possibility of revealing juror unfitness or even the hint of juror unfitness would not permit lawyers to indoctrinate jurors. After all, under the per se rule I favor, judges would still control the tenor and pace of voir dire.

against biased jurors. This deficiency, moreover, is not fully remedied by other means of protection—prohibiting racial appeals, instructing jurors to be impartial, or reviewing allegations of juror misconduct. As we shall see, these methods, too, are porous. (See chapter 8.) The way to address this large and urgent problem, however, is not to etch yet another race line in American law by allowing black but not white defendants to make racially discriminatory peremptory challenges. Such a line will attract the difficulties, misunderstandings, resentments, and countermobilizations that all other race lines have encountered. The better way is to enforce antidiscrimination norms stringently, demonstrating in practice as well as rhetoric a thoroughgoing commitment to treat all persons the same and with dignity before the law, regardless of race. Failure to do this will invite not only renewed calls for special racial protections for black defendants and hence the entrenchment of racial distinctions, but also subversion of the legal system, a problem to which I shall return. (See chapter 8.)

The Future of the Racially Discriminatory Peremptory Challenge

For all its faults, the Supreme Court has taken the country in the right direction by outlawing racially discriminatory peremptory challenges. Continuing to permit them would have allowed some prosecutors to use the strike as the functional equivalent of a law that excluded or minimized jury service by blacks for the purpose of confining authority to whites. Nothing could constitute a more flagrant violation of the nation's promise to treat all persons with equal respect. The Court has acted properly, too, in barring *all* racially discriminatory peremptory challenges, because, as *Swain* confirms, it is often difficult to disentangle prejudiced racial discrimination from strategic racial discrimination aimed at securing a desired result in a particular circumstance.

Even if it were possible for judges to distinguish easily and confidently between prejudiced racial discrimination and strategic racial discrimination, the Court would still be correct in outlawing *all* racial discrimination. The benefits of permitting strategic racial discrimination are not worth the costs. When both the defense and the prosecution have used their peremptory challenges in a racially discriminatory but strategically sensible way, it may be that they have accomplished a good: removing from the trial jury extremes of predilection, thereby creating a jury more likely to agree on one verdict or another than a jury formed without the molding of racially discriminatory peremptory challenges. Assuming that to be true, however, one must balance against that good the costs of permitting lawyers to exclude prospective jurors on a racial basis. A major cost is the public perception that the judicial system is unwilling to disentangle itself from the race line and that race not only matters but *should* matter in the adjudication of guilt or innocence. The case for prohibiting defendants' use of racially discriminatory peremptory challenges is weaker than the case for prohibiting prosecutors' use of racially discriminatory strikes.[104] That distinction, however, should not create a difference in result. The central problem, the toxic effects of racially discriminatory decisionmaking in our legal-political culture, is the same.

Although the Supreme Court has pointed the legal system in the right direction by prohibiting racially discriminatory peremptory challenges, how should that rule be enforced?

The current regime, which largely depends on objections raised by parties, imposes the heavy expense of case-by-case investigation and litigation.[105] One could reasonably conclude, however, that the present situation, although costly, cumbersome, and messy, is preferable to further reform in light of uncertainties about alternatives.

Another response might be to encourage or force trial judges to be more exacting in their review of the conduct of attorneys. Several thoughtful commentators maintain that judges tend to be far too willing to believe the race-neutral rationales offered to explain strikes which are allegedly racial.[106] They recommend, in part, that judges reject purely subjective rationales—a juror gave an attorney a "bad feeling" or made the lawyer feel "uncomfortable" or was too "casual"—unless the trial judge independently confirms that the juror in question acted noticeably differently from other eligible jurors or unless the subjective judgment is otherwise supported by some sort of tangible evidence in the record. Similarly, they recommend that judges examine the consistency of attorneys' race-neutral explanations. For instance, if an attorney strikes a black juror because of advanced age, the judge should determine whether other jurors as old or even older were left undisturbed by the attorney in question.

Some courts have already adopted these and similar recommendations. The negative side of this approach is that it raises court costs; the more scrutiny that trial judges give to attorneys and the more scrutiny that appellate judges give to trial judges, the more expensive trials become. The positive side is that intensification of scrutiny will likely reveal prohibited racial discrimination that might otherwise remain successfully camouflaged, deter racial discrimination that would otherwise surface, and openly signal to all that the legal system is committed to enforcing worthy norms that the Supreme Court has established.

A third response would be to decrease the number of peremptory challenges available to lawyers, thereby diminishing the power of attorneys to exclude an entire racial group, while simultaneously deregulating the peremptory challenge, thereby cutting down on monitoring costs.[107] The great drawback of this proposal is that it would formally permit racial discrimination. Due to the smaller number of peremptory challenges allotted, the resultant discrimination might have lessened impact, but the costs entailed by permitting *any* racial discrimination should doom this alternative. Legislators should not vote for it, and if they do, courts should strike it down as violative of the Equal Protection Clause.

A fourth response, proposed by Justice Marshall and others, is to abolish peremptory challenges.[108] The argument for abolition is propelled by three main points. First, even as modified by *Batson*, peremptory challenges offer attorneys an irresistible temptation to discriminate racially. Second, the effort to police *Batson*'s antidiscrimination rule, in addition to being foiled, adds considerable expense to the process of criminal adjudication. Third, basing peremptory challenges on the traits that many attorneys use as signals of disfavor—ethnicity, religion, residence, political affiliation, employment status—is also socially destructive.[109]

If one concludes, as I do, that the peremptory challenge should be abolished, the question then becomes whether courts or legislatures should extinguish it. As mentioned previously, the Supreme Court has interpreted the Constitution to forbid certain devices which permit the exercise of standardless, unconstrained power. (See pp. 183–84.) The Court, for instance, has invalidated municipal ordinances which permit officials to grant or withhold parade permits without any criteria for doing so. What makes such an ordinance unconstitutional in the Court's

view is that there is no good reason to leave the decisionmaker unconstrained, needlessly opening the door to arbitrariness or wrongful discriminations. By contrast, the peremptory challenge can serve a useful
social purpose, facilitating a quiet but effective means of excluding some
jurors (the proverbial three-dollar bills) who might otherwise avoid exclusion for cause. Moreover, in the post-*Batson* era, the peremptory challenge is no longer unconstrained; the Court has created standards for its
use. For these reasons, judges should not and probably will not take it
upon themselves to abolish the peremptory challenge.* Nor is it likely
that legislatures will abolish the peremptory challenge. Even though, on
balance, the negatives associated with the peremptory challenge outweigh the positives, there appears to be little in the way of effective, sustained political movement in the direction of abolition.

Assuming that the peremptory challenge will remain a part of criminal litigation for the foreseeable future, it is essential that courts enforce
the prohibition against racially discriminatory peremptory strikes more
consistently and forcefully than they have done thus far. If attorneys are
allowed easily to evade the prohibition, their success will generate destructive cynicism.

---

*In *Minetos* v. *City University of New York*, 925 F. Supp. 177 (S.D.N.Y. 1996), Judge
Constance Baker Motley held that peremptory challenges per se violate the Equal
Protection Clause:

> It is time to put an end to this charade. We have now had enough judicial
> experience with the *Batson* test to know that it does not truly unmask racial
> discrimination.... [L]awyers can easily generate facially neutral reasons for
> striking jurors and trial courts are hard pressed to second-guess them....
> After ten years, this court joins in Justice Marshall's call for an end to
> peremptory challenges and the racial discrimination they perpetuate.

Ibid. at 185. *Minetos* is a civil as opposed to a criminal case, but that distinction is immaterial to Judge Motley's conclusion.

Judge Motley's ruling will probably be overturned on appeal. Regardless of its
fate, however, its lineage is fitting: as an attorney (and protegé of Thurgood Marshall) Motley argued *Swain* v. *Alabama*.

7.

Race and the Composition of Juries:
From Antidiscrimination to Imposing Diversity

> *"If white America is too sick and shut in to see that lily-white juries in-spire black cynicism instead of confidence, then until further notice juries in racially charged cases should be half African American."*
> —Derrick Z. Jackson

> *"[B]alancing group bias on the jury is an invitation to jurors to abandon even the attempt to approach the evidence from a disinterested point of view."*
> —Jeffrey Abramson

A MAJOR QUESTION in the background of many present-day race relations controversies is whether merely ceasing to discriminate against racial minorities will suffice to establish racial justice. One camp contends that ceasing to discriminate is enough. Adherents to this view believe that anything more constitutes illicit reverse discrimination against whites.[1] A second camp contends that ceasing to discriminate against blacks, al-beit an essential first step, is insufficient to establish racial justice because blacks continue to be disadvantaged by prejudice and the vestiges of past racial oppression. At the same time, people in the second camp—and this is where I situate myself—are deeply reluctant to use racial criteria in efforts to redress racial disadvantage. This reluctance stems from a judgment about the present and a hope for the future. The judgment is that race-dependent policies are so toxic (producing or reinforcing re-sentments, feelings of superiority and inferiority, and incentives favoring sentiments of racial kinship and solidarity) that they are to be avoided in the absence of a clear showing that such policies are the only way to achieve immediately a goal of compelling importance. The hope is for a society in which color no longer serves as a uniform that places a person in one racial army or another, that no longer delimits the possibilities open to individuals, and that no longer constitutes an important social, moral, or political category. To deal with the problem of ongoing prejudice and the disadvantages bequeathed by past racial oppression, people in the second camp are more willing than people in the first camp to countenance race-dependent positive discriminations but strongly prefer relying on strict enforcement of antidiscrimination norms and nonracial policies that will aid the lower classes in general.[2] The U.S. Supreme Court has teetered for decades between these two camps.

A third camp contends, like the second, that merely ceasing to discriminate against blacks (and other racial minorities) is insufficient to establish racial justice. Unlike individuals in the second camp, however, people in the third enthusiastically embrace discriminations intended to help blacks and other racial minorities. They portray such policies as altogether different from those intended to oppress vulnerable racial groups and maintain that instead of seeking to repress racial consciousness, authorities should seek to manage fairly the interactions of racial groups while helping them retain their distinctive racial identities, perspectives, and sensibilities.[3]

These camps have clashed repeatedly over the role, if any, that racial criteria should play in the organization of schools, employment, business opportunities, and electoral districting. Here I examine the role, if any, that racial criteria should play in the organization of jury service.

Race, Juries, and the Problem of Unintended Underrepresentation

Even in the absence of illegal racial discrimination, traditional methods of jury selection often yield a substantial "underrepresentation" of blacks. By underrepresentation, I mean that the percentage of blacks serving on juries is lower than the percentage of blacks living in the jurisdictions from which jurors are drawn. The underrepresentation of blacks is attributable to a variety of factors.[4] Voter registration lists are the most commonly used source for lists of prospective jurors. For a wide range of reasons, including the systematic discouragement of black voting for many decades, blacks are consistently underrepresented on voter registration lists. Moreover, to be eligible for jury service, one must receive, complete, and return a questionnaire sent to all prospective jurors. Because blacks tend to move more often than whites, a larger percentage of blacks never receive questionnaires that have been mailed to outdated addresses. When receiving questionnaires, blacks, on average, return them at lower rates than whites. Among those who return the questionnaires, larger percentages of blacks than whites are disqualified by subjective and objective criteria. Some jurisdictions, for instance, authorize officials to exclude from consideration for jury service those whom they perceive to be deficient in the understanding of English, in "intelligence," in "integrity," or those who have been convicted of a felony. Subjective criteria open the door wide to the distortions of stereotyping or to the temptation to engage in camouflaged racial discrimination. Even when they are not racially excluded by means of subjective tests, however, blacks tend to be disproportionately excluded by objective tests. For example, larger percentages of blacks than whites fail to finish high school, which is important since some authorities use the completion of high school as a proxy for adequate "intelligence" to be a juror. Similarly, larger percentages of blacks than whites have been convicted for committing felonies, a certification of misconduct that precludes jury service in most (if not all) jurisdictions.

Critics of procedures that yield underrepresentations of blacks and other people of color have responded in several ways. One response has been to attack the constitutionality of criteria that disproportionately exclude blacks from jury service even if that effect is unintentional. Such attacks have been made on the basis of the Fourteenth Amendment and, more recently, the Sixth Amendment. The Fourteenth Amendment, as we have seen, enjoins the states (and by extension the federal government) to provide to all persons "the equal protection of the laws." The Sixth Amendment enjoins the federal government (and by extension the states) to provide to all defendants an impartial jury, which requires, according to the Supreme Court, that juries be selected from a representative cross-section of a given community.[5] Under either of these constitutional headings, the essential argument is the same: the criteria under attack should be invalidated because they disproportionately, albeit un-intentionally, bar blacks without a sufficiently good justification for their racially disparate consequence.

Courts have dismissed virtually all such attacks. They have dismissed complaints founded upon the Fourteenth Amendment because, as noted previously, the Supreme Court has determined that a disproportionate racial effect alone does not give rise to a constitutional violation of antidiscrimination norms. Rather, to be invalidated under the Fourteenth Amendment, a policy or decision must be shown to have been initiated or sustained with a racially discriminatory *intent*.[6]

Courts have also dismissed many complaints founded on the Sixth Amendment. Unlike the Fourteenth Amendment, the Sixth Amendment requires no showing of discriminatory intent. According to the Supreme Court, a person may establish a prima facie violation of the Sixth Amendment by showing that challenged criteria disproportionately bar a distinctive demographic group from jury service. The government, however, may rebut the complainant's prima facie case by showing that "a significant state interest [is] manifestly and primarily advanced" by criteria creating the disproportionate exclusion.[7] In most cases of attacks on objective criteria for jury service, such as being registered to vote, being a citizen, or having a record free of a felony conviction, courts have ruled that the criteria in question advance a significant governmental interest.[8]

Although many observers have criticized these rulings,[9] the courts have ruled correctly. In upholding the challenged criteria, courts have neither required nor endorsed them. In affirming the constitutionality of the criteria at issue, all that courts have declared is that these standards for eligibility are permissible. More substantively, it should be recognized that there is reason (albeit debatable reason) behind relying upon the challenged criteria: the belief that although jury service should be made widely available to members of the polity, it should not be made available to *all* but only to those who can meet certain minimal qualifications. The rhetoric of "inclusion" has induced some critics of existing policy to forget apparently that jury service entails (or should entail) the application of certain abilities that some persons, unfortunately, do not have. One would suppose that even the most enthusiastic inclusionist would concede that insane persons could properly be barred from the jury pool on the grounds that elected representatives should be permitted to declare that jurors need sanity to adjudicate the rights and liberties of their neighbors fairly. One would suppose that this concession would be made even if it were shown that this criterion—sanity—disproportionately excluded blacks or some other historically oppressed racial minority.

Federal law requires potential jurors to be able to speak English and to have sufficient proficiency in writing English to complete the juror qualification form satisfactorily. These criteria have attracted the condemnation of those who complain that it may "exclude disadvantaged groups that are disproportionately nonwhite, and serve little purpose in many cases because trial testimony is almost exclusively oral and jurors generally are not permitted to take notes."[10] Surely, however, elected representatives should be able to require jurors to speak, read, and understand the language in which the proceedings are conducted. It does not matter that in many cases the trial testimony is almost exclusively oral. What about those cases in which it is vital for jurors to examine written evidence? What about those cases in which it is unclear beforehand what sort of evidence will be presented? Can critics plausibly argue that the constitutionality of a requirement for jury service should vary according to the type of evidence that attorneys will present at trial? To argue that a racially disproportionate rate of exclusion should prohibit any literacy requirement for jurors as a matter of federal constitutional law is to carry concerns about racial disparities too far.

The same goes for the contention that prohibiting felons or people charged with committing felonies from jury service violates the Sixth or Fourteenth Amendment. True, the felony bar disproportionately excludes blacks. There is, however, a good reason for the exclusion. Those who have been charged with or convicted of committing felonies are likely to bear a grudge against the criminal justice system. Furthermore, in the vast majority of instances, committing a serious crime can properly be seen as a disturbing sign of personal irresponsibility.

A similar argument involves constitutional attacks on the practice of using voter registration lists as the sole source for jury pools. Critics complain that the practice merely spreads the problem of minority underrepresentation on voting lists to the jury system. Proponents defend exclusive use of voter registration lists on the grounds that doing so provides a prudent, unobtrusive, and inexpensive screening device that eliminates those persons insufficiently interested in civic affairs to vote or even to make themselves eligible to vote. Justice Stanley Mosk of the California Supreme Court pressed this point forcefully:

> Any citizen . . . who steadfastly ignores or avoids his simple civic duty to register and vote would be likely to ignore or avoid his more onerous civic duty to serve on a jury. And if he were by some means identified and reluctantly compelled to perform jury service he would in all likelihood not be a conscientious juror, a circumstance that might adversely affect a criminal defendant's right to be tried by a serious and objective trier of fact.[11]

Some critics of Mosk's position assert that there are no facts proving that people who register to vote are more likely to be conscientious jurors than those who fail or decline to register to vote.[12] That criticism is true. However, many of the most important and sound judgments that authorities make are based on intuitions nourished by experience rather than scientific empirical study. There are probably no empirical studies showing that recidivist bank robbers would be less likely than other persons to be conscientious jurors. Yet it cannot be seriously maintained that authorities cannot properly exclude recidivist bank robbers from jury service until this belief is supported by demonstrable evidence.

Racial disparities stemming from the operation of non-racial criteria do often reflect the vestiges of past racial discrimination. Nevertheless, so long as officials do not impose criteria for a discriminatory purpose, courts should permit them to determine whether, or to what extent, they wish to place jury selection procedures in the service of righting historic wrongs. In their rebellion against illicit selection schemes, some critics have gone to the untenable extreme of denouncing virtually all criteria in favor, apparently, of unbounded representation on juries. Critics of existing criteria sometimes sound as if they believe that inclusion or diversity or rectifying past racial injustice were the *only* values that should concern the citizenry. As important as these values are, however, they compete with others, including the value of a jury system peopled by citizens in whom society can confidently rely to bring knowledgeable and independent judgment to bear on decisions that directly affect the lives of all members of the community. To allow the flexibility and experimentation needed to attain an appropriate balance, courts considering claims under the Sixth and Fourteenth amendments should continue to do what they have essentially been doing: refrain from striking down existing rules of jury selection in the absence of a showing that a given selection scheme was or is animated by discriminatory intent.

Racially Reserved Seats on Juries?

Some people believe that a just system of jury selection requires not only the absence of discrimination against blacks as jurors but also affirmative measures to *ensure* their inclusion. The 1880 Supreme Court decision in *Virginia* v. *Rives*[13] provides an early illustration of this belief. *Rives* involved two black men charged with murder. The defendants argued that they were entitled to a jury on which at least one-third of the jurors would be black. According to the Court, the defendants "alleged that a strong prejudice existed in the community of the county against them, independent of the merits of the case, and based solely upon the fact that they are negroes, and that the man they were accused of having murdered was a white man. From that fact alone they were satisfied that they could not obtain an impartial trial before a jury exclusively composed of the white race."[14]

The defendants had reason to believe that their argument might prevail, that the Supreme Court might rule that, at least in cases involving allegations of interracial violence, defendants are entitled not only to a process that refrains from purposefully excluding people of the defendant's race but also to a process that intentionally includes some jurors of that race. For a long period in England certain sorts of litigants were entitled to juries composed of at least some people whom these litigants regarded as peers.[15] In twelfth-century England, for example, the Crown decided that Jews sued by Christians were entitled to juries on which 50 percent of the jurors were Jewish. Later, English authorities provided alien merchants with the right to have juries on which half the seats were occupied by their countrymen, if a sufficient number could be found. This tradition of mixed juries was brought to the English North American colonies. In 1674, in the Plymouth Colony, when several Indians were tried for murdering another Indian, six Indians were added to the jury that decided the defendants' fates. In 1823, at the trial of an alien charged with murder and piracy, Chief Justice John Marshall granted the defendant's motion for a mixed jury on which half the seats were reserved for aliens.*

Despite this history, the Supreme Court in *Rives* rejected the defendant's claim, stating that "[a] mixed jury . . . is not essential to the equal protection of the laws."[16] *Rives*, however, involved only the assertion that racially mixed juries are constitutionally obligatory; it did not reach the question of whether laws mandating racially mixed juries are constitutionally permissible. That question is of importance because currently a growing number of judges, jury commissioners, legislators, and scholars are instituting or proposing reforms that use racial criteria to require, or at least promote, racial diversity on American juries.[17] One proposal would instruct judges to take racial demographics into account in determining the locale to which cases should be transferred when they conclude that defendants cannot receive a fair hearing at the original place of trial. The impetus for this reform stems from the belief that,

---

*During Reconstruction, South Carolina passed a statute requiring the apportioning of jurors according to the number of black and white voters in a given locale, a provision that would have assured the presence of at least some blacks in most if not all parts of the state. See Eric Foner, *Reconstruction: America's Unfinished Revolution, 1863–1877*, 358 (1988); Charles S. Mangum, Jr., *The Legal Status of the Negro* 311 (1940).

A century later, the Black Panther party demanded that black defendants be tried by black juries, arguing that the only true peers of black defendants were other black people:

> We want black people when brought to trial to be tried by members of their peer group, and a peer group being one that comes from the same economic, social, religious, historical, and racial background . . . [we want] black people from the black community to sit upon the jury. [We want] them mothers who have been working twenty years in Miss Anne's Kitchen. . . . [We want] them hard-working fathers . . . some of them brothers who stand on the block out there wondering where they're going to get a gig.

Bobby Seale, "The Platform of the Black Panther Party," in *A Documentary History of the Negro People in the United States*, vol. 7, *From the Alabama Protests to the Death of Martin Luther King, Jr.*, 538–539 (Herbert Aptheker, ed., 1994). See also Note, "The Case for Black Juries," 79 *Yale Law Journal* 531 (1970); Diane Potash, "Mandatory Inclusion of Racial Minorities on Jury Panels," 3 *Black Law Journal* 80 (1973); Daniel W. Van Ness, "Preserving a Community Voice: The Case for Half-and-Half Juries in Racially-Charged Criminal Cases," 28 *John Marshall Law Review* 1 (1994).

especially in a case implicating racial conflict, it is unfair to move the trial of a person who would most likely be judged by a jury of a given racial composition to a locale where he will most likely be tried by a jury of a far different racial composition. Primarily, prompting this reform is dissatisfaction with a state of affairs in which white defendants facing trial in predominantly black or racially mixed areas are permitted to change venue to locales that are predominantly white.

A second reform involves the use of racially targeted mailing.[18] In some jurisdictions where racial minorities are underrepresented on jury rolls, officials have sent questionnaires to predominantly minority residential areas, organizations, and churches in an effort to elevate the number of minorities who complete the questionnaires.

A third proposal involves subtracting names of prospective jurors of a majority race in order to put the list in overall racial "balance." For instance, according to the Jury Selection Plan for the U.S. District Court for the Eastern District of Michigan,

> if the Court determines that a cognizable group of persons is sub-
> stantially overrepresented in the qualified jury wheel, the Chief
> Judge shall order the Clerk to remove randomly a specific number
> of names so that the population of each cognizable group in the
> qualified wheel closely approximates the percentage of the popula-
> tion of each group in the area of each place of holding court, accord-
> ing to the most recently published national census report.[19]

A fourth proposal involves a yet more direct effort to insure racially integrated juries. Under this proposal, judges would set aside a certain number of seats for racial minorities. At least one locale has already implemented this proposal with respect to *grand* juries. In Hennepin County, Minnesota, local authorities require judges to select at least two minority grand jurors for every grand jury.[20]* No legislature has

---

*The situation in Hennepin County bears noting. Although 9 percent of the county's adult population in 1990 were people of color, racial minorities constituted only 5.3 percent of the persons who sat on grand juries. In 40 percent of the cases, all-white grand juries determined whether to indict suspects; 71 percent of the criminal suspects were people of color; 66 percent of the victims of crime were people of color. See Albert W. Alschuler, "Racial Quotas and the Jury," 44 *Duke Law Journal* 704, 709 n.23 (1995).

yet enacted a law stipulating that *trial* juries must contain a certain minimum number of minority jurors. Some observers, however, insist that legitimacy and fairness demand a guarantee of racially integrated trial juries. Legislators in at least one state—Pennsylvania—have proposed a bill that would mandate a certain number of trial jurors who share the race of the defendant or victim.[21]

Proponents of these reforms argue that underrepresentation is a social evil in part because it increases the likelihood of all-white juries. Professor Albert W. Alschuler begins his argument in favor of racial quotas for juries by asserting that "few statements are more likely to evoke disturbing images of American criminal justice than this one: 'the defendant was tried by an all-white jury.' "[22] He and others find this prospect disturbing because, as we have seen, all-white juries have been complicit in terrible instances of racial injustice, convicting innocent black defendants because of Negrophobic animus or acquitting guilty white defendants because of feelings of white racial solidarity. Reformers fear, moreover, that even in the absence of mobilized racial bias, all-white juries will be far less able than juries that are racially mixed to perform appropriately the difficult tasks they are called upon to do. As editors of the *Harvard Law Review* put it, "Without the broad range of social experiences that a group of diverse individuals can provide, juries are often ill-equipped to evaluate the facts presented."[23]

The theory of reformers is that racial diversity in the jury room makes accessible to all the jurors useful knowledge, perspectives, and intuitions that may be absent from a monochromatic jury. Justice Marshall maintained, for example: "When any large and identifiable segment of the community is excluded from jury service, the effect is to remove from the jury room qualities of human nature and varieties of human experience, the range of which is unknown and perhaps unknowable."[24] A related belief is that racial diversity in the jury room inhibits the expression of prejudices—"I know he did it because that's the way niggers are"—which, left unchecked, tend to shortcut careful deliberation.[25] Justice O'Connor asserts, for instance, that there is substantial reason to believe that the distorting influence of race is minimized on a racially mixed jury.[26]

Some commentators also argue that, regardless of the performance of a jury, many onlookers will deny a verdict's legitimacy in any case involving interracial conflict if the jury contains no blacks. It is not simply the substance of verdicts that has led observers to doubt the guilt of many black defendants tried before all-white juries; it is also the absence of black participation on the juries that issued the verdicts. Similarly, it was not simply the substance of the verdict that triggered rioting in the aftermath of the first trial of the police officers who beat Rodney King; it was that no blacks participated in finding an absence of criminal wrongdoing on the part of the officers.

Another argument of some reformers is that underrepresentation of blacks on juries is harmful because jury service teaches habits of good citizenship and forges closer bonds to the civic order. Therefore, excluding blacks from jury service weakens an important sector in America's multiracial polity and harms the fabric of the society as a whole. Precisely because blacks have long suffered racial exclusion from governance, it is especially urgent to integrate them fully and quickly to counteract the cynicism, distrust, and hostility that invidious discrimination breeds in its victims (and often the children of its victims, even though these children are themselves no longer directly victimized).

Although these arguments are substantial, on balance they are outweighed by countervailing considerations. In the first place, officials could reduce much of the underrepresentation through policies that impose no formal racial distinctions. Since some (probably small) amount of underrepresentation stems from purposeful racial exclusion that is hidden from view by subjective, discretionary selection schemes, localities could switch to selection schemes that are more transparent and mechanical and thus less prone to racially motivated abuse. Since some (probably large) amount of underrepresentation stems from the exclusionary effect of race-neutral criteria such as appearance on a voter registration list, a locality could delete such criteria, make it easier for people to satisfy the criteria (e.g., make it easier to register to vote), or create other ways of obtaining names of potential jurors. For instance, a locality could supplement the list of registered voters with lists of persons who have obtained driver's licenses or paid local taxes. Localities could also make jury service less burdensome by paying greater compensation, prohibiting employers from retaliating against employees who serve on juries, and routinely following up on unreturned questionnaires and summonses—race-neutral reforms that would have the effect of enlarging the number of black (as well as other) jurors.

These measures, however, are hardly likely to satisfy reformers strongly committed to the abolition of the all-white jury. For one thing, under current constitutional understandings, local officials are not obligated to establish any of these measures. Furthermore, even if officials implement them, all-white juries would continue to emerge innocently in a certain number of cases because of blacks' relatively small numbers. In a jurisdiction that randomly selects its juries from a population that is 15 percent black, about 14 percent of the juries will contain no blacks.[27]

What about the fear that all-white juries, because of their racial character, render inaccurate verdicts? Professor Sherri Lynn Johnson, one of legal academia's most outspoken critics of the all-white jury, states that there is "strong" evidence "that racial bias frequently affects criminal trials" in which there is a paucity or absence of minority jurors.[28] She bases this conclusion on cases in which jurors explicitly stated that race played a part in their verdicts, on patterns of conviction and sentencing disparities, and most importantly in her view, on mock juror studies. She principally relies on experiments in which researchers found that the willingness of mock jurors of different races to ascribe guilt varies according to the race of defendants and victims. More specifically, these studies indicate that white jurors are more likely than black jurors to convict black defendants and to acquit defendants charged with crimes against black victims.

Although the racial composition of juries surely affects outcomes in certain trials, Professor Johnson overstates her point. Putting aside the methodological controversies that surround the studies that Johnson cites, it is simply impossible to say with confidence how frequently illicit racial concerns presently intrude on jury deliberations.[29] Professor Johnson herself concedes that the quality and quantum of evidence in a given case will likely condition the effect of a jury's racial demographics on a verdict. She hypothesizes that when the evidence is strong one way or another, the racial makeup of the jury probably does not matter. Concomitantly, she hypothesizes that typically it is only in marginal evidence cases that the jury's racial demography matters.[30]* Whether one

---

*Professor Johnson's hypothesis is consistent with similar hypotheses offered by other students of race relations in the administration of criminal law. Professor David C. Baldus hypothesizes, for instance, that racial selectivity in sentencing does not emerge in death penalty cases featuring either the most or the least atrocious

views the problem posed by the all-white jury as large or small will depend in part, then, on how many "marginal evidence cases" are brought to trial—a figure no one really knows.

If due regard is given to difficulties in measuring the risk of misjudgment by all-white juries, it becomes harder to decide whether the costs of the reforms in question will be worth the promised benefits. In order to refine the evaluation, one must ask what the potential costs are of prohibiting all-white juries.

One commentator suggested a cost by remarking that "jurors who have been selected according to race . . . may well believe that they were picked because race is somehow relevant to the process of deliberation and that each race is expected to be partisan along racial lines."[31] Professor J. Van Dyke echoed this concern when he observed: "A juror selected [by a computer selecting a mathematically correct number of members of demographic groups] might feel that she or he is filling some predetermined 'slot' and might attempt to give the view generally associated with those demographic characteristics rather than the juror's personal feelings about the case." Van Dyke identified another potential cost when he noted that "jurors might find it harder to work together as a group because they may be more conscious of their identified differences than the much stronger common bonds that unite them as people."[32] These are plausible risks that should be considered when calculating the desirability of the proposed reforms.

Another cost is the burden that would be associated with administering the suggested reforms. Professor Johnson proposes a reform under which defendants of a given race would have a right to a certain minimum number of "racially similar" jurors.[33] To implement this proposal, officials would have to ascertain the race of defendants and jurors.

---

scenarios (i.e., number of victims, method of killing, and so on). He suggests that racial selectivity emerges in the middle-range of cases where jurors perceive themselves as having the most discretion. For a discussion of the Baldus hypothesis see pp. 341–42. Similarly, Professor James J. Fyfe hypothesizes that racial selectivity does not emerge in police shootings of fleeing felons when police shoot at suspects who incontrovertibly pose a danger to officers or the general public. Fyfe argues that racial selectivity surfaces when police shoot at suspects in more ambiguous circumstances in which police discretion is maximized. See James J. Fyfe, "Blind Justice: Police Shootings in Memphis," 73 *Journal of Criminal Law & Criminology* 707 (1982).

Racial classification has always involved difficulties that our legal system has repressed.[34] In an increasingly multiracial society, controversies over racial classifications will become even more complex, frequent, and vexing. What does the judge do about the person who is part Asian and part black? Is such a defendant entitled to a minimum quota of Asian-Americans or a minimum quota of African-Americans? Is an Afro-Asian juror racially similar to a "plain" African-American? Is a Latino who traces his heritage back to Mexico "racially similar" to a Latino who traces his heritage back to Puerto Rico? Is a person who traces his heritage back to China "racially similar" to an individual who traces his heritage back to Vietnam? Even Professor Alschuler, a stalwart opponent of the all-white jury, concedes that the racial matching entailed by Professor Johnson's proposed reform would be "troublesome."[35]

Alschuler seeks to bypass this trouble with a proposal under which a minimum quota of self-identified "minority persons" would have to be present on all juries. As he recognizes, however, a variety of line-drawing controversies would certainly follow the implementation of such a plan. One controversy would stem from fights over who counts as a "minority person." If a black defendant is on trial in Los Angeles, will the presence of Korean-Americans or Latino-Americans suffice to fill the required quota of minority persons on a jury, despite the intense and widespread racial resentments and prejudices that have led to bitter conflicts among these groups?[36] Members of racial minority groups are frequently prejudiced against members of other minority racial groups.[37] Therefore, placing Latinos or Asian-Americans on a jury with whites trying a black defendant may fall short of the aims articulated by proponents of racial quotas for juries. First, the nonblack racial minorities may fail to protect the jury deliberations against racially selective indifference or hostility. Second, black observers may refrain from granting legitimacy to a guilty verdict rendered by a jury with no black members, even if the jury contains people identified with other racial minority groups.*

---

*For many people, a paradigmatic instance of the problem that the reformers seek to address is the jury in Simi Valley, California, that contained no blacks and that acquitted the police officers charged with criminally assaulting Rodney King. That jury did contain a Latino and an Asian-American. For many observers, however, those jurors did not count as "true" racial minorities; for them, only the presence of African-Americans would have counted. See Albert W. Alschuler, "Recital Quotes and the Jury," 44 *Duke Law Journal* 704, 733 (1995).

Alschuler acknowledges this difficulty. He writes that the appropriateness of grouping minority persons may depend partly on "the extent to which the members of racial and ethnic minorities sense commonalities with one another and on the extent to which other audiences perceive these commonalities." He also notes that "specification of the appropriate group for distinctive treatment may vary with the racial and ethnic characteristics and the social experiences of particular jurisdictions."[38] Alschuler is confident, however, that local officials can be entrusted with the delicate task of mapping the appropriate racial lines. I am not. I do not believe, as does Justice Thomas, that all racial lines are equally dangerous; clearly a race line aimed at excluding all racial minorities from the jury box is different from, and more objectionable than, a race line aimed at insuring the presence of a minimum number of racial minorities on every jury. At least an inclusionary race line has the virtue of indicating dramatically that authorities desire to break with the discredited exclusionary policies of the past. Still, fully conceding that Professor Alschuler's proposal is supported by strong arguments, I nonetheless conclude that, on balance, it would likely turn out to be more harmful than helpful. It would accentuate the significance of race in the minds of all by formally etching a new racial line into our body of laws. Moreover, it would do so on the basis of justifications that suggest that the intended duration of the race line would be permanent as opposed to temporary. After all, if obtaining diversity of viewpoint justifies racial quotas, that justification will always exist so long as America remains multiracial. Furthermore, insofar as the jury quota functions as a sort of insurance policy against whites' prejudice, it validates the charge that Americans of different hues cannot hope to entrust themselves to the fair judgments of one another. The jury quota would therefore likely deepen racial distrust at the very moment it attempts to establish a hedge against racial misconduct.

Race and Change of Venue
(Or, Is Anything Wrong with Simi Valley?)

One possible objection to the argument I am making is that I have focused too much on the most controversial race-sensitive reform proposals and not on race-sensitive reforms that have received the broadest political backing. To address that concern, I shall turn to the proposition that judges should take race into account in deciding where to try cases in circumstances in which the venue of the trial must be changed (typically because pretrial publicity prevents obtaining an impartial jury in the vicinity where the crime occurred).[39] According to this proposition's proponents, a judge should search for a locale that is demographically similar in racial and other terms to the original one. Some judges have already implemented this approach on their own.[40] Legislation enacted or pending in several states directs judges to attend to racial demographics in making trial venue determinations.*

Proponents of this reform point to several cases that, in their view, illustrate the dangers posed by permitting judges to choose the locations of trials without expressly taking into account racial demographics. The most famous of these cases is the initial prosecution of the police officers accused of criminally assaulting Rodney King. When those officers were indicted, they sought a change of venue on the grounds that unfavorable publicity negated the possibility of obtaining an impartial jury in Los

---

*A Florida statute provides that judges must "give priority to any county which closely resembles the demographic composition of the county wherein the original venue would lie." Fla. Laws, ch. 225 (1993). Although this statute does not expressly mention race, there can be no doubt that the legislature intended it to be a consideration and that judges view it as empowering them to consider race in making venue determinations. In 1993, for example, in a case involving the prosecution of white men accused of burning an African-American tourist, the trial judge rejected one city as the new home of the trial because that city's racial composition was insufficiently similar to that of the jurisdiction in which the trial was initially located. See "Trial Is Moved for 2 Charged in Burning of a Brooklyn Man," *New York Times*, June 22, 1993.

Similar legislation, some of which expressly refers to race, has been proposed in New York, New Jersey, Texas, and California, although most of it has failed thus far to win the political support necessary to become law. See Nancy J. King, "Racial Jurymandering: Cancer or Cure?" 68 *New York University Law Review* 720–721 (1993); M. Shanara Gilbert, "An Ounce of Prevention," 67 *Tulane Law Review* 1935–1942 (1993).

The American Bar Association Criminal Justice Standards provide that, in determining where to move a trial, the judge should consider "the racial, ethnic, religious, and other relevant demographic characteristics of the proposed venue, insofar as they may affect the likelihood of a fair trial by an impartial jury." "ABA Standards for Criminal Justice: Trial by Jury," reprinted in 53 *Criminal Law Report* (BNA) 2347, 2348 (September 29, 1993).

Angeles County, the place where the charges were brought. Initially, the trial judge denied the defendants' change of venue motion. A California appellate court, however, required a change of venue.[41] The trial judge then moved the case to the now infamous town of Simi Valley in Ventura County. Whereas Los Angeles County had a black population of about 11 percent, Ventura County had a black population of only about 2 percent. The prosecutor suggested that the judge should select a setting that would "reflect the demographics of the sending county," by which the prosecutor undoubtedly meant the *racial* demographics of the sending county.[42] The judge rejected this suggestion, however, declaring that he was ignoring demographics and considering only such matters as convenience in deciding the new place of trial. Ultimately, a Simi Valley jury of ten whites, a Latino, and an Asian-American acquitted the officers of the most serious charges, thus prompting a massive riot.

Another case reformers often cite is *Mallett* v. *State*.[43] Mallett, a black man, was accused of murdering a white state highway patrolman. Brought to trial initially in a county in southeast Missouri, Mallett's counsel moved for a change of venue. The defense and the prosecution were unable to agree on a new location. Defense counsel requested that the venue be moved to a community in which there would be at least a possibility of blacks sitting on the jury. The judge declined to move the trial to any of the sites recommended by either side. Instead, he transferred venue to a county far north of the original trial site—Schuyler County, a jurisdiction populated by about five thousand whites and *no* blacks. Mallett was convicted there and sentenced to death by an all-white jury.

In subsequent proceedings, a judge vacated Mallett's sentence and ordered that he be retried "in a venue where there is a possibility of blacks being on the jury." Justifying this order, the judge stated that he "need not find that [his colleague] acted with a discriminatory purpose." Instead he found that "an *inference* of discriminatory purpose exists" in the decision to move the case to Schuyler County.[44] He cited the following facts as relevant to his ruling:

> The case involves a cross-racial murder of a state trooper . . . counties which were of equal convenience to witnesses; equally free of pre-trial publicity; of equal, greater, or less distance; and included

blacks were [suggested to the trial judge] by the defense and prosecution; no specific or compelling reason existed to send the case to Schuyler County; there were no blacks living in Schuyler County at the time of trial; [the defendant] is a black man; the defense expressed [a desire that] the county chosen [as the new site for the trial would] include blacks.[45]

The Missouri Supreme Court reversed this ruling on the grounds that the facts listed above did not properly raise an inference that the trial judge had transferred the case to Schuyler County for racial reasons. "It can be assumed," the Missouri Supreme Court concluded, "that venue was changed to Schuyler County in order to get the case moved as far north as possible to a county where reports of [the murder] may have received less attention. There is not the slightest suggestion that race was a consideration in the decision to change the venue to Schuyler County."[46]

Some commentators roundly criticize the Missouri Supreme Court's view that judges need not (and perhaps legally cannot) take race into account in choosing the site for a trial. One objection is that this view fails to protect black defendants, like Mallett, from the prospect of being transferred from a trial site offering the possibility of some participation by black jurors to a trial site offering no such possibility. An accompanying concern is that some defendants might waive their right to seek a change of venue if a consequence of changing venue is the likelihood of standing trial in a locale where there is a much-diminished chance of obtaining racial minorities on the jury. For instance, in another Missouri case, *Young* v. *State*,[47] an attorney representing a black defendant withdrew a request for change of venue because of concern that the case would be transferred to a county containing few blacks.

Other opponents of the prevailing view are primarily mindful of the Rodney King episode. The principal object of their solicitude is not the defendant but rather the community losing jurisdiction over the trial. They contend that judges should take race into account in making venue changes because doing so permits the community where the trial was initially located to be represented in adjudicating the prosecution of persons accused of having violated that community's peace.

Another criticism is that, under the prevailing system, the judiciary fails to detect invidious racial discrimination manifested in venue selections. Justice Marshall's response to *Mallett* is illustrative. Joined by Justice Brennan, Marshall dissented from the Supreme Court's decision to decline to review the Missouri Supreme Court's resolution of the controversy. He contended that the circumstances in *Mallett* presented a prima facie case of purposeful discrimination, adding that the trial judge's decision was "particularly appalling because the defense counsel emphasized . . . that the venue should be one where members of Mallett's race resided, and because the judge should have selected other counties in Missouri that satisfied this valid concern."[48] Although Justice Marshall uses the rhetoric of purposeful discrimination to attack the ruling of the Missouri court, what he actually found "particularly appalling" was the trial judge's refusal to see racial demographics as an essential factor in venue selection. What animated Marshall's dissent was the view that federal constitutional law should (but does not) impose an affirmative obligation to take race into account in making change of venue decisions.

It would be odd, however, for constitutional law to demand that officials take race into account for purposes of deciding venue but not for purposes of deciding the racial composition of trial juries. If the value of racial diversity on juries is sufficiently important to trump federal constitutional law's presumptive prohibition against race-dependent decisionmaking by officials, why stop at only the *possibility* of obtaining black jurors, which is all that the venue decisions can offer? After all, even if judges steer cases to certain locales according to racial demographics, doing so does not *ensure* that blacks will be present on a given trial jury. Through some statistical fluke or a combination of strikes for cause and peremptory strikes, it is possible that an all-white jury could emerge even in a jurisdiction with a relatively large black population. If racial diversity is so important, the law should impose Professor Alschuler's solution of a jury quota, thereby obviating the need to tinker with the rules governing change of venue. On the other hand, if racial diversity is insufficiently important to justify the Alschuler solution, it would seem to be inadequate to justify drawing a race line for purposes of venue selection since the putative gains in racial diversity to be made from this reform would be attenuated by the possibility of ending up with an all-white jury anyway.

The claim that race-minded venue selection is needed to preserve the voice of the community from which a trial is being transferred is also dubious. After all, "every change of venue makes it impossible to have members of the aggrieved community hear the case and apply their values to the proceedings."[49] One reply is that if a racially similar community is chosen as the new venue, "local values might be approximated, thereby preserving . . . the key interests served by local community participation."[50] That *may* be true, but then again it may *not*. In the absence of demonstrable evidence that supports an exception, we should uphold the general rule prohibiting official racial distinctions. An assertion of controversial intuition should not suffice as the basis for etching a race line onto American law. Furthermore, assuming the empirical validity of the assertion, it is unclear why preserving the attenuated voice of an aggrieved community from which a trial has already been removed should be seen as sufficiently weighty to justify a race-minded procedure for selecting the new venue.

One reason might be the reassurance provided by an effort to signal unequivocally a desire to put to an end the days of white supremacy in the administration of criminal law. Such reassurance was poignantly forthcoming in the actions of Judge L. Breland Hilburn of the Hinds County, Mississippi, Circuit Court, when he presided over the trial of Byron De La Beckwith twenty-nine years after the defendant was alleged to have murdered Medgar Evers.[51] At the insistence of defense counsel, Judge Hilburn granted the defendant's motion for a change of venue on account of prejudicial pretrial publicity. Faced with the task of determining where to move the trial, Judge Hilburn stated forthrightly, but without any attempt at justification, that he would choose a new trial site with "close to the same racial balance" as Hinds County, where the killing occurred. Indeed, he said that he "would not consider any jurisdiction where the racial population [was] out of proportion with [Hinds County]."[52] He held the trial in DeSoto County, Mississippi, but held jury selection in Panola County, a jurisdiction with a racial composition similar to Hinds County. The jurors selected in Panola County were transported to and housed in the county where the trial took place. Unlike the two all-white juries that were unable in 1964 to reach a verdict, the 1992 jury composed of four whites and eight blacks convicted De La Beckwith of murder.

The sentiments behind Judge Hilburn's insistence upon finding a racial match for Hinds County are immeasurably better—more egalitarian, respectful, and just—than the sentiments which insured the lily-white character of the juries which judged the defendant in 1964. For that, all persons should be happy and grateful. Still, Hilburn's ruling, tellingly bereft of an articulated justification, is not one on which the legal system should confidently rest. Judge Hilburn accepted the proposition that racial demographics mattered in fact or appearance and then adapted the proceedings to that perceived reality with a race-minded ruling that treated certain jurisdictions differently from other jurisdictions because of racial composition. It is not unreasonable to think that this strategy of adaptation is the best way momentarily to deal with the daunting presence of racial conflict that continues to menace our society. In seeking to deal with that haunting menace by formally creating another race line, however, this adaptation may deepen the race-mindedness that both feeds and is fed by continuing racial conflict.*

What alternatives exist that would be both nonracial and reassuring to people who fear that the present regime permits judges to make subtle invidious racial discriminations harmful to blacks? One alternative would be a rule that strongly privileges the defendant's choice of venue in cases in which trials must be transferred.[53] Another alternative would be a procedure in which objective requirements are established, proposals meeting these requirements are offered by both sides, and a final choice is made by lot. There are probably other alternatives that could be tried that do not involve distinguishing between prospective jurors on the basis of race. In the absence of a detailed and thoroughly con-

---

*Another case from the civil rights era bears mentioning here. In the summer of 1972, Angela Davis, an outspoken black communist, was tried on charges that she had conspired to aid the attempted escape of several prisoners who seized hostages in a court house. An ensuing shoot-out left four persons dead and one seriously injured.

Ms. Davis requested that her trial be moved because of pre-trial publicity and that it be moved to a site that she preferred. The judge granted her motion for change of venue but sent the case to a county to which she had expressly objected. She was tried there. The jury was all white. It acquitted her on all charges. See Note, "Change of Venue in Criminal Cases: The Defendant's Right to Specify the County of Transfer," 26 *Stanford Law Review* 131, 131–132 (1973).

vincing argument that race-minded reforms would clearly improve matters, an argument which includes reasons why nonracial alternatives are inadequate, prudence and the constitutional disfavoring of race-dependent decisionmaking counsels rejecting the imposition of racial distinctions.

Arguing in favor of racial discrimination for the sake of assured racial diversity, Professor Alschuler turns for support to President Clinton's promise to appoint a cabinet that "looks like America."[54] Observing that "when Presidents are elected to office on the basis of promises to make their administrations look like America," Alschuler declares that "making [juries] look [like their jurisdictions] seems legitimate and appropriate."[55] The analogy, however, may not be as helpful as Alschuler hopes. Considerable discord surrounded President Clinton's implementation of his pledge, as certain groups complained that they did not receive their fair share of the available seats—difficulties of the very sort that any racially selective jury reform will invite.[56] Furthermore, there is the deeper question of whether the "looking like America" metaphor is an appropriate guiding aspiration. I do not think that it is. We should seek to look beyond looks. We should seek to require not that juries contain certain numbers of people who are white, brown, yellow, red, or black but simply that juries contain conscientious people committed to doing all that they can to bring about that mysterious quality we know as justice.

Some readers will undoubtedly contend that my rejection of race-dependent policies aimed at facilitating or insuring the presence of blacks on juries indicates that I am minimizing or ignoring the fact that race matters in the administration of criminal law. I agree that, in terms of the current situation, race matters. As I showed in some detail above, present illegal racial discriminations along with the vestiges of racial aggression in the past diminish the number of black jurors. In other words, I agree that, at present, the jury system, *like every American institution*, is affected by racial conflict. The question is what to do about it. Perhaps the most fundamental way in which I differ from at least some of those who back the reforms I oppose is that I believe that racial conflict is not inevitable, that it can be overcome, and that a morally good and politically realistic way to help in doing so is to decline to formalize race-mindedness in jury selection.

Courts and the Future of
Race-Dependent Jury Selection

I have argued that officials should reject proposals for race-dependent jury reforms. In the event that such reforms are implemented, however, how will courts, particularly the Supreme Court of the United States, likely respond?

Relevant case law is sparse. *Brooks* v. *Beto*[57] involved the prosecution of a black man, Willie B. Brooks, who was charged with raping a white woman in Van Zandt County, Texas, in 1959. Brooks was initially indicted by an all-white grand jury from which officials excluded blacks. After a federal appellate court invalidated a conviction in the same county because of the racial exclusion of blacks from a grand jury, the judge presiding over the *Brooks* case appointed new jury commissioners, one of whom was a black woman. The judge appointed her to insure that the names of blacks would be placed on the jury rolls. Two blacks were placed on the jury rolls, and the judge selected these individuals for the new grand jury that reindicted Brooks. In federal habeas corpus proceedings, Brooks attacked his conviction on the grounds that the purposeful *inclusion* of blacks on the grand jury violated the Equal Protection Clause.

The Fifth Circuit Court of Appeals, upholding a district court, affirmed the conviction. The court emphasized the practical difficulties that the state trial judge had faced, particularly the fact that, in the absence of any black grand jurors, the defendant would have had an excellent basis for challenging his conviction. Even if officials had used a race-neutral process to select his grand jury, the historical absence of any blacks on grand juries in the county would have given the defendant a strong basis for a prima facie claim of racial discrimination. The Fifth Circuit also emphasized that the race-dependent action taken by the trial judge and the jury commissioners in Van Zandt County and its acceptance of their action should be seen merely as a remedial response to a specific stubborn pattern of purposeful racial exclusion, similar to the race-specific orders that courts eventually decreed in the face of local resistance to desegregation of public schools. Rejecting the defendant's assertion that the local officials' race-dependent response was itself violative of equal protection, the Fifth Circuit declared:

Adhering to a formula which in words forbids conscious awareness of race in inclusion postpones, not advances, the day when this terrible blight of racial discrimination is exterminated. The challenge is to assure constitutional equality now. This often means, as it did in this case, eradication of the evils of the past. That evil of racial exclusion cannot be ignored. It must be reckoned with in terms which permit, indeed assure, equality for the immediate future. The evil and the evil practices are not theoretical. They are realities. The law's response must therefore be realistic.[58]

Although *Brooks* v. *Beto* can be read to support race-dependent jury selection policies in general, its particular factual situation supports a more limited reading. It emerged from a situation characterized by blatant, stubborn, purposeful racial exclusion and can thus be read as authorizing a race-specific remedy only in such circumstances. Those circumstances, however, are not the ones that spur the appeals of contemporary reformers, for they seek race-specific jury selection policies even in the absence of purposeful racial exclusion.

State v. *Moore*[59] is close to a repeat of *Brooks*. In *Moore*, a black defendant challenged the grand jury that indicted him for murder on the grounds that officials racially excluded blacks in selecting a foreman. Because of the recent overturning of a conviction on precisely these grounds, the judge presiding over Moore's case persuaded the white grand jury foreman to resign. The judge then appointed a black person as grand jury foreman. Under the black foreman, the grand jury reindicted Moore and a jury found him guilty of second-degree murder. The defendant then challenged the conviction on the grounds that the racially selective choice of the black grand jury foreman again invalidated the process under which he was tried. The North Carolina Supreme Court agreed, but did so under the *state* constitution, thereby shedding negligible light on the proper analysis of this issue outside of North Carolina.*

---

*In *Meders* v. *State*, 389 S.E. 2d 320 (1990), the Georgia Supreme Court was faced with a challenge to a jury selection scheme under which officials created "racial balance" by ensuring that every venire mirrored racially the jury list from which the venue was constituted. The Court avoided deciding the issue, ruling that the defen-

Over the past decade, the U.S. Supreme Court has become increasingly hostile to race-dependent public policies, even when they have been defended as efforts to include historically oppressed racial minorities in networks of economic opportunity and self-government. Hence, the Court has ruled that, pursuant to the Constitution, congressional contracting set-aside programs would be subject to a level of judicial scrutiny—"strict scrutiny"—that most, if not all, will probably fail to satisfy.[60] Similarly, the Court has invalidated as violative of the Equal Protection Clause congressional redistricting plans aimed at ensuring the electoral dominance of black voters in at least some number of districts.[61] A central feature of these and similar rulings is an insistence that racial distinctions of any sort are suspect and require exacting judicial examination. These decisions have come from a closely divided Court; only one of two changes in personnel could easily send the Court in a different direction. As things stand now, however, the Supreme Court would likely invalidate the reforms canvassed in this chapter.

In my view, courts should invalidate policies of the sort canvassed in this chapter. This is not to say that the reforms at issue are stupid or malevolent. To the contrary, these proposed reforms reflect good intentions and strong reasoning. They should still be invalidated, however, because courts should permit public racial discrimination only if officials can make a clear case that the discrimination in question is needed on an emergency basis to further a compelling societal interest. Fortunately, no such case can be made for race-dependent jury selection.

---

dant's attorney had failed to preserve it for appellate review. The Court urged officials to avoid manipulating the jury selection process and to be satisfied with a completely random process of selection. A concurring justice averred, however, that as a matter of federal constitutional law, he found nothing wrong with the challenged selection scheme. Distinguishing it from affirmative action plans that disadvantage whites, the justice asserted that the jury selection plan is "race neutral in that it does not give any group a distinct advantage over any other group." Ibid., 326.

8.

Playing the Race Card
in a Criminal Trial

Mulattos, negroes, Malays, whites, millionaires, paupers, princes, and kings, in the courts of Mississippi, are on precisely the same exactly equal footing. All must be tried on facts, and not on abuse. Only impartial trials can pass the Red Sea of this court without drowning. Trials are to vindicate innocence or ascertain guilt, and are not to be vehicles for denunciation.
—Supreme Court of Mississippi

Criminal justice is concerned with the pathology of the body politic. . . . A criminal trial . . . should have the atmosphere of the operating room.
—Felix Frankfurter

HOW SHOULD THE legal system respond if a prosecutor says in a closing argument, "Send these black men to jail for as long as you can; they had no business assaulting that good white woman." How should the system respond if a defense attorney says, "Send a message to the racist establishment by refusing to send your fellow black brother to prison." How should the system respond, in other words, to appeals to racial sentiments voiced by attorneys seeking to obtain desired results in criminal trials? Answering this and related questions is the burden of this chapter.

Prosecutors and Racial Appeals

Appealing to racial sentiments in a criminal proceeding is virtually always morally and legally wrong because doing so subverts the goal of the trial process to present to a judge or jury relevant evidence and ar-

guments upon which to determine fairly the culpability of a defendant.*
Appeals to racial sentiment—"playing the race card"—subvert this
process because they encourage juries to base their conclusions on
considerations irrelevant to the question of whether the prosecution has
proven beyond a reasonable doubt that the defendant committed the
crime with which he is charged. Racial appeals are not only a distraction
but a menace that can distort interpretations of evidence or even seduce
jurors into believing that they should vote in a certain way irrespective
of the evidence.

Although both prosecutors and defense attorneys have been known
to make racial appeals in trials,[1] virtually all of the pertinent case law
arises from allegations of misconduct against prosecutors. Because of the
Constitution's double jeopardy clause, only defendants have the opportunity to seek judicial review of a verdict.†

The most thoroughgoing and eloquent judicial condemnation of
prosecutorial appeals to prejudice is Judge Jerome N. Frank's dissenting
opinion in *United States* v. *Antonelli Fireworks Company.*[2] This was a case
decided during World War II that featured Italian-American businessmen who were alleged to have defrauded the government by covering
up their production of defective munitions. Arguing that the convictions at issue should be reversed because the prosecutor had made an illicit appeal to jurors' patriotism, Frank remarked that if a prosecutor is
"allowed to inflame the jurors by . . . arousing their deepest prejudices,
the jury may become in his hands a lethal weapon directed against the

---

*I decline to say that appealing to racial sentiments is *always* morally wrong only because I think that every principle has limits, that implicitly surrounding every good
idea—"thou shalt not kill"—are exceptions, that there are virtually no absolutes.
From here on, unless otherwise noted, my criticisms of playing the race card are subject to this qualification.

†Under the double jeopardy clause, the state's prosecution of a defendant must end
once he is acquitted in a state court. See Fifth Amendment, United States Constitution: "[N]or shall any person be subject for the same offence to be twice put in jeopardy of life or limb." See, generally, Wayne R. LaFave and Jerold H. Israel, *Criminal
Procedure*, 2nd ed., 1055–1086 (1991). A prosecution under federal law may follow an
acquittal in state court, however, even if the federal prosecution substantially overlaps with the state prosecution. See "Special Issue: The Rodney King Trials: Civil
Rights Prosecutions and Double Jeopardy," 41 *UCLA Law Review* 509 (1994).

defendants who may be innocent. He should not be permitted to summon that thirteenth juror, prejudice."[3]*

Although Frank's impassioned evocation of the thirteenth juror failed to convince his colleagues to void the conviction in *Antonelli*, there are scores of cases in which appellate courts have vacated convictions obtained by prosecutorial appeals to bias.† These include cases in which a prosecutor declared, "I am well enough acquainted with this class of niggers to know that they have got it in for the [white] race in their heart";[4] or, "Unless you hang this Negro, our white people living out in the country won't be safe";[5]‡ or, "You know the Negro race—how they stick up for each other when accused of crime and . . . get up an alibi [and] prove it by perjured testimony [from those of] their own color";[6] or, "Gentlemen, do you believe she would have had intercourse with this black brute?"[7]

All of these reversals of convictions were ordered prior to 1960. They demonstrate that judges (even white supremacist judges) have long been willing, in certain contexts, to vacate convictions that followed clear-cut and unimpeded appeals to jurors' racial prejudices. The rulings in this area, however, have never been uniform. In 1923, for instance, reviewing a conviction under a liquor law, the Court of Appeals

---

*At another point in the opinion, Frank refers to "Mr. Prejudice and Miss Sympathy . . . the names of witnesses whose testimony is not recorded, but must nevertheless be reckoned with." 155 F.2d 631, 658–659 (CA 2 1946) (Frank, J., dissenting).

†Attorneys have sought to enlist all varieties of religious, nationalistic, ethnic, and racial prejudices to sway decisionmakers. See, e.g., *Hiller* v. *State*, 50 S.W.2d 225 (Tenn. Sup. Ct. 1932) (reversing conviction for manslaughter in trial where prosecutor stated: "There came this dare-devil Jew, a speed fiend, a road hog at 60 miles an hour" and "other people have as much right on the roads . . . as this Jew from New Orleans"); *Honda* v. *People*, 141 P.2d 178 (Colo. Sup. Ct. 1943) (declining to reverse conviction for murder in trial where prosecutor declared that conduct by Japanese-American defendant was "a typical example of Oriental treachery"); *Marx* v. *State*, 150 S.W.2d 1014 (Tex. Crim. App. 1941) (reversing conviction for murder in trial where prosecutor describes defendant as a German "beast" who has "murdered a fine young citizen of your country"). Appeals to antiblack sentiments, however, constitute the great bulk of the cases involving appeals to prejudice.

‡In response to defense counsel's arguments in favor of the defendant, the prosecutor went on to remark, "I hope to God the day will never come in this country when the heel of the Ethiopian will be on the neck of the Caucasian." *Moulton* v. *State*, 199 Ala. 411 (1917).

of Alabama decided that a county solicitor did not commit reversible error when he asked a jury, "Are you gentlemen going to believe that nigger sitting over there . . . in preference to the testimony of . . . deputies?" According to the court, "It would probably be better if trial judges would eliminate as far as possible this character of argument." But even in the absence of any intervention by the trial judge, the court concluded that no relief was warranted because, at bottom, the statement objected to was merely "a question as to whether the jury would believe the defendant's testimony or that of the state."[8]

Numerous examples of similar judicial complacency are regrettably easy to unearth. During the trial of Dorothy Johnson for burglary, defense counsel strenuously objected and called for a mistrial when the county solicitor referred to the defendant, a black teenager, as a "nigger gal."[9] The trial judge overruled the objection, signaling apparently that he found nothing legally objectionable in the use of such language. In turn, the Alabama Court of Appeals affirmed the conviction with reasoning that was, if anything, more appalling than the prosecutor's initial affront:

> It was undisputed that defendant was a Negro. She took the stand in her own behalf and was before the jury. It is not every reference to a defendant as a negro, when he is a negro, that would be improper. It should appear that it was so made as to emphasize the difference in races, and thereby to appeal to race prejudice. The scanty recital in the record is insufficient to present the entire picture, as it was presented to the trial judge.[10]

First, the court of appeals' complaint about the state of the record rings hollow since the record was sufficiently complete to present all of the facts needed to adjudicate the issue at hand. Second, the prosecutor did not refer to the defendant's race for the legitimate purpose of identification. Rather, he insulted the defendant's race by carelessly using the degrading argot of a low-brow white supremacist to refer to this young black woman as she stood before the bar of justice.

Third, if one wrings out every drop of reasoning implicit in the appellate court's wretched opinion, one discerns the hint of an argument that runs like this: A problem would be posed by language which *appeals* to race prejudice, but here the prosecutor's remark simply exhibited his low opinion of Negroes. This argument raises the question of whether rhetoric that is "merely" racially insulting should be treated in the same way as language that is designedly inflammatory. The appropriate answer is in the affirmative and has been so viewed by many judges for a long time. Insults are not inert.[11] People use insulting language for a purpose, usually to put a person or group in an inferior "place." Contrary to what the Alabama Court of Appeals suggested, the prosecutor's reference to a "nigger gal" did "emphasize the difference in races." The prosecutor clearly signaled that, for racial reasons, he saw this defendant as a different type of defendant, a lower type, a "nigger gal" type, as distinct from a white teenager charged with the identical crime. By showing that he felt this way, the prosecutor implicitly invited the jurors to feel this way as well.

Since the 1960s, the rhetorical intensity of judicial condemnation of racial appeals and insults by prosecutors has generally increased (although, as we shall see, the case law remains variable). An example is *Miller* v. *North Carolina*.[12] *Miller* arose from the prosecution of three black men sentenced to death for raping a white woman.* After their convictions were affirmed in state court, the defendants sought federal habeas corpus relief, which they ultimately received in 1978 from a federal court of appeals that ordered officials either to retry or release the alleged assailants.

At trial, the defendants asserted that the complainant had consented to having sex with them. Repeatedly referring to the defendants as "these black men," the prosecutor attacked the plausibility of their claim on the grounds that the average white woman would never consent to have sex with a black man:†

---

*They were initially sentenced to death but later had their sentences reduced to life terms of imprisonment, probably because of *Coker* v. *Georgia*, 433 U.S. 584 (1977), which abolished the death penalty as a punishment for the rape of an adult woman. For commentary on the racial aspect of capital punishment for rape, see pp.312–26.

†This prosecutor was echoing a sentiment that has long been voiced by prosecutors seeking rape convictions against black suspects who defend themselves by asserting that the white complainant consented to sex. See, e.g., *State* v. *Washington*, 67 So. 930 (La. Sup. Ct. 1915) (reversing conviction gained after prosecutor declared to the jury "Gentlemen, do you believe that she would have had intercourse with this black

> If [consent] was the case [the complainant] could not come into this courtroom and relate the story that she has . . . to you good people, because I argue to you that the average white woman abhors anything of this type in nature that had to do with a black man. It is innate within us.[13]*

The court of appeals viewed these remarks as a "blatant appeal to racial prejudice" and concluded that when such an appeal is directed at an issue as "sensitive as consent to sexual intercourse in a prosecution for rape . . . the prejudice engendered is so great that automatic reversal is required."[14]

Another instructive case is *Withers* v. *United States*,[15] which involved the alleged kidnapping of a white man by two black men. The prosecutor noted in his closing argument that "not one white witness has been produced" who contradicts the alleged victim's rendition of what occurred. Later the prosecutor also stated, apparently without cause, that "we are not trying this case because these defendants are blacks."[16] The court of appeals vacated the convictions, holding that the prosecutor's words constituted an appeal to racial prejudice that may have had a substantial influence on the jury's decision.

---

brute"). See also *State* v. *Thomas*, 777 P.2d 445, 447–448 (Utah Sup. Ct. 1989); *People* v. *Cudjo*, 863 P.2d 635, 661 (Cal. Sup. Ct. 1993).

*The prosecutor argued that there was another reason that should persuade the jury to disbelieve the defendants' story:

> If she was [of] a mind to consent to intercourse, don't you know as reasonable men and women she was not going to consent whenever she was having her menstrual cycle. I argue to you that a person, white or black or yellow or any other color under the sun that would have intercourse with a woman during the time of her menstrual cycle is on the level of an animal, and only a person that would have such a deep desire to carry out the sex desire that he would do a thing like that. She told you that each of these black men had intercourse with her and that they passed the knife from one to another.

Apart from the prosecutor's effort to stigmatize any sexual intercourse during menstruation, it is worth noting his constant references to the color of peoples' skin— "white or black or yellow or any other color under the sun." *Miller* v. *North Carolina*, 583 F.2d 701, 704 n.3 (CA 4 1978).

Yet another example of an appellate court overturning a conviction on grounds of prosecutorial racial misconduct is *Johnson* v. *Rose*.[17] In *Johnson*, the state accused two black men of murder. At trial, one of the defendants attempted to establish an alibi for himself by claiming that at the time of the killing in question he was with a woman. The prosecutor was permitted, over objection, to ask whether the woman the defendant referred to was white, whether the defendant was the father of her children, and whether he had had intercourse with her the morning of the homicide. A federal court of appeals concluded that the inquiry into the sexual relationship between the defendant and the woman was "irrelevant and inflammatory . . . [so tainting] the entire trial that it denied both defendants that fundamental fairness which is the essence of due process."[18]

Reversals of convictions following prosecutorial appeals to bias are by no means routine. The case law is full of instances in which appellate courts conclude that a prosecutor's conduct, although objectionable, is adequately cured if the trial judge suitably admonishes the jury to disregard the prosecutor's wrongful statements; in which the issue has been lost to the defendant on appeal because his attorney failed at trial to object to the offending remarks; in which appellate courts rule that although a prosecutor acted wrongly, his action amounts to "harmless error," and in which appellate courts conclude that statements objected to as racially prejudiced should not be viewed as such. To get a better sense of these arguments and the contexts in which they arise, consider the following rulings.*

Curative Instructions at Trial

In *Thornton* v. *Beto*,[19] federal courts denied habeas corpus relief to a state prisoner who had been convicted of robbery even though it was conceded by everyone that at trial, the prosecutor referred to him and his co-defendant as "niggers" during the questioning of one of the robbery

---

*Deciphering the meaning of these decisions is often difficult because courts frequently list without ranking the different reasons for declining to overturn convictions. This leaves unclear the extent to which racial considerations as distinct from other factors influenced any given decision.

victims. The reviewing courts let the conviction stand in rulings that were silent on the issue of prosecutorial misconduct. It may have been that the courts did not deem the use of the term "nigger" as prejudicial in the sense of driving the jury to a verdict that it would not otherwise have reached; evidence of the defendant's guilt was strong. Or it may have been that the courts decided to refrain from disturbing the conviction because they believed that whatever harm the epithet did was erased by the trial judge's curative instruction. Or it may have been that the reviewing courts reached their conclusion on the basis of the cumulative weight of these two factors. Whatever the theory, it is telling that the judges involved apparently felt no need to chastise the prosecutor's use in court of the notorious N-word.

In *People* v. *Thomas*,[20] the Illinois Supreme Court explained its decision as if it turned, at least in part, on the curative power of the trial judge's instructions. That case stemmed from a prosecutor's statement during the penalty phase of a capital trial. The prosecutor told the jury that he would produce testimony indicating that the defendant had previously committed sexual assaults against two other "young white women."[21] The Illinois Supreme Court affirmed the death sentence handed down by the jury, rejecting the argument that the defendant was entitled to be resentenced because of the prosecutor's reference to the race of the victims:

> We must note first that no objection to this remark appears in the record. As such, the defendant has waived any challenge for the purpose of this appeal. We also must decline to notice this challenge under the plain error doctrine. While we agree that this remark was improper, it had no effect on the defendant's substantial rights....
>
> First, [the remark objected to] was an isolated statement. The prosecutor did not dwell on the victims' race. Second, the jury could plainly see that one of the victims that the prosecutor referred to is white because she testified, and it could plainly see that defendant is black because he was in the courtroom. Third, the jury was instructed to consider only the evidence, not the attorneys' remarks. It was also instructed that it could not be influenced by race. We cannot, therefore, say that there is a likelihood that the result would have been different had the prosecutor not made the statement.[22]

There is much in this statement that is complacent, evasive, and stupid. The Illinois Supreme Court says that the prosecutor did not "dwell" on the race of the victims. True, he did not *repeatedly* stress that they were white women. Mentioning it once was sufficient, however, to introduce the poisonous notion that the victims' race was relevant, that their whiteness somehow made the defendant's assault upon them more heinous than it would have been otherwise. (After all, for what other reason would the prosecutor mention their race?) True, the jury could see that one of the alleged victims was white because she testified. However, this commonly used defense for race-baiting should not be persuasive because the identity of the witness is irrelevant to the issue in question, that issue being whether the prosecutor engaged in reversible misconduct by mentioning the race of the witness, thereby attributing significance to her race.[23] Prior to the prosecutor's remark, jurors might have attached significance to the race of the witness. After his remark, the chances that they did so certainly increased. True, the trial judge did instruct the jurors to consider only the evidence presented and not the attorneys' remarks and specifically that they should not be influenced by race. Such instructions may exert a salutary influence in some instances,[24] but based upon my impression of the way in which people normally behave, I suspect that most of the time such instructions are futile in terms of performing their expressed purpose. How does one *un*influence jurors who have been influenced by a prosecutor's reference to the race of a young woman who testifies that she has been sexually assaulted by the defendant? As Albert Alschuler notes, "Juries are quite incapable of forgetting on command."[25]*

It is true that Thomas's attorney failed to object at trial, that such a failure constitutes a waiver under the state's procedural rules, and that waived objections need not typically be reviewed on appeal. But that point in favor of the court's conclusion should have been overwhelmed by the fact that the remark in question, which the court describes (all too

---

*In *Thornton* v. *Texas*, a prosecutor asked the victim of a robbery and kidnapping, "Would you have gotten out of this car for three nigger men at night if they hadn't had guns?" Without independently condemning the prosecutor's use of racial slurs, the Texas Court of Criminal Appeals affirmed the conviction, stating perfunctorily that "in view of the instruction of the [trial] court to disregard the remark, we conclude that no reversible error was committed." 451 S.W.2d 898, 902 (1970).

wanly) as "improper," was made during the penalty phase of a *capital sentencing hearing*. Someone's very life was on the line.

A dissenting justice rightly noted two reasons why the court should have reversed the defendant's death sentence and remanded the case for resentencing. First, "the possibility that racial prejudice will infect jury deliberations is especially great in the context of capital sentencing proceedings because a jury at such proceedings must make a highly subjective, unique, individualized judgment regarding the punishment that a particular person deserves." Second, "the risk that sentencing may have been based upon racial considerations is especially serious [in capital sentencing proceedings] in light of the complete finality of the death sentence."[26] Given the interest at stake (life itself), given the relative inexpensiveness of the remedy requested (resentencing, not retrial), given the concededly "improper" character of the remark in question (a reference to the whiteness of alleged victims of a black man accused of sexual assault, a crime notorious for bringing out the worst elements of racist obsession and revenge)—given all of this, it is profoundly unsettling to recognize that, in 1990 (not 1890), the highest court in the State of Illinois was sufficiently certain that the prosecution's misconduct had had no influence on the jury's judgment that it was willing to leave a death sentence undisturbed.

Failure to Object at Trial: The Perils of Lawyering

Related to the case law emphasizing the curative value of judicial admonitions to juries is the case law under which illicit statements by prosecutors are held to be insulated from appellate review because of the defense counsel's failure to object at the time the statement was made at trial. This rule forces attorneys to make their objections known at a time when relief can be given with the least expense and disruption—during the trial (instead of after it) and by the trial judge (instead of by appellate judges).[27] Three aspects of this rule bear noting. First, it is predicated on the questionable notion that judicial admonitions are significantly curative. From the point of view of defendants, however, strongly voiced judicial instructions that are supposedly curative may be counterproductive if they reinforce in the jurors' minds the very argument they are told to disregard. Second, this rule highlights the importance of defense attorneys, for their errors fall hard upon their clients. If the trial attorney neglects to object at the correct time, the objection is lost, maybe to the everlasting harm of a defendant.

Third, this rule (as most rules) is not absolute. It is qualified by the plain error doctrine, which holds that certain conduct is so blatantly and gravely injurious that judicial intervention is required even in the absence of an objection by defense counsel.[28] Hence, when an appellate court declines to review an instance of alleged prosecutorial misconduct at trial on the grounds that the objection has been waived by the failure of the defense counsel to object in a timely fashion, it is actually making two rulings: first, the character of the misconduct at issue was not so terrible as to require judicial intervention even in the absence of an objection; and second, even if the prosecutor's verbal conduct was improper, any opportunity for a judge to grant relief for that impropriety has been forfeited by defense counsel's default.

Seldom do appellate courts rely exclusively on a defense counsel's procedural default when they reject a claim of prosecutorial misconduct. In *Blair* v. *Armontrout*,[29] however, one glimpses this rarity in a ruling by an appellate court which seized upon the defense counsel's default in order to avoid the messy chore of grappling with the prosecutor's impropriety. Walter J. Blair was charged with murdering for pay a woman who was scheduled to testify against a man who had raped her. Blair, who is black, was tried before an all-white jury, which convicted him. Subsequently, the prosecutor convinced the jury that it should sentence Blair to death. In the course of making his argument, the prosecutor asked the jury, "Can you imagine [the victim's] state of mind when she woke up at 6 o'clock that morning, staring into the muzzle of a gun held by this black man?"[30]

Judge Gerald W. Heaney of the Federal Court of Appeals concluded that, in the circumstances of this case, the absence of an objection from defense counsel should not preclude review of the prosecutor's conduct but should instead prompt the court to determine whether Blair had been denied effective assistance of counsel. Responding to the prosecutor's remark, Heaney heatedly condemned it and associated it with a wide range of racial injustices:

> The prosecutor . . . introduced racial prejudice into the sentencing process by discussing the race of the defendant and speculating on

the victim's fear at seeing "this black man" with a gun. His argument carefully played upon white fear of crime and the tendency of white people to associate crime with blacks. This is an exceedingly powerful image in our society. It is perpetrated by the media and perpetrated by manipulative politicians. It leads white people to cross the street when they see an African American coming and to speed up when they walk nearby. It reinforced racial stereotypes that reverberate in employment decisions, housing decisions, and in the minds of African Americans who feel that they will never live to see a better day in this country.[31]

Judge Heaney's outrage was isolated, however; he was the lone dissenter. The court of appeals, affirming the death sentence, declined even to discuss the propriety of the prosecutor's statement in the absence of a properly preserved objection.

The plain error doctrine provides a device that judges can use, if so moved, to provide relief even in the face of a failure on the part of defense counsel to lodge a timely objection. But just suppose defense counsel keeps quiet not out of ignorance, laziness, or inattention but rather because of careful trial strategy? As Judge Simon Sobeloff once observed, "There may be instances where the failure to object to a grave violation manifestly stems from the attorney's fear that an objection will only focus attention on an aspect of the case unfairly prejudicial to his client."[32] Under those circumstances, defense counsel "is not likely to regard it as a favor when the judge himself, in an effort to correct the [offending] remark, reemphasizes it."[33] With this possibility in mind, Professor Alschuler has usefully suggested that in circumstances in which it is plausible that defense counsel may not want a curative admonition, a trial judge should "call both lawyers to the bench, chastise the prosecutor appropriately, and ask the defense attorney whether he wishes an instruction on the impropriety of the prosecutor's behavior."[34]

The Struggle over What Constitutes a Racially Improper Remark

Among the most interesting of the cases stemming from allegations of prosecutorial appeals to prejudice are those in which the government defends a conviction on the grounds that there was nothing wrong with the statements objected to. Two cases stand out, partly because of the brutality that gave rise to them and partly because of the way in which they were resolved by judges.

State of Missouri v. *Mayhue*[35] arose from a trial in which prosecutors charged three black men with committing a series of horrendous crimes against a white couple: kidnapping, robbery, rape, attempted murder, and murder. During the trial, the surviving victim of the attack was asked about conversations she had had with one of the suspects during his sexual assault upon her. She responded by saying that he had asked whether she was enjoying having sex with him and whether she had ever before had sex with a black man. She testified that she had answered in the negative to both of these questions. Later, during the prosecutor's closing argument, he remarked, "I suggest to you ladies and gentlemen [of the jury], that no person in their right mind would want to remember three black men getting on her naked body, dumping their seed in her vagina." Because defense counsel failed to object to this comment at trial, the Missouri Court of Appeals held that it would decline to grant relief to the defendant absent a showing of "a manifest injustice or miscarriage of justice." In the court's view, the defendant failed to make such a showing.

More pertinent to our present concern, the court of appeals set forth another basis for upholding the conviction. It concluded that the remark in question did not represent an attempt by the prosecutor to appeal to racial prejudice. "First and foremost," the court declared, "it was evident to everyone associated with this trial that appellant is black and the victims are white, so the racial relationship was of no surprise to anyone, including the jury."[36] This argument, which we have seen before, should be accorded no persuasive weight. Since the racial identities were "evident to everyone," why did the prosecutor feel called upon to mention the race of the defendants? Obviously *he* attached some importance to this fact and communicated his perception to the jury, thereby possibly tainting the jury's deliberation. The court's analysis misses or, more likely, evades the point of the defendant's argument on appeal. The defendant's complaint was not that the prosecutor informed the jury of something about which it had previously been unaware. The complaint was that the prosecutor's reference to the race of the defendants endowed that legally irrelevant fact with a new and potentially destructive prominence.

"Secondly," the court maintained, "there is medical evidence upon the record that live spermatozoa were obtained by swab from the victim's vagina."[37] This is a makeweight that continues the court's first contention that there was nothing wrong with the prosecutor's statement because it simply articulated facts about the case. Again, this amounts to nothing more than a rhetorical ploy to confuse and evade the real issue in question. The defendants did not challenge the prosecutor's statement regarding physical evidence obtained from the victim of the rape. Rather, they challenged the permissibility of the prosecutor's legally irrelevant reference to the race of the alleged assailants.

Third, the court implied that the prosecutor's statement represented an effort to reacquaint the jury with the complainant's testimony that during the assault one of the defendants had asked her whether she had ever previously had sex with a black man. This argument does not work either, though, for the prosecutor's statement does not refer to what one of the defendants allegedly said to the victim but refers instead to the psychic trauma that the victim was likely to continue to suffer.

The prosecutor's comment may have represented a mere verbal slip brought on by the excitement of a closing argument and the desire to convict three men who had apparently committed an atrocious crime. Nonetheless, one does not have to be a thoroughgoing Freudian to recognize that "slips" may be simultaneously accidental and tactical—accidental at the level of conscious conduct, tactical at the level of subconscious conduct.[38] Whatever the intentions of the prosecutor, moreover, the fact is that by expressly calling attention to the defendant's race he injected into the proceedings a racial element that was legally irrelevant and potentially prejudicial.

This does not end the matter. Perhaps a court would be justified in affirming the convictions notwithstanding the prosecutor's racially discriminatory remark, if it concluded that the remark reflected an inadvertent reflex rather than a calculated strategy[39] and also that the jury would almost certainly have rendered a guilty verdict in the absence of the remark because of the overwhelming evidence of guilt. However, an affirmance *criticizing* a racially discriminatory inadvertent reflex is different from an affirmance without any criticism at all. This difference is substantial, for in law as in all other areas of human interaction, language matters.

A similar controversy involving the propriety of a prosecutor's reference to race arose in *State of Louisiana* v. *Greene*.[40] Carlton R. Greene was convicted of aggravated burglary and rape. At his trial, a witness testified that the defendant had been at her apartment when they both noticed that a "white lady" was in the process of moving into an adjoining apartment. This "white lady" was raped that evening. In his summation, the prosecutor alluded to this testimony and referred to the victim as "the nice white lady" whom the defendant had reportedly noticed. Defense counsel objected and demanded a mistrial on the basis of a Louisiana statute that explicitly declares:

> Upon motion of a defendant, a mistrial shall be ordered when a remark or comment, made within the hearing of the jury by the judge, district attorney, or a court official, during the trial or in argument, refers directly or indirectly, to:
>
> (1) Race, religion, color, or national origin, if the remark or comment is not material and relevant and might create prejudice against the defendant in the mind of the jury.[41]

The statute goes on to declare that "an admonition to the jury to disregard the remark or comment shall not be sufficient to prevent a mistrial," although an admonition will be offered instead of a mistrial if that is what the defense desires.[42]

The trial judge apparently believed that the prosecutor's comment was improper because, upon defense counsel's objection, he admonished the jury to disregard any statement of the prosecutor "referring in any way, shape, or form to anyone's race."[43] However, the trial judge refused to grant the defense a mistrial and the jury proceeded to convict.

The Court of Appeals of Louisiana affirmed the conviction on the grounds that the prosecutor's remark had only recapitulated the testimony of the victim's neighbor. "There was no attempt," the court concluded, "to pursue a racial issue to prejudice [the] defendant."[44] The court's conclusion is plausible but probably erroneous (if not deceptive). After all, if the remark was a relevant recapitulation of a witness's testimony, why did the trial judge admonish the jury to disregard the comment? Perhaps the trial judge's admonition was itself a mistake, a mere sign of panic. More likely, however, is that the trial judge recognized the prosecutor's error, sought to give the defendant some relief for it, but was unwilling to follow wholly the dictates of the statute, which specifies that a mistrial is due whenever an irrelevant racial remark is uttered by a prosecutor within hearing of the jury. Likely, too, is that the court of appeals knew this but decided to join the trial judge in tacitly modifying the law, thereby engaging in a species of judicial statutory nullification.

Prosecutorial Misconduct vs. Clear Guilt: The Harmless Error Solution

Greene places into sharp relief a doctrine that judges often deploy in dealing with allegations of prosecutorial racial misconduct, the doctrine of harmless error.[45] The doctrine of harmless error stands for the proposition that a violation of a defendant's rights is excusable—"harmless"— if a reviewing court concludes that, given the evidence of guilt, the defendant would have been convicted anyway, even had the violation of his rights not occurred. The harmless error doctrine attempts to accommodate two powerful, conflicting considerations. One is protecting the rights of criminal defendants. The harmless error doctrine pays deference to this aim by placing upon the prosecution the burden of persuading a reviewing court that, absent the misconduct complained of, it would still have obtained a conviction. Moreover, judges have limited the harmless error doctrine, declaring that some misconduct is so inherently tainting that its presence should lead automatically to the reversal of a conviction. Examples include failing to provide counsel to a defendant charged with a felony, failing to provide a defendant with a public trial, and failing to provide a defendant with a trial presided over by an impartial judge.[46]

The other consideration is protecting the government from the expense of retrying a defendant in circumstances in which, absent the misconduct complained of, the conviction would still almost certainly have been obtained. The harmless error doctrine pays deference to this aim by providing the courts with a way to affirm a conviction even though the defendant's rights have been violated.

A small number of courts have held that the harmless error doctrine should not be applicable to racially inflammatory appeals by prosecutors because such conduct is so destructive of fairness and so important to eradicate that its mere presence should always be viewed as irredeemably prejudicial to the defendant. The Supreme Court of Delaware came to this conclusion in *Weddington* v. *State*,[47] a case in which a black man was convicted of attempting to murder a white woman with whom he had been carrying on an affair. During the cross-examination of the defendant, the prosecutor asked the following question: "Mr. Weddington, isn't it true that you got [two of your friends] to go up [to where the complainant was living] because you told them there [were] some loose white women up there?"[48] Defense counsel objected and demanded a mistrial. When the prosecutor confessed that he had no reason to believe that the defendant had acted on the basis implied by the question, the judge sustained the defense counsel's objection and instructed the jury to disregard what the prosecutor had asked. The trial judge declined, though, to declare a mistrial.

The Supreme Court of Delaware reversed the trial judge, ruling that the harm caused by the prosecutor's query could not be adequately cured by the trial judge's instruction. Furthermore, the court held that the prosecutor's violation was so inherently injurious that the harmless error doctrine should not be applied. "A question which improperly injects race as an issue before the jury," Justice Randy J. Holland declared, "violates the fundamental fairness which is essential to the very concept of justice." Therefore, the court decided that pursuant to the state and federal constitutions, "the right to a fair trial that is free of improper racial implications is so basic that an infringement upon that right can never be treated as harmless error."[49]

Weddington, however, is unusual. Most courts do apply the harmless error doctrine to prosecutorial racial misconduct. Consider, for example, *Herring* v. *State*,[50] a case with an interesting twist but an altogether conventional outcome. In *Herring*, a black man was convicted of raping a white woman. Unlike many of the cases we have encountered, this one was decided by a predominantly black jury. Eight blacks and four whites were selected to decide Ernest Herring's fate. The racial demographics of the jury clearly concerned the prosecutor and prompted him to make the following statement during his closing argument:

> Can you put race aside? Can you white members vote for a fair verdict? Can you black members vote for a fair verdict? You and I

know there are people in this county and this state and this city that would say—you are wasting your time. You can't have a jury with eight black people that are gonna vote for life for a black person raping a white person. Time will tell.

No matter if you've got his fingerprints all over the house. No matter if she's beaten. No matter if her vagina is bruised and torn. No matter if her door is forced open. You just can't get any black people who are gonna vote for life against a black defendant who does that to a white person.[51]

Defense counsel objected to the prosecutor's statement (although why he objected so late is a mystery) but did not request that the jury be instructed to disregard what it had heard. (Perhaps defense counsel decided not to do so fearing that such an instruction would only reinforce the prosecutor's remark.) The judge sustained the objection but did nothing else to signal to the jury the impropriety of the prosecutor's argument. The judge also declined to grant defense counsel's motion for a mistrial.

The Supreme Court of Mississippi affirmed the conviction while simultaneously asserting that the prosecutor's statement was "utterly reprehensible."[52] Unfortunately, the court did not clarify why it found this statement to be reprehensible. The matter is not obvious. One way of viewing the prosecution's statement is that far from being a racial appeal it was instead an attack upon racial appeals, a declaration that *all* jurors, blacks as well as whites, should pay attention only to the facts and the law, regardless of the race of the defendant. A less generous (and more realistic) view, however, is that the prosecutor was attempting to subject the largely black jury to a dose of reverse racial psychology, emphasizing the unfavorable impression that the white community would have of blacks as a whole if this particular jury failed to convict the black defendant.

Although the court failed to specify precisely why it found the prosecutor's remarks objectionable, it seems to have been saying that it disapproved not only of traditional racial appeals (i.e., appeals to the racial sentiments of whites) but of *any* injection of racial considerations into the proceedings. Having stated its disapproval, however, the court went on to conclude that the prosecutor's misconduct did not warrant a reversal. Deploying the harmless error doctrine, the court held that the prosecutor had shown beyond a reasonable doubt that the evidence of guilt was so overwhelming that, absent the prosecutor's remark, the jury would still have found the defendant guilty.

What Is to Be Done about Prosecutorial Racial Misconduct

Thus far, the discussion has focused mainly on the propriety of reversing a conviction to redress prosecutorial racial misconduct. Before returning to that subject with an evaluation and suggestions, however, I want to place our subject in a wider context by noting that there are other devices available for dealing with this problem and other decisionmakers who could play a useful role, starting with ordinary citizens.

The fundamental difficulty faced by opponents of prosecutorial racial misconduct is that the predominant weight of influential public opinion does not perceive misbehavior of this sort to be a scandal. It does not consistently make prosecutors who engage in racial misconduct pay a heavy political price. Officials are careful to avoid being labeled "soft on crime." They are careful because that label energizes the opposition of forces in society that are able to defeat them (or their sponsors) at the ballot box. The misconduct under discussion here seems to create no similar discreditation. As a general matter, making racial appeals or otherwise engaging in racial misconduct poses little or no hazard to prosecutors' careers. The case of Joseph Briley, district attorney of the Ocmulgee Judicial District Circuit in Georgia between 1974 and 1994, is illustrative. In 1978, civil rights attorneys discovered that Briley had instructed jury commissioners in one county in the circuit to limit the participation of blacks on juries to as low a percentage as could be defended in the event of a legal challenge.* Despite the uncovering of his plot, no

---

*Two other facts about Briley are worth noting. First, during his tenure as a prosecutor, he tried thirty-three death penalty cases, twenty-four of which were against black defendants. Stephen B. Bright, "Discrimination, Death and Denial: The Tolerance of Racial Discrimination in Infliction of the Death Penalty," 35 *Santa Clara Law Review* 925 (1995). Second, in cases in which defendants were black and victims were white, Briley used 94 percent of his peremptory challenges—96 out of 103—against black potential jurors. Ibid. Along with the irrefutable evidence of racial dis-

action was taken against Briley, and he remained in office until 1994, when he resigned while under investigation for sexual harassment.[53]

Although focused public disapproval backed up by a willingness to punish complacent politicians at the polls would be the best long-term antidote to the prosecutorial misbehavior under discussion, there are other sources of potential relief. Judges have at their disposal tools that could be used to discipline and deter prosecutorial misconduct. For the most part, however, they have been and remain excessively hesitant to deal vigorously with prosecutors who play the race card.

The most knowledgeable students of this subject argue, rightly, that "the ideal corrective for courtroom misconduct by prosecutors may be punishment for contempt of court" because "this sanction can be easily and quickly administered and . . . permits substantial flexibility in adjusting penalties to reflect the severity of the prosecutor's misconduct."[54] Judges wield this weapon against defense attorneys with some regularity. There are, however, extremely few instances in which trial judges have applied the same discipline to prosecutors (and in several of those rare instances courts of appeals have reversed).[55]

Judges could declare mistrials, fine prosecutors, reprimand them by name in published opinions, or suspend a prosecutor from practicing before their courts.[56] Judges, however, have tended to avoid applying these measures even in cases of egregious misconduct. As we have seen, appellate courts do sometimes chastise prosecutor's offices for "improper" and "unfortunate" remarks, but in case after case these boilerplate chastisements amount to nothing more than what Judge Frank decried as "purely ceremonial language" which not only fails to stem prosecutorial misbehavior but also "breeds a deplorably cynical attitude towards the judiciary."[57]

All of the disciplinary devices available to judges should be used to punish vigorously prosecutorial racial misconduct. At the very least, in deciding cases, appellate judges should describe fully the conduct at is-

---

crimination unearthed by the *Amadeo* litigation and the fact that Briley was permitted to keep his job after the revelation of his wrongdoing, these figures raise disturbing questions about the quality of public service offered by the prosecutor's office in the Ocmulgee Judicial District. Ibid., 901, 924–925, 935. See *Amadeo* v. *Zant*, 486 U.S. 214 (1988).

sue. If they decide that this conduct is improper, they should criticize it clearly, calibrating their rhetoric to the seriousness of the infraction.

In terms of affirming or upsetting convictions, what should appellate judges do? This is, of course, the most vexing aspect of the controversy.

As noted above, some jurists contend that prosecutorial appeals to racial bias should be among that class of errors that is exempt from the harmless error doctrine. Proponents of an automatic reversal rule maintain first that "once invoked, racial prejudice fatally compromises the impartiality of the jury . . . rendering unreliable its assessment of all evidence in the case." They contend, second, that "because of the high visibility of the prosecutor's actions, the failure to subject racially-biased prosecutorial conduct to automatic reversal [projects] an unacceptable public message concerning society's indifference to racial equality in the criminal justice system."[58]

Although courts should be more exacting and forceful in responding to prosecutorial racial appeals, I am unpersuaded that adopting an automatic reversal rule would be a good idea. Two concerns in particular bother me. One is the cost of opening up an opportunity for a defendant who is guilty in fact to escape reconviction because of the accidents that afflict litigation: the dimming of memories, the death of witnesses, the disappearance of physical evidence, and so on. A second concern is that an automatic reversal rule would be wrongly insensitive to the fact that racial misconduct by prosecutors varies in character. On the one hand, there is the inadvertent comment of negligible influence. On the other hand, there is the deliberate appeal to racial feeling that decisively affects a verdict or sentence. A properly enforced automatic reversal rule would collapse the distinctions between these various forms of misconduct.

I would support an automatic reversal rule if I believed that, under the prevailing, ad hoc, sliding scale approach, courts were wrongly declining to vacate convictions with intolerable frequency. My impression, though, is that with a notable exception, judges are typically balancing reasonably the competing values that are in tension with one another. The notable exception is the set of cases that involves misconduct in the context of a capital sentencing hearing.

Since putting a person to death is qualitatively different from other punishments, death sentences, if allowed at all, should require super-hygiene in application. In capital cases, all that the state can possibly "lose" is a reduction in sentence from execution to imprisonment for life. An automatic reversal rule in this limited setting is therefore morally essential.

Racial Misconduct by Jurors and Judges: The Problem of the Tainted Conviction

Another troubling area is marked by decisions addressing allegations that convictions and sentences were tainted by juror bias.[59] In *Spencer* v. *State*,[60] the Supreme Court of Georgia affirmed a death sentence imposed upon a black defendant despite the fact that a juror alleged in a posttrial affidavit that she overheard two other jurors making racially derogatory comments about the defendant during jury deliberations and the trial court refused even to consider the affidavit. To dramatize what it viewed as the insubstantiality of the defendant's claim, the Supreme Court of Georgia stated that it would decline to vacate the defendant's conviction or sentence even if it believed the affidavit. "Assuming the truth of the affidavit," the Court declared, "it shows only that two of the twelve jurors possessed some racial prejudice and does not establish that racial prejudice caused those two jurors to vote to convict [the defendant] and sentence him to die."[61] This is an egregious statement insofar as it suggests that there is not much wrong with a jury that includes two members who clearly harbor "some racial prejudice."

The situation would be different had the court, upon investigating the matter, concluded that racial bias had not, in fact, tainted the jury's decisionmaking. That, however, is not what the Georgia Supreme Court did. It affirmed a death sentence in the face of an unexamined affidavit which might have indicated that the state's ultimate punishment stemmed, at least in part, from racial bias.

Similarly regrettable is *Hance* v. *Zant*,[62]* a case in which two jurors

---

*The background facts of *Hance* v. *Zant* are nightmarish. In February and March 1978, William Henry Hance, a black soldier at Fort Benning in Columbus, Georgia, killed two prostitutes. In March and April, he sent letters to the Columbus police chief and a local newspaper claiming that "The Forces of Evil," a white supremacist organization, had kidnapped the two prostitutes, who were black. He claimed that "The Forces of Evil" had carried out the kidnappings to pressure the police to capture "the stocking strangler" who was then terrorizing the white women of the city.

claimed that they heard racially derogatory comments made about the defendant by fellow jurors and in which one juror asserted that she actually declined to vote in favor of capital punishment but that, when polled in court, she acquiesced to the will of her colleagues.* Prior to Hance's execution, no court examined the truthfulness of the jurors who belatedly revealed their sense that something amiss had influenced the jury on which they had served.

Any defendant who seeks to challenge his conviction on the basis of information regarding jury deliberations revealed by a juror faces two large obstacles. First, federal and state rules of evidence stringently exclude juror testimony that impeaches the jury's verdict. Federal Rule of Evidence 606(b) provides, for example, that:

> a juror may not testify as to any matter or statement occurring during the course of the jury's deliberations or to the effect of anything upon his or or any other juror's mind or emotions as influencing him to assent or dissent from the verdict ... except that a juror may testify on the question whether extraneous prejudicial information was

---

In these letters, Hance threatened to kill the two prostitutes unless the strangler was soon caught or unless $10,000 was given to the Forces of Evil. See *Hance* v. *Zant*, 696 F.2d 940 (CA 11 1983), *cert. denied,* 463 U.S. 1210 (1994); 114 S. Ct. 1392 (1994), denying application for stay of execution.

Since much will be made later of the claim that the criminal justice apparatus in Georgia tends to deal more harshly with white-victim murder cases than black-victim murder cases (see pp. 326–50), it is worth noting that *Hance* was a black-victim case.

*The only black juror claimed that her fellow jurors ultimately disregarded her vote as to punishment. She stated that the judge was apparently told that the jury vote for capital punishment was unanimous and that when the jury was polled as to its views, she indicated agreement with her colleagues only out of fear. She claimed that she felt afraid that she might be charged with perjury since she had said at voir dire that she would be willing to vote for a death sentence under appropriate circumstances. A white juror confirmed this account and added that during deliberations jurors referred to the defendant as a "typical nigger" and "just one more sorry nigger that no one would miss." See Bob Herbert, "Mr. Hance's 'Perfect Punishment,' " *New York Times*, March 27, 1994; Bob Herbert, "Jury Room Injustice," *New York Times*, March 30, 1994.

improperly brought to the jury's attention or whether an outside influence was improperly brought to bear upon any juror.[63]

Second, a requirement that the defendant show actual prejudice on account of juror misconduct strongly tends to doom the possibility of obtaining a new trial.

The vigor—the *excessive* vigor—with which courts protect the finality of jury verdicts against subsequent impeachment is suggested by the Supreme Court's decision in *Tanner* v. *United States*,[64] a nonracial case though one with dire implications for defendants alleging racial misconduct. In *Tanner*, two defendants were convicted of mail fraud and other crimes. After the conviction, two members of the jury informed defense attorney that throughout the trial, members of the jury imbibed liquor and other drugs. One result, they claimed, was that several members of the jury repeatedly slept during significant portions of the proceedings.

Defense attorneys requested the trial judge to hold a hearing to determine the accuracy of the charges and whether the alleged misconduct was of such a character that it deprived the defendants of their right to a competent jury. The judge refused. His refusal was upheld by a court of appeals and, finally, the Supreme Court.

The Court held that Federal Rule of Evidence 606(b) precluded consideration of the juror's testimony and that therefore the trial judge was correct in declining to hold a hearing to investigate further the veracity of the juror's confessions. The Court applied the Rule with excessive breadth. First, by its own terms, Rule 606(b) does not bar testimony concerning events occurring *prior* to jury deliberations. This would seem to have permitted testimony about juror intoxication during the trial. Second, Rule 606(b) expressly permits juror testimony about "an outside influence . . . improperly brought to bear upon any juror." Drugs could sensibly be seen as an outside influence.

Underlying the Court's broad reading of rule 606(b) is its concern to promote finality, to protect jurors from harassment by disappointed defense counsel, and to shield the privacy and independence of jury deliberations. There is, however, a poor fit between the Rule and these concerns. Rule 606(b) applies only to jurors; it does not apply to others who might have knowledge about the jurors. As interpreted by the

Supreme Court, therefore, Rule 606(b) prohibits jurors from testifying about their own intoxication but does not prohibit testimony from a bailiff who witnessed the intoxication. Yet "finality is disrupted as much by proof of juror misconduct from eavesdroppers, bartenders, and drug dealers as by proof from the jurors themselves."[65] Professor Alschuler rightly complains that the Rule promotes "finality in a haphazard, back-handed way, relying on the fact that no one other than jurors usually is able to testify to their misconduct."[66]

Rule 606(b) fares no better in terms of the other rationales invoked in its name. A better way to discourage harassment of jurors by attorneys or litigants would be to expressly forbid such harassment and to punish violators. As for protecting the privacy of jury deliberations, here the system encounters an embarrassing anomaly: It permits disclosure by jurors for the sake of informing or entertaining the public but withdraws any legal recognition to disclosures by jurors that reveal juror bias in deliberations.[67]

Regardless of competing views about the worthiness of Rule 606(b), one might have thought that there would at least be consensus in favor of the proposition that, at some point, even if the Rule expressly barred testimony, the Constitution would demand that the Rule give way so that the testimony in question could be heard and, if believed, acted upon. In *Tanner*, however, the Court raised the unsettling possibility that, in its view, the exclusion of testimony pursuant to Rule 606(b) *never* poses a constitutional difficulty because means other than juror testimony are available to protect a defendant's right to an impartial and unimpaired jury.[68]

Some judges continue to act on the assumption that, under certain circumstances, the Constitution would require a hearing for juror testimony barred by Rule 606(b) or its state law analogues.[69] On some of these occasions, however, judges have erected a virtually insuperable obstacle to relief: a requirement that a defendant show that juror misconduct created not simply a substantial risk of prejudice but a "substantial likelihood of prejudice" or a requirement that the defendant show not merely prejudice but prejudice of "such a magnitude" as to require a new trial.[70] Such formulations hold open the theoretical possibility that their authors may, in some cases, reverse a conviction because of juror bias. More important, though, these excessively demanding formulations further distort an unbalanced regime that is willing to invest huge amounts of energy into sifting prospective jurors prior to trial but is unwilling to invest even relatively small amounts of energy to examine jury verdicts where there is reason to suspect their integrity.[71]

Here, as in many areas, there is variability in case law. In *Powell* v. *Allstate Insurance Co.,*[72] for instance, the Florida Supreme Court approached the issue with a different attitude than most courts have shown. *Powell* stemmed from litigation between two motorists and an insurance company. Following a trial at which the motorists sued for money damages, a juror informed the judge that members of the (all-white) jury had made numerous racial jokes about the motorists. Based upon this disclosure, the motorists requested a new trial or, alternatively, a hearing to investigate further the juror's allegations. The trial judge denied both requests and was affirmed by an intermediate appellate court. The Florida Supreme Court, in an opinion by Judge Anstead, reversed. Acknowledging "the strong public policy against going behind a verdict to determine if juror misconduct had occurred," the Court nonetheless subordinated that policy to what Judge Anstead described as a "sacred trust to assure equal treatment before the law."[73] Ruling that the allegations, if true, described juror conduct that would violate the motorists' state and federal constitutional rights, the Florida Supreme Court directed the trial judge to hold a hearing to investigate the juror's charges. In contrast to the courts noted above, the Florida Supreme Court did not say that in order to win a new trial the motorists would have to show that the misconduct created a "substantial likelihood of prejudice." Rather, it held that prejudice would be presumed and declared that if the trial judge found the juror's allegations to be true, he should order a new trial. *Powell* is a civil and not a criminal case. The Florida Supreme Court has properly indicated, however, that the principles it articulated in *Powell* are applicable to criminal cases; after all, as important as fairness is in all courts, it is even more important in criminal courts where liberty (and sometimes life itself) is at stake.

An admirable decision, *Powell* is also an unusual one.* Reversals of

---

*The Florida Supreme Court also ordered a new trial in a tort case in which a member of an all-white jury reported the presence of racial slurs during deliberations and several statements by jurors to the effect that they did not want to award any damages to the plaintiff because "she was a fat, black woman on welfare and would blow

convictions are extremely rare even in light of troubling evidence of openly expressed racial prejudice in the jury box.* They will remain rare in part because *Tanner* rather than *Powell* reflects prevailing judicial attitudes.

Having discussed racial bias within the ranks of prosecutors and jurors, a word needs to be said about the problem of racially biased judges. That some judges are racially prejudiced is beyond dispute. The interesting questions are, to what extent is racial bias present within the ranks of the judiciary and, to what effect on the administration of the law. This is an area that has given rise to few large-scale, well-researched studies. Not surprisingly, impressions vary. There are instances in which judges have been censured, suspended, or even permanently removed because of racially biased statements made on or off the bench.[74] On occasion judges have recused themselves or had cases taken from them because of charges that their statements revealed racial bias. In *State* v. *Joseph*, for example, an Arizona state judge, Stanley Z. Goodfarb, conducted a postconviction hearing at which the defendant, a black man, argued that prosecutors had racially discriminated in their use of peremptory challenges.[75] Before taking evidence,

---

the money on liquor, cigarettes, Jai alai, bingo, or the dog track." *Wright* v. *Santos*, 679 So.2d 1233 (1996).

*In *United States* v. *Heller*, 785 F.2d 1524 (CA 11 1986), a court of appeals vacated a conviction handed down by a jury on which were seated several jurors who made anti-Jewish jokes and statements. According to the judges, "[t]he religious prejudice displayed by the jurors [was] so shocking to the conscience and potentially so damaging to public confidence in the equity of our system of justice, that we must act decisively to correct any harmful effects on this [defendant-appellant]." Ibid. at 1527. Considering this case with the limitations imposed by *Tanner* in mind, it is worth noting that the trial judge was put on notice of the offensive juror statements prior to the verdict.

In *Tobias* v. *Smith*, 468 F.Supp. 1287 (W.D. N.Y. 1979), notwithstanding the prohibitions of Rule 606(b), a judge ordered a postconviction hearing on the basis of a juror affidavit detailing racially prejudiced comments during deliberations. The judge indicated that he would order a new trial if he found the allegations to be true and if he found that the statements created "a probability of prejudice to the [defendant]," a lesser requirement than the "substantial probability of prejudice" required more recently in some federal courts. See *Shillcutt* v. *Gagnon*, 827 F.2d 1155, 1159 (CA 7 1987).

Judge Goodfarb met with the attorneys in his chambers without a court reporter present. During a discussion of the discrimination charge, the judge made a reference to "fucking niggers."[76] When the defense counsel insisted upon putting the remark on the record, the judge recused himself from further dealings with the case.*

A similar scenario emerged in *Peek* v. *State*,[77] a capital case in which it was established that the judge referred to the parents of the defendant as "niggers" during a recess between the guilt and penalty phases of a trial.† When the defense attorney moved to disqualify the judge on the basis of this remark, the judge recused himself from the remainder of the proceedings.

The rarest of rulings in this area is the reversal of a conviction or sentence on grounds of judicial racial bias. A case in which this did occur stemmed from the prosecution for a firearms violation of one of the most flamboyant black activists of the civil rights era. In *United States* v. *H. Rap Brown*,[78] a federal Court of Appeals vacated Brown's conviction on the grounds that he had been denied a fair tribunal. The evidence on which this conclusion was based came from a lawyer who had met the judge who presided over Brown's trial. This lawyer informed Brown's attorney that prior to the trial the judge told him "that he was going to get that nigger."[79] A different judge held a hearing to examine the lawyer's allegation and to determine what should be done in light of it. This judge found the lawyer's allegation to be credible but decided nonetheless to affirm the conviction and sentence. According to the second judge, the defendant received a fair trial notwithstanding the initial judge's remark and all that it may have signified about the judge's feelings toward H. Rap Brown or blacks in general.

---

*No action was taken against the judge for his comment. Not until four years later, after several other instances in which the judge used offensive language in judicial proceedings, did judicial authorities finally suspend Judge Goodfarb. See In re *The Matter of Stanley Z. Goodfarb*, 880 P.2d 620 (Ariz. Sup. Ct. 1994).

†According to the defense attorney, the judge said, "Since the nigger mom and dad are here anyway, why don't we go ahead and do the penalty phase today instead of having to subpoena them back at cost to the state." Another person heard the judge to have said, "Since the niggers are here, maybe we can go ahead with the sentencing phase." See *Peek* v. *State*, 488 So.2d 52, 56 (Fla. Sup. Ct. 1986).

The Court of Appeals reversed, noting that a federal statute requires the mandatory disqualification of a judge "in any proceeding in which his impartiality might reasonably be questioned" or "where he has a personal bias or prejudice concerning a party."[80] The Court of Appeals emphasized not only the virtue of actual impartiality but also the importance of the appearance of impartiality. Because the trial judge's remark did not comport with the appearance of justice and because the appellate tribunal could not determine from the trial record alone whether the defendant had received a fair trial, it vacated his conviction.

Brown is a triumph of sorts. On the other hand, one hastens to note that the Court of Appeals' decision did not prevent the offending judge from presiding over other cases in which the liberties, fortunes, and lives of other blacks were at stake. The same is true of the judge in *Peek*. The day after his recusal, he may well have presided over another case involving blacks.

Two main lessons emerge from the judicial bias case law. One is the inadequacy of the punishments imposed on judicial malefactors. Even when courts reverse their rulings or otherwise discipline them, a misplaced diffidence seems to prevent courts from publicly naming, strenuously denouncing, and effectively regulating judges who have sullied their posts by displaying racial bias.[81] The other lesson is the absolutely essential need for *all* persons to participate in the ongoing struggle to rid the criminal justice system of racial prejudice and other pollutants. Courts will, for the most part, grant at least some redress in cases in which judges have displayed overt racial bias. The biggest obstacle in such cases is not legal doctrine but the practical difficulty of documentation. This will require the same fortitude as that shown by the attorneys who, eschewing custom (and in some instances risking their careers), insisted upon bringing to light the racist comments of the judges who were caught in *Joseph, Peek*, and *Brown*.

The Defense Attorney and the "Race Card"

Thus far we have discussed racial misconduct by prosecutors, jurors, and judges. Now we shall turn to racial misconduct by defense attorneys. We have already encountered instances in which defense attorneys, with little or no interference from trial judges, unambiguously appealed to the racial sentiments of jurors on behalf of their clients. These cases involved attorneys who appealed to the racial feelings of white jurors sitting in judgment of white defendants accused of murdering blacks. Recall, for example, the attorney for the murderers of Emmett Till who, in addressing the jurors, noted his confidence that every last "Anglo-Saxon" one of them would have the courage to free his (obviously guilty) clients.[82]

Another type of appeal to racial bias arises in cases in which defense counsel make racially degrading comments about clients for the purpose of *helping* them. *Kornegay* v. *State* is illustrative.[83] In *Kornegay*, two black men were convicted of raping a white woman. The defendants claimed that the woman offered them sexual favors as partial payment for a car ride that they gave to the woman and her boyfriend, who were hitchhiking on a journey that had begun in Wisconsin. In his closing argument, counsel for the defendants maintained that all of the participants in this episode had acted badly but that the defendants had acted no worse than anyone else and had certainly committed no crime. Addressing the jury without interference of any sort from the trial judge, defense counsel declared:

> I told [my clients before trial] "Y'all are the sorriest bastards I have ever seen." . . . I said, "Y'all niggers 40 or 50 years ago would be lynched for something like this, but you're not under the law guilty of rape because these people [the complainants] are just as guilty as you are." . . . It just ain't right for them [the hitchhikers] to come through here doing what they did and it was not right for the two niggers to do what they did.[84]

The Georgia Court of Appeals maintained that "the repeated use of the racial epithet should have been stopped with a strong reprimand by the trial court, at the very least, even if counsel meant this line of argument as a trial tactic on defendants' behalf." The court then proceeded to reverse the convictions on the grounds that it was unsure whether the defense attorney's "unlawful characterizations [had allowed] the jury to regard defendants as racially inferior persons whose conviction for that reason would therefore be more easily reached."[85] This rationale for overturning the conviction is weak. After all, the court conceded that the defense counsel appears to have deliberately used the racial epithets to gain the jury's solicitude. Moreover, he appears to have been somewhat successful insofar as the jury acquitted the defendants of kidnapping and other serious charges. Hence, the court's stated reasons for reversing the convictions are at odds with the facts of the case. This disjunction leads me to speculate that the court did not really believe its own expressed rationale. A more likely motivation for the ruling is that the court believed that, even if the defense attorney's strategy was effective, trial judges must be encouraged to prohibit attorneys from using blatant racial appeals in their dealings with juries regardless of underlying tactical calculations.

Although *Kornegay* illustrates a fascinating twist on the mechanics of racial appeals, it is part of an old tradition: the appeal to the racial sentiments of whites. Defense counsel in *Kornegay* denounced his client as a "nigger" in order to help him, but the audience the defense attorney had in mind was a white audience.

Recently, discussion of racial appeals by defense counsel has focused as much (if not more) on the exploitation of the racial sentiments of black, as opposed to white, jurors. A key event behind this switch in focus was, of course, the trial of O.J. Simpson—"the trial of the century"—particularly the belief of many that his acquittal stemmed at least in part from a deliberate effort by his defense counsel to play the race card to the predominantly black jury.

Did Johnnie Cochran Use the "Race Card"? Problems of Interpretation

In the summer of 1994, prosecutors accused O.J. Simpson, a famous (now notorious) African-American athlete and entertainer, of murdering two white people: his former wife (Nicole Brown Simpson) and an acquaintance of hers (Ronald Goldman). Police allegedly found incriminating evidence at the murder site and at Simpson's residence, including a bloody glove presumably worn by the murderer. Simpson's attorneys maintained that the bloody glove had been planted by the police officer who claimed to have found it. That officer, Mark Fuhrman, was later shown to be prejudiced against blacks. On October 4, 1995, Simpson was acquitted by a jury composed of seven black women, two white women, one Hispanic man, and one black man.[86] After Simpson's acquittal, one of his attorneys, Robert Shapiro, complained, remarkably, that his co-counsel, Johnnie L. Cochran, Jr., had not only played the race card but "dealt it from the bottom of the deck."[87] Many observers concur with this appraisal (although many who do refuse to permit Shapiro to distance himself from Cochran).[88] Still others, however, contend that Cochran responded appropriately to circumstances that required a detailed examination of the racial views of a bigoted police officer.[89]

Although racial issues were present to some degree throughout the O.J. Simpson trial, on three occasions they completely dominated the proceedings. The first was when the prosecution requested Judge Lance Ito to prevent the defense from questioning Detective Fuhrman regarding his alleged use of the epithet "nigger."[90] The prosecution made a motion *in limine*, which is, essentially, a request by a party asking a judge for a protective order that prohibits the other party from voicing specified statements or questions that the moving party believes will be prejudicial. Motions *in limine* are typically made before trial in order to prevent the matters objected to from being brought to the attention of the jury.[91]

The prosecution argued that the judge should prevent the defense from examining Fuhrman about his alleged use of racial epithets on the ground that the information sought was irrelevant to the case and that, even if relevant, the information was more prejudicial than informative. Pleading for the judge to exclude inquiry into the history of the detective's use of the N-word, prosecutor Christopher Darden declared:

> If we really want the jury's attention focused on the evidence and on the legal and factual issues . . . we shouldn't let them hear this word, because if they hear this word they are going to focus their attention on the issue of race. They are going to be more concerned with whether Mark Fuhrman is a racist than they are with whether there was any way, any possibility . . . that Mark Fuhrman planted evidence. . . . That is what Mr. Cochran wants the jury to do. Skip the evidence.[92]

Darden asserted that permitting inquiry into the record of Fuhrman's use of the N-word would prejudice the state's case against Simpson because that word "is the filthiest, dirtiest, nastiest word in the English language" and would mainly accomplish one thing:

> It will upset the black jurors. It will issue a test . . . and the test will be: Whose side are you on? The side of the white prosecutors and the white policemen or on the side of the black defendant and his very prominent and black lawyer? That is what it is going to do. Either you are with the man or you are with the brothers. That is what it does.[93]

Summarizing the state's position, Darden told Judge Ito:

> If you allow Mr. Cochran to use this word and to play this race card, not only does the direction and the focus of the case change, but the entire complexion of the cases changes. It is a race case then. It is white versus black, African American versus Caucasian, us versus them, us versus the system.[94]

The defense, of course, objected and responded with a dual argument.[95] First, the defense contended that evidence relating to Fuhrman's racial views was relevant to its theory that, out of racial animus, he planted evidence suggestive of Simpson's guilt. Second, the defense contended that the evidence it sought would be more enlightening than confusing to the jury. Addressing himself directly to Darden's assertions regarding the blinding effect that the N-word would have on the black jurors, Cochran said that it was "demeaning" to suggest that "African Americans who have lived under oppression for 200 plus years in this country," who have lived with "offensive words, offensive looks, [and] offensive treatment every day," would be unable to deliberate fairly just because they heard the offensive N-word.[96]

The judge ultimately decided to permit the defense to ask Fuhrman whether, during the preceding ten years, he had used the N-word. Fuhrman denied that he had, a denial which, instead of ending the matter, set the stage for the second occasion on which racial conflict became the overwhelming consideration in the case.

Several months after Fuhrman's denial, audiotapes were unearthed in which he was heard to use the N-word liberally and with obvious relish. On the taped conversations, Fuhrman offered his interlocutor (an aspiring screenwriter) opinions and anecdotes that were not only laden with contempt for blacks but also laced with boasts that he had destroyed or otherwise tampered with evidence related to false charges he had lodged against blacks, particularly black men accompanying white women.[97] The defense, of course, sought to introduce the tapes into evidence in order to impeach Fuhrman's previous testimony. The prosecution sought to minimize, if not prevent, the jury's exposure to the tapes, arguing again that the issue of Fuhrman's racial attitudes was collateral to the central issue of the case and would serve more to confuse than to enlighten the jury.

The judge compromised. He permitted the jury to hear Fuhrman say the N-word twice and also permitted the defense to elicit from the person with whom Fuhrman had spoken the fact that over the course of their taped discussions Fuhrman had used the word "nigger" approximately forty-one times. Furthermore, Judge Ito permitted larger portions of the tape to be played in court, albeit outside the presence of the jury. This decision was important because it increased the possibility that members of the jury would be informed by relatives or spouses of the contents of the tape notwithstanding the judge's order that jurors refrain from exchanging information about the case with anyone. On the other hand, Judge Ito did not permit the defense to play the tape in its entirety to the jury. Moreover, in selecting what the jury would be permitted to hear, the judge excluded those portions of the tape that dealt with Fuhrman's boasts that, in dealing with blacks whom he disliked, he had previously tampered with evidence.[98]

The third time that race became the dominant focus of the trial was when defense counsel Johnnie Cochran presented a closing argument that, according to some observers, violated the rules of advocacy.[99] Two aspects of the closing will likely remain an important part of the folklore of this remarkable case. One was his demonizing characterization of Mark Fuhrman and another police officer as the "twin devils of deception."[100] The other was his plea to the jury suggesting that there were considerations other than evidence relating to the defendant's conduct that the jurors should take into account in determining their verdict. Referring to Fuhrman, Cochran stated, "This man could've been off the force long ago if [the authorities] had done their job, but they didn't . . . they did not have the courage. . . . That is what I am asking you to do. Stop this cover-up. . . . If you don't stop it, then who?" Later, Cochran declared, "And when you go back to the jury room, some of you may want to say, well, gee, you know, boys will be boys. . . . That is not acceptable as the conscience of this community. . . . You are empowered to say we are not going to take that anymore." Returning to the same theme, Cochran stated:

> Who then polices the police? You police the police. You police them by your verdict. You are the ones to send a message. Nobody else is going to do it in our society . . . nobody has the courage. . . . Maybe you are the right people at the right time at the right place to say: No more. We are not going to have this.[101]

Did the legal system (in the person of Judge Ito) respond appropriately to these controversies? The record is mixed. Ito ruled wrongly in initially permitting the defense to examine Fuhrman on his use of the N-word. The applicable rules of evidence permitted questions going to Fuhrman's credibility. Whether or not he used the N-word was irrelevant, however, at least initially, to the question of credibility. Asking Fuhrman whether in the past he had falsely testified or fabricated evidence would have related to credibility,* but asking him whether he was in the habit of referring to blacks as "niggers" did not. There is a sense, felt by many, that, in any event, it was relevant whether Fuhrman had referred to blacks as "niggers." This sense stems from the intuition that if Fuhrman used the N-word, it was a bit more probable that he was a bigot, and that if he was a bigot, it was a bit more probable that he might have planted evidence as the defense alleged. This chain of "ifs," however, highlights the initial tenuousness of the N-word inquiry. Properly applied, the law of evidence, which manifests considerable distrust of jurors' abilities to resist diversions, would have excluded the inquiry that Judge Ito permitted, especially in light of the impact that merely asking about the N-word would foreseeably have on at least some jurors.

---

*The defense was precluded from asking this question because, at the outset of the trial, it had no evidentiary basis for doing so.

Ironically, once Fuhrman denied using the N-word, the history of his racial language did become relevant to his credibility. Thus, Judge Ito rightly permitted the defense to requestion Fuhrman for purposes of impeachment and to play for the jury portions of the utterly discrediting audiotape.*

What about Johnnie Cochran's famous summation?

Some maintain that it was an improper call for jury nullification. Others maintain that it was a proper call for jurors to weigh heavily evidence suggesting that improper police behavior, including dishonesty, had deeply infected the prosecution's case. Both observations grasp a piece of a complicated reality. On the one hand, Cochran expressly denied that his client committed murder and challenged the factual basis of the prosecution's allegations. He did not adopt the stance of an advocate who conceded his client's guilt but pleaded for an acquittal nonetheless. On the other hand, it is possible to understand Cochran as saying that, even if jurors believed Simpson to be guilty beyond a reasonable doubt based on the evidence presented at trial, there was yet another reason to vote to acquit: the supposed need to "send a message" about police mendacity and racism, a need brought about by the inability or unwillingness of other authorities to "police the police."

I conclude that Judge Ito acted rightly by refraining from stopping or commenting upon Cochran's summation. Given the closeness of the issue, the leeway that should be given to attorneys in making arguments

---

*Judge Ito was wrong, however, in two other respects. First, he was wrong in excluding from the jury's attention Fuhrman's boasts about planting or destroying evidence. To quote Ito's most unforgiving critic, Vincent Bugliosi: "How in Ito's mind, could Fuhrman's mere use of the work 'nigger' in the past suggest he was more apt to have framed Simpson than if he claimed to have set up other criminal defendants in the past?" Vincent Bugliosi, *Outrage*, 73 (1996). Even worse was Ito's decision to play in open court portions of the tapes he excluded from the jury's consideration. The judge said that he did not want to be accused of suppressing information of vital public interest. If this was his concern, though, he could have addressed it by releasing the tapes *after* a verdict. What should have been his primary, overarching concern was not the public's thirst for information but rather the need for a fair trial. Judge Ito reversed those priorities, putting the fairness of the trial at risk for the sake of serving immediately mere curiosity. "In so far as the Fuhrman affair was concerned, Ito didn't know whether he was coming or going." Ibid.

to a jury, and the absence of a timely objection from the prosecution, Judge Ito's silence was prudent and fair.

The Neglected Problem of Neglectful (and Racially Prejudiced) Defense Attorneys

Simpson's attorneys were roundly criticized throughout the trial and after the verdict for "going too far" in defending their client. The journalist Fred Barnes spoke for many when he complained that Simpson's attorneys and other defense lawyers like them "are willing to make any arguments no matter how shameless or outrageous, on behalf of their clients."[102] It is a mistake, though, to generalize from an atypical episode. The great mass of persons charged with a serious criminal offense do not go to trial but instead plea-bargain.* Moreover, the average criminal defendant will not have several attorneys as did Simpson. The average defendant will have only one, frequently a person who is appointed by the court, and all too frequently a person who is ill equipped to represent his client effectively. Pathetically, the competence of appointed defense counsel is often lowest at precisely the point at which it should be highest—when the state seeks to extinguish a person's life for the commission of a crime.[103]

Consider the case of Wilburn Dobbs, who murdered the proprietor of a grocery store/gas station with a shotgun even though the victim apparently offered no resistance.[104] Fortunately, police succeeded in apprehending Dobbs. Unfortunately, the State of Georgia tried him in

---

*In 1989, 80 percent of all federal criminal cases were settled by guilty pleas. In 1988, in the seventy-five most populous counties in the United States, 91 percent of felony cases were settled by guilty pleas. See U.S. Department of Justice, *Sourcebook of Criminal Justice Statistics*, ed. Kathleen McGuire and Timothy J. Flanagan (1990).

Racial discrimination undoubtedly affects at least some of the highly discretionary decisions that prosecutors make in offering, accepting, and rejecting plea bargains, although the extent of this discrimination is unknown. See "Developments in the Law: Race and the Criminal Process," 101 *Harvard Review* (1988); Raymond Paternoster, "Prosecutorial Discretion in Requesting the Death Penalty: A Case of Victim-based Discrimination," 18 *Law and Society Review* 437 (1984); Michael L. Radelet and Glenn L. Pierce, "Race and Prosecutorial Discretion in Homicide Cases," 19 *Law and Society Review* 587 (1985).

proceedings that bring shame upon its administration of the law. A judge assigned Dobbs's defense to an attorney whose performance was so deficient that it deprived his client of what should constitute the bare minimum of representation required for a proper trial. This attorney did not know for sure whether he would actually conduct Dobbs's defense until the day of the trial. To his credit, the attorney did try to postpone the proceedings. Seeking a continuance, he told the court that he was, at that point, "in a better position to prosecute the case than defend it."[105] The judge, however, denied the request and the trial began. At trial, Dobbs's attorney failed to test the state's case in any substantial way. Most important, he failed to contest meaningfully the prosecutor's claim that his client should be executed. After conviction, during the sentencing phase of the trial, the defense attorney presented *no* evidence on Dobbs's behalf, contenting himself instead with merely reading to the jury part of a concurring opinion from a Supreme Court decision. To grasp the egregiousness of this conduct, one must recognize that in the penalty phase of a case in which a death sentence is sought, defense counsel is free to bring before a jury virtually anything that might move it to spare a defendant's life. Dobbs's defense counsel squandered this opportunity.

When subsequently challenged to explain his failure to offer any evidence in mitigation of his client's crime, the attorney claimed that the omission had been a tactical decision. He maintained that, because of his client's poor reputation in the community, he did not want to present "positive" character testimony for fear that it would be unpersuasive and, worse, provoke the prosecution to present damaging counterevidence.[106] That the attorney genuinely *decided* to forgo offering mitigating evidence is exceedingly doubtful. A different lawyer subsequently obtained affidavits from nineteen people who swore that they would have been willing to testify on Dobbs's behalf as character witnesses had they been contacted. The defense attorney did not contact them or anyone else who might have testified for Dobbs. This was not, then, a case in which a defense attorney attempted to unearth mitigating evidence and, upon evaluating it, decided to withhold the evidence. Rather, this is a case in which the attorney appears to have neglected to invest any energy in making even a preliminary inquiry.

To call what Dobbs's attorney did a "decision" is to dignify nothing more than lazy carelessness. This, however, is precisely what the courts did. In federal habeas corpus proceedings, a U.S. district court judge noted that Dobbs's attorney could have performed better in developing mitigating evidence, but concluded that the steps he took constituted "a reasonably substantial investigation." The court of appeals agreed that the defense attorney's investigation was "adequate."[107] In sum, in Dobbs's case the courts elevated no investigation into an adequate investigation.

This attitude toward the scandalously deficient performance of Dobbs's attorney is by no means unusual. Appellate courts have proven themselves willing to affirm routinely convictions and death penalties even when the laziness, inexperience, or ignorance of defense attorneys has severely compromised the adversarial character of trials.

The sector of the population most at risk of being saddled with inadequate legal counsel are those without the money to hire attorneys. The risk of inadequate representation has become more acute recently because legislatures have diminished or withdrawn funding from agencies that have heretofore represented indigent defendants, including those facing capital charges.[108] Here, as in many contexts, racial bias superimposes another layer of burden upon socioeconomic class inequities. In at least some instances, the lethal default of defense attorneys is related either to their own racial prejudices or to the racial prejudices of their peers, whom these attorneys are afraid of angering by fighting too hard on behalf of black clients.[109]

Racial bias of this sort probably played a role in the poor quality of representation that Dobbs received. Describing the testimony given by Dobbs's attorney in a postconviction hearing focusing on the attorney's performance, a district judge noted:

> Dobbs' trial attorney was outspoken about his [racial] views. He said that many blacks are uneducated and would not make good teachers, but do make good basketball players. He opined that blacks are less educated and less intelligent than whites either because of their nature or because "my granddaddy had slaves." He said that integration has led to deteriorating neighborhoods and schools, and referred to the black community in Chattanooga as "black boy jungle." He strongly implied that blacks have inferior morals by re-

lating a story about sex in a classroom. He also said that when he was young, a maid was hired with the understanding that she would steal some items. . . . He did say, however, that Martin Luther King, Jr., was "a great man."

The attorney stated that he uses the word "nigger" jokingly. He testified further that, in his experience as a criminal defense lawyer, a black accused of killing a white is more likely to be convicted than a black charged with killing a black, although he did not know why.[110]

It is difficult to draw hard and fast conclusions from this portrayal of the attorney's racial attitudes. Although these comments have a bad odor of racism about them, one must still acknowledge the gap that can separate attitudes from conduct. A racially biased attorney can nonetheless be skillful and committed, and an unprejudiced attorney can be inept and complacent. Here, as in so many areas we have discussed, complexity and uncertainty abound. What is clear, however, is that the plight of defendants stuck with attorneys who neglect their clients is a woefully underpublicized subject. O.J. Simpson's criminal trial showed much that is disturbing about the administration of law. Disturbing, too, however, is the character of Wilburn Dobbs's trial, including the inadequacy of the representation he received, a type of embarrassment to the legal profession about which many of Johnnie Cochran's critics are silent.

Black Power in the Jury Box?

Whatever message Johnnie Cochran intended to send with his famous summation, the fact is that a small but appreciable number of Americans believe that it is proper for them to engage in jury nullification.[111] Jury nullification means voting to acquit a defendant despite a belief beyond reasonable doubt that, based on proper evidence, the defendant is guilty of the crime with which he is charged. Nullification occurs when guilt is established but the jury decides to acquit based on its own sense of fairness, propriety, prejudice, or any other sentiment or concern. Race-conscious jury nullification has historically been exercised predominantly by whites. The focus of this discussion will be race-conscious nullification exercised by blacks, particularly the provocative encouragement of it voiced by Professor Paul Butler.

In "Racially Based Jury Nullification: Black Power in the Criminal Justice System," Professor Butler urges black jurors to refuse to vote to convict black defendants charged with certain crimes regardless of the evidence arrayed against them. He proposes this course of action because "the black community is better off when some nonviolent lawbreakers remain in the community rather than go to prison." More specifically, Butler argues that, absent special circumstances, black jurors should nullify convictions of guilty black defendants charged with what he describes as "nonviolent, *malum prohibitum* offenses, including victimless crimes like narcotics offenses."[112]

Butler does not argue in favor of nullification in all cases. He asserts that black jurors should vote to convict black defendants guilty of *violent* crimes like murder, rape, and assault. For an intermediate level of nonviolent crime, for example, theft or perjury, Butler contends that "nullification is an option that the [black] juror should consider, although there should be no presumption in favor of it." In this middle tier of cases, a black juror might appropriately vote for acquittal when a poor black woman steals from Tiffany's, but not when the same woman steals from her next-door neighbor. "The decision as to what kind of conduct by African-Americans ought to be punished is better made by African-Americans themselves," Butler writes, "based on the costs and benefits to their community, than by the traditional criminal justice process, which is controlled by white lawmakers and white law enforcers." It is "the moral responsibility of black jurors," Butler concludes, "to emancipate some guilty black outlaws."[113]

Butler's proposal rests on three main points. One is that a juror's power to vote to acquit a defendant who has been shown to be guilty is a power that may be put to laudable uses. He cites the refusal of a jury in *Bushnell's Case*[114] to convict a group of Quakers for unlawful assembly and disturbance of the peace, a landmark instance of resistance to governmental religious oppression. He cites the acquittal of Peter Zenger, who was accused of seditious libel for criticizing British colonial rule in North America, a landmark in the growth of freedom of expression. English law authorized the judge exclusively to determine whether statements made by the defendant were libelous. Yet, at trial, Zenger's attorney told the jury that it should ignore the judge's instructions and "make use of their own consciences and understandings, in judging of the lives, liberties, or estates of their fellow subjects."[115] Butler also cites *United States* v. *Morris* and other cases in which juries, prompted by defense attorneys, acquitted guilty defendants accused of violating the federal Fugitive Slave Act, which helped owners to recapture runaway slaves.[116]

Butler's second point is that a total breach of America's constitutional promises absolves blacks of a moral duty to obey the society's rules. " 'Democracy' as practiced in the United States," he writes, "has betrayed African Americans far more than they could ever betray it." According to Butler, the American power structure remains a pigmentocracy that condemns blacks to an inferior place in the social order and then punishes them harshly for antisocial conduct largely caused by the circumstances into which they have been thrown.[117] Butler's third point overlaps with the second. It is that white racism is the cause of much of the criminal conduct engaged in by blacks. "But for the (racist) environment," he writes, "the African American criminal would not be a criminal. . . . Racism creates and sustains the criminal breeding ground which produces the black criminal. Thus, when many African-Americans are locked up, it is because of a situation that white supremacy created."[118]

In Butler's view, blacks are subjected to "democratic domination" by a white majority that refuses to permit blacks to exercise a fair share of power. As a result, he contends, "African-Americans wield little influence over criminal law, state or federal."[119] Butler recognizes that, at least formally, blacks are protected against racial exclusion from participation in governance. To him, however, black participation is so limited that it amounts only to tokenism and reinforces the illusion that blacks are equal to whites in the eyes of the law. In light of their subjection to racist policies that they have had no fair opportunity to influence, blacks are morally justified, Butler concludes, in engaging in self-help, which means, in part, that they are ethically correct to exert black power in the jury box.

Professor Butler's essay brings into the open a clearly articulated version of a belief that had been known about previously only through furtive, vague, unnamed sources. Over the past few years, reports have surfaced of cases in which the evidence against black defendants being tried before predominantly black juries appeared to be so overwhelming that some observers speculated that jury nullification must account for acquittals or hung juries.[120] One example is the prosecution of Marion Barry, the mayor of Washington, D.C. After viewing a Federal Bureau of Investigation videotape that showed Barry smoking cocaine, and after listening to strong incriminating evidence from other sources, a predominantly black jury nonetheless declined to convict him of the most serious charges he faced.[121] Further evidence that black jurors engage in race-conscious nullification is provided by anonymous admissions of such conduct. In the District of Columbia, for instance, a person wrote an anonymous letter to court officials in which she identified herself as a juror who had recently declined to vote to convict a defendant charged with first degree murder. The letter writer stated that she and other members of the jury believed that the prosecution had proven the defendant's guilt but that they had voted to acquit anyway in deference to members of the jury who "didn't want to send any more Young Black Men to jail."[122]

The trial of O.J. Simpson, the most publicized criminal proceeding in American history, tremendously enlarged the specter (or hope) of race-conscious nullification by black jurors. Early on some commentators suggested that, in light of the intense anger felt by many blacks over racially discriminatory mistreatment by law enforcement officials, some black jurors might decline to vote to convict Simpson as a form of protest, regardless of the evidence in that particular case.[123] Those speculations were magnified when Johnnie Cochran focused jurors' attention on the infamous Mark Fuhrman.[124] Anxieties were heightened even more when, following Simpson's acquittal, some people celebrated in a fashion which suggested that they perceived the trial as a racial show of strength. Stating that he was happy with the acquittal even if Simpson did commit the murder, a black man in Boston ascribed his satisfaction to his perception that "we [blacks] never win *anything*." "A black man was charged with killing a white woman—a blond white woman at that," this man mused. "And the court said he didn't do it. Hell, that's worth celebrating."[125]

Butler published his essay against the backdrop of the Simpson acquittal. That timing, the provocativeness of its thesis, the identity of the author (a young black Harvard-trained law professor who is a former prosecutor), the prestige of the *Yale Law Journal*, anxieties over racial conflicts, and American culture's voracious appetite for controversial assured it a wide audience. Useful as a document that verifies and illuminates an important thread of thought and sensibility, Butler's essay is profoundly misleading as a guide to action. Not only is its destination regrettable, but along the way "Racially-Based Jury Nullification" gives voice to erroneous claims, dubious calculations, and destructive sentiments.

Butler's proposal rests on a seriously flawed assessment of the state of race relations within the administration of criminal law. According to Butler's portrayal, white racism is almost wholly triumphant in the criminal law system.[126] He sees black–white race relations as a narrative completely dominated by the continuity of African-American subordination, as opposed to a narrative marked by significant discontinuity—the leap from slavery to freedom, and from castelike stigmatization to an increasingly respected place in all aspects of American life. That explains why he feels justified in calling for subversion. He perceives blacks as occupying a place in the mind, soul, politics, and law of America that is essentially the same as that occupied by their enslaved or segregated forebears.

There is, to be sure, racial injustice in the administration of criminal law. In some instances, the injustices stem from the actions of officials who mistreat black suspects, defendants, and convicts, or offer ordinary black citizens less protection against criminality than is offered to whites (see chapters 2 and 3). In other instances, the law itself is racially unjust, as in the case law which broadly authorizes police officers to take race into account in making determinations of suspicion (see chapter 4). So, *yes*, Butler is correct when he notes with dissatisfaction that invidious racial discrimination remains a large and baleful presence in the criminal justice system.

Racial wrongdoing, however, is *all* that Butler sees. His portrayal of the criminal law system wholly omits any facts, developments, or tendencies that contradict, or even merely complicate, his preferred narrative. He portrays a static, one-dimensional system that is totally at odds with what black Americans need and want, a system that unequivocally represents and unrelentingly imposes "the white man's law." To illustrate his argument, Butler provides a long list of examples that document "racism in criminal justice":

inal Trial

case; the history of the criminalization of drug use; nporary administration of the death penalty; the use ing crime to race in the 1988 presidential campaign and other political campaigns; the beating of Rodney King and the acquittal of his police assailants; disparities between punishments for white-collar crimes and punishment for other crimes; more severe penalties for crack cocaine users than for powder cocaine users; the Charles Stuart and Susan Smith cases; police corruption scandals in minority neighborhoods in New York and Philadelphia; the O.J. Simpson case, including the extraordinary public and media fascination with it, the racist police officer who was the prosecution's star witness, and the response of many white people to the jury's verdict of acquittal; and, cited most frequently, the extraordinary incarceration of African-American men.[127]

A striking feature of Butler's presentation of this list is the absence of any acknowledgment that much of what he offers as evidence of racism also has a different side which evidences the long-standing struggle in American political culture *against* racism. True, the Scottsboro boys were subjected to a horrible, racially motivated persecution. It is also true, however, that courts at both the state and federal levels did ultimately prevent their executions, at times intervening in an extraordinary fashion.[128] Rodney King may have been victimized by officers in a police department that is rightly notorious for racism. Ultimately, however, several of his assailants were convicted and imprisoned pursuant to a federal criminal civil rights prosecution even after a state criminal trial in which they had largely prevailed.[129] Remarkably, Professor Butler lists the O.J. Simpson case among his examples of racism in the administration of criminal law. But, of course, in the end Simpson was *acquitted* despite the presence of considerable, if not overwhelming, incriminating evidence.

Butler's account withholds completely any recognition that restrictions on state power that define much of the constitutional law of criminal procedure are limits that emerged largely from struggles against racism.[130] Similarly, his account neglects to credit the significant presence of African-Americans in law enforcement, including those blacks in major urban areas who exercise power at the highest circles of executive police authority.* He speaks of the disparity in punishment between crack cocaine and powder cocaine as an example of "racism." Yet one would never suspect from his account that when the federal law that he criticizes was enacted, Charles Rangel, the African-American representative from Harlem, chaired the House Select Committee on Narcotics Abuse and Control and voted in favor of this law as did about half of the members of the Congressional Black Caucus.[131] In sum, Butler ignores or suppresses inconvenient facts, omitting significant parts of the story that cannot properly be overlooked if one seeks a comprehensive understanding of the place of race relations in the administration of criminal law. The criminal justice system is beset by racial problems, but they are by no means as large, immutable, or one-dimensional as Butler suggests. The problems we do face require judicious attention, not a campaign of defiant sabotage.

Another major failing of Butler's analysis is his failure to recognize that jury nullification is an exceedingly poor means for advancing the goal of a racially fair administration of criminal law. Two concerns are especially salient. First, as Professor Andrew C. Leipold notes, there is no reason to believe that a campaign of jury nullification will succeed in bringing about the broad social reforms that Butler demands. Jury nullification as typically implemented is a low-visibility, highly ambiguous protest unlikely to focus the attention of the public clearly on social problems in need of reform. "Because deliberations are secret and verdicts are opaque, it is hard to know why any particular jury decides to acquit"[132]—an observation vividly substantiated by the ongoing speculation over what animated the acquittal in the O.J. Simpson case. To publicize their aims, nullificationists would have to publicize their subversion of the criminal justice system, a route few have chosen to take.

That jury nullification is widely perceived as illegitimate under present circumstances suggests another reason for doubting the efficacy of

---

*"By the end of the 1980s, the number of African-American police chiefs had increaed to 130, and they served in six of the nation's largest cities (Baltimore, New York, Detroit, Chicago, Philadelphia, and Houston). This unprecedented phenomenon in American history represented a 180-degree change from the second-class status that African-Americans had traditionally held in American law enforcement." W. Marvin Dulaney, *Black Police in America* (1996).

Butler's proposal. Butler seems to believe that his proposal will move policymakers in the direction he desires, but there is little in the historical record to support this belief. Indeed, what evidence there is cuts the other way. When white Southern diehards made it clear that they would nullify criminal prosecutions of those who used racially motivated violence to resist reform in the aftermath of the Civil War, the ascendant political party in the national government responded with an unprecedented intervention of federal power in support of actions—the elevation of blacks to formal equality with whites—that the nullifiers abhorred.[133] A century later, when white Southern segregationist diehards again made it clear that they were prepared to nullify criminal prosecutions of violent criminals, large and powerful blocs in society again intervened in unprecedented ways, partly out of sympathy with those whom the nullifiers opposed, but also to show that they would not allow the legal order to be openly flouted.[134] In both of these instances, public opinion overwhelmed *white* nullifiers. An outspoken campaign of jury nullification carried on by blacks would reap no less of a reaction. The intimation that jury nullification explains, at least in part, several high-profile acquittals has already sparked tremendous condemnation that is likely to affect, for the worse, the fortunes of African-Americans. Referring to this danger, a columnist in the *New York Times* quoted a letter sent to him immediately before the Simpson acquittal. "When O.J. gets off," the writer declared, "the whites will riot the way we whites do: leave the cities, go to Idaho or Oregon or Arizona, vote for Gingrich . . . and punish the blacks by closing their day-care centers and cutting off their Medicaid."[135] Whether this prophecy will be borne out is unclear. Already, though, the perception that nullificationist sentiment is increasing has prompted calls for reaction. An example is the effort to replace the requirement that a jury be unanimous in order to convict with a less demanding standard under which convictions could be obtained with several jurors voting for acquittal. Critiques of the unanimity requirement have been around for a long time, and two states—Louisiana and Oregon—now permit convictions even with two or more jurors voting to acquit.[136] Fear of a perceived rise in nullificationist sentiments is giving new life to these criticisms.[137]

Changing the unanimity requirement does not exhaust the reactive possibilities that could ensue from implementation of Butler's proposal. If a large number of blacks clearly engage in "guerrilla warfare" as jurors, their action might call into question the right of blacks to be selected for jury service on precisely the same terms as others. Widespread adoption of Butler's proposal would likely give rise to measures designed to exclude prospective nullifiers from juries, measures that would result almost certainly in the disproportionate exclusion of blacks. Moreover, if adherents to the Butler program proved to be especially clever and relentless in their subversion, one can imagine (with horror) the emergence of demands that black prospective jurors show a special sign of allegiance to the legal system in return for the opportunity to be considered for jury service or, worse yet, demands that blacks be excused from jury service altogether during the pendency of the nullification crisis.

Professor Butler fails to mention the possibility that limiting the rights of blacks to sit on juries might be part of a reaction against his scheme. This is odd. Having called upon black jurors to sabotage the criminal justice system, he evinces little concern over the steps that might be taken in response. This omission may signal nothing more than a failure to think through the consequences of his proposal. I suspect, however, that it signals something more. I suspect that it signals, ironically, that despite all of his accusatory rhetoric, Professor Butler does not really believe that American society is as oppressively racist as he suggests. If a sufficient number of people were to follow his proposal, however, conditions might be brought into existence that would make his caricature of American society a self-fulfilling prophecy.

There are additional reasons to object to Butler's scheme and the reasoning and sensibility that it embodies. Butler suggests that black criminals should be exempt from *punishment* on the grounds that "but for the [racist] environment, the African-American criminal would not be a criminal."[138] Butler urges the conviction and incarceration of black *violent* criminals, but he claims to do so only for purposes of deterrence and incapacitation, not for purposes of retribution. Butler hints that he rejects retribution in general as a basis for coercive action.[139] However, as with every other significant aspect of his analysis, Butler develops a racial critique of retribution as applied to *black* criminals, maintaining that it is unfair to punish people for "negative" reactions to racist, oppressive conditions.[140]

This feature of Butler's analysis is significant for a variety of reasons. First, it both reflects and contributes to an argument made on behalf of people whose misconduct is said to be attributable to conditions that have so victimized them as to excuse their misdeeds.[141] This argument has been made on behalf of battered wives who have killed abusive husbands and battered children who have killed abusive parents. Butler simply extends the logic of these "abuse excuses" to people whom he perceives as having been battered by white racism—nearly *all* African-Americans.*

There is good reason to scrutinize closely all of the abuse excuses that have been advanced recently to absolve persons of criminal responsibility for acts typically viewed as criminal. Some appear to be of dubious merit. The racial oppression excuse that Butler offers is particularly ill-founded. Unlike other abuse excuses, Butler's is untethered to particular events or individuals. Rather, it refers to all of American history and embraces an entire race, *all* African-Americans, from Colin Powell on down.

The implications of Butler's theory for American race relations are staggering. If it were believed and acted upon, his conception of the irresponsibility of blacks would impose upon African-Americans a disability from which they were free even during the era of slavery: the disability of being perceived as people wholly devoid of moral choice and thus blameless for purposes of retribution, the same way that infants, the insane, and animals are typically viewed as morally blameless. The slave codes were based in part on a racially demeaning perception of blacks. As bad as those codes were, though, they all conceded that blacks were sufficiently human, moral, and responsible to be held accountable for their actions.[142]

Butler contends that African-Americans cannot afford to lock up African-Americans who engage in relatively minor, nonviolent infractions because, in doing so, "there is too little bang for the buck." "Black people have a community that needs building, and children who need

---

*Butler, of course, is not alone in pursuing this path. After Colin Ferguson shot twenty-five people on the Long Island Railroad on December 7, 1993, his attorneys announced that they would mount a black rage defense based on the idea that American racism had pushed their already unstable client into insanity. Ferguson fired his attorneys before they could present their theory. He represented himself, was convicted, and was sentenced to imprisonment for life. See Judd F. Sneirson, "Black Rage and the Criminal Law," 143 *University of Pennsylvania Law Review* 2251 (1995); Kimberly M. Copp, "Black Rage," 29 *John Marshall Law Review* 205 (1995).

rescuing, and as long as a person will not hurt anyone, the community needs him there to help." Assuming that the lawbreaker will help is a gamble, Butler concedes, "but not a reckless one, for the 'just' African-American community will not leave [him] be: It will . . . encourage his education and provide his health care . . . and, if necessary, sue him for child support."[143]

That is delusionary. If the communities Butler refers to possessed the resources he mentions, the crime problems they face would not be nearly so urgent; these communities could take care of these problems by themselves. Many poor, downtrodden communities, however, desperately weakened by social disorder and other ills, are apparently unable to address their crime problems adequately. That is why some of the residents in many of these communities clamor for curfews and even military intervention.* They want relief from criminals who both reflect and entrench social misery. Many of these criminal sowers of social decay are themselves victims of poverty, ignorance, joblessness, child abuse, and so on. Society ought to do more to prevent people from falling so low, and when people do fall, society ought to do more to attend to their plight. At the same time, however, society ought to insulate the neighbors of these victimized victimizers from criminal conduct.

Butler exudes keen sympathy for nonviolent drug offenders and similar criminals. By contrast, Butler is inattentive to the aspirations, frustrations, and fears of law-abiding people compelled by circumstances to live in close proximity to the criminals for whom he is willing to urge subversion of the legal system. Butler simply overlooks the sec-

---

*Recall that it was the African-American mayor of Washington, D.C., Sharon Pratt Kelly, who requested that President Clinton dispatch the National Guard to the nation's capital in order to quell spiraling violence. See B. Drummond Ayres, Jr., "Washington Mayor Seeks Aid on Guard in Combating Crime," *New York Times*, October 23, 1993. Prior to Mayor Kelly's request, other blacks had also called for extraordinary interventions on the part of law enforcement authorities, ranging from imposition of martial law to summary executions of drug dealers. See Michael Z. Letwin, "Report from the Front Line: The Bennett Plan, Street-Level Drug Enforcement in New York City and the Legalization Debate," 18 *Hofstra Law Review* 795, 797 n.13 (1990). Of African-Americans polled in February 1994, 25 percent designated crime the main problem facing the country today; 8 percent designated racism as the main problem. See William A. Henry, III, "How African Americans See It," *Time*, February 18, 1994.

tor of the black law-abiding population that desires *more* rather than *less* prosecution and punishment for *all* types of criminals. According to data collected by a 1993 Gallup Poll, 82 percent of the blacks surveyed believed that the courts in their area do not treat criminals harshly enough; 75 percent favored putting more police on the streets to combat crime; and 68 percent favored building more prisons so that longer sentences could be given.[144] One would never know from Butler's analysis that a large number of ordinary, grass-roots blacks embrace such views.*

If a large number of blacks have views on the administration of criminal law that are counter to Butler's, why worry about his proposal? Why not ignore his advice and simply wait for mass opinion within black and other communities to snub it? There are several reasons why it is worthwhile to oppose Butler's proposal openly and in detail. First, it would not take many people to wreak havoc with the jury system. The unanimity requirement renders juries uniquely susceptible to disruption by a resolute cadre of nullifiers. Since in most places it takes only one person to cause a hung jury, Butler would not need to convince an overwhelming number in order to succeed in creating substantial gridlock. Second, in terms of political significance, positioning, organization, and publicity are often more crucial than the popularity or unpopularity, intelligence or silliness, of a given viewpoint. Although many blacks hold views diametrically opposed to Butler's on nullification and related issues, *his* is the one that *60 Minutes* publicized and that will be deemed by many as the authentically "black" position.† Left un-

---

*Professor Butler does acknowledge the presence of those whom he refers to as African-American "law enforcement enthusiasts." He uses some of my writings to illustrate the views of that camp. See Butler, "Racially Based Jury Nullification: Black Power in the Criminal Justice System," 105 *Yale Law Journal* 677, 697–698 (1995). Nowhere, however, does he acknowledge the broad popularity of the views that he attributes to the law enforcement enthusiasts. To the contrary, although he writes that blacks "tend to be more worried about crime than whites," he asserts that "this enhanced concern . . . does not appear to translate into endorsement of tougher enforcement of traditional criminal law." Ibid., 699. As the polling data cited in the text and other evidence indicate, however, Butler's description of black public opinion is simply wrong. See Andrew D. Leipold, "The Dangers of Race-Based Jury Nullification," *UCLA Law Review* 109 (1996).

†See *60 Minutes,* 1996 WL 806 4808, March 10, 1996.

corrected, such misperceptions will gain currency, leading to the further isolation and stigmatization of Negroes in the eyes of many Americans.

Another reason to object to Butler's scheme is that it pays insufficient attention to excesses that Butler himself claims to oppose. Butler urges black jurors to nullify prosecution of black defendants only in cases involving nonviolent crime; he urges that they act normally, that is, vote based on their view of the evidence, in cases involving violent offenses. It is not all clear, however, why he draws the line at violent crime.* This vagueness suggests that Butler's primary concern is with protecting *blacks* against violence, and comments he made regarding the acquittal of O.J. Simpson raise doubts about the extent of his commitment to protecting *all* persons from criminal violence.

Explaining why nullification would be improper in a murder case, Butler says that black jurors should vote to convict (if the evidence points beyond reasonable doubt to guilt) because "there is a possibility that a guilty verdict will prevent another person from becoming a victim." "In effect," he notes, "I 'write off' the black person who takes a life . . . because the black community cannot afford the risks of leaving this person in its midst."[145] But just suppose that this murderer, objecting to black-on-black crime out of a sense of racial kinship, only kills white people? Not so long ago, after all, an entertainer-activist of note, Sister Souljah, suggested that "if black people kill black people every day, why not have a week [in which blacks] kill white people."[146] For black jurors to subvert openly a prosecution in such a case would surely send a powerful message, and to the extent that the hypothesized murderer self-consciously kills only white people, he poses no direct threat to black lives. This scenario would seem to present a difficult case for Butler. He concedes that he encounters problems deciding whether nullification is warranted in a case in which a black person burglarizes the home of a rich family. (Butler inexplicably omits the race of the rich family, but given the structure of his argument, it is fair to conclude that

---

*Indeed, Butler is inconsistent in drawing the line at violent crime. At one point, he concedes that under his analysis "this limitation is not morally required." Butler, "Racially Based Jury Nullification," 709. At other points, however, he draws the line at violent crime unequivocably. Ibid., 716 ("Under my proposal, violent lawbreakers would go to prison").

he is referring to a rich white family.) "I would encourage nullification here only in extreme cases (i.e., nonviolent theft from the very wealthy)," he writes, "and mainly for political reasons: If the rich cannot rely on criminal law for the protection of their property and the law prevents more direct self-help measures, perhaps they will focus on correcting the conditions that make others want to steal from them."[147] Having pushed the *property* of rich whites outside the protection of criminal law based on the supposition that doing so might scare them into supporting egalitarian social reforms, why not at least experiment with pushing the *lives* of rich whites outside the protection of criminal law, hoping for a similarly good result?

Butler shrinks from taking his jury nullification scheme this far, but he offers no reason why. Nor does he explain why anyone should have faith that those who follow his prescription will heed his (weak) admonition to draw the line at violent crime. He says that he is "confident that balancing the social costs and benefits of incarceration would not lead black jurors to release violent criminals simply because of their race."[148] Yet on the same page he concedes that "some violent offenders currently receive the benefits of jury nullification . . . from a misguided if well-intentioned attempt by racial critics to make a political point."* Moreover, in a revealing opinion-editorial piece published soon after the acquittal of O.J. Simpson, Butler expressed sentiments of the sort that would likely benefit some violent offenders through racially motivated exertions of black power in the jury box. Butler writes that, after hearing the verdict, "I danced my freedom dance along with my sisters and brothers all over the world." It would be one thing if Butler had danced his freedom dance upon a firm belief in Simpson's innocence, but that is not how Butler viewed the case. Butler writes that he believes that Simpson "probably did it,"[149] in other words, that Simpson probably murdered two human beings, one of whom was his former wife and the mother of his children. Butler properly notes that a perception of probable guilt is an inadequate basis for conviction, which requires a finding of guilt beyond reasonable doubt. Even assuming, however, that reasonable doubt was present, thereby rightly precluding a conviction, what is the character of the sentiment that would prompt one to *dance* after the

---

*Later in the essay he repeats the point, saying that "it appears that some black jurors now excuse some conduct—like murder—that they should not excuse." Ibid., 723.

acquittal of a defendant whom one believes to be probably guilty of a double murder? It is a sentiment that is morally repugnant and politically dangerous.

There are, as we have seen, reasons to object to Butler's proposal. First, the nature of the social injustice Butler rightly objects to is not of the sort that properly gives rise to revolutionary subversion. When blacks were enslaved, revolutionary means of redress were appropriate—including armed rebellion, not to mention jury nullification.[150] Today, however, blacks are not enslaved. In contrast to the period which witnessed the fugitive slave laws, blacks share in the shaping of governmental policies, including those that Butler portrays as the result of white domination.

Second, there remains the problem of efficacy. Because jury nullification is often opaque, it is ill suited as a vehicle for attacking widespread problems, as opposed to particular instances of injustice. Butler, moreover, limits his call for nullification only to prospective *black* jurors. This is strange. Butler himself recognizes that a much stronger message would certainly be sent if *all* prospective jurors pursued a campaign of nullification. Butler justifies limiting his call for nullification to black jurors on the grounds that blacks have a "unique history and position in the United States."[151] That is true as a matter of description. Why should that make a difference, however, as a matter of prescription? Perhaps Butler means to suggest that only black jurors have the moral right to engage in nullification because only their history and present circumstances relieve them of the duty to follow the rules of the legal order. If the rules of the legal order are fundamentally oppressive, however, then *all* citizens, whatever their race, should feel morally bound to disobey and change them. A black slave should not have felt bound by proslavery laws in the antebellum South, but neither should a white person have felt bound by those rules.

Perhaps Butler believes that only black jurors have a moral responsibility to address the plight of black communities, or (a variation on the theme) that only black jurors have a sufficiently strong responsibility to warrant the extraordinary step of nullification. Why, however, should the moral responsibility of whites to address the racial wrongs of American society be any less intense and exacting than the moral responsibility of blacks? Indeed, if anything, whites have *more* of a moral responsibility to act because of their greater ability to reform the society (and also perhaps because of having benefited, albeit involuntarily, from the society's privileging of white skin).

The most fundamental reason to oppose Professor Butler's call for racially selective jury nullification is that it is based on a sentiment that is regrettably widespread in American culture: an ultimately destructive sentiment of racial kinship that prompts individuals of a given race to care more about "their own" than people of another race. He expresses this sentiment throughout his essay by explicitly erecting racial boundaries around his conception of responsibility, community, and empathy.* Because of that sentiment, he assumes that it is proper for prospective black jurors to care more about black communities than white communities, that it is proper for black jurors to be more concerned with the fate of black defendants than white defendants, and that it is proper for the black juror to be more protective of the property (and perhaps the lives?) of black people than white people. Along that road lies moral and political disaster. The disaster includes not only increasing but, worse, *legitimizing* the tendency of people to privilege in racial terms "their own."† Some will say that this racial privileging has already happened and is, in any event, inevitable. The situation can and will get worse, however, if Butler's plan and the thinking behind it gain adherents. His program, although animated by a desire to challenge racial injustice, would demolish the moral framework upon which an effective, attractive, and compelling alternative can and must be built.

---

*He writes, for instance, that "African-American jurors should ... exercise their power in the best interests of the black community." Butler, "Racially-Based Jury Nullification," 715. If that is so, should white jurors exercise their power in the best interests of the white community? Some white jurors, judges, and legislators do exercise their power in what they perceive to be the best interest of the white community. They are wrong, however, to the extent that they do so on a racial basis. That correct sense of wrong is the basis upon which a moral critique of their actions must rest.

†One of the black members of the jury that acquitted O.J. Simpson reportedly stated after the verdict, "We've got to protect our own." See Jeffrey Toobin, *The Run of His Life: The People v. O.J. Simpson*, 431 (1996). One should be careful with this report; the author reporting it does not offer a specific source that permits an assessment of reliability. For my purposes, though, it is enough to note that the juror's alleged statement is wholly plausible because of the widespread existence of the racial sentiments I criticize.

9.

Race, Law, and Punishment:
The Death Penalty

"[T]he unconscious operation of irrational sympathies and antipathies, including racial, upon jury decisions and (hence) prosecutorial decisions is real , acknowledged in the decisions of this court, and ineradicable."
—Antonin Scalia

NO ISSUES CONCERNING race and criminal law are more sobering than those raised by allegations that racial selectivity affects the administration of capital punishment. First, sentencing a person to death as punishment for crime is a unique flexing of state power that inevitably reflects the society's deepest values, emotions, and neuroses. Second, the legal system has shown itself to be largely incapable of acknowledging the influence of racial sentiment in the meting out of punishment even in circumstances in which the presence of such bias is obvious. In no other area of criminal law have judges engaged in more obfuscation, delusion, evasion, and deception. Third, addressing racial discrimination in capital sentencing poses a daunting task for those seeking to craft appropriate remedies.

If a jurisdiction tends to punish more harshly murderers of whites than murderers of blacks, is the appropriate response to abolish capital punishment, to more narrowly limit the circumstances in which capital punishment is imposed, or to execute more people who murder blacks? Even if such a tendency exists, should it be the basis for granting relief to a convicted murderer who fails to show that racial discrimination affected the punishment meted out in his particular case? Is such a tendency a remediable wrong or, instead, an inevitable social trait whereby people unavoidably identify more with the victimization of "their own" as opposed to the victimization of "others"? If this tendency is a wrong, is remedying it within the capacity of courts or is remedying this wrong best left to the legislative and executive branches of government?

These and related questions are the subject of this chapter.

Rape, Capital Punishment, and the Politics of Denial

The clearest example of both the presence of racial discrimination in sentencing and the determination of judges to avoid acknowledging that presence is the case law that arose from efforts to save from execution black men convicted of raping white women.

The case of the Martinsville Seven, a group of black men condemned to death for raping a white woman in Martinsville, Virginia, in 1949, marked the first instance that death sentences for rape were seriously challenged on racial discrimination grounds.[1] The seven were tried and sentenced by all-white juries in proceedings that clearly established their guilt. On appeal, the defendants' attorneys showed that between 1908 and 1949, no white man had been executed for rape, although forty-five black men had been put to death.* During those same years, almost twice as many blacks as whites convicted for rape were sentenced to life imprisonment. Lawyers for the Martinsville Seven challenged their clients' death sentences on the grounds that this racial pattern represented a continuation of antebellum practices that the federal constitution had rendered illegal. They asserted that it was "the policy, practice, and custom of the Commonwealth of Virginia to inflict the death penalty upon negroes, because of their race and color, convicted of rape upon white women, while failing and refusing to in-

---

*One white man who had been sentenced to death for rape, received a commutation and pardon from the governor (for reasons I do not know). See Eric W. Rise, *The Martinsville Seven*, 120 (1995).

flict the death penalty upon white [men] convicted of rape of negro women."[2]

Virginia courts rebuffed the defendants' claim with arguments that have been repeated subsequently on numerous occasions. On direct review, the Supreme Court of Virginia took umbrage at the defendants' allegation, stating vehemently that there was "not a scintilla of evidence" in support of it and, indeed, that it was "contrary to fact."[3] The court noted two cases in which it set aside convictions and death sentences imposed on black men accused of raping white women. That response, however, failed to address the defendants' claim that, customarily, the criminal justice apparatus treated black men differently from white men convicted of rape. The defendants did not aver that the justices of the Supreme Court of Virginia treated blacks and whites differently on a racial basis. Rather, they argued that other, lower officials in the criminal justice hierarchy meted out racially discriminatory treatment in punishment. However, even if the defendants had charged the Virginia Supreme Court with complicity in the racial discrimination complained of, the two counterexamples that the court cited provide weak rebuttal evidence. Simply because the court ruled in favor of two black defendants did not mean that, as a class, black defendants accused of raping white women were not the targets of invidious racial discrimination. Even the two black defendants freed may have been discriminated against in the sense that similarly situated white men would not have been prosecuted or would have been freed more willingly by the courts pursuant to a different evidentiary standard. The charge of the Martinsville Seven was not that blacks were *invariably* discriminated against; their claim was that, for racial reasons, black men were typically sentenced to death for offenses which elicited less severe punishment when committed by white men. Furthermore, the cases cited by the Virginia Supreme Court were ones in which defendants' convictions were annulled for lack of evidence of guilt. Defendants' complaints, however, went to the question of punishment, not guilt. They maintained that even guilty defendants were entitled to be free of racial discrimination in the infliction of punishment.

The statistics offered by the defendants should have been deemed sufficiently arresting to require explanation in the same way that the prolonged absence of blacks from juries was deemed to require explanation in *Neal* and *Norris* (see pp. 169–177). Put more formally, the statistics should have been seen as constituting a prima facie case of racial discrimination. The Supreme Court of Virginia, however, gave the statistical evidence no credit and offered no reason for minimizing its significance so strongly. Nor did the court offer a counter-explanation that might plausibly explain why, over a forty-two–year period, forty-five of the forty-six men sentenced to death for rape were black.[4]

Rather than attempting to explain this pattern, the Virginia Supreme Court attacked the defendants' attorneys for even raising the issue, asserting that doing so was "an abortive attempt to inject into the proceedings racial prejudice."[5] To use a much noted current phrase, the Supreme Court of Virginia accused the lawyers of the Martinsville Seven of "playing the race card" in their efforts to save their clients from execution. As we have seen, defense attorneys do sometimes exploit racial sentiment. It is far-fetched to believe, however, that the attorneys for the Martinsville Seven were doing so. They raised the race question because the demographics of punishment for rape (and a social order openly devoted to a white supremacist pigmentocracy) gave good reason to believe that, for racial reasons, sentencing authorities characteristically treated blacks eligible for capital punishment more harshly than similarly situated whites.*

Further attempting to rebut the defendants' allegation, the Virginia Supreme Court admiringly highlighted the trial judge's admonition to the defense and prosecuting attorneys:

> Gentlemen of counsel, as you know, we are here called upon to try seven men charged with the most serious crime. . . . We here in the City and County have been entirely free from any trouble between

---

*At the time of the trial of the Martinsville Seven, Virginia required private firms to separate the races in places of public accommodation; required public authorities to separate the races in schools, hospitals, prisons, and other facilities; prohibited transracial marriage; excluded blacks from certain educational opportunities (e.g., medical and dental education) within the state (though the state did make available some limited funds for such education outside the state); and denied licenses to do business within Virginia to any fraternal beneficiary association, company, or society that accepted white and colored members. See Pauli Murry, *State's Laws on Race and Color* 46–490 (1950).

the races. We have in our community a negro population of splendid citizens and these good negro citizens deplore this unfortunate alleged happening as much, or more, than do the citizens of the white race. I here and now admonish you that this case must and will be tried in such a way as not to disturb the kindly feeling now locally existing between the races. It must be tried as though both parties were members of the same race.[6]

Putting aside the dubious notion that a jurisdiction governed by de jure segregation could be "entirely free from any trouble between the races," the trial judge's remarks, even if curative, were directed to the attorneys, not to the people who actually did the sentencing. Under Virginia law, it was left to the discretion of the jury to sentence persons convicted of rape to be "punished with death, or confinement in the penitentiary for life, or for any term not less than five years."[7] This law, the court declared, "applies to all alike, regardless of race or creed."[8] Of course, the defendants did not challenge the facial validity of the law; they challenged the way it was administered. The court claimed that variation in punishments handed down by juries "does not depend upon the race of the accused, but upon the circumstances, aggravation, and enormity of the crime proven in each case."[9] That observation, however, was more a declaration of faith than a description of reality. The court offered no factual support to substantiate its assertion.

Only briefly did the Supreme Court of Virginia respond with particularity to the defendants' charge:

There are no ameliorating circumstances shown in the records in these cases. On the contrary, the evidence shows that four men deliberately planned to waylay [the victim] and to ravish her. . . . [One defendant], a man 37 years of age, saw the four men attacking [the victim]. Instead of helping her, he left the scene, informed two others of what was taking place, the three went to the scene, and each, in turn, ravished [the victim]. One can hardly conceive of a more atrocious, a more beastly crime.[10]

The court seems to have been saying that, regardless of what had happened in other prosecutions, in this one there were sound, nonracial reasons for this jury or any jury to sentence these defendants to death. The court rejected defense attorneys' efforts to link this case to other rape cases. The court insisted that sentencing in other cases shed little or no light on the appropriateness of the punishment meted out in the case at hand.

After the Supreme Court of Virginia rejected their appeal, the Martinsville Seven pressed their claims anew in state habeas corpus proceedings. In addition to voicing arguments previously noted, the judges who rebuffed the defendants raised another concern worthy of notice: a belief that retaining the death penalty and eliminating racial disparities in sentencing would necessarily entail race consciousness in regulating punishment. That this concern was in the mind of at least one of the Virginia justices is shown by the worried musings of Justice John W. Eggleston, who suggested at oral argument that if the defendants' argument prevailed, "no Negroes could be executed unless a certain number of white people" were also sentenced to death.[11]

Soon after the Supreme Court of the United States declined to review the Virginia Supreme Court's denial of habeas corpus relief, the Martinsville Seven were executed by electrocution.* The arguments that their attorneys pioneeringly advanced, however, did not die. Other attorneys picked up and used these arguments in other jurisdictions where research unearthed clear, sharp, unexplained differences in the extent to which blacks as opposed to whites were sentenced to death for rape. In several cases in Florida, for example, defense attorneys challenged death sentences with racial discrimination claims based on evidence that, for a twenty-year period between 1935 and 1955, twenty-three blacks were executed for rape but only one white person.[12]

These challenges, too, however, proved unavailing. Characteristic is the following response by the Florida Supreme Court. The defendant's statistical evidence, the court declared,

---

*In addition to challenging the death sentences in court, those seeking to save the Martinsville Seven appealed for clemency to the governor of Virginia. Several letters pleading for mercy referred to an incident in which two white Richmond police officers convicted of raping a black woman received only seven-year prison terms. Nevertheless, Governor John S. Battle declined to commute the sentences of the Martinsville Seven. See Rise, *The Martinsville Seven*, 108.

is not shown to have any bearing on or relation to the case at bar. The historical fact that over a period of 20 years or more one white man and 23 Negroes have been tried and convicted for rape in Florida offers no lead to the correct determination of this case. The facts in none of these cases are shown to be remotely relevant to the case at bar and the points of law raised are not shown to be parallel in the slightest. To a sociologist or psychologist in some fields of research they would no doubt have value, but in a court of law as presented they are devoid of force or effect.[13]

The courts which rejected these and similar racial discrimination claims would have probably rejected *any* challenge to a punishment based primarily on a statistical study, regardless of its sophistication.* Notwithstanding judicial hostility, however, defense attorneys continued to press these claims. In the face of judicial rebukes, they persistently refined their evidence. There was considerable room for improvement, because the early statistical studies, although sufficiently disturbing to require an explanation from the state, did not precisely and systematically negate the possibility that disparities might, in fact, be explainable on other grounds. To remedy this deficiency, the NAACP Legal Defense and Educational Fund (LDF) organized a project to collect and assemble data about the administration of punishment for rape.[14] In one proceeding in which defense attorneys sought to make use of this information, a federal district judge reacted in a unique but noteworthy fashion.

In 1966, lawyers for Louis Moorer, a black man who raped a white woman in South Carolina, requested a sixty-day extension of a deadline

---

*Indeed, some judges came close to saying as much. In affirming the rejection of a racial discrimination challenge, a U.S. court of appeals remarked that "in light of the inviolability of the jury room, and in view of the uncontrolled character of the determinations that are confided to the jury, the trial court could not find that the statute here is unconstitutional in its application either to Negroes generally or to this appellant." *State* v. *Culver*, 253 F.2d 507, 508 (CA 5 1958), *cert. denied*, 358 U.S. 822 (1958). The notion that juries should possess a discretion in sentencing that is of an "uncontrolled character," along with a belief that the "inviolability of the jury room" entails refusing to review jury sentencing determinations, would appear to doom any and all equal protection attacks on sentences.

for submitting legal briefs on his behalf. He claimed that the state's administration of capital punishment for rape was racially discriminatory and that the extension was necessary in order to permit his attorneys the opportunity to buttress his case with information gathered by the LDF. U.S. District Judge Robert W. Hemphill denied the extension. Attorneys for Moorer then offered to introduce into evidence the raw data that had been gathered. Judge Hemphill refused to admit the documentation and instead took it into custody and ordered it sealed and subject to copying only with his permission. Moorer's attorney eventually succeeded in convincing a court of appeals to return the documentation to them (and indeed succeeded in winning a new trial for Moorer on grounds other than his racial discrimination claim).[15] But Judge Hemphill's order, albeit idiosyncratic, does illuminate the deep sense of affront felt by many judges when confronting the racial discrimination claims that desperate defense attorneys continued to assert.

The fullest airing of this issue occurred in a case from Garland County, Arkansas, which gave rise to several significant judicial opinions that rejected the defendant's claim.[16] In 1962, an all-white jury convicted a twenty-two-year-old black man, William L. Maxwell, of raping a thirty-five-year-old white woman, Stella Spoon, after breaking into her home, where she lived with her ninety-year-old father. Under Arkansas law, the jury could have either acquitted Maxwell, found him guilty with an affixed punishment of life imprisonment, or simply found him guilty, in which case the death penalty was mandatory. Because the jury selected the third alternative, it effectively condemned him to death.

Defense attorneys asserted that, by racial custom, Arkansas juries tended to deal more harshly with black men convicted of raping white women than any other class of convicted rapists. They charged that by more readily sentencing to death black male rapists of white women, the Arkansas authorities deprived that class of criminals of equality before the law. To advance this thesis, defense attorneys relied upon statistical studies directed by Professor Mervin Wolfgang.[17]

Using standard techniques, Wolfgang selected a random sample of counties to represent urban–rural and black–white demographic distributions. He examined information about every rape conviction in these counties between 1945 and 1965, not only the race of perpetrators and victims but a long list of other variables that would likely have had a bearing on the sentence rendered: offender characteristics (age, marital status, previous criminal record, etc.); victim characteristics (age, marital status, criminal record, reputation for chastity, children, etc.); nature of the relationship between the victim and the offender (were they strangers or had they had prior sexual relations); circumstances of the offense (was it related to a contemporaneous offense, was it carried out with a weapon, was the victim seriously physically injured, was the victim made pregnant by the attack, etc.); the circumstances of the trial (did the defendant plead guilty, was he represented by paid or appointed counsel, and so on).

Wolfgang's study found that of thirty-four blacks convicted of rape, ten (or 29 percent) were sentenced to death. By contrast, of twenty-one whites convicted of rape, only four (or 19 percent) were sentenced to death. When Wolfgang took the race of the victim into account, racial disparities widened and sharpened. Of the nineteen blacks convicted of raping white women, nine (or nearly 50 percent) were sentenced to death. By contrast, the incidence of the death penalty declined considerably in the remainder of the cases, all of which were intraracial (a black man charged with raping a black woman or a white man charged with raping a white woman). Juries imposed death sentences in only five (or 14 percent) of such cases.[18]

In the federal habeas corpus phase of the Maxwell litigation, U.S. District Court Judge J. Smith Henley gave the most detailed response to a racial discrimination challenge to a death sentence in a rape case that had ever been offered up to that point. Henley conceded that the sentencing pattern revealed by the Wolfgang study "could not be due to the operation of the laws of chance." Nonetheless, he concluded:

> the Court is not convinced that [the statistical evidence] is sufficiently broad, accurate, or precise as to establish satisfactorily that Arkansas juries in general practice unconstitutional racial discrimination in rape cases involving Negro men and white women or to require or justify the inference that the Garland County jury which tried petitioner was motivated by racial discrimination when it failed to assess a punishment of life imprisonment.[19]

Henley gave several reasons for his conclusion. First, in his view, the study covered too few counties and too few cases to make it convincing.

He noted that the counties examined contained only 47 percent of the state's population, questioned whether the counties studied were representative, and observed that the county in which the defendant was tried was not among those counties included in the Wolfgang study.

Henley also maintained that the Wolfgang study, although more extensive and sophisticated than its predecessors, failed to produce sufficient information about the rape cases examined to show convincingly that racial considerations as opposed to something else prompted the sentencing decisions of the juries studied. "Dr. Wolfgang's statistics," Henley remarked, "really reveal very little about the details of the cases of the . . . Negroes who received the death sentence for raping white women as compared to the details of the cases in which other racial situations were involved."[20]

Henley suggested, for instance, that the defense of consent in a rape case might play a role in the punishment handed down. Facing a consent defense, a jury might feel sufficiently sure of guilt to convict a defendant but insufficiently sure to condemn him to death. Defense counsel for a black defendant charged with raping a white woman might feel disabled, however, from using a consent defense for fear that it would alienate white jurors and judges.* Perceiving that a consent defense is infeasible (even if true), defense counsel for black defendants might have set forth other defenses that resulted in stiffer penalties than those given to defendants who did offer consent defenses. One response, of course, is to say that defense counsels' very fear of alienating white jurors is itself a testament to popular prejudices that infect the administration of the criminal law.† On the other hand, it might be said that defense attorneys misread judges and jurors and therefore mistakenly deprive their clients of a defense strategy that would have been helpful

---

*In Maxwell's case, however, the defense was consent. See *Maxwell* v. *Bishop*, 398 F.2d at 146–147 (CA 8 1968).

†On appeal, Maxwell's attorneys made just this point, writing that
> any experienced criminal lawyer in the South . . . well knows that the failure to present the defense of consent in interracial rape cases is itself a product of the discriminatory pattern of Southern justice. . . . Southern jury attitudes . . . have long impressed upon defense counsel the extreme unwisdom of advancing the consent defense on behalf of a Negro defendant where the complainant is white.

398 F.2d at 146. Did Maxwell's trial attorney behave foolishly?

to them. If this second hypothesis is true, it could be that, to a certain extent, racial disparities in sentencing reflect not racial discrimination by jurors but rather jurors' responses to black defendants whose attorneys have weakened their cases by offering fallacious defenses on the basis of misreadings of community sentiment.[21]

To buttress his ruling, Judge Henley quoted from the defendant's own expert witness. His analysis, Wolfgang had stated, "strongly suggests that racial discrimination is operative in the imposition of the death penalty for rape in Arkansas." Simultaneously, however, Wolfgang had heavily qualified his conclusion, writing that his "preliminary" analysis was neither "exhaustive nor conclusive," that his findings were merely "tentative" and "based upon an exploratory investigation of the available data," and that "interpreting the results must be done with caution." This rather remarkable equivocation of the defense's star witness, along with the momentum of precedent, eased the way for Judge Henley to hold that he was "simply not prepared to convict Arkansas juries of unconstitutional racial discrimination in rape cases."[22]

Henley intimated that he would probably *never* be persuaded to find a sentence unconstitutional on the basis of a statistical challenge of the sort relied upon by Maxwell. He doubted, he wrote, "that [racial] discrimination, which is a highly subjective matter, can be detected accurately by a statistical analysis. . . . Statistics are an elusive thing at best, and it is a truism that almost anything can be proved by them."[23]

Henley mentioned another consideration rather offhandedly that also figured into his decisionmaking. "There is no question," he remarked, "that the facts and circumstances surrounding [Maxwell's] offense were such as to justify the imposition of [capital punishment] entirely apart from any consideration of race."[24] Henley appears to have been saying (as did the Virginia Supreme Court in the Martinsville Seven case) that even if racial discrimination factored in other sentencing decisions, in the one before him the egregious character of the offense was more than sufficient to explain why a jury would impose the most severe punishment available.* This conclusion highlights one of

*The Supreme Court of Arkansas described the crime as follows based on evidence presented at trial:

> Once inside the home, the intruder subjected [the victim] to a literal nightmare of brutality and abuse. She fought and struggled, but to no avail. She

the great problems facing any advocate challenging a conviction or sentence for a serious violation on any grounds other than wrongful conviction—the impatience, annoyance, contempt, even hatred that many people, including appellate judges, feel for those who have perpetrated horrible crimes against society and then, after having done so, appeal to society's norms in order to avoid or lessen their punishment. Many people feel intuitively that defendants should receive no benefit even if they succeed in revealing abuses in the administration of the law. Compounding that ever-present difficulty is that, in *Maxwell* v. *Bishop*, defense attorneys were stuck with a client who had perpetrated an especially ugly version of an especially ugly crime.

The U.S. Court of Appeals upheld Judge Henley's ruling in an opinion written by Harry A. Blackmun, who would later play a pivotal role in struggles over the death penalty as a member of the U.S. Supreme Court.[25] The central theme of Blackmun's opinion was that the Wolfgang statistics were virtually irrelevant because they revealed nothing specific to Maxwell's sentencing. "What we are concerned with here," Blackmun declared, "is Maxwell's case and only Maxwell's case."[26]*

---

struck the intruder with a purse. When he forced his hand over her mouth to silence her screams she bit his finger, causing it to bleed. Her helpless father tried to aid her, but was struck and left bleeding. She tried to escape through the front door, but was caught. Her attacker kept threatening to kill her and her father as well. She was dragged and forced outside the house without shoes, and while clad only in her pajamas was forced to a remote spot some two blocks from her home, where battered, bruised, bleeding and exhausted she was overpowered and compelled against her will to suffer a deliberate and calculated rape of her person. After the ravage of her person had been accomplished, and before fleeing, her attacker threatened to kill her and her father if she told.

Maxwell v. *State*, 370 S.W.2d 113, 115 (1963).

*This theme emerges repeatedly:

We are not yet ready to condemn and upset the result reached in every case of a negro rape defendant in the State of Arkansas on the basis of broad theories of social and statistical justice.... Whatever value [the defendant's] argument may have as an instrument of social concern, whatever suspicion it may arouse with respect to southern interracial rape trials as a group over a long period of time, and whatever it may disclose with respect to other lo-

Blackmun also objected to the logic behind the defendant's proposed remedy. Blackmun noted that at oral argument Maxwell's lead attorney, Anthony Amsterdam, was asked whether agreement with his position would mean that it would be unconstitutional under the Equal Protection Clause for a black defendant in Arkansas ever to be properly sentenced to death if his victim was a white woman. Amsterdam had answered in the affirmative. He had also maintained that under his argument white men would still be able to be sentenced to death for rape. When Amsterdam was then asked whether this arrangement would create a new racial discrimination problem, he had replied that, once the situation immediately facing blacks was remedied, the situation facing whites "would take care of itself."[27]

This response touched a nerve. "The legal logic and the rightness of this totally escape us," Blackmun wrote. "The argument . . . turns back upon and defeats the very side which here proposes it."[28] The court of appeals, echoing the musing of Judge Eggleston in the Martinsville Seven case, was clearly bothered by the prospect of creating a formal racial distinction in the law as a remedy for what defense attorneys portrayed as an illicit, informal racial distinction in sentencing.

Nine years later, in 1976, the campaign to reform racially discriminatory sentencing for rape came to an ambiguous end when the Supreme Court, in *Coker v. Georgia*,[29] prohibited states from punishing rape with death. It did so, however, not on equality grounds but on the

---

calities, we feel that the statistical argument does nothing to destroy the integrity of Maxwell's trial.

Maxwell, 398 F. 2d at 147. According to Blackmun, moreover, the Wolfgang statistics failed to cast doubt on the Maxwell sentencing, in part because Garland County was not included among those that Wolfgang studied. Conceding that it was the state of Arkansas, not the county of Garland, that sought to execute Maxwell, Blackmun insisted that "nevertheless the county has a character and posture, too. . . . We are not yet ready to nullify this petitioner's Garland County trial on the basis of results generally, but elsewhere, throughout the South" Ibid. Blackmun also insisted that sentencing statistics in Garland County afforded "no local support for the petitioner's statistical argument" because, between 1954 and 1963, other than Maxwell's case, there were no death sentences handed down in that county. Ibid. "We are not certain," Blackmun concluded, "that statistics will ever be [Maxwell's] redemption." Ibid., 148.

grounds that the death penalty is so "excessive" in relation to rape that it violates the federal constitution's Eighth Amendment, which bans "cruel and unusual punishments."* Moreover, the Court did so without even mentioning the race question.†

There is some excuse for the Court's silence about race in *Coker*. The defendant and the victim were both white. That fact did not prevent Coker's attorney from mentioning at oral argument the Georgia authorities' "notorious and unsavory reputation for racial discrimination."[30] Nor did it prevent the American Civil Liberties Union, the Center for Constitutional Rights, the National Organization for Women, Legal Defense Fund, and other groups from contending, in a brief authored largely by Ruth Bader Ginsburg (now Justice Ginsburg), that "the death penalty for rape is an outgrowth of both male patriarchal views of women no longer seriously maintained by society and gross racial injustice created in part out of that patriarchal foundation."[31] Those references to race, however, were tangential to the main issue, at least as framed by the Supreme Court: whether a death sentence for rape is impermissibly harsh.

---

*That the Court would abolish capital punishment for rape but do so without grappling with the long-standing allegation of racial discrimination was foreshadowed by the first occasion on which several justices suggested that the death penalty for rape might be vulnerable to constitutional attack. In a 1963 case, *Rudolph* v. *Alabama*, 375 U.S. 889 (1963), Justice Arthur J. Goldberg (joined by Justices William O. Douglas and William J. Brennan) wrote a dissent from the Court's denial of review to a case in which a black man convicted of raping a white woman had been sentenced to death. Goldberg asserted that the Court should consider whether executing a person solely for rape is compatible with federal constitutional norms. In his published dissent, Goldberg made no mention of racial discrimination. It later surfaced, however, that in an earlier draft of the dissent he had briefly mentioned the race issue. Prohibiting capital punishment for sexual crimes not endangering human life, he had written, "would also eliminate the well-recognized disparity in the imposition of the death penalty for sexual crimes committed by whites and nonwhites." See Dennis D. Dorin, "Two Different Worlds: Criminologists, Justice and Racial Discrimination in the Imposition of Criminal Punishment in Rape Cases," 72 *Journal of Criminal Law and Criminology* 1667, 1694 (1981).

†"Excessive bail shall not be required, nor excessive fines imposed, nor cruel and unusual punishments inflicted." Constitution of the United States, Amendment VIII (1791).

Contrary to what some have suggested, therefore, the Court in *Coker* did not have to stretch greatly to avoid confronting the race question. Given the facts of the case and the Court's disposition of it, a comprehensive discussion of racial bias would have been somewhat gratuitous. On the other hand, it should be recognized that the justices are not passive figures who merely react to what comes before them. They select the cases they will adjudicate and in so doing either promote or subordinate issues competing for attention. It was probably no accident that, of the variety of cases involving convicted rapists on death row, the Supreme Court chose to review one involving a white defendant charged with an *intraracial* rape. The year before Ehrlich Anthony Coker was sentenced to death in Georgia, three black men were sentenced to death there.[32] These defendants were convicted of *interracial* rapes that would have posed squarely the racial discrimination issue.* The Court put them to the side while it dealt with Coker. Although a dodge of the race issue, the Court's action probably redounded to the black defendants' benefit. The Court would likely have ruled against them if it had adjudicated the racial issue. As it turned out, because of the *Coker* decision, the death sentences of *all* defendants condemned to die solely for rape were vacated and reduced.

Coker brought the campaign against racial discrimination in sentencing for rape to a standstill. It is by no means clear, however, that, in terms of racial equality, the underlying problem has been remedied. True, black rapists no longer are sent to death row at far greater rates than white rapists. It would not be at all surprising to learn, though, that a racial hierarchy still exists under which, in many locales, the black offender–white victim case elicits harsher punishment than any other racial dyad: black offender–black victim, white offender–white victim, or white offender–black victim. After all, that hierarchy continues to assert itself in capital sentencing for murder and other contexts suggestive of racially selective concern for the victims of crime.

---

*One of the cases would have posed the racial discrimination issue in an especially gripping context. The defendants badly beat a young woman, whom they accosted on a highway as she waited for assistance in repairing flat tires on her automobile. She testified that at least one of the men referred to her as a "honky bitch" and a "white bitch" as they beat and kidnapped her. See *Eberheart* v. *Georgia*, 206 S.E. 2d 12, 14 (1974).

In the absence of the death penalty, rights attorneys were less motivated to pursue the race issue in sentencing for rape. This is probably explainable in part by a justified disbelief that courts were likely to
respond affirmatively to racial discrimination claims in noncapital sentencing. It is also attributable in part to a sense that other concerns were
more worthy of investment. Jack Greenberg notes, for example, that
soon after LDF attorneys prevailed in *Coker*, the LDF Board of Directors "began asking questions about [the] capital punishment docket. It
wanted to know what proportion of our energies went into capital cases,
something board members asked about no other program." The questions, he notes, clearly "revealed discomfort" with the resources allocated to attacking capital punishment as opposed to other matters.[33]
Over time, a campaign that had begun as an attack against racial oppression in punishment evolved into more of a campaign against capital
punishment per se.* Hence, after *Coker*, when the specter of capital
punishment left the scene, death penalty abolitionists left the scene, too.
The scene that was left, however, the juncture at which sex, race, and violence meet, remains a place where the rape of a white woman by a
black man is often still considered to be a more serious affront to de-
cency than any other species of rape.[34]

Homicide, Race and Capital Punishment

The Supreme Court decided *Coker* at a critical moment in the history of
capital punishment. In 1972, in *Furman* v. *Georgia*,[35] a closely divided
(5 to 4) Court invalidated most existing state laws authorizing the death
sentence on the grounds that they violated the Eighth Amendment's

---

*The enlistment of the LDF in the campaign to abolish capital punishment
distorted [its] traditional focus on the treatment of the black American. Although the Fund's involvement at first stressed traditional issues of racial
discrimination, nonracial formulations soon crept into the campaign's arse-
nal. . . . [It became difficult] to determine whether, at very bottom, it was
the mere presence of racism in the capital process, or the ominous possibility of death at the end of the process, which was truly propelling the campaign.
    Eric L. Muller, "The Legal Defense Fund's Capital Punishment Campaign:
The Distorting Influence of Death," 4 *Yale Law and Policy Review* 158, 181 (1985).

prohibition against cruel and unusual punishments. All nine justices wrote opinions in *Furman*, prompting Professor Robert Weisberg to observe that it is not so much a ruling "as a badly orchestrated opera, with nine characters taking turns to offer their own arias."[36] Amid the cacaphony, however, a main chord is discernible—that the principal failing of then-existing capital sentencing regimes was the absence of a meaningful basis "for distinguishing the few cases in which [capital punishment] is imposed from the many cases in which it is not."[37] "These death sentences," Justice Potter Stewart complained, were "cruel and unusual in the same way that being struck by lightning is cruel and unusual."[38]

Furman suggested to some observers that the United States might join the trend of other advanced, Western, industrial democracies toward disavowal of capital punishment.* Many state legislatures responded to *Furman*, however, by enacting new death penalty statutes which they believed might overcome the Court's objections. In 1976, in yet another case from Georgia, *Gregg* v. *Georgia*,[39] the Supreme Court affirmed the constitutionality of at least some of these new "improved" capital punishment laws. The Court validated capital punishment as long as it was implemented by procedures that, in its view, "suitably directed and limited" the discretion of sentencers to preclude arbitrary or capricious punishment.[40] The most salient and significant feature of the approved death penalty statutes is the bifurcation of trials into a phase directed solely to determining whether the defendant is guilty and then a phase directed solely to determining whether he should be sentenced to death. At the sentencing phase, the defendant is given wide latitude to argue to a judge or jury that his life should be spared. The state, on the other hand, must persuade the judge or jury that the crime meets certain statutorily defined criteria that distinguish it from other crimes, and therefore justifies a death sentence.

In the aftermath of *Gregg*, and particularly as states began aggressively to seek the execution of condemned prisoners, civil rights activists

---

*France, Denmark, Germany, Spain, Italy, Switzerland, Sweden, and Australia, for example, do not permit capital punishment under any circumstances. Israel, Great Britain, South Africa, Canada, and Mexico permit capital punishment only for crimes under military law or crimes committed during wartime. See *The Death Penalty in America: Current Controversies* 78–83, ed. Hugo Adam Bedan (1997).

redoubled their efforts. A central feature of their attack, in courts of public opinion as well as courts of law, was and remains their allegation that death sentences tend to be applied in a racially discriminatory fashion. The Court declined to adjudicate the issue on several occasions[41] but finally agreed to consider it in 1987 in yet a third landmark case from Georgia, *McCleskey* v. *Kemp*.[42]

On May 13, 1978, Warren McCleskey, a black man, helped to rob the Dixie Furniture Store in Atlanta, Georgia. A white police officer, Frank Schlatt, attempted to foil the robbery but was killed by a shot to the head. Sometime later, McCleskey was arrested in connection with another armed robbery. Under questioning, he admitted to participating in the furniture store heist but denied shooting Officer Schlatt. After further investigation, it emerged that McCleskey had stolen a revolver capable of shooting the type of bullet that killed Officer Schlatt. McCleskey also reportedly admitted shooting Schlatt to both a codefendant and a neighboring inmate in jail, both of whom later testified against him.

A jury of eleven whites and one black sentenced McCleskey to life imprisonment for the robbery and death for the murder. His subsequent appeals followed the normal, dreary route of postconviction proceedings in capital cases. An aspect of his appeal, however, contained a challenge to the entire system of capital punishment in Georgia and beyond. Supported by the most comprehensive statistical analysis ever done on the racial demographics of sentencing in a single state, McCleskey's attorneys argued that their client's sentence should be invalidated because there was a constitutionally impermissible risk that both his race and that of his victim had played a significant role in the decision to sentence him to death.

McCleskey's claim was largely predicated on a study organized and overseen by David C. Baldus, an expert in the application of statistics to legal problems.[43] The Baldus study was derived from records involving the disposition of more than two thousand murder cases between 1973 and 1979. The Georgia Department of Pardons and Paroles and other state agencies provided Baldus with police reports, parole board records, prison files, and other items that evidenced the process by which state authorities handled criminal homicides.

Three findings of the Baldus study are especially pertinent. First, viewing the evidence on a statewide basis, Baldus found "neither strong nor consistent" evidence of discrimination directed against black defendants because of their race.[44] That did not prevent McCleskey's attorneys from asserting that "the race of the defendant—especially when the defendant is black and victim white—influences Georgia's capital sentencing process."[45] In their argument to the Supreme Court, however, McCleskey's attorneys clearly subordinated the claim of race-of-the-defendant discrimination to the claim of race-of-the-victim discrimination.

Second, Baldus found that among the variables that might plausibly influence capital sentencing—age, level of education, criminal record, military record, method of killing, motive for killing, relationship of defendant to victim, strength of evidence, and so forth—the race of the victim emerged as the most consistent and powerful factor. Initially, simple correlations suggested the importance of this variable. Without attempting to control for the possible effects of competing variables, Baldus found that perpetrators in white-victim cases were eleven times more likely to be condemned to death than perpetrators in black-victim cases.

Professor Baldus and his associates subjected this striking correlation to extensive statistical analysis to test whether the seemingly racial nature of this disparity was explainable in terms of hidden factors confounded with race. He eventually took into account some 230 nonracial variables that might have influenced the pattern of sentencing. He concluded that even after accounting for every nonracial variable that might have mattered substantially, the race of the victim continued to have a statistically significant correlation with the imposition of capital sentences. Applying a statistical model that included the thirty-nine nonracial variables believed most likely to play a role in capital punishment in Georgia, the Baldus study concluded that the odds of being condemned to death were 4.3 times greater for defendants who killed whites than for defendants who killed blacks, a variable nearly as influential as a prior conviction for armed robbery, rape, or even murder.[46]

Third, Baldus concluded that racial disparities in capital sentencing are most dramatic in that category containing neither the most aggravated nor the least aggravated homicides. Racial disparities are greatest, he argued, in the middle range of aggravated homicides. In the most aggravated cases, decisionmakers typically impose the death sentence regardless of racial variables, and in the least aggravated cases decisionmakers typically spare the defendant regardless of racial variables. In the middle range of aggravation, however, where a decision could go either way, the influence of racial variables emerges more powerfully. This hypothesis is particularly relevant to *McCleskey* because, in Baldus's view, McCleskey's crime was situated in the middle range of aggravated homicide.

After an evidentiary hearing, U.S. District Judge J. Owen Forrester rejected McCleskey's race discrimination claim primarily on the ground that the Baldus study did not represent "good statistical methodology."[47] He objected to what he viewed as significant omissions, errors, and inconsistencies in Baldus's data base and inadequacies in the design of Baldus's statistical models. Judge Forrester's findings were subsequently eclipsed because the court of appeals and the Supreme Court resolved the case without reviewing them; the appellate courts assumed arguendo that the Baldus study was valid. Judge Forrester's findings, however, continue to be relevant insofar as much of the criticism of *McCleskey* and support for legislative responses to it is premised on a belief in the validity of the Baldus study.

Although a comprehensive examination of the Baldus study would itself require a volume, several considerations pertinent to making an independent evaluation should be mentioned. First, the Baldus study is a product of the death penalty abolitionist wing of the academic community. Although Professor Baldus maintains that he would have published the results of his study no matter what its conclusions,[48] his study was partially financed by funds distributed by LDF—the employer of McCleskey's lawyers and an organization committed to erasing the death penalty. Baldus and his colleagues stated, moreover, that after a certain point, they began to conduct their research with litigation in mind. The Baldus study, in other words, is not the product of disinterested academic research subsequently used by a litigant's attorneys. Rather, the Baldus study is a species of sponsored research animated in part by sympathies with one side of a controversy. It should therefore be viewed with the skepticism that such research should always engender.

The methodology of the Baldus study has received high praise from many of the most distinguished researchers who have investigated the application of statistics to legal problems. Professor Richard Berk, a member of the National Academy of Sciences' Committee on Sentencing Research, testified that the Baldus study has "very high credibility" and "is far and away the most complete and thorough analysis of sentencing that [has] ever been done."[49] Similarly, several leading scholars in the field have collectively affirmed that the Baldus investigations "are among the best empirical studies on criminal sentencing ever conducted."[50] Such endorsements, however, must themselves be viewed skeptically against the backdrop of the propaganda war over capital punishment, because many, if not most, elite academics oppose capital punishment.

The factual core of the Baldus study withstands even a skeptical analysis, however. To some extent I am moved to this conclusion by the study's evident carefulness and its authors' insistence on making their data, premises, and calculations available and transparent to the public. I am also influenced by the sworn testimony of respected experts in Baldus's field, notwithstanding the risk of ideological taint identified above. The Baldus study, moreover, is consistent with findings published by a large body of prior research.[51] Even commentators who generally deride allegations of racial discrimination in the administration of criminal law concede that in the context of capital punishment the race of the victim consistently influences sentencing decisions.[52]

Although District Judge Forrester refused to credit the Baldus study, several distinguished specialists in applied statistics have brought the competence underlying his judgment into serious question.[53] Moreover, beyond the technical deficiencies noted by experts, Judge Forrester displayed a glaring, self-discrediting hostility to the Baldus study. Nothing better illustrates this than Judge Forrester's conclusion that Baldus's data base was irredeemably flawed because the questionnaires used to collect information "could not capture every nuance of every case."[54]* In the first place, Judge Forrester neglected to specify the significance of the omissions he deemed so important.[55] Second, and more fundamen-

---

*Subsequently Judge Forrester revealed contempt for the Baldus study by writing that the racial disparities it found were produced by "arbitrarily structured little rinky-dink regressions that accounted for only a few variables. . . . They prove nothing other than the truth of the adage that anything may be proved by statistics." *McCleskey* v. *Kemp,* No. C87-1517A 12 (N.D. Ga. Dec. 23, 1987) (order granting relief to McCleskey on other grounds).

tally, Judge Forrester's objection is premised upon a wildly perfectionist standard that is impossible to satisfy. "By insisting on a standard of 'absolute knowledge' about every single case, [Judge Forrester] implicitly rejected the value of all applied statistical analysis."[56]

The Court of Appeals for the Eleventh Circuit assumed the validity of the Baldus study but nevertheless affirmed the district court's race discrimination holding on the grounds that the statistical disparities and supplemental evidence failed to prove a constitutional violation.[57] The court declared that, in order to succeed, McCleskey would have to have produced evidence indicating that *his* sentence was the product of race-dependent decisionmaking. The Baldus study, however, "only" showed "that in a group involving blacks and whites, all of whose cases were virtually the same, there would be . . . more murderers of whites receiving the death penalty than murderers of blacks."[58] The court conceded that the statistics demonstrate that "there is a race-of-the-victim relationship with the imposition of the death sentence discernible in enough cases to be statistically significant in the system as a whole."[59] It concluded, however, that "no single petitioner could, on the basis of these statistics alone, establish that he received the death sentence because, and only because, his victim was white."[60]*

Justice Lewis Powell's opinion for a bare majority (5 to 4) of the Supreme Court largely followed the Eleventh Circuit's analysis.[61] The Supreme Court, too, assumed, arguendo, the validity of the Baldus study. Similarly, the Court insisted that the constitutionality of McCleskey's sentence must be determined by asking whether officials in *his* case purposefully discriminated on the basis of race. The Court concluded that no such inference could be drawn from the Baldus statistics. Justice Powell noted that in some contexts a "stark" pattern of statistical disparities may create a prima facie case which shifts onto the state the

*Three of the twelve judges who participated in the case dissented, including Judge Joseph W. Hatchett, the only black then on the Eleventh Circuit Court of Appeals, who dissented on the equal protection issue. See 753 F. 2d. at 907–927).

The other black jurist who participated in deciding *McCleskey*, Justice Thurgood Marshall, also dissented. I mention the racial backgrounds of Hatchett and Marshall not because their race presumptively endows them with greater insight but as a sociological datum that warrants further exploration and interpretation. Cf. Randall Kennedy, "Racial Critiques of Legal Academia," 102 *Harvard Law Review* 1745 (1989).

burden of rebutting an allegation of racial discrimination. He observed, however, that in the context of capital sentencing, "decisions at the heart of the State's criminal justice system," the Court would demand "exceptionally clear proof" before inferring that a sentencing authority had abused its discretion.[62] In the Court's view, the racial correlations revealed by the Baldus study did not meet that standard. Powell declared that "because of the risk that the factor of race may enter the criminal justice process, [the Court has] engaged in 'unceasing efforts' to eradicate racial prejudice from our criminal justice system."[63] In this instance, though, no clear showing had been made that racial prejudice animated the death sentence imposed upon McCleskey. Nor, according to Powell, did the Baldus statistics even show that racial prejudices played a significant role in other cases in Georgia. "At most," Powell averred, "the Baldus study indicates a discrepancy that appears to correlate with race."[64]

Justice Powell noted several reasons of policy that pushed the Court to rule as it did. One was the need to give ample latitude for sentencers to use their discretion in making the unique decision as to whether to end the life of a human being as punishment for a crime. Another concern was that accepting McCleskey's challenge would open a Pandora's box of litigation. "McCleskey's claim, taken to its logical conclusion," Powell remarked with alarm, "throws into serious question the principles that underlie our entire criminal justice system," because, if accepted, the Court "could soon be faced with similar claims as to other types of penalty" from members of other groups alleging bias.[65] Finally, Powell invoked considerations of judicial competence and judicial restraint as reasons for avoiding intervention. "McCleskey's arguments," he declared, "are best presented to legislative bodies. . . . It is the legislatures, the elected representatives of the people, that are constituted to respond to the will and consequently the moral values of the people."[66]

With the exception of Thurgood Marshall,* each of the dissenting justices (William J. Brennan, Harry A. Blackmun, and John Paul Stevens) wrote opinions explaining their disagreement with the Court.

---

*Although he joined Justice Brennan's dissent, it is striking that Justice Marshall declined to write an opinion of his own in *McCleskey* insofar as it constituted a major blow to his abolitionist hopes.

Maintaining that "we cannot pretend that in three decades we have completely escaped the trap of a historical legacy spanning centuries," Justice Brennan declared that "Warren McCleskey's evidence confronts us with the subtle and persistent influence of the past."[67]* Crediting the Baldus study "in light of both statistical principles and human experience," Brennan concluded that "the risk that race influenced McCleskey's sentence is intolerable by any imaginable standard."[68] Responding to the Court's concern that accepting McCleskey's claim would open the door to challenges attacking all aspects of criminal sentencing, Brennan remarked that it displayed "a fear of too much justice. . . . The prospect that there may be more widespread abuse than McCleskey documents may be dismaying, but it does not justify complete abdication of [the] judicial role."[69]

In his dissent, Justice Blackmun wrote that he was "disappointed with the Court's action not only because of its denial of constitutional guarantees to petitioner McCleskey individually, but also because of its departure from . . . well-developed constitutional jurisprudence."[70] Blackmun concluded that "the Court . . . sanctions the execution of a man despite his presentation of evidence that establishes a constitutionally intolerable level of racially based discrimination leading to the imposition of his death sentence."[71]†

Like Blackmun, John Paul Stevens did not consider the death

---

*According to Justice Blackmun:

> Unlike the evidence presented by Maxwell, which did not contain data from the jurisdiction in which he was tried and sentenced, McCleskey's evidence includes data from the relevant jurisdiction. Whereas the analyses presented by Maxwell did not take into account a significant number of variables and were based on a universe of 55 cases, the analyses presented by McCleskey's evidence take into account more than 400 variables and are based on data concerning all offenders arrested for homicide in Georgia from 1973 through 1978, a total of 2,484 cases. Moreover, the sophistication of McCleskey's evidence permits consideration of the existence of racial discrimination at various decision points in the process, not merely at the jury decision.

McCleskey, 481 U.S. at 354 n. 7 (Blackmun, J. dissenting).

†Ironically, the Eleventh Circuit Court of Appeals and, to a lesser extent, the Supreme Court argued that Baldus's ability to construct three tiers of sentencing for homicide in Georgia ws a *validation* of the state's new, post-*Furman*, death penalty regime. As Judge Paul H. Roney put it, "the Baldus study revealed an essentially ra-

penalty to be unconstitutional per se but did consider it to be unconstitutionally applied in Georgia in light of the Baldus study. In addition to criticizing the Court's judgment, Stevens proposed a reform aimed at lessening racial disparities in capital sentencing while simultaneously retaining the death penalty. Stevens (joined by Blackmun) proposed to limit the class of persons eligible for capital punishment to those who commit only the worst type of homicides. This proposal stemmed from his belief that "one of the lessons of the Baldus study is that there exist certain categories of extremely serious crimes for which prosecutors consistently seek, and juries consistently impose, the death penalty without regard to the race of the victim or the race of the offender."[72] He argued that "if Georgia were to narrow the class of death eligible defendants to those categories, the danger of arbitrary and discriminatory imposition of the death penalty would be significantly decreased, if not eradicated."*

A sign of the difficulties posed by *McCleskey* is that none of the justices' opinions is altogether satisfactory. The worst of the lot is also the one backed by the most power: Justice Powell's opinion for the Court. Powell strives to convey the impression that the conclusion he and his four associates reached is the only sensible alternative. He therefore gives the false impression that the case is easy. He responds to the parties' briefs, which one expects to be one-sided, with yet another tenden-

---

tional system, in which high aggravation cases were more likely to result in the death sentence than low aggravation cases. 753 F. 2d. at 879. See also 481 U.S. 313 n.36 ("The Baldus Study in fact confirms that the Georgia system results in a reasonable level of proportionality among the class of murderers eligible for the death penalty").

The Stevens-Blackmun proposal to execute only "worst case" perpetrators was vaguely anticipated by the judges who approved the death sentences in the Martinsville Seven case and *Maxwell* v. *Bishop* on the grounds that the crimes committed in those cases were so horrible that juries would likely have sentenced the defendants to death regardless of the racial sentiments of the juries.

*After the Supreme Court ruled against McCleskey's racial discrimination claim, his attorneys attacked his conviction on other grounds. This litigation also went to the Supreme Court, which again ruled against McCleskey. See *McCleskey* v. *Zant*, 499 U.S. 461 (1991). Georgia executed McCleskey on September 25, 1991. See Lyle V. Harris and Mark Curriden, "McCleskey Is Executed for '78 Killing; Marietta Native Paces His Cell, Consoles Family in Final Hours," *Atlanta Constitution*, September 25, 1991.

tious brief, although his is styled an "opinion" and thus part of the constitutional law of the United States.

Two features of Powell's opinion are especially troubling. One is his minimization of the facts behind McCleskey's claim. Confronted by statistics indicating that people who kill whites in Georgia are four times more likely to be sentenced to death than people who kill blacks, Powell blandly remarked that "at most [this] indicates a discrepancy that appears to correlate with race"[73]—a statement as vacuous as one declaring, say, that "at most" studies on lung cancer indicate a discrepancy that appears to correlate with smoking. Another example of the resolute evasiveness that emerges time and again in Powell's opinion is his statement that the Court should "decline to assume that what is unexplained is invidious."[74] The petitioner, of course, was not asking the Court to make any such assumption. Rather, McCleskey's attorneys offered into evidence a comprehensive study showing that certain patterns in capital sentencing cannot plausibly be explained by any variable other than race.

A willful refusal to grant any credence whatsoever to the petitioner's arguments also characterizes Powell's handling of historical evidence. Prior to the Civil War, Georgia, like most slave states, enacted laws that expressly imposed racially discriminatory capital punishments. In the aftermath of slavery, Southern officials continued to administer the death penalty and indeed the entire apparatus of the criminal law in a patently racist fashion. In 1972, when the Court struck down the Georgia capital sentencing statute in *Furman* v. *Georgia*, a number of justices acknowledged the existence of credible evidence indicating that race had continued to serve as a basis for inflicting death sentences.[75] Moreover, if one views capital punishment in Georgia in light of experience derived from other contemporaneous aspects of the state's criminal justice system, the historical argument in favor of McCleskey's contention gains even more force.[76] The Court, however, curtly dismissed McCleskey's reference to historical context:

[McCleskey's "historical evidence"] focuses on Georgia laws in force during and just after the Civil War. Of course, the historical background of the decision is one evidentiary source for proof of intentional discrimination. But unless historical evidence is reasonably contemporaneous with the challenged decision, it has little probative value. Although the history of racial discrimination in this country is undeniable, we cannot accept official actions taken long ago as evidence of current intent.[77]

This comment misrepresents McCleskey's evidence and argument. McCleskey did not call attention solely to laws in force "during and just after the Civil War." Rather, he focused attention on certain historical continuities that illuminate the statistical data that constituted the core of his case. As Justice Brennan rightly observed, it is "unrealistic to ignore the influence of history in assessing the plausible implications of [the statistical] evidence."[78] The Court's suggestion that the legacy of Georgia's history shines *no* light on the Baldus statistics is both laughable and tragic.

The second outstanding feature of Powell's opinion is his resolute unwillingness to recognize the uniqueness of two distinctions that the Court had previously periodically acknowledged. One was that *McCleskey* involved a peculiarly irrevocable punishment; as various justices have noted, "death is different."[79] The other is that the case involved an allegation that capital punishment in Georgia was systematically meted out according to an especially toxic social demarcation, the race line. Powell refused to recognize these two distinctions as limiting boundaries, probably because doing so would undercut his demagogic assertion that accepting McCleskey's claim would necessarily open a Pandora's box from which limitless disruption would ensue. Fretting that an acceptance of McCleskey's racial claim would invite members of other groups—"even" women[80]—to launch equal protection challenges, Powell and the Court majority resolutely shut the door to any statistics-driven, class-based challenge to the administration of punishment. To justify this action in the context of a case involving blacks, the paradigmatic "out-group" in American political culture, Powell argued that no "logical" reason exists for distinguishing racial or gender bias from any other sort of bias—a bias, for instance, against facial unattractiveness.[81] The life of the law, however, includes not only logic but also experience, and experience teaches that in the United States, racial sentiment displays an intensity and persistence that is distinguishable from all other biases. There exists, moreover, a textual warrant in the Constitution for distinguishing racial and, to a lesser extent, gender bias from other sorts of preference and prejudice.

A similar slamming of the door greeted the oft-voiced claim that allegations of unfairness with respect to death penalties are entitled to special judicial solicitude.[82] As Blackmun complained in dissent, Powell's opinion for the Court gave "new meaning" to the notion that death is different by applying *lesser* scrutiny to the decisionmaking process that leads to death sentences than to decisions affecting employment or the selection of juries.[83]

Powell's *McCleskey* opinion was haunted by anxiety over the consequences of acknowledging candidly the large influence of racial sentiment in the administration of capital punishment in Georgia. Powell did not want to concede facts that might prompt the Court to question the racial fairness of capital sentencing, trigger additional *McCleskey*-like challenges, and perhaps even lead to judicially directed reforms of sentencing in general. Nor did he want to concede facts that indicate that the Court was knowingly willing to countenance a regime of capital punishment in which race significantly influenced decisions as to who would be spared and who would be killed. So Powell and his associates acted as if the Baldus study uncovered a minor discrepancy as opposed to an alarming anomaly. It would have been better if the Court openly declared that, for reasons of policy, it declined to grant relief to McCleskey notwithstanding the disturbing facts revealed by the Baldus study.* Doing so would have performed the tremendous benefit of edu-

---

*Several years after *McCleskey*, Justice Powell revealed that his "understanding of statistical analysis . . . ranges from limited to zero." See John C. Jeffries, Jr., *Justice Lewis F. Powell, Jr.*, 439 (1994). One might wonder whether a person with such limited knowledge should have played a pivotal role in a case so dependent on a statistical analysis. Judicial ignorance of various sorts, however, is a fact of life. See Dennis D. Dorin, "Two Different Worlds: Criminologists, Justices, and Racial Discrimination in the Imposition of Capital Punishment in Rape Cases," 72 *Journal of Criminal Law and Criminology* 1667 (1981).

After retiring from the Court, Powell indicated that he no longer believed that states should be allowed to inflict capital punishment. See Jeffries, *Powell* at 435. Some have lauded Powell for publicly disclosing his change of mind. I am more impressed by the poignant fact that the learning and experience which prompted this conversion came too late to be put to direct use by Powell in his capacity as a Justice.

cating the public about the real world of capital sentencing and the real world of Supreme Court decisionmaking.*

Dissent in McCleskey:
The Perils of Sentimentality

The dissenters rebuked the *McCleskey* Court for what they saw as its betrayal of established traditions. Justice Blackmun maintained, for instance, that he was "disappointed with the Court's action . . . because of its departure from . . . well-developed constitutional jurisprudence."[84] There is much in the claim of disappointment, however, that smells of rank sentimentality. True, the Court could have decided differently; had there been the will, available precedent could have lit the way. In the context of equal protection challenges to jury commissioners authorized to select jury pools on the basis of vague standards, for example, the Supreme Court has shown a marked skepticism toward unexplained racial disparities. It has shifted the burden of explanation to the state when presented with evidence indicating significant discrepancies between the percentage of the population of eligible racial minorities in a given jurisdiction and the percentage of racial minorities selected for

---

*Soon after reading an early draft of Justice Powell's opinion, Justice Scalia wrote a memorandum to his colleagues in which he stated that he believed that racial discrimination did affect capital sentencing and that he would nonetheless vote to uphold it. He wrote that he did not "share the view, implicit in [Powell's draft opinion] that an effect of racial factors upon sentencing, if it could be shown by sufficiently strong statistical evidence, would require reversal. Since it is my view," he continued, "that the unconscious operation of irrational sympathies, including racial, upon jury decision and (hence) prosecutorial [ones], is real, acknowledged by the [cases] of this court, and ineradicable, I cannot honestly say that all I need is more proof."

One cannot know for certain whether Justice Scalia remained committed to this view. If he did, it is unfortunate that he decided not to publish his perspective on *McCleskey*. Because his comments surely represent the viewpoint of at least some policymakers, making them widely accessible would have sharpened and deepened public debate. Justice Scalia's memo became public when it was found among the papers Justice Thurgood Marshall gave to the Library of Congress. See Dennis D. Dorin, "Far Right of the Mainstream: Racism, Rights, and Remedies from the Perspective of Justice Antonin Scalia's *McCleskey* Memorandum," 45 *Mercer Law Review* 1035 (1994).

possible jury service. The Court could have deployed this same methodology in *McCleskey*—if it had possessed the will to do so. On the other hand, Powell's opinion for the Court was well within the ambit of expectations reasonably derived from prior rulings. *McCleskey* did not begin the Supreme Court's deregulation of the death penalty; it reflected and accelerated a process that had already begun and developed momentum.[85] Although some justices had intimated that the Court should subject to special rigor death sentences challenged on grounds of racial fairness, a stronger tradition, exemplified by the Martinsville Seven case, favored the ethos that prevailed.

If *McCleskey* disappoints, it should do so on some basis other than tradition, for the majority cannot rightly be accused of promulgating a startling ruling. To the contrary, *McCleskey* was all too predictable. Its critics must face the fact that, as far as reported cases disclose, defendants rarely, verging on never, succeed in challenging punishments using arguments of the sort voiced by Warren McCleskey's attorneys.[86]

The Problem of Remedy

The central concern that dictated the Court's resolution of *McCleskey* was anxiety about what judges might have to face if it acknowledged that the influence of racial sentiment in sentencing represents a distortion and unfairness of constitutional dimension. Pretend for a moment, however, that the Supreme Court reversed the district court's rejection of the Baldus study and, based on the study's conclusions, declared a violation of the Equal Protection Clause. Assuming that the Court could have reached this point, what should it have done next?

One alternative would have been to abolish capital punishment entirely on the grounds that racial selectivity is an inextricable part of the administration of capital punishment in the United States and that it would be better to have no death penalty than one unavoidably influenced consistently by racial sentiment.

A more reserved variant would have involved vacating all death sentences in Georgia. Such a response would have fallen short of the ultimate aim of abolitionists since it would apply only to a single state. However, this response would surely have given a tremendous boost to the abolitionist movement by placing a large question mark over the le-

gitimacy of any death penalty system generating unexplained racial disparities of the sort at issue in *McCleskey*. Since studies suggest that
McCleskey-like statistics exist in several death penalty states, especially
those with the largest death rows, the implementation of even a limited
abolitionist remedy would have been significant indeed.

For those opposed to capital punishment anyway, abolishing it to
vindicate the norms of equal protection is a costless enterprise. Abolition, however, is a costly prospect to the extent that one views the death
penalty—as most Americans do—as a useful and highly valued public
good. Polls indicate that, at least since the 1980s, upwards of 70 percent
of Americans indicate that they favor capital punishment.[87] Moreover,
since 1988, the number of crimes punishable by death has increased dramatically, mainly as a result of federal legislation.[88] From the perspective of a proponent of capital punishment, abolition as a remedy for
race-of-the victim discrimination is equivalent to reducing to darkness a
town in which streetlights have been provided on a racially unequal basis.[89] From this perspective, it would make more sense to remedy the inequality by installing lights in the parts of town which have been
wrongly deprived of illumination. Carrying on the analogy, it would be
better to remedy the problem outlined by the Baldus statistics by leveling up—increasing the number of people executed for murdering
blacks—rather than leveling down—abolishing capital punishment
altogether.

Before turning to the level-up solution, however, notice should be
paid to still other possibilities. One is the idea, embraced by Justices
Stevens and Blackmun, of limiting the class of persons eligible for execution to those who commit only the most aggravated homicides. The
problem with this proposal is that it seems merely to replicate what the
Court sought to accomplish by permitting the revival of capital punishment pursuant to procedures that, theoretically, limited and informed
sentencers so that similarly situated criminals would be punished according to some tolerably coherent pattern. One point upon which both
death penalty deregulators and death penalty abolitionists agree is that
"the task of selecting in some objective way those persons who should be
condemned to die . . . remains beyond the capacities of the criminal justice system."[90] The facts of *McCleskey* itself highlight this problem with
the Stevens and Blackmun proposal. According to Professor Baldus,

McCleskey's murder was located in the middle range of aggravated murders. In his view, the crime was not among the most heinous murders for which people have been condemned to death in Georgia. It is difficult, however, to see why this is so. McCleskey's crime involved, after all, the murder of a policeman during a robbery by a recidivist who is said to have boasted of the killing. Surely there are many, including potential judges and jurors, who would rank this crime in the same category of heinousness as some of the murders which Professor Baldus does place in the "worst case" category.*

Another alternative would be for the Court to retract its rejection of mandatory death sentences. As we have seen, in 1972 the Court struck down all existing state death penalty statutes on the grounds that, by delegating unguided discretionary power to sentencing authorities, they provided insufficient protection against arbitrariness or discrimination. Ten states responded by enacting statutes prescribing capital punishment as the mandatory sentence for the commission of certain crimes. In 1976, the Court invalidated these laws on the grounds that they were inconsistent with fundamental trends in social mores, encouraged juries to shape their verdicts to avoid the harshness of mandatory sentences, and that the procedures established by mandatory sentencing failed to consider each defendant in a sufficiently individualized manner.[91] The justices imposed a constitutional requirement that sentencers in capital trial be provided with discretion to extend mercy.[92] Yet it is precisely this power to grant leniency that opens the door to the *McCleskey* problem. As Kenneth Culp Davis observes, "The discretionary power to be lenient has a deceptive quality that is dangerous to justice.... The power to be lenient is the power to discriminate."[93]

---

*For example, Professor Baldus and his associates ranked as a worst case crime a murder committed during a robbery that the defendant and his co-perpetrator were hired to perform. The defendant was apparently designated as the triggerman, although the co-perpetrator seems to have actually done the killing. The defendant had only one prior offense on his record, and that was nonviolent. It is not at all clear to me, however, that the murder for which McCleskey was sentenced to die warrants less punishment than this murder which Baldus and his colleagues place in the worst case category. See Kennedy, *"McCleskey v. Kemp:* Race, Capital Punishment, and The Supreme Court," *Harvard Law Review* 1388, 1431–1433 (1988).

It is by no means clear, moreover, that mandatory capital sentencing would affect racial disparities. First, even if mandatory capital sentencing were allowed, there would remain the possibility that juries would continue to extend relatively more leniency to the killers of blacks, declining more frequently to convict such killers of crimes that trigger automatic death sentences. Second, and probably more important, the institutional actors who have the most to do with the prevalence and incidence of capital sentences are prosecutors, not jurors. Prosecutors decide whether and for what to charge a defendant. Prosecutors further decide whether to charge a person with a capital crime or to accept a plea bargain for a noncapital offense.[94] That prosecutors can be strongly influenced by racial bias is clear.[95] Yet mandatory sentencing schemes do little to address the problem of race-dependent leniency on the part of prosecutors. Although mandatory sentencing provisions would limit, to some extent, the discretion of jurors or judges in responding to choices framed by prosecutors, such laws would do nothing to constrain the prior exercise of prosecutorial discretion.

In his *McCleskey* dissent, Justice Blackmun noted that prosecutors in Georgia are governed by virtually no authoritative instructions regarding how they should decide whom to charge with capital crimes. He suggested that a second possible remedy for racial disparities in capital sentencing would be the establishment of "guidelines" setting forth the appropriate bases for exercising prosecutorial discretion in homicide cases that potentially implicate capital punishment.[96] Blackmun was silent, however, about the substantive content of the guidelines he had in mind. In light of the failure of statutory guidelines that supposedly channel juror discretion, it is difficult to imagine instructions to prosecutors that would compel, or even facilitate, the consistency that Justice Blackmun envisioned.*

---

*At the time of Justice Blackmun's dissent in *McCleskey*, he believed that it was possible to administer capital punishment in a constitutionally acceptable way. In the waning days of his tenure as an active Justice, however, he changed his mind and became a death penalty abolitionist. See *Callins* v. *Collins*, 114 S. Ct. 1127, 1128 (1994) (Blackmun, J., dissenting from denial of certiorai).

The Level-up Solution to Racial Discrimination in Capital Sentencing

The level-up solution to the *McCleskey* problem would entail purposefully securing more death sentences against murderers of blacks. One way to pursue this aim would be to impose a choice upon jurisdictions with *McCleskey*-like sentencing patterns: Either respond as vigorously to the murders of blacks by condemning perpetrators of such crimes to death (as is done to murderers of whites), or relinquish the power to put anyone to death.

One problem with using race-conscious measures to reform the administration of capital punishment is that to many observers doing so will seem bizarre at first blush. That reaction, however, is likely to be based, at least in part, upon an exaggerated perception of the extent to which notions of individual dessert currently infuse sentencing practices. Sentencing is typically keyed not only to the perceived moral dessert of individual defendants but also to utilitarian calculations regarding society's needs. Punishment is used by those pronouncing sentence upon convicted defendants to instruct an onlooking society.

Another problem with the level-up alternative is that even those who favor, or at least tolerate, race-conscious remedies in some contexts reach a point where they find that such remedies are simply too severe to impose upon individuals who themselves played no direct part in inflicting the initial injury. The Supreme Court, for instance, has drawn a bright line of prohibition against affirmative action in the context of employment layoffs.[97] Affirmative action for racial minorities that decreases the chances that white applicants will be *hired* is sometimes allowable, because the burden to be borne "is diffused to a considerable extent among society generally."[98] Affirmative action that results in the *layoff* of white workers, however, is deemed a burden that is "too intrusive" to accept.[99] Transposed to the death penalty context, the argument would run that sentencing individuals to death pursuant to a race-conscious plan to equalize the provision of death penalty services is simply too harsh a social tax to impose even upon convicted murderers who are, because of their own conduct, "eligible" for execution.

This argument, however, rests heavily upon the "death is different" distinction. It loses considerable force to the extent that one sees the death penalty as part of a continuum of punishments rather than a unique phenomenon occupying a wholly different moral plane. For those who eschew the "death is different" idea, it is not self-evident why, if race can and should be taken into account in redressing racial injustice in employment, housing, voting, and education, race cannot also be taken into account in reforming capital sentencing. They might well recognize the real danger of creating incentives to sentence certain defendants to death primarily to create "good" statistics. They might conclude, however, that this is a danger worth risking in order to encourage officials to take more seriously the security and suffering of black communities and in order to symbolize the affirmative constitutional obligation to insure some rough measure of substantive racial equality in every sphere of American life—including the provision of law enforcement resources.*

The Racial Justice Act

In 1988, Representative John Conyers (D.-MI) and Senator Edward Kennedy (D.-MA) proposed legislation, the Racial Justice Act (RJA), that would have established as prima facie evidence of racial discrimination the very type of statistical evidence that Warren McCleskey had relied upon.[100] In *McCleskey* the Supreme Court held that, in order to prevail on a constitutional claim, a petitioner would have to show purposeful racial discrimination in his own particular case. By contrast, the

---

*Several readers of drafts of this chapter have asked where I stand on the question of the constitutionality of capital punishment. This question is different from the one I address in the text, which is the narrower issue of racial fairness in the administration of capital punishment. Still, I shall answer their question, albeit in a necessarily summary fashion. I do not regard capital punishment as unconstitutional per se. I oppose capital punishment as a matter of policy because of anxiety over the risks of error, my sense that the benefits derived from capital punishment are quite matginal, and my fear of the lethal, collective, bureaucratic anger that the state displays when it puts a person to death. I am not, however, a fervent abolitionist. To put the matter plainly, many other concerns rank higher on my political agenda than abolishing capital punishment. I was much more deeply committed to the abolition of capital punishment before I clerked for Justice Thurgood Marshall in 1982. Constantly reading about the horrible crimes perpetrated by murderers sentenced to death gave me a better understanding of the sentiments that prompt many to insist upon retaining, and in some instances, inflicting capital punishment.

proposed RJA required no showing of purposeful discrimination and created for a petitioner the rebuttable presumption that a statistically significant racial disparity in death sentences in a given locale meant that wrongful racial discrimination tainted his sentence too.

Under the RJA, a petitioner would have confronted an uphill climb in order to prevail. The RJA put the initial burden of proof on petitioners. Moreover, even if a petitioner succeeded in making out a prima facie case, the RJA allowed the government to rebut the charge by showing by a preponderance of the evidence either (a) that there are nonracial reasons that persuasively explain the apparently racial sentencing disparities or (b) that even in the absence of racial discrimination the petitioner at issue would still have been sentenced to death in light of the enormity of his crime.

Despite these moderating features, the RJA has failed thus far to receive sufficient political support to become law. It twice passed the House of Representatives. The second time it did so, some supporters in Congress threatened to torpedo a massive and electorally sensitive anti-crime bill unless the RJA was included.[101] When the smoke cleared, however, the crime bill passed without the RJA. The RJA lacked the support of Democratic President Bill Clinton[102] and would have faced unyielding resistance from opponents (mainly Republicans) in the Senate.*

Many motivations activated opposition to the RJA. One is merely a crass desire by politicians to be perceived as "tough" on crime, a stance that has become identified with support for capital punishment. Politicians in this camp go where the political winds blow.

Another motivation is a covert desire to vent or exploit the antiblack

---

*The remarks in opposition of Senator Orrin Hatch (R.-UT) are representative:
  The so-called Racial Justice Act has nothing to do with racial justice and everything to do with abolishing the death penalty. [The RJA] would instead impose an unreliable and manipulable statistical quota on imposition of the death penalty. It would convert every death penalty case into a massive sideshow of statistical squabbles and quota quarrels.

Cong. R. S4602 (April 21, 1994). See also Cong. R. S5210 (May 5, 1994) (remarks of Senator Grassley); Cong. R. 4328 (May 6, 1994) (remarks of Senator D'Amato). Another statement that articulates objections to the RJA is found in the dissent to the Report of the House Committee on the Judiciary which supported the RJA. See Report 103-458, 103D Congress, 2d Session.

racism that animates a hard to measure but appreciable number of Americans who remain committed to the notion that blacks are racially inferior to whites and who abhor the racial egalitarianism that has become the official ideology of the United States. For this community, the death penalty retains an assuring symbolic association with the racial hierarchies of the past and becomes even more significant symbolically when challenged directly on grounds of racial justice.

Another motivation is a sincere belief in three propositions: (a) that some people commit crimes that are so awful that justice demands extinguishing their lives; (b) that the RJA would pose a large threat to the ability of some jurisdictions to implement capital punishment; and (c) that racial justice would not be substantially furthered by the RJA. Holders of this set of beliefs disapprove of racial discrimination but are unwilling to support a law that would offer a reprieve to a murderer based on statistical evidence of racial discrimination in cases other than his own. These policymakers place at the center of their concern the horror wreaked upon society by a convicted murderer. They demand that priority be given to avenging that horror.

They also argue that "leveling up" is the logical response to complaints of race-of-the-victim racial discrimination. They do not raise that prospect to embrace it; leveling up would entail a mode of formal race-conscious decisionmaking to which they simply disapprove.[103] Rather, they raise the prospect of leveling up to highlight the fact that the RJA's supporters do not advance *that* solution. Dissenting from the favorable report on the RJA promulgated by the House of Representatives Committee on the Judiciary, Henry Hyde (R.-IL) and others maintained that if the RJA were really designed to remedy race-of-the-victim discrimination, "the solution would be to seek the death penalty in more cases in which black defendants murder black defendants."[104] The inference Hyde and others draw is that the total neglect of the leveling-up alternative by supporters of the RJA evidences a concern not so much with racial justice as with impeding the administration of capital punishment by all available means.

Of these three camps of opponents to the RJA, only the third warrants an extended response; the other two are virtually impervious to argument. The great failing of this camp is complacency in the face of what should certainly be disturbing evidence that, in fact, in some jurisdictions, authorities do respond with less vigor and empathy to black-victim homicides than white-victim homicides. One feature of this complacency takes the form of denying that a problem exists. The following statement by congressional opponents of the RJA is representative: "While it may be true that killers of white victims are more likely to receive the death penalty than killers of blacks, this statistical disparity is easily explained by the presence of mitigating or aggravating factors which account for the differences in sentences."[105] In light of the experience with capital punishment for rape and the Baldus study and the many other investigations that have consistently reached similar conclusions, it cannot sensibly be said that the racial disparities revealed are "*easily* explained" by nonracial factors. Indeed, given the past and present realities of racial conflict in the United States, it would be absolutely extraordinary if racial bias did not affect sentencing, including (or maybe especially) capital sentencing. I am not ignoring or minimizing the changes that have significantly bettered race relations over the past half-century. But alongside notable discontinuities in American race relations are ugly continuities as well, including willful blindness to invidious racial discrimination in punishment.

One could acknowledge the presence of racial discrimination but nonetheless oppose the RJA on the grounds that the benefits of capital punishment outweigh the costs created by racial distortions in its administration. Opponents of the RJA, however, obsessively committed to making no concessions useful to the other side, decline even to acknowledge the obvious. In this regard they mirror the deniers who refuse to admit that blacks do in fact commit a disproportionate share of street crime. The opponents of the RJA refuse to admit that, on a racial basis, in a substantial (albeit hard to specify) number of instances, individuals in America—police and prosecutors, judges and jurors, editors and readers—react more to the murder of white than black persons. Recognizing this obvious but repressed fact is an essential step toward creating a more decent and equitable administration of criminal law.*

---

*During the same period that Congress repeatedly rejected the RJA, it made scores of federal offenses into capital crimes. See Bureau of Justice Statistics Bulletin, "Capital Punishment 1994," 11–13, February 1996. Thus far, racial minorities hare predominated among those for whom death sentences have been sought,. Of the first thirty-seven federal death penalty prosecutions brought under the new statutes, all

Race, Parochialism, and the Marketplace of Emotion

The statistics revealed by the Baldus study pose a difficult set of problems in part because Americans are deeply ambivalent about the social dynamics that give rise to these statistics. On the one hand, many subscribe to the idea that racial sentiments should play no role in social judgments. They say that they share the vision of a society in which people are judged solely on the quality of their character and not the color of their skin. On the other hand, many of these same people believe that it is proper for race to serve as a basis for pride, solidarity, loyalty, and affection. Every true man, Justice John Marshall Harlan declared, "has pride of race."[106] That many people of all hues agree is illustrated by racially exclusive private clubs, racial selectivity in advertisements for companionship, demonstrations such as the Million Man March, and the entire gamut of cultural practices by which individuals, on a racial basis, prefer "their people" over others. It should come as no surprise, then, that the enforcement of criminal law in jurisdictions dominated politically by whites would generate statistics suggesting that, in these locales, officials respond more empathetically to white than black victims of crime. That response is simply a reflection of a race-conscious society which continually reproduces a racially stratified marketplace of emotion.

This stratification stems from America's tragic history of race relations. It also stems, however, from a wider, perhaps even universal

---

but four were against people of color. (Staff Report by the Subcommittee on Civil and Constitutional Rights of the Committee of the Judiciary, U.S. House of Representatives, Racial Disparities in Federal Death Penalty Prosecutions 1988–1994, H.R. 458, 103d Cong. 2d Sess. 3 [March 1994]). The new federal death penalty legislation does offer one concession to those concerned about racial discrimination in sentencing. 18 U.S.C. § 3593 (1994) directs a judge to instruct a jury that "in considering whether a sentence of death is justified, it shall not consider the race, color, religious beliefs, national origin, or sex of the defendant or of any victim." The statute also provides that, in the event a jury sentences a defendant to death, every member of the jury must submit to the court a signed affidavit stating that no consideration of race or any other prohibited identification was involved in reaching his or her decision.

problem. Thousands of people die every day, yet most of us grieve only for those few with whom we most identify: parents, children, siblings, spouses, friends. In a sense, we all devalue the rest of the world in relation to our own small circle of loved ones; hence Jean Jacques Rousseau's charge that the preferences of friendship are "thefts" against humanity.[107] Typically, when we speak in sorrow about those killed in war, we refer to the casualties on *our* side. When an airplane disaster occurs, local newspapers typically highlight only the lives of *local* victims. The *McCleskey* statistics, in other words, do not represent something confined to race relations. Along many dimensions, we all engage in differential valuations of human life according to clannish criteria—family, locality, nationality. Recognizing the extent to which the *McCleskey* problem is related to a universal dilemma in human relations might help to facilitate a more candid discussion of this problem, a discussion in which judges, legislators, and other influential policymakers might more easily acknowledge, reflect upon, and change the realities of racial sentiment in American life.

10.

Race, Law,
and Punishment:
The War on Drugs

THE "WAR ON DRUGS" refers to a policy that attempts to reduce the supply, distribution, and use of illicit narcotics by increasingly punitive criminal measures.[1] This policy figures prominently in discussions about race relations and the administration of criminal law because its enforcement has greatly enlarged the numbers of blacks subjected to arrest, prosecution, and imprisonment. The war on drugs has thus dramatically accentuated the suspicion with which police authorities regard blacks. Incidents generated by the war on drugs account for a large proportion of the cases discussed in chapter 4 concerning the propriety of using race as a signal of risk. The war on drugs, moreover, largely explains why, in recent years, the incarceration rate among blacks has exponentially superseded the rate among whites.[2] Some observers claim that these results are not merely unintended side-effects of a nonracial policy but are instead the consequences of something far more malevolent: a racially biased design. One theory is that authorities do not really desire to stop the drug trade (at least among blacks) but desire instead to use drugs as a means of corrupting and disabling black communities.[3] Another is that the war on drugs is designed to imprison as many blacks as possible (particularly young black men), partly to incapacitate them and partly to make them into a particularly serviceable scapegoat—the Negro as Criminal.[4] A third is that the war on drugs, although truly aimed against illicit narcotics, is conducted in a fashion that is negligently indifferent to the war's collateral damage to blacks. According to this theory, if the war on drugs did to white communities what it is doing to black communities, white policymakers would long ago have called a truce in order to pursue some other, less destructive, course.[5]

I explore the racial critique of the war on drugs in two related contexts. In one, critics allege that officials single out black women for prosecution on charges of introducing their babies to cocaine. In the other, critics allege that Congress engaged in racial discrimination when it enacted, or retained, a law that punishes crack cocaine offenders much more harshly than powder cocaine offenders.

I make two main arguments. First, to a large extent, allegations of racial discrimination have been insufficiently substantiated to delineate a constitutional violation under governing law. Second, these allegations are not only unpersuasive in courts but also counterproductive in legislatures. They divert the discussion from the broad ground of whether a given policy is wise to the narrower, more treacherous ground of whether a given policy is racially discriminatory. The allegations are also counterproductive in that they trigger an especially stubborn defensiveness in support of existing policy from politicians who take umbrage at being accused of having engaged in racial misconduct. There is an important difference between saying that a policy is wrong, or misguided, or mistaken, or imprudent, or even silly and saying that a policy is "racist."

Race, Selective Prosecution, and "Crack Babies"

Is it true, as some scholars, activists, and journalists allege, that law enforcement authorities have engaged in racial discrimination in their prosecution of certain women for exposing fetuses or newborns to illicit drugs?[6]

The beginnings of this controversy can be traced to July 1989, when Jennifer Clarise Johnson, a twenty-three-year-old black crack addict,

became the first woman in the United States to be convicted for exposing a baby to illicit drugs via pregnancy. Florida officials brought
charges against Johnson after her two children tested positive for cocaine at birth. The prosecution contended that she "distributed" crack to
her infants during the brief interval after birth and before the umbilical
cord was severed.[7]

Prosecutors attempting to bring such cases have encountered a wel-
ter of moral, political, and legal objections. One objection is that the
statutes barring the distribution of cocaine were not meant to be used
against mothers who unintentionally passed the drug to their newborns;
Johnson's conviction was overturned on this ground.[8] Other objections
include the argument that these prosecutions deprive defendants of due
process of law inasmuch as no one could reasonably have known that
merely passing cocaine through one's umbilical cord could serve as the
basis of a criminal offense, that these prosecutions wrongly encroach
upon the right of a woman to control her reproductive life, and that fear
of prosecution will drive addicted women either to abort fetuses or to
avoid obtaining medical care.[9] The objection with which we shall be
principally concerned, however, is the claim that, for illicit racial reasons, officials have targeted women of color for prosecution.

Professor Dorothy Roberts articulates the most extensive and influential elaboration of this charge: "Poor black women have been selected
for punishment as a result of an inseparable combination of their gender, race, and economic status." "Poor Black women are the primary
targets of prosecutors, not because they are more likely to be guilty of fetal abuse, but because they are Black and poor." "The state's decision to
punish drug addicted mothers rather than help them stems from the
poverty and race of the defendants and society's denial of their full dignity as human beings."[10]

Roberts bases her allegations on two main grounds. The first is historical. She points to the sexual abuse of slave women, the undermining
of the slave family, and the harsh treatment of black women by social
welfare agencies. According to Roberts, prosecuting black women for
fetal abuse is simply a recent episode in "the systematic, institutionalized
denial of reproductive freedom that has uniquely marked Black
women's history in America."[11] The second ground is statistical. The argument is that, of the women prosecuted, the percentage who are black

so far outstrips blacks' percentage of pregnant women generally that the disparity creates a presumption of racially selective prosecution. By 1990, of fifty-two women prosecuted, thirty-five were black, fourteen white, two Latino, and one Native American. In Florida, ten out of eleven criminal cases were brought against black women. In South Carolina, seventeen of the eighteen cases brought for either criminal neglect of a child or distribution of drugs to a minor were brought against black women.[12]

What should one make of Roberts's charges?

First of all, her charges are surely plausible. Given the long and sad history of documented, irrefutable racial discrimination in the administration of criminal law, including discrimination initiated or tolerated by prosecutors, no informed observer should be shocked by the suggestion that some prosecutors treat black pregnant women more harshly than identically situated white pregnant women.

Secondly, that no judicial decisions support Professor Roberts's charge should not be viewed itself as a decisive refutation of her claim. The legal system is as hostile to charges of racial discrimination in prosecutorial decisionmaking as it is hostile to charges of racial discrimination in sentencing. That at least some officials have engaged in racially selective prosecutions is beyond doubt. Research has uncovered no cases, however, in which a court has ruled that, on grounds of racial discrimination, a prosecutor abused his discretion.*

---

*Some jurists might contend that the reversal of the conviction in *Yick Wo* v. *Hopkins*, 118 U.S. 356 (1886) represents an instance in which the courts invalidated a prosecution on grounds of racial discrimination, In *Yick Wo* the Supreme Court granted habeas corpus relief to a Chinese laundryman who was prosecuted for failing to obtain permission for exemption from the requirements of a local ordinance governing the type of buildings in which laundries could be located. The record clearly showed that while officials gave permission to nearly all of the whites who applied for it, they withheld permission from nearly all of the Chinese people who applied. The Supreme Court held in favor of Yick Wo, establishing that the Fourteenth Amendment applied to alienage as well as race. The ruling also established that the Court would recognize an individious administration of a statute as a violation of equal protection as well as a statute that facially discriminates against persons unjustifiably. In the Court's oft-cited words, "Though the law itself be fair on its face and impartial in appearance, yet, if it is applied and administered ... with an evil eye and

Three cases illustrate the judiciary's hostility to claims of racial discrimination in prosecution. In 1905, in *Ah Sin* v. *Wittman*,[13] a defendant sought to overturn a conviction for illicit gambling on the grounds that, for racial reasons, only Chinese people were prosecuted for this offense. The Supreme Court affirmed the conviction. Although Chinese were the only persons who had been prosecuted under the city's ordinance, no evidence indicated that others (e.g., whites) had violated the law. The Court concluded that, in the absence of such evidence, there was a possibility that the monochromatic statistics resulted not from racial selectivity in prosecution but, from the predominance of Chinese violators of

---

an unequal hand, so as practically to make unjust and illegal discrtiminations between persons in similar circumstances, material to their rights, the denial of equal justice is still within the prohibition of the Constitution." Ibid., 373–374. In *Yick Wo*, however, the officials who were shown to have engaged in wrongful discrimination were not the prosecutors but rather the officers in charge of awarding exemptions. See *United States* v. *Falk*, 479 F.2d 616, 618–619 (CA 7 1973) for a useful discussion of this point.

In *People* v. *Winters*, 342 P.2d 538 (Sup.Ct., App. Div 1959), a trial judge dismissed gambling charges against a group of blacks on the grounds that the gambling laws in Los Angeles were enforced in a racially discriminatory manner. An appellate court, however, reversed this decision.

In *People* v. *Ochoa*, 15 65 Cal. App.3d 885 (CA App. Ct. 1985), an intermediate state court of appeal dismissed a prosecution when officials refused to follow a judicial order to produce information to defense attorneys bearing on the question of prosecutorial intent. But that is not the same as a final judgment that a prosecutor illicitly went after a defendant on racial grounds.

The case that is closest to this description is *Duncan* v. *Perez*, 445 F.2d 557 (CA 5 1971). This case involved the prosecution of a black man for simple battery. Attempting to break up a fight between black and white youngsters near a recently desegregated public school, the defendant purportedly slapped the arm of one of the white boys. The defendant was tried and sentenced to prison and a fine before his conviction was reversed by the Supreme Court, which held that he had been unconstitutionally denied a jury trial. See *Duncan* v. *Louisiana*, 391 U.S. 145 (1968). When the local prosecutor, a notorious white supremacist, attempted to retry the defendant, the federal district court, enjoined a retrial on the grounds that the prosecution was maintained in bad faith and for purposes of harassment, that there existed no legitimate state interest in a reprosecution for simple battery in the circumstances of this case, and that reprosecution would deter and suppress the exercise of federally secured rights by blacks in the parish where this controversy arose.

the antigambling ordinance. "No latitude of intention should be indulged in a case like this," Justice Joseph McKenna declared on behalf of the Court. "There should be certainty to every intent. . . . This is a matter of proof, and no fact should be omitted to make it out completely, when the power of a Federal court is invoked to interfere with the course of criminal justice of a State."[14]

The second case is *Butler* v. *Cooper*, which arose in 1977 in Portsmouth, Virginia.[15] Police arrested Esther Butler for selling two cans of beer in her home without the appropriate license. On three occasions she appeared in court for a scheduled hearing. Each time, over her objection, the case was continued on motion of the prosecution. After the last continuance, a police officer suggested that she plead guilty to a lesser offense. After she refused, she was convicted, fined $200, and sentenced to jail for sixty days, although ultimately her conviction was vacated because of the failure of the police to follow certain procedural technicalities.

Butler charged that she was prosecuted in bad faith because she actively supported blacks' advancement, that the continuances were typical of trial delays imposed on black defendants to force them to accede to plea bargains, and that all of these measures were part of a larger pattern of official mistreatment of the black community. She filed a suit seeking damages from various law enforcement officials, who, she alleged, had conspired to deprive her and all black Americans in Portsmouth of the equal protection of the laws. More specifically, she complained that these officials engaged in racially selective enforcement of the state's liquor laws. She claimed that although one-third of Portsmouth's population was black, 98 percent of those arrested for illegal liquor sales were black. She claimed that although undercover operatives were used to infiltrate black social clubs in order to facilitate such prosecutions, infiltration was not used against white social clubs. Finally, she claimed that although there existed no such disparity for related offenses such as drunk driving and public drunkenness.

The federal district court, affirmed by the court of appeals, granted the municipality's motion for summary judgment, ruling that the plaintiff's allegations were insufficient to warrant a trial. According to the trial judge, "Assuming . . . that plaintiff's contention is true [that 98 percent of the arrests were of blacks], that fact alone is wholly inadequate to support the conspiracy charge in this case. [S]he offers no other factual material of any type in support of her allegations."[16] Affirming this ruling, the U.S. Court of Appeals declared that "without more proof, we cannot permit this plaintiff to pursue an unfounded grudge . . . There is no genuine issue of any material fact."[17] This judgment was surely wrong. As Judge John D. Butzner pointed out in a strong dissent, the existence of the racial disparity was uncontested and unexplained, and there was direct conflict between the plaintiff's charge and the city's denial that it used undercover agents to infiltrate black social organizations. This is not to say that Butler should necessarily have prevailed at trial. It is to say that her allegations at least warranted a trial. Given that all reasonable inferences are to be drawn in favor of the party resisting summary judgment, the refusal of the courts to provide a trial to test Butler's allegations constituted a flagrant error.

United States v. *Armstrong*[18] provides a third illustration of the judicial system's hostility to charges of racially prejudiced prosecution (and indeed *any* type of challenge to the exercise of prosecutorial discretion). *Armstrong* arose from the prosecution of five black men charged with, among other crimes, dealing crack cocaine. Authorities chose to prosecute them under federal law as opposed to state law, a significant decision since federal penalties far exceeded state penalties.*

The defendants claimed that officials racially discriminated in subjecting them to prosecution under federal law. In support of their allegations, the defendants submitted an affidavit that indicated that blacks were the defendants in *all* of the twenty-four federal crack prosecutions faced in 1991 by the Federal Public Defender's Office for the Central District of California. They also made a discovery motion requesting information from the prosecutor about the criteria used to decide what type of charges to bring against defendants. A federal district judge granted the defendant's discovery motion after a prosecutor initially told her that he could offer "no explanation" for the racial demographics

---

*If convicted under federal law, one defendant, Christopher Armstrong, faced a prison term of fifty-five years to life. Under California law he would have faced a sentence of three to nine years. Another defendant, Aaron Hampton, would have faced a maximum term of fourteen years under state law but a *mandatory* life term under federal law. See Brief for Respondents Shelton Auntwan Martin, Aaron Hampton, Christopher Lee Armstrong, and Freedi Mack, at 2, *Armstrong*, 116 S.Ct. 1480 (No: 96-157), available in 1996 WL 17111, at 2.

noted by the defendants' affidavit. After a bit more skirmishing between the parties, the district judge insisted upon enforcing her discovery order.[19] When the prosecutor refused to comply, the judge dismissed the indictments, which opened the way to an appeal.

Although the U.S. Court of Appeals for the Ninth Circuit upheld the district court,[20] the Supreme Court disagreed. The Court concluded that the *Armstrong* defendants would not be entitled to discovery until they could first produce some evidence that similarly situated defendants of other races could have been but were not prosecuted under federal law for crack offenses. This requirement was predicated on the Court's reaffirmation of its holding in *Ah Sin* that, in order to make out a selective prosecution claim, the defendant-claimant "must show that similarly situated individuals of different race were not prosecuted."[21]

The Supreme Court's decision was based on an eight to one vote, with Justice Stevens as the lone dissenter. Albeit outvoted, Stevens was correct in concluding that the Court should have permitted the trial judge the latitude to order discovery. Such decisions are typically left to the sound discretion of trial judges, and in this case the defendants offered sufficient evidence of rightfully disturbing statistics and testimony to warrant the trial judge's order. Justice Stevens pointedly remarked:

> Even if respondents failed to carry their burden of showing that there were individuals who were not black but who could have been prosecuted in federal court for the same offenses, it does not follow that the District Court abused its discretion in ordering the discovery. There can be no doubt that such individuals exist, and indeed the Government has never denied the same. In these circumstances, I fail to see why the District Court was unable to take judicial notice of the obvious fact and demand information from the Government's files to support or refute respondents' evidence.[22]

The defendants in *Armstrong* were not seeking discovery based on naked assertions. They were seeking discovery based upon preliminary indications that should have been seen as raising a substantial question regarding the racial evenhandedness of a U.S. Attorney's Office. The prosecutors simply wanted to avoid the burden of explanation, a burden that could have been regulated reasonably by means other than attenuating the already inadequate judicial oversight of prosecutorial discretion.* Although the U.S. Attorney's Office may well have been able to rebut the defendants' charges,[23] Justice Stevens was right in concluding that the Court was wrong to bar the trial judge from ordering the government to produce information relevant to the allegation.

The failure of the judicial system to police prosecutors adequately, however, does not automatically validate a claim of racial (or any other) misconduct. Professor Roberts's thesis (at least her initial presentation of it) is that prosecutors do not simply target women who happen mainly to be black and poor but target these women *because* they are black and poor.[24] Is Professor Roberts's thesis persuasive? Does she offer a concrete instance that substantiates her broad-brush allegation? Does she offer an example of a prosecutor treating a black pregnant woman more punitively than a similarly situated white woman?

The answer is no.

One piece of evidence upon which Roberts relies heavily is a study indicating that in Pinellas County, Florida, black women were ten times more likely than whites to be reported to public health authorities for substance abuse during pregnancy.[25] This disparity is especially significant, according to Roberts, because "little difference existed in the prevalence of substance abuse by pregnant women along either racial or

---

*The solicitor general of the United States reported that providing detailed information to rebut racial selective prosecution allegations in a case analogous to *Armstrong* had cost the government approximately 1000 attorney-hours. See Petition for a Writ of Certiorari, *United States* v. *Armstrong*, 48 F.3d 1508 (CA 9 1995) (No. 95-157) at 23 n.3. Presumably, however, the need for extensive research could, in many instances, be obviated by a clear, straightforward response on the part of prosecutors to question-raising demographic patterns. Recall that in *Armstrong* an assistant United States Attorney stated that he could offer "no explanation" for the exclusively black class of defendants prosecuted by his office for crack trafficking offenses. When a cogent explanation cannot be offered, it is probably a prudent investment of resources for the government to uncover information that sheds light on the validity or invalidity of racial discrimination claims. The fear of overburdening the prosecutors is mistaken. After all, federal district judges are on hand to regulate the discovery process. The trial judge in *Armstrong* was one of the few who has ever ordered the government to respond to a discovery motion on behalf of a selective prosecution claim. It is unwise to prevent judges from issuing such orders in circumstances in which they reasonably perceive an appreciable likelihood that allegations of prosecutorial racial discrimination are true.

economic lines."[26] This statement is accurate, however, only if one ignores different sorts of substance abuse and instead bundles all of the cases together, treating cocaine users identically with alcohol drinkers and marijuana smokers. Roberts herself acknowledges that the pool of black women studied in Pinellas County differed in their drug usage from the pool of white women studied. Although the white pregnant women tested positive more frequently for marijuana (14.4 percent versus 6 percent for black women), the black pregnant women tested positive more frequently for cocaine (7.5 percent versus 1.8 percent for white women).[27]

The authors of the study on which Roberts relies suggest that the racial disparity in reporting rates might reflect not racially motivated disparate treatment but the interaction of two other considerations: more severe symptoms in newborns arising from exposure to cocaine and a pattern of preferences such that black pregnant women are more likely than white pregnant women to be addicted to cocaine. Roberts fails inexplicably to grapple with these hypotheses. Instead, she simply insists that "racial prejudice and stereotyping must be a factor" in the racially disparate pattern of reporting by the medical personnel in Pinellas County.[28]

Commenting on the decision of prosecutors to bring fetal endangerment cases against crack cocaine users as opposed to users of other drugs, Roberts states:

> The selection of crack addiction for punishment can be justified neither by the number of addicts nor the extent of the harm to the fetus. Excessive alcohol consumption during pregnancy, for example, can cause severe fetal injury, and marijuana use may also adversely affect the unborn. . . . Although different forms of substance abuse prevail among pregnant women of various socioeconomic levels and racial and ethnic backgrounds, inner-city Black communities have the highest concentration of crack addicts. Therefore, selecting crack abuse as the primary fetal harm to be punished has a discriminatory impact that cannot be medically justified.[29]

This statement is riddled with problems. Medical research on fetal endangerment by mothers' drug usage is ongoing and, as Roberts herself indicates, is marked by differences in opinion.[30] In such a setting,

Roberts's confident, rigid condemnation of those who give first priority to cocaine abuse is misguided. Perhaps her position that crack is no more of a danger to babies than other drugs will eventually be vindicated by medical science. Even so, all this may indicate is that those whom she attacks were wrong; it would not alone show that they were racists. Her response, moreover, is wholly unresponsive to the argument that prosecutors justifiably gave priority to cocaine cases because babies exposed to it *displayed* more severe symptoms than those generated by exposure to other illicit drugs. Maybe that belief, too, was erroneous. But here, again, erring in good faith is different from racially invidious decisionmaking.

Roberts's response also fails to address satisfactorily those who believe that cocaine use poses more of an overall danger to society than other sorts of illicit drug use and thus that cocaine abuse in all areas, including fetal endangerment, warrants relatively more of an investment in law enforcement. She simply ignores this plausible alternative to her theory of a campaign of prosecutions animated by an amalgam of racial and class biases.

Another difficulty with Roberts's theory is that she abandons it herself. She plays bait-and-switch. She initially claims that "poor Black women . . . are the primary targets of prosecutors . . . because they are Black and poor."[31] This statement, buttressed by similar ones, articulates a claim of disparate treatment: prosecutors have either consciously or unconsciously treated black pregnant women differently than similarly situated white pregnant women. Later, however, Roberts changes ground:

> It is unlikely that [any legislators, prosecutors, nurses, or doctors] intentionally singled out Black women for punishment based on a conscious devaluation of their motherhood. The disproportionate impact of the prosecutions on poor Black women does not result from such isolated, individualized decisions. Rather, it is a result of two centuries of systematic exclusion of Black women from tangible and intangible benefits enjoyed by white society.[32]

In other words, she retreats altogether from the assertion that prosecutors have *targeted* certain persons for prosecution because of their identity as poor black women and instead alleges that these women are victims of "systemic exclusion" and its consequences, a state of affairs some people refer to as "institutional racism": the perpetuation of circumstances that oppress black people even in the absence of current racial discrimination.

The unintentional perpetuation of past oppression is a phenomenon that warrants much more attention and redress than it has heretofore received. This phenomenon will only receive clarification and attention, however, if commentators are careful to distinguish it from disparate treatment: dealing with some people differently than others because of their race. Often, as in Professor Roberts's article, commentators do not. Sometimes this omission is due to sloppiness. Sometimes it is attributable to a strategy of obfuscation pursuant to which complainants designedly make vague, ambiguous allegations. Sometimes it amounts to a tactic of stigmatization pursuant to which accusers attempt to mold public opinion by making allegations that sectors of the public are predisposed to believe whether or not the accusations are true. Whatever the explanation, a cost in public education is exacted by this blurring of analytical categories.

There is yet another difficulty with Roberts's thesis. It is premised on the belief that the prosecution of black women for fetal endangerment represents a devaluation of black women as mothers. She does not satisfactorily explain, however, the basis for her inference. She writes:

> Prosecutions represent one of two possible responses to the problem of drug-exposed babies. The government may choose either to help women have healthy pregnancies or to punish women for their prenatal conduct. Although it might seem that the state could pursue both of these avenues at once, the two responses are ultimately irreconcilable. Far from deterring injurious drug use, prosecution of drug-addicted mothers in fact deters pregnant women from using available health and counseling services because it causes women to fear that, if they seek help, they could be reported to government authorities and charged with a crime.[33]

Although Professor Roberts asserts that there exists an "irreconcilable" difference between prosecuting women for fetal endangerment and helping women to have healthy pregnancies, she does not explain why that must be so. In several locales, officials use criminal prosecution as a method to pressure a person into participating in a drug treatment program.[34] Roberts responds that even the threat of criminal prosecution is objectionable insofar as it will likely scare away some women from visiting health services. That prospect is a large and important concern that decisionmakers should carefully weigh. There are other concerns, however, to be weighed as well. Should public authorities be prohibited from using the threat of criminal process to push a woman into treatment no matter what the character of her drug abuse, no matter what the consequence to herself and her babies, and no matter how adamantly she refuses to seek treatment otherwise? Perhaps the answer is yes on the grounds that such women will be few and far between, while larger numbers of women will injure themselves and their babies by forgoing treatment if there is any chance that seeking treatment will make prosecution more likely. But reaching a different conclusion should not automatically make a person either unreasonable or a bigot.[35]

A final point to be made about Roberts's analysis is that it shows no attentiveness to the problem of *underprotection* of the law. She complains because black women have been subjected to prosecutions for fetal endangerment at rates considerably higher than white women. But just suppose that the racial demographics of prosecution were reversed. Indeed, to dramatize the point, imagine that officials brought drug abuse, fetal endangerment cases solely against white women. Would that not rightly prompt suspicion of racially selective devaluation of black babies on the grounds that withholding prosecution deprives black babies of the equal *protection* of the laws?[36] Roberts's analysis has little to say about this hypothetical situation because her complaint is trapped by a reflexive animosity to law enforcement and an inattentiveness to its essential function as a protector of the weak.

Before proceeding, I want to emphasize what I have and have not said. I have not spoken in favor of prosecuting pregnant drug abusers (although there are surely some instances when irresponsible conduct by pregnant persons cries out for a punitive response). I have simply argued that the allegations of unconstitutional racial discrimination that are often made by opponents of prosecutions have not been persuasively substantiated. This is more than a legal point (as important as such points are). It is also a political matter. Deficient allegations of racial discrimination further debase the already diminished currency of such claims, marginalize well-grounded criticisms of punitive sanctions, and elicit stubborn defensiveness from officials who can concede having been mistaken but cannot abide the charge that racial bias determined their conduct.

Race and Differences in Sentencing for Crack Cocaine vs. Powder Cocaine

Professor Roberts attacked the administration of a criminal punishment. We turn now to an attack on a punishment itself: provisions which impose a much higher penalty for dealing or possessing crack cocaine than powder cocaine.* Under the federal Anti-Drug Abuse Act of 1986,[37] a person convicted of possession with intent to distribute fifty grams or more of crack cocaine must be sentenced to no less than ten years in prison. By contrast, only if a person is convicted of possession with intent to distribute at least 5,000 grams of powder cocaine is he subject to a mandatory minimum of ten years—a 100:1 ratio in terms of intensity of punishment. Moreover, under the federal Anti-Drug Abuse Act of 1988,[38] a person caught merely possessing one to five grams of crack cocaine is subject to a mandatory minimum sentence of five years in prison. Crack cocaine is the only drug for which there exists a mandatory minimum penalty for a first offense of simple possession.

Many see this dramatic difference in punishment in racial terms because of the confluence of two considerations. The first is the apparent similarity of the underlying offenses; all involve cocaine. Because crack cocaine is derived from powder cocaine, some observers maintain that trafficking in one is essentially the same as trafficking in the other. Cocaine is cocaine, they assert. The second is the difference in the racial composition of the pools of people arrested, prosecuted, and imprisoned. In 1992, 92.6 percent of the defendants convicted for crack cocaine offenses nationally were black and only 4.7 percent white. In comparison,

---

*Powder cocaine is a white substance that is a potent anesthetic and a powerful stimulant. It can be administered in a variety of ways, including injection and snorting. Crack cocaine is derived from powder cocaine and is taken into the body when it is vaporized and inhaled. See United States Sentencing Commission, *Special Report to the Congress: Cocaine and Federal Sentencing Policy* 7–30 (1995).

45.2 percent of defendants sentenced for powder cocaine offenses were white, and only 20.7 percent black.[39]

Some argue that by punishing crack cocaine offenses much more harshly than powder cocaine offenses federal and state governments violate the Equal Protection clause of the U.S. Constitution and other legal protections.[40] This claim has had some influence with journalists and other molders of public opinion.[41] It helped to move the Minnesota Supreme Court to invalidate Minnesota's drug sentencing law under the state constitution.[42] Moreover, concerns over racial fairness prompted the United States Sentencing Commission to recommend that Congress narrow the crack–powder sentencing differential.[43]

Several federal judges have also castigated the crack sentencing statute as racially unjust.[44] One judge invalidated the sentencing regime in a Missouri case that arose from Edward Clary's conviction, pursuant to a guilty plea, of possessing with intent to distribute 67.76 grams of crack cocaine.[45] Because Clary was caught with over 50 grams of crack, he was subject under federal law to a mandatory minimum sentence of ten years' imprisonment. To "qualify" under federal law for the same ten-year minimum sentence, he would have had to have been caught with 5,000 grams of powder cocaine.

Clary, an eighteen-year-old black man with no prior convictions, charged that this penalty differential had a disproportionate and unjustifiable impact on him and other blacks because blacks are much more likely than whites to traffic in crack. Everyone concedes that there exists a striking and racially identifiable pattern in the demographics of the drug trade. In the Eastern District of Missouri, between 1988 and 1992, blacks constituted 98.2 percent of the defendants convicted of crack cocaine charges.[46] The disagreement is over the inferences which should be drawn from such statistics in light of all that has surrounded the origins and ongoing ratification of the sentencing statute at issue.

Concluding that the sentencing provision in the Anti-Drug Abuse Act was a product of "unconscious racism" as well as "irrational and arbitrary" decisionmaking, Judge Clyde S. Cahill refused to sentence Clary in accordance with it.[47]* His ruling, which was subsequently re-

---

*According to Judge Cahill:

The totality of the facts in this case converge to support the conclusion that racial discriminatory influences, at least unconsciously, played an apprecia-

versed, emphasizes three points. First, racism has historically influenced the formulation of drug policy. Fear and hatred of Asians was part of what mobilized punitive legal measures against the distribution or use of opium, a drug associated in the public mind with the Chinese. Similarly, fear and hatred of blacks was part of what led to the criminalization of marijuana, cocaine, and heroin, drugs that were said to incite the dangerous instincts of African-Americans. Judge Cahill notes, for example, that "the Harrison Act of 1914, the first federal law to prohibit distribution of cocaine and heroin, was passed on the heels of overblown media accounts depicting heroin-addicted black prostitutes and criminals in the cities."[48] To Cahill, these historical episodes put the current demonization of crack into an alarming light:

> Almost every major drug has been, at various times in America's history, treated as a threat to the survival of America by some minority segment of society. Panic based on media reports which incited racial fears has been used historically in this country as the catalyst for generating racially biased legislation. The association of illicit drug use with minorities and the threat of it "spreading to the higher ranks" is disturbingly similar to the events which culminated in the "100 to 1" ratio enhancement in the crack statute.[49]

Cahill's second point is that the crack trade largely stems from terrible social conditions which are permitted to fester because of a racially selective failure to adequately aid America's black ghettos:

> Picture a city where it is easier to buy cocaine than it is to purchase a loaf of bread. . . . Think of a community where mothers, barely

---

ble role in promulgating the enhanced statutory scheme for possession and distribution of crack. Legislators' unconscious racial aversion towards blacks, sparked by unsubstantiated reports of the effects of crack, reactionary media prodding, and an agitated constituency, motivated the legislators to enhance the punishment scheme to produce a dual system of punishment in the application of this statute.
846 F.Supp. 796–797 (E.D. Mo.), rev'd., 34 F.3d 709 (CA 8 1994), cert. denied, 115 S.Ct. 1172 (1995).

more than children themselves, serve as one-parent heads of house-holds in a world without fathers. Consider a neighborhood without effective leaders because they all have fled to suburbia. . . . Remember the children who rarely see a doctor, lawyer, or teacher as a neighbor and whose only source of inspiration is a chain-bedecked drug peddler.

These portraits of misery and degradation are the daily world of the inner city resident and are all . . . products of unconscious racism. Is it any wonder that there is no motivation, no happiness, no hope?[50]

Cahill's third point is that there exists in American political culture widespread "unconscious racism." Relying heavily on an influential article by Professor Charles R. Lawrence, III,[51] Cahill declares:

Racism goes beyond prejudicial discrimination and bigotry. It arises from outlooks, stereotypes, and fears of which we are vastly un-aware. Our historical experience has made racism an integral part of our culture even though society has more recently embraced an ideal that rejects racism as immoral. . . . The root of unconscious racism can be found in the latent psyches of white Americans that were inundated for centuries with myths and fallacies of their superiority over the black race. So deeply embedded are these ideas, that their acceptance . . . from generation to generation [has] become a mere routine. . . . A benign neglect for the harmful impact or fallout upon the black community that might ensue from decisions made by the white community for the "greater good" of society has replaced intentional discrimination. . . . Most Americans have grown beyond the evils of overt racial malice, but still have not completely shed the deeply rooted cultural bias that differentiates between "them" and "us."[52]

In Cahill's view, Congress's 100-to-1 sentencing disparity between crack and powder cocaine is an instance of unconscious racism at work, an example of "racial influences which unconsciously seeped into the legislative decisionmaking process." According to him, an important aspect of this process was racist media coverage, which misinformed legislators and inflamed their constituencies. The media, he wrote,

"created a stereotype of a crack dealer as a young black male, unemployed, gang affiliated, gun toting, and a menace to society." "Not all
young black men are drug dealers," he asserted, yet "the broad brush of
uninformed public opinion paints them all the same."[53]*

Compounding the problem of exaggeration, Cahill argued, was the
problem of influence. In his view, the media's

> stereotypical images undoubtedly served as the touchstone that in-
> fluenced racial perceptions held by legislators and the public as re-
> lated to the "crack epidemic." . . . The prospect of black crack
> migrating to the white suburbs led the legislators to reflexively pun-
> ish crack violators more harshly than their white, suburban, powder
> cocaine dealing counterparts.[54]†

To substantiate his conclusion that Congress acted at least partially on
the basis of racial reflexes triggered by racist reporting, Judge Cahill
notes that the legislation was developed speedily, that the Senate conducted only a single hearing dedicated to examining crack cocaine, and
that, according to the then counsel to the House Subcommittee on
Crime, important figures in the House of Representatives, without deliberation, "arbitrarily doubled [the punishment for crack cocaine] simply to symbolize Congressional seriousness." The judge quotes the aide
as remarking that "if the ratio selected had been 20 to 1, 3 to 1, or 5 or 10
to 1, it might have been a logical demarcation. But the exaggerated effect of a 100 to 1 ratio is illogical and not rational."[55]

Judge Cahill found wholly unsatisfactory the justifications articulated by the U.S. Justice Department to support the crack–powder distinction. The Justice Department argued that Congress acted within its
authority by punishing crack offenses more harshly than powder offenses because it reasonably viewed the former as more dangerous than
the latter. It viewed crack as more dangerous because, in its opinion,

---

*In the midst of his polemic against the news media Judge Cahill declares, jarringly,
that "these stereotypical descriptions of drug dealers may be accurate." 846 F.Supp.
783 (E.D. Mo. 1995).

†Judge Cahill also declared that "media reports associating blacks with the horrors of
crack cocaine caused the Congress to react irrationally and arbitrarily." 846 F.Supp.
784 (E.D. Mo. 1995).

crack is more potent, more addictive, and more accessible to more people because of pricing and the way it is typically marketed. Judge Cahill rejected the first two justifications on the basis of experts who testified at congressional hearings and in hearings before him. On the basis of their testimony, Cahill concluded, "There is no evidence that the use of crack makes the user physiologically or psychologically more prone to violence or other antisocial behavior than does the use of powder cocaine." With respect to the third prong of Congress's asserted justification, Cahill maintained that "crack is no cheaper than cocaine powder because cocaine is the essential product of crack."[56]

In sum, according to Judge Cahill, Congress had no reasonable basis to distinguish sharply the penalties for powder and crack cocaine. In the most impassioned section of his opinion, Judge Cahill declared:

> It would be far more fair and just, in keeping with the "get tough" rhetoric . . . to require that both black and white violators serve the same 10 years imprisonment, be it "crack" or powder cocaine. Cocaine is, really, cocaine!! No crack could exist without cocaine powder. Eliminate cocaine and crack disappears!! This would be simple and fair and would eliminate racial injustice. Of paramount value would be the enhanced respect for the judiciary and the nation by bringing about equal justice for all—not merely punishment for "JUST US."[57]

According to the judge, "Although intent *per se* may not have entered Congress' enactment of the crack statute, its failure to account for a foreseeable disparate impact which would affect black Americans in grossly disproportionate numbers would nonetheless violate the spirit and letter of equal protection."[58] He asserted, moreover, that Congress would have acted differently if Congress knew that it was mainly whites rather than mainly blacks who stood to suffer such draconian punishment. "If young white males were being incarcerated at the same rate as young black males," he concluded, "the statute would have been amended long ago."[59]

Judge Cahill's opinion evidences an admirable abhorrence of racial inequities in American life and a laudable desire to better the situation. It also exemplifies, however, much of what this book debunks. Angered by racism and indifference to it, Judge Cahill seizes the moment to deliver a polemic against racial injustice despite features of the case that belie his assertions. Careless about facts, the opinion evades facing realities that pose a challenge to its conclusions. Indifferent to the discipline of legal analysis, the opinion reads as if it were a caricature created to serve the purposes of those who denounce the supposed imperialism of the federal judiciary.

Part of Judge Cahill's historical point is valid. Prohibitionists of various sorts have excited racial sentiments to demonize drug usage they have sought to criminalize.[60] At the same time, it is also true that authorities have neglected vices that have menaced black communities, thereby depriving them of the equal *protection* of the law. Although Judge Cahill pays little attention to this side of the story, black legislators in Congress did when they initiated efforts to isolate crack as a peculiarly dangerous newcomer to the drug market.

One might have thought that for those who are suspicious of the aims and sentiments that guided the design of the Anti-Drug Abuse Act, the positions and statements of *black* members of Congress would be of some importance. But Judge Cahill and virtually all of the rest of the critics who have condemned as racist the crack–powder distinction have failed to take into account the opinions of the members of Congress who concerned themselves most intently and consistently with elevating the fortunes of African-Americans, namely the black members of Congress.[61] They have rendered the blacks in Congress invisible. This is not to say that the opinions of black members of Congress should be viewed as dispositive. Persons of any hue can be wrong, opportunistic, or racially prejudiced even with respect to people of their own racial background. Still, it would be useful to some extent to know where the black members of Congress have stood on the matter. The claim that illicit racial beliefs and perceptions animated the enactment of the crack–powder distinction would surely be strengthened if all or even most of the black members of Congress had objected to the statute on racial grounds.

The fact is, however, that eleven of the twenty-one blacks who were then members of the House of Representatives voted in favor of the law which created the 100-to-1 crack–powder differential. It is difficult to interpret precisely the meaning of a vote. A representative might be against certain portions of a bill but favor others sufficiently to support the legislation overall. Or one might even vote in favor of a bill while inwardly opposing it. Still, in light of charges that the crack–powder distinction was enacted partly because of conscious or unconscious racism, it is noteworthy that *none* of the black members of Congress made that claim at the time the bill was initially discussed. Still more striking is that some of the black members of Congress who did vote for the bill expressed views regarding crack cocaine that strongly support the logic of the crack–powder differential.

Charles Rangel, an African-American liberal Democratic representative from Harlem, New York, chaired the House Select Committee on Narcotics Abuse and Control when the federal crack–powder differential was enacted. In March 1986, he became the first person in Congress to draw attention to crack as a new and special danger, noting that "what is most frightening about crack is that it has made cocaine widely available and affordable for abuse among our youth."[62] Five months later, Major Owens, a liberal Democratic representative from the predominantly black Bedford-Stuyvesant section of Brooklyn, New York, introduced legislation to increase punishment for trafficking in cocaine. He did this to rectify what he viewed as "preferential treatment for cocaine." At that time, trafficking in cocaine was punished much less harshly than trafficking in heroin. Owens's proposed legislation lowered the amount of cocaine presumed to signal that a person is a distributor and raised the penalties substantially—twenty years and a $250,000 fine for the first offense and forty years and a $500,000 fine for a subsequent offense. "We must make it perfectly clear," Owens declared, "that we view this drug as highly dangerous and that we will not tolerate its importation, possession, or sale."[63]

Soon thereafter, Representative Owens returned to this subject, observing:

> There is a groundswell in the neighborhoods . . . all across America . . . which demands that effective steps be taken to end the drug trafficking and the drug abuse epidemic. . . . None of the press accounts really have exaggerated what is actually going on. It is as bad as any articles have stated. It is as bad as anything you have read about. It is as bad as anything you have seen on television or heard on radio."[64]

Complaining again about what he viewed as insufficient punishment for cocaine-related offenses, Owens maintained:

Current law does not take cocaine seriously. It is not surprising [therefore] that we have an epidemic now which is heightened by the appearance of a purified form of cocaine which is called crack.... Whereas the law requires stiff penalties for other narcotics, the law does not require very stiff penalties in the case of the possession of a considerable amount of cocaine."[65]

Representative Owens was followed on the floor of the House by Alton Waldon, another African-American liberal Democratic representative from a predominantly black district in New York. His message was much the same as Owens's but with a bit more punitive bite and a more focused attention on crack:

The madness which is crack has no respect for social, professional or economic status. Crack usage is the evidence that our society may in fact be losing control of itself. For those of us who are black this self-inflicted pain is the worst oppression we have known since slavery.... Let us ... pledge to crack down on crack.[66]

The comments of Rangel, Owens, and Waldon were made before the 100-to-1 crack–powder differential was proposed as legislation. They are, however, consistent with that legislation and helped to prepare the ground for it. After all, if crack trafficking represents, in Waldon's words, "the worst oppression we have known since slavery," one reasonable response might well be to impose severe mandatory minimum sentences on those guilty of such antisocial conduct.

The absence of any charge by black members of Congress that the crack–powder differential was racially unfair speaks volumes; after all, several of these representatives had long histories of distinguished opposition to any public policy that smacked of racial injustice. That several of these representatives demanded a crackdown on crack is also significant. It suggests that the initiative for what became the crack–powder distinction originated to some extent *within* the ranks of African-American congressional officials. All of these facts are relevant in evaluating whether the crack–powder distinction should be prohibited on racial justice grounds. All of them militate against Judge Cahill's conclusion. None is mentioned in his opinion.

Judge Cahill concluded that Congress lacked any reasonable basis for punishing crack more harshly than powder and that subsequent study confirmed the lack of a reasonable basis for distinguishing between crack and powder. This assertion is preposterous. Congress acted on the basis of the same information that prompted Representatives Rangel, Owens, and Waldon to urge their colleagues to "crack down on crack," information which suggested that crack cocaine was more dangerous than powder cocaine along several dimensions: more addictive, more closely linked to criminal violence, more perilous to the health of users, and more widely accessible. Some of these claims have been challenged. However, even with respect to those that are most controversial, one cannot fairly say—as did Judge Cahill—that Congress had *no* reasonable basis for embracing them. One might disagree with the experts Congress chose to credit and the conclusions Congress chose to reach. To say, though, that those conclusions are bereft of rationality is clearly wrong.

Some opponents of the crack–powder distinction acknowledge this point. Thus, Professor David A. Sklansky, in a careful critique of the crack–powder distinction, writes, "The force of Judge Cahill's protest was unfortunately undercut by his own failure to recognize and respect . . . the genuine and important differences between crack and powder cocaine."[67]* This, however, puts the matter all too nicely. Judge Cahill's opinion represents a willed refusal to acknowledge something that cannot be properly avoided: that whatever one's view about the wisdom of punishing crack cocaine offenses more harshly than powder cocaine offenses, it is simply irrefutable that crack and powder are distinct forms of narcotics, even though they share the same root. Putting to the side the controverted scientific testimony about the relative addictiveness and toxicity of powder and crack, one difference between the two appears to be accepted universally: crack is typically sold in smaller quantities at lesser prices in a more convenient form and is therefore more accessible to larger groups of people. Crack democratized the co-

---

*At another point in his article, Sklansky describes as "demonstrably incorrect" Judge Cahill's claim that "there is no reliable medical evidence that crack cocaine is more addictive than powder cocaine." David A. Sklansky, "Cocaine, Race, and Equal Protection," 47 *Stanford Law Review* 1283 (1995).

caine high. It "reinvigorated the cocaine market and greatly increased the population of cocaine abusers."[68]* That alone provided a sufficient basis for distinguishing between crack and powder, notwithstanding their common cocaine lineage. Even if crack and powder were otherwise identical, the greater marketability of crack means that it has more potential reach than powder and can thus be reasonably perceived as more of a social danger.†

Judge Cahill and other critics contend that even if crack is more dangerous than powder, it is not so much more dangerous as to justify the difference in punishment meted out by Congress. This complaint has two dimensions, one procedural, the other substantive. The procedural complaint is that Congress acted hurriedly and haphazardly. This is true. These flaws in the lawmaking process, however, are blemishes that constitutional law (fortunately) tolerates. Judge Cahill made much of the Congress bypassing routine procedures in its haste to legislate. But with the exception of certain constitutional requirements, there is nothing that compels Congress to follow any set course. Sometimes crises properly move legislators to streamline their typical procedures, as Congress did in 1964 when it enacted the Civil Rights Act.[69] The substantive complaint is that Congress's draconian punishment for crack offenses are simply too harsh to permit. The constitutional grounding for that challenge, however, is the Eighth Amendment's prohibition against cruel and unusual punishment not the Equal Protection clause's insistence upon equality of treatment. Several defendants have challenged the crack sentencing regime on Eighth Amendment grounds. But these claims, too, have been uniformly and rightly rejected by the federal courts.[70]

Two other features of *Clary* warrant comment. One has to do with

---

*"In 1978, cocaine was something between a curiosity and a menace. . . . By 1988, cocaine had become the drug problem par excellence, with a retail market nearly equal to those for heroin and marijuana combined. . . . How did a minor drug become so major, a seemingly benign drug so horrible? In a word, crack happened." Mark A. R. Kleiman, *Against Excess: Drug Policy for Results*, 295–296 (1992).

†Addressing this point, Judge Cahill utters a non sequitur: "Crack is no cheaper than cocaine powder because cocaine is the essential product of crack." 846 F.Supp at 792 (E.D. Mo. 1995). Assuming that "cocaine is the essential product of crack," drug pushers can and do market powder and crack differently, a difference that lawmakers can reasonably take into account in establishing punishments.

Judge Cahill's portrayal of enhanced punishment for crack offenses as an increased burden on blacks as a class. The other has to do with his comments regarding the influence of the media in shaping public opinion regarding crack.

Although Cahill assumes that punishing black crack offenders is a burden upon blacks as a class, the basis for this assumption is questionable. After all, it could be that increasing the punishment of crack offenders correspondingly benefits those who obtain relief when those offenders are incarcerated. As Professor Kate Stith keenly observes:

> While it appears true that the enhanced penalties for crack cocaine more often fall upon black defendants, the legislature's action might also have been a laudatory attempt to provide enhanced protection to those communities—largely black . . . —who are ravaged by abuse of this potent drug. . . . [I]f dealers in crack cocaine have their liberty significantly restricted, this will afford greater liberties to the majority of citizens who are the potential victims of drug dealing and associated violent behaviors. *This is the logic of the criminal law,* and it is distressing that [judicial opponents of the crack–powder distinction] recognize[] only half of this logic—the denial of liberty to lawbreakers.[71]

In his zeal to protect that mainly black pool of persons convicted of crack offenses, Cahill almost completely ignores those, also mainly black, who must share space on streets and in buildings with crack traffickers.

His neglectfulness is facilitated by two important holes in his analysis. First, he appears to be unmindful that imprisonment is both a burden and a benefit—a burden for those imprisoned and a good for those whose lives are bettered by the confinement of criminals who might otherwise prey upon them. Second, he appears to be unmindful of what properly constitutes a racially discriminatory burden. Among the reasons he struck down the federal crack–powder sentencing distinction is that, in his view, it imposed a racially discriminatory burden upon blacks as a class. But what is racially discriminatory about the crack–powder distinction? Enhanced penalties for trafficking in crack fall upon *anyone* convicted of such conduct, regardless of race. Without explaining why, Cahill writes as if black crack convicts represent blacks as a whole. They do not. To the extent that the enhanced punishment for crack offenses falls upon blacks, it falls not upon blacks as a class but only upon a distinct subset of the black population—those in violation of the crack law.

There have been laws, silent as to race, that directly burdened only a subset of the black population but were intentionally aimed at disadvantaging blacks as a class. For example, one of the methods used by Alabama to minimize the electoral power of blacks as a class was a state constitutional provision, silent with respect to race, that permanently disenfranchised those convicted of committing certain crimes. The authors of the provision designed it to be a weapon useful for removing from voting lists as many blacks as possible by designating as disenfranchising crimes only those offenses that blacks were thought most likely to commit. Because unjustified racial considerations animated the Alabama officials, the Supreme Court rightly voided that law.[72] If there existed persuasive evidence that in 1986 or subsequently Congress had as one of its purposes the aim to imprison blacks longer than whites, then that too would be an instance of unconstitutional racial discrimination. Evidence supporting such a conclusion is scarce, however, which is precisely why Judge Cahill had to go beyond, indeed *against*, the evidence and perform various doctrinal contortions in order to conjure a violation of the Equal Protection Clause.

Like many who condemn the crack–powder distinction, Judge Cahill attributes much of the blame to the media. "Congress' decision was based, in large part," he writes, "on the racial imagery generated by the media which connected the 'crack problem' with blacks in the inner city." He maintains that "legions of newspaper articles regarding the crack cocaine epidemic depicted racial imagery of heavy involvement by blacks in crack cocaine. Practically every newspaper account featured a black male either using crack, selling crack, involved in police contact due to crack, or behind bars because of crack."[73]

Cahill is right to consider as relevant evidence of motive materials that members of Congress entered into the *Congressional Record*. One might, in some instances, be able to draw inferences from sources to which a legislator appreciatively refers. As with much else in his opinion, however, Judge Cahill takes this point too far by automatically attributing to the legislators the motives he discerns in the journalists. News reporting or scholarship that is admittedly racist can be put to all manner of uses depending on the user's aims. Newspaper stories generated by journalists who reflexively link blackness with crime can be read and acted upon by a legislator who rejects the journalists' racial premise but nonetheless believes that, for nonracial reasons, punishments need to be enhanced to discourage crack trafficking more firmly.

Judge Cahill is also right to question the monochromatic portraiture of crack usage that often emerges in newspaper and television accounts. Such accounts typically link crack and blacks. As Dorothy Lockwood, Anne E. Pottieger, and James A. Inciardi observe, "Journalists have portrayed crack use and crack-related crime as essentially problems of blacks in inner city neighborhoods." These researchers conclude, however, that "the crack/crime/black connection repeatedly portrayed in the popular media . . . is an overstatement." There does appear to be disproportionate crack use among blacks. Statistics from the National Institute of Drug Abuse (NIDA) Household Survey in 1991 show, for instance, that while 4.3 percent of blacks surveyed had used crack, only 1.5 percent of whites and 2.1 percent of Hispanics reported having used the drug. But as Lockwood, Pottieger, and Inciardi point out, "because whites represent the majority of the U.S. population, these percentage estimates still imply that most crack users are *not* black." Extrapolating from the NIDA estimates, they estimate that of 479,000 crack users in 1991, 49.9 percent (238,000) were white, 14.2 percent (68,000) were Hispanic, and 35.9 percent (172,000) were black.[74]

Judge Cahill asks why it is that so few white crack users and dealers appear in media coverage when whites appear to constitute the plurality of crack abusers. His answer is "racism." The deep-seated association between blackness and criminality may indeed have fixed the expectations of those responsible for creating "the news" such that they are more willing and able to see and report drug abuse by blacks as opposed to drug abuse by whites. Perhaps managers of news media also pander to certain expectations in order to create news that will fit comfortably into the assumptions held by large numbers of consumers.

These are plausible hypotheses that resonate with what we know about recurrent patterns in the production of news. Much more detailed, systemic analysis will be required, however, for an authoritative conclusion. First of all, there are plausible alternative explanations that warrant investigation. One is that journalists, like police, gravitate toward drug scenes that are simultaneously dramatic and accessible. It might be that crack abuse is peculiarly concentrated and open in black neighborhoods and that therefore they have been the locales most attractive to journalists interested in reporting the crack story.* Invidious racial discrimination is not absent as a consideration in this hypothesis. Racial discrimination helps to explain why so many black communities suffer from peculiarly intense levels of social isolation, communal deterioration, and hyper-concentrations of poverty.[75] Under this hypothesis, however, the main locus of objectionable discrimination resides not in the media that report the problem of crack abuse but rather in the com-

---

*Commenting on police practices, Michael Tonry observes that urban police departments often focus on disadvantaged minority neighborhoods in combating the trade in illegal narcotics:

For a variety of reasons it is easier to make arrests in socially disorganized neighborhoods, as contrasted with urban blue-collar and urban or suburban white-collar neighborhoods. First, more of the routine activities of life, including retail drug dealing, occur on the streets and alleys in poor neighborhoods. In working-class and middle-class neighborhoods, many activities, including drug deals, are likelier to occur indoors. This makes it much easier to find dealers from whom to make an undercover buy in a disadvantaged urban neighborhood than elsewhere.

Second, it is easier for undercover narcotics officers to penetrate networks of friends and acquaintances in poor urban minority neighborhoods than in more stable and closely knit working-class and middle-class neighborhoods. The stranger buying drugs on the urban street corner or in an alley or overcoming local suspicions by hanging around for a few days and then buying drugs is commonplace. The substantial increases in the numbers of black and Hispanic police officers in recent decades make undercover narcotics work in such neighborhoods easier. . . .

Both these differences between socially disorganized urban neighborhoods and other neighborhoods make extensive drug-law enforcement operations in the inner city more likely and, by police standards, more successful. Because urban drug dealing is often visible, individual citizens, the media, and elected officials more often pressure police to take action against drugs in poor urban neighborhoods than in other kinds of neighborhoods

Tonry, *Malign Neglect: Race, Crime, and Punishment in America*, 105–106 (1995).

plex and diffuse array of actors—national politicians, urban mayors, voters, bankers, developers, and so forth—whose actions over decades have contributed significantly to creating and perpetuating criminogetic ghettos.

Another hypothesis is that much of the news media linkage between crack and black communities stems not from bigotry but, to the contrary, from an impulse to *help* those communities precisely because of their racial identity. This hypothesis is consistent with Cahill's complaint that news media racially discriminate in making judgments about the portrayal of the crack story. It is inconsistent with Cahill's complaint insofar as it attributes a benign motivation to the media's racial discrimination. In evaluating this possibility, recall the claim of Congressman Rangel that news media were paying insufficient attention to the havoc crack was wreaking in black neighborhoods.

Determining whether cultural imagery is good or bad politically for blacks or any other group is difficult and unavoidably open to disputation. In December 1993, the *New York Times Magazine* ran a series of photographs by Eugene Richards that focused on hard-core cocaine addicts and the ugliness and desperation that surrounded the lives of his subjects.[76] The most controversial of the photos showed a black female crack addict reaching for a man's zipper with the purpose of exchanging oral sex for money. A toddler clings to her back and in the background on the wall of her apartment are portraits of Malcolm X, Martin Luther King, Jr., and W.E.B. DuBois. Richards and the *Times* were harshly criticized in some quarters for publishing the photo. A spokesman for the Committee to Eliminate Media Offensive to African People (CEMOTAP), echoing Judge Cahill's theme of unconscious racism, labeled Richards "a racist who doesn't seem to know he's a racist."[77] In a review of Richards's photographs, Brent Staples asked plaintively: "Couldn't [he] have found a setting where most or at least half of the drug addicts were white?"*

There is an important and legitimate criticism articulated by these comments. As was noted above, there does exist a striking disjuncture

---

*Staples goes on to say that he was "not asking for equal opportunity representation of drug abuse." That seems implicitly, however, to be precisely what he demanded. See Brent Staples, "Coke Wars," *New York Times Book Review*, February 6, 1994.

between the racial demographics of *actual* illicit drug use (which is mainly white in absolute numbers) and the racial demographics of *portrayed* illicit drug use (which is mainly black). Also reflected in these comments, however, is a tendency to blame the messenger for bad news. Eugene Richards did not fabricate the conditions he photographed; he publicized them. The Congress of the United States did not fabricate a distinction between crack cocaine and powder cocaine; it recognized the difference and chose to respond to it by imposing disparate punishments.

The Future of the Crack–Powder Distinction

Judge Cahill's ruling in *Clary* was promptly overturned by a U.S. Court of Appeals, which joined all of the other federal courts of appeal that had previously rejected equal protection attacks on the crack–powder sentencing differential.[78] The essential message of all of these rulings is that, in order to prevail, a defendant must show that Congress punished crack more harshly than powder for racial reasons. It is not enough to show that Congress initially passed the law or has kept it in place with the knowledge that the law would give rise to a racial disparity among those prosecuted for drug offense. Rather, the courts demand that a defendant show that Congress acted with the intention of bringing about the racial results anticipated. To paraphrase the Supreme Court, a defendant must show that the government acted because of and not simply despite foreseen racial consequences. Since there is no substantial evidence indicative of such intent on the part of Congress courts have rightly rejected claims of the sort articulated by Mr. Clary's lawyers.

Given that most courts have already reached this conclusion, why do I invest space, time, and energy defending their rulings?* I do so because their rulings, although currently ascendant, are nonetheless controversial. In influential circles—the newspaper editorial page, the law review, the constitutional law class, and the statements of distinguished jurists—the rulings I defend are condemned as illegitimate. Unre-

---

*I am responding here to a question posed by Professor David Cole. See "The Paradox of Race and Crime: A Comment on Randall Kennedy's 'Politics of Distinction,'" 73 *Georgetown Law Journal* 2547, 2548–2549 (1995).

butted, these attacks will gather momentum and influence and spread the errors so vividly displayed in Judge Cahill's opinion. An example of this danger is offered by the U.S. Sentencing Commission.

In 1995, the Commission took steps to "equalize[] sentences for offenses involving similar amounts of crack cocaine and powder cocaine."[79] The Commission sought to amend the sentencing guidelines it promulgates and recommended that Congress eliminate the statutory differential distinguishing crack and powder. The Commission suggested a level-down equalization pursuant to which traffickers in crack cocaine would be sentenced identically with traffickers in powder cocaine. The Commission's amendments to the sentencing guidelines would have gone into effect automatically absent specific disapproval from both houses of Congress. However, with the support of President Clinton, Congress did disapprove, the first time it had done so in the Commission's history.[80]

Congress and the president probably took the action they did not so much on the basis of a careful review of the Commission's recommendation but instead on the basis of a political dynamic that has captured both the Republican and Democratic parties, a political dynamic that rewards perceived "toughness" and punishes perceived "softness" in the war on crime. Given that crack has become the well-recognized epitome of the drug menace, the likely political fallout from lowering penalties against crack offenses would alone have discouraged most electoral politicians from pursuing that course.*

In *Cocaine and Federal Sentencing Policy*, a report published by the

---

*Commenting on President Clinton's support for the congressional override of the Sentencing Commission's recommendations, Professor Christopher Edley, Jr., observes that

> from the president's perspective the question of crack sentencing seemed quite simple because the politics were so compelling. Whatever the substantive merits of reducing the disparities in sentencing, it would have been impossible from a *communications* standpoint to explain to the American people that it was anything but a soft-on-crime retreat in the war on drugs. One of President Clinton's singular political achievements was to eliminate the national GOP's almost thirty-year edge in opinion polls as the party that is tough on crime. I suppose it was thought [by the Clinton administration] that nothing should be done to destroy that achievement.

Not All Black and White: Affirmative Action and American Values, 236–237 (1996).

Commission several months before its ill-fated attempt to amend the crack–powder disparity, the Commission set forth several reasons in favor of reducing the magnitude of the crack–powder distinction. One was that sentencing guidelines enacted subsequent to Congress's establishment of the crack–powder distinction could provide judges with a more finely calibrated means of either imposing or declining to impose enhanced punishments as certain prescribed circumstances warranted. Another was that the existing crack–powder distinction created undesirable anomalies. "One premise of the mandatory minimum sentencing structure," the Commission noted, "is that, all other things being equal, a drug dealer's danger to society is in direct proportion to the quantity of the drug in which he/she deals. Yet, as a result of the [crack–powder] differential, a large-scale powder cocaine dealer who traffics in 500 grams (2,500–5,000 dosage units) of powder cocaine will receive the same sentence as a crack dealer who has sold only 5 grams (10–25 doses) of crack cocaine; that is a five-year sentence of imprisonment."[81] The Commission conceded that this massive difference in the quantity of drug necessary to trigger the same sentence would be acceptable if crack cocaine was that much more dangerous than powder cocaine. The Commission stated, however, that it did not view crack as being multiply more dangerous. The commission suggested that crack cocaine may be somewhat more socially harmful than powder cocaine but indicated quite firmly that it did not believe that this marginal difference justified Congress's dramatically enhanced punishment of crack offenses.

For reasons already mentioned, it is doubtful that any conceivable set of arguments offered by the Commission would have persuaded the Congress or the president to lessen punishments imposed on crack offenders. The Commission did not help its case, however, with its statement setting forth the reasons behind its recommendations for reform. The Commission's statement differs in significant ways from its previous report to Congress. Most important, in the previous report, concern over racial disparities did not drive the analysis. The Commission recognized that much of the opposition to the crack–powder distinction stemmed from a perception that it was racially discriminatory.[82] But the Commission report suggests neither that a desire to mollify those holding that impression determined the Commission's recommendation nor that the Commission itself believed the crack–powder distinction to be racially biased. By contrast, the Commission's subsequent statement to Congress clearly suggests that the Commission had been won over by those advancing a racial critique of the crack–powder distinction. Race took center stage, with the Commission averring that it "was deeply concerned that almost ninety percent of offenders convicted of crack cocaine offenses in the federal courts are blacks" and that in its view an insufficient policy basis existed to justify a penalty differential that was having a severe impact on a particular minority group.[83]

The appearance of justice is a proper and important consideration in policymaking. That the crack–powder distinction appears to many to be racially unfair (and will be viewed as such by many even after explanations have been offered) is an important negative factor to consider in determining whether to reform or eliminate the crack–powder distinction. The Commission's statement, however, went beyond this point to imply that, in substance as well as appearance, the existing crack–powder distinction is racially unjust.

In making this claim, the Commission adopted some of the most self-discrediting stances taken by opponents of the crack–powder distinction. Without explanation, the Commission asserted, for example, that "the fact that crack cocaine is typically sold in smaller amounts, which may make it more readily available among lower-income groups, [does not] justify increased punishment compared to a form of the drug that is more commonly sold in amounts available only to more affluent persons."[84] This assertion is much in need of defense. One of the strongest reasons *favoring* the crack–powder distinction is precisely that crack is more accessible and, for that reason alone, more dangerous. As Representative Rangel observed, "what is most frightening about crack is that it has made cocaine widely available and affordable for abuse among our youth."[85] Surely it would be just and sensible for a government to punish more severely a person knowingly distributing a poison in a low-priced (say $5) container as opposed to a high-priced (say $50) container even if the poison in the two containers was otherwise identical. It would be just and sensible on the grounds that because the $5 container is less expensive it is more affordable to more people and thus more potentially accessible. The same logic supports distinguishing crack cocaine from powder cocaine. Because it is relatively inexpensive, crack helped tremendously to democratize cocaine use, a dubious "achievement" that the government should surely be able to "reward" with a punitive response without eliciting the charge that doing so is racially discriminatory.

The congressional debate over the Commission's recommendation produced no new insights. Proponents of maintaining the crack–powder distinction repeated familiar refrains: Drugs are evil; crack is especially evil; lessening the penalties on crack would signal failure of nerve in the war on drugs, and so on. Opponents did much the same. A few resorted to open accusations that the crack–powder distinction represented purposeful racial discrimination. "Is there a conspiracy," Representative Bobby Rush asked rhetorically, "to incarcerate as many African American males as possible?" Others were a bit more subtle. "I have never suggested that the motivation ten years ago . . . was a racist motivation," Representative Mel Watt remarked. But "the impact of this law has been very, very, very substantially racist."[86]

In all likelihood, nothing could have been said which would have changed the mind of the Congress. I suspect, though, that a turnabout was made even more improbable by allegations branding existing policy (and by implication its backers) as racist. That is because allegations of racism put into question more than a person's judgment; they put into question a person's basic moral fitness. Once the racism charge is voiced, considerations of personal honor and public reputation elevate the stakes and polarize the antagonists. Moreover, once a charge of racism is lodged, it tends to dominate all other concerns. Instead of determining on a broad basis the relative merits of a policy, discussion is channeled toward the narrow question of whether the policy at issue is "racist." During the congressional debate, for example, the Commission's nonracial reason for sentencing reform was eclipsed. Focused on loud allegations of racism, many members of Congress, including the proponents of reform, overlooked the fact that, under current law, low-level crack dealers sometimes receive longer sentences than their high-level, powder-selling suppliers.

Those propounding a racial critique of the crack–powder distinction often assert that the situation would be different if the racial shoe were on the other foot, if over 90 percent of crack offenders were white instead of black. If that were so, the argument runs, white policymakers would be prompted to change course because of the clamorings of constituents terrified by the prospect of a son, daughter, or friend facing five- and ten-year mandatory minimum prison sentences. The plausibility of this scenario is itself disturbing. For the more plausible this counterfactual proposition, the more it suggests the possibility that racially selective empathy is presently at work, silently prompting legislators to pursue a strategy in attacking drug use that they would not pursue if whites were in the same position that blacks occupy.*

On the other hand, there are indications that cut the other way. Trafficking and use of methamphetamine is dominated by whites. Yet recently a bill was enacted that enhanced the punishment for dealing this drug to levels comparable to that imposed on crack dealers.[87] After the state supreme court invalidated Minnesota's crack–powder distinction under the Minnesota Constitution, the state legislature was put to the test of either leveling up—raising the criminal penalty on powder offenses (to that reserved for crack offenses)—or leveling down—lowering the penalty on crack offenses (to that reserved for powder offenses). The legislature chose to level up. Pushed to move one way or another, President Clinton and many in the U.S. Congress would also choose to level up.[88] Arguably this would be a good result. It would erase, for many, the appearance of a racial double standard.† On the

---

*Arguing that racially selective sympathy plays a role in deciding criminal punishments for drug offenses, Alfred Blumstein avers:

> A major factor contributing to [the de facto decriminalization of marijuana] was undoubtedly a realization that the arrestees were much too often the children of individuals, usually white, in positions of power and influence. Those parents certainly did not want the consequences of a drug arrest to be visited on their children, and so they used their leverage to achieve a significant degree of decriminalization.

See Alfred Blumstein, "Making Rationality Relevant: The American Society of Criminology 1992, Presidential Address," 31 *Criminology* 1 (1993).

†Equalization of punishments, however, would not completely negate the suspicions of some skeptics that racially selective sympathies are still present in the decision to continue the war on drugs. That is because the numbers of whites adversely affected by a leveling up of punishments would remain very small in comparison with the total white population. Skeptics contend that this relatively small number of marginalized whites would serve as a sacrifice to legitimate a policy that would continue to disproportionately burden blacks.

other hand, the cost of purchasing this assurance of evenhandedness would be a rise in the numbers of people being sent to prison for long stays—a steep price, indeed, but one that ascendant political forces are likely willing to pay.

Again I want to stress what I have and have not said. I have not endorsed the current crack-powder sentencing differential. Perhaps it should be rejected. After all, it perversely permits some large-scale traffickers in powder to be punished less severely than some small-scale traffickers in crack. More important, the crack-powder sentencing differential is part of a war against drugs that should be reconsidered. There is force to the argument that policing prohibition with draconian laws is inefficient, the cause of avoidable misery, and inferior to alternative models of regulation.[89] Maybe the crack–powder distinction and, indeed, the entire war on drugs is mistaken. But even if these policies are misguided, being mistaken is different from being racist, and the difference is one that greatly matters.

Afterword

I HOPE THAT readers will take from this book two overriding impressions.

First, much remains to be done to make the administration of criminal law racially just. Authorities need to commit themselves more vigorously to the idea that government must accord to persons, regardless of race, equal treatment before the law. Established securely in some areas, this fundamental idea should be advanced in all. The context in which equal treatment is most openly and notably absent, both in terms of legal formalities and actual practice, is police surveillance. The legal doctrines that permit police to treat blackness as a mark of increased risk of criminality generates large pools of distrust, anger, and discord. Blacks are keenly aware that their constitutional protection against unwarranted police intrusion is of a decidedly inferior sort than the protection enjoyed by whites. This racially disparate treatment is wrong. Instead of continuing to place a racial tax on blacks for purposes of carrying out the war against crime, judges (and ordinary citizens too!)

should demand that the burdens of this war be imposed on a nonracial basis.

Authorities, moreover, should enforce the law's promises. If the law promises trials in which racially discriminatory peremptory challenges are barred, judges should see to it that that prohibition is obeyed. If satisfactorily enforcing such a prohibition becomes impossible, legislators should change the procedures altogether—i.e., abolish the peremptory challenge—in order to obviate the discrimination issue. To declare a legal norm and then permit it to be ignored or evaded is to create the grounds for corrosive cynicism.

For this same reason, authorities should be candid. This book's tour of the administration of criminal law has revealed numerous instances in which officials have denied facts that cannot sensibly be denied: the facts behind lynching and the failure to address it, the facts behind the wholesale and long-standing racial exclusion of blacks from the jury box, the fact that until rather recently certain jurisdictions reserved capital punishment for certain sorts of black criminals (i.e., the alleged black assailant of a white woman). Denials of real racial discrimination continue. We see it in judicial decisions that implausibly portray racial insults or appeals as innocuous rhetoric with no ill effects. We see it in assertions by jurists and scholars that there exists no credible evidence that racial discrimination plays an ongoing and large (though difficult to isolate) role in the allocation of capital punishment.

True, it is sometimes genuinely difficult to determine an appropriate remedial response. The proper way to address that difficulty, however, is to acknowledge and grapple with it, not bury it beneath unbelievable assertions that, in fact, no real problem exists. Whitewashing racial wrongs (especially while simultaneously proclaiming that courts are doing everything reasonably possible to combat racially invidious government action) corrupts officials and jades onlookers, nourishing simplistic, despairing, and defeatist critiques of the law that are profoundly destructive.

The second impression that I want to leave with readers should serve as an antidote to these overwrought, defeatist critiques by acknowledging that the administration of criminal law has changed substantially for the better over the past half century and that there is reason to believe that, properly guided, it can be improved even more. Today there are more formal and informal protections against racial bias than ever before, both in terms of the protections accorded to blacks against criminality and the treatment accorded to black suspects, defendants, and convicts. That deficiencies, large deficiencies, remain is clear. But comparing racial policies today to those that prevailed in 1940 or 1960 or even 1980 should expose the fallacy of asserting that nothing substantial has been changed for the better.

This point is worth stressing because of the prevalence and prominence of pessimistic thinking about the race question in American life. Some commentators maintain, in all seriousness, that there has been no significant improvement in the overall fortunes of black Americans during the past half century, that advances that appear to have been made are merely cosmetic, and that the United States is doomed to remain a pigmentocracy. This pessimistic strain often turns paranoid and apocalyptic in commentary about the administration of criminal law.

It is profoundly misleading, however, to focus exclusively on the ugliest aspects of the American legal order. Doing so conceals real achievements: the Reconstruction Constitutional Amendments, the Reconstruction civil rights laws, *Strauder* v. *Alabama, Dempsey* v. *Moore, Brown* v. *Mississippi, Powell* v. *Alabama, Norris* v. *Alabama, Batson* v. *Kentucky*, the resuscitation of Reconstruction by the civil rights movement, the changing demographics of the bench, bar, and police departments—in sum, the stigmatization (albeit incomplete) of invidious racial bias. Neglecting these achievements robs them of support. Recent sharp attacks upon basic guarantees bequeathed by the New Deal ought to put everyone on notice of the perils of permitting social accomplishments to lose their rightful stature in the public's estimation. Moreover, one-dimensional condemnations of the racial situation in America renders attractive certain subversive proposals that are, given actual conditions, foolish, counterproductive, and immoral. I think here in particular of the call for racially selective jury nullification. Such proposals should be openly challenged on the grounds that they fundamentally misperceive the racial realities of American life.

The most salient feature of race relations in America at the end of the twentieth century is its complexity—a complexity that renders unfit as guides to action either the claim that racial bias no longer constitutes a major problem or the claim that racial bias is as dominant now as it once was. Any reliable guide to a better future must carefully take into account what has been accomplished and build upon it, using as a lodestar the uncompromisable ideal of treating all persons equally regardless of race, an aspiration best sought by responding to persons strictly on the basis of conduct not color.

Notes

1. The Race Question in Criminal Law

1. See David C. Anderson, *Crime and the Politics of Hysteria: How the Willie Horton Story Changed American Justice* (1995); Dan T. Carter, *The Politics of Rage: George Wallace, the Origins of the New Conservatism, and the Transformation of American Politics*, 375, 378 (1995); Thomas E. Cronin, Tania Z. Cronin, and Michael E. Milakovich, *United States* v. *Crime in the Streets* (1981); Lawrence M. Friedman, *Crime and Punishment in American History*, 274–276 (1993); Fred P. Graham, *The Self-Inflicted Wound*, 10–26, 86–101 (1970).

   For the period of 1964 to 1992, Christopher Jencks was correct when he quipped that, "like rain on election day, crime is good for the Republicans," because when "crime seems to be increasing, significant numbers of Americans tend to blame liberal permissiveness and turn to conservative political candidates." *Rethinking Social Policy: Race, Poverty and the Underclass*, 92–93 (1992).

2. See Bill Clinton and Al Gore, *Putting People First: How We Can All Change America*, 71–80 (1992); Barney Frank, *Speaking Frankly: What's Wrong with*

the Democrats and How to Fix It, 119–134 (1992); Adam Nagourney, "Politics: The Candidates; Dole Attacks on Crime, but Clinton Is Ready," *New York Times*, September 17, 1996.

3. See, e.g., Susan B. Garland, "The Law-and-Order Democrats," *Business Week*, October 25, 1993; Blaine Harden and Peter Baker, "Candidates Mine Crime Issue for Votes; Clinton Tries to Counter Sting of Dole's Attacks While Competing for Tough Image," *Washington Post*, September 17, 1996; Kathy Lewis and G. Robert Hillman, "Clinton, Dole Hammer Crime: New Report Shows Decline," *Dallas Morning News*, September 18, 1996; Marianne Means, "Clinton, Dole and the Ever-escalating War on Crime," *San Diego Union Tribune*, September 19, 1996; Mike Oliver, "Even Republicans Enjoy Chiles' Anti-Crime Message," *Orlando Sentinel*, September 19, 1996.

4. See Carter, *Politics of Rage*.

5. See Ellis Cose with Allison Samuels, "The Darden Dilemma," *Newsweek*, March 25, 1996; Clarence Page, "Black Crime and the Darden Dilemma," *Baltimore Sun*, February 9, 1995.

6. See Benjamin A. Holden, Laurie P. Cohen, and Eleena de Lisser, "Color-Blinded? Race Seems to Play an Increasing Role in Many Jury Verdicts," *Wall Street Journal*, October 4, 1995; Randall Kennedy, "The Angry Juror," *Wall Street Journal*, September 30, 1994; Michael D. Weiss and Karl Zinsmeister, "When Race Trumps Truth in Court," *American Enterprise*, January–February 1996. In "Racially Based Jury Nullification: Black Power in the Criminal Justice System," 105 *Yale Law Journal* 677 (1995), Professor Paul Butler agrees with the proposition that some black jurors are engaging in racially selective nullification. Unlike many commentators, however, he largely applauds the practice. (For more on this issue, see pp. 295–310.)

7. Here I imagine myself speaking to the editoral boards of *The National Review*, *The American Enterprise*, the *Weekly Standard*, and *Commentary* magazines, as well as to the board of directors of the Federalist Society.

8. See, e.g., Elizabeth Gleick, "The Crooked Blue Line," *Time*, September 11, 1995; Jack E. White, "Fuhrman Is No Surprise," *Time*, Septmber 11, 1995. For an instructive, detailed exploration of the broader phenomenon of which the Fuhrman controversy is but a vivid episode, see Morgan Cloud, "The Dirty Little Secret," 43 *Emory Law Journal* 1311 (1994).

9. See, e.g., Clint Bolick, *The Affirmative Action Fraud—Can We Restore the American Civil Rights Vision?* (1996); Terry Eastland, *Ending Affirmative Action: The Case for Colorblind Justice* (1996); Antonin Scalia, "The Disease as Cure," *Washington University Law Quarterly* 147 (1979).

10. *Adarand Constructors, Inc.* v. *Pena*, 115 S.Ct. 2097, 2119 (1995) (Thomas, J., concurring).

11. Compare the federal government's briefs in *Wygant* v. *Jackson Bd. of Educ.*, 476 U.S. 267 (1986) and *Richmond* v. *J.A. Croson*, 488 U.S. 469 (1989), challenging affirmative action programs with the federal government's brief in *Batson* v. *Kentucky*, 476 U.S. 79 (1986), supporting the permissibility of racially discriminatory peremptory challenges.

12. See Edward C. Banfield, *The Unheavenly City: The Nature and Future of Our Urban Crisis*, 67–87 (1970); Dinesh D'Souza, *The End of Racism: Principles for a Multicultural Society* (1995); Samuel Jared Taylor, *Paved with Good Intentions: The Failure of Race Relations in Contemporary America*, 63–108 (1992); William Wilbanks, *The Myth of a Racist Criminal Justice System* (1987). I disagree with much that is in these books, but have learned much from them with respect to my main point: the perils of making exaggerated or unsubstantiated claims of racism.

13. On the Tawana Brawley controversy, see Grand Jury of the Supreme Court, State of New York, County of Dutchess, *Report of the Grand Jury and Related Documents Concerning the Tawana Brawley Investigation* (1988); Robert D. McFadden, et al., *Outrage: The Story behind the Tawana Brawley Hoax* (1990); Mike Taibbi and Anna Sims-Phillips, *Unholy Alliances: Working the Tawana Brawley Story* (1989).

14. Barbara Omolade, *The Rising Song of African American Women*, 186 (1994). Omolade's statement was initially published in her article "Black Women, Black Men and Tawana Brawley," 12 *Harvard Women's Law Journal* 12, 16 (1989). Cf. Patricia Williams, *The Alchemy of Race and Rights*, 168–178 (1991).

15. William Kunstler interview with Jon Kalish, *New York Newsday*, June 23, 1988.

16. See, e.g., Sam V. Meddis, "Drug War Claiming 'Entire Generation' of Young Blacks," *USA Today*, July 27, 1993 (quoting A. J. Kramer, chief of the Federal Public Defender Office in Washington, D.C.); John A. Powell and Eileen B. Hershenov, "Hostage to the Drug War: The National Purse, the Constitution and the Black Community," 24 *University of California at Davis Law Review* 557, 616 (1991) ("Now is the time to factor in the cost of our current strategy and to redirect our efforts towards assisting the hostages of [the war on drugs]—minority populations. To do otherwise is to passively bear witness to something increasingly akin to genocide").

17. See David Tuller, "Surgeon General's Remarks: Debate Changing in War on Drugs," *San Francisco Chronicle*, December 11, 1993 (quoting Representative Rangel as saying that he was "shocked" by the surgeon general's sug-

gestion to study the efficacy of drug legalization); see also A. M. Rosenthal, "On My Mind: Captive Neighborhood," *New York Times*, July 10, 1992 (stating that the legalization of drugs "would amount to genocide against the major drug victims—blacks and Hispanics").

18. The statement in the text is undisturbed by charges that the Central Intelligence Agency aided drug trafficking U.S.-sponsored Nicaraguan contras during the 1980s. Though charges published in the *San Jose Mercury News* in the summer of 1996 initially appeared to substantiate the rumors of conspiracy that have long circulated, especially in black communities, critical examination quickly revealed that the charges were overblown. See Douglas Farah and Walter Pincus, "CIA, Contras and Drugs: Questions on Links Linger," *Washington Post*, October 31, 1996; Tim Golden, "In Stories Linking CIA to Drug Pushers, Blacks Are Quick to Believe; Cynicism Aimed at White Establishment," *Chicago Tribune*, October 22, 1996; Tim Golden, "Though Evidence Is Thin, Tale of CIA and Drugs Has a Life of Its Own," *New York Times*, October 21, 1996; Charles Lane, "An Imaginary Conspiracy," *Baltimore Sun*, November 8, 1996.

According to the Genocide Convention of the United Nations, genocide refers to acts "committed with intent to destroy, in whole or in part, a national, ethnical, racial or religious group, as such." The Convention on Genocide, December 9, 1948, 78 U.N.T.S. 277.

19. See Paul Shepard, "Elders, Drug Czar Disagree on Study; Legalization Part of Crime Discussion," *Cleveland Plain Dealer*, January 8, 1994.

20. See, e.g., David C. Baldus and James W.L. Cole, *Statistical Proof of Discrimination* (1980).

21. A book that is notably marred by this tendency—beginning with its title— is Jerome G. Miller's *Search and Destroy: African-American Males in the Criminal Justice System* (1996).

22. For example, throughout "The Death of Discretion? Reflections on the Federal Sentencing Guidelines," 101 *Harvard Law Review* 1938 (1988), Professor Charles Ogletree uses "disparity" and "discrimination" as if they were synonyms.

23. See Douglas S. Massey and Nancy Denton, *American Apartheid: Segregation and the Making of the Underclass* (1993); Douglas S. Massey, "Getting Away with Murder: Segregation and Violent Crime in Urban America," 143 *University of Pennsylvania Law Review* 1203 (1995).

24. See Jeffrey Rosen, "The Bloods and the Crits: O. J. Simpson, Critical Race Theory, the Law, and the Triumph of Color in America," *The New Republic*, December 9, 1996.

25. See Willem Adriaan Bonger, *Race and Crime* (1943).

26. See Salvatore J. La Gumina, ed., *Wop! A Documentary History of Anti-Italian Discrimination in the United States* (1973).

27. See Howard M. Sachar, *A History of the Jews in America*, 170 (1992).

28. Quoted in George M. Fredrickson, *The Black Image in the White Mind: The Debate on Afro-American Character and Destiny, 1817–1914* (1971).

29. See Glenn C. Loury, "Racial Fixations on the Right," *Washington Times*, November 3, 1995 ("Conservatives talk incessantly nowadays about 'black crime,' 'black illegitimacy,' 'black school failure,' 'black social pathology.' But what has race to do with these problems, per se?"). John DiIulio, however, rejects criticism of the term "black crime," describing it as an "empty word game." See Letters, *City Journal*, 128 (Summer 1996).

30. See Stuart A. Scheingold, *The Politics of Street Crime: Criminal Process and Cultural Obsession* (1991). Marred by exaggeration, William J. Chambliss, "Crime Control and Ethnic Minorities: Legitimizing Racial Oppression by Creating Moral Panic," in *Ethnicity, Race and Crime: Perspectives across Time and Space* (Darnell F. Hawkins, ed., 1995), nonetheless contains useful information and insight on this point.

31. See William Julius Wilson, *When Work Disappears: The World of the New Urban Poor* (1996); Alex Kotlowitz, *There Are No Children Here: The Story of Two Boys Growing up in the Other America* (1991); Nicholas Lemann, *The Promised Land: The Great Black Migration and How It Changed America* (1991). For an extraordinary cinematic analysis, see the documentary *Hoop Dreams* (Steve James, James F. Marx, Peter Gilbert, 1994), and for an illuminating exploration of this terrain in fiction, see Richard Price, *Clockers* (1992).

32. See Jill S. Quadagno, *The Color of Welfare: How Racism Undermined the War on Poverty* (1994); Lawrence Bobo and Ryan A. Smith, "Antipoverty Policy, Affirmative Action, and Racial Attitudes," in *Confronting Poverty: Prescriptions for Change*, 390–394 (Sheldon H. Danziger, Gary D. Sandefur, and Daniel H. Weinberg, eds., 1994).

33. Thomas Byrne Edsall with Mary D. Edsall, *Chain Reaction: The Impact of Race, Rights and Taxes on American Politics*, 236 (1991).

34. See Paul Glastris and Jeannye Thornton, "A New Civil Rights Frontier," *U.S. News and World Report*, January 17, 1994. See also Hanna Rosin, "Action Jackson: Jesse's Volte-face on Crime," *New Republic*, March 21, 1994.

35. See Terrence D. Meithe, "Fear and Withdrawal from Urban Life," 539 *The Annals of the American Academy of Political and Social Science [The Annals]* 14 (1995); Wesley G. Skogan, "Crime and the Racial Fears of White Americans," 539 *The Annals* 59 (1995).

36. Joleen Kirschenmen and Kathryn M. Neckerman, " 'We'd Love to Hire

Them, but . . .': The Meaning of Race for Employers," in *The Urban Underclass* (Christopher Jencks and Paul E. Peterson, eds., 1991).

37. Douglas S. Massey, "Getting away with Murder: Segregation and Violent Crime in Urban America," 143 *University of Pennsylvania Law Review* 1203 (1995).

38. See also Nathan Glazer, "A Tale of Two Cities," *New Republic*, August 2, 1993; Charles Murray, "Class and Underclass," *New York Times*, May 21, 1993.

39. See Anderson, *Crime and the Politics of Hysteria*; Edsall and Edsall, *Chain Reaction*, 224; Graham, *Self-Inflicted Wound*, 86–101; Scheingold, *Politics of Street Crime*.

40. See Evelyn Brooks Higginbotham, *Righteous Discontent: The Women's Movement in the Black Baptist Church, 1880–1920*, 185–230 (1993). See also Regina Austin, " 'The Black Community,' Its Lawbreakers, and a Politics of Identification," 65 *Southern California Law Review* 1769 (1992).

41. See W.E.B. DuBois, "The Talented Tenth," in Henry Louis Gates, Jr., and Cornel West, *The Future of the Race*, 133 (1996).

42. Higginbotham, *Righteous Discontent*, 197.

43. See Staughton Lynd and Roberta Yancey, "The Unfamiliar Campus," *Dissent*, Winter 1964. The inner civil war that erupted within black America during the civil rights era remains to be chronicled.

44. See Higginbotham, *Righteous Discontent*, 199–201, quoting one black Baptist women's leader who decried "the poison generated by Jazz music" and another who condemned dance halls as places of "unbridled criminality" where Negroes made "a voluntary return to the jungle." Reactions against this ethos became loud and extravagant in the 1960s and 1970s. See William L. Van Deburg, *New Day in Babylon: The Black Power Movement and American Culture, 1965–1975* (1992)

45. See Glenn C. Loury, *One by One from the Inside Out*, 301–302 (1995). ("For many of these people the hard edge of judgment and retribution is tempered by sympathy for and empathy with the perpetrators.")

46. See Roger Lane, *William Dorsey's Philadelphia and Ours: On the Past and Future of the Black City in America*, 55 (1991). That same year, the redoubtable Kelly Miller, one of the country's most incisive commentators on racial problems, stated that ceasing to rape was the key to ending lynching. Ibid.

47. Ibid.

48. See John DiIulio, Jr., "The Question of Black Crime," 117 *The Public Interest* 7 (1994); Adam Walinsky, "The Crisis of Public Order," *Atlantic Monthly*, July 1995; Miller, *Search and Destroy*, 38.

49. See Massey, "Getting away with Murder," 1204, 1205.

50. See Walinsky, "Crisis of Public Order," 48.

51. See "Reflections on the King Verdict," in *Reading Rodney King/Reading Urban Uprising*, 244 (Robert Gooding-Williams, ed., 1993).

52. See Mark V. Tushnet, *Making Civil Rights Law: Thurgood Marshall and the Supreme Court, 1936–1961*, 28 (1994).

53. For an alternative viewpoint which conceives of virtually all black convicts as "political prisoners," see Eldridge Cleaver, *Soul on Ice* (1968); George Jackson, *Soledad Brother: The Prison Letters of George Jackson* (1970), and *Blood in My Eye* (1972). For a good description and analysis of this viewpoint and how it grew in influence during the 1960s and 1970s, see Eric Cummins, *The Rise and Fall of California's Radical Prison Movement* (1994).

54. An example of the difference that reputation can make is provided by the differing fates of the Communist Party and the NAACP when both faced repression in the 1950s and both sought to use the First Amendment to the federal constitution as a shield against governmental investigations. "Sympathetic to the aims, methods, and personnel of the NAACP, the Supreme Court extended to the nation's leading civil rights organization a measure of protection against legislative harassment that it declined to grant to the Communist Party. Legal doctrine did not compel such disparate treatment. A political judgment did—one that cautiously embraced the NAACP and fearfully rejected the Communist Party." See Randall Kennedy, "Contrasting Fates of Repression: A Comment on Gibson v. Florida Legislative Investigation Committee," in Secret Agents: *The Rosenberg Case, McCarthyism & Fifties America* 227 (Marjorie Garber and Rebecca L. Walkowitz, eds., 1995).

55. See, e.g., Coramae Richey Mann, *Unequal Justice: A Question of Color* (1993); "Developments in the Law: Race and the Criminal Process," 101 *Harvard Law Review*, 1472 (1988); Patricia Williams, "Spirit-Murdering the Messenger: The Discourse of Fingerpointing as the Law's Response to Racism," 42 *University of Miami Law Review*, 127–130 (1987).

56. See, e.g., James J. Kilpatrick, *The Southern Case for School Segregation*, 63–70 (1962).

57. Frank, *Speaking Frankly*, 124. See also Graham, *Self-Inflicted Wound*, 86–88; Charles E. Silberman, *Criminal Violence, Criminal Justice*, 160 (1978) ("whites of good will . . . and blacks have avoided talking about [the fact that black offenders account for a disproportionate number of the crimes that evoke the most fear] lest they provide ammunition to bigots").

58. See Michael H. Tonry, *Malign Neglect—Race, Crime, and Punishment in America*, 64–65 (1995).

59. See ibid., 68 ("Most modern empirical analyses of sentencing conclude that

when legitimate differences among individual cases are taken into account, little or no systematic difference in contemporary sentencing outcomes appears to be attributable to race.")

60. Ibid.

61. See Jonathan Alter and Mark Starr, "Race and Hype in a Divided City," *Newsweek*, January 22, 1990; Margaret Carlson, "Presumed Innocent," *Time*, January 22, 1990; Lee A. Daniels, "The American Way: Blame a Black Man," *Emerge*, February 28, 1995; Richard Lacayo, "Stranger in the Shadows," *Time*, November 14, 1994. For additional examples see Katheryn K. Russell, "The Racial Hoax as Crime," 71 *Indiana Law Journal* 593 (1996).

62. See, e.g., Michael Hildelang, "Race and Involvement in Common Law Personal Crimes," 43 *American Sociological Review* 93 (1978).

63. According to the U.S. Department of Justice Bureau Criminal-Victimization Study of 1992, victims reported blacks as the perpetrators in 29 percent of the violent crimes suffered. See U.S. Department of Justice, Bureau of Justice Statistics, 1992. See also DiIulio, "Question of Black Crime;" Hacker, *Two Nations*, 179–198; Martin Kasindorf, " '92 Violent Crime Hit 1 in 10 Blacks, a Record," *Newsday*, November 15, 1993.

64. Tonry, *Malign Neglect*, 79.

65. See, e.g., Robert J. Sampson and William Julius Wilson, "Toward a Theory of Race, Crime, and Urban Inequality," in John Hagan and Ruth D. Peterson, eds., *Crime and Inequality* (1995).

66. Myrdal, *An American Dilemma*, II: 52.

67. See "A Special Section: The Central Park Rape," *Village Voice*, May 8, 1989, especially Greg Tate, "Leadership Follies."

68. In the aftermath of his arrest, "Hastings, Florida's first African American federal judge, immediately garnered support from the African American community. . . . [A] group of black businessmen named Judge Hastings its man of the year, the state NAACP gave the judge its top award, then Hastings was asked to be the principal speaker at the Florida National Bar Association annual dinner." Todd D. Peterson, "The Role of the Executive Branch in the Discipline and Removal of Federal Judges," 1993 *University of Illinois Law Review* 809, 822.

69. "I feel them to be heroes," remarked community activist Paul Parker, speaking of Damian Williams and Henry Watson, the two men who were filmed severely beating Reginald Denny. See Dervy Murdock, "Hoods in the 'Hood: Getting Tough on Crime," *Ethnic NewsWatch*, February 28, 1994.

70. See Kimberle Crenshaw, "Mapping the Margins: Intersectionality, Identity Politics, and Violence against Women of Color," 43 *Stanford Law Review* 1241, 1273–1274 (1991) ("Tyson was the beneficiary of the longstanding practice of using antiracist rhetoric to deflect the injury suffered by Black women victimized by Black men").

71. *See* Jeffrey Toobin, *The Run of His Life: The People v. O.J. Simpson* (1996).

72. See Henry Louis Gates, Jr., "Thirteen Ways of Looking at a Black Man," *New Yorker*, October 23, 1995. Gates quotes Amiri Baraka as exclaiming: "To see [Simpson] get all of this God-damned support from people he has historically and steadfastly eschewed just pissed me off. He eschewed black people all his life and then, like Clarence Thomas, the minute he gets jammed up he comes talking about 'Hey, I'm black.' " See also Jonathan Alter, "Black and White and Read All Over," *Newsweek*, August 1, 1994; Kenneth B. Noble, "The Simpson Defense: Source of Black Pride," *New York Times*, March 6, 1995; Jill Smolowe, "Race and the O.J. Case," *Time*, August 1, 1994.

73. Quoted in Patricia Smith, "A Victory O.J. Didn't Deserve," *Boston Globe*, October 4, 1995.

74. See James Baldwin, "A Report from Occupied Territory," *The Nation*, July 11, 1966, reprinted in *Law and Resistance: American Attitudes toward Authority* (Laurence Veysey, ed., 1970).

75. See Silberman, *Criminal Violence, Criminal Justice*, 192–224; D'Souza, *The End of Racism*, 99–100, 503–510.

76. Austin, " 'The Black Community,' " 1776. See also, Jack Katz, *Seductions of Crime: Moral and Sensual Attractions in Doing Evil*, 237–273 (1988); Silberman, *Criminal Violence, Criminal Justice*, 159–224. On the widespread tendency to celebrate criminals, see Martha Grace Duncan, " 'A Strange Liking': Our Admiration for Criminals," 1991 *University of Illinois Law Review* 1.

77. Quoted in John Edgar Wideman, *Brothers and Keepers*, 57 (1984).

78. This statement rests upon my own impressions as well as information and views set forth in the following materials: Butler, "Racially Based Jury Nullification," Sam Greenlee, *The Spook Who Sat By the Door* (1969); Richard Majors and Janet Mancini Billson, *Cool Pose: The Dilemmas of Black Manhood in America* 33–34 (1992); Mark Naison, "Outlaw Culture and Black Neighborhoods," *Reconstruction*, 4 (1992); William G. Blair, "Jury Acquits Larry Davis in Shooting of Six Police Officers," *New York Times*, November 21, 1988; Amy Singer, "Larry Davis Beats The Rap," *American Lawyer*, May 1990.

79. Dorothy E. Roberts, "Crime, Race, and Reproduction," 67 *Tulane Law Review* 1945, 1947 (1993). For writing which reflects this same general point of view, see Mann, *Unequal Justice*; Butler, "Racially Based Jury Nullification"; Gary Peller, "Criminal Law, Race, and the Ideology of Bias: Transcending the Critical Tools of the Sixties," 67 *Tulane Law Review* 2231 (1993).

2. History: Unequal Protection

1. William Goodell, *The American Slave Code in Theory and Practice: Its Distinctive Features Shown by Its Statutes, Judicial Decisions, and Illustrative Facts*, 309 (1968 [1853]).

2. See Ira Berlin, *Slaves without Masters: The Free Negro in the Antebellum South* (1975); Winthrop Jordan, *White over Black: American Attitudes toward the Negro, 1550–1812* (1969); Leon F. Litwack, *North of Slavery: The Negro in the Free States, 1790–1860* (1961); Thomas D. Morris, *Southern Slavery and the Law, 1619–1860*, 17–36 (1996); Mark V. Tushnet, *The American Law of Slavery, 1810–1860*, 139–156 (1981).

3. See Andrew Fede, "Legitimized Violent Slave Abuse in the American South 1619–1865: A Case Study of Law and Social Change in Six Southern States," 29 *American Journal of Legal History* 93, 95 (1985) (hereinafter, "Slave Abuse"). See also Andrew Fede, *People without Rights: An Interpretation of the Fundamentals of the Law of Slavery in the U.S. South* (1992).

4. Fede, "Slave Abuse," 118.

5. See *Oliver v. State*, 39 Miss. 526, 540 (1860).

6. *Souther v. The Commonwealth*, 48 Va. 338, 344 (1851). For another example of a master convicted for the unlawful killing of a slave, see *State v. Hoover*, 20 N.C. 395 (1839).

7. Fede, "Slave Abuse," 113.

8. 8 N.C. 210 (1820).

9. Ibid., at 213.

10. Ibid.

11. Ibid., 217

12. Ibid.

13. 13 N.C. 263 (1829). *State v. Mann* has attracted considerable attention over the years. See, e.g., Morris, *Southern Slavery and the Law*, 190–193; Mark V. Tushnet, *The American Law of Slavery 1810–1860: Considerations of Humanity and Interest*, 54–65 (1981); Robert M. Cover, *Justice Accused: Antislavery and the Judicial Process*, 78 (1975); Orlando Patterson, *Slavery and Social Death: A Comparative Study*, 3–4 (1982); Harriet Beecher Stowe, *The Key to Uncle Tom's Cabin*, 78–79 (1853).

14. Ibid., 263.
15. Ibid., 264.
16. Ibid., 267.
17. Ibid., 266.
18. Ibid.
19. See Fede, "Slave Abuse." Eugene D. Genovese, *Roll, Jordan, Roll: The World the Slaves Made* (1974).
20. W.E.B. DuBois, *Black Reconstruction in America*, 10 (1995 [.935]).
21. *The Souls of Black Folk*, 6 (1989 [1903]).
22. *The Autobiography of Malcolm X*, 2 (1965). Malcolm X's maternal forebears lived in the Caribbean before the Civil War, but his sentiment certainly reflects that felt by many blacks whose forebears were raped by whites in the American antebellum South. See also Eldridge Cleaver, *Soul on Ice* (1968). Describing the motivations behind his raping of white women, Cleaver writes he "was very resentful over the historical fact of how the white man used the black woman." Ibid., 14.
23. See, e.g., Adele Logan Alexander, " 'She's No Lady, She's a Nigger': Abuses, Stereotypes, and Realities from the Middle Passage to Capitol (and Anita) Hill," in *Race, Gender, and Power in America: The Legacy of the Hill-Thomas Hearing* (Anita Faye Hill and Emma Coleman Jordan, eds., 1995); Catherine Clinton, "With a Whip in His Hand: Rape, Memory, and African-American Women," in *History and Memory in African American Culture* (Geneviève Fabre and Robert O'Meally, eds., 1994); bell hooks, *Ain't I a Woman: Black Women and Feminism* (1981); Toni Morrison, *Beloved* (1987); Patricia J. Williams, *The Alchemy of Race and Rights* (1991).
24. Ice Cube, *Death Certificate* (Priority Records, 1993).
25. See Morris, *Southern Slavery and the Law*, 303–321.
26. According to Professor Genovese, "Some [black] drivers forced the slave woman in much the same way as did some masters and overseers. It remains an open question which of these powerful white and black males forced the female slaves more often." Genovese, *Roll, Jordan, Roll*, 371.
27. 37 Miss. Rep. 316, 318 (1859).
28. Ibid., 320. In colonial Virginia, however, there were a few instances, albeit rare, in which slaves were prosecuted for raping other slaves. See Morris, *Southern Slavery and the Law*, 306.
29. 37 Miss. Rep. 320.
30. See Susan Brownmiller, *Against Our Will: Men, Women and Rape*, 217 (1975); Karen A. Getman, "Sexual Control in the Slaveholding South: The Implementation and Maintenance of a Racial Caste System," 7 *Harvard*

Women's Law Journal 115 (1984); Jennifer Wriggins, "Rape, Racism, and the Law," 6 *Harvard Women's Law Journal* 103 (1983).

31. Harriet A. Jacobs, *Incidents in the Life of a Slave Girl. Written by Herself*, 77 (Jean Fagan Yellin, ed., 1987 [1861]).

32. See Morris, *Southern Slavery and the Law*, 305 (stating that in the eyes of the law "no white could ever rape a slave woman").

33. See Melton A. McLaurin, *Celia: A Slave* (1991); A. Leon Higginbotham, Jr., "Race, Sex, Education and Missouri Jurisprudence: *Shelley v. Kraemer* in a Historical Perspective," 67 *Washington University Law Quarterly* 673, 680–685 (1989).

34. Quoted in McLaurin, *Celia*, 92–93.

35. See Morris, *Southern Slavery and the Law*, 306–307.

36. See *Grandison (a slave) v. State*, 21 Tenn. 451–452 (Tenn. 1841).

37. See U.S. Congress, Senate Committee on Slavery and the Treatment of Freedmen, "Equality Before the Law in the Courts of the United States," S. Rep. No. 25, 38th Cong., 1st Sess. 35 (1964). Hereinafter, "Equality Before the Law."

38. See Morris, *Southern Slavery and the Law*, 229–248; Berlin, *Slaves Without Masters*, 96; Paul Finkelman, "Prelude to the Fourteenth Amendment: Black Legal Rights in the Antebellum North," 17 *Rutgers Law Journal* 415 (1986).

39. *Jordan v. Smith*, 14 Ohio 199, 201 (1846).

40. According to the pro-slavery scholar Thomas R.R. Cobb, *An Inquiry into the Law of Negro Slavery in the United States of America*, 233 (1858), the mendacity of the Negro "is a fact too well established to require the production of proof, either from history, travels or craniology." See also Daniel J. Flanigan, "Criminal Procedure in Slave Trials in the Antebellum South," in *The Law of American Slavery: Major Historical Interpretations* (Kermit L. Hall, ed., 1987). "While slaves were considered too untrustworthy to influence whites' fates, their testimony was so often absolutely necessary to convict their own kind that it was admitted without much hesitation." Ibid., 210.

41. "Equality Before the Law."

42. See Flanigan, "Criminal Procedure," 237–241.

43. Eric Foner, *Reconstruction: America's Unfinished Revolution, 1863–1877*, 425 (1988). See also George C. Rable, *But There Was No Peace: The Role of Violence in the Politics of Reconstruction* (1984); Allen W. Trelease, *White Terror: The Ku Klux Klan Conspiracy and Southern Reconstruction* (1971).

44. Foner, *Reconstruction*, 428.

45. Ibid., 120.
46. Ibid., 262.
47. Ibid., 263.
48. Michael R. Belknap, *Federal Law and Southern Order: Racial Violence and Constitutional Conflict in the Post-Brown South*, 4–5 (1995), quoting Charles W. Ramsdell, *Reconstruction Texas*, 164 (1964 [1910]).
49. Rable, *But There Was No Peace*, 21, quoting telegram from General Phillip H. Sheridan to J. A. Rawlins, November 4, 1866, Sheridan Papers.
50. See Foner, *Reconstruction*, 458. See also Robert J. Kaczorowski, *The Politics of Judicial Interpretation: The Federal Courts, Department of Justice and Civil Rights, 1866–1876* (1985).
51. See Foner, *Reconstruction*, 444–459. See also Lou Falkner Williams, *The Great South Carolina Ku Klux Klan Trials, 1871–1872* (1996); Kermit L. Hall, "Political Power and Constitutional Legitimacy: The South Carolina Ku Klux Klan Trials, 1871–1872," 33 *Emory Law Journal* 921 (1984).
52. Foner, *Reconstruction*, 458, quoting letters from Amos T. Akerman, Attorney General, to General Alfred H. Terry, November 18, 1871, Akerman Papers.
53. William Safire, "Judge Bork Stands up to the Lynch Mob," *Chicago Tribune*, October 13, 1987.
54. See Ruth Marcus, "Hill Describes Details of Alleged Harassment; Thomas Categorically Denies All the Charges; Court Nominee Calls Ordeal 'Lynching for Uppity Blacks,' " *Washington Post*, October 12, 1991. See also James J. Kilpatrick, "Lynch Mob Assembles to Keep Thomas off the Supreme Court," *Orlando Sentinel Tribune*, August 8, 1991. Similarly, George Will likened opposition to the nomination of William Lucas as assistant attorney general for civil rights as a "lynching." See "The Lucas Matter: A Liberal Lynching," *Washington Post*, July 25, 1989.
55. See Sheryl McCarthy, "Chavis: Victim of His Own Arrogance," *Newsday*, August 24, 1994; Clarence Page, "The Race Card Still Gets Played Again and Again," *Chicago Tribune*, August 24, 1994.
56. This definition is a simplified version of that suggested by James H. Chadbourn at the end of a careful review of competing statutory definitions of lynching. See *Lynching and the Law*, 47 (1933). Much controversy has surrounded definitions of lynching. After considerable debate, one group of antilynching activists stipulated in 1940 that for an event to properly be termed a lynching "there must be legal evidence that a person has been killed, and that he met his death illegally at the hands of a group acting under the pretext of service to justice, race, or tradition." W. Fitzhugh

Brundage, *Lynching in the New South: Georgia and Virginia, 1880–1930*, 17 (1993). The state of Alabama defined lynching as follows: "Any number of persons assembled for any unlawful purpose and intending to injure any person by violence and without authority of law shall be regarded as a mob, and any act of violence exercized by such mob upon the body of any person shall, when such crime results in the death of the injured person, constitute the crime of lynching." See Chadbourn, 149.

57. There is a large and growing literature on lynching. The work I have found most useful includes Brundage, *Lynching*, 62; Chadbourn, *Lynching*, 64; *Lynching, Racial Violence, and Law* (Paul Finkelman, ed., 1992); Ralph Ginzburg, *100 Years of Lynching* (1962); Jacquelyn Dowd Hall, *Revolt against Chivalry: Jessie Daniel Ames and the Women's Campaign against Lynching* (rev. ed., 1993); Barbara Holden-Smith, "Lynching, Federalism, and the Intersection of Race and Gender in the Progressive Era," 8 *Yale Journal of Law and Feminism* 31 (1996); Neil R. McMillen, *Dark Journey: Black Mississippians in the Age of Jim Crow*, 224–253 (1989); Arthur Raper, *The Tragedy of Lynching* (1933); Stacy Capman Saravay, "Lawmakers, Reformers, and Apologists Respond to Lynching: A Critical Survey of the Literature," Third Year Paper, Harvard Law School (1990); Stewart E. Tolnay and E. M. Beck, *A Festival of Violence: An Analysis of Southern Lynchings, 1882–1930* (1995); Walter White, *Rope and Faggot* (1929); Stephen J. Whitfield, *A Death in the Delta: The Story of Emmett Till*, 1–14 (1988); George C. Wright, *Racial Violence in Kentucky, 1865–1940* (1990); Robert L. Zangrando, *The NAACP Crusade against Lynching, 1909–1950* (1980).

58. See Zangrando, *NAACP Crusade*, 4.

59. For a useful compilation of figures, see ibid., 4. Zangrando notes that the prevalence of lynching was undoubtedly greater than these statistics indicate, since they account neither for unreported lynchings nor for "legal" executions carried out in order to preempt mob killings.

60. National Association for the Advancement of Colored People, *Thirty Years of Lynching in the United States, 1889–1918*, 11 (1969 [1919]).

61. Ibid., 12.

62. Ibid., 12–13.

63. Ibid., 13.

64. Ibid., 14.

65. Ibid., 15.

66. Ibid., 17.

67. Ibid.

68. Ibid., 18.

69. Whitfield, *Death in the Delta*, 2, quoting Philip Alexander Bruce, *The Plantation Negro as a Freeman*, 83–84 (1889).

70. "Lynching: A Southern View," *Atlantic Monthly*, 155, February 1904.

71. In 30 percent of Southern lynchings between 1882 and 1930, researchers have found traces of accusations of sexual misconduct. See Tolnay and Beck, *Festival of Violence*, 48.

72. W. J. Cash, *The Mind of the South* (1991 [1941]).

73. Whitfield, *Death in the Delta*, 3, quoting Bob Ward, "William Bradford Huie Paid for Their Sin," *Writer's Digest*, 54, September 1974.

74. McMillen, *Dark Journey*, 240, quoting Theodore Bilbo to Louise Kates, December 9, 1938, Box 138, Post-1040, NAACP.

75. Ibid., 224, quoting *Jackson Daily Clarion-Ledger*, September 10, 1908.

76. Richard Wright, *Black Boy* 190 (1945). "Like whipping under slavery," Jacquelyn Dowd Hall writes, "lynching was an instrument of social discipline intended to impress not only the immediate victim but all who saw or heard about the event." *Revolt against Chivalry*, 136.

77. McMillen, *Dark Journey*, 239. See also Brundage, *Lynching*, 49 ("Most [Southern whites] agreed that the crimes that posed the greatest menace to the racial hierarchy fell within the jurisdiction of the lynch mob.")

78. McMillen, *Dark Journey*, 224.

79. See Joel Williamson, *The Crucible of Race*, 188 (1984). Cole Blease is also reported to have said: "Whenever the Constitution comes between me and the virtue of the white women of South Carolina, I say 'to hell with the Constitution!' " Howard Smead, *Blood Justice: The Lynching of Mack Charles Parker* xi (1986).

80. Chadbourn, *Lynching*, 114, quoting *Mississippi Senate Journal* 88 et seq. (1900). Some have credited the vocal and active opposition to lynching shown by Virginia Governor Charles O'Ferrall and North Carolina Governor Cameron Morrison with decreasing the numbers of lynchings in those states. See Brundage, *Lynching*, 176; William H. Richardson, "No More Lynchings! How North Carolina Solved the Problem," 64 *Review of Reviews* 401, 402 (1924).

81. See Chadbourn, *Lynching*, 25–26.

82. Ibid., 13.

83. See James L. Crouthamel, "Springfield Race Riot of 1908," 45 *Journal of Negro History* 164 (July 1960). This article is conveniently reprinted in Finkelman, *Lynching, Racial Violence, and Law*, 76.

84. See Charles Flint Kellogg, *NAACP: A History of the National Association for the Advancement of Colored People*, vol. 1, 1909–1920, 11 (1967).

85. Between 1882 and 1951, opponents of lynching introduced 248 bills. Not one passed. See Belknap, *Federal Law*, 18.

86. See George C. Rable, "The South and the Politics of Antilynching Legislation, 1920–1940," 51 *Journal of Southern History* 201 (1985).

87. See Nancy J. Weiss, *Farewell to the Party of Lincoln: Black Politics in the Age of FDR*, 119 (1983).

88. See Trudier Harris, *Exorcising Blackness: Historical and Literary Lynching and Burning Rituals* (1984).

89. See William B. Hixson, Jr., "Moorfield Storey and the Defense of the Dyer Anti-lynching Bill," 42 *New England Quarterly* 65 (March 1969). Storey changed his mind and fervently supported federal antilynching legislation in the face of a frightening rise in antiblack violence after World War I.

90. Compare *Brzonkala v. Virginia Polytechnic and State Univ.*, 935 F. Supp. 779 (W.D. Va. 1996) striking down as unconstitutional the Violence Against Women Act (VAWA) with *Doe v. Doe*, 929 F. Supp. 608 (D. Conn. 1996) upholding constitutionality of VAWA.

91. See Eugene Gressman, "The Unhappy History of Civil Rights Legislation," 50 *Michigan Law Review* 1323, 1339 (1952).

92. See Michael Les Benedict, "Preserving the Constitution: The Conservative Basis of Radical Reconstruction," 61 *Journal of American History* 65 (1974); Michael Les Benedict, "Preserving Federalism: Reconstruction and the Waite Court," 1978 *Supreme Court Review* 39.

93. See Benedict, "Preserving Federalism," 47.

94. Foner, *Reconstruction*, 530.

95. Outraged by the massacre, President Grant issued an executive order directing the military to bring order to Colfax and apprehend those who perpetrated the killings. Many Southern whites, on the other hand, subscribed to the view of *The Shreveport Times*, which described the massacre as a "wholesome lesson the negroes have been taught." See Frederick M. Lawrence, "Civil Rights and Criminal Wrongs: The Mens Rea of Federal Civil Rights Crimes," 67 *Tulane Law Review* 2113, 2155 n.168 (1993).

96. 203 U.S. 1 (1906), overruled by *Jones v. Alfred H. Mayer Co.*, 392 U.S. 409 (1968).

97. 325 U.S. 91 (1945).

98. 203 U.S. 5.

99. Ibid., 4.

100. Ibid., 14.

101. Charles Fairman, *Reconstruction and Reunion, 1864–88*, vol. 7, 266 (1987). Taking pains to limit federal jurisdiction under the Thirteenth and Fif-

teenth amendments only to cases of racially motivated violence, Bradley went on to say that "any outrages, atrocities, or conspiracies . . . which do not flow from [the war of race] but spring from the ordinary felonious or criminal intent which prompts to such unlawful acts are not within the jurisdiction of the United States." Ibid.

102. *Screws*, 325 U.S. 92–93 (1945).

103. Lawrence, "Civil Rights," 2171 n.261.

104. Ibid., 2171–2172.

105. *Screws*, 325 U.S. 138.

106. Ibid.

107. Ibid., 139.

108. Ibid., 137–138.

109. See Lawrence, "Civil Rights," 2174. For additional commentary on *Screws*, see Woodford Howard and Cornelius Bushoven, "The *Screws* Case Revisited," 29 *Journal of Politics* 617 (1967); Julius Cohen, "The Screws Case: Federal Protection of Negro Rights," 46 *Columbia Law Review* 104 (1946).

110. H.R. 13, 67th Cong., 1st Sess. §1 (1921).

111. Holden-Smith, "Lynching," 55, quoting 62 *Congressional Record* 468 (1921).

112. Ibid., 56.

113. Ibid.

114. Ibid., 57.

115. Ibid.

116. Ibid., 59.

117. White Slave Traffic (Mann) Act, ch. 395, 36 Stat. 825, 825 (1910), codified as amended at 18 U.S.C. §§2421–2424 (1988).

118. H.R. Rep. No. 47, 61st Cong., 2d Sess. 11 (1909).

119. Holden-Smith, "Lynching," 68, quoting 45 *Congressional Record* 809, 811 (1910).

120. Ibid., 70, quoting 45 *Congressional Record* 1040 (1910).

121. Ibid., quoting 45 *Congressional Record* 811 (1910).

122. Harrison Narcotics Act of 1914, ch. 1, 38 Stat. 785 (1914) [later ratified at 26 U.S.C. §691–708 (1928)], repealed by Comprehensive Drug Abuse Prevention and Control Act of 1970, Pub. L. No. 91–513, §110 (b) (3)-(A), 38 Stat. 1236, 1292 (1970).

123. Act of July 30, 1912, ch. 263, 37 Stat. 240 (1912).

124. Holden-Smith, "Lynching," 76.

125. See Dan Streible, "Race and the Reception of Jack Johnson Fight Films," in *The Birth of Whiteness: Race and the Emergence of U.S. Cinema*, 170, 186–187 (Daniel Bernardi, ed., 1996).

126. See Zangrando, *NAACP Crusade*, 169. See also Harvard Sitkoff, "Racial Militancy and Interracial Violence in the Second World War," 58 *Journal of American History* 661 (1971).

127. See Zangrando, *NAACP Crusade*, 7.

128. See Mary L. Dudziak, "Desegregation as a Cold War Imperative," 41 *Stanford Law Review* 61 (1988); Doug McAdam, *Political Process and the Development of Black Insurgency, 1930–1970* (1982).

129. For the most comprehensive examination of the murder of Emmett Till and its place in American history, see Whitfield, *Death in the Delta*. The continuing resonance of this case is reflected in the novels that have used it as a point of departure. See Bebe Moore Campbell, *Your Blues Ain't Like Mine* (1992), and Lewis Nordan, *Wolf Whistle* (1993).

130. Whitfield, *Death in the Delta*, 20, quoting Edward L. Ayers, *Vengeance and Justice: Crime and Punishment in the 19th Century American South*, 244 (1984). Till's mother testified that, prior to her son's visit to Mississippi, she had warned him of the need to observe what Richard Wright called the ethics of living Jim Crow. "I told him," his mother said, "to be very careful how he spoke, and to say 'yes, sir' and 'no, ma'am,' and not to hesitate to humble yourself if you had to get down on your knees." Quoted in Whitfield, *Death in the Delta*, 40.

131. See William Bradford Huie, *Three Lives for Mississippi* (1965).

132. Whitfield, *Death in the Delta*, 24, quoting *Jackson Clarion-Ledger*, September 2, 1955.

133. Ibid., 26, quoting *Jackson Daily News*, September 1, 1955.

134. Ibid., 24, quoting William M. Simpson, "Reflections on a Murder: The Emmett Till Case," in *Southern Miscellany: Essays in History in Honor of Glover Moore*, 184–195 (1981).

135. Ibid., 41.

136. Ibid.

137. Ibid., 42 quoting Hugh Steven Whitaker, "Case Study in Southern Justice: The Emmett Till Case," 154–155, M.A. thesis, Florida State University (1963).

138. Ibid., 46, quoting the European Headquarters of American Jewish Committee, Survey of Public Opinion in France, Italy, Belgium, Switzerland, Germany, Tunisia on the Emmett Till Case (October 1955), Archives of the American Jewish Committee (copy in possession of author).

139. Ibid., 42.

140. Ibid., 46–47.

141. Ibid., 49, quoting David Halberstam, "Tallahatchie County Acquits a Peckerwood," *Reporter*, April 19, 1956.

142. The best single source on this subject is Belknap, *Federal Law*. Additional sources on which I have relied include Charles M. Payne, *I've Got the Light of Freedom: The Organizing Tradition and the Mississippi Freedom Struggle* (1995); John Dittmer, *Local People: The Struggle for Civil Rights in Mississippi* (1994).

143. Belknap, *Federal Law*, 29.

144. See Dittmer, *Local People*, 109, 215.

145. See Belknap, *Federal Law*, 108.

146. See Maryanne Vollers, *Ghosts of Mississippi: The Murder of Medgar Evers, the Trials of Byron De La Beckwith, and the Haunting of the New South* (1995).

147. See Belknap, *Federal Law*; Victor S. Navasky, *Kennedy Justice* (1971). See also Burke Marshall, *Federalism and Civil Rights* (1964); Richard A. Wasserstrom, 33 *University of Chicago Law Review* 406 (1966) (reviewing *Federalism and Civil Rights*).

148. See Doug McAdam, *Freedom Summer* (1988); Clayborne Carson, *In Struggle: SNCC and the Black Awakening of the 1960s* (1981).

149. Seth Cagin and Philip Drey, *We Are Not Afraid: The Story of Goodman, Schwerner, and Chaney and the Civil Rights Campaign for Mississippi*, 354 (1988).

150. See Belknap, *Federal Law*, 165–168.

151. For commentary on the racist obstructionism of Judge Cox, see Gerald M. Stern, "Judge William Harold Cox and the Right to Vote in Clarke County, Mississippi," in *Southern Justice*, 165 (Leon Friedman, ed., 1965).

152. See *United States* v. *Price*, 383 U.S. 787 (1966).

153. See Belknap, *Federal Law*, 161.

154. Ibid., 186–190.

155. Ibid., 187.

156. Ibid., 140. (Quoting telegram from Nhagwin M. Jackson, District Attorney, State of Mississippi, to Robert Kennedy, May 14, 1964).

157. Ibid., at 201.

158. Ibid., 201–202.

159. Ibid., 202.

160. Belknap, *Federal Law*, 204.

161. Ibid., 236.

162. 18 U.S.C. §245 (2)(b)(1)(1994).

163. 18 U.S.C. §245 (2)(b)(2)(1994).

164. Belknap, *Federal Law*, 217.

165. See Patricia A. Turner, *I Heard It Through the Grapevine: Rumor in African-American Culture*, 108–122 (1993).

166. See Clayborne Carson, "Malcolm and the American State," in *Malcolm X:*

The FBI File (David Gallen, ed., 1991); Michael Friedly, *Malcolm X: The Assassination* (1992); David J. Garrow, *The FBI and Martin Luther King, Jr.* (1981).

167. See *Racially-Motivated Violence: Litigation Strategies* (Randolph M. Scott-McLaughlin, ed., 1984); Charles H. Jones, Jr., "An Argument for Federal Protection against Racially Motivated Crimes: 18 U.S.C. §241 and the Thirteenth Amendment," 21 *Harvard Civil Rights–Civil Liberties Law Review* 689 (1986).

168. On the other hand, for an example of a successful prosecution under Section 245, see *United States v. Franklin*, 704 F.2d 1183 (10 CA 1983).

169. McMillen, *Dark Journey*, 204.

170. Ibid.

171. Ibid.

172. Ibid.

173. Ibid., 203.

174. Ibid.

175. Ibid.

176. See Myrdal, *An American Dilemma*, 551.

177. *Kelley v. Stone*, 514 F.2d 18, 19 (CA 9 1975).

178. *The Kerner Report: The 1968 Report of the National Advisory Commission on Civil Disorders*, 307 (1988 [1968]).

179. Steven B. Duke and Albert C. Gross, *America's Longest War*, 163 (1993).

180. See Kimberle Williams Crenshaw, "Mapping the Margins: Intersectionality, Identity Politics, and Violence against Women of Color," 43 *Stanford Law Review* 1241, 1266–1269 (1991).

181. See "Race Tilts the Scales of Justice. Study: Dallas Punishes Attacks on Whites More Harshly," *Dallas Times Herald*, August 19, 1990. See also Gary D. LaFree, *Rape and Criminal Justice: The Social Construction of Sexual Assault* (1989).

182. LaFree, *Rape and Criminal Justice*, 239.

183. Ibid., 219–220.

184. Charles S. Mangum, Jr., *The Legal Status of the Negro*, 368–370 (1940).

185. See studies discussed in Randall Kennedy, "McCleskey v. Kemp: Race, Capital Punishment, and the Supreme Court," 101 *Harvard Law Review* 1388, 1395–1397 (1988).

186. See *McCleskey v. Kemp*, 481 U.S. 279 (1987); David C. Baldus, George Woodward, and Charles A. Pulaski, Jr., *Equal Justice and the Death Penalty* (1990).

3. History: Unequal Enforcement

1. See Daniel J. Flanigan, *The Criminal Law of Slavery and Freedom, 1800–1863* (1987); and Thomas D. Morris, *Southern Slavery and the Law, 1619–1860* (1996).
2. Flanigan, *Criminal Law*, 31–32.
3. Ibid., 18.
4. *State* v. *Tom*, 13 N.C. 569, 572 (1830). For a subtle discussion of conflict within the community of ideas embraced by the master class, see William W. Fisher III, "Ideology and Imagery in the Law of Slavery," 68 *Chicago-Kent Law Review* 1051 (1993).
5. Flanigan, *Criminal Law*, 15–16.
6. *Luke* v. *State*, 5 Fla. 185, 195 (1853).
7. See Judith Kelleher Schafer, *Slavery, the Civil Law, and the Supreme Court of Louisiana*, 65 (1994), quoting *State* v. *Kentucky* 8 La. Ann. 308 (1853).
8. See Philip J. Schwarz, *Twice Condemned: Slaves and the Criminal Laws of Virginia, 1705–1865*, 52–54 (1988); Michael S. Hindus, "Black Justice under White Law: Criminal Prosecutions of Blacks in Antebellum South Carolina," in *Race Relations and the Law in American History*, 183–184 (Kermit L. Hall, ed., 1987).
9. See A. E. Keir Nash, "Fairness and Formalism in the Trials of Blacks in the State Supreme Courts of the Old South," 56 *Virginia Law Review* 64 (1970). See also Nash, "A More Equitable Past? Southern Supreme Courts and the Protection of the Antebellum Negro," 48 *North Carolina Law Review* 197 (1970), reprinted in *Race Relations and the Law in American History*, 406 (Kermit L. Hall, ed., 1987); Nash, "Reason of Slavery: Understanding the Judicial Role in the Peculiar Institution," 32 *Vanderbilt Law Review* 7 (1979); Nash, "Texas Justice in the Age of Slavery: Appeals Concerning Blacks and the Antebellum State Supreme Court," 8 *Houston Law Review* 438 (1971); Nash, "The Texas Supreme Court and the Trial Rights of Blacks, 1845–1860," 58 *Journal of American History* 622 (1971).
10. See *Nelson* v. *State*, 6 Ala. 394 (1844); *Grandison (a slave)* v. *State*, 21 Tenn. 451 (1841).
11. See *Spence* v. *State*, 17 Ala. 192 (1850).
12. 30 Tenn. 159 (1850).
13. Ibid., 163.
14. *Peter* v. *State*, 12 Miss. 31 (1844).
15. *Brown* v. *State*, 173 Miss. 542 (1935). The U.S. Supreme Court reversed the

conviction, however. See *Brown* v. *Mississippi*, 297 U.S. 278 (1936). (For a discussion of *Brown* see pp. 104–107.)

16. On the history of the controversy over the Negro Seamen Acts, see Henry Wilson, *History of the Rise and Fall of the Slave Power in America*, III, 578–586 (1872); Andrew Kull, *The Color-Blind Constitution*, 11–15 (1992).

17. Ira Berlin, *Slaves without Masters*, 96 (1975). For a period in the late eighteenth century, Delaware, too, prohibited free blacks from testifying against whites. Ibid., 91.

18. Ibid., 96.

19. Ibid., 95.

20. See Arthur Zilversmit, *The First Emancipation: The Abolition of Slavery in the North* (1967).

21. See Leon F. Litwack, *North of Slavery* (1961). See also Paul Finkelman, "Prelude to the Fourteenth Amendment: Black Legal Rights in the Antebellum North," 17 *Rutgers Law Review* 415 (1986).

22. Litwack, *North of Slavery*, 96.

23. Ibid., 71.

24. See Thomas D. Morris, *Free Men All: The Personal Liberty Laws of the North, 1780–1861* (1974).

25. 41 U.S. 539 (1842).

26. Act of September 18, 1850, 9 Stat. 462.

27. See Stanley W. Campbell, *The Slave Catchers: Enforcement of the Fugitive Slave Law, 1850–1860* (1970).

28. *Civil Rights Cases*, 109 U.S. 3, 30 (1883) (Harlan, J., dissenting).

29. This is the text of a handbill dated April 24, 1851, found in the archives of the Library of Congress.

30. Campbell, *Slave Catchers*, 207.

31. See Flanigan, *Criminal Law*, 273–275.

32. See 42 U.S.C. § 1981 (1994).

33. See Eric Foner, *Reconstruction: America's Unfinished Revolution*, 362 (1988).

34. See Donald G. Nieman, "Black Political Power and Criminal Justice: Washington County, Texas, 1868–1884," 55 *Journal of Southern History* 391 (1989).

35. See William Cohen, "Negro Involuntary Servitude in the South, 1865–1940: A Preliminary Analysis," 42 *Journal of Southern History* 31 (1976).

36. Foner, *Reconstruction*, 363, quoting *Selma Southern Argus*, February 3, 1870.

37. William Archer, *Through Afro-America*, 35 (1910).

38. Neil R. McMillen, *Dark Journey: Black Mississippians in the Age of Jim Crow*, 201–202 (1989), quoting *Dixon* v. *Mississippi*, 74 Miss. 271, 275 (1896).

39. See Andrew L. Shapiro, "Challenging Criminal Disenfranchisement under the Voting Rights Act: A New Strategy," 103 *Yale Law Journal* 537 (1993).

40. *Ratliff* v. *Beale*, 74 Miss. 247, 265, 266–267 (1896).

41. 170 U.S. 213 (1898).

42. 471 U.S. 222 (1985).

43. *Williams*, 170 U.S. at 222

44. Ibid.

45. Ibid.

46. Jennifer Wriggins, "Rape, Racism, and the Law," 6 *Harvard Women's Law Journal* 103, 109 (1983), quoting *State* v. *Petit* 119 La. 1013, 1016 (1907).

47. *Carraway* v. *Mississippi*, 163 Miss. 639 (1932), quoted in McMillen, *Dark Journey*, 207. See also Martha Myers, "The New South's 'New' Black Criminal: Rape and Punishment in Georgia, 1870–1940," in *Ethnicity, Race, and Crime: Perspectives across Time and Place* (Darnell F. Hawkins, ed., 1995).

48. 34 S.E. 135 (1899).

49. Ibid., 136.

50. See Wriggins, "Rape, Racism, and the Law," 120–121.

51. Ibid., 708.

52. 36 Ala. App. 707 (1953).

53. Ibid.

54. Ibid.

55. Cohen, "Negro Involuntary Servitude," 33.

56. Ibid., 35.

57. Ibid., 46.

58. Ibid., 48–49.

59. Ibid., 48.

60. Ibid., 51.

61. Ibid., 50. Investigating this report, the U.S. Department of Justice learned that fifty-five blacks had been arrested and seventeen convicted of vagrancy. Although no whites were arrested, federal officials refused to conclude that the vagrancy law was being administered in a racially discriminatory manner. Ibid.

62. Ibid., 54.

63. Ibid.

64. See *Code of Alabama*, Vol. II, Criminal Sec. 3812 (1886). "Any person, who, with intent to injure or defraud his employer, enters into a contract in writing for the performance of any act or service, and thereby obtains money or other personal property from such employer, and with like intent, and without just cause, and without refunding such money, or paying for such

property, refuses to perform . . . must, on conviction, be punished as if he had stolen it." Pete Daniel, "Up from Slavery and down to Peonage: The Alonzo Baily Case," 57 *Journal of American History* 654 (1970), reprinted in *Race Relations and the Law in American History*, 59 (Kermit C. Hall, ed., 1987).

65. Ibid., 61, quoting notes from Erastus J. Parsons to Charles J. Bonaparte, March 7, 1908, on file with General Records of Department of Justice, file 50-162-5.

66. See Alexander M. Bickel and Benno C. Schmidt, *The Judiciary and Responsible Government: 1910–1921* (1984).

67. 219 U.S. 219 (1911).

68. Ibid., 244–245.

69. Bickel and Schmidt, *The Judiciary*, 862, quoting Brief for the United States as Amicus Curiae, *Bailey* v. *Alabama*, 219 U.S. 219 (1911).

70. *Bailey*, 219 U.S. at 231.

71. Ibid.

72. See *Taylor* v. *Georgia*, 315 U.S. 25 (1942); *Pollock* v. *Williams*, 322 U.S. 4 (1944).

73. See Richard C. Cortner, *A Mob Intent on Death: The NAACP and the Arkansas Riot Cases*, 11 (1988).

74. Cortner, *Mob Intent*, 24–25, quoting Charles Flint Kellogg, *NAACP: A History of the National Association for the Advancement of Colored People*, 163 (1967).

75. Ibid., 26, quoting Walter White, *A Man Called White: The Autobiography of Walter White*, 51 (1948).

76. Ibid., 75, quoting *Arkansas Gazette*, April 16, 1920.

77. *Barks* v. *State*, 132 Ark. 154 (1920).

78. *Ware* v. *State*, 146 Ark. 321 (1920).

79. *Ware* v. *State*, 159 Ark. 540 (1923).

80. 237 U.S. 309 (1915).

81. See Leonard Dinnerstein, *The Leo Frank Case* (1968).

82. *Hicks* v. *State*, 143 Ark. 158, 162 (1920).

83. 261 U.S. 86, 91 (1923).

84. Robert M. Cover, "The Origins of Judicial Activism in the Protection of Minorities," 91 *Yale Law Journal* 1287, 1306 (1982).

85. See Dan T. Carter, *Scottsboro: A Tragedy of the American South* (rev. ed., 1969); James Goodman, *Stories of Scottsboro* (1994).

86. Carter, *Scottsboro*, 297, quoting *New York Times*, December 1, 1993.

87. Ibid., 235.

88. Ibid., 237.

89. 287 U.S. 45 (1932).

90. 294 U.S. 587 (1935).

91. Carter, *Scottsboro*.

92. *Powell*, 287 U.S. at 56.

93. Carter, *Scottsboro*, at 344–345.

94. Ibid., 347.

95. For an interesting analysis of racial hoaxes featuring false claims of criminality by blacks, see Katherine K. Russell, "The Racial Hoax as Crime: The Law as Affirmation," 71 *Indiana Law Journal* 593 (1996). Professor Russell describes the prosecution of the Scottsboro Boys as "the most notorious racial hoax case in our history." Ibid. at 597.

96. 297 U.S. 278 (1936). For an excellent description of the case, see Richard C. Cortner, *A "Scottsboro" Case in Mississippi: The Supreme Court and Brown v. Mississippi* (1986).

97. *Brown*, 297 U.S. at 284.

98. *Brown* v. *State*, 173 Miss. 542 (1935).

99. Ibid., at 572.

100. *Brown*, 173 Miss. at 574.

101. Ibid., 578.

102. Ibid.

103. 297 U.S. 278, 285–286 (1936).

104. Cortner, *A "Scottsboro" Case*, 155.

105. See Michael L. Radelet, Hugo Adam Bedau, and Constance E. Putnam, *In Spite of Innocence: Erroneous Convictions in Capital Cases* (1992). See also pp. 125–128.

106. See Kenneth O'Reilly, *Racial Matters: The FBI's Secret File on Black America, 1960–1972* (1989); David J. Garrow, *The FBI and Martin Luther King, Jr.* (1981); Clayborne Carson, *Malcolm X: The FBI File* (1991).

107. O'Reilly, *Racial Matters*, 14.

108. Ibid., 13.

109. For a careful discussion of the prosecution that is sensitive to the complicated racial politics that surrounded it, see Judith Stein, *The World of Marcus Garvey: Race and Class in Modern Society*, 186–208 (1986).

110. Stein, *Marcus Garvey*, 192.

111. See Garrow, *The FBI and Martin Luther King, Jr.*

112. Ibid., 126.

113. See ibid., 336. See also Senate Select Committee to Study Governmental Operations with Respect to Intelligence Activities, Final Report, S. Rep. No. 94–755, 94th Cong., 2d Sess. (1976).

114. See, e.g., Stokely Carmichael, *Stokely Speaks: Black Power back to Pan*

Africanism (1971); Eldridge Cleaver, *Post-Prison Writings and Speeches* (Robert Scheer, ed., 1969); *The Black Panthers Speak* (Philip S. Foner, ed., 1970); *Off the Pigs! The History and Literature of the Black Panther Party* (G. Louis Heath, ed., 1976); Huey P. Newton, *To Die for the People: The Writings of Huey P. Newton* (1972); Bobby Seale, *Seize the Time: The Story of the Black Panther Party and Huey P. Newton* (1970).

115. See Hugh Pearson, *The Shadow of the Panther* (1994).

116. O'Reilly, *Racial Matters*, 309.

117. Ibid., 307.

118. See *Hampton* v. *Hanrahan*, 600 F.2d 600 (7th Cir. 1979).

119. Gunnar Myrdal, *An American Dilemma*, 535, Vol. II, 1962 (rev. ed. [1994]).

120. Ibid., 536.

121. Ibid., 541.

122. East St. Louis Riots: Report of the Special Committee Authorized by Congress to Investigate the East St. Louis Riots, reprinted in *Racial Violence in the United States*, 69 (Allen D. Grimshaw, ed., 1969).

123. Allen D. Grimshaw, "Actions of Police and the Military in American Race Riots," in *Racial Violence in the United States* 275 [quoting Herbert Seligman, "Race War?" *New Republic* 49 (1919)].

124. Ibid., 123.

125. Thurgood Marshall, "The Gestapo in Detroit," reprinted in ibid., 141.

126. *Report of the National Advisory Commission on Civil Disorders* 115 (1968).

127. Ibid., 299.

128. Ibid., 302–303. See also Robert Blauner, "Internal Colonialism and Ghetto Revolt," in *Racial Oppression in America* (1972). Echoing Myrdal, Blauner asserted (albeit without reference to documentation) that "[o]f all establishment institutions, police departments probably include the highest proportion of individual racists." Ibid., 97–98.

129. See Bruce Porter and Marvin Dunn, *The Miami Riot of 1980: Crossing the Bounds*, 27 (1984).

130. Ibid.

131. For books and articles I have relied upon in discussing the litigation surrounding the beating of Rodney King, see Independent Commission on the Los Angeles Police Department, *Report of the Independent Commission of the Los Angeles Police Department* (1991) (hereinafter Christopher Commission Report), Stacey C. Koon, with Robert Dietz, *Presumed Guilty: The Tragedy of the Rodney King Affair* (1992); Laurie L. Levenson, "The Future of State and Federal Civil Rights Prosecutions: The Lessons of the Rodney King Trial," 41 *UCLA Law Review* 509 (1994); Roger Parloff, "Maybe the Jury Was Right," *American Lawyer*, June 1992.

132. See Staff of the *Los Angeles Times, Understanding the Riots: Los Angeles before and after the Rodney King Case* (1992); Institute for Alternative Journalism *Inside the L.A. Riots* (1992).

133. See Parloff, "Maybe the Jury Was Right"; David Nicholson, "Presumed Guilty: The Cops and Rodney King," 2 *Reconstruction*, no. 2 (1993).

134. Christopher Commission Report. See also Joe Domanick, *To Protect and to Serve: The LAPD's Century of War in the City of Dreams* (1994); Mike Davis, *City of Quartz: Excavating the Future in Los Angeles*, 265–322 (1990).

135. Christopher Commission Report, xii.

136. Ibid., 72.

137. Peter L. Davis, "Rodney King and the Recriminalization of Police Brutality in America: Direct and Judicial Access to the Grand Jury as Remedies for Victims of Police Brutality When the Prosecution Declines to Prosecute," 53 *Maryland Law Review* 271, 281–283 (1994).

138. See 42 U.S.C. §1983 (1994) originally enacted as §1 of the Ku Klux Klan Act of 1871, ch. 22, §1, 17 Stat. 13.

139. See David Rudovsky, "Police Abuse: Can the Violence Be Contained?" 27 *Harvard Civil Rights–Civil Liberties Law Review* 465 (1992).

140. See Davis, "Rodney King."

141. 423 U.S. 362 (1976).

142. 461 U.S. 95 (1983).

143. See *Council of Organizations on Philadelphia Police Accountability and Responsibility* v. *Rizzo*, 357 F. Supp. 1289 (E. D. Penn. 1973).

144. Ibid., 1319.

145. See *Goode* v. *Rizzo*, 506 F.2d 542 (CA 3 1994).

146. 423 U.S. 366 (1976).

147. For an illuminating, detailed critique of the Supreme Court's handling of the case, see Richard H. Fallon, Jr., "Of Justiciability, Remedies, and Public Law Litigation: Notes on the Jurisprudence of *Lyons*," 59 *New York University Law Review* 1 (1984).

148. *Lyons*, 461 U.S. 114–115 (1983) (Marshall, J., dissenting).

149. Ibid., 116.

150. Ibid., 137.

151. An additional example of this trend in the judiciary is *McCleskey* v. *Kemp*, 481 U.S. 279 (1987) (upholding the constitutionality of the administration of capital punishment in Georgia). See pp. 326–345. An example of this trend in Congress is the Prison Reform Litigation Act, Pub. L. No. 104–134, 110 Stat. 1321 (1996), limiting the authority of federal judges in legal challenges to prison conditions. See also Donald L. Horowitz, *The Courts and Public Policy* (1977).

152. The precursor to the book was Hugo Adam Bedau and Michael L. Radelet, "Miscarriages of Justice in Potentially Capital Cases," 40 *Stanford Law Review* 21 (1987). For a critique see Steven J. Markman and Paul G. Cassell, "Protecting the Innocent: A Response to the Bedau-Radelet Study," 41 *Stanford Law Review* 121 (1991).

153. See Michael L. Radelet, Hugo Adam Bedau, and Constance E. Putnam, *In Spite of Innocence: Erroneous Convictions in Capital Cases*, 124 (1992).

154. *Ex Parte Brandley*, 781 S.W.2d 886, 926 (Tx. Ct. Crim. App., 1989).

155. Ibid., 887.

156. Ibid., 933. After the Texas Court of Criminal Appeals affirmed the district judge, state authorities declined to re-try Brandley.

157. See, e.g., Linn Washington, *Black Judges on Justice* (1994).

158. David M. Oshinsky, *"Worse Than Slavery": Parchman Farm and the Ordeal of Jim Crow Justice*, 34 (1996).

159. Edward L. Ayers, *Vengeance and Justice: Crime and Punishment in the 19th-Century American South*, 197 (1984).

160. Ibid., 198.

161. See Ronald L. Goldfarb and Linda R. Singer, *After Conviction*, 411–414 (1973); Desmond King, *Separate and Unequal: Black Americans and the U.S. Federal Government*, 142–171 (1995); Michael Mushlin, *Rights of Prisoners*, 193–196 (2d. ed., 1993).

162. *Nicholds v. McGee*, 169 F.Supp. 721, 724 (N.D. Cal.), appeal dismissed, 361 U.S. 6 (1959).

163. See, e.g., *Lee v. Washington*, 390 U.S. 333 (1968); *Gates v. Collier*, 349 F. Supp. 881 (N.D. Miss. 1972) affd, 501 F.2d 1291 (CA 5 1974); *United States v. Wyandotte County, Kansas*, 480 F.2d 969 (CA 10 1973) *cert. denied* 414 U.S. 1068 (1973). For an incisive critical examination of desegregation in prisons see James B. Jacobs, "The Limits of Racial Integration in Prison," 18 *Criminal Law Bulletin* 117 (1982).

164. Ayers, *Vengeance and Justice*, 193.

165. Quoted in Alex Lichtenstein, "Through the Rugged Gates of the Penitentiary: Convict Labor and Southern Coal, 1870–1900," in *Race and Class in the American South Since 1890* (Melvyn Stokes and Rick Halpern, eds., 1994).

166. Ibid., 4–5.

167. James B. Jacobs, "The Limits of Racial Integration in Prison," 18 *Criminal Law Bulletin* 117 (1982).

168. See *Santiago v. Miles*, 774 F. Supp. 775 (W.D.N.Y., 1991).

169. Ibid., 794.

170. Ibid., 783.

171. Ibid., 785.

172. Michael B. Mushlin, *Rights of Prisoners* (2d. ed., vol. 1, 1993).

173. *Stroud* v. *Swope*, 187 F. 2d 850 CA 9 1951), *cert. denied* 342 U.S. 829 (1951). For an excellent examination of the hands-off doctrine, see Note, "Beyond the Ken of the Courts: A Critique of Judicial Refusal to Hear the Complaints of Convicts," 72 *Yale Law Journal* 506 (1963).

174. See Kathleen Engel and Stanley Rothman, "The Paradox of Prison Reform: Rehabilitation, Prisoners' Rights, and Violence," 7 *Harvard Journal of Law and Public Policy* 413 (1984).

175. See Michael Tonry, *Malign Neglect—Race, Crime and Punishment in America*, 58–59 (1995).

176. Ibid., 58.

177. See David M. Siegal, "Rape in Prison and AIDS: A Challenge for the Eighth Amendment Framework of *Wilson v. Seiter*," 44 *Stanford Law Review* 1541 (1992). For a vivid account by a watchful inmate-observer see Wilbert Rideau, "The Sexual Jungle," in *Life Sentences: Rage and Survival Behind Bars* (Wilbert Rideau and Ron Wikberg, eds., 1992).

178. Leo Carroll, *Hacks, Blacks, and Cons: Race Relations in a Maximum Security Prison*, 184–185 (1974). In his study of the Rhode Island Adult Correctional Institution, Carroll found that 75 percent of the homosexual rapes there involved black perpetrators and white victims, though blacks constituted only 25 percent of the inmate population. See also James B. Jacobs, *New Perspectives on Prisons and Imprisonment*, 72–74 (1983); Daniel Lockwood, *Prison Sexual Violence*, 28 (1980). *Stroman* v. *Griffin*, 331 F. Supp. 226, 228 (S.D. Ga. 1971) recounts circumstances of interracial sexual assaults that prompted him to uphold the prison authorities' practice of racially segregating inmates. For a grisly fictional account of this phenomenon see Donald Goines, *White Man's Justice, Black Man's Grief*, 49–74 (1973).

179. Tonry, *Malign Neglect*, 61.

180. See "Recent Legislation: Criminal Law—Prison Labor—Florida Reintroduces Chain Gangs," 109 *Harvard Law Review* 876 (1996).

181. See Norval Morris, "The Contemporary Prison, 1965–Present," in *The Oxford History of the Prison: The Practice of Punishment in Western Society*, 242, Norval Morris and David J. Rothman, eds., 1995. ("Whatever the causes, many of the prisons and jails in the United States . . . appear to be institutions designed to segregate from society a young black and Hispanic male underclass.")

4. Race, Law, and Suspicion

1. Larry Alexander, "What Makes Wrongful Discrimination Wrong?" 141 *University of Pennsylvania Law Review* 149, 167 (1992).

2. In considering the problem of police use of race in making determinations of suspiciousness, I have benefited enormously from the following: Arthur Isak Applebaum, "Racial Generalization, Police Discretion and Bayesian Contractualism," in *Handled with Discretion* (John Kleinig, ed., 1996); Jody D. Armour, "Race Ipsa Loquitur: Of Reasonable Racists, Intelligent Bayesians, and Involuntary Negrophobes," 46 *Stanford Law Review* 781 (1994); Elizabeth A. Gaynes, "The Urban Criminal Justice System: Where Young + Black + Male = Probable Cause," 20 *Fordham Urban Law Journal* 621 (1993); Ericka L. Johnson, " 'A Menace to Society': The Use of Criminal Profiles and Its Effects on Black Males," 38 *Howard Law Journal* 629 (1995); David A. Harris, "Factors for Reasonable Suspicion: When Black and Poor Means Stopped and Frisked," 69 *Indiana Law Journal* 659 (1994); Sheri Lynn Johnson, "Race and the Decision to Detain a Suspect," 93 *Yale Law Journal* 214 (1983); Tracey Maclin, " 'Black and Blue Encounters': Some Preliminary Thoughts about Fourth Amendment Seizures: Should Race Matter?" 26 *Valparaiso University Law Review* 243 (1991); Adina Schwartz, " 'Just Take Away Their Guns' ": The Hidden Racism of *Terry v. Ohio*," 23 *Fordham Urban Law Journal* 317 (1996); Carol S. Steiker, "Second Thoughts about First Principles," 107 *Harvard Law Review* 820, 838–844 (1994).

3. See Ira Berlin, *Slaves without Masters: The Free Negro in the Antebellum South*, 93 (1975).

4. *Korematsu* v. *United States*, 323 U.S. 214, 216 (1944).

5. Ibid., 219.

6. See, e.g., Nanette Dembitz, "Racial Discrimination and the Military Judgment: The Supreme Court's *Korematsu* and *Endo* Decisions," 45 Columbia Law Review 175 (1945); Morton Grodzins, *Americans Betrayed* (1949); Peter Irons, *Justice at War* (1983); Eugene Rostow, "The Japanese American Cases: A Disaster," 54 *Yale Law Journal* 489 (1945).

7. See 323 U.S. 214, 236 (1944) (Murphy, J., dissenting).

8. Ibid., 233.

9. See Civil Liberties Act of 1988, codified at 50 U.S.C. 1989 (1988). See also Commission on Wartime Relocation and Internment of Civilians, *Personal Justice Denied* (1982); Leslie T. Hatamiya, *Righting a Wrong: Japanese Americans and the Passage of the Civil Liberties Act of 1988* (1993).

10. See *State* v. *Dean*, 543 P.2d 425, 427 (Arizona 1975).

11. See *United States* v. *Weaver*, 966 F.2d 391 (CA 8 1992), *cert. denied*, 506 U.S. 1040 (1992).

12. See *United States* v. *Martinez-Fuerte*, 428 U.S. 543, 563–564 (1976).

13. This hypothetical is based on the events following the murder of Carol Stuart in Boston in 1989. As it turns out, Stuart's (white) husband almost certainly killed her. He committed suicide after suspicion finally settled on him. See Jonathan Alter and Mark Starr, "Race and Hype in a Divided City," *Newsweek*, January 22, 1990; Margaret Carlson, "Presumed Innocent," *Time*, January 22, 1990; Andrew Kopkind, "The Stuart Case: Race, Class, and Murder in Boston," *The Nation*, February 5, 1990.

14. This hypothetical is based on what happened to Earl Graves, Jr., a young black business executive educated at Yale College and the Harvard Business School. Reflecting on the incident, Graves observed, "Regardless of your status in this life, you are viewed first as a black male. And with that comes a variety of assumptions, most of them negative, that unfortunately white people sometimes have—you're a threat, a suspect, you're less than they are." Lisa Genasci, "Success Is No Shield for Racism Discrimination: No Matter What Positives They Hold, Blacks Say They Daily Confront Adversity That Their White Counterparts Cannot Imagine," *Los Angeles Times*, June 14, 1995.

15. *Dean*, 543 P.2d at 427.

16. 966 F.2d at 394, n.2.

17. Ibid., 394.

18. 428 U.S. 543 (1976).

19. Ibid., 563–564.

20. Ibid., 564, n.17.

21. See *Lowery* v. *Virginia*, 388 S.E.2d 265 (Va. Ct. App., 1990).

22. See, e.g., *United States* v. *Laymon*, 730 F.Supp. 332 (D. Colo. 1990); *United States* v. *Taylor*, 956 F.2d. 572, 580–583 (CA 6 1992) (Keith, J., dissenting); ibid., 591–592 (Jones, J., dissenting).

23. See, e.g., William Ryan, *Blaming the Victim*, 192–218 (rev. ed., 1976); "Developments in the Law: Race and the Criminal Process," 101 *Harvard Law Review* 1472, 1507–1511 (1988); Patricia Williams, "Spirit Murdering the Messenger: The Discourse of Fingerpointing as the Law's Response to Racism," 42 *University of Miami Law Review* 127, 127–130 (1987); Loren Page Ambinder, "Dispelling the Myth of Rationality: Racial Discrimination in Taxicab Service and the Efficacy of Litigation under 42 U.S.C. 1981," 64 *George Washington Law Review* 342 (1996); Johnson, " 'A Menace to Society,' " 629.

24. Williams, "Spirit Murdering the Messenger," 129.

25. See, e.g., *Judgment under Uncertainty: Heuristics and Biases* (Daniel Kahnemann, Paul Slovic, and Amos Tversky, eds., 1982); *The Rational Choice Controversy: Economic Models of Politics Reconsidered*, ed. Jeffrey Friedman (1996).

26. See pages 19–20.

27. Cornel West, *Race Matters* (1993).

28. Measures discriminating *against* racial minorities have been subject typically to a scrutiny that has been " 'strict' in theory [but] fatal in fact." Gerald Gunther, "Foreword: In Search of Evolving Doctrine on a Changing Court: A Model for a Newer Equal Protection," 86 *Harvard Law Review* 1, 8 (1972). For cases illustrating this point, see *McLaughlin* v. *Florida*, 379 U.S. 184 (1964) (invalidating prohibition of interracial cohabitation); *Loving* v. *Virginia*, 388 U.S. 1 (1967) (invalidating prohibition of interracial marriage); *Palmore* v. *Sidoti*, 466 U.S. 429 (1984) (reversing child custody order based, in part, on remarriage of white mother to a black man).

29. See, e.g., *Shaw* v. *Hunt*, 116 S.Ct. 1894, 1902 (1996); *Miller* v. *Johnson*, 115 S.Ct. 2475, 2490 (1995). Ironically, strict scrutiny is understood now to have originated in *Korematsu* v. *United States* (see pp. 138–140).

30. Paul Brest, "Foreword: In Defense of the Antidiscrimination Principle," 90 *Harvard Law Review* 1, 7 (1976).

31. See page 147.

32. 966 F.2d 391, 396–397.

33. See, e.g., *United States* v. *Travis*, 62 F.3d 170, 174–176 (CA 6 1995).

34. In a constitutional setting, a complaining party who proves that he has been subjected to racial discrimination prevails unless the defendant can show that for legitimate nonracial reasons it would have taken the same course absent the wrongful motive. See *Arlington Heights* v. *Metropolitan Housing Development Corporation*, 429 U.S. 252, 270–271, n.21 (1977); *Hunter* v. *Underwood*, 471 U.S. 222, 228 (1985). Statutory civil rights law also acknowledges the problem of mixed motives. See, e.g., 42 U.S.C. § 2000e-5 (G)(2)(B) (Supp. V 1993) (describing procedures for determining liability in mixed motive cases under the Civil Rights Act of 1991).

35. *Arlington Heights* v. *Metropolitan Housing Development Corporation*, 429 U.S. 252, 265–266 (1977).

36. See *Bush* v. *Vera*, 116 S.Ct. 1941 (1996). *Miller* v. *Johnson*, 115 S.Ct. 2475, 2488 (1995).

37. See Jerome H. Skolnick, *Justice without Trial*, 80 (1966).

38. Henry Louis Gates, Jr., "Thirteen Ways of Looking at a Black Man," *New Yorker*, October 23, 1995.

39. *New York Times*, January 23, 1989.

40. Ibid.
41. Don Wycliff, "Blacks and Blue Power," *New York Times*, February 8, 1987.
42. See, e.g., Peter S. Canellos, "Police Force a Confidence Gap, Many Blacks Worried Officers Cover for Own," *Boston Globe*, October 17, 1997; Brent Staples, "The Rodney King 'Soundtrack,' " *New York Times*, September 11, 1995. For an excellent theatrical exploration of this phenomenon, see Charles Fuller, *Zooman and the Sign* (1980).
43. See Douglas S. Massey and Nancy A. Denton, *American Apartheid: Segregation and the Making of the Underclass* (1993); *Race, Poverty, and American Cities* (John Charles Roger and Judith Welch Wagner, eds., 1996).
44. See note 37.
45. Such an officer might say:

    I'm sorry for interrupting your evening, sir, but a crime has been committed by someone who fits your general description. For the protection of all law-abiding members of society, the police have a policy of stopping and questioning those who resemble suspected criminals. Even though I have stopped you, I continue to presume that you are a law-abiding member of society, and so I hope that you can see that you and your neighbors are protected by such a policy. I trust that, upon reflection, you will find it reasonable to assume this burden. We do not suspect *you* of committing a crime, we suspect someone who resembles you. Help us confirm our presumption that you are yourself, and not the suspect you resemble, and we will trouble you no more. It is true that you were picked out for questioning in part because your skin color matches the described skin color of the suspect. . . . I simply am supposing that individuals with your skin color are more likely to be the particular person for whom we are searching.

    See Applebaum, "Racial Generalization," 151.
46. 428 U.S. at 563–564, n.16.
47. Ibid., 564, n.17.
48. *United States* v. *Prendy-Binett*, 995 F.2d 1069, 1075 (CA DC 1993) (Edwards, J., dissenting).
49. See, e.g., *Morgan* v. *Woessner*, 975 F.2d 629 (CA 9 1992); *Washington* v. *Lambert*, 1996 WL 617358 (CA 9 1996).
50. 730 F.Supp. 332 (D. Colo. 1990).
51. Ibid., 333–338.
52. See Morgan Cloud, "The Dirty Little Secret," 43 *Emory Law Journal* 1311 (1994).
53. According to the officer, the defendant signed a form indicating that the

defendant consented to a search. According to the court, the defendant's signature was obtained by coercion. 730 F.Supp. at 340–342 (D. Colo. 1990).

54. Ibid., 336.

55. 428 U.S. at 557–558 (1976).

56. Consider the case of Edward Lawson, a black man who was detained or arrested on approximately fifteen occasions between March 1975 and January 1977 while walking at night, often in predominantly white neighborhoods. *Kolender* v. *Lawson*, 461 U.S. 352 (1983) (invalidating the vagrancy law under which Lawson was arrested).

57. See, e.g., *Morgan* v. *Woessner*, 975 F.2d 629 (CA 9 1992) (describing altercation between police officers and baseball superstar Joe Morgan); Robyn Meredith, "White Officer's Acquittal Brings Protest March," *New York Times*, November 15, 1996 (describing acquittal of white police officer charged with manslaughter following death of black motorist fatally injured during scuffle that attended stop for traffic violation).

58. Reprinted in *Speech and Power: The African-American Essay and Its Cultural Content, from Polemics to Pulpit*, 397 (Gerald Early, ed., 1993).

59. Ibid., 399.

60. Ibid.

61. See, e.g., Barbara Bergmann, *In Defense of Affirmative Action* (1996); Terry Eastland, *Ending Affirmative Action* (1996); Christopher Edley, Jr., *Not All Black and White: Affirmative Action, Race, and American Values* (1996).

62. Compare *Richmond* v. *Croson Co.*, 488 U.S. 469 (1989), with *United States* v. *Martinez-Fuerte*, 428 U.S. 543 (1976).

63. See, e.g., *Wygant* v. *Jackson Board of Education*, 476 U.S. 267 (1986); *Adarand Constructors, Inc.* v. *Pena*, 515 U.S. 200 (1995).

64. See, e.g., *United States* v. *Laymon*, 730 F.Supp. 332 (D. Colo. 1990).

65. Jake Lamar, *Bourgeois Blues*, 128–129 (1991).

66. See George P. Fletcher, *A Crime of Self-Defense: Bernhard Goetz and the Law on Trial* (1988).

67. See, e.g., Dorothy Gilliam, "Law of the Monster," *Washington Post*, June 18, 1987 ("just try to imagine whether a pistol-toting black man would have had such a sweeping vindication had he shot four white teenagers" in similar circumstances).

68. See Fletcher, *Crime of Self-Defense*, 206.

5. Race and the Composition of Juries: Setting the Ground Rules

1. See Paul Finkelman, "Prelude to the Fourteenth Amendment: Black Legal Rights in the Antebellum North," 17 *Rutgers Law Journal* 415 (1986).
2. For useful commentary on the early history of African American jury service, see Albert W. Alschuler and Andrew G. Deiss, "A Brief History of the Criminal Jury in the United States," 61 *University of Chicago Law Review* 867 (1994); Jeffrey S. Brand, "The Supreme Court, Equal Protection, and Jury Selection: Denying That Race Still Matters," 1994 *Wisconsin Law Review* 511; Douglas L. Colbert, "Challenging the Challenge: Thirteenth Amendment as a Prohibition against the Racial Use of Peremptory Challenges," 76 *Cornell Law Review* 1 (1990); Benno C. Schmidt, Jr., "Juries, Jurisdiction and Race Discrimination: The Lost Promise of *Strauder v. West Virginia*," 61 *Texas Law Review* 1401 (1983).
3. Alschuler and Deiss, "Brief History," 887 (quoting *Colored Tribune*, June 3, 1876).
4. 100 U.S. 303 (1879).
5. 103 U.S. 370 (1880).
6. *Strauder*, 100 U.S. at 304.
7. Ibid., 307–308.
8. Ibid.
9. Ibid., 309.
10. Ibid.
11. Ibid., 393.
12. 100 U.S. 310 (1879).
13. Neal, 103 U.S. at 397.
14. See Gilbert Thomas Stephenson, *Race Distinctions in American Law*, 254 (1969 [1910]).
15. Ibid., 256.
16. Ibid., 257.
17. Ibid., 265.
18. Ibid., 268.
19. 287 U.S. 45 (1932).
20. See, e.g., *Gideon* v. *Wainwright*, 372 U.S. 335 (1963), holding that state must appoint counsel to represent indigents in all felony prosecutions.
21. See *United States ex rel Goldsby* v. *Harpole*, 263 F.2d 71, 82 (CA 5 1959). The judges went on to write that "the very prejudice which causes the dominant race to exclude members of what it may assume to be an inferior race from

jury service operates with multiplied intensity against one who resists such exclusion." Community pressures continue to dissuade some defense attorneys from raising jury discrimination claims. See *Gates* v. *Zant* 863 F.2d 1492, 1497–1499 (CA 11 1989), rehearing denied (per curiam), 880 F.2d 293, cert. denied, 493 U.S. 945 (1989). See also Stephen B. Bright, "Discrimination, Death and Denial: The Tolerance of Racial Discrimination in the Infliction of the Death Penalty," 35 *Santa Clara Law Review* 433, 468 (1995).

22. See Schmidt, "Juries," 1462–1472.
23. 75 So. 199 (1917).
24. 236 P. 68 (Cr. Ct. App., 1925).
25. Ibid., 71.
26. Ibid.
27. Ibid., 72.
28. See, e.g., *Murray* v. *Louisiana*, 163 U.S. 101 (1896); *Thomas* v. *Texas*, 212 U.S. 278 (1909); *Williams* v. *Mississippi*, 170 U.S. 213 (1898). See also Schmidt, "Juries," 1462–1472.
29. See, e.g., *Carter* v. *Texas*, 177 U.S. 442 (1900); *Rogers* v. *Alabama*, 192 U.S. 226 (1904).
30. 294 U.S. 587 (1935).
31. Ibid., 591.
32. Schmidt, "Juries," 1479.
33. See Dan T. Carter, *Scottsboro: A Tragedy of the American South* 194–195 (Rev. ed. 1979 [1969]).
34. *Norris*, 294 U.S. at 598–599.
35. Ibid., 599.
36. Ibid., 598.
37. See Colbert, "Challenging the Challenge," 83.
38. 303 U.S. 613 (1938).
39. 311 U.S. 128 (1940).
40. Ibid., 132.
41. 316 U.S. 400 (1942).
42. Cf. Carter, 326 (noting newspaper reactions to *Norris*). The Charleston [South Carolina] *News and Courier* declared that selecting blacks for jury service was simply "out of the question" and that *Norris* "can and will be evaded." Ibid.
43. 325 U.S. 398 (1945).
44. Ibid., 409.
45. Ibid.

46. Ibid.

47. Ibid., 410 (Murphy, J., dissenting).

48. See Jack Bass, *Unlikely Heroes* (1981); John Andrew Martin, "The Fifth Circuit and Jury Selection Cases: The Negro Defendant and His Peerless Jury," 4 *Houston Law Review* 448 (1966). See also J. W. Peltason, *Fifty-eight Lonely Men* (1971 [1961]).

49. *Harper* v. *State*, 171 So. 2d. 129, 134 (Sup. Ct. Miss., 1965). See also *Bass* v. *State*, 182 So.2d 591 (Sup. Ct. Miss., 1966). See, generally, Roger S. Kuhn, "Jury Discrimination: The Next Phase," 41 *Southern California Law Review* 235, 236 n.9 (1968).

50. See *Brooks* v. *Beto*, 366 F. 2d 1 (CA 5 1966).

51. See Howard Smead, *Blood Justice: The Lynching of Mack Charles Parker* (1986).

52. 486 U.S. 214 (1988). See also Bright, "Discrimination," 467–468.

53. See Jon M. Van Dyke, *Jury Selection Procedures*, 86–87 (1977). For critiques of the key-man system of jury selection, see Charles R. DiSalvo, "The Key-Man System for Composing Jury Lists in West Virginia: The Story of Abuse, the Case for Reform," 87 *West Virginia Law Review* 219 (1985); Kuhn, "Jury Discrimination," 235, 260–264; "Arkansas' Key-Man Jury Selection Procedures: Opportunity for Discrimination," 30 *Arkansas Law Review* 527 (1977).

54. See V. Hale Starr and Mark McCormick, *Jury Selection*, 445–457 (2nd ed., 1993).

55. For an especially instructive article on this subject, see Barbara Allen Babcock, "Voir Dire: Preserving 'Its Wonderful Power,' " 27 *Stanford Law Review* 545 (1975).

56. Pub. L. No. 90-274, § 101, 82 Stat. 54 (codified as amended at 28 U.S.C. §§ 1861–1869 (1988)).

57. 396 U.S. 320 (1970).

58. Ibid., 327–328.

59. Ibid., 332.

60. See 100 U.S. at 310. See also *Fay* v. *New York* 332 U.S. 261 (1947), upholding law under which state chose as prospective "blue ribbon" jurors those deemed to be especially well qualified to judge especially difficult or prominent cases.

61. 396 U.S. at 333 (1969).

62. Ibid. at 337 (1969) ("We cannot conclude, even on so compelling a record as that before us, that the guarantees of the Constitution can be secured only by the total invalidation of the challenged provisions.").

63. Ibid., 336–337.
64. See *Shuttlesworth* v. *City of Birmingham*, 394 U.S. 147 (1969).
65. For useful commentary on the vice of vagueness, see Anthony Amsterdam, "The Void-for-Vagueness Doctrine in the Supreme Court," 109 *University of Pennsylvania Law Review* 67 (1960). On the legitimacy of the Supreme Court taking prophylactic measures in order to avoid the necessity of case-by-case adjudication of measures that invite abuse, see David A. Strauss, "The Ubiquity of Prophylactic Rules," 55 *University of Chicago Law Review* 190 (1988).
66. 430 U.S. 482 (1977).
67. Ibid., 497.
68. 339 U.S. 282 (1950).
69. Ibid., 302.
70. Ibid., 304.
71. See Daniel J. Meltzer, "Deterring Constitutional Violations by Law Enforcement Officials: Plaintiffs and Defendants as Private Attorneys General," 88 *Columbia Law Review* 247 (1988).
72. Ibid., 286.
73. *Vasquez*, 474 U.S. at 262.
74. 443 U.S. 545 (1979).
75. 468 U.S. 339 (1984).
76. Ibid., 341.
77. When *Hobby* was decided, it was unclear whether the Court would grant relief to a white defendant who could show that officials had racially excluded blacks from his jury. Subsequently, though, in *Powers* v. *Ohio*, 499 U.S. 400 (1991), the Court held that a white defendant would be entitled to relief if he could prove that a prosecutor; using peremptory challenges, had racially excluded blacks from his jury.
78. Ibid., 342. The Fifth Amendment prohibits the federal government from depriving anyone of life, liberty, or property without due process of law. When the Fifth Amendment became part of the Constitution in 1791, it was certainly not intended to prohibit racial discrimination. Over time, however, the egalitarian aspirations of the Fourteenth Amendment have been read into the Fifth Amendment. Hence, when the Supreme Court belatedly invalidated de jure segregation in public education, *Brown* v. *Board of Education*, 347 U.S. 483 (1954), it simultaneously invalidated de jure segregation in the federal enclave of the District of Columbia, *Bolling* v. *Sharpe* 347 U.S. 497 (1954). Observing that "it would be unthinkable that the same Constitution would impose a lesser duty on the Federal Government [than

the States]," the Court held that de jure segregation represented a denial of the due process clause of the Fifth Amendment. Ibid., 500.

79. *Hobby*, 468 U.S. at 349 (1984).

80. See, e.g., *State* v. *Cofield*, 357 S.E.2d 622, 631 (N.C. 1987) (Webb, J., dissenting).

81. 468 U.S. at 361–362 (Marshall, J., dissenting).

82. Ibid., 353–354.

83. Compare *State* v. *Cofield*, 357 S.E.2d 622, 626 (N.C. 1987) (racial discrimination in selection of grand jury foreman in North Carolina entitles defendant to relief under Equal Protection Clause of federal constitution) with *State* v. *Ramseur* 524 A.2d 188, 244 (N.J. 1987) (racial discrimination in selection of grand jury foreman in New Jersey does not entitle defendant to relief under Equal Protection Clause of federal constitution).

6. Race and the Composition of Juries

1. 380 U.S. 202 (1965).

2. See ibid., 231 (Goldberg, J., dissenting).

3. *Swain*, 380 U.S. at 222, 223.

4. Ibid., 212, 221–222.

5. Ibid., 224.

6. Ibid., 223.

7. Ibid., 241 (Goldberg, J., dissenting).

8. Jeffrey S. Brand, "The Supreme Court, Equal Protection, and Jury Selection: Denying That Race Still Matters," 1994 *Wisconsin Law Review* 511, 564 (quoting "Alabama Seeks End of Scottsboro Case," *New York Times*, November 17, 1935).

9. "Comment, *Swain v. Alabama*: A Constitutional Blueprint for the Perpetuation of the All-White Jury," 52 *Virginia Law Review* 1157, 1174–1175 (1966).

10. 421 F.Supp. 467 (D. Conn., 1976).

11. Ibid., 473.

12. See *United States* v. *Newman*, 549 F.2d 240 (CA 2 1977).

13. Ibid., 251.

14. 583 P.2d 748 (Cal., 1978).

15. Ibid., 762.

16. Ibid., 768.

17. 387 N.E.2d 499 (Mass., 1979).

18. Ibid., 505.

19. Ibid., 515.

20. See *Gilliard* v. *Mississippi*, 464 U.S. 867, 871 (1983) (Marshall, J., dissenting from denial of certiorari).

21. See Randall Kennedy, "Doing What You Can With What You Have: The Greatness of Justice Marshall," 80 *Georgetown Law Journal* 2081 (1992).

22. See Peter Linzer, "The Meaning of Certiorari Denials," 79 *Columbia Law Review* 1227 (1979).

23. *McCray* v. *New York*, 461 U.S. 961 (1983) (Marshall, J., dissenting from denial of certiorari).

24. See *McCray* v. *Abrams*, 576 F.Supp. 1244, 1245 (E.D.N.Y. 1983).

25. *People* v. *McCray*, 443 N.E.2d 915, 916 (N.Y. App. Div. 1982).

26. 461 U.S. 964–965 (1983) (emphasis added).

27. Ibid., 961 (Stevens, J.).

28. 464 U.S. 867 (1983) (Marshall, J., dissenting from denial of certiorari).

29. Ibid., 869–870.

30. See *Williams* v. *Illinois*, *Dixon* v. *Illinois*, *Yates* v. *Illinois*, 466 U.S. 981 (1984) (Marshall, J., dissenting).

31. See *Illinois* v. *Williams*, 454 N.E.2d 220 (1983).

32. *Dixon*, 466 U.S. at 984.

33. See *Harris* v. *Texas*, 467 U.S. 1261 (1984), (Marshall, J., dissenting from denial of certiorari).

34. Ibid., 1264.

35. *McCray* v. *Abrams*, 576 F.Supp. 1244, 1249 (E.D.N.Y. 1983).

36. See *McCray* v. *Abrams*, 750 F.2d 1113 (CA 2 1984).

37. Ibid., 1131.

38. Compare *Booker* v. *Jabe*, 775 F.2d 762 (CA 6 1985), vacated sub nom. *Michigan* v. *Booker*, 478 U.S. 1001 (1086) (following *McCray*), with *United States* v. *Leslie*, 783 F.2d 541 (CA 5 1986), vacated 479 U.S. 1074 (1987) (following *Swain*).

39. See *Batson* v. *Kentucky*, 476 U.S. 79 (1986).

40. Ibid., 101 (White, J., concurring).

41. *Batson*, 476 U.S. at 95, quoting *Arlington Heights* v. *Metropolitan Housing Development Corporation*, 429 U.S. 252, 266 n.14 (1977).

42. Ibid., 95–96, citing *McCray* v. *New York*, 461 U.S. 965 (1983) (Marshall, J., dissenting from denial of certiorari).

43. Ibid., 96–98.

44. Ibid., 125 (Burger, C.J., dissenting).

45. Ibid., 138 (Rehnquist, J., dissenting).

46. Ibid., 105 (Marshall, J., concurring).

47. Ibid., 106.

48. See E. Vaughn Dunnigan, "Discrimination by the Defense: Peremptory Challenges after *Batson v. Kentucky*," 88 *Columbia Law Review* 355 (1988); Katherine Goldwasser, "Limiting a Criminal Defendant's Use of Peremptory Challenges," 102 *Harvard Law Review* 808 (1989); Toni Massaro, "Peremptories or Peers? Rethinking Sixth Amendment Doctrine, Images, and Procedures," 64 *North Carolina Law Review* 501 (1986).

49. See *Batson*, 476 U.S. 91 (1986); *Swain*, 380 U.S. 202, 219 (1965); *Stilson v. United States*, 250 U.S. 583, 586 (1919).

50. See, e.g., *Pace v. Alabama*, 106 U.S. 583 (1882); *Plessy v. Ferguson*, 163 U.S. 537 (1896).

51. See *Powers v. Ohio*, 499 U.S. 400, 410 (1991) ("racial classifications do not become legitimate on the assumption that all persons suffer them in equal degree") quoting *Loving v. Virginia*, 388 U.S. 1, 87 (1967); *Shaw v. Reno*, 509 U.S. 630, 65 (1993) ("racial classifications receive close scrutiny even when they may be said to burden or benefit the races equally").

52. See Kenneth J. Melilli, "*Batson* in Practice: What We Have Learned about *Batson* and Peremptory Challenges," 71 *Notre Dame Law Review* 447, 462–464 (1996) (analyzing post-*Batson* challenges to the use of peremptory strikes in cases from 1986 to 1993); Jere W. Morehead, "When a Peremptory Challenge Is No Longer Peremptory: *Batson*'s Unfortunate Failure to Eradicate Invidious Discrimination from Jury Selection," 43 *DePaul Law Review* 625, 629–635 (1994) (reporting post-*Batson* cases in which prosecutors have successfully asserted nonracial bases for their peremptory challenges); Michael J. Raphael and Edward J. Ungvarsky, "Excuses, Excuses: Neutral Explanations under *Batson v. Kentucky*," 27 *University of Michigan Journal of Law Reform* 229 (1993); Brian J. Serr and Mark Maney, "Racism, Peremptory Challenges, and the Democratic Jury: The Jurisprudence of a Delicate Balance," 79 *Journal of Criminal Law and Criminology* 1, 43–47 (1988) (chronicling the ease with which prosecutors meet the challenge of offering nondiscriminatory reasons for their peremptory challenges).

53. But see *United States v. Thompson*, 827 F.2d 1254, 1256 n. 1, 1260 (CA 9 1987) (prosecutor expressly mentioned race as basis for peremptory challenge); *Lee v. State*, 747 S.W.2d 57, 59 (Tex. Ct. App. 1988) (same). Despite having mentioned race as a basis for striking jurors, the prosecutors in these cases later claimed that race had nothing to do with their selection of peremptory strikes. See generally Raphael and Ungvarsky, "Excuses," 326.

54. See Melilli, "*Batson* in Practice," 459.

55. 530 N.E.2d 1351 (Ill. 1988).

56. See *Griffith* v. *Kentucky*, 479 U.S. 314 (1987). In *Griffith*, the Supreme Court also expressly extended *Batson* to federal prosecutions.
57. 357 S.E.2d 792 (Ga. 1987).
58. Ibid., 795.
59. See Albert W. Alschuler, "The Supreme Court and the Jury: Voir Dire, Peremptory Challenges, and the Review of Jury Verdicts," 56 *University of Chicago Law Review* 153, 171 (1989).
60. See Melilli, "*Batson* in Practice," 470–478. Note that the South Carolina Supreme Court has urged trial courts to require prosecutors to supply reasons *whenever* they exclude members of a defendant's race from a jury. *State* v. *Jones*, 358 S.E.2d 701, 703 (S.C., 1987). See also *State* v. *Holloway* 553 A.2d 166, 170–171 (Conn. 1989).
61. See *United States* v. *Montgomery*, 819 F.2d 847, 851 (CA 8 1987) ("The fact that the government accepted a jury which included two blacks, when it could have used its remaining peremptory challenges to strike these potential jurors, shows that the government did not attempt to exclude all blacks, or as many blacks as it could, from the jury"). By contrast, see the much better reasoned opinion in *United States* v. *Battle*, 836 F.2d 1084, 1086 (CA 8 1987) ("the striking of a single black juror for racial reasons violates the equal protection clause, even though other black jurors are seated"). See generally Melilli, "*Batson* in Practice," 470–478.
62. See *Purkett* v. *Elem*, 115 S.Ct. 1769, 1770–1771 (1995).
63. 526 So.2d 605 (Ala. Crim. App. 1986).
64. Ibid., 615.
65. Ibid., 616.
66. The Alabama Court of Criminal Appeals affirmed the trial judge, asserting that he had applied *Batson* "with extreme caution and sensitivity." Ibid., 608.
67. 368 S.E.2d 838, 839 (1988).
68. Ibid., 839.
69. Ibid., 843 (Frye, J., concurring).
70. 505 U.S. 42 (1992).
71. See Laurence Tribe, *American Constitutional Law*, 1688–1720 (2nd ed., 1988).
72. *McCollum*, 505 U.S. at 54.
73. Ibid. (quoting *Edmonson* v. *Leesville Concrete Co., Inc.*, 500 U.S. 614, 625) (1991). But see ibid., 62–69 (O'Connor, J., dissenting).
74. Goldwasser, "Limiting a Criminal Defendant's Use of Peremptory Challenges," 808.
75. *McCollum*, 505 U.S. at 49.

76. Ibid., 49.
77. See, e.g., *Government of Virgin Islands* v. *Forte*, 865 F.2d 59, 64 (CA 3 1989) ("we will not read *Batson* to make a distinction between white and black defendants"); *State* v. *Carr*, 427 S.E. 2d 273 (Ga. 1993); *State* v. *Knox*, 609 So. 2d 803 (La. 1992). See also Justice Thomas's comment that given the holding and reasoning in *McCollum*, "it is difficult to see how the result would be different if the defendants . . . were black." *McCollum*, 505 U.S. at 62., n.2 (Thomas, J., dissenting).
78. *McCollum*, 505 U.S. at 68 (O'Connor, J., dissenting).
79. Ibid., 69 (quoting Brief of NAACP Legal Defense Fund as Amicus Curiae, *McCollum* v. *Georgia*).
80. Ibid., 60 (Thomas, J., dissenting). On another occasion, Justice Scalia also voiced this point, stating that the Court's regulation of the peremptory challenge creates a situation in which "the minority defendant can no longer seek to prevent an all-white jury, or to seat as many jurors of his own race as possible." *Edmonson* v. *Leesville Concrete Co.*, 500 U.S. at 644 (1990) (Scalia, J., dissenting).
81. As the LDF Brief put it, "whether white defendants can use peremptory challenges to purge minority jurors presents quite different issues from whether a minority defendant can strike majority group jurors." Brief of the NAACP Legal Defense Fund as Amicus Curiae. *McCollum*, at 4–5.
82. Ibid., 7.
83. *Batson*, 476 U.S. at 102, 106 (Marshall, J., concurring).
84. See *Holland* v. *Illinois*, 493 U.S. 474, 497 (Marshall, J., dissenting) (1990).
85. Batson, 476 U.S. at 89.
86. William T. Pizzi, "Batson v. Kentucky: Curing the Disease but Killing the Patient," *Supreme Court Review* 97, 126 (1987).
87. On voir dire, see V. Hale Starr and Mark McCormick, *Jury Selection: An Attorney's Guide to Jury Law and Methods* (1985); Babcock, "Voir Dire: Preserving 'Its Wonderful Power'; Sheri Lynn Johnson, "Black Innocence and the White Jury," 1671–1676; Albert W. Alschuler, "The Supreme Court and the Jury," 157–163; "Developments in the Law—Race and the Criminal Process," 1577–1580.
88. See Barbara Allen Babcock, Voir Dire: Preserving Its Wonderful Power," 27 *Stanford Law Review* 545 (1975). For a manual on aggressive voir dire, see *Minimizing Racism in Jury Trials: The Voir Dire Conducted by Charles R. Garry in People of California v. Huey P. Newton* (Ann Fagan Ginger, ed., 1969).
89. In thirteen states the judge alone conducts voir dire. In eighteen states attorneys are mainly responsible for voir dire. In nineteen states, attorneys

and judges share the responsibility. Under the Federal Rules of Criminal Procedure 24 (a), judges determine who shall conduct voir dire and how it shall be conducted. As of 1985, 75 percent of federal judges conducted voir dire themselves, permitting attorneys only to submit questions for the judges' consideration. See Starr and McCormack, *Jury Selection* 39–40.

90. 409 U.S. 524 (1973). The Court relied heavily upon its decision forty years earlier in *Aldridge* v. *United States*, 283 U.S. 308 (1931) (reversing conviction in federal case in which the trial court refused to permit inquiry into racial prejudice; the defendant was black and the victim white).

91. *Dukes* v. *Waitkevitch*, 393 F. Supp 253, 255 (D. Mass. 1975) *rev'd, Dukes* v. *Waitkevitch*, 536 F. 2d 469 (CA 1 1976), cert. denied, 429 U.S. 932 (1976).

92. 424 U.S. 589 (1976).

93. Ibid., 597.

94. Ibid., 597, n. 9.

95. 476 U.S. 28 (1986).

96. Ibid., 30–31.

97. Ibid., 36–37.

98. Ibid., 53.

99. Ibid., 39.

100. Ibid., 42–43.

101. See, e.g., *Commonwealth* v. *Christian*, 389 A.2d 545, 549 n.11 (Pa. Supreme Ct. 1978); *Commonwealth* v. *Holland*, 444 A2d. 1179 (Pa. Superior Ct. 1982). See also *State* v. *Jones*, 486 N.E. 2d 179 (Ohio App. Ct. 1984) (holding the questioning of racial bias must be made available to defendants upon request).

102. *State* v. *Jones*, 233 S.E. 2d 287 (S.C. 1977).

103. Ibid., 288.

104. See Massaro, "Peremptories or Peers?"; Goldwasser, "Limiting a Criminal Defendant's Use of Peremptory Challenges."

105. See Pizzi, "*Batson* v. *Kentucky*."

106. See David D. Hopper, "*Batson* v. *Kentucky* and the Prosecutorial Peremptory Challenge: Arbitrary and Capricious Equal Protection?" 74 *Virginia Law Review* 811, 826–831 (1988); Melilli, "*Batson* in Practice"; Raphael and Ungvarsky, "Excuses"; Paul H. Schwartz, "Equal Protection in Jury Selection? The Implementation of *Batson v. Kentucky* in North Carolina," 69 *North Carolina Law Review* 1533, 1564–1566 (1991); Joshua E. Swift, "*Batson*'s Invidious Legacy: Discriminatory Juror Exclusion and the 'Intuitive' Peremptory Challenge," 78 *Cornell Law Review* 336, 361–366 (1993).

107. See George Fletcher, *With Justice for Some: Victims' Rights in Criminal Trials*, 251 (1995).

108. See *Batson* v. *Kentucky*, 476 U.S. 79, 107–108 (1986) (Marshall, J., concurring). See also Alschuler, "The Supreme Court and the Jury," 202–211; Note, "The Case of Abolishing Peremptory Challenges in Criminal Trials," 121 *Harvard Civil Right–Civil Liberties Law Review* 227 (1986).

109. The Supreme Court invalidated peremptory challenges based on gender in *J.E.B.* v. *Alabama*, 114 S. Ct. 1419 (1994). Lower courts have extended *Batson* to cover Italian Americans, see *United States* v. *Biaggi*, 673 F. Supp. 96 (E.D.N.Y. 1987), *aff'd*, 853 F.2d 89 (CA 2 1988), *cert. denied*, 489 U.S. 1052 (1989); Native Americans, see *United States* v. *Chalan*, 812 F. 2d 1302 (CA 10 1987); Hispanics, see *United States* v. *Alcantar*, 832 F. 2d 1175 (CA 9 1987), *appeal after remand*, 897 F.2d 436 (CA 9 1990) and still other ethnic groups. Some courts, however, have declined to extend *Batson* to religion, see *Minnesota* v. *Davis*, 504 N.W. 2d 767 (Minn. 1993) or age, see *United States* v., *Cresta*, 825 F. 2d 538 (CA 1 1983).

7. Race and the Composition of Juries

1. See, e.g., Lino A. Graglia, "The 'Remedy' Rationale for Requiring or Permitting Otherwise Prohibited Discrimination: How the Court Overcame the Constitution and the 1964 Civil Rights Act," 22 *Suffolk University Law Review* 569 (1988); U.S. Department of Justice, Office of Legal Policy, *Report to the Attorney General: Redefining Discrimination: "Disparate Impact" and the Institutionalization of Affirmative Action* (1988).

2. See, e.g., Paul Brest, "The Supreme Court, 1975 Term—Foreword: In Defense of the Antidiscrimination Principle," 90 *Harvard Law Review* 1 (1976).

3. See, e.g., T. Alexander Aleinikoff, "A Case for Race-Consciousness," 91 *Columbia Law Review* 1060 (1991); Neil Gotanda, "A Critique of 'Our Constitution Is Color Blind,' " 44 *Stanford Law Review* 1 (1991).

4. See Hiroshi Fukurai, Edgar W. Butler, and Richard Krooth, *Race and the Jury: Racial Disenfranchisement and the Search for Justice* (1993); Nancy J. King, "Racial Jurymandering: Cancer or Cure? A Contemporary Review of Affirmative Action in Jury Selection," 68 *New York University Law Review* 707, 712–719 (1993); National Jury Project, *Jurywork: Systematic Techniques* (2nd ed., 1987) ("American jury systems tend to overrepresent white, middle-aged, suburban, middle-class people and underrepresent other groups"); Cynthia A. Williams, "Jury Source Representativeness and the

Use of Voter Registration Lists," 65 *New York University Law Review* 590 (1990). See also J. Van Dyke, *Jury Selection Procedures* 28 (1977); "Developments in the Law—Race and the Criminal Process," 101 *Harvard Law Review* 1472, 1558 (1988).

5. See *Duren* v. *Missouri,* 439 U.S. 357 (1979); *Taylor* v. *Louisiana,* 419 U.S. 522 (1975).

6. *Washington* v. *Davis,* 426 U.S. 229 (1976).

7. See *Duren,* 439 U.S. 367–368 (1979).

8. See, e.g., *United States* v. *Greene,* 995 F.2d 793 (CA 8 1993), upholding disqualification of felons; *United States* v. *Cecil,* 836 F.2d 1431 (CA 4) (en banc), upholding use of voter registration list as sole source names for potential jurors, *cert. denied,* 487 U.S. 1205 (1988).

9. See, e.g., David Kairys, Joseph B. Kadane, and John P. Lehoczky, "Jury Representativeness: A Mandate for Multiple Source Lists," 65 *California Law Review* 776 (1977); Williams, "Jury Source Representativeness"; "Developments in the Law—Race and the Criminal Process"; Van Dyke, *Jury Selection Procedures.*

10. See "Developments in the Law—Race and the Criminal Process," 1564; Van Dyke, *Jury Selection Procedures,* 133. See also *United States* v. *Benmuhar,* 658 F.2d 14 (CA 1 1981), *cert. denied,* 457 U.S. 117 (1982).

11. *People* v. *Harris,* 679 P.2d 433 (Cal. 1984) (Mosk, J., dissenting). *Harris* is virtually unique in holding that exclusive reliance on voter registration lists as sources for prospective jurors violates the federal Constitution's Sixth Amendment.

12. See Kairys, Kadane, and Lehoczky, "Jury Representativeness," 809–810.

13. 100 U.S. 313 (1880).

14. Ibid., 315.

15. See Marianne Constable, *The Law of the Other: The Mixed Jury and Changing Conceptions of Citizenship, Law, and Knowledge* (1994); Deborah A. Ramirez, "The Mixed Jury and the Ancient Custom of Trial by Jury de Medietate Linguae: A History and a Proposal for Change," 74 *Boston University Law Review* 777 (1994).

16. *Rives,* 100 U.S. at 323.

17. The key articles on this subject are King, "Racial Jurymandering"; and Alschuler, "Racial Quotas."

18. See King, "Racial Jurymandering," 724 n.55.

19. Ibid., 723 n.53, quoting U.S. District Court, Eastern District of Michigan, Jury Selection Plan (1992).

20. See Alschuler, "Racial Quotas."

21. See King, "Racial Jurymandering," 728 n.75.

22. Alschuler, "Racial Quotas," 704.

23. "Developments in the Law—Race and the Criminal Process," 1559. See also Valerie P. Hans and Neil Vidmar, *Judging the Jury*, 138–140 (1986).

24. *Peters* v. *Kiff*, 407 U.S. 493, 503–504 (1972).

25. See Jeffrey Abramson, *We, the Jury: The Jury System and the Ideal of Democracy* 101 (1994).

26. *Georgia* v. *McCollum*, 505 U.S. 42, 68 (O'Connor, J., dissenting).

27. See Stephen J. Schulhofer, "The Trouble with Trials. The Trouble with Us," 105 *Yale Law Journal* 825, 836 (1995).

28. See Johnson, "Black Innocence," 1695.

29. Although Professor King believes that the studies show persuasively that jurors' race can and does matter in decisionmaking in certain contexts, she also rightly notes that the social scientific research on juror conduct "must be viewed with caution." Nancy J. King, "Postconviction Review of Jury Discrimination: Measuring the Effects of Juror Race on Jury Decisions," 92 *Michigan Law Review* 63, 75 (1993). See also Jeffrey E. Pfeifer, "Reviewing the Empirical Evidence on Jury Racism: Findings of Discrimination or Discriminatory Findings?" 69 *Nebraska Law Review* 230 (1990).

30. Johnson, "Black Innocence and the White Jury," 83 *Michigan Law Review* 1611, 1699.

31. Note, "The Defendant's Challenge to a Racial Criterion in Jury Selection: A Study in Standing, Due Process and Equal Protection," 74 *Yale Law Journal* 919, 924–925 (1965).

32. Van Dyke, *Jury Selection Procedures*, 18.

33. See Johnson, 1695–1700.

34. See Ian F. Haney Lopez, *White by Law: The Legal Construction of Race* (1996); F. James Davis, *Who Is Black: One Nation's Definition* (1991); Christopher A. Ford, "Administering Identity: The Determination of 'Race' in Race-Conscious Law," 82 *California Law Review* 1231 (1994).

35. See Alschuler, "Racial Quotas," 733.

36. See, e.g., Bill Ong Hing, "In the Interest of Racial Harmony: Revisiting the Lawyer's Duty to Work for the Common Good," 47 *Stanford Law Review* 901 (1995); Lisa C. Ikemoto, "Traces of the Master Narrative in the Story of African American/Korean American Conflict: How We Constructed 'Los Angeles,'" 66 *Southern California Law Review* 1581 (1993).

37. See, e.g., Jack Levin and William C. Levin, *The Functions of Discrimination and Prejudice,* 74–75 (1982); George Eaton Simpson and J. Milton Yinger, *Racial and Cultural Minorities: An Analysis of Prejudice and Discrimination,* 195–198 (5th ed., 1985).

38. Alschuler, "Racial Quotas," 734.

39. For useful commentary on this issue, see M. Shanara Gilbert, "An Ounce of Prevention: A Constitutional Prescription for Choice of Venue in Racially Sensitive Criminal Cases," 67 *Tulane Law Review* 1855 (1993); Laurie L. Levenson, "Change of Venue and the Role of the Criminal Jury," 66 *Southern California Law Review* 1533 (1993); Note, "Out of the Frying Pan or into the Fire? Race and Choice of Venue after Rodney King," 106 *Harvard Law Review* 705 (1993). All of these commentators argue in favor of racially selective venue procedures which I oppose.

40. See pages 258–259. See also Lewis L. Douglass, "Race, Jury Composition and Change of Venue Applications," *New York Law Journal* 1 (October 1, 1992).

41. See *Powell* v. *Superior Court,* 283 Cal. Rptr. 777 (Cal. Ct. App. 1991).

42. See "Excerpts: L.A. Hearing on Venue of Police Trial," *National Law Journal* 35, June 1, 1992.

43. See *Mallett* v. *State,* 769 S.W.2d 77 (Mo. S.Ct.), *cert. denied*, 494 U.S. 1009 (1990).

44. Ibid., 78.

45. Ibid., 81.

46. Ibid.

47. 770 S.W.2d 243 (Mo. 1989). See also *United States* v. *Bryant,* 471 F.2d 1040, 1043 (CA DC 1972), *cert. denied*, 409 U.S. 1112 (1973).

48. See 494 U.S. 1009, 1012 (1990).

49. "Out of the Frying Pan," 715.

50. Ibid.

51. See Gilbert, "Ounce of Prevention," 1882–1886.

52. Ibid.

53. See Andrew L. Faber, Note, "Change of Venue in Criminal Cases: The Defendant's Right to Specify the County of Transfer," 26 *Stanford Law Review* 131 (1973).

54. See Jack Nelson and David Lauter, "Clinton Vows to Rebuild U.S.," *Los Angeles Times,* October 20, 1992.

55. See Alschuler, "Racial Quotas," 742–743.

56. See, e.g., David Lauter, "Angry Clinton Defends His Cabinet Selections . . . He Attacks Criticism by 'Bean Counters,' " *Los Angeles Times,* December 22, 1992; Julia Malone, "Scuffing up the Cabinet Some Claim Clinton Fails at Diversity," *Atlanta Journal and Constitution,* December 18, 1992; Daniel Seligman, "How to Count Beans," *Fortune,* March 8, 1993.

57. 366 F.2d 1 (CA 5 1966), *cert. denied*, 386 U.S. 975 (1967). For useful commentary on *Brooks* and related cases, see Kuhn, 315–322; Martin, "Recent

Decisions, Conscious Inclusion of Negroes on Grand Jury Venire Is Not Violative of Negro Defendant's Right to Equal Protection: *Brooks* v. *Beto*," 366 F.2d 1 (5th Cir. 1966)," 55 *Georgetown Law Journal* 942 (1967).

58. 366 F. 2d 24 (CA 5 1966).

59. 404 S.E.2d 845 (N.C. 1991).

60. See *Adarand Constructors Inc.* v. *Pena,* 115 S.Ct. 2097 (1995).

61. See *Miller* v. *Johnson,* 115 S.Ct. 2475 (1995); *Bush* v. *Vera,* 116 S. Ct. 1941 (1996); *Shaw* v. *Hunt,* 116 S. Ct. 1894 (1996).

8. Playing the Race Card in a Criminal Trial

1. See Bennett L. Gershman, *Prosecutorial Misconduct,* 6th ed. (1991); Charles S. Mangum, Jr., *The Legal Status of the Negro,* 356–363 (1940); Albert W. Alschuler, "Courtroom Misconduct by Prosecutors and Trial Judges," 50 *Texas Law Review* 629 (1972); Steven D. DeBrota, "Arguments Appealing to Racial Prejudice: Uncertainty, Impartiality, and the Harmless Error Doctrine," 64 *Indiana Law Journal* 375 (1989); Michael T. Fisher, "Harmless Error, Prosecutorial Misconduct, and Due Process: There's More to Due Process than the Bottom Line," 88 *Columbia Law Review* 1298 (1988); Sheri Lynn Johnson, "Racial Imagery in Criminal Cases," 67 *Tulane Law Review* 1739 (1993); Debra T. Landis, "Annotation, Prosecutor's Appeals in Criminal Cases to Racial, National, or Religious Prejudice as Ground for Mistrial, New Trial, Reversal, or Vacation of Sentence: Modern Cases," 70 *American Law Review* 4th 664 (1991); Eva S. Nilsen, "The Criminal Defense Lawyer's Reliance on Bias and Prejudice," 8 *Georgetown Journal of Legal Ethics* 1 (1994); Note, "Banishing the Thirteenth Juror: An Approach to the Identification of Prosecutorial Racism," 92 *Columbia Law Review* 1212 (1992); Note, "The Nature and Consequences of Forensic Misconduct in the Prosecution of a Criminal Case," 54 *Columbia Law Review* 946 (1954).

2. See 155 F.2d 631, 642–666 (CA 2 1946).

3. Ibid., 658–659.

4. *Taylor* v. *State,* 50 Tex. Criminal Reports 560 (1907).

5. *Moulton* v. *State,* 199 Ala. 411 (1917).

6. *Tannehill* v. *State,* 159 Ala. 51 (1909).

7. *Marshall* v. *State,* 85 Tex. Crim. 131 (1919).

8. See *James* v. *State,* 92 So. 909, 910 (Ala. Ct. App. 1922).

9. See *Johnson* v. *State,* 51 So.2d 901 (Ala. Ct. App. 1951).

10. Ibid. (internal quotation marks and citations omitted).

11. See Shari L. Kirkland et al., "Further Evidence of the Deleterious Effects of Overheard Derogatory Ethnic Labels: Derogation beyond the Target," 13 *Personality and Social Psychology Bulletin* 216 (1987). In this widely cited study, researchers concluded that racial slurs overheard by mock jurors affected their judgment to the detriment of defendants even though the mock jurors expressed disapproval of the remarks.

12. *Miller* v. *North Carolina*, 583 F.2d 701 (CA 4 1978).

13. Ibid., 704.

14. Ibid., 708.

15. 602 F.2d 124 (CA 6 1979).

16. Ibid., 125, 126.

17. 546 F.2d 678 (CA 6 1976).

18. Ibid., 679.

19. 470 F.2d 657 (CA 5), *cert. denied*, 93 S.Ct. 1560 (1973). See also *Thornton* v. *Texas*, 451 S.W.2d 898 (Tex. Ct. Crim. App. 1970).

20. 561 N.E.2d 57 (Ill. 1990).

21. Ibid.

22. Ibid.

23. See *Brent* v. *White*, 398 F.2d 503 (CA 5), *cert. denied*, 393 U.S. 1123 (1969); *State* v. *Bell*, 209 S.E.2d 890 (S.C. Sup. Ct.), *cert. denied*, 420 U.S. 1008 (1975); *Rhoden* v. *State*, 274 So.2d 630 (Ala. Ct. Crim. App. 1973).

24. See Alschuler, "Courtroom Misconduct," 652. ("It would be unfair to assert that curative instructions have no amelioration effect whatever.")

25. Ibid.

26. 561 N.E.2d 57, 79 (Ill. 1990) (internal quotation marks and citations omitted).

27. See Alschuler, "Courtroom Misconduct," 648.

28. See *Lawn* v. *United States*, 355 U.S. 339, 359–360 n.15 (1958); *Viereck* v. *United States*, 318 U.S. 236, 248 (1943). See also Federal Rule of Criminal Procedure 52(b) ("Plain errors or defects affecting substantial rights may be noticed although they were not brought to the attention of the Court").

29. 916 F.2d 1310 (CA 8 1990).

30. Ibid., 1347.

31. Ibid., 1351.

32. See *United States* v. *Sawyer*, 347 F.2d 372, 374 (CA 4 1965).

33. Alschuler, 650, "Courtroom Misconduct."

34. Ibid. For a case where this procedure was followed, see *Lucear* v. *State*, 146 S.E.2d 316 (Ga. Sup. Ct. 1965).

35. 653 S.W.2d 227 (Mo. 1983).

36. Ibid., 237.

37. Ibid.

38. See Charles R. Lawrence III, "The Id, the Ego, and Equal Protection: Reckoning with Unconscious Racism," 39 *Stanford Law Review* 317 (1987).

39. See Alschuler, "Courtroom Misconduct," 645 (judges "have frequently attached significance to whether the prosecutor's misconduct was intentional").

40. 542 So.2d 156 (La. 1989).

41. Ibid., 157.

42. Ibid.

43. Ibid., 158.

44. Ibid.

45. The commentary on the doctrine of harmless error is voluminous. Writings on which I rely include Roger J. Traynor, *The Riddle of Harmless Error* (1970); Harry T. Edwards, "To Err Is Human, but Not Always Harmless: When Should Legal Error Be Tolerated?" 70 *New York University Law Review* 1167 (1995); DeBrota, "Arguments Appealing to Racial Prejudice"; Fisher, "Harmless Error."

46. See *Arizona v. Fulminante*, 499 U.S. 279, 294 (White, J., dissenting).

47. 645 A.2d 607 (Del. 1988).

48. Ibid., 610.

49. Ibid., 613, 614–615.

50. 522 So.2d 745 (Miss. 1988).

51. Ibid., 746.

52. Ibid., 747.

53. Briley's resignation does not end this obscene tale, however. When he resigned, he was allowed to retire with a pension. Stephen B. Bright, "Discrimination, Death and Denial," 35 *Santa Clara Law Review* 433, 483 n.197 (1995). See also, "The Briley File," *Fulton County Daily Reporter*, November 7, 1994.

54. Alschuler, "Courtroom Misconduct," 673. See also Gershman, *Prosecutorial Misconduct*, 13-13.

55. See Gershman, *Prosecutorial Misconduct*, 13-13.

56. Ibid., 13-14, 13-16.

57. *Antonelli*, 155 F.2d 661. (CA 2 1946).

58. "Developments in the Law—Race and the Criminal Process," 1595.

59. See Alschuler, "The Supreme Court and the Jury," 211–229; "Developments in the Law—Race and the Criminal Process," 1595–1603; Johnson, "Black Innocence and the White Jury," 1679–1680.

60. 398 S.E. 2d 179 (Ga. 1990).
61. Ibid., 184.
62. 696 F.2d 940 (CA 11 1983), *cert. denied*, 463 U.S. 1210 (1983); 114 S. Ct. 1392 (1994) (denying application for stay of execution).
63. Federal Rules of Evidence 606(b).
64. 483 U.S. 107 (1987).
65. Alschuler, "The Supreme Court and the Jury," 225.
66. Ibid.
67. See ibid., 226 ("Our legal system fosters confidentiality by forbidding disclosure only when disclosure would save a defendant from wrongful punishment").
68. See *Tanner*, 483 U.S. at 127.
69. See, e.g., *Shillcutt* v. *Gagnon*, 827 F. 2d 1155, 1158–1159 (CA 7 1987).
70. See *Shillcutt* v. *Wisconsin*, 350 N.W.2d 686, 695 (Wis. 1984); *Shillcutt* v. *Gangnon*, 827 F.2d. 1155, 1159 (CA 7 1987). By contrast, in *In re Murchison*, 349 U.S. 133, 136 (1955), the Supreme Court asserted that "our system of law has always endeavored to prevent even the probability of unfairness."
71. See Alschuler, "The Supreme Court and the Jury," 154–155, 226.
72. 652 So.2d 354 (Fla. 1995).
73. Ibid., 358.
74. See Jeffrey M. Shaman, Steven Lubet, and James J. Alfini, *Judicial Conduct and Ethics*, 74–82 (2d ed. 1995).
75. *In re The Matter of Stanley Z. Goodfarb*, 880 P.2d 620 (Ariz. 1994).
76. Ibid., 621.
77. *Peek* v. *State*, 488 So.2d 52 (Fla. 1986).
78. 539 F.2d 467 (CA 5 1976).
79. Ibid., 468.
80. Ibid., 469–470 (quoting 28 U.S.C. §455 (a) and (b)).
81. See Stephen B. Bright, "Discrimination, Death, and Denial: The Tolerance of Racial Discrimination in Infliction of the Death Penalty," 35 *Santa Clara Law Review* 433 (1995); Bryan A. Stevenson and Ruth E. Friedman, "Deliberate Indifference: Judicial Tolerance of Racial Bias in Criminal Justice," 51 *Washington & Lee Law Review* 509 (1994).
82. See pp. 59–63.
83. 329 S.E.2d 601 (Ga. Sup. Ct. 1985).
84. Ibid., 603.
85. Ibid., 605–606.
86. For varying perspectives on the O.J. Simpson case, see Jeffrey Abramson, ed., *Postmortem: The O.J. Simpson Case: Justice Confronts Race, Domestic Vi-*

olence, Lawyers, Money, and the Media (1996); Vincent Bugliosi, *Outrage: The Five Reasons O.J. Simpson Got Away with Murder* (1996); Johnnie L. Cochran, Jr., *Journey to Justice* (1996); Christopher A. Darden, *In Contempt* (1996); Alan M. Dershowitz, *Reasonable Doubts* (1996); Tom Elias and Dennis Schatzman, *The Simpson Trial in Black and White* (1996); Robert L. Shapiro, *The Search for Justice* (1996); Jeffrey Toobin, *The Run of His Life: The People v. O.J. Simpson* (1996).

87. See Sally Ann Stewart, "Shapiro Lashes out at Cochran over 'Race Card,'" *USA Today*, October 4, 1995.

88. See, e.g., Toobin, *Run of His Life;* Bugliosi, *Outrage;* Fred Barnes, "The Shame of Lance Ito," *Weekly Standard*, October 16, 1996.

89. See, e.g., Dershowitz, *Reasonable Doubts*, 165; William Raspberry, "Reasonable Doubt Not Unreasonable," *Detroit News*, October 11, 1995.

90. See "People's Motion *in limine* to Exclude from Trial Remote, Inflammatory, and Irrelevant Character Evidence Regarding L.A.P.D. Detective Mark Fuhrman," 1994 WL 737963 (Cal. Super. Doc.) (filed December 12, 1994).

91. See Douglas L. Colbert, "The Motion in *limine* in Politically Sensitive Cases: Silencing the Defendant at Trial," 39 *Stanford Law Review* 1271 (1987); Chaya Weinberg-Brodt, "Jury Nullification and Jury-Control Procedures," 65 *New York University Law Review* 825 (1990).

92. 1995 WL 15923, 23.

93. Ibid., 20.

94. Ibid., 23–24.

95. See "Defense Response to People's Motion *in limine* to Exclude Evidence Regarding the Credibility of L.A.P.D. Detective Mark Fuhrman," 1994 WL 737960 (Cal. Super. Doc.) (filed December 30, 1994).

96. 1995 WL 15923, 26.

97. See Adam Pertman, "Fuhrman Tapes Reveal Raw, Racist Remarks," *Boston Globe*, August 30, 1995; Jessica Siegel, "Former Cop's Slurs Stun Simpson Trial; L.A., Nation Shocked by Violence, Bigotry," *Chicago Tribune*, August 30, 1995.

98. Mark Fuhrman later accepted a plea bargain to settle criminal charges that he committed perjury with his testimony in the Simpson trial. A judge sentenced him to three years' probation and a $200 fine. See Alan Abrahamson, "Fuhrman Enters Plea of No Contest to Perjury," *Los Angeles Times*, October 3, 1996.

99. See, e.g., Bugliosi, *Outrage*.

100. 1995 WL 697928, 15 (Cal. Super. Trans.) (September 28, 1995).

101. Ibid., at 10–13.

102. See Barnes, "The Shame of Lance Ito." See also, "The Unreasonable Doubt," *New Republic*, October 23, 1995 (Johnnie Cochran is a "repulsive and compelling" symbol because "he exploits the basest of the human psyche for money").

103. See Stephen B. Bright, "Counsel for the Poor: The Death Sentence Not for the Worst Crime, but for the Worst Lawyer," 103 *Yale Law Journal* 1835 (1994); Gary Goodpaster, "The Trial for Life: Effective Assistance of Counsel in Death Penalty Cases," 58 *New York University Law Review* 299 (1983); Marcia Coyle, "Fatal Defense: Trial and Error in the Nation's Death Belt," *National Law Journal* 30 (June 11, 1980).

104. *Dobbs* v. *State*, 224 S.E.2d 3 (Ga. 1976); *Dobbs* v. *Zant*, 720 F.Supp. 1566 (N.D. Ga 1989), *aff'd*, 963 F.2d 1403 (CA 11 1991), rev'd 506 U.S. 357 (1993); *Dobbs* v. *Zant* (N.D. Ga.) (order of July 29, 1994). See also Bright, "Counsel for the Poor," 912–915.

105. Quoted in Bright, "Counsel for the Poor," 913.

106. *Dobbs* v. *Kemp*, 790 F.2d 1499, 1513–1514 (CA 11 1986).

107. Ibid., 1513 (quoting the district court).

108. See "Death Penalty Legal Centers Are Closing," *Columbus Dispatch*, February 26, 1926 (describing closure of federal post-conviction defender organizations on account of defending by Congress); "Shortchanging Inmates on Death Row," *New York Times*, October 13, 1995 (criticizing defunding); Anthony Lewis, "Cruel and Reckless," *New York Times*, August 11, 1995. See, generally, Rebecca Marcus, "Racism in Our Courts: The Underfunding of Public Defenders and Its Disproportionate Impact upon Racial Minorities," 22 *Hastings Constitutional Law Quarterly* 219, 222–233 (1994).

109. See Bright, "Counsel for the Poor."

110. 720 F.Supp. 1566, 1576–1577 (N.D. Ga. 1989).

111. See Andrew D. Leipold, "Rethinking Jury Nullification," 82 *Virginia Law Review* 253, 253–257 (1996). Professor Leipold notes that jury nullification even has its own lobby, the Fully Informed Jury Association (FIJA).

112. 105 *Yale Law Journal* 677, 679, 715 (1995).

113. Ibid., 715, 679.

114. 124 Eng. Rep. 1006 (C.P. 1670).

115. See Butler, "Racially Based Jury Nullification: Black Power in the Criminal Justice System," 105 *Yale Law Journal* 677 (1995). See ibid., 702, quoting James Alexander, *A Brief Narration of the Case and Trial of John Peter Zenger Printer of the New York Weekly Journal*, ed. Stanley N. Katz, 93 (1963 [1736]).

116. 26 F.Cas. 1323, 702–703 (C.C.D. Mass. 1851) (No. 15,815).

117. See Butler, "Racially Based Jury Nullification," 693.

118. Ibid., 694. At another point, Butler writes, "Criminal conduct among African-Americans is often a predictable reaction to oppression. Sometimes black crime is a symptom of internalized white supremacy; other times it is a reasonable response to the racial and economic subordination every African-American faces every day." Ibid., 680.

119. Ibid., 712.

120. See, e.g., Michael D. Weiss and Karl Zinsmeister, "When Race Trumps Truth in Court," 7 *American Enterprise* 54 (January–February 1996); Randall Kennedy, "The Angry Juror," *Wall Street Journal*, September 30, 1994; Benjamin A. Holden, et al., "Race Seems to Play an Increasing Role in Many Jury Verdicts," *Wall Street Journal*, October 4, 1995.

121. See Butler, "Racially Based Jury Nullification," 678–679.

122. E. Barton Gellman and Sari Horwitz, "Letter Stirs Debate after Acquittal: Writer Says Jurors Bowed to Racial Issue in D.C. Murder Case," *Washington Post*, April 22, 1990.

123. See Kennedy, "The Angry Juror."

124. See, e.g., Carl Rowan, "Fuhrman Tips the Scale at Simpson Trial," *Chicago Sun-Times*, September 10, 1995 ("A sickeningly racist, sexist, lying sociopath named Mark Fuhrman has virtually guaranteed the outcome of America's explosive double-murder trial, whether he did or did not murder [the victims]. O.J. Simpson will not be convicted by a jury . . . mostly because the jury knows of Fuhrman's perjury and racism").

125. See Patricia Smith, "A Victory O.J. Didn't Deserve," *Boston Globe*, October 4, 1995. See also Paul Butler, "O.J. Reckoning: Rage for a New Justice," *Washington Post*, October 8, 1995.

126. See Butler, "Racially Based Jury Nullification," 693 ("Like other American law, [criminal law] is an instrument of white supremacy").

127. Ibid., 695.

128. See *Powell* v. *Alabama*, 287 U.S. 56 (1932); *Norris* v. *Alabama*, 294 U.S. 587 (1935); Dan T. Carter, *Scottsboro: A Tragedy of the American South*, rev. ed. (1979); James Goodman, *Stories of Scottsboro* (1994).

129. See "Special Issue: The Rodney King Trials," 509.

130. See, e.g., *Moore* v. *Dempsey*, 261 U.S. 86 (1923); *Brown* v. *Mississippi*, 297 U.S. 278 (1936); *Chambers* v. *Florida*, 309 U.S. 227 (1940). Substantive limits on the punitive power of the state have also emerged from struggles against racism. See, e.g., *Coker* v. *Georgia*, 433 U.S. 584 (1977); *Bailey* v. *Alabama*, 219 U.S. 219 (1911).

131. See Randall Kennedy, "Is Everything Race?" *New Republic*, January 1, 1996.

132. See Andrew D. Leipold, "The Dangers of Race-Based Jury Nullification: A Response to Professor Butler," 44 *UCLA Law Review* 109, 16 (1996).

133. See Eric Foner, *Reconstruction: America's Unfinished Revolution, 1863–1877* (1988).

134. See Michal R. Belknap, *Federal Law and Southern Order: Racial Violence and Constitutional Conflict in the Post-Brown South* (1995).

135. Frank Rich, "The L.A. Shock Treatment," *New York Times*, October 4, 1995, quoting Ben Stein.

136. See *Johnson* v. *Louisiana*, 406 U.S. 356 (1972), upholding state law requiring nine of twelve jurors to vote for conviction; *Apodaca* v. *Oregon*, 406 U.S. 404 (1972) (upholding state law requiring ten of twelve jurors to vote for conviction).

137. See, e.g., Mark Curriden, "Jury Reform: No One Agrees on Whether the System Is Broken, but Everyone Is Trying to Change It," *ABA Journal* 72, November 1995; Maura Dolan, "Key State Panel to Consider Major Changes for Trial," *Los Angeles Times*, October 31, 1995, describing recommendation of California governor Pete Wilson to modify unanimity requirement in criminal trials.

138. Butler, "Racially Based Jury Nullification," 594.

139. Ibid., 716 ("Even if just deserts (*sic*) were susceptible to accurate measure, I would reject the idea of punishment for retribution's sake").

140. Ibid.

141. See Alan M. Dershowitz, *The Abuse Excuse* (1994); Kimberly M. Copp, "Black Rage: The Illegitimacy of a Criminal Defense," 29 *John Marshall Law Review* 205 (1995); Patricia J. Falk, "Novel Theories of Criminal Defense Based upon the Toxicity of the Social Environment: Urban Psychosis, Television Intoxication, and Black Rage," 74 *North Carolina Law Review* 731 (1996); Judd F. Sneirson, "Black Rage and the Criminal Law: A Principled Approach to a Polarized Debate," 143 *University of Pennsylvania Law Review* 2251 (1995).

142. See Thomas D. Morris, *Southern Slavery and the Law, 1619–1860* (1996).

143. Ibid., 716, 717.

144. See U.S. Department of Justice, Bureau of Justice Statistics, *1994 Sourcebook of Criminal Justice Statistics*, 172, 178 (1994).

145. Butler, "Racially Based Jury Nullification," 719.

146. See "In Her Own Disputed Words: Transcript of Interview That Spawned Souljah's Story," *Washington Post*, June 16, 1992; David Mills, "Sister Soul-

jah's Call to Arms: The Rapper Says the Riots Were Payback. Are You Paying Attention?" *Washington Post*, May 13, 1992.
147. Butler, "Racially Based Jury Nullification," 719, 722.
148. Ibid., 716.
149. See Butler, "O.J. Reckoning."
150. Compare Michael Walzer, "The Obligations of Oppressed Minorities," in *Obligations: Essays on Disobedience, War, and Citizenship* (1970).
151. Butler, "Racially Based Jury Nullification," 706 n.158.

9. Race, Law, and Punishment: The Death Penalty

1. This notable case has been unfortunately neglected even within the ranks of death penalty abolitionists. Perhaps it will begin to receive the attention it warrants in light of Professor Eric Rise's recent and excellent study of the case. See Eric W. Rise, *The Martinsville Seven: Race, Rape, and Capital Punishment* (1995).
2. *Hampton* v. *Commonwealth*, 58 S.E.2d 288, 298 (Va. Sup.Ct. 1950).
3. Ibid.
4. See Rise, *The Martinsville Seven*, 120.
5. *Hampton*, 58 S.E. 2d at 298.
6. Ibid.
7. Ibid.
8. Ibid., 299.
9. Ibid.
10. Ibid.
11. See Rise, *The Martinsville Seven*, 125.
12. See *State ex rel. Copeland* v. *Mayo*, 87 So.2d 501 (Fla. Sup. Ct. 1956); *Thomas* v. *State*, 92 So.2d 621 (Fla. Sup. Ct. 1957). See also *Williams* v. *State*, 110 So.2d 654 (1959) (thirty-three blacks but only one white executed for rape between 1925 and 1959).
13. *State ex rel. Copeland*, 87 So.2d at 503.
14. See Michael Meltsner, *Cruel and Unusual: The Supreme Court and Capital Punishment*, 86–87 (1973). Meltsner's book offers a close and vivid look at the LDF's campaign against capital punishment by an insightful participant-observer.
15. See *Moorer* v. *State of South Carolina*, 368 F.2d 458 (CA 4 1966).
16. See *Maxwell* v. *State*, 370 S.W.2d 113 (Ark. Sup. Ct. 1963); *Maxwell* v. *Stephens*, 229 F.Supp. 205 (E.D. Ark. 1964); *Maxwell* v. *Stephens*, 348 F.2d 325 (CA 8 1965), *cert. denied*, 382 U.S. 944 (1965); *Maxwell* v. *Bishop*, 257

F.Supp. 710 (E.D. Ark. 1966); *Maxwell* v. *Bishop*, 398 F.2d 138 (CA 8 1968), *vacated and remanded*, 398 U.S. 262 (1970).

17. See Marvin E. Wolfgang and Marc Riedel, "Rape, Racial Discrimination, and the Death Penalty," in *Capital Punishment in the United States*, eds., Hugo Adam Bedau and Chester M. Pierce (1976); Wolfgang, "The Social Scientist in Court," 65 *Journal of Criminal Law and Criminology* 239 (1974); Wolfgang, "The Death Penalty: Social Philosophy and Social Science Research," 14 *Criminal Law Bulletin* 18 (1978).

18. *Maxwell*, 257 F.Supp. at 718.

19. Ibid., 719.

20. Ibid., 720.

21. Ibid., 720–721. On this point, Judge Henley was largely following the lead of Judge Gordon E. Young, who had raised this issue at an earlier proceeding. *Maxwell* v. *Stephens*, 229 F.Supp. at 216–217. A useful discussion of this matter is provided by Dennis B. Dorin in his excellent article, "Two Different Worlds: Criminologists, Justices and Racial Discrimination in the Imposition of Criminal Punishment in Rape Cases," 72 *Journal of Criminal Law and Criminology* 1667 (1981). Wolfgang suggests that he accounted for the consent defense variable, but as Dorin notes, without interviewing all defense lawyers in all of the rape cases studied—something that does not seem to have been done (and even if it were done, one would still face the problem of how much to credit the recollections of losing counsel)—it is impossible to test the alternative hypothesis that Judge Henley suggested. Ibid., 1678–1679.

22. *Maxwell* v. *Bishop*, 257 F.Supp. 720.

23. Ibid., 720.

24. Ibid., 719 n.9.

25. Blackmun had earlier written an opinion upholding the initial denial of federal habeas corpus relief to Maxwell. See *Maxwell* v. *Stephens*, 348 F.2d 325 (CA 8 1965).

26. *Maxwell* v. *Bishop*, 398 F.2d at 147.

27. Ibid., 148.

28. Ibid.

29. 433 U.S. 584 (1977).

30. See Gerhard Casper and Phillip Kurland, eds., *Landmark Briefs and Arguments of the Supreme Court of the United States: Constitutional Law*, vol. 97, 1976 Term Supplement, 891 (1978).

31. Ibid., 871.

32. See *Eberheart* v. *Georgia*, 206 S.E.2d 12 (1974), and *Hooks* v. *Georgia*, 210

S.E.2d 668 (1974). The U.S. Supreme Court vacated the death sentences in both of these cases. See 433 U.S. 917 (1977).

33. Ibid.

34. See Kimberle Crenshaw, "Mapping the Merging: Intersectionality, Identity Politics, and Violence against Women of Color," 43 *Stanford Law Review* 1241, 1265–1282 (1991).

35. 408 U.S. 238 (1972).

36. Robert Weisberg, "Deregulating Death," *Supreme Court Review* 305, 315 (1983).

37. *Furman*, 408 U.S. at 313 (White, J., concurring).

38. Ibid., 309 (Steward, J., concurring).

39. 428 U.S. 153 (1976). See also *Proffitt* v. *Florida*, 428 U.S. 242 (1976); *Jurek* v. *Texas*, 428 U.S. 262 (1976).

40. *Gregg*, 428 U.S. at 189.

41. See, e.g., *Sullivan* v. *Wainwright*, 464 U.S. 109 (1983) (denying application for stay of execution for a petitioner raising a claim of racial discrimination in application of capital punishment); *Shaw* v. *Martin*, 733 F.2d 304, 311–314 (CA 4 1984), *rehearing denied*, 469 U.S. 1067 (1984); *Smith* v. *Balkcom*, 660 F.2d 573, 584–585 (CA 5 1981), *modified*, 671 F.2d 858, 859–860 (CA 5), *cert. denied*, 459 U.S. 882 (1982); *Spinkelink* v. *Wainwright*, 578 F.2d 582, 612–616 (CA 5 1978), *cert. denied*, 440 U.S. 976 (1979).

42. 481 U.S. 279 (1987).

43. For judicial descriptions of the Baldus study, see *McCleskey* v. *Kemp*, 481 U.S. at 286–289. *McCleskey* v. *Kemp*, 753 F.2d 887 (CA 11 1987); and *McCleskey* v. *Zant*, 580 F.Supp. 338, 352–379 (N.D. Ga. 1984). For a view of the Baldus study from the perspective of McCleskey's attorneys, see Petitioner's Post-Hearing Memorandum in Support of His Claims of Arbitrariness and Racial Discrimination, 3–41, 54–56, *McCleskey* v. *Zant*, 580 F.Supp. 338 (N.D. Ga. 1984) (No. C81-2434A) [hereinafter, Petitioner's Post-Hearing Memorandum]; and Brief for Petitioner, *McCleskey* v. *Kemp*, 107 S.Ct. 1756 (1987) (No. 84-6811). For a defense of the Baldus study by its authors, seeD. Baldus, G. Woodworth, and C. Pulaski, *McCleskey v. Zant and McCleskey v. Kemp: A Methodological Critique* (supplement to D. Baldus and J. Cole, *Statistical Proof of Discrimination* (1988)) [hereinafter, *A Methodological Critique*]. For published research by Professor Baldus and his associates related to the testimony they offered on behalf of McCleskey, see David C. Baldus, Charles Pulaski, and George Woodworth, "Comparative Review of Death Sentences: An Empirical Study of the Georgia Experience," 74 *Journal of Criminal Law and Criminology* 661 (1983); David C.

Baldus, Charles A. Pulaski, Jr., George Woodworth, and Frederick D. Kyle, "Identifying Comparatively Excessive Sentences of Death: A Quantitative Approach," 33 *Stanford Law Review* 1 (1980); David C. Baldus, Charles Pulaski, and George Woodworth, "Arbitrariness and Discrimination in the Administration of the Death Penalty: A Challenge to State Supreme Courts," 15 *Stetson Law Review* 133 (1986); and Baldus, "Monitoring and Evaluating Contemporary Death Sentencing Systems: Lessons from Georgia," 18 *University of California at Davis Law Review* 1375 (1985).

44. See Baldus, Woodworth, and Pulaski, "Arbitrariness," 158.

45. See Brief for Petitioner, *McCleskey* v. *Kemp*, in Casper and Kurland, eds., *Landmark Briefs*, Vol. 171, 597, 646 (1988).

46. See 431 U.S. 355 (Blackmun, J., dissenting).

47. 580 F.Supp. at 379.

48. See David C. Baldus, George Woodworth, and Charles A. Pulaski, Jr., *Equal Justice and the Death Penalty: A Legal and Empirical Study* (1990).

49. Brief for Petitioner, 67, *McCleskey* v. *Kemp*, 107 S.Ct. 1756 (1987) (No. 84-6811), quoting Federal Trial Transcript at 1740, *McCleskey* v. *Zant*, 580 F.Supp. 338 (N.D. Ga. 1984).

50. Brief Amici Curiae for Dr. Franklin M. Fisher, Dr. Richard O. Lempert, Dr. Peter W. Sperlich, Dr. Marvin E. Wolfgang, Professor Hans Zeisel, and Professor Franklin E. Zimring in Support of Petitioner Warren McCleskey, 3. *McCleskey* (No. 84-6811) [hereinafter, Brief Amici Curiae for Dr. Fisher].

51. For commentary on this research, see William J. Bowers, with Glenn L. Pierce and John F. McDevitt, *Legal Homicide*, 67–102 (1984); Sarah T. Dike, *Capital Punishment in the United States*, 30–51 (1982); Samuel R. Gross and Robert Mauro, "Patterns of Death: An Analysis of Racial Disparities in Capital Sentencing and Homicide Victimization," 37 *Stanford Law Review* 27, 38–49 (1984); and Gary Kleck, "Racial Discrimination in Criminal Sentencing: A Critical Evaluation of the Evidence with Additional Evidence on the Death Penalty," 46 *American Sociological Review* 783 (1981).

One exception to the agreement with Baldus is a study conducted by the *Stanford Law Review* which found that neither the race of the defendant nor the race of the victim was associated with patterns of capital sentencing in California between 1958 and 1966. See "A Study of the California Penalty Jury in First-Degree Murder Cases," 21 *Stanford Law Review* 1297, 1421 (1967). The contrast between the *Stanford Law Review* study and most of the other research on capital sentencing may reflect real differences in the jurisdictions examined or methodological deficiencies in the Stanford study, which might have obscured racial influences upon capital sentencing in California. See Gross and Mauro, "Patterns of Death," 41 n.55.

Studies consistent with Baldus's findings include William Bowers, G. Pierce, and J. McDevitt, *Legal Homicide* (1984) (covering sentencing patterns in Florida, Georgia, Ohio, and Texas from the effective date of each state's post-*Furman* capital sentencing statute until 1978); Harold Garfinkel, "Research Note on Inter- and Intra-Racial Homicides," 27 *Social Forces* 369 (1949) (studying ten counties in North Carolina between 1930 and 1940); Gross and Mauro, "Patterns of Death" (examining racial patterns in capital sentencing in Arkansas, Florida, Georgia, Illinois, Mississippi, North Carolina, Oklahoma, and Virginia between 1976 and 1980); Michael L. Radelet, "Racial Characteristics and the Imposition of the Death Penalty," 46 *American Sociological Review* 918 (1981) (studying twenty counties in Florida between 1976 and 1977); Marc Riedel, "Discrimination in the Imposition of the Death Penalty: A Comparison of the Characteristics of Offenders Sentenced Pre-Furman and Post-Furman," 49 *Temple Law Quarterly* 291 (1976) (finding continued disproportionate death sentencing of nonwhites after the *Furman* decision); Hans Zeisel, "Race Bias in the Administration of the Death Penalty: The Florida Experience," 95 *Harvard Law Review* 466–468 (1981); Franklin E. Zimring, Joel Eigen, and Sheila O'Malley, "Punishing Homicide in Philadelphia: Perspectives on the Death Penalty," 43 *University of Chicago Law Review* 227 (1976) (reporting on response to homicides in Philadelphia during a portion of 1970); Note, "Discrimination and Arbitrariness in Capital Punishment: An Analysis of Post-*Furman* Murder Cases in Dade County, Florida, 1973–1976," 33 *Stanford Law Review* 75 (1980).

52. See, e.g., William Wilbanks, *The Myth of a Racist Criminal Justice System*, 120 (1987).

53. Brief Amici Curiae for Dr. Fisher, 3, stating that Judge Forrester's critique of the Baldus study was "uninformed and indefensible"; see also Gross and Mauro, "Patterns of Death," 91–92, arguing that several of Judge Forrester's forays into statistical methodology were "ill-informed and wrong." Professors Gross and Mauro highlight five instances in which the judge's assertions are contradicted by academic authorities.

54. 580 F.Supp. at 356.

55. See 753 F.2d 914–917 (Johnson, J., dissenting).

56. See Brief Amici Curiae for Dr. Fisher, 23.

57. Ibid., 896.

58. Ibid., 895.

59. Ibid., 897.

60. Ibid.

61. 481 U.S. 279 (1987).

62. Ibid., 297.

63. Ibid., 309.

64. Ibid., 277, 312.

65. Ibid., 315.

66. Ibid., 319 (internal citations omitted).

67. Ibid., 344 (Brennan, J., dissenting).

68. Ibid., 325.

69 Ibid., 339.

70. Ibid., 345 (Blackmun, J., dissenting).

71. Ibid., 367.

72. Ibid., 367 (Stevens, J., dissenting).

73. Ibid., 312.

74. Ibid., 313.

75. See *Furman*, 408 U.S. at 249–251 (Douglas, J., concurring); ibid., 310 (Stewart, J., concurring).

76. See, e.g., *Amadeo* v. *Kemp*, 486 U.S. 214 (1988) (describing covert effort by prosecutor to minimize jury service of women and blacks).

77. *McCleskey*, 481 U.S. at 298 (internal quotation marks omitted).

78. Ibid., 332 (Brennan, J., dissenting).

79. Ibid., 347 (Blackmun, J., dissenting).

80. Ibid., 316–317.

81. Ibid.

82. For examples of special solicitude, see *Reid* v. *Covert*, 354 U.S. 1, 77 (1957) (Harlan, J., concurring) ("So far as capital cases are concerned, I think they stand on quite a different footing than other offenses. In such cases the law is especially sensitive to demands for . . . procedural fairness"); and *Stein* v. *New York*, 346 U.S. 156, 196 (1953) ("When the penalty is death, we, like state court judges, are tempted to strain the evidence and even, in close cases, the law in order to give a doubtfully condemned man another chance"). See also *Hamilton* v. *Alabama*, 368 U.S. 52, 55 (1961); *Williams* v. *Georgia*, 349 U.S. 375, 391 (1955); *Andres* v. *United States*, 33 U.S. 740, 752 (1948); *Powell* v. *Alabama*, 287 U.S. 45, 71–72 (1932); *Diaz* v. *United States*, 223 U.S. 442, 455 (1912).

83. *McCleskey*, 481 U.S. at 347–348 (Blackmun, J., dissenting); Anthony Amsterdam, "In Favorem Mortis: The Supreme Court and Capital Punishment," *Human Rights* 14 (Winter 1987).
84. *McCleskey*, 481 U.S. at 344.
85. See Weisberg, "Deregulating Death."
86. Cf. *District Attorney for the Suffolk District* v. *Watson*, 381 Mass. 648 (1962) (invalidating state death penalty law in part on grounds of racial discrimination).
87. See U.S. Department of Justice, Bureau of Justice Statistics, *1994 Sourcebook of Criminal Justice Statistics*, 200–201 (1994), noting that 72 percent of Americans in 1993 favored the death penalty for murder while 21 percent opposed it. Clearly, though, most Americans, including many who are highly mobilized politically, support the retention of capital punishment. See Phoebe C. Ellsworth and Samuel R. Gross, "Hardening of the Attitudes: Americans' Views on the Death Penalty," in *The Death Penalty in America*, Hugo Adem Bedan, ed. (1997).
88. See, e.g., Violent Crime Control and Law Enforcement Act of 1994, Pub. L. No. 103-322, 108 Stat. 1796, Title VI (codified as included in scattered sections of 18 U.S.C.).

    Capital punishment has also made gains at the state level. In 1995, New York became the thirty-eighth state to provide for capital punishment. See James Dao, "Death Penalty in New York Reinstated after 18 Years; Pataki Sees Justice Served," *New York Times*, March 8, 1995.

    Because support for the death penalty is so widespread and intense, many officials work hard to court proponents of capital punishment or at least avoid offending them. See Stephen B. Bright and Patrick Keenan, "Judges and the Politics of Death: Deciding between the Bill of Rights and the Next Election in Capital Cases," 75 *Boston University Law Review* 759 (1995).
89. See *Hawkins* v. *Town of Shaw*, 461 F.2d 1171 (CA 5 1972) (en banc) (per curiam); Michael Ratner, "Inter-Neighborhood Denials of Equal Protection in the Provision of Municipal Services," 4 *Harvard Civil Rights–Civil Liberties Law Review* 1 (1968).
90. *Godfrey* v. *Georgia*, 446 U.S. 420, 442 (1980) (Marshall, J., concurring). Compare, e.g., *Woodson* v. *North Carolina*, 428 U.S. 280, 316 (1976) (Rehnquist, J., dissenting) (arguing that appellate review of death sentences will not afford meaningful protection against vagaries or biases set loose by jury discretion in sentencing), with *Godfrey* v. *Georgia*, 446 U.S. at 437–442 (1980) (Marshall, J., concurring) (arguing that appellate review of capital sentenc-

ing cannot assure objectivity and evenhandedness). For a prescient warning against attempts to inject due process within the anarchical domain of capital sentencing, see *McGautha* v. *California*, 402 U.S. 183, 204 (1971), in which Justice Harlan observed that "to identify before the fact those characteristics of criminal homicides and their perpetrators which call for the death penalty and to express these characteristics in language which can be fairly understood and applied by the sentencing authority, appear to be tasks which are beyond present human ability."

For a scathing abolitionist attack on the Court's attempts to rationalize capital sentencing, see C. Black, Jr., *Capital Punishment: The Inevitability of Caprice and Mistake*, 2d ed., 111–156 (1981). But it is Professor Weisberg who provides the most rounded evaluation of the attempt to affirm legal formality within the death penalty context:

> Capital punishment is at once the best and worst subject for legal rules. The state's decision to kill is so serious, and the cost of error so high, that we feel impelled to discipline the human power of the death sentence with rational legal rules. Yet a judge or jury's decision is an intensely moral, subjective matter that seems to defy the designers of general formulas for legal decision.

Weisberg, "Deregulating Death" at 308.

91. See, e.g., *Roberts* v. *Louisiana*, 428 U.S. 325 (1976); *Woodson* v. *North Carolina*, 428 U.S. 280 (1986).

92. Underlining the insistence that sentencing authorities must be allowed to extend mercy, the Court has held that sentencers must also be allowed to consider any mitigating evidence that a defendant seeks to introduce. See *Eddings* v. *Oklahoma*, 455 U.S. 104, 113–114 (1982); *Lockett* v. *Ohio*, 438 U.S. 586, 604 (1978).

93. Kenneth Culp Davis, *Discretionary Justice*, 170 (1969). Compare *Gregg* v. *Georgia*, 428 U.S. 153, 199 (1976) (plurality opinion) ("Nothing in any of our cases suggests that the decision to afford an individual defendant mercy violates the Constitution").

94. On the power of prosecutors in Georgia's system of capital punishment, see Ursula Bentele, "The Death Penalty in Georgia: Still Arbitrary," 62 *Washington University Law Quarterly* 573, 609–620 (1985). See also Barry Nakell and Kenneth Hardy, *The Arbitrariness of the Death Penalty*, 152–158 (1987). The influence of prosecutors in the context of capital cases is only the most dramatic instance of their extraordinary power in the administration of criminal justice as a whole. See, generally, James Vorenberg, "Decent Restraint of Prosecutorial Power," 94 *Harvard Law Review* 1521 (1981); "De-

velopments in the Law—Race and the Criminal Process," 101 *Harvard Law Review* 1472, 1520–1557, 1588–1595 (1988).

95. See, e.g., Joseph E. Jacoby and Raymond Paternoster, "Sentencing Disparity and Jury Packing: Further Challenges to the Death Penalty," 73 *Journal of Criminal Law and Criminology* 379 (1982); Raymond Paternoster, "Race of Victim and Location of Crime: The Decision to Seek the Death Penalty in South Carolina," 74 *Journal of Criminal Law and Criminology* 754 (1983); Michael L. Radelet and Glenn L. Pierce, "Race and Prosecutorial Discretion in Homicide Cases," 19 *Law and Society Review* 587 (1985).

96. *McCleskey*, 481 U.S. at 365 (Blackmun J., dissenting).

97. See *Wygant* v. *Jackson Board of Education*, 476 U.S. 267 (1986).

98. Ibid., 282.

99. Ibid., 283.

100. See Vada Berger, et al., "Too Much Justice: A Legislative Response to *McCleskey* v. *Kemp*," 24 *Harvard Civil Rights–Civil Liberties Law Review* 437 (1989); Paul Schoeman, "Easing the Fear of Too Much Justice: A Compromise Proposal to Revise the Racial Justice Act," 30 *Harvard Civil Rights–Civil Liberties Law Review* 543 (1995).

101. See Naftali Bendavid, "Black Lawmakers Hold Balance on Crime; Legislative Endgame Reveals Caucus's Power, Divisions," *Legal Times*, August 22, 1994; Harvey Berkman, "Race and Death Stymie Crime Bill," *National Law Journal*, August 1, 1994.

102. The evolution of Bill Clinton's views on capital punishment, from evident disapproval to open embrace, vividly reflects the growing influence of public sentiment favoring retention and enforcement of capital punishment. See Marshall Frady, "Annals of Law and Politics: Death in Arkansas," *New Yorker* 105 (February 22, 1993); George E. Jordan, "Campaign '92: Clinton and Crime; Supports Capital Punishment as Sign of Toughness," *Newsday*, May 4, 1992. Clinton neither openly opposed nor openly supported the RJA, a remarkable stance that reflects the tortured state of public opinion over race relations and the death penalty. See William Douglas, "Clinton Won't Back Racial Justice Act," *Newsday*, July 15, 1994; Mitchell Locin, "Clinton's Crime Bill Gamble; President Shunts Aside Black Allies, Wows Right," *Chicago Tribune*, July 25, 1994; Katherine Q. Seelye, "White House Offers Compromise to Free Logjam on Crime Measure," *New York Times*, July 21, 1994; "The Silent White House," *New York Times*, July 15, 1994.

103. Many of those who opposed the RJA on the grounds that it would inevitably create pressures for race-norming in prosecutorial decisionmaking have similarly opposed other measures that define racial discrimination

more broadly than the intent to discriminate and that shift burdens of persuasion upon showings of racial disparity. One significant episode of opposition culminated in President George Bush's veto of antidiscrimination legislation in 1990, on the grounds that it encouraged racial quotas in hiring. See Message to the Senate Returning without Approval the Civil Rights Act of 1990, 26 Weekly Compilation of Presidential Documents 1632 (October 22, 1990).

104. See Dissenting Views on Racial Justice Act, Report 103-458, House Committee on the Judiciary, 103d Congress, 2d Sess., March 24, 1994, at 13.

105. Ibid., 14.

106. *Plessy* v. *Ferguson*, 163 U.S. 537, 554 (Harlan, Jr., dissenting) (1896).

107. "We are justly punished for those exclusive attachments which make us blind and unjust, and limit our universe to the persons we love. All the preferences of friendship are thefts committed against the human race and the fatherland. Men are all our brothers, they should all be our friends." J. Rousseau, *Correspondence générale*, IV:82 (1925), quoted in Sanford Levinson, "Testimonial Privileges and the Preferences of Friendship," 1984 *Duke Law Journal* 631.

10. Race, Law, and Punishment: The War on Drugs

1. See Eva Bertram, Morris Blachman, Kenneth Sharpe, and Peter Andreas, *Drug War Politics: The Price of Denial* (1996); Steven B. Duke and Albert C. Gross, *America's Longest War: Rethinking Our Tragic Crusade against Drugs* (1993).

2. See Michael Tonry, *Malign Neglect: Race, Crime, and Punishment in America*, 81–124 (1995); Alfred Blumstein, "Prisons," in *Crime*, ed., James Q. Wilson and Joan Petersilia, 398–401 (1995).

3. See Patricia A. Turner, *I Heard It through the Grapevine: Rumor in African-American Culture*, 180–201 (1993). A poll conducted in New York City in 1990, for instance, found that of the blacks interviewed, one quarter said that "the government deliberately makes sure that drugs are easily available in poor black neighborhoods in order to harm black people." See Jason DeParle, "Talk of Government Being out to Get Blacks Falls on More Attentive Ears," *New York Times*, October 29, 1990. Louis Farrakhan holds this view. He has stated that "the epidemic of drugs and violence in the black community stems from a calculated attempt by whites to foster black self-destruction." See Howard Kurtz, "Conspiracy or Paranoia? Some Think Drugs Are Allowed to Hurt Black Communities," *Seattle Times*, January 7, 1990.

This view has been reinforced by allegations that the Central Intelligence Agency facilitated the importation of cocaine into the United States by opponents of the Sandanista Nicaraguan regime, which the United States sought to topple in the 1980s. See, e.g., Gregory L. Vistica and Vern E. Smith, "Was the CIA Involved in the Crack Epidemic?" *Newsweek* 72 (September 30, 1996); Jack E. White, "Crack, Contras and Cyberspace: When It Comes to the CIA and Drugs, Are the Paranoids on the Right Track?" *Time* 59 (September 30, 1996).

4. Diana R. Gordon, *The Return of the Dangerous Classes: Drug Prohibition and Policy Politics* (1994); Clarence Lusane, *Pipe Dream Blues: Racism and the War on Drugs* (1991); Jerome G. Miller, *Search and Destroy: African-American Males in the Criminal Justice System*, 80–86 (1996).

5. See, e.g., Tonry, *Malign Neglect*, 81–124.

6. See Jacqueline Berrien, "Pregnancy and Drug Use: The Dangerous and Unequal Use of Punitive Measures," 2 *Yale Journal of Law and Feminism* 239 (1990); Dawn Johnsen, "Shared Interests: Promoting Healthy Births without Sacrificing Women's Liberty," 43 *Hastings Law Journal* 569, 611–613 (1992); Dorothy Roberts, "Punishing Drug Addicts Who Have Babies: Women of Color, Equality, and the Right of Privacy," 104 *Harvard Law Review* 1419 (1991).

7. See Roberts, "Punishing Drug Addicts Who Have Babies," at 1420.

8. See *Johnson* v. *Florida*, 602 So.2d 1288 (1992). For similar rulings, see *Commonwealth* v. *Welch*, 864 S.W.2d 280 (Ky. 1993); *State* v. *Gray*, 584 N.E.2d 710 (Ohio 1992). For a ruling reaching the opposite conclusion, see *Whitner* v. *State of South Carolina*, 1996 S.C. Lexis 120.

9. See, e.g., Janet Gallagher, "Prenatal Invasions and Interventions: What's Wrong with Fetal Rights," 10 *Harvard Women's Law Journal* 9 (1987); Susan Goldberg, "Medical Choices during Pregnancy: Whose Decision Is It Anyway?" 41 *Rutgers Law Review* 591 (1989); Note, "Pregnancy Police: The Health Policy and Legal Implications of Punishing Pregnant Women for Harm to Their Fetuses," 16 *New York University Review of Law and Social Change* 277 (1988).

10. See Roberts, "Punishing Drug Addicts," 1424, 1432, 1481.

11. Ibid., 1436–1444, 1436.

12. Ibid., 1421 n.6.

13. 198 U.S. 500 (1905).

14. Ibid., 508. Clearly federalism concerns also influenced the Court's response.

15. 554 F.2d 645 (CA 4 1977).

16. Ibid., 647.

17. Ibid., 648.

18. 116 S.Ct. 1480 (1995).
19. In an attempt to assuage the court's concerns, the government produced a list of 3,500 defendants prosecuted for federal drug crimes in the preceding three years. Blacks were the defendants in all but eleven instances, and in these cases the defendants were also of color. See 116 S.Ct. at 1495 n.6 (Stevens, J., dissenting).
20. See *United States* v. *Armstrong*, 48 F.3d 1508 (CA 9 1995).
21. *Armstrong*, 116 S.Ct. at 1487 (1996).
22. Ibid., 1494 (Stevens, J., dissenting).
23. See Drew S. Days III, "Race and the Federal Criminal Justice System: A Look at the Issue of Selective Prosecution," 48 *Maine Law Review* 179, 184–189 (1996) (suggesting that nondiscriminatory explanations account for disparities that appear initially to arise from racially selective decision-making by law enforcement officials). But see the Supreme Court 1995 Term, "Race-Based Selective Prosecution," 110 *Harvard Law Review* 165 (1996).
24. See Roberts, "Punishing Drug Addicts," 1432 ("Poor black women . . . are the primary targets of prosecutors, not because they are more likely to be guilty of fetal abuse, but because they are black and poor").
25. See Chasnoff, Lendress, and Barrett, "The Prevalence of Illicit Drug or Alcohol Use during Pregnancy and Discrepancies in Mandatory Reporting in Pinelles County, Florida," 322 *New England Journal of Medicine* 1201 (1990).
26. Roberts, "Punishing Drug Addicts," 1433–1434.
27. Ibid., 1435 n.85.
28. Ibid., 1434 n.78.
29. Ibid., 1434–1435.
30. Ibid. at 1429 ("Data on the extent and potential severity of maternal cocaine use [on infants] are controversial.") Compare, e.g., Linda C. Mayes, Richard H. Granger, Mark H. Bornstein, and Barry Zuckerman, "The Problem of Prenatal Cocaine Exposure: A Rush to Judgment," *Journal of the American Medical Association*, January 15, 1992, with Joseph J. Volpe, "Mechanisms of Disease: Effect of Cocaine Use on the Fetus," *New England Journal of Medicine*, August 6, 1992.
31. Ibid., 1432.
32. Ibid., 1454.
33. Ibid., 1422.
34. See Paul A. Logli, "The Prosecutor's Role in Solving the Problem of Prenatal Drug Use and Substance Abused Children," 43 *Hastings Law Journal*

559 (1992); Charles M. London, "Clinton's Cocaine Babies," *Policy Review* (Spring 1995).

35. For arguments in favor of using prosecution as part of a strategy for deterring illicit drug use by pregnant women, pressuring drug users to participate in rehabilitation programs, or placing women in circumstances in which drugs are inaccessible (i.e., prison), see Logli, "Prosecutor's Role"; Louise M. Chan, "S.O.S. from the Womb: A Call for New York Legislation Criminalizing Drug Use during Pregnancy," 21 *Fordham Urban Law Journal* 199 (1993); Lisa M. Noller, "Taking Care of Two: Criminalizing the Ingestion of Controlled Substances during Pregnancy," *University of Chicago Law School Roundtable* 367 (1995).

36. Compare Randall Kennedy, "*McCleskey* v. *Kemp*: Race, Capital Punishment, and the Supreme Court," 101 *Harvard Law Review* 1388 (1988) (criticizing failure of legal system to protect African-Americans from criminality) with Stephen L. Carter, "When Victims Happen to Be Black," 97 *Yale Law Journal* 420 (1988) (same).

37. Pub. L. No. 99-570, 100 Stat. 3207 (1986).

38 Pub. L. No. 100-690, 102 Stat 4181 (1988).

39. See *United States* v. *Clary*, 846 F.Supp. 768, 786 (E.D. Mo.), rev'd, 34 F.3d 709 (CA 8 1994), *cert. denied*, 115 S.Ct. 1172 (1995).

40. See, e.g., Matthew F. Leitman, "A Proposed Standard of Equal Protection Review for Classifications within the Criminal Justice System That Have a Racially Disparate Impact: A Case Study of the Federal Sentencing Guidelines' Classification between Crack and Powder Cocaine," 25 *University of Toledo Law Review* 215 (1994); Knoll D. Lowney, "Smoked Not Snorted: Is Racism Inherent in Our Crack Cocaine Laws?" 45 *Washington University Journal of Urban and Contemporary Law* 121 (1994); David A. Sklansky, "Cocaine, Race, and Equal Protection," 47 *Stanford Law Review* 1283 (1995).

41. See, e.g., "Race and Drug Laws," *San Francisco Chronicle*, October 23, 1995; "Equal Before the Law," *The Atlanta Constitution*, October 20, 1995; "The Sentence Guidelines Straitjacket," *Chicago Tribune*, September 5, 1993; "Even among Drug Peddlers, Justice Isn't Blind," *St. Louis Post-Dispatch*, December 24, 1991. See also Diana Gordon, "Crack in the Penal System," *The Nation*, December 4, 1995; Sam V. Meddis, "Is the Drug War Racist? Disparities Suggest that the Answer is Yes," *U.S.A. Today*, July 23, 1993; Salim Muwakkil, "Young Black Men Victims in War on Drugs," *Chicago Sun-Times*, March 13, 1996; Carl Rowan, "Racism in Drug Sentencing Laws Puts Black America Behind Bars," *Chicago Sun-Times*, November 10, 1995.

42. *State* v. *Russell*, 477 N.W.2d 886 (Minn. 1991).

43. See Amendments to the Sentencing Guidelines for United States Courts, 60 Fed. Reg. 25,074 (May 10, 1995).

44. See, e.g., *United States* v. *Dumas*, 64 F.3d 1427 (Boochever, J., concurring) (CA 9 1995) (describing the crack-powder differential as "an unjustified distinction with appalling racial effects"); *United States* v. *Then*, 56 F.3d 464 (Calabresi, J., concurring) (CA 2 1995) ("The unfavorable and disproportionate impact that the 100-to-1 crack/cocaine sentencing ratio has on members of racial minority groups is deeply troubling"); *United States* v. *Willis*, 967 F.2d 1220, 1226–1227 (Heaney, J., and Lay, J., concurring) (CA 8 1992). See also Robert L. Carter, "The Criminal Justice System Is Infected with Racism," *Vital Speeches*, March 1, 1996.

45. *United States* v. *Clary*, 846 F.Supp. 768 (E.D. Mo.), rev'd, 34 F.3d 709 (CA 8 1994), *cert. denied*, 115 S.Ct. 1172 (1995).

46. Ibid., 786.

47. Ibid., 796–797.

48. Ibid., 775.

49. Ibid., 775–776.

50. Ibid., 778.

51. "The Id, the Ego, and Equal Protection: Reckoning with Unconscious Racism," 39 *Stanford Law Review* 317 (1987).

52. 846 F.Supp. 778–779 (E.D. Mo. 1995).

53. Ibid., 782, 783.

54. Ibid., 784.

55. Ibid., 784.

56. Ibid., 792.

57. Ibid.

58. Ibid., 782.

59. Ibid., 792.

60. See, e.g., David Musto, *The American Disease: Originals of Narcotic Control*, expanded ed. (1987); Denise Heard, "Prohibition, Racism and Class Politics in the Post Reconstruction South," 13 *Journal of Drug Issues* 77 (1983).

61. Remarkably little has been written about the initial response of the black members of Congress to the advent of crack cocaine. For an exception see Ted Gest, "New War Over Crack; Racism Wasn't An Issue When Laws First Passed," *U.S. News & World Report*, November 6, 1995. See also Randall Kennedy "Is Everything Race?" *New Republic*, January 1, 1996.

62. See "The Urgent Need to Attack 'Crack,' " E 132 Cong. Rec. 944, March 21, 1986.

63. 132 Cong. Rec. H 2705, August 1, 1986.

64. 132 Cong. Rec. H 5939, August 11, 1986.

65. Ibid.

66. Ibid.

67. See Sklansky, "Cocaine," 49.

68. Duke and Gross, *America's Longest War*, 69.

69. See Charles and Barbara Whalen. *The Longest Debate: A Legislative History of the 1964 Civil Rights Act* (1985).

70. See, e.g., *United States* v. *Thompson*, 27 F.3d 671 (CA DC 1994), *cert. denied*, 115 S.Ct. 650 (1994); *United States* v. *Frazier*, 981 F.2d 92 (CA 3 1992), *cert. denied*, 113 S.Ct. 1661 (1993); *United States* v. *Colbert*, 894 F.2d 373 (CA 10 1990), *cert. denied*, 496 U.S. 911 (1990). In *United States* v. *Walls*, 841 F.Supp. 24, 31 (D.D.C. 1994), a district court judge found the crack sentencing scheme to be in violation of the Eighth Amendment. That ruling, however, was subsequently reversed. See *United States* v. *Walls*, 70 F.3d 1323 (CA D.C. 1995).

71. See Kate Stith, "The Government Interest in Criminal Law: Whose Interest Is It, Anyway?" in *Public Values in Constitutional Law*, ed. Stephen E. Gottlieb, 137, 158 (1993). Professor Stith's comments were specifically directed at the decision of the Minnesota Supreme Court in *State* v. *Russell*, 477 N.W.2d 886 (Minn. 1991), in which the Minnesota Supreme Court reached the same conclusions as did Judge Cahill in *Clary*. For a critique of *Russell*, see Randall Kennedy, "The State, Criminal Law, and Racial Discrimination: A Comment," 107 *Harvard Law Review* 1255, 1261–1270 (1994).

72. *Hunter* v. *Underwood*, 471 U.S. 222 (1985).

73. 846 F.Supp. 785, 787 (E.D. Mo. 1995). See also Jimmie L. Reeves and Richard Campbell, *Cracked Coverage: Television News, the Anti-Cocaine Crusade, and the Reagan Legacy* (1994).

74. "Crack Use, Crime by Crack Users, and Ethnicity," in *Ethnicity, Race, and Crime: Perspectives across Time and Space*, ed. Darnell F. Hawkins, 212, 231, 214 (1995).

75. See Douglas S. Massey and Nancy A. Denton, *American Apartheid: Segregation and the Making of the Underclass* (1993); Douglas S. Massey, "Getting away with Murder: Segregation and Violent Crime in Urban America," 143 *University of Pennsylvania Law Review* 1203 (1995).

76. See Richard B. Woodward, "Under Their Skin," *New York Times Magazine*, December 5, 1993.

77. See Tim Appelo, "Are These Photographs Racist, or Real?; 'Cocaine True':

The Furor over Crack's Color," *Washington Post*, April 10, 1994. See also Barbara Carton, "Photographer Accused of Shooting with a Biased Lens; Eugene Richards' Pictorial of Addicts Sparks a Furor," *Boston Globe*, March 14, 1994.

78. See *United States* v. *Clary*, 34 F.3d 709 (CA 8 1994), cert. denied, 115 S.Ct. 1172 (1995). See also U.S. Sentencing Commission, *Special Report to the Congress: Cocaine and Federal Sentencing Policy*, 214–215 (1995), noting that as of February 1995, all final judicial rulings had concluded that the crack–powder distinction did not violate the federal Equal Protection Clause.

79. Amendments to the Sentencing Guidelines for United States Courts, 60 Fed. Reg. 25,074, 25,075–25,077 (May 10, 1995).

80. See Pub. L. 104–38, 109 Stat. 334 (October 30, 1995); Ann Devory, "Clinton Retains Tough Law on Crack Cocaine; Panel's Call to End Disparity in Drug Sentencing Is Rejected," *Washington Post*, October 31, 1995.

81. U.S. Sentencing Commission, 197.

82. Ibid., 192.

83. See U.S. Sentencing Commission, Amendments, 25074, 25076.

84. Ibid., 25077.

85. See "The Urgent Need to Attack 'Crack,'" E 132 Cong. Rec. 944, March 21. 1986.

86. See 141 Cong. Rec. H 10255, 10273, 10260 (October 18, 1995).

87. See Comprehensive Methamphetamine Control Act of 1996, 21 U.S.C. § 801, Pub.L. 104–237, 101 Stat. 3099 (October 3, 1996). See also Paul M. Barrett, "FBI's Antiviolence Campaign in Los Angeles Is Again Raising Issue of Racial Discrimination," *Wall Street Journal,* February 1, 1996 (noting that whites constituted 72.9 percent of the persons prosecuted for methamphetamine offenses in 1994, while blacks constituted only 1.6 percent of the persons prosecuted). See Minn. Stat. §§152.021-.023 (Supp. 1993); see also Debra L. Dailey, "Prison and Race in Minnesota," 64 *University of Colorado Law Review* 761, 776–777 (1993), explaining that, in order to preserve severe punishment of crack cocaine offenses in the face of *Russell*, the Minnesota legislature increased penalties for powdered cocaine offenses to the same level of severity.

88. President Clinton has suggested addressing the racial disparities complained about by increasing the penalty for distributing powder cocaine. See Ann Devroy, "Clinton Retains Tough Law on Crack Cocaine; Panel's Call to End Disparity in Drug Sentencing Is Rejected," *Washington Post*, October 31, 1995. Representative Gerald B. H. Solomon (R.-NY) has also proposed leveling up punishments for powder cocaine offenses to the same

severity as punishments for crack cocaine offenses. See Cong. Rec. No. 2128 (November 8, 1995).

89. See Duke and Gross, *America's Longest War*; Bertram, Blaichman, Sharpe, and Andreas, *Drug War Politics*; Ethan A Nadelmann, "Thinking Seriously About Alternatives to Drug Prohibition," *Daedalus: Journal of the American Academy of Arts and Sciences* (Summer 1992); Kurt L. Schmoke, "An Argument in Favor of Decriminalization," 18 *Hofstra Law Review* 501 (1990).

Bibliography

Cases

Adarand Constructors, Inc. v. *Pena.* 515 U.S. 200 (1995).

Ah Sin v. *Wittman.* 198 U.S. 500 (1905).

Akins v. *Texas.* 325 U.S. 398 (1945).

Aldridge v. *United States.* 283 U.S. 308 (1931).

Amadeo v. *Zant.* 486 U.S. 214 (1988).

Andres v. *United States.* 333 U.S. 740 (1948).

Ann v. *State.* 30 Tenn. 159 (1850).

Apodaca v. *Oregon.* 406 U.S. 404 (1972).

Arizona v. *Fulminante.* 499 U. S. 279 (1991).

Bailey v. *Alabama.* 219 U.S. 219 (1911).

Banks v. *State.* 143 Ark. 154 (1920).

Bass v. *State.* 182 So.2d 591 (Miss. 1966).

Batson v. *Kentucky.* 476 U.S. 79 (1986).

Battle v. *Anderson.* 376 F.Supp. 402 (E.D. Okla. 1974).

Blair v. *Armontrout.* 916 F.2d 1310 (CA 8 1990).

Blevins v. *Brew.* 593 F.Supp. 245 (W.D. Wis. 1984).

Booker v. *Jabe.* 775 F.2d 762 (CA 6 1985), *vacated sub. nom Michigan* v. *Booker*, 478 U.S. 1001 (1986).

Bounds v. *Smith.* 430 U.S. 817 (1977).

Branch v. *State.* 526 So.2d 605 (Ala. Crim. App. 1986).

Brent v. *White.* 398 F.2d 503 (CA 5 1968), *cert. denied*, 393 U.S. 1123 (1969).

Brooks v. *Beto.* 366 F.2d 1 (CA 5 1966), *cert. denied*, 386 U.S. 975 (1967).

Brown v. *Mississippi.* 297 U.S. 278 (1936).

Brown v. *State.* 173 Miss. 542 (1935).

Brzonkala v. *Virginia Polytechnic and State University.* 935 F.Supp. 779 (W.D. Va. 1996).

Bush v. *Vera.* 116 S.Ct. 1941 (1996).

Bushnell's Case. 124 Eng. Rep. 1006 (Ct. Comm. Pleas 1670).

Butler v. *Cooper.* 554 F.2d 645 (CA 4 1977).

Callins v. *Collins.* 510 U.S. 1141 (1994).

Carraway v. *State.* 163 Miss. 639 (1932).

Carter v. *Jury Commission of Greene County.* 396 U.S. 320 (1970).

Carter v. *Texas.* 177 U.S. 442 (1900).

Cassell v. *Texas.* 339 U.S. 282 (1950).

Castanada v. *Partida.* 430 U.S. 482 (1977).

Chambers v. *Florida.* 309 U.S. 227 (1940).

City of Los Angeles v. *Lyons.* 461 U.S. 95 (1983).

City of Mobile v. *Bolden.* 446 U.S. 55 (1980).

Civil Rights Cases. 109 U.S. 3 (1883).

Coker v. *Georgia.* 433 U.S. 584 (1977).

Commonwealth v. *Christian.* 389 A.2d 545 (Pa. Sup. Ct. 1978).

Commonwealth v. *Holland.* 444 A.2d 1179 (Pa. Super. Ct. 1982).

Commonwealth v. *Soares.* 387 N.E.2d 499 (Mass. Sup. Ct. 1979).

Commonwealth v. *Welch*, 864 S.W. 2d 280 (Ky. Sup. Ct. 1993).

Cooper v. *Aaron.* 358 U.S. 1 (1958).

Currin v. *State.* 638 N.E.2d 1319 (Ind. Ct. App. 1994).

Diaz v. *United States.* 223 U.S. 442 (1912).

Dobbs v. *State.* 224 S.E.2d 3 (Ga. Sup. Ct. 1976).

Dobbs v. *Zant.* 720 F.Supp. 1566 (N.D. Ga. 1989), *aff'd* 963 F.2d 1403 (CA 11 1991), *rev'd* 506 U.S. 357 (1993).

Dobbs v. *Zant.* No. 4:80 -cv- 247-HLM (N.D. Ga. Aug. 7, 1989).

Doe v. *Doe.* 929 F.Supp. 608 (D. Conn. 1996).

Dorsey v. *State.* 108 Ga. 477 (1899).

Dukes v. *Waitkevitch*. 393 F.Supp. 253 (D. MA 1975).

Dupree v. *State*. 33 Ala. 380 (1859).

Duren v. *Missouri*. 439 U.S. 357 (1979).

Eberheart v. *State*. 206 S.E.2d 12 (Ga. Sup. Ct. 1974).

Eddings v. *Oklahoma*. 455 U.S. 104 (1982).

Edmonson v. *Leesville Concrete Co., Inc*. 500 U.S. 614 (1991).

Ex parte Brandley. 781 S.W.2d 886 (Tex. Crim. App. 1989).

Ex parte Endo. 323 U.S. 283 (1944).

Ex parte Hollman. 79 S.C. 9 (1907).

Ex parte Virginia. 100 U.S. 339 (1879).

Fay v. *New York*. 332 U.S. 261 (1947).

Frank v. *Mangum*. 237 U.S. 309 (1915).

Franklin v. *South Carolina*. 218 U.S. 161 (1910).

Furman v. *Georgia*. 408 U.S. 238 (1972).

Gamble v. *State*. 357 S.E.2d 792 (Ga. Sup. Ct. 1987).

Gates v. *Collier*. 349 F.Supp. 881 (N.D. Miss. 1972).

Gates v. *Zant*. 863 F.2d 1492 (CA 11 1989), *reh'g denied,* 880 F.2d 293 (per curiam), *cert. denied*, 493 U.S. 945 (1989).

Georgia v. *McCollum*. 505 U.S. 42 (1992).

Gideon v. *Wainwright*. 372 U.S. 335 (1963).

Gilliard v. *Mississippi*. 464 U.S. 867 (1983).

Godfrey v. *Georgia*. 446 U.S. 420 (1980).

Government of Virgin Islands v. *Forte*. 865 F.2d 59 (CA 3 1989).

Grandison (a slave) v. *State*. 21 Tenn. 451 (Sup. Ct.. 1841).

Gregg v. *Georgia*. 428 U.S. 153 (1976).

Griffith v. *Kentucky*. 479 U.S. 314 (1987).

Guice v. *Fortenberry*. 722 F.2d 276 (CA 5 1984).

Hale v. *Kentucky*. 303 U.S. 613 (1938).

Hall v. *Pennsylvania State Police*. 570 F.2d 86 (CA 3 1978).

Hamilton v. *Alabama*. 368 U.S. 52 (1961).

Ham v. *South Carolina*. 409 U.S. 524 (1973).

Hampton v. *Commonwealth*. 58 S.E.2d 288 (1950).

Hampton v. *Hanrahan*. 600 F.2d 600 (CA 7 1979).

Hampton v. *State*. 88 Miss. 257 (1906).

Hance v. *Zant*. 696 F.2d 940 (CA 11 1983), *cert. denied*, 463 U.S. 1210 (1993);

Hance v. *Zant*, 981F.2d 1180 (CA 11) (denial of habeas corpus), *reh'g denied*, 988 F2d 1220 (CA 11), *cert. denied*, 510 U.S. 920 (1993).

Harper v. *State*. 171 So.2d. 129 (Miss. Sup. Ct. 1965).

Harris v. *Texas*. 467 U.S. 1261 (1984).

Hawkins v. *Town of Shaw*. 461 F.2d 1171 (CA 5 1972).

Herring v. *State*. 522 So.2d 745 (Miss. Sup. Ct. 1988).

Hicks v. *State*. 143 Ark. 158 (1920).

Hill v. *Texas*. 316 U.S. 400 (1942).

Hiller v. State. 50 S.W.2d 225 (Tenn. Sup. Ct. 1932).

Hirabayashi v. *United States*. 320 U.S. 81 (1943).

Hobby v. *United States*. 468 U.S. 339 (1984).

Hodges v. *United States*. 203 U.S. 1 (1906), *overruled in part by Jones* v. *Alfred H. Mayer Co.*, 392 U.S. 409 (1968).

Holland v. *Illinois*. 493 U.S. 474 (1990).

Honda v. *People*. 141 P.2d 178 (Colo. Sup. Ct. 1943).

Hooks v. *State*. 210 S.E.2d 668 (Ga. Sup. Ct. 1974).

Hunter v. *Underwood*. 471 U.S. 222 (1985).

Illinois v. *Williams*. 454 N.E.2d 220 (Ill. Sup. Ct. 1983).

Inmates of Attica Correctional Facility v. *Rockefeller*. 453 F.2d 12 (CA 2 1971).

In re Murchison. 349 U.S. 133 (1955).

In re the Matter of Stanley Z. Goodfarb. 880 P.2d 620 (Ariz. Sup. Ct. 1994).

James v. *State*. 92 So. 909 (Ala. Ct. App. 1922).

J.E.B. v. *Alabama*. 114 S.Ct. 1419 (1994).

Johnson v. *Florida*, 602 So.2d 1288 (Fla. Sup. Ct. 1992).

Johnson v. *Louisiana*. 406 U.S. 356 (1972).

Johnson v. *Puckett*. 929 F.2D 1067 (CA 5 1991), *cert. denied*, 502 U.S. 898 (1991).

Johnson v. *Rose*. 546 F.2d 678 (CA 6 1976).

Johnson v. *State*. 51 So.2d 901 (Ala. Ct. App. 1951).

Johnson v. *State*. 404 So.2d 553 (Miss. Sup. Ct. 1981).

Jordan v. *Smith*. 14 Ohio 199 (1846).

Jurek v. *Texas*. 428 U.S. 262 (1976).

Kelly v. *Stone*. 514 F.2d 18 (CA 9 1975).

King v. *County of Nassau*. 581 F.Supp. 493 (E.D. N.Y. 1984).

Kolender v. *Lawson*. 461 U.S. 352 (1983).

Korematsu v. *United States*. 323 U.S. 214 (1944).

Kornegay v. *State*. 329 S.E.2d 601 (Ga. Ct. App. 1985).

Lawn v. *United States*. 355 U.S. 339 (1958).

Lee v. *State*. 747 S.W.2d 57 (Tex. Ct. App. 1988).

Lee v. *Washington*. 390 U.S. 333 (1968).

Lockett v. *Ohio*. 438 U.S. 586 (1978).

Loving v. *Virginia*. 388 U.S. 1 (1967).

Lowery v. *Virginia*. 388 S.E.2d 265 (Va. Ct. App. 1990).

Lucear v. *State*. 146 S.E.2d 316 (Ga. Sup. Ct. 1965).

Luke (a slave) v. *State*. 5 Fla. 185 (1853).

Mallett v. *State*. 769 S.W.2d 77 (Mo. Sup. Ct), *cert. denied*, 494 U.S. 1009 (1990).

Malloy v. *Hogan*. 378 U.S. 1 (1964).

Marshall v. *State*. 210 S.W. 798 (Tex. Crim. App. 1919).

Marx v. *State*. 150 S.W.2d 1014 (Tex. Crim. App. 1941).

Maxwell v. *Bishop*. 257 F.Supp. 710 (E.D. Ark. 1966); *aff'd* 398 F.2d 138 (CA 8 1968), *vacated and remanded*, 398 U.S. 262 (1970).

Maxwell v. *State*. 370 S.W.2d 113 (Ark. Sup. Ct. 1963).

Maxwell v. *Stephens*. 229 F.Supp. 205 (E.D. Ark. 1964); *aff'd*, 348 F.2d 325 (CA 8 1965), *cert. denied*, 382 U.S. 944 (1965).

McCleskey v. *Kemp*. 753 F.2d 877 (CA 11 1985).

McCleskey v. *Kemp*. 481 U.S. 279 (1987).

McCleskey v. *Kemp*. No. C87-1517A (N.D. Ga. Dec. 23, 1987).

McCleskey v. *Zant*. 580 F.Supp. 338 (N.D. Ga. 1984).

McCray v. *Abrams*. 576 F. Supp. 1244 (E.D.N.Y. 1983); *aff'd in part, vacated in part*, 750 F.2d 1113 (CA 2 1984).

McCray v. *Abrams*, 576 F. Supp. 1244 (E.D. N.Y. 1983); *aff'd* 756 F. 2d 277 (CA 2 1985); *cert. granted*, judgment vacated, 478 U.S. 1001 (1986).

McCray v. *New York*. 461 U.S. 961 (1983).

McGautha v. *California*. 402 U.S. 183 (1971).

McLaughlin v. *Florida*. 379 U.S. 184 (1964).

McMillian v. *State*. 616 So.2d 933 (Ala. Crim. App. 1993).

McQuirter v. *State*. 63 So.2d 388 (Ala. Ct. App. 1953).

Meders v. *State*. 389 S.E.2d 320 (Ga. Sup. Ct. 1990).

Michigan v. *Booker*. 478 U.S. 1001 (1986).

Miller v. *Johnson*. 115 S.Ct. 2475 (1995).

Miller v. *North Carolina*. 583 F.2d 701 (CA 4 1978).

Minnesota v. *Davis*. 504 N.W.2d 767 (Minn. Sup. Ct. 1993).

Monell v. *New York Department of Social Services*. 436 U.S. 658 (1978).

Monroe v. *Pape*. 365 U.S. 167 (1961).

Moore v. *Dempsey*. 261 U.S. 86, 91 (1923).

Moorer v. *South Carolina*. 368 F.2d 458 (CA 4 1966).

Morgan v. *Woessner*. 975 F.2d 629 (CA 9 1992).

Moulton v. *State*. 199 Ala. 411 (1917).

Murray v. *Louisiana*. 163 U.S. 101 (1896).

Neal v. *Delaware*. 103 U.S. 370 (1880).

Nelson (a slave) v. *State*. 6 Ala. 394 (1844).

Nichols v. *McGee*. 169 F.Supp. 721 (N.D. Cal. 1959).

Norris v. *Alabama*. 294 U.S. 587 (1935).

Oliver v. *State*. 39 Miss. 526 (High Ct. of Errors and App. 1860).

Palmore v. *Sidoti*. 466 U.S. 429 (1984).

Peek v. *State*. 488 So.2d 52 (Fla. Sup. Ct. 1986).

People v. *Cudjo*. 863 P.2d 635 (Cal. Sup. Ct. 1993).

People v. *Hall*. 4 Cal. 399 (1854).

People v. *Harris*. 679 P.2d 433 (Cal. Sup. Ct. 1984).

People v. *McDonald*. 530 N.E.2d 1351 (Ill. Sup. Ct. 1988).

People v. *Thomas*. 561 N.E.2d 57 (Ill. Sup. Ct. 1990).

People v. *Wheeler*. 583 P.2d 748 (Cal. Sup. Ct. 1978).

People v. *Williams*. 454 N.E.2d 220 (Ill. Sup. Ct. 1983).

Peter (a slave) v. *State*. 12 Miss. 31 (1844).

Peters v. *Kiff*. 407 U.S. 493 (1972).

Plessy v. *Ferguson* 163 U.S. 537 (1896).

Pollock v. *Williams*. 322 U.S. 4 (1944).

Powell v. *Alabama*. 287 U.S. 45 (1932).

Powell v. *Allstate Insurance Co*. 652 So.2d 354 (Fla. 1995).

Powell v. *Superior Court*. 283 Cal.Rptr. 777 (Cal. Ct. App. 1991).

Powers v. *Ohio*. 499 U.S. 400 (1991).

Prigg v. *Pennsylvania*. 41 U.S. 539 (1842).

Proffitt v. *Florida*. 428 U.S. 242 (1976).

Purkett v. *Elem*. 514 U.S. 765 (1995).

Ratliff v. *Beale*. 74 Miss. 247 (1896).

Reid v. *Covert*. 354 U.S. 1 (1957).

Rentfrow v. *Carter*. 296 F.Supp. 301 (N.D. Ga. 1968).

Rhoden v. *State*. 274 So.2d 630 (Ala. Crim. App. 1973).

Richmond v. *J.A. Croson Co*. 488 U.S. 469 (1989).

Rizzo v. *Goode*. 423 U.S. 362 (1976).

Roberts v. *Louisiana*. 428 U.S. 325 (1976).

Rogers v. *Alabama*. 192 U.S. 226 (1904).

Rose v. *Mitchell*. 443 U.S. 545 (1979).

Rostker v. *Goldberg*. 453 U.S. 57 (1981).

Royals v. *State*. 75 So. 199 (Fla. Sup. Ct. 1917).

Rudolph v. *Alabama*. 375 U.S. 889 (1963).

Sacher v. *United States*. 343 U.S. 1 (1952).

Santiago v. *Miles*. 774 F.Supp. 775 (W.D. N.Y. 1991).

Screws v. *United States*. 325 U.S. 91 (1945).

Shaw v. *Hunt*. 116 S.Ct. 1894 (1996).

Shaw v. *Martin*. 733 F.2d 304 (CA 4 1984).

Shaw v. *Reno*. 509 U.S.. 630 (1993).

Shillcutt v. *Gagnon*. 827 F.2d 1155 (CA 7 1987).

Shillcutt v. *Wisconsin*. 350 N.W.2d 686 (Wis. Sup. Ct. 1984).

Shuttlesworth v. *City of Birmingham*. 394 U.S. 147 (1969).

Smith v. *Balkcom*. 660 F.2d 563 (CA 5 1981), *modified*, 671 F.2d 858 (Ca 5 1981), *cert. denied*, 459 U.S. 882 (1982).

Smith v. *Kemp*. 464 U.S. 1032 (1983).

Smith v. *Texas*. 311 U.S. 128 (1940).

Souther v. *Commonwealth*. 48 Va. 338 (1851).

Spence (a slave) v. *State*. 17 Ala. 192 (1850).

Spencer v. *State*. 398 S.E.2d 179 (Ga. Sup. Ct. 1990).

Spinkellink v. *Wainwright*. 578 F.2d 582 (CA 5 1978), *cert. denied*, 440 U.S. 976 (1979).

State ex rel. Copeland v. *Mayo*. 87 So.2d 501 (Fla. Sup. Ct. 1956).

State v. *Greene*. 542 So.2d 156 (La. Ct. App. 1989).

State v. *Mayhue*. 653 S.W.2d 227 (Mo. Ct. App. 1983).

State v. *Bell*. 209 S.E.2d 890 (S.C. 1974), *cert. denied*, 420 U.S. 1008 (1975).

State v. *Carr*. 427 S.E.2d 273 (Ga. Sup. Ct. 1993).

State v. *Cofield*. 357 S.E.2d 622,(N.C. Sup. Ct. 1987).

State ex rel. Thomas v. *Culver*. 253 F.2d 507 (CA 5), *cert. denied*, 358 U.S. 822 (1958).

State v. *Dean*. 543 P.2d 425 (Ariz. Sup. Ct. 1975).

State v. *Gray*. 584 N.E.2d 710 (Ohio Sup. Ct. 1992).

State v. *Holloway*. 553 A.2d 166 (Conn. 1989).

State v. *Hoover*. 20 N.C. 365 (1839).

State v. *Jackson*. 368 S.E.2d 838 (N.C. Sup. Ct. 1988).

State v. *Jacobs*. 50 N.C. 259 (1858).

State v. *Jones*. 358 S.E.2d 701 (S.C. Sup. Ct. 1987).

State v. *Jones*. 486 N.E.2d 179 (Ohio Ct. App. 1984).

State v. *Jones*. 233 S.E.2d 287 (S.C. Sup. Cr. 1977).

State v. *Knox.* 609 So.2d 803 (La. Sup. Ct. 1992).

State v. *Mann.* 13 N.C. 263 (1829).

State v. *Moore.* 404 S.E.2d 845 (N.C. Sup. Ct. 1991).

State v. *Petit.* 119 La. 1013 (1907).

State v. *Ramseur.* 524 A.2d 188 (N.J. Sup. Ct. 1987).

State v. *Russell.* 477 N.W.2d 886 (Minn. Sup. Ct. 1991).

State v. *Smith.* 791 S.W.2d 744 (Mo. Ct. App. 1990).

State v. *Tackett.* 8 N.C. 210 (1820).

State v. *Thomas.* 250 Mo. 189 (1913).

State v. *Thomas.* 777 P.2d 445 (Utah Sup. Ct. 1989).

State v. *Tom (a slave).* 13 N.C. 569 (1830).

State v. *Washington.* 136 La. 855 (1915).

Stein v. *New York.* 346 U.S. 156 (1953).

Stilson v. *United States.* 250 U.S. 583 (1919).

Story v. *State.* 133 Miss. 476 (1923).

Strauder v. *West Virginia.* 100 U.S. 303 (1879).

Stroman v. *Griffin.* 331 F.Supp. 226 (S.D. Ga. 1971).

Stroud v. *Swope.* 187 F.2d 850 (CA 9 1951), *cert. denied* 342 U.S. 829 (1951).

Sullivan v. *Wainwright.* 464 U.S. 109 (1983).

Swain v. *Alabama.* 380 U.S. 202 (1965).

Tannehill v. *State.* 159 Ala. 51 (1909).

Tanner v. *United States.* 483 U.S. 107 (1987).

Taylor v. *Georgia.* 315 U.S. 25 (1942).

Taylor v. *Louisiana.* 419 U.S. 522 (1975).

Taylor v. *State.* 50 Tex. Criminal Reports 560 (Tex. Crim. App. 1907).

Tennessee v. *Garner.* 471 U.S. 1 (1985).

Thomas v. *State.* 92 So.2d 621 (Fla. Sup. Ct. 1957).

Thomas v. *Texas.* 212 U.S. 278 (1909).

Thornton v. *Beto.* 470 F.2d 657 (CA 5 1972), *cert. denied*, 411 U.S. 920 (1973).

Thornton v. *Texas.* 451 S.W.2d 898 (Tex. Crim. App. 1970).

Tobias v. *Smith.* 468 F.Supp. 1287 (W.D. N.Y. 1979).

Turner v. *Murray.* 476 U.S. 28 (1986).

United States v. *Alcantar.* 832 F.2d 1175 (CA 9 1987).

United States v. *Alcantar.* 897 F.2d 436 (CA 9 1990).

United States v. *Antonelli Fireworks Co.* 155 F.2d 631 (CA 2 1946), *cert. denied*, 329 U.S. 742 (1946).

United States v. *Battle.* 836 F.2d 1084 (CA 8 1987).

United States v. *Benmuhar.* 658 F.2d 14 (CA 1 1981), *cert. denied*, 457 U.S. 1117 (1982).

United States v. *Biaggi.* 853 F.2d. 89 (CA 2 1988).

United States v. *Brown.* 539 F.2d 467 (CA 5 1976).

United States v. *Bryant.* 471 F.2d 1040 (CA DC 1972), *cert. denied*, 409 U.S. 1112 (1973).

United States v. *Cecil.* 836 F.2d 1431 (CA 4 1988), *cert. denied*, 487 U.S. 1205 (1988).

United States v. *Chalan.* 812 F.2d 1302 (CA 10 1987).

United States v. *Clary.* 846 F.Supp. 768 (E.D. Mo. 1994), *rev'd*, 34 F.3d 709 (CA 8 1994), *cert. denied*, 513 U.S. 1182 (1995).

United States v. *Cresta.* 825 F.2d 538 (CA 1 1987).

United States v. *Dumas.* 64 F.3d 1427 (CA 9 1995).

United States v. *Franklin.* 704 F.2d 1183 (CA 10 1983).

United States v. *Greene.* 995 F.2d 793 (CA 8 1993).

United States v. *Heller.* 785 F.2d 1524 (CA 11 1986).

United States v. *Laymon.* 730 F.Supp. 332 (D. Colo. 1990).

United States v. *Leslie.* 783 F.2d 541 (CA 5 1986), *vacated*, 479 U.S. 1074 (1987).

United States v. *Martinez-Fuerte.* 428 U.S. 543 (1976).

United States v. *Montgomery.* 819 F.2d 847 (CA 8 1987).

United States v. *Morris.* 26 F.Cas. 1323 (Cir. Ct. D. Mass. 1851).

United States v. *Newman.* 549 F.2d 240 (CA 2 1977).

United States v. *Nicholas.* 448 F.2d 622 (CA 8 1971).

United States v. *Prandy-Binett.* 995 F.2d 1069 (CA D.C. 1993).

United States v. *Price.* 383 U.S. 787 (1966).

United States v. *Robinson.* 421 F.Supp. 467 (D. Conn. 1976).

United States v. *Sawyer.* 347 F.2d 372 (CA 4 1965).

United States v. *Taylor.* 956 F.2d 572 (CA 6 1992).

United States v. *Then.* 56 F.3d 464 (CA 2 1995).

United States v. *Thompson.* 827 F.2d 1254 (CA 9 1987).

United States v. *Travis.* 62 F.3d 170 (CA 6 1995).

United States v. *Weaver.* 966 F.2d 391 (CA 8 1992).

United States v. *Wyandotte County, Kansas.* 480 F.2d 969 (CA 10 1973).

United States ex rel. Goldsby v. *Harpole.* 263 F.2d 71 (CA 1959).

Vasquez v. *Hillery.* 474 U.S. 254 (1986).

Viereck v. *United States.* 318 U.S. 236 (1943).

Village of Arlington Heights v. *Metropolitan Housing Development Corporation.* 429 U.S. 252 (1977).

Virginia v. *Rives.* 100 U.S. 313 (1879).

Ware v. *State.* 146 Ark. 321 (1920).

Washington v. *Davis.* 426 U.S. 229 (1976).

Washington v. *Lambert.* 98 F.3d 1181 (CA 9 1996).

Weddington v. *State.* 545 A.2d 607 (Del. Sup. Ct. 1988).

Welch v. *State.* 30 Okla.Cr.Rep. 330 (1925).

Whitner v. *State.* 1996 S.C. Lexis 120 (S.C. Sup. Ct. 1996).

Whitus v. *Balkcom.* 333 F.2d 496 (CA 5 1964), *cert. denied*, 379 U.S. 931 (1964).

Williams v. *Georgia.* 349 U.S. 375 (1955).

Williams v. *Illinois.* 466 U.S. 981 (1984).

Williams v. *Mississippi.* 170 U.S. 213 (1898).

Williams v. *State.* 110 So.2d 654 (Fla. Sup. Ct. 1959).

Withers v. *United States.* 602 F.2d 124 (CA 6 1979).

Woodson v. *North Carolina.* 428 U.S. 280 (1976).

Wright v. *CTL Distribution, Inc.* 679 So.2d 1233 (Fla. Dist. Ct. App. 1996).

Wygant v. *Jackson Bd. of Educ.* 476 U.S. 267 (1986).

Young v. *State.* 770 S.W.2d 243 (Mo. Sup. Ct. 1989).

Books

Abramson, Jeffrey. *We, the Jury: The Jury System and the Ideal of Democracy* (1994).

Abramson, Jeffrey, ed. *Postmortem: The O.J. Simpson Case: Justice Confronts Race, Domestic Violence, Lawyers, Money, and the Media* (1996).

Amnesty International. *United States of America: The Death Penalty* (1987).

Anderson, David C. *Crime and the Politics of Hysteria: How the Willie Horton Story Changed American Justice* (1995).

Aptheker, Herbert, ed. *A Documentary History of the Negro People in the United States*, Volume 7, *1960–1968: From the Alabama Protests to the Death of Martin Luther King, Jr.* (1994).

Archer, William. *Through Afro-America: An English Reading of the Race Problem* (1910).

Ayers, Edward L. *Vengeance and Justice: Crime and Punishment in the 19th Century American South* (1984).

Baldus, David C., and James W.L. Cole. *Statistical Proof of Discrimination* (1980).

Baldus, David C., George Woodworth, and Charles A. Pulaski, Jr. *Equal Justice and the Death Penalty: A Legal and Empirical Analysis* (1990).

Banfield, Edward C. *The Unheavenly City: The Nature and Future of Our Urban Crisis* (1970).

Bass, Jack. *Unlikely Heroes: The Dramatic Story of the Southern Judges of the Fifth Circuit Who Translated the Supreme Court's Brown Decision into a Revolution for Equality* (1981).

Beck, E.M., and Stewart E. Tolnay. *A Festival of Violence: An Analysis of Southern Lynchings, 1882–1930* (1995).

Bedau, Hugo Adam, Michael L. Radelet, and Constance E. Putnam. *In Spite of Innocence: Erroneous Convictions in Capital Cases* (1992).

Belknap, Michael R. *Federal Law and Southern Order: Racial Violence and Constitutional Conflict in the Post-Brown South* (1995).

Bell, Malcolm. *The Turkey Shoot: Tracking the Attica Cover-Up* (1995).

Bergmann, Barbara. *In Defense of Affirmative Action* (1996).

Berlin, Ira. *Slaves without Masters: The Free Negro in the Antebellum South* (1975).

Bernardi, Daniel, ed. *The Birth of Whiteness: Race and the Emergence of U.S. Cinema* (1996).

Bertram, Eva, Morris Blachman, Kenneth Sharpe, and Peter Andreas. *Drug War Politics: The Price of Denial* (1996).

Bickel, Alexander M., and Benno C. Schmidt, Jr. *The Judiciary and Responsible Government, 1910–1921* (1984).

Billson, Janet Mancini, and Richard Majors. *Cool Pose: The Dilemmas of Black Manhood in America* (1992).

Black, Charles L., Jr. *Capital Punishment: The Inevitability of Caprice and Mistake.* 2d ed. (1981).

Blauner, Robert. *Racial Oppression in America* (1972).

Boger, John Charles, and Judith Welch Wegner, eds. *Race, Poverty, and American Cities* (1996).

Bolick, Clint. *The Affirmative Action Fraud—Can We Restore the American Civil Rights Vision* (1996).

————. *Unfinished Business: A Civil Rights Strategy for America's Third Century* (1990).

Bonger, Willem Adriaan. *Race and Crime* (1943).

Bowers, William J., with Glenn L. Pierce and John F. McDevitt. *Legal Homicide: Death as Punishment in America, 1864–1982* (1984).

Brown, H. Rap. *Die, Nigger, Die* (1969).

Brownmiller, Susan. *Against Our Will: Men, Women and Rape* (1975).

Brundage, W. Fitzhugh. *Lynching in the New South: Georgia and Virginia, 1880–1930* (1993).

Bugliosi, Vincent. *Outrage: The Five Reasons Why O.J. Simpson Got away with Murder* (1996).

Cagin, Seth, and Philip Dray. *We Are Not Afraid: The Story of Goodman, Schwerner, and Chaney and the Civil Rights Campaign for Mississippi* (1988).

Campbell, Bebe Moore. *Your Blues Ain't Like Mine* (1992).

Campbell, Stanley W. *The Slave Catchers: Enforcement of the Fugitive Slave Law, 1850–1860* (1970).

Carmichael, Stokely. *Stokely Speaks: Black Power Back to Pan-Africanism* (1971).

Carroll, Leo. *Hacks, Blacks, and Cons: Race Relations in a Maximum Security Prison* (1974).

Carson, Clayborne. *In Struggle: SNCC and the Black Awakening of the 1960s* (1981).

Carter, Dan T. *The Politics of Rage: George Wallace and the Origins of the New Conservatism and the Transformation of American Politics* (1995).

———. *Scottsboro: A Tragedy of the American South*. Rev. ed. (1979).

Cash, W. J. *The Mind of the South* (1991 [1941]).

Catterall, Helen Tunnicliff, ed. *Judicial Cases Concerning American Slavery and the Negro*. 5 vols. (1968).

Chadbourn, James Harmon. *Lynching and the Law* (1933).

Cleaver, Eldridge. *Soul on Ice* (1968).

———. *Post Prison Writings and Speeches*, edited by Robert Scheer (1969).

Clinton, Bill, and Al Gore. *Putting People First: How We Can All Change America* (1992).

Cobb, Thomas R.R. *An Inquiry into the Law of Negro Slavery in the United States of America* (1858).

Cochran, Johnnie L., Jr. *Journey to Justice* (1996).

Constable, Marianne. *The Law of the Other: The Mixed Jury and Changing Conceptions of Citizenship, Law, and Knowledge* (1994).

Cortner, Richard C. *A Mob Intent on Death: The NAACP and the Arkansas Riot Cases* (1988).

———. *A "Scottsboro" Case in Mississippi: The Supreme Court and Brown* v. *Mississippi* (1986).

Cose, Ellis. *The Rage of a Privileged Class* (1993).

Cover, Robert M. *Justice Accused: Antislavery and the Judicial Process* (1975).

Cronin, Tania Z., Thomas E. Cronin, and Michael E. Milakovich. *United States* v. *Crime in the Streets* (1981).

Cross, Brian. *It's Not about a Salary . . . Rap, Race and Resistance in Los Angeles* (1993).

Cummins, Eric. *The Rise and Fall of California's Radical Prison Movement* (1994).

Currie, Elliott. *Confronting Crime: An American Challenge* (1985).

Curtis, Lynn A. *Violence, Race, and Culture* (1975).

Darden, Christopher A. *In Contempt* (1996).

Dash, Leon. *Rosa Lee: A Mother and Her Family in Urban America* (1996).

Davis, F. James. *Who Is Black? One Nation's Definition* (1991).

Davis, Kenneth Culp. *Discretionary Justice* (1969).

Davis, Mike. *City of Quartz: Excavating the Future in Los Angeles* (1990).

Dershowitz, Alan M. *The Abuse Excuse* (1994).

———. *Reasonable Doubts: The O.J. Simpson Case and the Criminal Justice System* (1996).

Dike, Sarah T. *Capital Punishment in the United States* (1982).

Dinnerstein, Leonard. *The Leo Frank Case* (1968).

DiPerna, Paula. *Juries on Trial* (1984).

Dittmer, John. *Local People: The Struggle for Civil Rights in Mississippi* (1994).

Domanick, Joe. *To Protect and to Serve: The LAPD's Century of War in the City of Dreams* (1994).

D'Souza, Dinesh. *The End of Racism: Principles for a Multicultural Society* (1995).

DuBois, W.E.B. *Black Reconstruction in America* (1995); originally *Black Reconstruction* (1935).

———. *The Souls of Black Folk* (1989 [1903]).

Duke, Steven B., and Albert C. Gross. *America's Longest War: Rethinking Our Tragic Crusade against Drugs* (1993).

Dulaney, W. Marvin. *Black Police in America* (1996).

Earley, Pete. *Circumstantial Evidence: Death, Life, and Justice in a Southern Town* (1995)

Early, Gerald, ed. *Speech and Power: The African-American Essay and Its Cultural Content from Polemics to Pulpit* (1993).

Eastland, Terry. *Ending Affirmative Action: The Case for Colorblind Justice* (1996).

Edley, Christopher. *Not All Black and White: Affirmative Action, Race, and American Values* (1996).

Edsall, Thomas Byrne, with Mary D. Edsall. *Chain Reaction: The Impact of Race, Rights, and Taxes on American Politics* (1991).

Elias, Tom, and Dennis Schatzman. *The Simpson Trial in Black and White* (1996).

Epstein, Richard. *Forbidden Grounds: The Case Against Employment Discrimination Laws* (1992).

Fabre, Genevieve, and Robert O'Meally, eds. *History and Memory in Afro-American Culture* (1994).

Fairman, Charles. *Reconstruction and Reunion, 1864–88.* 2 vols. (1971–1987).

Fede, Andrew. *People without Rights: An Interpretation of the Fundamentals of the Law of Slavery in the U.S. South* (1992).

Finkelman, Paul, ed. *Lynching, Racial Violence, and Law* (1992).

Flanigan, Daniel J. *The Criminal Law of Slavery and Freedom, 1800–1868* (1987).

Fletcher, George P. *A Crime of Self-Defense: Bernhard Goetz and the Law on Trial* (1988).

———. *With Justice for Some: Victims' Rights in Criminal Trials* (1995).

Foner, Eric. *Reconstruction: America's Unfinished Revolution, 1863–1877* (1988).

Foner, Philip S., ed. *The Black Panthers Speak* (1970).

———. *The Life and Writings of Frederick Douglass* (1955).

Frank, Barney. *Speaking Frankly: What's Wrong With the Democrats and How to Fix It* (1992).

Frederickson, George M. *The Black Image in the White Mind: The Debate on Afro-American Character and Destiny, 1817–1914* (1971).

Friedly, Michael. *Malcolm X: The Assassination* (1992).

Friedman, Jeffrey, ed., *The Rational Choice Controversy: Economic Models of Politics Reconsidered* (1996).

Friedman, Lawrence M. *Crime and Punishment in American History* (1993).

Friedman, Leon, ed. *Southern Justice* (1965).

Fukurai, Hiroshi, Edgar W. Butler, and Richard Krooth. *Race and the Jury: Racial Disenfranchisement and the Search for Justice* (1993).

Fuller, Charles. *Zooman and the Sign* (1980).

Garber, Marjorie, and Rebecca L. Walkowitz, eds. *Secret Agents: The Rosenberg Case, McCarthyism and Fifties America* (1995).

Garrow, David J. *The FBI and Martin Luther King, Jr.* (1981).

Gates, Henry Louis, Jr., and Cornel West. *The Future of the Race* (1996).

Genovese, Eugene D. *Roll, Jordan, Roll: The World the Slaves Made* (1974).

Gershman, Bennett L. *Prosecutorial Misconduct*. 6th ed. (1991).

Gilmore, Al-Tony. *Bad Nigger! The National Impact of Jack Johnson* (1975).

Ginger, Ann Fagan. *Minimizing Racism in Jury Trials: The Voir Dire Conducted by Charles R. Garry in People of California v. Huey P. Newton* (1969).

Ginzburg, Ralph. *100 Years of Lynching* (1962).

Goines, Donald. *White Man's Justice, Black Man's Grief* (1973).

Goldfarb, Ronald L., and Linda R. Singer. *After Conviction* (1973).

Goodell, William. *The American Slave Code in Theory and Practice* (1968 [1853]).

Gooding-Williams, Robert, ed. *Reading Rodney King/Reading Urban Uprising* (1993).

Goodman, James. *Stories of Scottsboro* (1994).

Gordon, Diana R. *The Return of the Dangerous Classes: Drug Prohibition and Policy Politics* (1994).

Gordon, Linda. *Pitied but Not Entitled: Single Mothers and the History of Welfare, 1890–1935* (1994).

Gottlieb, Stephen E., ed. *Public Values in Constitutional Law* (1993).

Graham, Fred P. *The Self-Inflicted Wound* (1970).

Greenberg, Cheryl Lynn. *"Or Does It Explode?" Black Harlem in the Great Depression* (1991).

Greenberg, Jack. *Crusaders in the Courts* (1994).

Greenlee, Sam. *The Spook Who Sat By the Door* (1969).

Grimshaw, Allen D., ed. *Racial Violence in the United States* (1969).

Grodzins, Morton. *Americans Betrayed* (1949).

Guadagno, Jill. *The Color of Welfare: How Racism Undermined the War on Poverty* (1994).

Hacker, Andrew. *Two Nations: Black and White, Separate, Hostile, Unequal* (1992).

Hall, Jacquelyn Dowd. *Revolt against Chivalry: Jessie Daniel Ames and the Women's Campaign against Lynching*. Rev. ed. (1993).

Hall, Kermit L., ed. *Civil Rights in American History: Major Historical Interpretations.* (1987).

———. *The Law of American Slavery: Major Historical Interpretations* (1987).

———. *Race Relations and the Law in American History: Major Historical Interpretations* (1987).

Halpern, Rick, and Melvyn Stokes, eds. *Race and Class in the American South Since 1890* (1994).

Haney-Lopez, Ian F. *White by Law: The Legal Construction of Race* (1996).

Hans, Valerie P., and Neil Vidmar. *Judging the Jury* (1986).

Harris, Trudier. *Exorcising Blackness: Historical and Literary Lynching and Burning Rituals* (1984).

Harwell, Fred. *A True Deliverance* (1979).

Hatamiya, Leslie T. *Righting a Wrong: Japanese Americans and the Passage of the Civil Liberties Act of 1988* (1993).

Hawkins, Darnell F., ed. *Ethnicity, Race, and Crime: Perspectives across Time and Place* (1995).

Heath, Louis G., ed. *Off the Pigs! The History and Literature of the Black Panther Party* (1976).

Higginbotham, Evelyn Brooks. *Righteous Discontent: The Women's Movement in the Black Baptist Church, 1880–1920* (1993).

Hill, Anita Faye, and Emma Coleman Jordan, eds. *Race, Gender, and Power in America: The Legacy of the Hill-Thomas Hearing* (1995).

Hooks, Bell. *Ain't I a Woman: Black Women and Feminism* (1981).

Horwitz, David. *The Courts and Public Policy* (1977).

Huie, William Bradford. *Wolf Whistle and Other Stories* (1955).

Institute for Alternative Journalism. *Inside the L.A. Riots* (1992).

Irons, Peter. *Justice at War* (1983).

Isaacs, Harold R. *The New World of Negro Americans* (1963).

Jackson, George. *Blood in My Eye* (1972).

———. *Soledad Brother: The Prison Letters of George Jackson* (1970).

Jacobs, Harriet A. *Incidents in the Life of a Slave Girl*, Written by Herself (Jean Fagan Yellin, ed. [1987] 1861).

Jacobs, James B. *New Perspectives on Prisons and Imprisonment* (1983).

Jeffries, John C., Jr. *Justice Lewis F. Powell, Jr.* (1994).

Jencks, Christoper. *Rethinking Social Policy: Race, Poverty, and the Underclass.* (1992).

Jencks, Christopher, and Paul E. Peterson, eds. *The Urban Underclass* (1991).

Jordan, Winthrop D. *White over Black: American Attitudes toward the Negro, 1550–1812* (1969).

Kaczorowski, Robert J. *The Politics of Judicial Interpretation: The Federal Courts, Department of Justice and Civil Rights, 1866–1876* (1985).

Kahneman, Daniel, Paul Slovic, and Amos Tversky, eds. *Judgment Under Uncertainty: Heuristics and Biases* (1982).

Kellogg, Charles Flint. *NAACP: A History of the National Association for the Advancement of Colored People*, Volume 1, *1909–1920* (1967).

Kelly, Mike. *Color Lines: The Troubled Dreams of Racial Harmony in an American Town* (1995).

Kilpatrick, James J. *The Southern Case for School Segregation* (1962).

King, Desmond. *Separate and Unequal Black Americans and the U.S. Federal Government* (1995).

Kleinig, John, ed. *Handled With Discretion* (1996).

Kleiman, Mark, A.R. *Against Excess: Drug Policy for Results* (1992).

Koon, Stacey C., with Robert Deitz. *Presumed Guilty: The Tragedy of the Rodney King Affair* (1992).

Kotlowitz, Alex. *There Are No Children Here: The Story of Two Boys Growing Up in the Other America* (1991).

Kull, Andrew. *The Color-Blind Constitution* (1992).

LaFave, Wayne R., and Jerold H. Israel. *Criminal Procedure*. 2nd ed. (1992).

LaFree, Gary D. *Rape and Criminal Justice: The Social Construction of Sexual Assault* (1989).

LaGumina, Salvatore J., ed. *Wop! A Documentary History of Anti-Italian Discrimination in the United States* (1973).

Lamar, Jake. *Bourgeois Blues: An American Memoir* (1991).

Lane, Roger. *Roots of Violence in Black Philadelphia, 1860–1900* (1986).

———. *William Dorsey's Philadelphia and Ours: On the Past and Future of the Black City in America* (1991).

Lemann, Nicholas. *The Promised Land: The Great Black Migration and How It Changed America* (1991).

Levin, Jack, and William C. Levin. *The Functions of Discrimination and Prejudice* (1982).

Levy, Leonard W., Kenneth L. Karst, and Dennis J. Mahoney, eds. *Encyclopedia of the American Constitution* (1986).

Liebman, James S., and Randy Hertz. *Federal Habeas Corpus Practice and Procedure*, 2d ed. (1994).

Litwack, Leon F. *North of Slavery: The Negro in the Free States, 1790–1860* (1961).

Lockhart, William B., Yale Kamisar, Jesse H. Choper, and Steven H. Shiffrin. *Constitutional Law*. 6th ed. (1986).

Lockwood, Daniel. *Prison Sexual Violence* (1980).

Loury, Glenn C. *One by One from the Inside Out: Essays and Reviews on Race and Responsibility in America* (1995).

Lusane, Clarence. *Pipe Dream Blues: Racism and the War on Drugs* (1991).

Lynch, Michael J., and E. Britt Patterson, eds. *Race and Criminal Justice* (1991).

Madhubuti, Haki R., and Maulana Karenga, eds. *Million Man March/Day of Absence: A Commemorative Anthology: Speeches, Commentary, Photography, Poetry, Illustrations, and Documents* (1996).

Malcolm X. *The Autobiography of Malcolm X* (1965).

Mangum, Charles S., Jr. *The Legal Status of the Negro* (1940).

Mann, Coramae Richey. *Unequal Justice: A Question of Color* (1993).

Mars, Florence, with Lynn Eden. *Witness in Philadelphia* (1977).

Marshall, Burke. *Federalism and Civil Rights* (1964).

Massey, Douglas S., and Nancy A. Denton. *American Apartheid: Segregation and the Making of the Underclass* (1993).

McAdam, Doug. *Freedom Summer* (1988).

McFadden, Robert D., et al. *Outrage, The Story behind the Tawana Brawley Hoax* (1990).

McLaurin, Melton A. *Celia, a Slave* (1991).

McMillen, Neil R. *Dark Journey: Black Mississippians in the Age of Jim Crow* (1989).

Meltsner, Michael. *Cruel and Unusual: The Supreme Court and Capital Punishment* (1973).

Miller, Jerome G. *Search and Destroy: African-American Males in the Criminal Justice System* (1996).

Morris, Norval, and David J. Rothman, eds. *The Oxford History of the Prison: The Practice of Punishment in Western Society* (1995).

Morris, Thomas D. *Free Men All: The Personal Liberty Laws of the North, 1780–1861* (1974).

———. *Southern Slavery and the Law, 1619–1860* (1996).

Morrison, Toni. *Beloved* (1987).

Mushlin, Michael. *Rights of Prisoners*, 2nd ed. (1993).

Musto, David. *The American Disease: Origins of Narcotic Control.* Expanded ed. (1987).

Myrdal, Gunnar. *An American Dilemma: The Negro Problem and Modern Democracy.* 2 vols. (1995 [1944]).

Nakell, Barry, and Kenneth A. Hardy. *The Arbitrariness of the Death Penalty* (1987).

Navasky, Victor S. *Kennedy Justice* (1971).

Newton, Huey P. *To Die for the People: The Writings of Huey P. Newton* (1972).

Nordan, Lewis. *Wolf Whistle: A Novel* (1993).

Omolade, Barbara. *The Rising Song of African American Women* (1994),.

O'Reilly, Kenneth. *Racial Matters: The FBI's Secret File on Black America, 1960–1972* (1989).

Oshinsky, David M. *"Worse Than Slavery": Parchman Farm and the Ordeal of Jim Crow Justice* (1996).

Patterson, Orlando. *Slavery and Social Death* (1982).

Payne, Charles M. *I've Got the Light of Freedom: The Organizing Tradition and the Mississippi Freedom Struggle* (1995).

Pearson, Hugh. *The Shadow of the Panther: Huey Newton and the Price of Black Power in America* (1994).

Peltason, J. W. *Fifty-eight Lonely Men: Southern Federal Judges and School Desegregation* (1971 [1961]).

Porter, Bruce, and Marvin Dunn. *The Miami Riot of 1980: Crossing the Bounds* (1984).

Price, Richard. *Clockers* (1992).

Quadagno, Jill. *The Color of Welfare: How Racism Undermined the War on Poverty* (1994).

Rable, George C. *But There Was No Peace: The Role of Violence in the Politics of Reconstruction* (1984).

Radelet, Michael L., Hugo Adam Bedau, and Constance E. Putnam. *In Spite of Innocence: Erroneous Convictions in Capital Cases* (1992).

Raper, Arthur. *The Tragedy of Lynching* (1933).

Reeves, Jimmie L., and Richard Campbell. *Cracked Coverage: Television News, the Anti-Cocaine Crusade, and the Reagan Legacy* (1994).

Reston, James, Jr. *The Innocence of Joan Little: A Southern Mystery* (1977).

Rideau, Wilbert, and Ron Wikberg. *Life Sentences: Rage and Survival Behind Bars* (1992).

Rise, Eric W. *The Martinsville Seven: Race, Rape, and Capital Punishment* (1995).

Roberts, Paul Craig, and Lawrence Stratton. *The New Color Line* (1996).

Rose, Harold M., and Paula D. McClain. *Race, Place, and Risk: Black Homicide in Urban America* (1990).

Ryan, William. *Blaming the Victim.* Rev. ed. (1976).

Sachar, Howard M. *A History of the Jews in America* (1992).

Schafer, Judith Kelleher. *Slavery, the Civil Law, and the Supreme Court of Louisiana* (1994).

Scheingold, Stuart A. *The Politics of Law and Order: Street Crime and Public Policy* (1984).

———. *The Politics of Street Crime: Criminal Process and Cultural Obsession* (1991).

Schwarz, Philip J. *Twice Condemned: Slaves and the Criminal Laws of Virginia, 1705–1865* (1988).

Scott-McLaughlin, Randolph M., ed. *Racially-Motivated Violence: Litigation Strategies* (1984).

Seale, Bobby. *Seize the Time: The Story of the Black Panther Party and Huey P. Newton* (1970).

Shaman, Jeffrey M., Steven Lubet, and James J. Alfini. *Judicial Conduct and Ethics.* 2d. ed. (1995).

Shapiro, Robert. *The Search for Justice* (1996).

Silberman, Charles E. *Criminal Violence, Criminal Justice* (1978).

Simms, Margaret C., and Samuel L. Myers, Jr., eds. *The Economics of Race and Crime* (1988).

Simpson, George Eaton, and J. Milton Yinger. *Racial and Cultural Minorities: An Analysis of Prejudice and Discrimination.* 5th ed. (1985).

Skolnick, Jerome H. *Justice without Trial* (1966).

Smead, Howard. *Blood Justice: The Lynching of Mack Charles Parker* (1986).

Staff of the Los Angeles Times. *Understanding the Riots: Los Angeles Before and After the Rodney King Case* (1992).

Starr, V. Hale, and Mark McCormick. *Jury Selection.* 2nd ed. (1993).

Stein, Judith. *The World of Marcus Garvey: Race and Class in Modern Society* (1986).

Stephenson, Gilbert Thomas. *Race Distinctions in American Law* (1969 [1910]).

Stowe, Harriet Beecher. *The Key to Uncle Tom's Cabin* (1853).

Stuckey, Sterling. *Slave Culture: Nationalist Theory and the Foundations of Black America* (1987).

Taibbi, Mike, and Anna Sims-Phillips. *Unholy Alliances: Working the Tawana Brawley Story* (1969).

Taylor, Samuel Jared. *Paved with Good Intentions: The Failure of Race Relations in Contemporary America* (1992).

Tonry, Michael. *Malign Neglect: Race, Crime, and Punishment in America* (1995).

Toobin, Jeffrey. *The Run of His Life: The People v. O.J. Simpson* (1996).

Traynor, Roger J. *The Riddle of Harmless Error* (1970).

Trelease, Allen W. *White Terror: The Ku Klux Klan Conspiracy and Southern Reconstruction* (1971).

Tribe, Laurence H. *American Constitutional Law*. 2nd ed. (1988).

Turner, Patricia A. *I Heard It Through the Grapevine: Rumor in African-American Culture* (1993).

Tushnet, Mark V. *The American Law of Slavery 1810–1860: Considerations of Humanity and Interest* (1981).

———. *Making Civil Rights Law: Thurgood Marshall and the Supreme Court, 1936–1961* (1994).

Van Deburg, William L. *New Day in Babylon: The Black Power Movement and American Culture, 1965—1975* (1992).

Van Dyke, Jon M. *Jury Selection Procedures: Our Uncertain Commitment to Representative Panels* (1977).

Veysey, Laurence, ed. *Law and Resistance: American Attitudes toward Authority* (1970).

Vollers, Maryanne. *Ghosts of Mississippi: The Murder of Medgar Evers, the Trials of Byron de la Beckwith, and the Haunting of the New South* (1995).

Washington, Linn. *Black Judges on Justice: Perspectives from the Bench* (1992).

Weiss, Nancy J. *Farewell to the Party of Lincoln: Black Politics in the Age of FDR* (1983).

West, Cornel. *Race Matters* (1993).

Wheeler, Stanton, Kenneth Mann, and Austin Sarat. *Sitting in Judgment: The Sentencing of White-Collar Criminals* (1988).

Wheeler, Stanton, Elin Waring, and Nancy Bode. *Crimes of the Middle Classes: White-Collar Offenders in the Federal Courts* (1991).

White, Walter. *Rope and Faggot: A Biography of Judge Lynch* (1929).

Whitfield, Stephen J. *A Death in the Delta: The Story of Emmett Till* (1988).

Wicker, Tom. *A Time to Die: The Attica Prison Revolt* (1994).

Wideman, John Edgar. *Brothers and Keepers* (1984).

Wilbanks, William. *The Myth of a Racist Criminal Justice System* (1987).

Williams, Patricia J. *The Alchemy of Race and Rights: Diary of a Law Professor* (1991).

Williamson, Joel. *The Crucible of Race: Black/White Relations in the American South since Emancipation* (1984).

Wilson, Henry. *History of the Rise and Fall of the Slave Power in America.* 3 vols. (1872–1877).

Wilson, James Q., and Richard J. Herrnstein. *Crime and Human Nature* (1985).

Wilson, James Q., and Joan Petersilia, eds. *Crime* (1995).

Wilson, William Julius. *The Truly Disadvantaged: The Inner City, the Underclass, and Public Policy* (1987).

———. *When Work Disappears: The World of the New Urban Poor* (1996).

Wolfe, Tom. *The Bonfire of the Vanities* (1987).

Wolfgang, Marvin E., and Bernard Cohen. *Crime and Race: Conceptions and Misconceptions* (1970).

Wright, George C. *Racial Violence in Kentucky, 1865–1940: Lynchings, Mob Rule, and "Legal Lynchings"* (1990).

Wright, Richard. *Black Boy: A Record of Childhood and Youth* (1945).

———. *Uncle Tom's Children* (1965 [1940]).

Zangrando, Robert L. *The NAACP Crusade against Lynching, 1909–1950* (1980).

Zilversmit, Arthur. *The First Emancipation: The Abolition of Slavery in the North* (1967).

Journal Articles and Book Chapters

Aleinikoff, T. Alexander. "A Case for Race-Consciousness." 91 *Columbia Law Review* 1060 (1991).

Alexander, Adele Logan. " 'She's No Lady, She's a Nigger': Abuses, Stereotypes, and Realities from the Middle Passage to Capitol (and Anita) Hill." In *Race, Gender, and Power in America: The Legacy of the Hill-Thomas Hearings*, edited by Anita Faye Hill and Emma Coleman Jordan (1995).

Alexander, Larry. "What Makes Wrongful Discrimination Wrong?" 141 *University of Pennsylvania Law Review* 149 (1992).

Alschuler, Albert W. "Racial Quotas and the Jury." 44 *Duke Law Journal* 704 (1995).

———. "The Supreme Court and the Jury: Voir Dire, Peremptory Challenges, and the Review of Jury Verdicts." 56 *University of Chicago Law Review* 153 (1989).

———. "Courtroom Misconduct by Prosecutors and Trial Judges." 50 *Texas Law Review* 629 (1972).

Alschuler, Albert W., and Andrew G. Deiss. "A Brief History of the Criminal Jury in the United States." 61 *University of Chicago Law Review* 867 (1994).

Ambinder, Loren Page. "Dispelling the Myth of Rationality: Racial Discrimination in Taxicab Service and the Efficacy of Litigation Under 42 U.S.C. 1981." 64 *George Washington Law Review* 342 (1996).

Amsterdam, Anthony. "In Favorem Mortis: The Supreme Court and Capital Punishment." *Human Rights* (Winter 1987).

———. "The Void-for-Vagueness Doctrine in the Supreme Court." 109 *University of Pennsylvania Law Review* 67 (1960).

Applebaum, Arthur Isak. "Racial Generalization, Police Discretion and Bayesian Contractualism." In *Handled with Discretion*, ed. John Kleinig. (1996).

"Arkansas' Key-Man Jury Selection Procedures: Opportunity for Discrimination." 30 *Arkansas Law Review* 527 (1977).

Arkin, Steven D. "Discrimination and Arbitrariness in Capital Punishment: An Analysis of Post-Furman Murder Cases in Dade County, Florida, 1973–1976." 33 *Stanford Law Review* 75 (1980).

Armour, Jody D. "Race Ipsa Loquitur: Of Reasonable Racists, Intelligent Bayesians, and Involuntary Negrophobes." 46 *Stanford Law Review* 781 (1994).

Austin, Regina. "Beyond Black Demons and White Devils: Antiblack Conspiracy Theorizing and the Black Public Sphere." 22 *Florida State University Law Review* 1021 (1995).

———. " 'A Nation of Thieves': Securing Black People's Right to Shop and to Sell in White America." 1994 *Utah Law Review* 147 (1994).

———. " 'The Black Community,' Its Lawbreakers, and a Politics of Identification." 65 *Southern California Law Review* 1769 (1992).

Babcock, Barbara Allen. "Voir Dire: Preserving 'It's Wonderful Power.' " 27 *Stanford Law Review* 545 (1975).

Bailey, D'Army. "The Role of Race in the Memphis Courts." 51 *Washington and Lee Law Review* 529 (1994).

Baldus, David C. "Monitoring and Evaluating Contemporary Death Sentencing Systems: Lessons from Georgia." 18 *University of California at Davis Law Review* 1375 (1985).

Baldus, David C., Charles Pulaski, and George Woodworth. "Arbitrariness and Discrimination in the Administration of the Death Penalty: A Challenge to State Supreme Courts." 15 *Stetson Law Review* 133 (1986).

———. "Comparative Review of Death Sentences: An Empirical Study of the Georgia Experience." 74 *Journal of Criminal Law and Criminology* 661 (1983).

Baldus, David C., Charles A. Pulaski, Jr., George Woodworth, and Frederick D. Kyle. "Identifying Comparatively Excessive Sentences of Death: A Quantitative Approach." 33 *Stanford Law Review* 1 (1980).

Baldus, David C., George Woodworth, and Charles A. Pulaski, Jr. "Reflections on the 'Inevitability' of Racial Discrimination in Capital Sentencing and the 'Impossibility' of Its Prevention, Detection, and Correction." 51 *Washington and Lee Law Review* 359 (1994).

Baldwin, James. "A Report from Occupied Territory," reprinted in *Law and Resistance: American Attitudes toward Authority*, edited by Laurence Veysey (1970).

Becton, Charles L. "The Drug Courier Profile: 'All Seems Infected That th'Infected Spy, as All Looks Yellow to the Jaundic'd Eye.' " 65 *North Carolina Law Review* 417 (1987).

Bedau, Hugo Adam, and Michael L. Radelet. "Miscarriages of Justice in Potentially Capital Cases." 40 *Stanford Law Review* 21 (1987).

Benedict, Michael Les. "Preserving Federalism: Reconstruction and the Waite Court." *Supreme Court Review* 39 (1978).

———. "Preserving the Constitution: The Conservative Basis of Radical Reconstruction." 61 *Journal of American History* 65 (1974).

Bentele, Ursula. "The Death Penalty in Georgia: Still Arbitrary." 62 *Washington University Law Quarterly* 573 (1985).

Berger, Vada, et al. "Too Much Justice: A Legislative Response to McCleskey v. Kemp." 24 *Harvard Civil Rights–Civil Liberties Law Review* 437 (1989).

Berkman, Harvey. "Race and Death Stymie Crime Bill." *National Law Journal* (August 1, 1994).

Berrien, Jacqueline. "Pregnancy and Drug Use: The Dangerous and Unequal Use of Punitive Measures." 2 *Yale Journal of Law and Feminism* 239
(1990).

Blumstein, Alfred. "Making Rationality Relevant: The American Society of
Criminology 1992, Presidential Address." 31 *Criminology* 1 (1993).

Brand, Jeffrey S. "The Supreme Court, Equal Protection, and Jury Selection:
Denying That Race Still Matters." 1994 *Wisconsin Law Review* 511 .

Brest, Paul. "In Defense of the Antidiscrimination Principle." 90 *Harvard
Law Review* 1 (1976).

Bright, Stephen B. "Discrimination, Death and Denial: The Tolerance of
Racial Discrimination in the Infliction of the Death Penalty." 35 *Santa
Clara Law Review* 433 (1995).

———. "Counsel for the Poor: The Death Sentence Not for the Worst
Crime, but for the Worst Lawyer." 103 *Yale Law Journal* 1835 (1994).

Bright, Stephen B., and Patrick Keenan. "Judges and the Politics of Death:
Deciding between the Bill of Rights and the Next Election in Capital
Cases." 75 *Boston University Law Review* 759 (1995).

Butler, Paul. "Racially Based Jury Nullification: Black Power in the Criminal
Justice System." 105 *Yale Law Journal 677 (1995)*.

Carson, Clayborne. "Malcolm and the American State." In *Malcolm X: The
FBI File* (1991).

Carter, Stephen L. "When Victims Happen to Be Black." 97 *Yale Law Journal* 420 (1988).

Chan, Louise M. "S.O.S. from the Womb: A Call for New York Legislation
Criminalizing Drug Use during Pregnancy." 21 *Fordham Law Journal*
199 (1993).

Chasnoff, Ira J., Harvey J. Landress, and Mark E. Barrett. "The Prevalence
of Illicit Drug or Alcohol Use during Pregnancy and Discrepancies in
Mandatory Reporting in Pinellas County, Florida." 322 *New England
Journal of Medicine* 1201 (1990).

Clinton, Catherine. "With a Whip in His Hand: Rape, Memory, and
African-American Women." In *History and Memory in African-American
Culture*, edited by Genevieve Fabre and Robert O'Meally (1994).

Cloud, Morgan. "The Dirty Little Secret." 43 *Emory Law Journal* 1311
(1994).

Cohen, Julius. "The Screws Case: Federal Protection of Negro Rights." 46
Columbia Law Review 94 (1946).

Cohen, William. "Negro Involuntary Servitude in the South, 1865–1940: A

Preliminary Analysis." 42 *Journal of Southern History* 31 (1976), reprinted in *Race Relations and the Law in American History*, edited by Kermit L. Hall (1987).

Colbert, Douglas L. "Challenging the Challenge: Thirteenth Amendment as a Prohibition against the Racial Use of Peremptory Challenges." 76 *Cornell Law Review* 1 (1990).

———. "The Motion in Limine in Politically Sensitive Cases: Silencing the Defendant at Trial." 39 *Stanford Law Review* 1271 (1987).

Cole, David. "The Paradox of Race and Crime: A Comment on Randall Kennedy's 'Politics of Distinction.' " 83 *Georgetown Law Journal* 2547 (1995).

"Comment: *Swain* v. *Alabama*: A Constitutional Blueprint for the Perpetuation of the All-White Jury." 52 *Virginia Law Review* 1157 (1966).

Copp, Kimberly M. "Black Rage: The Illegitimacy of a Criminal Defense." 29 *John Marshall Law Review* 205 (1995).

Cover, Robert M. "The Origins of Judicial Activism in the Protection of Minorities." 91 *Yale Law Journal* 1287 (1982).

Crenshaw, Kimberle Williams. "Mapping the Margins: Intersectionality, Identity Politics, and Violence against Women of Color." 43 *Stanford Law Review* 1241 (1991).

Crouthamel, James L. "Springfield Race Riot of 1908." 45 *Journal of Negro History* 164 (July 1960), reprinted in *Lynching, Racial Violence, and Law*, edited by Paul Finkelman (1992).

Curriden, Mark. "Jury Reform: No One Agrees on Whether the System Is Broken, But Everyone Is Trying to Change It." 81 *ABA Journal* 72 (1995).

Dailey, Debra L. "Prison and Race in Minnesota." 64 *University of Colorado Law Review* 761 (1993).

Daly, Kathleen. "Criminal Law and Justice System Practices as Racist, White, and Racialized." 51 *Washington and Lee Law Review* 431 (1994).

Daniel, Pete. "Up from Slavery and down to Peonage: The Alonzo Bailey Case." 57 *Journal of American History* 654 (1970), reprinted in *Race Relations and the Law in American History*, edited by Kermit L. Hall (1987).

Davis, Peter L. "Rodney King and the Decriminalization of Police Brutality in America: Direct and Judicial Access to the Grand Jury as Remedies for Victims of Police Brutality When the Prosecution Declines to Prosecute." 53 *Maryland Law Review* 271 (1994).

Days, Drew S., III. "Race and the Federal Criminal Justice System: A Look at the Issue of Selective Prosecution." 48 *Maine Law Review* 179 (1996).

DeBrota, Steven D. "Arguments Appealing to Racial Prejudice: Uncertainty, Impartiality, and the Harmless Error Doctrine." 64 *Indiana Law Journal* 375 (1989).

Delgado, Richard. "Rodrigo's Eighth Chronicle: Black Crime, White Fears—On the Social Construction of Threat." 80 *Virginia Law Review* 503 (1994).

Dembitz, Nanette. "Racial Discrimination and the Military Judgment: The Supreme Court's *Korematsu* and *Endo* Decisions." 45 *Columbia Law Review* 175 (1945).

"Developments in the Law: Race and the Criminal Process." 101 *Harvard Law Review* 1472 (1988).

DiIulio, John J., Jr. "The Question of Black Crime." 117 *The Public Interest* 3 (1994).

DiSalvo, Charles R. "The Key-Man System for Composing Jury Lists in West Virginia: The Story of Abuse, the Case for Reform." 87 *West Virginia Law Review* 219 (1985).

Dorin, Dennis D. "Far Right of the Mainstream: Racism, Rights, and Remedies from the Perspective of Justice Antonin Scalia's *McCleskey* Memorandum." 45 *Mercer Law Review* 1035 (1994).

———. "Two Different Worlds: Criminologists, Justices and Racial Discrimination in the Imposition of Criminal Punishment in Rape Cases." 72 *Journal of Criminal Law and Criminology* 1667 (1981).

DuBois, W.E.B. "The Talented Tenth," reprinted in Henry Louis Gates, Jr., and Cornel West, *The Future of the Race* (1996).

Dudziak, Mary L. "Desegregation As a Cold War Imperative." 41 *Stanford Law Review* 61 (1988).

Duncan, Martha Grace. "'A Strange Liking': Our Admiration for Criminals." 1991 *University of Illinois Law Review* 1 (1991).

Dunnigan, E. Vaughn. "Discrimination by the Defense: Peremptory Challenges after Batson v. Kentucky." 88 *Columbia Law Review* 355 (1988).

Earle, Elizabeth L. "Banishing the Thirteenth Juror: An Approach to the Identification of Prosecutorial Racism." 92 *Columbia Law Review* 1212 (1992).

Edwards, Harry T. "To Err Is Human, but Not Always Harmless: When Should Legal Error Be Tolerated?" 70 *New York University Law Review* 1167 (1995).

Engel, Kathleen, and Stanley Rothman. "The Paradox of Prison Reform:

Rehabilitation, Prisoners' Rights, and Violence." 7 *Harvard Journal of Law and Public Policy* 413 (1984).

Fair, Brian K. "Using Parrots to Kill Mockingbirds: Yet Another Racial Prosecution and Wrongful Conviction in Maycomb," 45 *Alabama Law Review* 404 (1994).

Falk, Patricia. "Novel Theories of Criminal Defense Based Upon the Toxicity of the Social Environment: Urban Psychosis, Television Intoxication, and Black Rage." 74 *North Carolina Law Review* 731 (1996).

Fallon, Richard H., Jr. "Of Justiciability, Remedies, and Public Law Litigation: Notes on the Jurisprudence of Lyons." 59 *New York University Law Review* 1 (1984).

Fede, Andrew. "Legitimized Violent Slave Abuse in the American South, 1619–1865: A Case Study of Law and Social Change in Six Southern States." 29 *American Journal of Legal History* 93 (1985).

Finkelman, Paul. "The Crime of Color." 67 *Tulane Law Review* 2063 (1993).

———. "Prelude to the Fourteenth Amendment: Black Legal Rights in the Antebellum North." 17 *Rutgers Law Journal* 415 (1986).

Fisher, Michael T. "Harmless Error, Prosecutorial Misconduct, and Due Process: There's More to Due Process than the Bottom Line." 88 *Columbia Law Review* 1298 (1988).

Fisher, William W., III. "Ideology and Imagery in the Law of Slavery." 68 *Chicago-Kent Law Review* 1051 (1993).

Flanigan, Daniel J. "Criminal Procedure in Slave Trials in the Antebellum South." 40 *Journal of Southern History* 537 (1974), reprinted in *The Law of American Slavery*, edited by Kermit L. Hall (1987).

Ford, Christopher A. "Administering Identity: The Determination of 'Race' in Race-Conscious Law." 82 *California Law Review* 1231 (1994).

Fyfe, James J. "Blind Justice: Police Shootings in Memphis." 73 *Journal of Criminal Law and Criminology* 707 (1982).

Gallagher, Janet. "Prenatal Invasions and Interventions: What's Wrong with Fetal Rights." 10 *Harvard Women's Law Journal* 9 (1987).

Garfinkel, Harold. "Research Note on Inter- and Intra-Racial Homicides." 27 *Social Forces* 369 (1949).

Gaynes, Elizabeth A. "The Urban Criminal Justice System: Where Young + Black + Male = Probable Cause." 20 *Fordham Urban Law Journal* 621 (1993).

Getman, Karen A. "Sexual Control in the Slaveholding South: The Implementation and Maintenance of a Racial Caste System." 7 *Harvard Women's Law Journal* 115 (1984).

Gilbert, M. Shanara. "An Ounce of Prevention: A Constitutional Prescription for Choice of Venue in Racially Sensitive Criminal Cases." 67 *Tulane Law Review* 1855 (1993).

Goldberg, Susan. "Medical Choices during Pregnancy: Whose Decision Is It Anyway?" 41 *Rutgers Law Review* 591 (1989).

Goldwasser, Katherine. "Limiting a Criminal Defendant's Use of Peremptory Challenges: On Symmetry and the Jury in a Criminal Trial." 102 *Harvard Law Review* 808 (1989).

Goodpaster, Gary. "The Trial for Life: Effective Assistance of Counsel in Death Penalty Cases." 58 *New York University Law Review* 299 (1983).

Gotanda, Neil. "A Critique of Our Constitution Is Colorblind." 44 *Stanford Law Review* 1 (1991).

Goulding, Jill. "Race, Sex, and Genetic Discrimination in Insurance: What's Fair." 80 *Cornell Law Review* 1646 (1995).

Graglia, Lino A. "The 'Remedy' Rationale for Requiring or Permitting Otherwise Prohibited Discrimination: How the Court Overcame the Constitution and the 1964 Civil Rights Act." 22 *Suffolk University Law Review* 569 (1988).

Greene, Dwight L. "Justice Scalia and Tonto, Judicial Pluralistic Ignorance, and the Myth of Colorless Individualism in Bostick v. Florida." 67 *Tulane Law Review* 1979 (1993).

Gressman, Eugene. "The Unhappy History of Civil Rights Legislation." 50 *Michigan Law Review* 1323 (1952).

Grimshaw, Allen D. "Actions of Police and the Military in American Race Riots." In *Racial Violence in the United States* 275, edited by Allen D. Grimshaw (1969).

Gross, Samuel R., and Robert Mauro. "Patterns of Death: An Analysis of Racial Disparities in Capital Sentencing and Homicide Victimization." 37 *Stanford Law Review* 27 (1984).

Gunther, Gerald. "In Search of Evolving Doctrine on a Changing Court: A Model for a Newer Equal Protection." 86 *Harvard Law Review* 1 (1972).

Hall, Kermit L. "Political Power and Constitutional Legitimacy: The South Carolina Ku Klux Klan Trials, 1871–1872." 33 *Emory Law Review* 921, (1984).

Harris, David A. "Factors for Reasonable Suspicion: When Black and Poor Means Stopped and Frisked." 69 *Indiana Law Journal* 659 (1994).

Heard, Denise. "Prohibition, Racism and Class Politics in the Post Reconstruction South." 13 *Journal of Drug Issues* 77 (1983).

Herman, Susan N. "Why the Court Loves Batson: Representation-Reinforcement, Colorblindness, and the Jury." 67 *Tulane Law Review* 1807 (1993).

Higginbotham, A. Leon, Jr. "Race, Sex, Education and Missouri Jurisprudence: Shelley v. Kraemer in a Historical Perspective." 67 *Washington University Law Quarterly* 673 (1989).

Hindelang, Michael J. "Race and Involvement in Common Law Personal Crimes." 43 *American Sociological Review* 93 (1978).

Hindus, Michael S. "Black Justice under White Law: Criminal Prosecutions of Blacks in Antebellum South Carolina." 63 *Journal of American History* 575 (1976), reprinted in *Race Relations and the Law in American History*, edited by Kermit L. Hall (1987).

Hing, Bill Ong. "The Interest of Racial Harmony: Revisiting the Lawyer's Duty to Work for the Common Good," 47 *Stanford Law Review* 901 (1995).

Hixson, William B., Jr. "Moorfield Storey and the Defense of the Dyer Anti-lynching Bill." 42 *New England Quarterly* 65 (1969).

Hobbs, Fay Wilson. "Building Bridges: A Personal Reflection on Race, Crime, and the Juvenile Justice System." 51 *Washington and Lee Law Review* 535 (1994).

Holden-Smith, Barbara. "Lynching, Federalism, and the Intersection of Race and Gender in the Progressive Era." 8 *Yale Journal of Law and Feminism* 31 (1996).

Hopper, David D. "Batson v. Kentucky and the Prosecutorial Peremptory Challenge: Arbitrary and Capricious Equal Protection?" 74 *Virginia Law Review* 811 (1988).

Howard, Woodford, and Cornelius Bushoven. "The *Screws* Case Revisited." 29 *Journal of Politics* 617 (1967), reprinted in *Civil Rights in American History*, edited by Kermit L. Hall (1987).

Ikemoto, Lisa C. "Traces of the Master Narrative in the Story of African American/Korean American Conflict: How We Constructed 'Los Angeles.' " 66 *Southern California Law Review* 1581 (1993).

Jacobs, James B. "The Limits of Racial Integration in Prison." 18 *Criminal Law Bulletin* 117 (1982).

Jacoby, Joseph E., and Raymond Paternoster. "Sentencing Disparity and Jury Packing: Further Challenges to the Death Penalty." 73 *Journal of Criminal Law and Criminology* 379 (1982).

Johnsen, Dawn. "Shared Interests: Promoting Healthy Births without Sacrificing Women's Liberty." 43 *Hastings Law Journal* 569 (1992).

Johnson, Ericka L. "A Menace to Society: The Use of Criminal Profiles and Its Effects on Black Males." 38 *Howard Law Journal* 629 (1995).

Johnson, Sheri Lynn. "Racial Imagery in Criminal Cases." 67 *Tulane Law Review* 1739 (1993).

———. "The Language and Culture (Not to Say Race) of Peremptory Challenges." 35 *William and Mary Law Review* 21 (1993).

———. Comment. "Unconscious Racism and the Criminal Law." 73 *Cornell Law Review* 1016 (1988).

———. "Black Innocence and the White Jury." 83 *Michigan Law Review* 1611 (1985).

———. "Race and the Decision to Detain a Suspect." 93 *Yale Law Journal* 214 (1983).

Jones, Charles H., Jr. "An Argument for Federal Protection against Racially Motivated Crimes: 18 U.S.C. §241 and the Thirteenth Amendment." 21 *Harvard Civil Rights–Civil Liberties Law Review* 689 (1986).

Kairys, David, Joseph B. Kadane, and John P. Lehoczky. "Jury Representativeness: A Mandate for Multiple Source Lists." 65 *California Law Review* 776 (1977).

Katz, Jack. "Of Hardmen and 'Bad Niggers': Gender and Ethnicity in the Background of Stickup." In Jack Katz, *Seductions of Crime: Moral and Sensual Attractions in Doing Evil* (1988).

Kelley, Robin D.G. "Kickin' Reality, Kickin' Ballistics: 'Gangsta Rap' and Postindustrial Los Angeles." In Robin D. G. Kelley, *Race Rebels: Culture, Politics, and the Black Working Class* (1994).

Kennedy, Randall. "The State, Criminal Law, and Racial Discrimination: A Comment." 107 *Harvard Law Review* 1255 (1994).

———. "Doing What You Can with What You Have: The Greatness of Justice Marshall." 80 *Georgetown Law Journal* 2081 (1992).

———. "*McCleskey* v. *Kemp:* Race, Capital Punishment, and the Supreme Court." 101 *Harvard Law Review* 1388 (1988).

King, Nancy J. "Racial Jurymandering: Cancer or Cure? A Contemporary Review of Affirmative Action in Jury Selection." 68 *New York University Law Review* 707 (1993).

————. "Postconviction Review of Jury Discrimination: Measuring the Effects of Juror Race on Jury Decisions." 92 *Michigan Law Review* 63 (1993).

Kirkland, Shari L., et al. "Further Evidence of the Deleterious Effects of Overheard Derogatory Ethnic Labels: Deregulation Beyond the Target." 13 *Personality and Social Psychology Bulletin* 216 (1987).

Kirschenman, Joleen, and Kathryn M. Neckerman. " 'We'd Love to Hire Them, but . . .': The Meaning of Race for Employers." In *The Urban Underclass*, edited by Christopher Jencks and Paul E. Peterson (1991).

Kleck, Gary. "Racial Discrimination in Criminal Sentencing: A Critical Evaluation of the Evidence with Additional Evidence on the Death Penalty." 46 *American Sociological Review* 783 (1981).

Kuhn, Roger S. "Jury Discrimination: The Next Phase." 41 *Southern California Law Review* 235 (1968).

Landis, Debra T. "Annotation, Prosecutor's Appeals in Criminal Cases to Racial, National, or Religious Prejudice as Ground for Mistrial, New Trial, Reversal, or Vacation of Sentence: Modern Cases." 70 *American Law Review* 664. (1991).

Lawrence, Charles R., III. "The Id, the Ego, and Equal Protection: Reckoning with Unconscious Racism." 39 *Stanford Law Review* 317 (1987).

Lawrence, Frederick M. "Civil Rights and Criminal Wrongs: The Mens Rea of Federal Civil Rights Crimes." 67 *Tulane Law Review* 2113 (1993).

Leipold, Andrew D. "The Dangers of Race-Based Jury Nullification: A Response to Professor Butler." 44 *UCLA Law Review* 109 (1996).

————. "Rethinking Jury Nullification." 87 *Virginia Law Review* 753 (1996).

Leitman, Matthew F. "A Proposed Standard of Equal Protection Review for Classifications within the Criminal Justice System That Have a Racially Disparate Impact: A Case Study of the Federal Sentencing Guidelines' Classification between Crack and Powder Cocaine." 25 *University of Toledo Law Review* 215 (1994).

Letwin, Michael Z. "Report from the Front Line: The Bennett Plan, Street-Level Drug Enforcement in New York City and the Legalization Debate." 18 *Hofstra Law Review* 795 (1990).

Levenson, Laurie L. "The Future of State and Federal Civil Rights Prosecutions: The Lessons of the Rodney King Trial." 41 *UCLA Law Review* 509 (1994).

————. "Change of Venue and the Role of the Criminal Jury." 66 *Southern California Law Review* 1533 (1993).

Levinson, Sanford. "Testimonial Privileges and the Preferences of Friendship." 1984 *Duke Law Journal* 631 (1984).

Lind, Michael. "Jury Dismissed." In *Postmortem: The O.J. Simpson Case: Justice Confronts Race, Domestic Violence, Lawyers, Money, and the Media*, edited by Jeffrey Abramson (1996).

Linzer, Peter. "The Meaning of Certiorari Denials." 79 *Columbia Law Review* 1227 (1979).

Lockwood, Dorothy, Anne E. Pottieger, and James A. Inciardi. "Crack Use, Crime by Crack Users, and Ethnicity." In *Ethnicity, Race, and Crime: Perspectives across Time and Place*, edited by Darnell F. Hawkins (1995).

Logli, Paul A. "The Prosecutor's Role in Solving the Problem of Prenatal Drug Use and Substance Abused Children." 43 *Hastings Law Journal* 559 (1992).

London, Charles M. "Clinton's Cocaine Babies." *Policy Review* (Spring 1995).

Lowney, Knoll D. "Smoked Not Snorted: Is Racism Inherent in Our Crack Cocaine Laws?" 45 *Washington University Journal of Urban and Contemporary Law* 121 (1994).

Maclin, Tracey. "Justice Thurgood Marshall: Taking the Fourth Amendment Seriously." 77 *Cornell Law Review* 723 (1992).

———. " 'Black and Blue Encounters: Some Preliminary Thoughts About Fourth Amendment Seizures: Should Race Matter?" 26 *Valparaiso University Law Review* 243 (1991).

———. "Book Review: Seeing the Constitution from the Backseat of a Police Squad Car." 70 *Boston University Law Review* 543 (1990).

———. "The Decline of the Right of Locomotion: The Fourth Amendment on the Streets." 75 *Cornell Law Review* 1258 (1990).

Mann, Coramae Richey. "A Minority View of Juvenile 'Justice.' " 51 *Washington and Lee Law Review* 465 (1994).

Marcus, Rebecca. "Racism in Our Courts: The Underfunding of Public Defenders and Its Disproportionate Impact upon Racial Minorities." 22 *Hastings Constitutional Law Quarterly* 219 (1994).

Markman, Steven J., and Paul G. Cassell. "Protecting the Innocent: A Response to the Bedau–Radelet Study." 41 *Stanford Law Review* 121 (1991).

Martin, Ben L. "From Negro to Black to African American." 106 *Political Science Quarterly* 83 (1991).

Martin, John Andrew. "The Fifth Circuit and Jury Selection Cases: The Negro Defendant and His Peerless Jury." 4 *Houston Law Review* 448 (1966).

Martin, Phillip W.D. "Understanding Black Rage." 2, no. *Reconstruction* 12 (1992).

Massaro, Toni M. "Peremptories or Peers? Rethinking Sixth Amendment Doctrine, Images, and Procedures." 64 *North Carolina Law Review* 501 (1986).

Massey, Douglas S. "Getting away with Murder: Segregation and Violent Crime in Urban America." 143 *University of Pennsylvania Law Review* 1203 (1995).

Melilli, Kenneth J. "Batson in Practice: What We Have Learned about Batson and Peremptory Challenges." 71 *Notre Dame Law Review* 447 (1996).

Meltzer, Daniel J. "Deterring Constitutional Violations by Law Enforcement Officials: Plaintiffs and Defendants as Private Attorneys General." 88 *Columbia Law Review* 247 (1988).

Merton, Robert K. "The Self-Fulfilling Prophecy." *Antioch Review* (Summer 1948), reprinted in Robert K. Merton, *Social Theory and Social Structure* (1949).

Miethe, Terance D. "Fear and Withdrawal from Urban Life." 539 *The Annals of the American Academy of Political and Social Science* 14 (1995).

Morehead, Jere W. "When a Peremptory Challenge Is No Longer Peremptory: Batson's Unfortunate Failure to Eradicate Invidious Discrimination from Jury Selection." 43 *De Paul Law Review* 625 (1994).

Muller, Eric L. "The Legal Defense Fund's Capital Punishment Campaign: The Distorting Influence of Death." 4 *Yale Law and Policy Review* 158 (1985).

Myers, Martha A. "The New South's 'New' Black Criminal: Rape and Punishment in Georgia, 1870–1940." In *Ethnicity, Race, and Crime: Perspectives across Time and Place*, edited by Darnell F. Hawkins (1995).

Nash, A. E. Keir. "A More Equitable Past? Southern Supreme Courts and the Protection of the Antebellum Negro." 48 *North Carolina Law Review* 197 (1970), reprinted in *Race Relations and the Law in American History*, edited by Kermit L. Hall (1987).

———. "Reason of Slavery: Understanding the Judicial Role in the Peculiar Institution." 32 *Vanderbilt Law Review* 7 (1979).

———. "Texas Justice in the Age of Slavery: Appeals Concerning Blacks and the Antebellum State Supreme Court." 8 *Houston Law Review* 438 (1971).

————. "The Texas Supreme Court and Trial Rights of Blacks, 1845–1860." 58 *Journal of American History* 622 (1971).

————. "Fairness and Formalism in the Trials of Blacks in the State Supreme Courts of the Old South." 56 *Virginia Law Review* 64 (1970).

Nicholson, David. "Presumed Guilty: The Cops and Rodney King." *Reconstruction* 2, no. 2 (1993).

Nieman, Donald G. "Black Political Power and Criminal Justice: Washington County, Texas, 1868–1884." 55 *Journal of Southern History* 391 (1989).

Nilsen, Eva S. "The Criminal Defense Lawyer's Reliance on Bias and Prejudice." 8 *Georgetown Journal of Legal Ethics* 1 (1994).

Note. "Banishing the Thirteenth Juror: An Approach to the Identification of Prosecutorial Racism." 92 *Columbia Law Review* 1212 (1992).

Note. "Beyond the Ken of the Courts: A Critique of Judicial Refusal to Hear the Complaints of Convicts." 72 *Yale Law Journal* 506 (1963).

Note. "The Case of Abolishing Peremptory Challenges in Criminal Trials." 121 *Harvard Civil Rights–Civil Liberties Law Review* 227 (1986).

Note. "The Case for Black Juries." 79 *Yale Law Journal* 531 (1970).

Note. "Change of Venue in Criminal Cases: The Defendant's Right to Specify the County of Transfer." 26 *Stanford Law Review* 131 (1973).

Note. "Conscious Inclusion of Negroes on Grand Jury Venire Is Not Violative of Negro Defendant's Right to Equal Protection." 55 *Georgetown Law Journal* 942 (1967).

Note. "The Defendant's Challenge to a Racial Criterion in Jury Selection: A Study in Standing, Due Process and Equal Protection." 74 *Yale Law Journal* 919 (1965).

Note. "Discrimination and Arbitrariness in Capital Punishment: An Analysis of Post-Furman Murder Cases in Dade County, Florida, 1973–1976." 33 *Stanford Law Review* 75 (1980).

Note. "Judicial Right Declaration and Entrenched Discrimination." 94 *Yale Law Journal* 1741 (1985).

Note. "Making the Violation Fit the Remedy: The Intent Standard and Equal Protection Law." 92 *Yale Law Journal* 328 (1982).

Note. "The Nature and Consequences of Forensic Misconduct in the Prosecution of a Criminal Case." 54 *Columbia Law Review* 946 (1954).

Note. "Negro Defendants and Southern Lawyers: Review in Federal Habeas Corpus of Systematic Exclusion of Negroes from Juries." 72 *Yale Law Journal* 559 (1963).

Note. "Out of the Frying Pan or into the Fire? Race and Choice of Venue after Rodney King." 106 *Harvard Law Review* 705 (1993).

Note: "Pregnancy Police: The Health Policy and Legal Implications of Punishing Pregnant Women for Harm to Their Fetuses." 16 *New York University Review of Law and Social Change* 227 (1988).

Ogletree, Charles. "The Death of Discretion? Reflections on Federal Sentencing Guidelines." 101 *Harvard Law Review* 1938 (1988).

Paternoster, Raymond. "Prosecutorial Discretion in Requesting the Death Penalty: A Case of Victim-based Racial Discrimination." 18 *Law and Society Review* 437 (1984).

———. "Race of Victim and Location of Crime: The Decision to Seek the Death Penalty in South Carolina." 74 *Journal of Criminal Law and Criminology* 754 (1983).

Peller, Gary. "Criminal Law, Race, and the Ideology of Bias: Transcending the Critical Tools of the Sixties." 67 *Tulane Law Review* 2231 (1993).

Peterson, Todd D. "The Role of the Executive Branch in the Discipline and Removal of Federal Judges." 1993 *University of Illinois Law Review* 809.

Pfeifer, Jeffrey E. "Reviewing the Empirical Evidence on Jury Racism: Findings of Discrimination or Discriminatory Findings?" 69 *Nebraska Law Review* 230 (1990).

Pizzi, William T. "*Batson* v. *Kentucky:* Curing the Disease but Killing the Patient." *Supreme Court Review* 97 (1987).

Potash, Diane. "Mandatory Inclusion of Racial Minorities on Jury Panels." 3 *Black Law Journal* 80 (1973).

Powell, John A., and Eileen B. Hershenov. "Hostage to the Drug War: The National Purse, the Constitution and the Black Community." 24 *University of California at Davis Law Review* 557 (1991).

Rable, George C. "The South and the Politics of Antilynching Legislation, 1920–1940" 51 *Journal of Southern History* 201 (1985).

Radelet, Michael L. "Racial Characteristics and the Imposition of the Death Penalty." 46 *American Sociological Review* 918 (1981).

Radelet, Michael L., and Glenn L. Pierce. "Race and Prosecutorial Discretion in Homicide Cases." 19 *Law and Society Review* 587 (1985).

Ramirez, Deborah A. "The Mixed Jury and the Ancient Custom of Trial by Jury de Medietate Linguae: A History of a Proposal for Change." 74 *Boston University Law Review* 777 (1994).

Raphael, Michael J., and Edward J. Ungvarsky. "Excuses, Excuses: Neutral

Explanations under Batson v. Kentucky." 27 *University of Michigan Journal of Law Reform* 229 (1993).

Ratner, Michael. "Inter-Neighborhood Denials of Equal Protection in the Provision of Municipal Services." 4 *Harvard Civil Rights–Civil Liberties Law Review* 1 (1968).

Reynolds, William Bradford. "The Reagan Administration's Civil Rights Policy: The Challenge for the Future." 42 *Vanderbilt Law Review* 993 (1989).

Richardson, William H. "No More Lynchings! How North Carolina Solved the Problem." 64 *Review of Reviews* 401 (1924).

Riedel, Marc. "Discrimination in the Imposition of the Death Penalty: A Comparison of the Characteristics of Offenders Sentenced Pre-Furman and Post-Furman." 49 *Temple Law Quarterly* 261 (1976).

Roberts, Dorothy E. "Crime, Race, and Reproduction." 67 *Tulane Law Review* 1945 (1993).

———. "Punishing Drug Addicts Who Have Babies: Women of Color, Equality, and the Right of Privacy." 104 *Harvard Law Review* 1419 (1991).

Rostow, Eugene. "The Japanese American Cases: A Disaster." 54 *Yale Law Journal* 489 (1945).

Rudovsky, David. "Police Abuse: Can the Violence Be Contained?" 27 *Harvard Civil Rights–Civil Liberties Law Review* 465 (1992).

Russell, Katheryn K. "The Racial Hoax as Crime: The Law as Affirmation." 71 *Indiana Law Journal* 593 (1996).

Scalia, Antonin. "The Disease as Cure." *Washington University Law Quarterly* 147 (1979).

Schmidt, Benno C., Jr. "Juries, Jurisdiction and Race Discrimination: The Lost Promise of *Strauder* v. *West Virginia*." 61 *Texas Law Review* 1401 (1983).

Schoeman, Paul. "Easing the Fear of Too Much Justice: A Compromise Proposal to Revise the Racial Justice Act." 30 *Harvard Civil Rights–Civil Liberties Law Review* 543 (1995).

Schulhofer, Stephen J. "The Trouble with Trials, the Trouble with Us." 105 *Yale Law Journal* 825 (1995).

Schwartz, Adina. " 'Just Take away Their Guns': The Hidden Racism of *Terry* v. *Ohio*." 23 *Fordham Urban Law Journal* 317 (1996).

Schwartz, Paul H. "Equal Protection in Jury Selection? The Implementation of *Batson* v. *Kentucky* in North Carolina." 69 *North Carolina Law Review* 1533 (1991).

Serr, Brian J., and Mark Maney. "Racism, Peremptory Challenges, and the Democratic Jury: The Jurisprudence of a Delicate Balance." 79 *Journal of Criminal Law and Criminology* 1 (1988).

Shapiro, Andrew L. "Challenging Criminal Disenfranchisement under the Voting Rights Act: A New Strategy." 103 *Yale Law Journal* 537 (1993).

Sheley, Joseph F. "Structural Influences on the Problem of Race, Crime, and Criminal Justice Discrimination." 67 *Tulane Law Review* 2273 (1993).

Siegal, David M. "Rape in Prison and AIDS: A Challenge for the Eighth Amendment Framework of *Wilson* v. *Seiter*." 44 *Stanford Law Review* 1541 (1992).

Sitkoff, Harvard. "Racial Militancy and Interracial Violence in the Second World War." 58 *Journal of American History* 661 (1971).

Sklansky, David A. "Cocaine, Race, and Equal Protection." 47 *Stanford Law Review* 1283 (1995).

Skogan, Wesley G. "Crime and the Racial Fears of White Americans." 539 *The Annals of the American Academy of Political and Social Science* 59 (1995).

Sneirson, Judd F. "Black Rage and the Criminal Law: A Principled Approach to a Polarized Debate." 143 *University of Pennsylvania Law Review* 2251 (1995).

"Special Issue: The Rodney King Trials: Civil Rights Prosecutions and Double Jeopardy." 41 *UCLA Law Review* 509 (1994).

"Special Issue: A Study of the California Penalty Jury in First-Degree-Murder Cases." 21 *Stanford Law Review* 1297 (1969).

Spencer, Gary. "Attica Inmates Win $1.3 Million from State." *New York Law Journal* (October 26, 1989).

Steiker, Carol S. "Pretoria, Not Peoria." 74 *Texas Law Review* 1285 (1996).

———. "Second Thoughts about First Principles." 107 *Harvard Law Review* 820 (1994).

Stern, Gerald M. "Judge William Harold Cox and the Right to Vote in Clarke County, MIssissippi." In *Southern Justice*, edited by Leon Friedman (1965).

Stevenson, Bryan A., and Ruth E. Friedman. "Deliberate Indifference: Judicial Tolerance of Racial Bias in Criminal Justice." 51 *Washington and Lee Law Review* 509 (1994).

Stith, Kate. "The Government Interest in Criminal Law: Whose Interest Is It, Anyway?" In *Public Values in Constitutional Law*, edited by Stephen E. Gottlieb (1993).

Strauss, David A. "The Ubiquity of Prophylactic Rules." 55 *University of Chicago Law Review* 190 (1988).

Streible, Dan. "Race and the Reception of Jack Johnson Fight Films." In *The Birth of Whiteness: Race and the Emergence of U.S. Cinema*, edited by Daniel Bernardi (1996).

Sunstein, Cass R. "Three Civil Rights Fallacies." 79 *California Law Review* 751 (1991).

Swift, Joel H. "Defendants, Racism and the Peremptory Challenge." 22 *Columbia Human Rights Law Review* 177 (1991).

Swift, Joshua E. "Batson's Invidious Legacy: Discriminatory Juror Exclusion and the 'Intuitive' Peremptory Challenge." 78 *Cornell Law Review* 336 (1993).

Tanford, J. Alexander. "Racism in the Adversary System: The Defendant's Use of Peremptory Challenges." 63 *Southern California Law Review* 1015 (1990).

Thomas, Kendall. "*Rouge et Noir* Reread: A Popular Constitutional History of the Angelo Herndon Case," 65 *Southern California Law Review* 2599 (1992).

Van Ness, Daniel W. "Preserving a Community Voice: The Case for Half-and-Half Juries in Racially-Charged Criminal Cases." 28 *John Marshall Law Review* 1 (1994).

Vorenberg, James. "Decent Restraint of Prosecutorial Power." 94 *Harvard Law Review* 1521 (1981).

Walton, Anthony. "Willie Horton and Me." In *Speech and Power: The African-American Essay and Its Cultural Content from Polemics to Pulpit*, edited by Gerald Early Vol. 2. (1993).

Walzer, Michael. "The Obligations of Oppressed Minorities." In *Obligations: Essays on Disobedience, War, and Citizenship* (1970).

Wasserstrom, Richard A. Book Review (Burke Marshall, *Federalism and Civil Rights*). 33 *University of Chicago Law Review* 406 (1966).

Watts, Jerry G. "Reflections on the Rodney King Verdict and the Paradoxes of the Black Response." In *Reading Rodney King/Reading Urban Uprising*, edited by Robert Gooding-Williams (1993).

Weinberg-Brodt, Chaya. "Jury Nullification and Jury-Control Procedures." 65 *New York University Law Review* 825 (1990).

Weisberg, Robert. "Deregulating Death." *Supreme Court Review* 305 (1983).

Weisburd, David, Elin Waring, and Stanton Wheeler. "Class, Status, and the Punishment of White Collar Criminals." 15 *Law and Social Inquiry* 223 (1990).

Wheeler, Stanton, David Weisburd, and Nancy Bode. "Sentencing the White Collar Offender: Rhetoric and Reality." 47 *American Sociological Review* 641 (1982).

Williams, Cynthia A. "Jury Source Representativeness and the Use of Voter Registration Lists." 65 *New York University Law Review* 590 (1990).

Williams, Patricia. "Spirit-Murdering the Messenger: The Discourse of Fingerpointing as the Law's Response to Racism." 42 *University of Miami Law Review* 127 (1987).

Wolfgang, Marvin E. "The Death Penalty: Social Philosophy and Social Science Research." 14 *Criminal Law Bulletin* 18 (1978).

———. "The Social Scientist in Court." 65 *Journal of Criminal Law and Criminology* 239 (1974).

Wolfgang, Marvin E., and Marc Riedel. "Rape, Racial Discrimination, and the Death Penalty." In *Capital Punishment in the United States*, edited by Hugo Adam Bedau and Chester M. Pierce (1976).

Wriggins, Jennifer. "Rape, Racism, and the Law." 6 *Harvard Women's Law Journal* 103 (1983).

Zeisel, Hans. "Race Bias in the Administration of the Death Penalty: The Florida Experience." 95 *Harvard Law Review* 456 (1981).

Zeisel, Hans, and Shari Seidman Diamond. "The Effect of Peremptory Challenges on Jury and Verdict: An Experiment in a Federal District Court." 30 *Stanford Law Review* 491 (1978).

Zimring, Franklin E., Joel Eigen, and Sheila O'Malley. "Punishing Homicide in Philadelphia: Perspectives on the Death Penalty." 43 *University of Chicago Law Review* 227 (1976).

Miscellaneous

ABA Standards for Criminal Justice: Trial by Jury, 53 *Criminal Law Report* (BNA) 2347 (September 29, 1993).

"Attica: The Official Report of the New York State Special Commission on Attica" (1972).

Bureau of Justice Statistics. *Sourcebook of Justice Statistics 1993*, Kathleen Maquire and Ann L. Pastore, eds. (1994).

Commission on Wartime Relocation and Internment of Civilians. *Personal Justice* (1982).

Grand Jury of the Supreme Court, State of New York, County of Dutchess. *Report of the Grand Jury and Related Documents Concerning the Tawana Brawley Investigation* (1988).

Independent Commission on the Los Angeles Police Department (Christopher Commission). *Report of the Independent Commission on the Los Angeles Police Department* (1991).

Institute for Alternative Journalism. *Inside the L.A. Riots: What Really Happened, and Why It Will Happen Again* (1992).

The Kerner Report: The 1968 Report of the National Advisory Commission on Civil Disorders (1988 [1968]).

National Association for the Advancement of Colored People. *Thirty Years of Lynching in the United States, 1889–1918* (1969 [1919]).

National Jury Project. *Jurywork: Systematic Techniques*. 2nd ed. (1987).

Saravy, Stacy Capman. "Lawmakers, Reformers and Apologists Respond to Lynching: A Critical Survey of the Literature." Third Year Paper *Harvard Law School* (1990).

Seale, Bobby. "The Platform of the Black Panther Party." In *A Documentary History of the Negro People in the United States*, Volume 7, *1960–1968: From the Alabama Protests to the Death of Martin Luther King, Jr.*, edited by Herbert Aptheker (1994).

Senate Select Committee to Study Governmental Operations with Respect to Intelligence Activities. *Final Report*, S.Rep. No. 94-755, 94th Cong., 2d. Sess. (1976).

Staff of the *Los Angeles Times*. *Understanding the Riots: Los Angeles before and after the Rodney King Case* (1992).

U.S. Congress, Senate Committee on Slavery and the Treatment of Freedmen. "Equality Before the Law in the Courts of the United States. "S.Rep. No. 25, 38th Congress, 1st Sess. 35 (1864).

U.S. Department of Justice, Bureau of Justice Statistics. *Sourcebook of Criminal Justice Statistics* (1994).

U.S. Department of Justice. *Criminal Victimization in the United States* (1993).

U.S. Department of Justice. *A National Crime Victimization Survey Report* (May 1996).

U.S. Department of Justice, Office of Legal Policy. *Report to the Attorney General: Redefining Discrimination: "Disparate Impact" and the Institutionalization of Affirmative Action* (1987).

U.S. Sentencing Commission. *Special Report to the Congress: Cocaine and Federal Sentencing Policy* (1995).

Newspapers and Magazine Stories

Abrahamson, Alan. "Fuhrman Enters Plea of No Contest to Perjury." *Los Angeles Times*. October 3, 1996.

Alter, Jonathan. "Black and White and Read All Over." *Newsweek*, August 1, 1994.

Alter, Jonathan, and Mark Starr. "Race and Hype in a Divided City." *Newsweek*, January 22, 1990.

"Angry Clinton Defends His Cabinet Selections. . . . He Attacks Criticism by 'Bean Counters.' " *Los Angeles Times*, December 22, 1992.

Appelo, Tim. "Are Those Photographs Racist, or Real?; 'Cocaine True': The Furor over Crack's Color." *Washington Post,* April 10, 1994.

Ayres, B. Drummond, Jr. "Washington Mayor Seeks Aid of Guard in Combating Crime." *New York Times*, October 23, 1993.

Baker, Peter, and Blaine Harden. "Candidates Mine Crime Issue for Votes." *Washington Post*, September 17, 1996.

Barnes, Fred. "The Shame of Lance Ito." *The Weekly Standard*, October 16, 1995.

Bendavid, Naftali. "Black Lawmakers Hold Balance on Crime: Legislative Endgame Reveals Caucus's Power, Divisions." *Legal Times*, August 22, 1994.

Benjamin, Playthell. "Fare Deal for All: Catching a New York Cab Is Easy—If You're White." *The Independent*, February 8, 1995.

Blair, William G. "Jury in Bronx Acquits Larry Davis in Shooting Six Police Officers." *New York Times,* November 21, 1988.

Borg, Gary. "Jackson Rips Clinton on Drug Penalty." *Chicago Tribune*, November 3, 1995.

Bradley, Bill. "Race and the American City." 138 *Congressional Record* S. 4241, March 26, 1992.

"The Briley File," *Fulton County Daily Rep.*, November 7, 1994.

Brown, Keith M. "The Shades of Racism." *Newsday*, May 7, 1993.

Brown, Reginald J. Letter to the Editor, *Washington Times*, October 27, 1996.

Butler, Paul. "O.J. Reckoning: Rage for a New Justice." *Washington Post*, October 8, 1995.

"Cab Company Wary of Blacks Faces Sanction." *New York Times*, February 2, 1995.

Canellos, Peter S. "Police Face a Confidence Gap, Many Blacks Worried, Officers Cover for Own," *Boston Globe*, October 17, 1996.

Carlson, Margaret. "Presumed Innocent." *Time*, January 22, 1990.

Carton, Barbara. "Photographer Accused of Shooting with a Biased Lens; Eugene Richards' Pictorial of Addicts Sparks a Furor." *Boston Globe*, March 14, 1994

Cose, Ellis, with Allison Samuels. "The Darden Dilemma." *Newsweek*, March 25, 1996.

Coulson, Crocker. "The Cabbie's Eye." In "The Jeweler's Dilemma." *New Republic*, November 10, 1986.

Coyle, Marcia. "Fatal Defense: Trial and Error in the Nation's Death Belt." *National Law Journal* 30, June 11, 1980.

Daley, Steve. "House Rivals Unite to Soften Anti-Terror Bill." *Chicago Tribune*, March 14, 1996.

Daniels, Lee A. "The American Way: Blame a Black Man." *Emerge*, February 28, 1995.

Dao, James. "Death Penalty in New York Reinstated after 18 Years; Pataki Sees Justice Served." *New York Times*, March 8, 1995.

"Death Penalty Legal Centers Are Closing." *Columbus Dispatch*, February 26, 1996.

DeParle, Jason. "Talk of Government Being Out to Get Blacks Falls on More Attentive Ears," *New York Times*, October 29, 1990.

DiIullio, John J., Jr. "My Black Crime Problem, and Ours." *City Journal*, Spring 1996.

Dolan, Maura. "Key State Panel to Consider Major Changes for Trials." *Los Angeles Times*, October 31, 1995.

Douglas, Lewis L. "Race, Jury Composition and Change of Venue Applications." *New York Law Journal* 1, October 1, 1992.

Douglas, William. "Clinton Won't Back Racial Justice Act." *Newsday*, July 15, 1994.

D'Souza, Dinesh. "The 'Rational' Discrimination of Cab Drivers," *Washington Times*, October 21, 1996.

Emery, Richard. "The Even Sadder New York Police Saga." *New York Times*, December 12, 1987.

"Even among Drug Peddlers, Justice Isn't Blind." *St. Louis Post-Dispatch*, December 24, 1991.

"Excerpts: L.A. Hearing on Venue of Police Trial." *National Law Journal*, June 1, 1992.

Farah, Douglas, and Walter Pincus. "CIA, Contras and Drugs: Questions on Links Linger." *Washington Post*, October 31, 1996.

Frady, Marshall. "Annals of Law and Politics: Death in Arkansas." *New Yorker*, February 22, 1993.

Gates, Henry Louis, Jr. "Thirteen Ways of Looking at a Black Man." *New Yorker*, October 23, 1995.

Gellman, Barton, and Sari Horwitz. "Letter Stirs Debate after Acquittal: Writer Says Jurors Bowed to Racial Issue in D.C. Murder Case." *Washington Post*, April 22, 1990.

Genasci, Lisa. "Success Is No Shield for Racism; Discrimination: No Matter What Positives They Hold, Blacks Say They Daily Confront Adversity That Their White Counterparts Cannot Imagine." *Los Angeles Times*, June 14, 1995.

"Georgia Pardons Victim 70 Years After Lynching." *New York Times,* March 12, 1986.

Gilliam, Dorothy. "Law of the Monster." *Washington Post*, June 18, 1987.

Glastris, Paul, and Jeannye Thornton. "A New Civil Rights Frontier." *U.S. News & World Report*, January 17, 1994.

Glazer, Nathan. "A Tale of Two Cities." *New Republic*, August 2, 1993.

Gleick, Elizabeth. "The Crooked Blue Line." *Time*, September 11, 1995.

Henry, William A., III. "How African Americans See It." *Time*, February 28, 1994.

Herbert, Bob. "Jury Room Injustice." *New York Times*, March 30, 1994.

———. "Mr. Hance's 'Perfect Punishment,' " *New York Times*, March 27, 1994.

Hevesi, Dennis. "Cab Hailed by Dinkins Rides on By." *New York Times*, December 4, 1994.

Holden, Benjamin, Laurie P. Cohen, and Eleena de Lisser. "Color Blinded: Race Seems to Play an Increasing Role in Many Jury Verdicts." *Wall Street Journal*, October 4, 1995.

"Hot Line for Discriminating Taxicabs." *Washington Post*, August 10, 1994.

"In Her Own Disputed Words: Transcript of Interview That Spawned Souljah's Story." *Washington Post*, June 16, 1992.

Jackson, Derrick Z. "Intentional Injustice." *Boston Globe*, December 11, 1996.

Jackson, Don. "Police Embody Racism to My People." *New York Times*, January 23, 1989.

"The Jeweler's Dilemma: How Would You Respond?" *New Republic*, November 10, 1986.

Johnson, Mary A. " 'Plot' a Ploy, Farrakhan Says; Minister Charges U.S. Out to Discredit Him." *Chicago Sun-Times,* January 18, 1995.

Jordan, George E. "Campaign '92: Clinton and Crime; Supports Capital Punishment as Sign of Toughness." *Newsday*, May 4, 1992.

Kalish, Jon. "Interview with William Kunstler." *Newsday*, June 23, 1988.

Kasindorf, Mark. " '92 Violent Crime Hit 1 in 10 Blacks, a Record," *Newsday*, November 15, 1993.

Kennedy, Randall. "Is Everything Race?" *New Republic*, January 1, 1996.

———. "The Angry Juror." *Wall Street Journal*, September 30, 1994.

Kilpatrick, James J. "Lynch Mob Assembles to Keep Thomas Off the Supreme Court." *Orlando Sentinel Tribune*, August 8, 1991.

Kopkind, Andrew. "The Stuart Case: Race, Class, and Murder in Boston." *The Nation*, February 5, 1990.

Kurtz, Howard. "Conspiracy or Paranoia? Some Think Drugs Are Allowed to Hurt Black Communities." *Seattle Times*, January 7, 1990.

Lacayo, Richard. "Stranger in the Shadows." *Time*, November 14, 1994.

Lane, Charles. "An Imaginary Conspiracy." *Baltimore Sun*, November 8, 1996.

Lewis, Anthony. "Cruel and Reckless." *New York Times*, August 11, 1995.

Lewis, Kathy, and Robert G. Hillman. "Clinton, Dole Hammer Crime: New Report Shows Decline." *Dallas Morning News*, September 18, 1996.

Loury, Glenn C. "Racial Fixations on the Right." *Washington Times*, November 3, 1995.

Lynd, Staughton, and Roberta Yancey. "The Unfamiliar Campus." *Dissent*, Winter 1964.

Malone, Julia. "Scuffing up the Cabinet: Some Claim Clinton Fails at Diversity." *Atlanta Journal and Constitution*, December 18, 1992.

Mathews, Jay. "Use of Testers to Fight Bias Stirs Backlash." *Washington Post*, December 14, 1992.

Maxwell, Bill. "An Ugly Truth about Young Black Males." *St. Petersburg Times*, February 12, 1995.

McCarthy, Sheryl. "Chavis: Victim of His Own Arrogance." *Newsday*, August 24, 1994.

Means, Marianne. "Clinton, Dole and the Ever-Escalating War on Crime." *San Diego Union-Tribune*, September 19, 1996.

Meddis, Sam V. "Drug War Claiming 'Entire Generation' of Young Blacks." *USA Today*, July 27, 1993.

————. "Is the Drug War Racist? Disparities Suggest the Answer Is Yes." *USA Today*, July 23, 1993.

Meredith, Robyn. "White Officer's Acquittal Brings Protest March," *New York Times*, November 15, 1996.

Mersey, William. "Why Cabbies Pass up Blacks." *New York Times*, January 1, 1995.

Mills, David. "Sister Souljah's Call to Arms: The Rapper Says the Riots Were Payback. Are You Paying Attention?" *Washington Post*, May 13, 1992.

Mitchell, Locin. "Clinton's Crime Bill Gamble; President Shunts Aside Black Allies, Woos Right." *Chicago Tribune*, July 25, 1994.

Murdock, Dervy. "Hoods in the 'Hood: Getting Tough on Crime." *Ethnic NewsWatch*, February 28, 1994.

Murray, Charles. "Class and Underclass." *New York Times*, May 21, 1993.

Nagourney, Adam. "Politics: The Candidates: Dole Attacks on Crime, But Clinton Is Ready." *New York Times*, September 17, 1996.

Naison, Mark. "Outlaw Culture and Black Neighborhoods." *Reconstruction* no. 4 (1994).

Nelson, Jack, and David Lauter. "Clinton Vows to Rebuild U.S." *Los Angeles Times*, October 20, 1992.

Noble, Kenneth B. "The Simpson Defense: Source of Black Pride." *New York Times*, March 6, 1995.

Oliver, Mike. "Even Republicans Enjoy Chiles' Anti-Crime Message." *Orlando Sentinel*, September 19, 1996.

Clarence. "Shabazz Case Shows FBI Can Abuse Powers It Now Has." *ndo Sentinel*, May 9, 1995.

Black Crime and the Darden Dilemma." *Baltimore Sun*, February

————. "The Race Card Still Gets Played Again and Again," *Chicago Tribune*, August 24, 1994.

————. "Talk of 'The Plan' Is a Paranoid View of Black Problems." *Chicago Tribune*, January 24, 1990.

Parloff, Roger. "Maybe the Jury Was Right." *American Lawyer,* June 1992.

Pasternak, Judy. "U.S. Settles Case Against Daughter of Malcolm X." *Los Angeles Times*, May 2, 1995.

Pertman, Adam. "Fuhrman Tapes Reveal Raw, Racist Remarks." *Boston Globe*, August 30, 1995.

Poe, Clarence H. "Lynching: A Southern View." *Atlantic Monthly*, February 1904.

Purdum, Todd S. "Prosecuting Officers: False-Arrest Case Shows It Can Take Time and Publicity to Redress Wrongs." *New York Times*, March 16, 1989.

"Questions About Plot to Kill Farrakhan Show Blacks' Mistrust of Legal System." *Rocky Mountain News*, January 19, 1995.

"Race and Drug Laws." *San Francisco Chronicle*, October 23, 1995.

"Race and Racism: American Dilemma Revisited." *Salmagundi*, nos. 104, 105 (1994–1995).

"Race Tilts the Scales of Justice. Study: Dallas Punishes Attacks on Whites More Harshly." *Dallas Times Herald*, August 19, 1990.

Raspberry, William. "Reasonable Doubt Not Unreasonable." *Detroit News*, October 11, 1995.

————. "It's Business, Not Racism." *Washington Post*, June 28, 1989.

Rezendes, Michael. "Billing Incident Revives Images of Racism." *Boston Globe*, December 22, 1992.

Rich, Frank. "The L.A. Shock Treatment." *New York Times*, October 4, 1995.

Rosenbaum, David E. "John C. Stennis, 93, Longtime Chairman of Powerful Committees in the Senate Dies." *New York Times*, April 24, 1995.

Rosenthal, A. M. "Captive Neighborhood." *New York Times*, July 10, 1992.

Rosin, Hanna. "Action Jackson: Jesse's Volte-face on Crime." *New Republic*, March 21, 1994.

Rowan, Carl. "Fuhrman Tips the Scale at Simpson Trial." *Chicago Sun-Times*, September 10, 1995.

Safire, William. "Judge Bork Stands Up to the Lynch Mob." *Chicago Tribune,* October 13, 1987.

Scales, Ann, and Charles M. Sennott. "Cab Firm's Policy May Mean Separate, Unequal Service." *Boston Globe*, February 28, 1995.

Seelye, Katherine Q. "White House Offers Compromise to Free Logjam on Crime Measure." *New York Times*, July 21, 1994.

Seligman, Daniel. "How to Count Beans." *Fortune*, March 8, 1993.

Seligman, Herbert. "Race War?" *The New Republic* 49 (1919).

"The Sentence Guidelines Straitjacket." *Chicago Tribune*, September 5, 1993.

Shales, Tom. "TV Preview." *Washington Post*, July 19, 1994.

"Shapiro Lashes out at Cochran and Tactics." *Boston Globe*, October 4, 1995.

Shepard, Paul. "Elders, Drug Czar Disagree on Study: Legalization Part of Crime Discussion." *Cleveland Plain Dealer*, January 8, 1994.

"Shortchanging Inmates on Death Row." *New York Times*, October 13, 1995.

Seigel, Jessica. "Former Cop's Slurs Stun Simpson Trial: L.A., Nation Shocked by Violence, Bigotry." *Chicago Tribune*, August 30, 1995.

"The Silent White House." *New York Times*, July 15, 1994.

Singer, Amy. "Larry Davis Beats the Rap." *American Lawyer*, May 1990.

Smith, Patricia. "A Victory O.J. Didn't Deserve." *Boston Globe*, October 4, 1995.

Smolowe, Jill. "Race and the O.J. Case." *Time*, August 1, 1994.

Special Section. "The Park Rape." *Village Voice*, May 8, 1989.

Tate, Greg. "Leadership Follies." *Village Voice*, May 8, 1989.

Terry, Don. "After 18 Years in Prison, 3 Are Cleared of Murders, *New York Times*, July 3, 1996.

"Trial Is Moved for 2 Charged in Burning of a Brooklyn Man." *New York Times*, June 23, 1993.

"Trouble at the Taxi Stand." *Boston Globe*, December 22, 1992.

Tuller, David. "Surgeon General's Remarks: Debate Changing in War on Drugs." *San Francisco Chronicle*, December 11, 1993.

"The Unreasonable Doubt." *New Republic* October 23, 1995.

Vistica, Gregory L., and Vern E. Smith. "Was the CIA Involved in the Crack Epidemic?" *Newsweek* 72 (September 30, 1996).

Walinsky, Adam. "The Crisis of Public Order." *Atlantic Monthly*, July 1995.

Weiss, Michael D., and Karl Zinmeister. "When Race Trumps Truth in Court." *American Enterprise*, January–February 1996.

Whitaker, Barbara. "Philadelphia Still Reeling from Police Scandal." *Dallas Morning News*, September 3, 1995.

White, Jack E. "Crack, Contras and Cyberspace: When It Comes to the CIA and Drugs, Are the Paranoids on the Right Track?" *Time* 59 (September 30, 1996).

———. "Fuhrman Is No Surprise." *Time*, September 11, 1995.

Will, George F. "The Lucas Matter: A Liberal Lynching." *Washington Post*, July 25, 1989.

Williams, Juan. "Closed Doors." *New Republic*, November 10, 1986.

Woodward, Richard B. "Under Their Skin." *New York Times Magazine*, December 5, 1993

Wright, Gregory. "Fare Game." *Washington Post*, June 20, 1993.

Wycliff, Don. "Blacks and Blue Power." *New York Times*, February 8, 1987.

Zehren, Charles Z. "A Year After Oklahoma City—Unkept Promises—Still No Pact on Anti-Terror Bill." *Newsday*, April 15, 1996.

Index

abuse excuse, 303–4

Adarand Constructors, Inc. v. *Pena,*
    393*n*10, 424*n*63, 439*n*60

affirmative action, 6–7, 344, 393*n*11
    jury selection and, 178
    race-dependent policing, compari-
        son with, 159–61

Against Excess: Drug Policy for Results
    (Kleiman), 374*n*

Ah Sin v. *Wittman,* 355–56

Akerman, Amos T., 41

Akins v. *Texas,* 178–79

Alabama
    Black Code, 85
    blacks as a class, racist legislation
        targeting, 376
    jury selection, 173, 176–77, 182
    labor exploitation of blacks, 92,
        93–94, 413*n*64

lynchings, 42, 404*n*56

peremptory challenges based on
    racial criteria, 194–95

prosecutorial racial misconduct,
    258–60

rape cases, 90, 100–104

slavery laws, 78–79

vagrancy laws, 86, 91

Alabama Court of Appeals, 90,
    258–60

Alabama Supreme Court, 78–79, 102,
    176, 195

Aldridge v. *United States,* 434*n*90

Alexander, Larry, 137

Allen, Henry J., 97

Allen, Louis, 63

Alschuler, Albert W., 210, 221*n*, 226*n*,
    240, 244–45, 252, 264, 267, 280

Amadeo v. *Kemp,* 452*n*76